A Modern Dictionary of
SOCIOLOGY

1. Differentiate between biological Needs and instincts. Illustrate any Answer

2. Criticize the belief that all women have material Instincts.

3. Identify your major personality traits and Account for their development in terms of (a) Cultural Norm prevalent in my family And/or other intimate groups in which I was reared (b) games when young

Looking glass Self
generalized other

A Modern Dictionary of
SOCIOLOGY

GEORGE A. THEODORSON

and ACHILLES G. THEODORSON

Thomas Y. Crowell Company

NEW YORK   ESTABLISHED 1834

To Lucille

Preface

There has been a long-standing need for a comprehensive dictionary of sociology, a fact recognized by those new to the field as well as by those sociologists concerned with the need for an assembling of concepts and a greater clarification and interrelating of them. In writing the dictionary, the authors' first concern was to meet the needs of undergraduate and graduate students by providing them with an aid to the understanding of the concepts they are most likely to encounter. It has also been our aim to provide a dictionary useful to professionals in related fields and to the general public, who are finding an increasing number of sociological terms in popular books, magazines, newspapers, on the radio, and on television.

Since there are diverse approaches to the field of sociology, we have chosen to include as many concepts as possible. However, the difficulties involved in defining the concepts of a relatively young, complex, and rapidly changing discipline are obvious. Despite seven years of intensive research, we probably have inadvertently omitted some concepts that should have been included. On the other hand, a few sociologists will undoubtedly feel that certain of the terms we have included, such as "in-group" and "out-group," might better have been omitted. Our judgment was that if some sociologists find or have found such terms useful, either in their writing or lecturing, it is wise to define them. However, when a concept is clearly obsolete or rarely used, this is indicated to the reader. Where more than one usage is given, the preferred, more widely accepted, or in some cases more sociologically relevant, usage is listed first.

We have included concepts from a variety of conceptual levels and historical periods and from different theoretical and methodological approaches. In selecting concepts from related fields—such as cultural anthropology, psychology, statistics, economics, political science, and philosophy—two criteria have been emphasized. First of all, it has been our intent to choose those concepts that the student of sociology is most likely to encounter in the literature of the field, especially in such branches as social psychology, demography, and political sociology. Secondly, related concepts have been included if they seem important to an understanding of the assumptions and various approaches of sociology, or if they clarify the sociological point of view by way of contrast. In order to aid the reader in tying together the concepts and ideas of the discipline, we have made what we hope are useful cross-references and have added short discussions to some definitions.

One of the major hindrances to the study of sociology has been the special language that has developed over the years. For the professional sociologist this language is a necessity, but for the person new to the field it is sometimes frustrating. We hope that the dictionary will help those new to sociology to venture forth into the professional journals and more sophisticated sociological literature without fear or confusion. In the past, simply learning the language of sociology was a long ordeal. This volume may help to speed the process of mastering the essential insights and procedures of the discipline, and perhaps thereby bring new contributions to the study of society to earlier fruition.

We should like to thank the following colleagues for reading the manuscript and for commenting on the whole manuscript or on specific definitions: David Westby, Rex Warland, Benjamin Nelson, Gian Sarup, Joan Kirschner, John Kosa, Llewellyn Gross, and Gordon DeJong. We would like to give special thanks to Rex Warland for his conscientious examination of the statistical terms and his valuable suggestions, and to David Westby, whose wide knowledge of sociological literature enabled him to provide helpful suggestions for additions and modifications. The editorial suggestions of Margaret Miner were of great value and are much appreciated. The assistance of Edward Tripp, editor of the Thomas Y. Crowell reference division, is also acknowledged. His cooperation, patience, and tact helped speed the work to its conclusion.

The encouragement and good cheer of Anna Theodorson and her assistance, in so many ways, are fully appreciated. Carol Jean Theodorson's tolerance of an unreasonably preoccupied father is hereby acknowledged and some overdue restitution promised. Lucille Theodorson worked closely with us throughout both the research and writing phases of this project. Her optimistic nature provided an additional contribution without which this volume might never have been completed.

A Modern Dictionary of
SOCIOLOGY

A

abandoned selves. See SELVES, ABANDONED.

aberrant behavior. See DEVIANCE.

ability. A quality possessed by an individual that enables him to perform an act, solve a problem, or make an adjustment. Ability refers to potential performance, that is, whether or not an individual can at a given time act in a specified manner or learn certain skills or knowledge. It is not used with reference to the source of the individual's potentiality for accomplishment. Whether this potentiality is based on inherited traits or previous learning, or a combination of both, is irrelevant. Intelligence tests are tests of ability. See APTITUDE; CAPACITY.

ability, primary mental. A mental ability that occurs relatively independently of other mental abilities. In other words, primary mental abilities are not highly correlated with each other. In an intelligence test a person may score high in one primary mental ability and low in another. L. L. Thurstone hypothesized that the primary mental abilities are the basic components of intelligence. Among those that he hypothesized are memorization, reasoning, numerical ability, and verbal comprehension. FACTOR ANALYSIS may be used to identify statistically independent abilities.

abnormal behavior. Deviation from expected patterns of behavior. Abnormality of social or psychological behavior may be defined differently in different cultures, in different historical periods, and in different social situations. Sociologists study what individuals and groups consider abnormal behavior. Abnormal behavior as defined within a given society usually interferes with an individual's ability to function in that society, but under specific conditions within a particular culture or in certain types of situations, abnormal behavior may be encouraged, or at least temporarily tolerated. Many sociologists avoid the use of the term. See CONFORMITY; DEVIANCE.

1

abnormal psychology. See PSYCHOLOGY, ABNORMAL.

abreaction. The process of reducing or removing emotional tension by re-experiencing in some way the original situation that produced the tension. PSYCHOANALYSIS, PSYCHODRAMA, and SOCIODRAMA are techniques used to bring about abreaction.

abscissa. The horizontal or x axis on a graph. The abscissa is perpendicular to the ORDINATE or vertical axis. See COORDINATE AXES.

absentee ownership. The ownership of the means of production or distribution by persons who are not regularly present to supervise or otherwise be involved in the productive (or distributive) enterprise. The term may refer to the absentee ownership of land that is worked by tenant farmers, sharecroppers, or laborers supervised by local managers or overseers. It also refers to the absentee ownership of factories or other businesses. This includes not only businesses that are branches of large, national companies with their headquarters in another city, but all large CORPORATIONS in which there is inherent a divorce of ownership from management, with the owners consisting of widely scattered stockholders, most of whom are in no way involved in the operation of the company.

absenteeism. The rate of absence from work of an individual or a work force in a given period of time. Absenteeism may be studied for any specified number or category of individuals (for example, for the entire labor force of a nation, for the employees in a particular factory, for the women employees of a certain company, for a specified age range) as well as for a single individual.

absolute, cultural. A VALUE or social norm that people in a particular culture feel is universally applicable and correct for all peoples and for all times. For example, if the monogamous form of marriage were regarded as the only natural and moral form of family organization, this would be a cultural absolute. In some societies the value of democracy or communism may be a cultural absolute. On the other hand, a strong cultural proscription against eating a certain food would not be a cultural absolute if it is held to be applicable to group members only and not considered necessary for nonmembers. No FOLKWAY is a cultural absolute. In modern, complex societies the number of cultural absolutes has tended to decline with the growth of CULTURAL RELATIVISM. See NORM, SOCIAL.

absolute scale. See RATIO SCALE.

absolute value of a number. The value of a number without regard to positive or negative (plus or minus) sign. The absolute value of both $+5$ and -5 is 5.

abstract social class. A class of persons, or SOCIAL CATEGORY, whose members have some sense of self-awareness as a unit and feeling of common interests. They do not have sufficient unity or organization to be considered a GROUP or even a COLLECTIVITY. On the other hand, the abstract social class differs from those social categories that are merely classifications of an investigator, categories of which persons are often not even aware of being a part. Examples of abstract social classes would be cat lovers, gardeners, housewives, and teen-agers. The term was introduced by George Herbert Mead, who distinguished it from CONCRETE SOCIAL CLASS. (G. H. Mead, *Mind, Self and Society,* University of Chicago Press, Chicago, 1934.)

abstraction. An intellectual process using selective perception to reach generalizations. In the process of abstraction perception is focused on a certain aspect of reality. This aspect or element is selected from a variety of perceived phenomena, and, through the use of symbols, is analyzed and stated in terms of generalizations that are derived from some of the concrete contexts in which the element occurs and are assumed to be applicable to all similar cases, while not completely descriptive of any one of them. Through abstraction common elements may be seen in a wide variety of objects and events, thus facilitating classification and analysis.

accidental sample. See SAMPLE, ACCIDENTAL.

accommodation. A process of social adjustment in which groups in conflict with each other agree to terminate or prevent further conflict by temporarily or permanently establishing peaceful interaction. This type of social interaction allows antagonistic groups to maintain their separate identities and attitudes, with the exception of those attitudes that would lead to disruptive conflict. The degree of cooperation and domination of one group over the other may vary considerably. Conciliation, compromise, arbitration, contract, and truce are forms of this adjustment. Sometimes the term includes the adjustment of individuals, as well as of groups and societies. The Swiss Confederation of diverse communities of Protestants, Catholics, Germans, French, and Italians and the political attitude embodied in the slogan "peaceful coexistence" are examples of accommodation.

acculturation. 1. The modification of the culture of a group or an individual through contact with one or more other cultures and the acquiring or exchanging of culture traits.

2. The transmission of culture from one generation to another within the same culture. In this sense the term has the same meaning as SOCIALIZATION.

See ASSIMILATION. Pg 17

achievement. See ASCRIPTION-ACHIEVEMENT; ROLE, ACHIEVED; STATUS, ACHIEVED.

acquired motive pattern. A concept developed by Theodore M. Newcomb to refer to the new motives and goals that an individual acquires as a result of his occupancy of a particular role. These acquired motives contribute to the satisfactory performance of the role. They result primarily from the new self-conception that the individual develops because of his new role and from his need to maintain this new self-conception.

action. Behavior which has meaning to the individual, that is, behavior which he directs toward a goal. See ACTION, SOCIAL; BEHAVIOR.

action, social. 1. ACTION oriented to or influenced by another person or persons. It is not necessary for more than one person to be physically present for action to be regarded as social action. In social action the behavior or anticipated behavior of others is taken into account in the action. Max Weber pointed out that the failure to act, or the passive acquiescence to the actions of others, is included as a part of social action. See BEHAVIOR, SOCIAL.

2. An organized attempt to solve a social problem.

action anthropology. See ANTHROPOLOGY, ACTION.

action frame of reference. The FRAME OF REFERENCE of social action theory used to analyze social and personality systems. It focuses on the actor (or actors), his values and goals, in specific situations. (See T. Parsons and E. A. Shils, eds., *Toward a General Theory of Action,* Harvard University Press, Cambridge, Mass., 1951.) See ACTION THEORY, SOCIAL.

action research. Research concerned primarily with discovering the most effective means of bringing about a desired social change. Here, the discovery of scientific principles is of secondary or incidental interest. Action research is a type of applied research. See RESEARCH, APPLIED.

action theory, social. A theoretical development within social behaviorism which has focused upon the concept of social action, interpreted as the value-motivated behavior of individuals, in attempting to construct a systematic explanation of human behavior. The foremost influence in the development of social action theory was the work of Max Weber. Other outstanding contributors include Karl Mannheim, Robert M. MacIver, Florian Znaniecki, and Talcott Parsons. Social action theory rejects rigid BEHAVIORISM by emphasizing the importance of the subjective meaning attached to a situation by an individual actor. The subjective meaning is analyzed in terms of the actor's internalized values and his expectations of the reactions of others. In social action theory, human behavior is studied in terms of persons acting in culturally defined situations and in systems of social relationships. See BEHAVIORISM, SOCIAL; VALUE.

activity. Observable physical action. One of the three principal concepts used by George C. Homans in his analysis of groups. (G. C. Homans, *The Human Group*, Harcourt, Brace, New York, 1950.) See INTERACTION; SENTIMENT.

adaptation. In the general biological sense, the adjustment of an organism to its environment. In the process of adaptation the organism's activity may be modified to suit it to a changing environment, or genetic changes may occur in the organism which contribute to the survival of its kind.

adaptation, modes of individual. See RETREATISM; RITUALISM.

adaptation, sensory. Adjustment of the sense organs to a certain level of stimulation after prolonged experience with that level, so that the effect on the organism is less marked. For example, persons who regularly eat spicy foods are less sensitive to spices than those who rarely eat them; those who live in an environment with a certain strong odor or high level of noise become less aware of and disturbed by the odor or noise than a newcomer would be.

adaptation, social. The process by which a group or an individual adjusts his behavior to suit his social environment, that is, other groups or the larger society. Many sociologists prefer to reserve the term adaptation for the biological adjustment of an individual to his environment. See ACCOMMODATION; ACCULTURATION; ADJUSTMENT; AMALGAMATION; ASSIMILATION.

adaptive culture. See CULTURE, ADAPTIVE.

addiction. Dependence upon a particular substance (e.g., drug, alcohol, tobacco) that the individual feels he must have. The dependence may be either physiological or psychological in nature. See ADDICTION, DRUG.

addiction, drug. A "state of periodic or chronic intoxication, detrimental to the individual and to society, produced by a repeated consumption of the drug (natural or synthetic). Its characteristics include: (1) an overpowering desire or need (compulsion) to continue taking the drug and to obtain it by any means; (2) a tendency to increase the dose; (3) a psychic (psychological) and sometimes, a physical dependence on the effects of the drug." (United Nations Expert Committee on Drugs Liable to Produce Addiction, World Health Organization Report 21, Geneva, 1950.)

addition theorem. The principle holding that the PROBABILITY that either or any one of two or more mutually exclusive events will occur in a given trial or occurrence is the sum of the individual probabilities. For example, in randomly selecting a card from a deck, the probability of obtaining a queen is 4/52, since there are four queens, each with a probability of 1/52. This is also known as the rule of addition. See PRODUCT THEOREM.

adhesion. See CULTURE ADHESION.

adjustment. A relatively harmonious relationship within and between individuals and groups. The term is not used by sociologists in any consistent technical sense, and it is usually defined with reference to a stated analytic problem or system of values. Because of the complexity and dynamic nature of human interaction, what appears from one frame of reference to be adjustment often may be perceived as maladjustment from another perspective. Hence, when sociologists use the term they usually apply it operationally for the solution of an immediate analytic problem. For some specific forms of social adjustment between groups, see ACCOMMODATION; ACCULTURATION; AMALGAMATION; ASSIMILATION.

administrative region or **area.** A territorial unit, such as a town, city, or state, as defined by its political boundaries. Ecologists have used the term to contrast with NATURAL AREA.

adolescence. A period of physical transition to maturity that begins usually at the age of twelve or thirteen. The child becomes capable of bearing or begetting children. Attitudes toward this phenomenon differ in different cultures, and the social and psychological impact on the adolescent varies according to cultural and social patterns.

affect. Emotion or feeling.

affective neutrality. The restraint of the desire for immediate satisfaction of an impulse in order to further a more distant goal. See AFFECTIVITY; AFFECTIVITY-AFFECTIVE NEUTRALITY.

affectivity. The experiencing and expressing of emotion, used especially with reference to the satisfaction of an immediate need or impulse. See AFFECTIVE NEUTRALITY; AFFECTIVITY-AFFECTIVE NEUTRALITY.

affectivity-affective neutrality. The opposition between the demands of an impulse or immediate need and the possible benefits of restraint and discipline. For the individual in a given situation, this is the dilemma of whether to give primacy to an impulse or to other values and more distant goals. Affectivity-affective neutrality is one of the five PATTERN VARIABLES proposed by Talcott Parsons. (T. Parsons and E. A. Shils, eds., *Toward a General Theory of Action,* Harvard University Press, Cambridge, Mass., 1951.)

affinal relative. A relative by marriage (or adoption), rather than by consanguineal ties.

agamy. The absence of regulations either requiring group members to marry within the group or prohibiting such marriages. The group does not require either ENDOGAMY or EXOGAMY on the part of its members, being indifferent as to whether they marry persons within or outside of the group. This term was introduced into cultural anthropology by Robert H. Lowie, who took it from biology. (R. H. Lowie, *Social Organization*, Routledge & Kegan Paul, London, 1950.)

age, mental. See MENTAL AGE.

age-and-area hypothesis. The hypothesis that CULTURE TRAITS found at the periphery of a CULTURE AREA tend to be older forms than those found at the CULTURE CENTER, and that these older forms had spread from the center to the periphery at an earlier time. Therefore, the age of a culture trait may be determined by studying its distance from the culture center, combined with archaeological investigation of the culture center. Presumably archaeological investigation of the culture center would uncover evidence of the older form of the culture trait found at the periphery of the culture area. There is disagreement among cultural anthropologists as to the validity of this hypothesis.

age-grading. Division of a society into different status levels based on age groupings. At each age level members of the society are expected to conform to culturally defined behavior patterns, usually according to their sex-age grouping.

age-sex pyramid. A chart showing in one diagram the age distribution of males and females in a particular population. It is actually two histograms, placed back to back, with the bars lying horizontally, rather than standing vertically. A vertical line divides the chart into two parts. The left side of the chart, with its bars extending to the left from the vertical line, usually indicates the number or percentage of males in the particular age category represented by each bar. The right side, with bars extending to the right from the mid-line, provides the same information for females. This type of chart is sometimes called an age-and-sex triangle. See HISTOGRAM; POPULATION PYRAMID.

agelicism. The sociological position, represented most typically by Émile Durkheim, which maintains that social phenomena have an independent reality and cannot be reduced to or explained in merely individual terms. The social group is seen as more than a sum of the individuals who comprise it. It has an existence of its own which precedes and survives the individual member. Moreover, the group is seen as the primary causal factor in individual behavior, for it shapes the individual and provides him with his beliefs, values, and motivations. See GESTALT PSYCHOLOGY; REDUCTIONISM; SOCIAL FACT.

agglomeration. 1. The process by which two or more cities, towns, or other such units grow together to form one ecological or population cluster, although the administrative units comprising the agglomeration may remain separate. Large cities usually expand to form large areas of population concentration which include many smaller and formerly independent settlements.

2. Any clustering of population that extends beyond the political boundaries of the administrative unit.

3. A METROPOLITAN AREA. The term is used in this sense in the *United Nations Demographic Yearbook*.

aggregate. 1. A gathering of persons in physical proximity who have come together temporarily and lack any organization or lasting pattern of interrelationships. An AUDIENCE, a CROWD, and a MOB are types of aggregates. See COLLECTIVITY; GROUP.

2. A number of persons who share certain social characteristics (occupation, for example) but are not socially organized. This usage is synonymous with SOCIAL CATEGORY.

aggression. A hostile act intended to harm a person or object, often the result of frustration. The term also refers to the desire or tendency to perform hostile acts. See FRUSTRATION-AGGRESSION HYPOTHESIS.

aggression, displaced. Aggression that is not directed at the source of the individual's frustration, either because he is unaware of the source or because the source is inaccessible or too threatening, but which instead is directed at another person or object that serves as a substitute target. This process is referred to as displacement.

aggression, free-floating. Aggressive feelings the cause of which is unrecognized by the individual and which are not limited to a specific object or objects. These uncrystallized feelings of hostility, resulting from underlying tensions, are aroused in numerous and varied situations, rather than attached to a limited number of more or less appropriate objects. The aggression is called free-floating because it is ever present in the individual, ready at any time to be directed at a new object.

agnate. A relative whose relationship is traced through the male line of descent.

Agricultural Revolution. The change from agriculture based on human labor and simple, animal-driven machinery to a highly mechanized agriculture based on the use of complex, power-driven machinery. The Agricultural Revolution also involved the application of scientific knowledge to agriculture in areas such as plant and animal breeding, the development of chemical fertilizers, insect control, etc. The result of the use of the new machinery and scientific knowledge is greatly increased production per unit of land and per man-hour, and consequently a much smaller percentage of the population is engaged in agricultural pursuits. The Agricultural Revolution has accompanied the INDUSTRIAL REVOLUTION.

aleatory element. See RELIGION, ALEATORY ELEMENT IN.

alienation. A feeling of noninvolvement in and estrangement from one's society and culture. The values and social norms shared by others seem meaningless to the alienated individual. Thus he feels isolated and frustrated. Alienation also involves a feeling of powerlessness. The individual feels unable to control his own destiny or to have any significant effect on the important events of the world through his actions. It is generally agreed that meaninglessness and powerlessness are both important aspects of alienation, although some writers stress one more than the other. These complementary factors tend to reinforce each other. Meaninglessness involves alienation from values and norms, while the feeling of powerlessness involves alienation from roles, but the meaninglessness of norms necessarily results in lack of concern for the proper performance of roles, and conversely alienation from roles necessarily results in the rejection of the norms and values supporting those roles. Thus meaninglessness and powerlessness together contribute to the individual's estrangement from the culture and social interrelationships of his society.

The term alienation has had long and varied use in many fields besides sociology, including philosophy, theology, law, and psychiatry. Important treatments of the concept may be found in the writings of Georg Hegel, Ludwig Feuerbach, Karl Marx, and Sigmund Freud.

alienation, coefficient of. See COEFFICIENT OF ALIENATION.

allopatric group. A cultural group with its own geographic territory shared with no other cultural group. See SYMPATRIC GROUPS.

alpha error. See ERROR, ALPHA.

alternatives, cultural. Two or more forms of behavior that, in a particular society, are acceptable in a given situation. These alternatives "represent different reactions to the same situations or different techniques for achieving the same ends." (R. Linton, *The Study of Man*, Appleton-Century-Crofts, New York, 1936.) In simple cultures the range of cultural alternatives is more likely to be familiar to and agreed upon by all members of society than in a complex culture. In a complex culture, such as the United States, the range of acceptable alternative norms of behavior often varies from one subgroup to another. Members of one subgroup may reject the legitimacy of certain alternatives accepted by members of other subgroups. See SPECIALTIES, CULTURAL; UNIVERSALS, CULTURAL.

altruism. 1. Behavior in which the individual gives primacy to the welfare or happiness of another or others above his own welfare or happiness. He suppresses his own desires or impulses in order to make possible the other person's satisfaction of his desires. See SELF-ORIENTATION—COLLECTIVITY-ORIENTATION.

2. The state of society or a social group in which the individual is com-

pletely merged with the group and has no interests apart from those of the group. Members are trained to renounce individualism and to value duty and obedience to the group welfare above all else. This use of the term is made in Émile Durkheim's analysis of suicide. See SUICIDE, ALTRUISTIC.

amalgamation. The biological process of two or more racial or sub-racial stocks interbreeding or intermarrying, so that originally distinct groups fuse into new racial stocks. Sometimes the term is used to refer to the biological union of ethnic or nationality groups.

ambience. The unorganized network of persons who interact with a designated individual in a designated context. In discussing the neighborhood ambience, Theodore Caplow, Sheldon Stryker, and Samuel E. Wallace state that "all the neighbors with whom a given subject sustains interaction above a stated minimum level comprise a meaningful collectivity, whose members are not necessarily in interaction with each other. In some cases the members of these collectivities are completely disconnected and have no mutual relationships except through the subject. In other instances, each member may sustain interaction with many others." (T. Caplow, S. Stryker, and S. E. Wallace, *The Urban Ambience*, Bedminster Press, New York, 1964.)

ambivalence. A state of contradictory emotions or impulses that follows from the recognition by a person that his performance of an act or role will result in negative outcomes or violation of normative standards no matter which of the alternatives he chooses from those he judges to be open to him in the particular situation. Thus, ambivalence involves conflicting feelings of attraction and repulsion toward a given object, person, or action.

amitate. 1. A pattern of special relationships between a child and his or her paternal aunt (the child's father's sister) found in certain societies.
2. Sometimes limited to a culturally patterned special relationship between a nephew and his paternal aunt.
See AVUNCULATE.

anaclitic depression. See DEPRESSION, ANACLITIC.

analogue model. See MODEL, ANALOGUE.

analytic psychology. See PSYCHOLOGY, ANALYTIC.

anarchism. The doctrine that any form of politically organized government is unnecessary and undesirable. Anarchism assumes the basic goodness of man, and maintains that if society were properly organized there would be no need for coercion. Most anarchists reject the institution of private property, advocating instead communal ownership. Usually Pierre Proudhon is regarded as the founder of modern anarchism, while

Mikhail Bakunin was probably its most famous advocate. Bakunin is associated with the development of the use of terroristic acts (e.g., bombs in
places frequented by the well-to-do, assassination of prominent persons)
as an anarchistic technique. However, many anarchists repudiated the use
of terror and violence. There has been a wide variety in the views held by
anarchists ranging from a belief in extreme individualism to SYNDICALISM.
Anarchist activity reached its peak in the 1890's and early 1900's.

ancestor worship. A religious cult found in some societies (e.g., China,
Dahomey) based upon the belief that the spirits of deceased ancestors can
influence events in the lives of the living. Culturally defined ceremonies
and rituals are practiced to honor a family's ancestors (or the ancestors of
another designated group such as a clan, household, etc.) and to encourage the spirits of the ancestors to protect and help the group or individual.

ancestry. See under DESCENT.

anchorage. A point of reference used by an individual in making a
judgment. The term is synonymous with "anchoring point." See FRAME OF
REFERENCE.

animal society. See INSECT SOCIETY.

animatism. The belief that a supernatural force or power exists in persons, animals, and inanimate objects. This essence is believed to be trans-
ferable from one person or object to another. The power, while having a
supernatural character, is impersonal, and thus is not a ghost, soul, or
spirit. The power itself is sometimes called MANA. The concept of animatism was introduced by Robert R. Marett, who sought to distinguish it
from Edward B. Tylor's concept of ANIMISM. Marett maintained that animatism preceded animism. (R. R. Marett, *The Threshold of Religion,*
Methuen, London, 1914.)

animism. The belief that all objects, both animate and inanimate, are
permanently or temporarily inhabited by spirits or souls. The spirits are
conceived of as beings with an existence distinct from, and therefore
capable of surviving the death or destruction of, the persons, animals,
plants, or objects they inhabit. Often all activity is believed to be caused
by these spirits. Usually there is also a belief in the existence of other spirit
beings with powers over the lives of men. The spirits inhabiting objects of
nature as well as those in the spirit world may be worshiped or treated
with fear or respect. Edward B. Tylor maintained that animism was man's
earliest form of religion. (See E. B. Tylor, *Primitive Culture,* John Murray,
London, 1871.) See ANIMATISM.

anomia. See ANOMIE.

anomic division of labor. See DIVISION OF LABOR, ANOMIC.

anomie. 1. A condition characterized by the relative absence or confusion of values in a society or group. As originally developed by Émile Durkheim, "this concept referred to a property of the social and cultural structure, not to a property of individuals confronting that structure." Anomie involves "a breakdown in the cultural structure, occurring particularly when there is an acute disjunction between cultural norms and goals and the socially structured capacities of members of the group to act in accord with them." (R. K. Merton, *Social Theory and Social Structure,* Free Press, Glencoe, Ill., 1957.) Anomie is the "strict counterpart of the idea of social solidarity. Just as social solidarity is a state of collective ideological integration, anomie is a state of confusion, insecurity, 'normlessness.' The collective representations are in a state of decay." (D. Martindale, *The Nature and Types of Sociological Theory,* Houghton Mifflin, Boston, 1960.) Evidence of anomie may be found in some modern urban slums composed of recent migrants from rural backgrounds, who no longer accept their traditional values and norms and who yet remain unassimilated into the social and cultural life of the complex and inhospitable urban community.

2. A social psychological condition characterized by a similar breakdown in values and a feeling of isolation. It is "a result of the high degree of specialization in mass society and that loss of intimacy found in closely knit primary groups." (K. Young, *Personality and Problems of Adjustment,* Appleton-Century-Crofts, New York, 1952.)

Some writers have preferred to reserve the term *anomie* for the sociological conception defined in 1. above, and have suggested the alternate *anomia* (L. Srole, *American Sociological Review,* December 1956; D. L. Meier and W. Bell, *American Sociological Review,* April 1959) or *anomy* (R. M. MacIver, *The Ramparts We Guard,* Macmillan, New York, 1950) for the psychological concept defined in 2. See SUICIDE, ANOMIC.

anomie, acute. A term used by Sebastian DeGrazia to refer to a severe form of anomie in which the value and belief systems of a society or group disintegrate, order collapses for the individual, and he is gripped by extreme anxiety. (S. DeGrazia, *The Political Community,* University of Chicago Press, Chicago, 1948.) See ANOMIE, SIMPLE.

anomie, simple. A term used by Sebastian DeGrazia to refer to a milder form of anomie in which there are conflicting values and beliefs in a society or group, and the individual experiences confusion and apprehension. See ANOMIE, ACUTE.

anomy. See ANOMIE.

anonymity. The condition of an individual in modern urban society when impersonal SECONDARY RELATIONS predominate. Anonymity occurs when large populations, heterogeneity, and high mobility hinder the development of close PRIMARY RELATIONS in which there is a lasting personal involvement. In the majority of interpersonal relationships individuals are unknown to each other as total personalities, and the effectiveness of informal social controls is decreased. Anonymity is an important element in urban life, and for some individuals (e.g., in rooming-house districts) it may extend to almost all social relationships, leading to social isolation. See GESELLSCHAFT; SPECIFICITY.

anthropogeography. See GEOGRAPHY, HUMAN.

anthropoid. Manlike; of or pertaining to the primate suborder that includes man and the tailless apes.

anthropology. A broad scientific discipline dedicated to the comparative study of mankind, from its first appearance to its present stage of development. The major subdivisions of anthropology are discussed under the headings ANTHROPOLOGY, CULTURAL; ANTHROPOLOGY, PHYSICAL; ARCHAEOLOGY; and LINGUISTICS.

anthropology, action. A branch of applied anthropology that attempts to use the principles of cultural anthropology to aid a people in attaining goals that they have set for themselves.

anthropology, applied. The application of the findings of scientific anthropology to the solution of a wide range of practical problems.

anthropology, cultural. The study of the culture and social structure of a community or society. Cultural anthropology emphasizes the understanding of the total configuration and interrelationships of culture traits, complexes, and social relationships in a particular geographic environment and historical context. Thus it is concerned with the influence of geographic and historical as well as social and psychological factors in the analysis of the development of a culture, its present characteristics, and the changes it is undergoing. Very many of the investigations of cultural anthropologists have been studies of nonliterate and non-Western societies; however, in recent years there has been a tendency to extend the approach of cultural anthropology to the study of modern Western society. Cultural anthropology is generally considered synonymous with social anthropology (the name preferred in Britain) and ethnology.

anthropology, functional. An approach to cultural anthropology, within the theoretical framework of FUNCTIONALISM, that analyzes culture traits and social interrelationships in terms of their function in maintaining a sociocultural system.

anthropology, linguistic. See LINGUISTICS.

anthropology, meta-. See META-ANTHROPOLOGY.

anthropology, physical. The branch of anthropology that is concerned with man as a biological organism. Physical anthropology deals with the origin of man, the comparative study of racial and subracial groups, the measurement and classification of anatomical differences among men, problems of heredity, the influence of differences in the physical environment on the human organism, and the interrelationship between biological and cultural differences among men. Physical anthropology is sometimes referred to as somatic anthropology or as somatology.

anthropology, prehistoric. See ARCHAEOLOGY.

anthropology, social. See ANTHROPOLOGY, CULTURAL.

anthropology, somatic. See ANTHROPOLOGY, PHYSICAL.

anthropometry. The division of physical anthropology that is concerned with the measurement and classification of anatomical differences among men.

anthropomorphism. The attribution of human characteristics to that which is not human.

anticipation. See SOCIALIZATION, ANTICIPATORY.

antisocial behavior. 1. Behavior believed by the members of a group to be against the interests of their group. The behavior reflects a rejection of social norms and values accepted and considered important by group members.

2. Behavior that is disruptive or potentially disruptive to the smooth functioning or survival of a group, regardless of whether or not group members recognize that the group's welfare is threatened. In this sense antisocial behavior is determined by outside observers and may include behavior not disapproved by group members.

anxiety. An emotional state characterized by extreme apprehensiveness. Anxiety is a learned emotional response related to fear but differing from fear in that it tends to be of longer duration, of disproportionate intensity, more pervasive of the personality, and lacking a clear focus on a specific object.

aphasia. A disorder, usually resulting from brain damage, that involves some type of loss or impairment of the ability to use or comprehend language. There may be an impairment of the ability to speak, to read, to write, or to understand the spoken word.

aphasia, sensory. See SENSORY APHASIA.

Apollonian culture. A culture that places high value on moderation, sobriety, and restraint. The term was used by Ruth Benedict to designate a culture like that of the Pueblo Indians, whose basic values and world view, she maintained, were in marked opposition to those of most other Indian cultures of North America. In particular, Apollonian values reject the view that excess and frenzy bring insight and wisdom and hold that disruptive psychological states and individualism are of no benefit to the society or the individual. By contrast, the Dionysian culture that characterizes most other North American Indian tribes (for example, the Plains Indians and the Indians of Mexico) holds philosophical values that approve the desire for personal experience, recklessness, exaltation, states of emotional excess, and a general passion to break through the usual sensory routine of everyday life, sometimes by the use of drugs. The terms Apollonian and Dionysian had previously been used by Friedrich Nietzsche in his study of Greek tragedy to distinguish analogous world views. (R. Benedict, *Patterns of Culture*, Mentor, New York, 1948.)

applied sciences. See ANTHROPOLOGY, APPLIED; PSYCHOLOGY, APPLIED; SCIENCE, APPLIED; SOCIOLOGY, APPLIED.

aptitude. The potentiality of an individual for learning a certain skill or a particular type of knowledge. The term aptitude differs from ABILITY in that it is generally used in a more limited sense to refer to a specific skill or type of knowledge. It entails the concept of a potentiality for performance prior to specific training. However, it does not imply that this potential is necessarily inherited. The aptitude may result from environmental influences that provide appropriate attitudes or related knowledge or skills, or to a combination of hereditary and environmental factors. Aptitudes are usually measured by specifically devised tests. See CAPACITY.

aptitude test. A standardized test designed to predict an individual's probability of success if given training in a particular field. Aptitude tests attempt to measure not only inherited CAPACITY but also interest and relevant, previously learned skills and knowledge. Prediction from aptitude test scores always is based on statistical probability.

arbitration. A form of ACCOMMODATION in which parties in conflict agree to accept the decision of an impartial third party in settling their dispute.

archaeology. A branch of anthropology concerned with the study of past cultures through the analysis of material remains. Since archaeology does not depend primarily on written records it can include the study of cultures that were not literate and are therefore outside the scope of history. Thus archaeology includes the analysis of prehistoric cultures of the distant past as well as nonliterate cultures of the recent past. In addition, archaeology provides information about past civilizations to supplement the knowledge gained through written records. Archaeologists study cultural artifacts, such as the remains of buildings, tools, pottery, art objects, as well as other material objects found at the site of the culture, such as animal bones. Many of these objects are uncovered through excavation.

area diagram. A type of graphic presentation in which a figure, such as a circle or rectangle, is divided into sections, each proportional in area to the size of the quantity it represents. The PIE CHART is a common type of area diagram.

area of deterioration. See ZONE IN TRANSITION.

area sample. See SAMPLE, AREA.

area under the curve. On a LINE GRAPH the area between the line of the graph (the curve) and the horizontal axis. This would be the total area under the curve. In addition the area under the curve between any two specified points on the horizontal axis can be determined.

argot. Slang peculiar to a particular group. Possession of this special language reflects the unique experiences of the group and also functions to increase the distinctiveness of the IN-GROUP in contrast to the OUT-GROUP. Originally, the term was used to refer to the special language of criminal groups.

aristocracy. 1. A hereditary UPPER CLASS.

2. A form of government based on rule by an upper class, usually hereditary, or an elite.

arithmetic mean. See MEAN, ARITHMETIC.

art. 1. The expression of perceptions and emotions in an aesthetic form that conveys meaning and similar feelings to others. Art forms are always culturally standardized to some extent, but within the cultural framework the amount of individual expression permitted varies greatly from one culture or historic period to another. Art tends to reflect societal values. However in a complex society some forms of aesthetic expression reflect the values of a specialized group of artists.

2. Skill in performing a task that results from a combination of knowledge, experience, and the understanding of the subtle influences of a variety of factors. The task itself may be relatively concrete or abstract; for example, art may be embodied in both carpentry and teaching.

art, sociology of. See SOCIOLOGY OF ART.

art institution. Patterns of behavior primarily concerned with providing perceptual, emotional, and expressional satisfactions. See INSTITUTION, SOCIAL.

artifact, cultural. Any object made or modified by man which has a culturally defined and standardized form and use. Artifacts include tools, buildings, clothing, weapons, art objects, etc. An artifact is a material CULTURE TRAIT.

artifact, statistical. A statistical inference resulting from BIAS in the collection or treatment of data.

asceticism. A way of life based on devotion to certain nonmaterial values or ideals with a renunciation of physical pleasures and an emphasis on simplicity, discipline, and self-denial.

ascription. See ASCRIPTION-ACHIEVEMENT; ROLE, ASCRIBED; STATUS, AS-
CRIBED.

ascription-achievement. The opposition between two modes of relating to a person in a given situation: according to a status that is ascribed in
the situation, or in terms of his achievement or performance in relevant
situations. In other words, this is the dilemma of whether to treat a person
according to who he is or in terms of what he is doing or may be expected
to do in the given situation. Thus, treating an individual in terms of a position he holds which is irrelevant to the given situation (for example, asking
the president of a college to call plays in a football game) would be ascription even if the position were an achieved position. Probably because of
this difference from the usual distinction between ascribed and achieved
status this dilemma has more recently been called quality-performance. It
is one of the five PATTERN VARIABLES proposed by Talcott Parsons. (T. Parsons
and E. A. Shils, eds., *Toward a General Theory of Action*, Harvard University Press, Cambridge, Mass., 1951.)

aspiration, differential. See DIFFERENTIAL ASPIRATION.

aspiration, level of. The standard of achievement which an individual
sets for himself and which he expects to attain. The term may be used to
refer to anything from an individual's expectation of his performance on a
test to the over-all position in life toward which he is striving.

aspirational reference group. See REFERENCE GROUP, ASPIRATIONAL.

assimilation. 1. The complete merging of groups or individuals with
separate cultures and identifications into one group with a common culture and identity. In most sociological usage, assimilation may refer to
both the one-way absorption of an individual or group into another group
and the mutual absorption or blending of divergent cultures. Assimilation
is similar to ACCULTURATION, in which a culture is modified through contact
with one or more other cultures, but assimilation involves the complete
elimination of cultural differences and differentiating group identifications. Unlike AMALGAMATION, assimilation does not require a biological fus-
ing of groups.

2. A one-way process in which an individual or group takes over the
culture and identity of another (usually larger) group and becomes a part
of that group.

3. A process of mutual absorption or blending of divergent cultures in
which each incorporates elements of the other.

association. 1. A formal group organized for a specialized and specifically stated purpose. An association has established rules of organization and procedure, a formalized system of leadership, and certain common interests among its members. Because of the limited involvement of
the members, impersonal or SECONDARY RELATIONS predominate. An asso-

ciation differs from other formal groups in the sharply defined and specialized nature of its goals. Modern society is characterized by a large variety
of associations, including business organizations, labor unions, schools,
political parties, athletic clubs, and a vast array of special interest groups
ranging from the American Philatelic Society to the National Association
for the Advancement of Colored People.

2. A relatively enduring pattern of interaction. This definition would
include all groups, ranging from informal small groups to associations as
defined above.

association, compulsory. See ASSOCIATION, INVOLUNTARY.

association, differential. See DIFFERENTIAL ASSOCIATION, OCCUPATIONAL.

association, involuntary. An ASSOCIATION or specialized, formally organized group in which membership is based on birth or compulsion
rather than on choice—for example, a conscripted army.

association, statistical. A statistical relationship in which two or more
variables occur or vary together. Any of a variety of statistical techniques
may be used to measure the extent to which a change in one variable results in a corresponding change in another variable (or variables). The
selection of a particular technique depends upon such factors as whether
the variables are qualitative or quantitative, the number of variables, and
the nature of the data. For examples of techniques for measuring statistical
association, see CONTINGENCY COEFFICIENT C; CORRELATION, LINEAR; COR-
RELATION, RANK DIFFERENCE; PHI COEFFICIENT. See also CONTINGENCY;
CORRELATION; REGRESSION, STATISTICAL.

association, voluntary. An ASSOCIATION, or specialized formally organized group, in which membership is based on deliberate choice and from
which members may resign—for example, a professional association such
as the American Sociological Association.

associationism. A psychological theory in which all mental processes,
no matter how complex, are seen as eventually reducible to certain simple,
basic elements or sensations. Learning and mental development, for
example, then would basically involve the combining and recombining of
numerous discrete, simple elements according to certain laws. See
ATOMISM.

atomism. A type of theory in which simple, basic units are regarded as
the ultimate elements of reality. In sociology, atomism refers to the theoretical view that all social phenomena—groups, institutions, social
classes, and so forth—must be regarded as the sum of the acts of individuals. Thus, the acts of individual people are regarded as the basic concep-

tual units for the analysis of all social phenomena. See BEHAVIORISM; BE-HAVIORISM, SOCIAL; REDUCTIONISM.

atomization. The breakdown of group ties, especially those within the family, neighborhood, or other primary group, resulting in unattached individuals whose social relationships are largely or entirely secondary, impersonal, and transient. The ANONYMITY of modern urban life provides a milieu in which atomization may occur. See ANOMIE.

attenuation, statistical. The reduction in the size of a CORRELATION through errors of measurement. Because of errors the correlation obtained in a study is lower than the true correlation that exists in the population. A correction for attenuation may be used to estimate the size of the correlation without the chance errors. The obtained correlation is divided by the square root of the product of the reliability coefficients of the two variables. The resulting value is the maximum probable correlation between the variables. It should be remembered, however, that this is a theoretical and not an obtained value. See COEFFICIENT OF RELIABILITY.

attitude. 1. An orientation toward certain objects (including persons —others or oneself) or situations that is emotionally toned and relatively persistent. An attitude is learned, and may be regarded as a more specific expression of a VALUE or BELIEF in that an attitude results from the application of a general value to concrete objects or situations. An attitude involves a positive or negative evaluation and a readiness to respond to related objects or situations in a characteristic and predictable manner. See OPINION.
2. A tendency to act in a consistent manner toward certain related objects and situations. This more operationalized definition is preferred by some writers on the grounds that attitudes can be inferred only from observed behavior, even though the attitude precedes the behavior. Most attitude studies, however, deal with verbal responses rather than observations of behavior. It should be recognized, though, that many behaviorists regard verbal response as a form of behavior. Bert F. Green distinguishes among elicited verbal attitudes (responses to attitude questionnaires), spontaneous verbal attitudes ("opinions expressed by individuals in normal conversations with friends"), and action attitudes ("verbal or nonverbal behavior directed toward an object in the referent class"). He concludes: "Emphasis on the validity of verbal attitude scales for predicting action attitudes often obscures the fundamental issue in attitude research. We are interested in the relation of attitudes to other variables, such as socioeconomic status, education, exposure to propaganda, or other attitudes. If we wish to study the relation of elicited verbal attitudes to such variables, then we need a scale that measures elicited verbal attitude.

. . . It is only when we attempt to use a scale based on elicited verbal attitude as an indicant of action attitude that this question of validity is paramount." (B. F. Green in *Handbook of Social Psychology*, edited by G. Lindzey, Addision-Wesley Press, Reading, Mass., 1954.)
See SCALE, ATTITUDE.

attitude, categorical. See CATEGORICAL ATTITUDE.

attitude, ideational. An attitude expressed by a speaker or writer. The term was used by Florian Znaniecki to distinguish attitude expressed in this way from attitude expressed through action. (F. Znaniecki, *Cultural Sciences*, University of Illinois Press, Urbana, Ill., 1952.) See ATTITUDE, REALISTIC.

attitude, realistic. An attitude expressed by the way in which a person perceives and reacts to a situation, that is, in the way he defines it in the course of his actions. Florian Znaniecki used the term to distinguish this from formal expressions of attitude. See ATTITUDE, IDEATIONAL; DEFINITION OF THE SITUATION.

attitude change, negative. An attitude change in a subject or subjects in a direction opposite to that sought or expected by the instigator of the change (for example, a propagandist or experimenter). This is sometimes referred to as the boomerang effect.

attitude change, positive. An attitude change in a subject or subjects in a direction desired or expected by the instigator of the change (for example, a propagandist or experimenter).

attitude cluster. Two or more attitudes held by an individual that are highly interrelated, support each other, and are distinct from his other attitudes. For example, attitudes concerning a given ethnic group may form an attitude cluster that is consistent in itself but unrelated to other attitudes, such as political persuasion. An attitude may be part of a cluster or may be held in relative isolation from other attitudes. A person usually has both attitude clusters and relatively isolated individual attitudes.

attitude scale. See SCALE, ATTITUDE.

attitudes, latent structure of. See LATENT STRUCTURE ANALYSIS; LAZARSFELD LATENT-DISTANCE MODEL.

attribute. 1. A CATEGORY of a qualitative VARIABLE. Thus, Christian, Jewish, Moslem, Buddhist, and Hindu would be attributes of the variable religion, and male and female would be attributes of the variable sex. See VARIATE.

2. The dominant CATEGORY of a dichotomous qualitative VARIABLE. The variable is stated in terms of the presence or absence of the attribute.

Thus, for example, religiosity would be the attribute measured by the dichotomy religious and not religious.

audience. 1. A number of persons subject to a common source of communication, but with minimal or no communication with each other. An audience may be an AGGREGATE in physical proximity, as in the case of an audience in a theater, or it may be widely dispersed, as in the case of a television audience. Similar responses of persons in an audience result from similar reactions to the same stimuli and not from agreement reached through interaction. It may be noted that the sociological usage of the term differs from the general usage in that a GROUP (as sociologically defined) listening to a speaker would not be considered an audience.

2. An AGGREGATE (persons in physical proximity) subject to a common source of communication.

See CROWD; MASS COMMUNICATION; PUBLIC.

authoritarian leadership. See LEADERSHIP, AUTHORITARIAN.

authoritarian personality. A personality type characterized by extreme conformity, rigidity, suppression of emotional feelings, submissiveness to authority, and arrogance toward those considered inferior. It is a basically insecure personality which seeks security in social hierarchies and in strong in-group identification, accompanied by the ethnocentric belief that the highest values are exclusively embodied in one's own group. The concept of the authoritarian personality has been used extensively in studies of prejudice, and findings that indicate that this personality type is highly prejudiced against out-groups have been used to explain prejudice, at least in part, in terms of the personality syndrome of the authoritarian personality.

The authoritarian personality is an abstract or IDEAL TYPE. Actual personalities may have various combinations of the elements of this ideal type, each element to a greater or lesser degree. The utility of this concept depends on the extent to which the elements comprising the authoritarian personality are found to be correlated under various circumstances and in a variety of cultural contexts.

authority. Power that is legitimized and institutionalized in a society or other social system. This form of power is attached to a social STATUS and is accepted as proper and legitimate by all members of the social system. Subordinates comply with the directives of those in authority because they accept their control as justified and proper. As a rule, authority inheres in the status itself and does not depend on the personal qualities of the occupant of the status. Systems of authority are particularly characteristic of formal organizations but positions of authority are also found in small groups. See AUTHORITY, CHARISMATIC; POWER.

authority, charismatic. AUTHORITY legitimized by the extraordinary characteristics of a leader and the inspired or sanctified nature of his mission. Authority is normally based on STATUS rather than on personal qualities, and charismatic authority is unique in that it depends on the ability of the leader to inspire devotion in his followers and manifest the "divine" or special nature of his mission. Although the concept of charisma comes from a religious source, charismatic authority is not necessarily religious in the traditional sense. The "divine" mission may be based on nationalism, and the leader regarded as the embodiment of the mysterious spirit of the people—for example, the authority of Hitler as *Führer* in Nazi Germany. Like all forms of authority, charismatic authority is institutionalized, although often much less securely than other forms of authority, and embedded in a formalized pattern of rules and behavior. Max Weber distinguished charismatic authority from traditional authority and legal authority. (R. Bendix, *Max Weber*, Doubleday, Garden City, N.Y., 1960.) See CHARISMA; CHARISMATIC LEADERSHIP.

authority, legal. Authority legitimized by a system of formal laws specifically enacted to regulate conduct rationally and achieve designated goals. Max Weber distinguished legal authority from traditional authority and charismatic authority. (R. Bendix, *Max Weber*, Doubleday, Garden City, N.Y., 1960.)

authority, professional. See PROFESSIONAL AUTHORITY.

authority, rationalistic. See AUTHORITY, LEGAL.

authority, traditional. Authority legitimized by the sanctity of tradition. Max Weber distinguished traditional authority from charismatic authority and legal authority. (R. Bendix, *Max Weber*, Doubleday, Garden City, N.Y., 1960.)

autism. See AUTISTIC THINKING.

autism, socially shared. A belief held by a social group that is perpetuated mainly because it is shared among the members of the group and satisfies certain needs, rather than because the belief has any objective validity. An example would be Muzafer Sherif's study of the AUTOKINETIC EFFECT, in which a group of subjects established a shared belief about the distance a light moved, and reinforced this belief among themselves, even though in fact the light was stationary. (M. Sherif, *The Psychology of Social Norms*, Harper, New York, 1936.) Another example of socially shared autism is found when the administrators of a large bureaucratic organization believe that the shortcomings of their organization are due to the "personality types" of their subordinates, who need only to be more efficiently "managed." This belief acts as a protective device that hides the role played by a failure of administration. Such socially shared autism often leads to arbitrary rules and pressures upon subordinates, entirely contrary to the real need for administrative reform, and also to a growing lack of communication, coordination, and harmony. Often those in power have a tendency to believe that most of the failures of their organization are due to their (powerless) subordinates, and that basically the individual and collective successes of their subordinates are due to the triumph of their administrative skills. The term *socially shared autism* was introduced by Gardner Murphy. See AUTISTIC THINKING.

autistic thinking. Highly subjective or individualistic thinking that is based on a withdrawal from reality into fantasy. It is a form of wishful thinking that protects the needs of the person's ego from frustrating situations. Autistic thinking is a symptom of schizophrenia, but it is also a common phenomenon among normal people, and especially children, for short periods of time. Normally, however, autism is limited by social interaction that involves constant social sanctioning for individuals who are not conforming to normative patterns of thought and behavior. Social sanctions tend to maintain common modes of thought and frames of reference in social groups and in human life in general. Autistic thinking is, of course, necessary for creativity and innovation and even beneficial as a temporary withdrawal from the pressures of some aspects of social and cultural realities. But in those areas of human behavior that are exposed to the examination of other human beings, conformity is an essential in order to make communication possible and to ensure order and stability in social groups and in the personality structure of individuals. Persons isolated from social interaction for long periods of time are less subject to social validation and normative corrections of autistic thinking, and thus such persons are prone to mental disorder. See CONSENSUAL VALIDATION.

autocracy. A form of government in which ultimate authority resides in one person (the autocrat) who occupies the top position in a hierarchy of power and from whom authority descends to the bottom of the hierarchy. The autocrat is not accountable for his decisions to his subordinates or his subjects. An autocracy can be an absolute monarchy or a dictatorship. The autocrat may gain his position through heredity, the seizure of power by military force or the threat of force, or manipulation within a bureaucratic organization (e.g., within a political party that controls the government in a one-party state). An autocracy may be, but is not necessarily, a totalitarian state. See TOTALITARIANISM.

autokinetic effect. An illusion of movement of a visual stimulus. For example, in a completely darkened room a stationary pinpoint of light will appear to move because there is no spatial frame of reference. Muzafer

Sherif has used this phenomenon to study experimentally the formation of group norms and their effect in creating shared perceptions about the direction of the movement of the objectively stationary point of light. (M. Sherif, *The Psychology of Social Norms*, Harper, New York, 1936.)

automation. The process of advanced mechanization in which complex machines perform tasks formerly performed by men, often replacing men who operated simpler machines. The development and use of sophisticated electronic and mechanical devices decreases the need for a wide variety of human labor, and machines may even be used to supervise and control other machines. Automation may permit greatly increased production at reduced cost per unit (bringing particularly great savings where labor costs are high or a labor shortage exists) and increased leisure time, but also may increase the problem of technological unemployment and the need for retraining of personnel.

autonomy. The ability of an individual to select personal values and to withstand social pressures for conformity in a given situation. An autonomous individual is able to act independently of the norms of an immediate group situation in favor of his own personal norms or convictions. See INNER-DIRECTED SOCIETY; OTHER-DIRECTED SOCIETY.

autonomy, functional. See FUNCTIONAL AUTONOMY.

average. A numerical value that is a central point about which other values in a series are dispersed. An average provides a single, summary measure of a distribution of numerical values. In statistical terms it is usually referred to as a measure of central tendency, for it summarizes in one value the central tendency of all the variations in a distribution taken as a whole. There are different types of averages, or different measures of central tendency, each of which may result in a different average value for the same series of values. See CENTRAL TENDENCY, MEASURE OF; see also the various entries listed under MEAN, ARITHMETIC; MEDIAN; and MODE.

average deviation. See MEAN DEVIATION.

avoidance relationship. An ETIQUETTE found in some societies, prescribing that interaction between certain relatives be either highly formalized or minimal. This sociocultural arrangement, with either partial or complete restriction of social interaction, may occur, for example, between son-in-law and mother-in-law.

avoidance rituals. Prescribed restrictions on behavior and formalized patterns of behavior that function to maintain social distance between persons. Avoidance rituals limit the degree of involvement of individuals in a social relationship, help to maintain a certain level of formality in the relationship, and preserve some degree of individual autonomy for the participants in the situation. Avoidance rituals are the basis of one of the two types of DEFERENCE BEHAVIOR distinguished by Erving Goffman. (E. Goffman, *American Anthropologist,* June 1956.) See PRESENTATIONAL RITUALS.

avunculate. An institutionalized social relationship in which an especially close tie exists between a mother's brother and her son, with authority over the son falling on the maternal uncle rather than upon the father. The uncle often transmits his property to his nephew rather than to his son. See AMITATE.

avunculocal residence. The custom that prescribes that a married couple reside with or in the locality of the husband's maternal uncle.

axiate hypothesis of urban growth. The hypothesis, proposed by Charles J. Galpin, that as cities grow outward from the center, growth tends to follow the highways and other major lines of transportation, thus forming a pattern similar to that of spokes radiating out from the axle of a wheel. Galpin emphasized the importance of commercial and industrial land use in urban growth. According to his hypothesis, commercial and industrial establishments steadily push residential land use farther and farther out along the main arteries of transportation, until finally residential land use starts to fill in the interstitial areas between the main lines of transportation, beginning in the area closer to the inner city. (C. J. Galpin, *Rural Life,* Century, New York, 1918.) See CONCENTRIC ZONE HYPOTHESIS, BURGESS'; ECOLOGY, HUMAN; SECTOR HYPOTHESIS.

axiom. A statement whose truth is either self-evident or so well established that it is unquestioned and universally accepted within a scientific discipline, or a statement true by definition (or assumption) within a logical system and used to derive other propositions.

axis. One of two perpendicular lines used in the construction of a graph. See COORDINATE AXES.

B

band. A territorially based community that is smaller than a tribe. It is the most elementary form of community and is often found among nomadic and seminomadic peoples. Its size is determined by the availability of grazing land or the availability of game and other food sources. Its social organization is relatively simple and its forms of SOCIAL CONTROL are informal.

band wagon technique. A PROPAGANDA device by which the purported acceptance of an idea, product, or the like by a large number of people is claimed in order to win further public acceptance.

bar chart. See BAR GRAPH.

bar diagram. See BAR GRAPH.

bar graph. A type of graphic presentation of data in which either horizontal or vertical bars are drawn to represent a distribution of cases. The bars are drawn to scale and represent proportionately the quantities being compared. The bar graph is most often used to portray the FREQUENCY DISTRIBUTION of a qualitative VARIABLE, with each bar representing a CATEGORY of the variable, its height or length indicating the number of cases in that category. Bar graphs are also used to portray TIME SERIES, with the height or length of each bar indicating the frequency or magnitude of the variable in each time period. They may also be used with quantitative variables, with the height or length indicating the number of cases in each CLASS INTERVAL. See FREQUENCY DISTRIBUTION CURVE; GRAPH; HISTOGRAM.

bar graph, divided. A BAR GRAPH in which the bars are divided into segments that show the number of cases in two or more subdivisions of each CATEGORY. For example, if the bars in a graph represented the categories of the variable marital status, each might be divided into two segments representing males and females, thus showing the proportion of each sex in each category as well as the total distribution of cases among the categories.

bargaining, collective. See COLLECTIVE BARGAINING.

bargaining power. See BILATERAL POWER RELATION.

barter. Trading by the direct exchange of goods, rather than by buying and selling with some type of money or medium of exchange. In simple societies it is often the only form of economic exchange.

base line. See ABSCISSA.

base map. A map that shows the location of important geographic and economic features of an area, and is used to plot the distribution of social phenomena, such as income levels. It is also called social base map.

beena marriage. See MARRIAGE, BEENA.

behavior. Any response or reaction of an individual, including not only bodily reactions and movements, but also verbal statements and subjective experiences. Although some writers have used the terms behavior and ACTION interchangeably, in the most widely accepted usage behavior is a broader term that applies to anything an individual does, says, thinks, or feels, regardless of whether it is purposive and meaningful to the individual. See BEHAVIORISM.

behavior, aberrant or **deviant.** See DEVIANCE.

behavior, abnormal. See ABNORMAL BEHAVIOR.

behavior, antisocial. See ANTISOCIAL BEHAVIOR.

behavior, collective. See COLLECTIVE BEHAVIOR.

behavior, conventional. See CONVENTIONAL BEHAVIOR.

behavior, covert. The behavior of an individual that is not directly observable by other people. Covert behavior, which includes feelings and thoughts, may be inferred from the individual's overt behavior or from his description of his experiences.

behavior, innate. See INNATE BEHAVIOR.

behavior, mass. See MASS BEHAVIOR.

behavior, overt. The readily observable behavior of an individual, as contrasted with covert behavior. See BEHAVIOR, COVERT.

behavior, rational. See RATIONAL BEHAVIOR.

behavior, role. See ROLE BEHAVIOR.

behavior, social. Behavior on the part of a person or persons that is in response to the behavior or expected reaction of other persons. The persons influencing the individual's behavior need not necessarily be physically present. Thus social behavior, while a response to other persons or groups, may or may not involve the physical presence of more than one person.

behavior mechanism. See DEFENSE MECHANISM.

behavior pattern. A relatively uniform and observable sequence of actions of either persons or groups in response to a given type of situation.

behavioral science. A scientific discipline that is concerned with the development of a body of principles that will contribute to the understanding of human behavior. Usually included among the behavioral sciences are sociology, psychology, cultural anthropology, and some aspects of economics and political science.

behaviorism. A school of psychology based upon the study of observable behavior. Behaviorism developed as an attempt to make psychology more objective and closer to the physical sciences. Its early development was strongly influenced by the work of John B. Watson. It rejected the use of concepts such as consciousness and will that could not be studied in terms of specific, observable behavior, and placed great emphasis upon OPERATIONAL DEFINITIONS. It also rejected the use of insight or subjective experience as nonscientific techniques in studying human behavior. The stimulus-response approach to learning became characteristic of most psychological behaviorists. Attempts were made to maximize the use of laboratory and experimental procedures. The more extreme behaviorists attempted to focus exclusively on overt behavior and eliminate all concepts referring to mental states (such as value, belief, or attitude) or to levels of abstraction beyond the individual (such as culture, social institution). Such extreme behaviorism is of course inherently rejected by sociologists. In modified form, behaviorism has had a great deal of influence on the development of sociology. See BEHAVIORISM, SOCIAL. See also CONDITIONED RESPONSE; VERSTEHEN, METHOD OF.

behaviorism, social. A theoretical position within sociology that views the individual and his interaction with other individuals as the basic unit of sociological analysis. Social behaviorism, however, is not atomistic since social concepts and generalizations on the group or societal level are definitely not rejected, but are regarded as valid and meaningful in so far as they are based upon the behavior of individuals. Social behaviorism embraces a variety of approaches including SYMBOLIC INTERACTIONISM and social action theory. See ACTION THEORY, SOCIAL.

belief. 1. A statement about reality that is accepted by an individual as true. A belief differs from a VALUE, in that while a value concerns what a person regards as good or desirable, a belief is a statement of what he regards as true and factual. A belief may be based upon empirical observation, logic, tradition, acceptance by others, or faith. Thus, it is possible to speak of scientific and nonscientific beliefs. Beliefs form the basic structure of the individual's conception of the world (his cognitive structure) and the framework within which his perceptions occur.

2. A statement about reality that is at least partially based on faith. In this sense, statements based totally upon empirical observations are not considered beliefs.

See ATTITUDE; OPINION.

bell-shaped curve. See FREQUENCY DISTRIBUTION CURVE, NORMAL.

belt graph. A type of segmented LINE GRAPH in which several line graphs, combined in a single chart, show the component elements being depicted as well as their total. The belt graph is the linear counterpart of the divided BAR GRAPH. It shows the distribution of the component parts individually and together. For example, a belt graph may show the distribution of several income categories over a period of years, with each belt of the graph showing the number of cases in each income category over the years, and all the belts combined indicating the total number of cases in the population during that period of years. See BAR GRAPH, DIVIDED.

beta error. See ERROR, BETA.

bias. 1. Systematic distortion occurring in the course of research which influences the outcome of the research, increasing the likelihood of one outcome rather than another. It may have its source in the selection of the sample to be studied, in the wording of the questions used in the study, in the appearance, attitudes, or methods of the interviewers, or in the analysis of the data. See SAMPLE, BIASED.

2. See PREJUDICE.

bias, theoretic. See THEORETIC BIAS.

biased sample. See SAMPLE, BIASED.

"big animal" theory of society. A theoretical model of society as essentially a biological organism. An example would be Thomas Hobbes' *Leviathan,* in which he conceptualized the state as a great artificial man or monster. See ORGANISM.

bilateral or **bilineal descent.** Descent or inheritance regarded as determined equally by the mother's and the father's line. One's mother's and one's father's relatives are accepted equally as kin. The culture determines which relatives (that is, how far removed or how wide a circle) are socially significant, but social significance extends to the same degree of relationship on the father's and mother's side. Bilateral descent is the custom in American society. See UNILATERAL or UNILINEAL DESCENT.

bilateral kinship system. See KINSHIP SYSTEM, BILATERAL.

bilateral power relationship. See POWER RELATIONSHIP, BILATERAL.

bilineal descent. See BILATERAL or BILINEAL DESCENT.

bilocal residence. A custom that allows married couples to have the choice of living with or in the locality of either the husband's or the wife's family. See MATRILOCAL RESIDENCE; PATRILOCAL RESIDENCE.

bimodal curve. See FREQUENCY DISTRIBUTION, BIMODAL.

binomial distribution. The theoretically expected distribution of a series of random samples drawn from a population with two categories or classes. A binomial distribution would show the theoretical frequency with which one would expect to obtain random samples with each of a series of proportions of cases in one of the two categories. For example, if 50 random samples were drawn from a population half male and half female, the binomial distribution could give the theoretically expected number of samples that would be all male, 90% male, 80% male, 70% male, etc. The binomial distribution is one of the important mathematical models used in statistics. See POISSON DISTRIBUTION; SAMPLE, RANDOM.

binomial test. A nonparametric statistical test that may be used when research data are divided into just two categories (e.g., male and female, favorable responses and unfavorable responses, over 21 years of age and under 21 years of age). The binomial test uses the BINOMIAL DISTRIBUTION to test whether the distribution of cases in the sample studied differs significantly from the distribution that would be expected if the sample were drawn randomly from a particular two-class population. It is a GOODNESS-OF-FIT TEST.

biogenic motive. An impulse to act that stems from the biological nature of the organism, for example impulses arising from hunger, thirst, or sex and uninfluenced by learning. Since the concept excludes social and cultural influences, it is rarely used in the analysis of social behavior, except perhaps with reference to infants or to an attempted theoretical distinction between hereditary and environmental factors in human behavior. In psychobiological research the concept, of course, has greater utility.

biological heritage. The sum total of the biological characteristics transmitted from parents to offspring. The term is used in contrast with *cultural heritage.* See CULTURE; HEREDITY.

biological imperative. An activity essential to the survival of an organism or the continued existence of its species. See CULTURAL IMPERATIVE; FUNCTIONAL REQUISITE.

biologism. The tendency to apply the theoretical framework of biology to the study of human behavior. The use of the term is usually disparaging, implying that another theoretical model (the social or psychological) would be more appropriate and fruitful.

biosocial. A term referring to those characteristics of an organism that result from the interaction of biological and social influences, e.g., sexual behavior.

biotic community. A hypothesized subsocial and nonrational aspect of human community. The term was taken from plant and animal ecology and applied to the study of human communities by Robert E. Park and other early human ecologists, who distinguished between a biotic level and a cultural level of human organization. The biotic level was regarded as subsocial, based on nonthoughtful adjustments made in the struggle for existence and reflected in the spatial distribution of persons and services. The cultural level, based on communication and consensus, was regarded as a superstructure resting on the biotic level. The biotic level was also referred to as "community" and the cultural level as "society." The study of the biotic community was considered the proper field for human ecology. The distinction between a biotic level and a cultural level of human organization came under severe attack in the late thirties and forties, and is no longer maintained by human ecologists. The term biotic community is seldom found in the writings of human ecologists today. (See G. A. Theodorson, *Studies in Human Ecology*, Harper and Row, New York, 1961.)

birth rate, crude. The number of live births per 1,000 persons in a population within a given period of time, usually one year. The formula for the crude birth rate is the number of live births in a population during a given year divided by the total population of the area or group at the midpoint of the year (July 1). This figure is then multiplied by 1,000 to yield a more manageable figure. The crude birth rate is often called simply the birth rate.

birth rate, differential. See FERTILITY, DIFFERENTIAL.

birth rate, nuptial. The number of live legitimate births in a population during a year period, divided by the number of married females of childbearing age (usually 15–44) in the population. This figure is then multiplied by 1,000.

birth rate, specific. The number of live births per 1,000 persons in any given category of a particular population. The most common specific birth rate is the age-sex specific rate, usually the number of births per 1,000 women of childbearing age (usually 15–44, but sometimes 20–44, 20–49, or 15–49) in the population. However, it is also possible to obtain the birth rate for any other category or combination of categories in a population. See FERTILITY RATE.

biserial correlation. See CORRELATION, BISERIAL.

bivariate data. Data in which there are two measurements for each item, for example, the income and years of education of each subject studied.

bivariate distribution. See FREQUENCY DISTRIBUTION, BIVARIATE.

blighted area. An urban district that is deteriorating economically and is characterized by a growing number of dilapidated buildings and a general decline in the upkeep of the area. Such a district is not considered to be beyond rehabilitation, but is on its way to becoming a SLUM. See ZONE IN TRANSITION.

blue collar worker. A manual worker, one whose work is primarily physical and dealing with things, rather than mental or social. The category includes skilled, semiskilled, and unskilled workers, and includes farm workers as well as factory workers, miners, construction workers, etc. The term is used to differentiate the manual worker from the WHITE COLLAR WORKER.

body-type theories. Schemes of classification that attempt to show a relationship between the physical structure of the body and the personality structure of the individual. Such theories have never been validated, and are generally rejected by sociologists today. See LOMBROSIAN THEORY; SHELDON'S BODY TYPES.

Bogardus social distance scale. A technique for scaling attitudes to measure the social-psychological distance between a person and various racial and nationality groups. The individual is given a series of graded categories and asked to indicate the closest social intimacy he would accept with each group: 1) exclude from my country, 2) admit only as a visitor to my country, 3) admit to citizenship, 4) admit to employment in my occupation, 5) admit to my school as a classmate, 6) admit to my street as a neighbor, 7) admit to my club as a chum, 8) admit to my family through marriage. (E. S. Bogardus, *Sociology and Social Research*, January–February 1933.)

bolshevism. A branch of Marxian COMMUNISM, developed in Russia under the leadership of Lenin, that gained control of the country in the Revolution of October (November by the Western calendar) 1917. The Bolsheviks emerged as the radical faction in a split in the Russian Social Democratic Labor Party in 1903. The name derives from the fact that the Bolsheviks received a majority of the votes for the Central Committee at the Party Congress, while the Mensheviks, a more moderate faction, received a minority. The Bolsheviks were concerned with the practical application of Marxism to their current situation, the development of a disciplined party organization, emphasis upon the indoctrination and leadership of the PROLETARIAT by a radical intelligentsia, and the seizure of power by revolution. An independent party named the Social Democratic Labor Party (Bolsheviks) was formed in 1912. In 1918 the name was changed to Communist Party (Bolsheviks). In 1952 the word Bolsheviks was dropped from the party name. See SOCIALISM; TOTALITARIANISM.

boomerang effect. See ATTITUDE CHANGE, NEGATIVE.

Bossard's law of family interaction. A principle stating that for every increase in the number of persons in a family there is more than a corresponding increase in the number of personal interrelationships. That is, with each additional person "the number of persons increases in the simplest arithmetical progression in whole numbers, while the number of personal interrelationships within the group increases in the order of triangular numbers." (H. S. Bossard, *American Journal of Sociology*, January 1945.)

bourgeoisie. The owners of the means of production and distribution in a capitalist society, ranging from wealthy capitalists to small shopowners. The term originally referred to the urban middle class which emerged in Europe in the late Middle Ages, as a class of businessmen distinct from the nobility and the peasantry, and sometimes is still used to refer to the middle class. However, after its use by Karl Marx and his followers, the term increasingly became associated with Marxian doctrine. Marx regarded the bourgeoisie as the class that controls capitalist societies and suppresses the working class or PROLETARIAT. It is the bourgeoisie that must be overthrown by the revolution of the proletariat in order to establish a socialist society. Marx distinguished between the grand bourgeoisie, or large-scale capitalists such as financiers, large industrialists, and large landowners, and the petit (or petty) bourgeoisie, or small shopkeepers. See COMMUNISM; DIALECTICAL MATERIALISM; SOCIALISM.

brachycephalic. Round-headed or broad-headed, with a CEPHALIC INDEX of 80 to 84.9, so that the skull is at least 80% as broad as it is long. See DOLICHOCEPHALIC; MESOCEPHALIC.

break-in-transportation hypothesis. A hypothesis of Charles H. Cooley stating that, with regard to the location of urban settlement, population and wealth tend to appear where there is a break in transportation or interruption in the flow of goods. Cities tend to develop where lines of transportation (such as roads, rivers, railroads) meet, where goods are stored, broken up into smaller units, loaded or unloaded, or transferred to other forms of transportation (from water to land transport, wagon to railroad, etc.). (C. H. Cooley, *Publication of the American Economic Association*, May 1894.) See CENTRAL PLACE THEORY.

building, density of. See DENSITY, BUILDING.

bureaucracy. 1. A large-scale, formal organization that is highly differentiated and efficiently organized by means of formal rules and departments or bureaus of highly trained experts whose activities are coordinated by a hierarchical chain of command. This type of organization is also characterized by a centralization of authority, and emphasis on discipline, rationality, technical knowledge, and impersonal procedures. Bureaucracy is an abstract, or IDEAL TYPE, which actual formal organizations may approach to varying degrees. Thus no formal organization is ever completely rational, efficient, and formalized in its organization and operation, but insofar as these ideals are dominant in practice, the organization is usually regarded as a bureaucracy. With the contemporary growth of a great many very large, formal secondary groups established to attain specific goals, bureaucracy has become the characteristic form of organization in many fields, including industrial corporations, labor unions, governmental agencies, schools, hospitals, and military organizations.

2. The administrative aspects of a formal organization, that is, the hierarchical apparatus of control, as distinguished from the formal organization itself, even as an IDEAL TYPE. Thus the workers in a factory, because they are not part of the administration, would not be considered part of the bureaucracy even though they are part of the formal organization.

bureaucrat, functional. See BUREAUCRATIC TYPES.

bureaucrat, job. See BUREAUCRATIC TYPES.

bureaucrat, service. See BUREAUCRATIC TYPES.

bureaucrat, specialist. See BUREAUCRATIC TYPES.

bureaucratic leader. See LEADER, BUREAUCRATIC.

bureaucratic types. Characteristic personality types within a bureaucracy differentiated by Leonard Reissman on the basis of their involvement in their professional group versus the bureaucracy. They are: the functional bureaucrat—oriented to a professional group; the specialist bureaucrat—also oriented to a professional group but has some identification with the bureaucracy; the service bureaucrat—somewhat oriented to a professional group but primarily obtains satisfaction by serving the bureaucracy; and the job bureaucrat—entirely immersed in the bureaucracy with his profession providing only the qualifications and skills for his job. (L. Reissman, *Social Forces,* March 1949.)

bureaucratization. The process in which a formal organization increasingly takes on the characteristics of a bureaucracy. A central aspect of this process is the formalization of rules and regulations. Bureaucratization may proceed to any degree for a given organization. See BUREAUCRACY.

Burgess' concentric zone hypothesis. See CONCENTRIC ZONE HYPOTHESIS, BURGESS'.

business cycle. Cyclical fluctuations in business activity, in which periods of depression or recession (contractions) alternate with periods of prosperity or INFLATION (expansions). The alternating high and low phases of the business cycle follow each other in regular succession, but do not follow any fixed pattern of duration or intensity. These changes in levels of production, employment, prices, and wages are not fully understood. See CYCLICAL MOVEMENT; DEFLATION; FLUCTUATION, PERIODIC.

business district. See CENTRAL BUSINESS DISTRICT.

business union. See UNION, BUSINESS.

C

calendrical rites. Ceremonies performed regularly according to the occurrence of predictable, natural events, such as the onset of a season, a special position of the moon or sun, or the like. Such seasonal ceremonies are distinguished from noncalendrical or CRISIS RITES that are performed in response to immediate group or personal anxieties or needs. See RITES DE PASSAGE.

calibration. The process of adjusting the units of a scale to conform to a standard series of values, usually in an attempt to obtain an INTERVAL SCALE.

canalization. The psychological process in which a generalized tension or need becomes attached to a specific object (or objects) as a source of satisfaction. During the process of SOCIALIZATION a child learns the culturally defined sources of satisfaction, and general needs are canalized to become specific needs. For example, hunger, which is at first a generalized need for any type of food, is canalized during socialization into a need for certain foods regarded as desirable in the individual's culture or subculture.

capacity. A biologically inherited, innate potentiality for learning within an individual. This psychological concept of assumed inherited differences in intelligence, aptitudes, etc., thus far has been of little value to sociologists because of the great difficulty of distinguishing inherited influences from social and cultural influences in accounting for variations in human personality and intelligence. See ABILITY; APTITUDE.

capital. Goods or other forms of wealth not needed for immediate consumption, which can be used to produce further capital or other goods or services.

capitalism. An economic system based upon the accumulation and investment of CAPITAL by private individuals who then become the owners of the means of production and distribution of goods and services. Capitalism is also characterized by economic motivation through private profit, competition, the determination of prices and wages primarily through supply and demand, an extensive system of credit, freedom of contract, and a free labor market. LAISSEZ-FAIRE capitalism has been severely modified by the rise of MONOPOLIES and OLIGOPOLIES, INSTITUTIONAL CAPITALISTS, government regulations, and labor unions.

capitalism, spirit of. See PROTESTANT ETHIC.

capitalist, institutional. See INSTITUTIONAL CAPITALIST.

card stacking. A PROPAGANDA technique in which an audience is presented with only those selected facts and arguments that support a particular position. Those facts and arguments that do not support, or that tend to weaken, the propagandist's position are ignored or suppressed.

cardinal scale. See RATIO SCALE.

career. A progression of related occupational roles through which a person moves during his working life. A career comprises a socially recognized patterned sequence of occupational roles, often with increasing prestige and rewards. Thus, individuals in a given occupation in a particular society tend to follow the same or one of a few standard patterns of role progression.

cargo cult. A religious movement that developed in New Guinea and surrounding islands, resulting in a great variety of similar cults. Cargo cults are based on the expectation that a great cargo ship (or in later cults, airplane) will be brought by the spirits of deceased ancestors, loaded with modern machines, tools, and other goods for the native population. With the aid of this cargo and the help of the spirits, the Europeans will be killed or driven out, and the native people will have the products and standard of living currently enjoyed by the Europeans. The cargo cults are classified as millennarian movements because they are directed toward a millennium, a day when a sudden supernatural event will occur that will radically change the members' lives. The cargo cults began to appear in the late nineteenth century, but became more widespread after World War I, particularly in the 1930's. See CULT; MILLENNARIAN MOVEMENT.

cartel. 1. An agreement among two or more business organizations to limit competition among themselves in certain specified ways, such as limiting production, fixing prices, establishing a geographic marketing area for each, and so forth. The members of a cartel retain their organizational independence, and do not merge. Companies forming a cartel may be from the same or different nations.

2. An agreement among two or more independent business organiza-

tions from at least two different nations to limit competition in specified ways. In the first usage, given above, this would be referred to as an international cartel.

case history. An intensive study of an individual's life from his earliest childhood years to the present. Case histories may be compiled in a variety of ways, including the use of autobiographies, letters, diaries, legal documents, and interviews with the individual and/or with others who know him. Case histories are used to understand the behavior of a person and to shed light on the character of particular social statuses and roles, career patterns, social groups, and the like. Case history is a more limited term than *case study*. The case history technique when used by itself is one type of case study; however, it may also be used along with other techniques as part of a larger case study. See CASE STUDY METHOD.

case study method. A method of studying social phenomena through the thorough analysis of an individual case. The case may be a person, a group, an episode, a process, a community, a society, or any other unit of social life. All data relevant to the case are gathered, and all available data are organized in terms of the case. The case study method gives a unitary character to the data being studied by interrelating a variety of facts to a single case. It also provides an opportunity for the intensive analysis of many specific details that are often overlooked with other methods. This approach rests on the assumption that the case being studied is typical of cases of a certain type, so that through intensive analysis generalizations may be made which will be applicable to other cases of the same type.

caste. 1. A closed social stratum based on heredity that determines its members' prestige, occupation, place of residence, and social relationships. The castes of a society form a hierarchy of superior-subordinate ranks and relationships that is justified by religion, law, and magic. Each caste is endogamous, and social relations between members of different castes are severely limited and formalized. There are some who prefer to restrict the term to refer only to the traditional system of stratification in India.

2. Any rigid system of social stratification based on heredity. When the caste system is regarded as an abstract or IDEAL TYPE to which actual societies correspond to a greater or lesser degree, then many societies are seen as having castelike elements. W. Lloyd Warner, for example, considered the relations between whites and Negroes in the South as castelike.
See STRATIFICATION, SOCIAL.

categorical attitude. The tendency, characteristic of all human thought and inherent in the use of language, to classify objects and events into categories. The categorical attitude enables man to see similarities in separate objects, to group objects into types, to name these types, and to generalize. Thus man never reacts to an object or event in isolation, but rather as part of a total system of classification. This attitude is basic to man's use of SYMBOLS and makes possible his abstract manipulation of his environment. See ABSTRACTION; STEREOTYPE.

categorical contact. Contact between individuals solely on the basis of the social category or group membership of each. See SECONDARY RELATIONS; SPECIFICITY.

categorization. See CATEGORICAL ATTITUDE.

category. 1. A concept used for the purpose of classification. See CATEGORICAL ATTITUDE.

2. In statistics, a subdivision of a VARIABLE used in classifying data. Usually the term is limited to the subdivisions of a qualitative variable, although sometimes it is also used to refer to the class intervals of a quantitative variable. See CLASS INTERVAL; VARIABLE, QUALITATIVE; VARIABLE, QUANTITATIVE.

category, social. See SOCIAL CATEGORY.

catharsis. The process of reducing anxiety or emotional conflict by the release of emotions through the verbalization or acting out of frustrations.

cathexis. A positive or negative emotional response to an object (a person, a group, a thing, a situation). A positive cathexis is an emotional attraction to an object. The object is desired by the individual, and he is motivated to try to attain it. A negative cathexis is an emotional repulsion from an object, and the individual is motivated to try to avoid it. The term was originally used by Sigmund Freud, who sought to make an analogy between an electric charge and an individual's attachment of psychic energy to an object.

causal explanation. See CAUSE; CAUSATION.

causal system. See CAUSATION.

causation. The concept that the occurrence of events is determined by cause and effect relationships. Causation assumes that events do not occur in a random fashion nor are they associated with each other in a two-way (symmetrical) relationship. The assumption of causation is that events are associated in a one-way (asymmetrical) relationship so that the occurrence of one leads to the occurrence of the other. If the principle of causation is accepted, the function of science is then seen as uncovering laws of cause and effect relationships. See CAUSE; LAW, SCIENTIFIC; RELATIONSHIP, SYMMETRICAL.

causation, cumulative. See CUMULATION, PRINCIPLE OF.

causation, multiple. The ascription of more than one possible cause to a given event. In sociology multiple causation assumes that one cannot attribute a single cause to any behavior or complex of behaviors or to any aspect of a sociocultural system because of the complex configuration of conditions under which social phenomena occur. Multiple causation may mean either that several causes in combination bring about a given effect or that any one of several causes may bring about the effect. See CAUSE.

causation, social. The concept that social behavior and social patterns are subject to causal laws and can be explained in terms of cause and effect. See CAUSATION.

cause. An event (or events) that precedes and results in the occurrence of another event. Whenever the first event (the cause) occurs, the second event (the effect) necessarily or inevitably follows. Moreover, in simple causation the second event does not occur unless the first event has occurred. Thus the cause is both the SUFFICIENT CONDITION and the NECESSARY CONDITION for the occurrence of the effect. However, with the conception of MULTIPLE CAUSATION, various possible causes may be seen for a given event, any one of which may be a sufficient but not necessary condition for the occurrence of the effect, or a necessary but not sufficient condition. In the case of multiple causation, then, the given effect may occur in the absence of all but one of the possible sufficient but not necessary causes; and, conversely, the given effect would not follow the occurrence of some but not all of the various necessary but not sufficient causes. See CAUSATION.

cause, effective. The immediate cause of an event. When a sequence of events occurs that may be regarded as a linked chain of causes, each resulting in the following event, the effective cause of any given event is the event immediately preceding it.

cell. In a STATISTICAL TABLE, the place for each entry of data. The cells provide for all the possible combinations of the rows and columns of the table.

cenogamy. A rare form of marriage in which two or more men are married to two or more women.

censorship. The arbitrary regulation or control of the communication of ideas and information by individuals or groups in positions of POWER or AUTHORITY.

census. The enumeration and collection of information about a population. Usually the term refers to a complete count of all persons in the population being studied. However, the U.S. Census Report, originally collected to fulfill the United States constitutional requirement of arranging for the apportionment of members of the House of Representatives, takes both a total enumeration of the population and a sampling of the total population for additional information considered essential for planning in government, business, and other spheres of activity in a complex society.

census, de facto. An enumeration of a population according to the actual location of people at the moment they were counted. This is opposed to a *de jure* census, which is "an allocation according to where the people normally or legally belong. The *de facto* census, favored by Great Britain, records all 'warm bodies' wherever they are found, whether their presence in that place be permanent or temporary. It has the advantage of providing a literal accounting of the populace exactly where they are at a given moment, without the sometimes arbitrary reallocation of people temporarily away from home. Its disadvantage is that population figures may be inflated or deflated by tourists, traveling salesmen and other transients. . . . United States census officials have traditionally used the *de jure* scheme." (R. Thomlinson, *Population Dynamics,* Random House, New York, 1965.)

census, de jure. See CENSUS, DE FACTO.

census tract. A small subdivision of a city or metropolitan area devised to facilitate the tabulation and analysis of census data. In the United States, cities, and often adjacent areas, are divided into census tracts by the Census Bureau in cooperation with the local community. Usually a census tract has a population between 3,000 and 6,000. Census tracts are used both for statistical research and for local administrative purposes.

centile point. See PERCENTILE.

central business district. The central retail shopping area and dominant commercial district of a city. This is the first or inner zone of Ernest W. Burgess' five concentric urban zones. Sometimes referred to as the downtown business district, it is the ecological center of large American cities—the area of highest land values and greatest accessibility, where communication and transportation lines converge. Railroad stations, hotels, department stores, theaters, banks, etc., are concentrated here. Except for hotel transients, few people reside in this district. It is densely populated only during the working hours of the day. See CONCENTRIC ZONE HYPOTHESIS, BURGESS'; ECOLOGY, HUMAN.

central limit theorem. A statistical theorem stating that the SAMPLING DISTRIBUTION of a mean approaches the normal distribution as the number of random samples becomes very large, even if the values that comprise the sample means and the population from which the random samples are drawn do not form a normal distribution. See FREQUENCY DISTRIBUTION CURVE, NORMAL.

central place theory. A geographical and ecological theory that explains the distribution of urban sites in terms of the functions cities perform for the rural areas surrounding them. According to this theory, urban sites are central places that evolve as service centers for the surrounding countryside. The larger the city the larger is its tributary area. Hypothetically, one could draw a circle to indicate the rural area that serves and is served by each city.

central position. See CENTRAL TENDENCY, MEASURE OF.

central tendency, measure of. Any of various statistical measures used to obtain a single number that is considered the most representative value of a series of data. Commonly referred to as an AVERAGE, this number is the central point in the frequency distribution of a single variable about which the other values are distributed. The center of the distribution may vary according to the particular measure of central tendency used—the mean, MEDIAN, or MODE. See the entries beginning with MEAN.

centralization. 1. An ecological process in which services tend to cluster in a limited area, usually at a focal point of lines of transportation and communication. The term refers to the tendency for retail businesses, banks, factories, recreational, health, and educational centers, and other types of service facilities to congregate in a central and readily accessible section of an urban area, such as the CENTRAL BUSINESS DISTRICT. In the technical, ecological usage the term refers to the clustering of services only and not to residences. See CONCENTRATION; DECENTRALIZATION.

2. The clustering of either services or residences. In this usage no distinction is made between centralization and CONCENTRATION.

centrogram. A map in which statistical techniques are used to present various aspects of the spatial distribution of a population or community. The technique most commonly used in centrograms is the computation of the mean center, usually the mean population center or the point about which the population of a designated area is equally distributed in all directions. Other types of centrograms may be based on other types of central points (for example, median center), on proportionate dividing lines (such as quartilides dividing the population of an area into quarters), or on isopleths (lines showing the distribution of rates or magnitudes, used in ISOMETRIC MAPS). A centrogram may also show changes in a population distribution over a period of time. The study of the application of statistics to cartography, that is, the construction of centrograms, is sometimes referred to as centrography. The terms centrogram and centrography were first introduced by the Mendelew Centrographical Laboratory in Leningrad.

cephalic index. A measurement of head type used by physical anthropologists in the attempt to classify the races and subraces of mankind. Maximum head width is divided by maximum head length and multiplied by 100. The more broad-headed a person is, the higher will be his cephalic index. See BRACHYCEPHALIC; DOLICHOCEPHALIC; MESOCEPHALIC.

ceremonial coyness. A rule of behavior that prescribes a degree of symbolic reluctance or modesty in certain sociocultural situations. Brides often are expected to exhibit such a response.

ceremony. A formal, established sequence of behavior that symbolically expresses the importance of a particular event, occasion, or belief. Ceremonies are usually celebrated collectively and function to reinforce for the participants the sanctity and special meaning of the event being celebrated. Ceremonies may also function to strengthen group cohesiveness. Ceremony is usually distinguished from RITUAL in two respects. First, in the most accepted usage, a ceremony is regarded as necessarily social and involving the participation of more than one person, whereas a ritual may be either collective or individual. A single individual may perform a private ritual, but not a ceremony. Second, the term ceremony usually implies a more elaborate sequence of behavior than a ritual, and usually consists of a standardized series of ritual acts. Marriage, graduation, the inauguration of government officials, church services, and group initiations are examples of ceremonies.

chance factors. Varied and unknown factors, regarded as irrelevant to a given study, that influence the outcome of the study to some extent but not in a way or degree considered significant. It is never possible to control or even to know all the factors that may influence a given outcome. Thus, for example, it is not possible to have a SAMPLE that is perfectly representative of the POPULATION from which it was drawn, nor is it usually possible to know precisely all of the minute ways in which the sample differs from the population. Therefore, if a random sample of a population is measured in a certain way, the measurement obtained will not be exactly the same as if the entire population had been measured, nor will two random samples from the same population yield precisely the same measurement. These variations among samples or between a sample and a population, if they are small, are considered insignificant. See PROBABILITY; SAMPLE, RANDOM; SIGNIFICANCE, STATISTICAL.

chance variation. Differences among samples from the same population that are due to CHANCE FACTORS.

change, cultural. See CULTURE CHANGE.

change, cyclical. See CYCLICAL MOVEMENT.

change, rate of. See RATE OF CHANGE.

change, social. See SOCIAL CHANGE.

change, telic. See TELIC CHANGE.

Chapin social status scale. A RATING SCALE devised by F. S. Chapin to measure a family's socioeconomic status primarily on the basis of the material equipment of their living room. The scale (as revised in 1933) lists seventeen items, for each of which a specified plus or minus score is given. For example, eight points are added for a fireplace with three or more utensils and two points are subtracted if there is a sewing machine in the living room. Points also are added for subscriptions to newspapers and periodicals. In the second part of the scale the condition of the living room is rated and points are added or subtracted for cleanliness, orderliness, etc. A total score is obtained for each home rated, and mean scores may then be found for groupings based on occupation and other measures of socioeconomic status. (F. S. Chapin, *Contemporary American Institutions,* Harper, New York, 1935.) Louis Guttman has presented a revised weighting of the items in the Chapin scale based on a FACTOR ANALYSIS of the items (*American Sociological Review,* June 1942).

character. 1. A relatively enduring and consistent pattern of values, attitudes, and behavior of an individual that conforms to and is based on the values and the norms, especially the mores, of a group with which he identifies. Thus, in this sense, character is essentially regarded as the moral and ethical aspect of personality, as determined by the moral standards of one's group. This term, however, is not often used in a technical sense by sociologists.

2. In psychological usage, PERSONALITY. The term "character structure" is also used with this meaning.

character, national. See NATIONAL CHARACTER.

charisma. A mystical quality of personality that makes an individual seem to possess certain extraordinary (often superhuman or supernatural) abilities and advantages. Max Weber borrowed this term, literally meaning "gift of grace," from the Christian concept of special power inherent in the priesthood. See AUTHORITY, CHARISMATIC; CHARISMATIC LEADERSHIP.

charismatic authority. See AUTHORITY, CHARISMATIC.

charismatic leadership. A type of leadership that is based primarily on the heroic, sacred, or other compelling personality characteristic of the leader, rather than upon official position, whether attained or inherited. Joan of Arc, for example, was a charismatic leader. A charismatic leader may or may not hold a position of authority in a formal organization. Jesus and Buddha, for example, were charismatic religious leaders, neither holding a formal position in a hierarchy. See CHARISMA.

chart. An arrangement of numerical data in graphic or pictorial form. See GRAPH.

childhood. The period of life from birth to adulthood. The duration of childhood varies from one culture to another. In some cultures childhood is considered ended at PUBERTY, in others at marriage, in still others at some arbitrary age. In the United States legal definitions usually place the end of childhood at 18 or 21 years of age.

chi-square test. A statistical test used to determine the probability of differences between observed and theoretical, or expected, frequencies being due only to chance or being large enough to be statistically significant. The chi-square test may be used with one sample, in which instance it is a GOODNESS-OF-FIT TEST. More often it is used with two or more samples to determine if the samples differ significantly in the relative frequency of cases in each of a series of (two or more) categories. The actual number of cases in each category for each sample is compared with the number that would be expected on the basis of the marginal totals (the sums for each variable and each sample) alone, that is, if there were no real difference among the samples. If the size of the samples is small, resulting in table entries of five or less, Yates' correction for continuity is used. This correction involves subtracting .5 from each difference between observed and expected frequencies, thus reducing the size of the differences. While the chi-square test is usually regarded as a nonparametric test, some writers maintain that it actually is parametric because the use of the observed marginal totals often implies certain parametric assumptions. See NON-PARAMETRIC STATISTICS; PARAMETRIC STATISTICS; PROBABILITY; SIGNIFICANCE, STATISTICAL.

choice-status. A sociometric term referring to the position of an individual in a group or community based on the number of positive and negative choices he receives in a SOCIOMETRIC TEST. See SOCIOMETRY.

choropleth map. A map in which geographical subdivisions (regions, districts, census tracts, etc.) are shaded in various degrees from white to black to indicate relative frequencies, densities, or rates of a specified phenomenon, such as a certain type of crime. A darker shading indicates a greater relative frequency. This kind of map is also referred to as a shaded map. See also CROSS-HATCHED MAP.

church. A formal organization serving as a channel or focal point for religious activity. It may be regarded as the organizational manifestation of religion, or the RELIGIOUS INSTITUTION. As a formal organization it has a system of authority, explicitly stated values and goals, and regulations governing the qualifications for membership and the rights and obligations of its members. A church also is characterized by a set of beliefs, a system of interrelated roles, a system of social norms, certain rituals and ceremonies, and buildings or meeting places. National or international churches are secondary groups comprised of local units, which may be either secondary groups themselves, as in the case of a large urban church, or primary groups, as in the case of a small rural church. See CHURCH-SECT TYPOLOGY; GROUP, PRIMARY; GROUP, SECONDARY.

church-sect typology. A TYPOLOGY, or schema for differentiating types, formulated by Ernst Troeltsch, that distinguishes between two generalized or ideal types of religious organization—church and sect. It has been widely used in the classification and analysis of religious groups. Basically, church, as opposed to sect, is defined as a religious organization that accepts the social structure and the secular culture in which it exists. It is integrated into society, and is conservative and respectable. It seeks to influence the secular world through the existing order. Its religious practice is formalized and traditional, and membership is largely through birth. In contrast, sect is defined as a religious group that rejects much of the secular society and culture in which it exists. Its members, usually drawn from the lower classes, do not try to influence the existing social order, but rather withdraw from it and seek to carry out their religious beliefs in their own lives in a literal and radical manner. In a sect emphasis is placed on the active participation and involvement of all members, and membership is frequently by conversion. The distinction between clergy and laity is not emphasized, and often the clergy are not full-time professionals. The typology has been criticized, and various modifications have been proposed. Critics maintain that the various elements comprising each type are not inherently interrelated or necessarily correlated. However, many sociologists have found the typology useful in studying religious groups. See CULT; DENOMINATION; ECCLESIA; SECT.

circle graph or chart. See PIE CHART.

circular interaction or **reaction.** A type of interaction in which two or more individuals continuously reinforce a given type of response in each other. The reaction of one individual elicits a response in the other individual that in turn reinforces the original reaction of the first individual, and so on.

city. A dense concentration of people settled in a relatively small geographic area and engaged in nonagricultural pursuits. The activities of a city's population are specialized and functionally interrelated, and governed by a formalized political system. A functional definition of city would focus on the predominance of nonagricultural activities (e.g., manufacturing, commerce, administration, education) among the inhabitants. By legal definition, a city is a place incorporated or granted a charter and proclaimed a city by a higher political authority. Census definitions of a city are usually based on a minimum population, for example, 2,500 in the United States, 2,000 in France, 11,000 in Egypt, 30,000 in Japan. Some ecological studies define a city by a minimum population density per square mile. See METROPOLIS; URBAN PLACE.

city, commerical. A CITY with little manufacturing, especially of durable goods, that serves primarily as a center for the distribution and exchange of economic goods and the provision of related services.

city, dormitory. See CITY, RESIDENTIAL.

city, industrial. A CITY that serves predominantly as a manufacturing or mining center. Industrial cities usually are small, with one or two dominant industries. Although the industrial city does provide retail and other services for its inhabitants and a limited surrounding area, its location or other factors inhibit it from serving as an important commercial or financial center. Frequently the industries are branches of larger companies that have their headquarters and carry on their major commercial and financial operations elsewhere.

city, inner. See INNER CITY.

city, metropolitan. See METROPOLIS.

city, nucleated. A city with one dominant commercial center on which the major lines of transportation and communication converge, and about which the rest of the city is organized and oriented. Chicago is an example of a nucleated city. See CITY, POLYNUCLEATED.

city, overbounded. A city whose political limits extend beyond the area of urban settlement, thereby including within the city limits an area that is rural in character. In most industrial countries, cities are usually underbounded rather than overbounded. See CITY, UNDERBOUNDED.

city, polynucleated. A city that does not have a single dominant commercial center but is instead divided into sections, each with its own commercial center and pattern of ecological organization. Peking is an example of a polynucleated city. See CITY, NUCLEATED.

city, residential. A city that is primarily a residential suburb of a larger city. The residential city is economically dependent on the larger central city, which provides employment for many of its inhabitants. The residential city thus lacks the economic base of other cities of the same size that are not part of a metropolitan HINTERLAND. See CITY, SATELLITE; SUBURB, RESIDENTIAL.

city, satellite. A city located near a larger city, and part of its METROPOLITAN AREA, but not totally dependent on it for employment. The satellite city has industry or other sources of employment for its inhabitants as well as for others in the metropolitan area. See CITY, RESIDENTIAL; SUBURB, EMPLOYING.

city, underbounded. A city that includes within its political boundaries only a portion of the area of urban settlement. The underbounded city is surrounded by an urban area with which it forms one economic and ecological unit. A central city in a METROPOLITAN AREA is an underbounded city. In most industrial countries cities are usually underbounded. See CITY, OVERBOUNDED.

city government. See COMMISSION PLAN OF CITY GOVERNMENT; COUNCIL-MANAGER PLAN OF CITY GOVERNMENT; MAYOR-COUNCIL PLAN OF CITY GOVERNMENT.

city land use, multiple nuclei pattern of. See MULTIPLE NUCLEI PATTERN.

city-manager form of municipal government. See COUNCIL-MANAGER PLAN OF CITY GOVERNMENT.

city planning. See PLANNING, URBAN SOCIAL.

city-state. A city that is an independent STATE, and not subordinate to any larger political unit. The jurisdiction of a city-state typically extends beyond the city to include smaller cities, villages, and rural areas in a band of territory surrounding the city. Examples of city-states are ancient Athens and Sparta, and, in the late Middle Ages, Venice and Genoa.

civil law. 1. Most often used in contrast to CRIMINAL LAW, to refer to laws dealing with property disputes between persons or groups.
2. Sometimes used to refer to Roman law, in contrast to English common law or the common law of other nations.
3. In earlier usage, secular law or the law of the state or municipality in contrast to canon law or natural or divine law.

civil liberties. Rights recognized as properly belonging to all individuals in a society that has a formal legal system. While civil liberties are subject to specified limits, usually justified in terms of the common good or the rights of others, they are considered not subject to arbitrary denial by other persons or the state. Some usage defines civil liberties primarily in terms of the rights of individuals in relation to the state.

civilization. 1. Generally refers to a highly complex, as contrasted with a relatively simple, culture. The term "advanced" is sometimes substituted for complex. Some writers consider the possession of writing, the existence of cities, a complex division of labor, advanced technology, and "advanced" states of political, religious, philosophical, and artistic institutions as indicators of civilization.
2. A culture that has developed writing, domesticated animals, and formed a stable, settled agricultural complex.
3. Some writers, such as Arnold Toynbee, define civilization in terms of the institutionalization of a system of ethical and religious traditions and ideologies that dominates a society or a number of related societies. An example would be Western civilization.

civilization, preindustrial. A civilization, such as that of ancient Athens or Rome, or nineteenth-century China or India, having a highly advanced and sophisticated level of artistic, literary, philosophical, and technological development, but in which urban life has not developed the characteristic qualities of modern urban industrial society. See INDUSTRIAL REVOLUTION.

clan. 1. A unilateral kin group, based on either matrilineal or patrilineal descent. The members of a clan believe they are descended from a common ancestor through the culturally accepted line of descent (matrilineal or patrilineal). Whether or not they in fact share a common biological ancestor, all members of a clan believe that they do. Clans usually practice EXOGAMY and frequently have religious, political, economic, and other functions.

2. A matrilineal descent group. When clan is defined in this way, the term SIB would be used for the group defined in 1. above, and thus a clan would be a matrilineal sib.

3. A kin group that not only claims unilateral descent but also practices UNILOCAL RESIDENCE.

See GENS; UNILATERAL DESCENT.

class. See CATEGORY; SOCIAL CLASS.

class, closed. See CLOSED-CLASS SYSTEM.

class, economic. A stratum of society that has been differentiated from other strata on the basis of economic factors. An economic class is comprised of persons who have a similar level and source of income and type of occupation, and a similar share of societal wealth and economic and occupational power and authority. See SOCIAL CLASS; SOCIOECONOMIC STATUS.

class, lower. See LOWER CLASS.

class, middle. See MIDDLE CLASS.

class, open. See OPEN-CLASS IDEOLOGY; OPEN-CLASS SYSTEM.

class, political. SOCIAL CLASS defined primarily in terms of degree of influence or control over the political organization of a society.

class, social. See SOCIAL CLASS.

class, socioeconomic. See SOCIAL CLASS; SOCIOECONOMIC STATUS.

class, statistical. See CLASS INTERVAL.

class, status. SOCIAL CLASS defined in terms of hierarchical status or prestige. A status class consists of persons who have a similar level of prestige symbols in a society. The prestige symbols may be based on style of life, type of occupation, social activities, ethnic or family background, or other factors considered significant in a particular society. Status class really represents a way of looking at, or one approach to, social class.

class, upper. See UPPER CLASS.

class, working. See WORKING CLASS.

class conflict. See CLASS STRUGGLE.

class consciousness. Awareness of belonging to and identification with a given SOCIAL CLASS, accompanied by a feeling of some degree of solidarity with other persons of the same class, and the feeling that one's personal interests are dependent upon the position and attainments of the social class as a whole. Werner S. Landecker distinguished three major aspects of class consciousness: CLASS-STATUS CONSCIOUSNESS, CLASS-STRUC-TURE CONSCIOUSNESS, and CLASS-INTEREST CONSCIOUSNESS.

class consciousness, false. Identification with a social class to which one does not belong. The individual supports policies and class interests that are not in accordance with his objective self-interests.

class crystallization. The coinciding of various criteria of social rank in a society to form a system of social classes. When there is a high degree of class crystallization, persons who have a high rank on one criterion also rank high on other criteria (such as income, occupation, education, family lineage, style of life, and so forth). Social classes then are fairly distinct, and there is a minimum of overlap among the separate classes. When class crystallization is low, various criteria of social rank contradict each other and class lines are blurred. See SOCIAL CLASS.

class frequency. In statistics, the number of occurrences in a given CLASS INTERVAL of a VARIABLE. For example, if the variable were age, and 115 respondents were in the class interval 20 through 24 years of age, the class frequency would be 115. See FREQUENCY DISTRIBUTION.

class identification. See CLASS CONSCIOUSNESS.

class-interest consciousness. A type of CLASS CONSCIOUSNESS distin-guished by Werner S. Landecker that is characterized by an awareness of class structure coupled with a sense that each class tends to act in its own interest. "By 'class interest consciousness' we mean a series of beliefs, ranging from an identification of personal interests with class interests and a distinction between the interests of different classes to the extreme view that class conflict is the necessary result of conflicting class interests." (W. S. Landecker, *American Sociological Review*, April 1963.) See CLASS-STATUS CONSCIOUSNESS; CLASS-STRUCTURE CONSCIOUSNESS.

class interval. An arbitrary, convenient subdivision of a quantitative VARIABLE. The total RANGE of the variable is divided into class intervals, preferably equal in size. Both continuous and discrete variables are so divided to facilitate analysis. For example, for the continuous variable weight, ranging in a given sample from 101 pounds to 200 pounds, the intervals might be 10 pounds and there would be ten class intervals; the first class interval would then be 101 pounds through 110 pounds. For the discrete variable group size, the interval might be 5, and the first class interval would then be 2 through 6 members. Class intervals are used in presenting the FREQUENCY DISTRIBUTION of a quantitative variable. See CATEGORY; VARIABLE, CONTINUOUS; VARIABLE, DISCRETE.

class law. A law that benefits the upper class and is detrimental to the interests of the majority of the members of a society.

class society. A society in which there is a sharp differentiation of social classes with a high degree of CLASS CRYSTALLIZATION. In a class society, each class is characterized by certain distinctive attitudes, values, and other cultural characteristics, thus forming a subculture within the larger culture of the society as a whole.

class-status consciousness. A type of CLASS CONSCIOUSNESS distinguished by Werner S. Landecker that is characterized by a strong identification with one's own class. "The 'class status consciousness' of a person has as its object his actual position in a class system and his relationship to others who share that position. This type of class consciousness includes a person's self-identification with a particular class, if corroborated by some kind of reality check; a preference for members of one's own class as friends and leisuretime associates . . . , manifestations of allegiance to one's class . . . , and conceptions of one's class as a local, regional, or national entity . . . , or as cutting across national boundaries." (W. S. Landecker, *American Sociological Review*, April 1963.) See CLASS-INTEREST CONSCIOUSNESS; CLASS-STRUCTURE CONSCIOUSNESS.

class-structure consciousness. A type of CLASS CONSCIOUSNESS distinguished by Werner S. Landecker that is characterized by a general awareness of the structure of social classes in one's society. "'Class structure consciousness' has as many facets as does class structure itself. Questions as to whether there are different classes in a given community or society, asked in a number of opinion surveys, provide limited evidence of this kind. Other aspects of class structure consciousness are: a recognition of the class positions characteristic of various occupations . . . ; the belief that there are class barriers which keep some men of personal ability from getting ahead . . . ; knowing the location of boundary lines between different classes . . . ; a sense of class differences in power or privilege . . . ; and conceptions of class structure as a system of two, three or more strata." (W. S. Landecker, *American Sociological Review*, April 1963.) See CLASS-INTEREST CONSCIOUSNESS; CLASS-STATUS CONSCIOUSNESS.

class-structure hypothesis. The assumption that the hierarchically ordered statuses of a community or society tend to form relatively distinct major groupings which may be termed social classes. The analysis of a society in terms of social classes assumes that the various status rankings are relatively consistent with each other and that there are fairly clear-cut distinctions between the major hierarchical levels into which the status rankings fall. See STATUS-CONTINUUM HYPOTHESIS.

class struggle. An inevitable struggle between social classes resulting from their conflicting interests. The term is used in various types of CONFLICT THEORY (both Marxist and non-Marxist) and implies that the process of social stratification engenders potential or actual attempts on the part of whole social classes, or segments of them, to maintain or redistribute existing arrangements of power, wealth, and prestige. The terms *class struggle* and *class conflict* are often used interchangeably. The term is not widely used in American sociological theory.

classical economic theory. A body of economic theory developed primarily in England in the eighteenth and nineteenth centuries, and associated with such men as Adam Smith, David Ricardo, Thomas R. Malthus, John Stuart Mill, Jeremy Bentham, and others. It was based on the assumption that man's behavior is essentially rational and governed by the attempt to attain his self-interest. The classical economists generally supported the idea that the pursuit of self-interest by the individual members of society in a free economic system would lead to the greatest possible prosperity for the society. They therefore supported private property and individual economic freedom, and tended to favor the limiting of government interference in the economic realm to minimal and clearly necessary functions. See ECONOMIC MAN; LAISSEZ-FAIRE; LIBERALISM.

classification. 1. The process of arranging data into categories or class intervals to facilitate the comprehension and analysis of the data. See CATEGORY; CLASS INTERVAL; TABULATION.

2. See CATEGORICAL ATTITUDE.

classificatory scale. See NOMINAL SCALE.

classificatory kinship system. See KINSHIP TERMINOLOGY, CLASSIFICATORY.

classless society. 1. A society not divided into a hierarchy of social classes.

2. A society in which social classes are ill-defined, blurred, and overlapping. There is little CLASS CONSCIOUSNESS and a low degree of CLASS CRYSTALLIZATION. Criteria of social rank vary independently of each other, and quite commonly a person will have contradictory ranks according to differing criteria. There are no subcultures based on social class. See CLASS SOCIETY; SOCIAL CLASS.

cleavage. A process in which the interdependent subdivisions of a large group (frequently a formal organization) form subgroups, characterized by in-group loyalty and identification within each subgroup and rivalry and social distance among the subgroups.

climatic determinism. A theory of human behavior holding that climate is the most important causal factor determining patterns of human behavior and the structure of societies. Cultural differences are explained primarily in terms of adjustment to climatic conditions. An example would be the fallacy that temperate climates cause greater industriousness and lead to the development of higher levels of civilization. Because of the great variety of cultural forms that are found under any given set of climatic conditions and man's capacity to modify climatic influences through technology, climatic determinism is not accepted by sociologists today. See GEOGRAPHIC DETERMINISM.

climax, culture. See CULTURE CENTER.

climax stage. A hypothesized stage in the development of an urban area in which the ecological relationships within the area are in a state of equilibrium. This involves a stable set of relationships between a metropolitan center, or center of dominance, and its surrounding area, or HINTERLAND. The term climax stage was originally taken from plant ecology, where it meant a balance among the forms of vegetation in an area. It is used today primarily by writers with a more economics-oriented approach to human ecology. See DOMINANCE, ECOLOGICAL; ECOLOGY, HUMAN.

clinical psychology. See PSYCHOLOGY, CLINICAL.

clinical sociology. See SOCIOLOGY, CONCRETE.

clique. 1. A relatively small, informal, voluntary group (two persons or more), without a formal structure, based on mutual interests and usually friendship. The relationships among members of the clique are usually intimate and cooperative. The clique may or may not be formed from among the members of a larger group. Often cliques are composed of people from the same general social class. In such a case, the clique is the smallest unit of a social class.

2. A small, informal group existing within a larger, formal organization. The members of a clique share certain common interests that may be at variance with the structure or goals of the larger organization. The structure of social relationships within the clique is not part of and may to some extent run counter to the formal social structure of the organization.

closed-class system. A class system or society in which social class is based primarily on family status rather than on personal abilities and achievements. A closed-class system is usually contrasted with an OPEN-

CLASS SYSTEM. A closed-class system may be regarded as an intermediate form between an open-class system and a CASTE system (which has even less social mobility than a closed-class system). More often, however, a caste system is regarded as one form of a closed-class system. The ESTATE system is another form.

closed population. See POPULATION, CLOSED.

closed shop. A plant or enterprise that employs only union labor. See OPEN SHOP; UNION SHOP.

cluster sample. See SAMPLE, CLUSTER.

coalition. A temporary alliance of two or more groups or individuals for the purpose of limited cooperative activity.

Cochran Q test. A statistical test that is an extension of the McNEMAR TEST, and that is used with three or more matched samples to determine whether the samples differ significantly in the proportion of cases in each of two categories. It is a nonparametric statistical test. See NONPARAMETRIC STATISTICS; PROBABILITY; SIGNIFICANCE, STATISTICAL.

code. Any system of group standards (for example, beliefs, rules, laws) that tends to regulate and integrate the behavior of group members.

codification of the rules stage, Piaget's. The fourth and final of Jean Piaget's stages of a child's development in terms of the RULES OF THE GAME. In this stage, which appears at about the age of eleven to twelve, the child not only becomes familiar with all the details of the rules, but also gains an understanding of their logic that enables him to apply them to a wide variety of situations. (J. Piaget, *The Moral Judgment of the Child,* Harcourt, Brace, New York, 1932.)

coding. A research procedure in which the data collected (for example, by questionnaire) are prepared for counting and tabulation by classification and codification. Categories or classes are devised so that each observation (for example, each answer from a questionnaire) will fall into one or another of a predetermined set of categories. The raw data are transferred into symbols (usually numerical) and can then, for example, be transferred to punched cards and be rapidly processed with an electronic computer. Determining the categories to be used in the analysis of data prior to the collection of the data is called precoding.

coefficient. A summarizing measure that provides in one mathematical value information about the relationship between two (or more) variables. The most commonly used coefficient is the COEFFICIENT OF CORRELATION. See all entries under COEFFICIENT.

coefficient of alienation. A measure of the lack of relationship (or error) that exists between two variables with a CORRELATION of a given size. Symbolized by the letter k, it is obtained by the formula $\sqrt{1-r^2}$; that is, by taking the square root of 1 minus r^2 (r is the Pearson product-moment correlation). The higher the correlation between two variables, the lower will be the coefficient of alienation. If the coefficient of alienation is high, one can rely very little on predictions of the values of one variable from those of the other variable. The coefficient of alienation is used in obtaining the STANDARD ERROR OF ESTIMATE. See COEFFICIENT OF CORRELATION; CORRELATION, PEARSON PRODUCT-MOMENT; REGRESSION, STATISTICAL.

coefficient of concordance. See KENDALL COEFFICIENT OF CONCORDANCE W.

coefficient of contingency. See CONTINGENCY COEFFICIENT C.

coefficient of correlation. A summary measure of the degree and direction of relationship between two (or occasionally more) variables. It indicates in one numerical value the extent to which a change in one variable is associated with a corresponding change (in the same or the opposite direction) in the other variable. The correlation coefficient may range in size from 1 to −1. A plus value indicates a positive correlation, a minus value indicates a negative correlation. The higher the value (either positive or negative) of the coefficient (the closer to 1 or −1) the greater is the association between the variables. A coefficient of 0 indicates that there is no correlation between the variables; that is, their variations are totally independent of each other. There are various coefficients of correlation, each symbolized by a letter, which represent different types of correlation. See entries listed under CORRELATION.

coefficient of correlation, point biserial. See CORRELATION, BISERIAL.

coefficient of determination. A measure of the proportion of the variation of one quantitative variable that is associated with (or explained by) the variation of another quantitative variable in a linear relationship. The coefficient of determination, symbolized by r^2, is the square of the Pearson product-moment correlation coefficient, r. It may range from 0 to 1. Thus if r were −.7, r^2 would be .49, and this would mean that 49% of the variation of each variable could be accounted for by the other. See CORRELATION, LINEAR; CORRELATION, PEARSON PRODUCT-MOMENT; REGRESSION, LINEAR.

coefficient of regression. See REGRESSION COEFFICIENT.

coefficient of reliability. A COEFFICIENT OF CORRELATION that is used to judge the RELIABILITY of a measuring instrument such as a test or questionnaire. The reliability coefficient may be the COEFFICIENT OF CORRELATION between two administrations of a test to the same subjects, or between two forms of the same test administered to a group randomly divided into two parts, or between halves of a test. See SPEARMAN-BROWN FORMULA.

coefficient of reproducibility. See REPRODUCIBILITY COEFFICIENT.

coefficient of validity. The coefficient of correlation between a measuring device and an independent, accepted measure of the characteristic the device is supposed to measure. It is simply the coefficient obtained in correlating a measuring device with another measure in order to test the VALIDITY of the device.

coefficient of variability. See COEFFICIENT OF VARIATION.

coefficient of variation. A measure of statistical dispersion that expresses variation in terms of a value that is not dependent on the size of the units of a variable. For example, a low-income group may have as much or more variation in income as a high-income group, but if the STANDARD DEVIATION of each group were stated in dollars the standard deviation of the high income group would appear to be greater because of the higher income level of the group. By using the coefficient of variation, the degree of variation (or dispersion) of incomes in the two groups can be compared without regard to or interference from the difference in the income levels of the groups. The coefficient of variation, symbolized by V, is obtained by multiplying the standard deviation (σ) by 100 and then dividing by the arithmetic mean ($V = \frac{\sigma\ 100}{\bar{x}}$). It is sometimes referred to as the coefficient of relative variation (CRV) or the coefficient of variability. See DISPERSION, STATISTICAL.

coefficient, phi. See PHI COEFFICIENT.

coercion. See FORCE.

cognate. A blood relative through the mother's side of the family.

cognition. The process by which an individual comes to know and interpret his environment. Cognition comprises all the processes by which an individual acquires knowledge, including perceiving, thinking, remembering, wondering, imagining, generalizing, and judging.

cognitive consonance. A consistency among the beliefs, ideas, perceptions, and other items and aspects of knowledge that form a COGNITIVE SYSTEM such that the system stands as an integrated and harmonious whole without internal contradictions. Cognitive consonance is not an absolute quality, but varies in degree, so that cognitive systems may be relatively more or less consonant.

cognitive dissonance hypothesis. The hypothesis, developed by Leon Festinger, that when a COGNITIVE SYSTEM comprises inconsistent items of knowledge (that is, contradictory perceptions, beliefs, or other forms of information) about a person, object, situation, or event (a condition referred to as cognitive dissonance) the individual experiences discomfort or tension that motivates him to reduce the dissonance by modifying one or more aspects of the system. (L. Festinger, *A Theory of Cognitive Dissonance*, Row, Peterson, Evanston, Ill., 1957.) See COGNITIVE CONSONANCE.

cognitive map. A mental image of an external object. The mental image (internalized object) represents the external object more or less accurately but is never an exact duplication of it. The internalized object is a SYMBOL of the external object that it represents.

cognitive process. See COGNITION.

cognitive selectivity. The tendency of an individual to include among his cognitions those items of knowledge that are in agreement with his beliefs, attitudes, values, and needs, and to exclude those that are not. Selectivity occurs in perception, interpretation, and remembering. Thus, even without deliberate intent, information that is in accordance with an individual's intellectual and emotional view of the world is more likely to be perceived, emphasized, and remembered than information that he finds incongruent and disturbing. See PERCEPTION, SELECTIVE.

cognitive system. A number of interrelated cognitions (items of knowledge) held by an individual. A cognitive system may consist of knowledge about a person, a group, an event, a type of behavior, a class of objects, or any subject, concrete or abstract. An individual has a number of cognitive systems which vary in complexity and in the degree to which they are interrelated. An IDEOLOGY is characterized by a high degree of interconnection among major cognitive systems.

cognitive theory. A theoretical approach in psychology that emphasizes the role of COGNITION in behavior and that regards the cognitive processes as important foci of psychological analysis. Cognitive theory stands in contrast to the radical BEHAVORISM of the stimulus-response approach in which behavior is analyzed in terms of CONDITIONING and in which cognitive mental processes are excluded as explanatory concepts on the grounds that their influence on behavior is nonobservable and nonmeasurable. Cognitive theory is holistic in its approach and therefore related to GESTALT PSYCHOLOGY. Cognitive theorists include Jean Piaget, Gordon W. Allport, Kurt Lewin, David Krech, Richard S. Crutchfield, and many others. See HOLISM; PHENOMENOLOGICAL APPROACH; SYMBOLIC-INTERACTIONISM.

cohesion, social. The integration of group behavior as a result of social bonds, attractions, or "forces" that hold members of a group in interaction over a period of time. When there is a high level of social cohesion the group is attractive to its members. Members have strong positive feelings toward the group, want to remain in the group, and like each other. They have high ESPRIT DE CORPS. In addition, social cohesion involves agreement with and acceptance by the members of the group's goals, norms, and role structure, that is, the distribution of rights and responsibilities. A high or low level of social cohesion may be found in large groups and small groups, formal groups and informal groups.

cohesiveness. See COHESION, SOCIAL.

cohort. As used in demography, a number of people having a common characteristic, for example, all persons in a given population who were born in 1940, or all persons suffering from a particular disease. See COHORT ANALYSIS.

cohort analysis. The study of a number of people with some common characteristic over a long period of time. For example, all persons in a particular community who are known to have attempted to commit suicide in a given year could form a cohort which is analyzed through the years to see how many repeatedly attempt suicide and how many eventually succeed in taking their own lives. In demographic analysis women are grouped according to their date of birth or marriage to form cohorts. The number of children born to the women in each cohort throughout the entire reproductive period of their lives is recorded and different cohorts are compared. In demography cohort analysis is useful in indicating long-term trends in population change. Moreover, it shows changes in the pattern of reproduction (for example, changes in the number and timing of births) much sooner after the changes occur than does the net reproduction rate. See REPRODUCTION RATE, NET.

collective, social. See SOCIAL COLLECTIVE.

collective bargaining. A process of ACCOMMODATION in which the members of a union negotiate through representatives with management to achieve higher wages, better working conditions, and the solution of other grievances. Collective bargaining, as opposed to each employee's bargaining separately with management, is the prime technique by which labor exerts POWER to counterbalance the power of the employer.

collective behavior. 1. Interrelated and similar, but unstructured, reactions and patterns of behavior on the part of a number of persons who are responding to a common influence or stimulus. Collective behavior is nontraditional, in the sense that it is not subject to clearly defined, culturally established norms. Cultural definitions and social norms, of course, to a certain extent determine and limit all social behavior, but in the case of collective behavior the cultural expectations are general and nonspecific and may be contradictory, leaving the situation largely undefined. Collective behavior is not group behavior, for there is not sufficient organization and interaction for the persons involved to be considered a social group. Forms of collective behavior are manifest in various types of crowd behavior, the spread of fads and fashions, the formation of public opinion, and the rise of social movements. See AGGREGATE; AUDIENCE; COLLECTIVITY; CRAZE; CROWD; FAD; FASHION; GROUP; MASS BEHAVIOR; MOB; PUBLIC; SOCIAL MOVEMENT.

2. Behavior involving two or more persons.

collective excitement. See SOCIAL CONTAGION.

collective mind. See GROUP MIND.

collective representation. A term introduced by Émile Durkheim to refer to a symbol having a common intellectual and emotional meaning to the members of a group. Collective representations reflect the history of the group, that is, the collective experience of the group over time. They include not only symbols in the form of objects, such as a flag, but also the basic concepts that determine the way in which one views and relates to the world. "Now it is unquestionable that language, and consequently the system of concepts which it translates, is the product of a collective elaboration. What it expresses is the manner in which society as a whole represents the facts of experience. The ideas which correspond to the diverse elements of language are thus collective representations. . . . In fact, there are scarcely any words among those which we usually employ whose meaning does not pass, to a greater or less extent, the limits of our personal experience. Very frequently a term expresses things which we have never perceived or experiences which we have never had or of which we have never been the witnesses. . . . Thus there is a great deal of knowledge condensed in the word which I never collected, and which is not individual." Collective representations "add to that which we can learn by our personal experience all that wisdom and science which the group has accumulated in the course of centuries." Collective representations express collective sentiments and ideas which give the group its unity and unique character. Thus they are an important factor contributing to the solidarity of a society or other social group. (É. Durkheim, *The Elementary Forms of Religious Life*, tr. by J. W. Swain, Free Press, Glencoe, Ill., 1947.)

collective responsibility. The social norm holding that a family or larger social group (for example, clan or village) is responsible for the behavior of its members and may be held accountable for their misdeeds.

collectivism. The doctrine that economic activity should be controlled through collective action and not left to the unregulated actions of individuals in pursuit of their self-interests. It is the opposite of the philosophy of LAISSEZ-FAIRE. The term is usually defined in a broad sense to include both systems of collective ownership of the means of production and distribution and systems of private ownership with strong state or other collective regulation. However, the term is sometimes used as the equivalent of SOCIALISM or COMMUNISM.

collectivity. 1. A plurality of persons who share certain common values and interests, have some feeling of solidarity, and some pattern of ROLE relationships. In this sense collectivity is a broad term including both groups and those pluralities that lack sufficient structure and interaction to be considered groups but are not merely aggregates. See GROUP.

2. A plurality of persons having a degree of social structure, collective consciousness, and interaction that would be classified as intermediate between an AGGREGATE (having no such structure) and a GROUP. See CROWD; PUBLIC; SOCIAL CATEGORY.

collectivity-orientation. See SELF-ORIENTATION—COLLECTIVITY-ORIENTATION.

column. In statistical tables a vertical listing of categories all of which have a common classification.

column heading. In statistical tables a title that descriptively indicates the common classification of the data listed in a column.

combination. In statistics, a collection of objects considered without reference to their order in forming a SET or subset. See PERMUTATION.

combinations, instinct for. See INSTINCT FOR COMBINATIONS AND INSTINCT FOR GROUP PERSISTENCES.

commensalism. Interaction among individuals or groups that perform similar functions. This functional similarity may promote a feeling of social solidarity and provide the basis for joint action. On the other hand, it also can lead to competition for the same position—competition that can become quite severe. Organizations such as labor unions and professional associations attempt to control commensalistic competition among their members. The term commensalism has been used primarily in human ecology to refer to the relationships within a community between functionally similar groups or categories of persons. See ECOLOGY, HUMAN; SYMBIOSIS.

commercial revolution. A series of economic and social changes that occurred in Europe, particularly western Europe and northern Italy, in late medieval and early modern times. These changes included the decline of the manorial system and the freeing of men from their bonds to the land, the expansion of cities, the development of systems of credit, the growth of international trade with exchange between areas specializing in the production of different goods, the development of an open market with wealth increasingly in the form of money and credit rather than land.

With the commercial revolution a new class, neither peasantry nor nobility, the merchant class, became economically dominant and of increasing political importance. The commercial revolution preceded the INDUSTRIAL REVOLUTION.

commission plan of city government. A form of city government headed by a small, frequently a five-man, commission elected from the city at large. One of the members is chosen by the commissioners themselves to serve as presiding officer, and he is usually referred to as mayor. Each commissioner is in charge of administering a particular department of the city government. In the commission form of government, instead of a separation of powers there is a concentration of all legislative and executive authority in one body. The commission plan, originally proposed about the turn of the century as an effort to reform corrupt municipal governments, represents an attempt to apply the principles of business administration to city government and to minimize politics. The commission form spread rapidly in the United States in the early years of the twentieth century, with the greatest number of cities using the plan at the time of World War I. Since then in its pure form it has declined greatly in popularity. The commission plan may be found in a number of communities in modified form, combined with aspects of another plan of city government, for example, a commission and a separately elected mayor. See COUNCIL-MANAGER PLAN OF CITY GOVERNMENT; MAYOR-COUNCIL PLAN OF CITY GOVERNMENT.

commitment. A feeling of obligation to follow a particular course of action or to seek a particular goal. As a result, freedom of choice and the number of alternatives in social action are limited.

common factor. See FACTOR.

common sense. Cultural traditions or folk knowledge constituting a body of shared and relatively standardized explanations and interpretations of a variety of phenomena (from natural occurrences to social behavior) and containing solutions to everyday problems. Belief in the wisdom of such folk knowledge is rooted in the feeling that it represents the fruit of one's own personal experience and the accumulated experience of one's culture. In fact, common sense is rooted in widely shared views and interpretations based on traditional beliefs and theories. However, the common sense of today represents not only the wisdom of the past, but also very often the discarded theories of yesterday's scholars. It may also include a large number of beliefs based on superstition and ignorance.

communality. A number of persons who share a common interest and come together periodically to pursue this interest. A communality may or may not have the social structure and cohesiveness of a GROUP. It may be short-lived and of little importance to those involved in its activities, or it may be of long duration and deeply involve its members. If it is a group, it may be a small, close-knit, informal group or a large, formal, secondary group. The members of a communality need not live near one another, but must be able to gather from time to time at a common place to pursue their joint activity. Examples would be a Rotary club, a chess club, and a professional society. See GROUP, INFORMAL; GROUP, SECONDARY.

communication. The transmission of information, ideas, attitudes, or emotions from one person or group to another (or others) primarily through symbols. In effective communication the meaning conveyed to the recipient corresponds closely to that intended by the sender. Communication forms the basis for all social interaction; it enables the transmission of cumulative knowledge and makes possible the existence of empathic understanding among individuals. See LANGUAGE; MASS COMMUNICATION; SYMBOL.

communication, mass. See MASS COMMUNICATION.

communication, pseudo-. See PSEUDO-COMMUNICATION.

communication, subliminal. See SUBLIMINAL COMMUNICATION.

communication, symbolic. COMMUNICATION through conventional symbols with shared meanings, primarily in the form of language. Human communication is primarily symbolic. See LANGUAGE; SYMBOL.

communication, unconscious. COMMUNICATION through culturally conventionalized gestures which individuals with the same cultural background make and respond to without reflection. A smile, a shrug, a nod of the head are examples of this form of communication.

communication channel. A term used in the study of groups to refer to a relatively regularized relationship of communication between two or more persons. Communication between persons in such a relationship is frequent, and information is often passed on from one to the other, in either a one- or two-way relationship.

communication distortion. The tendency for information to become changed in content or partially lost in the process of communication.

communication net or **network.** The pattern of COMMUNICATION among the members of a GROUP. Communication is never equal in amount or intensity among all the members of a group. Certain individuals communicate more with each other than with others. Patterns of communication are influenced by such factors as the formality or informality of the group and the degree of structuring of relationships among members, the purpose of the group, status differences among members, and personal preferences. The pattern of communication channels in a group may change according to changes in the group's activity. See COMMUNICATION CHANNEL.

communication system. In a formal organization, the interrelated system of communication channels. See COMMUNICATION CHANNEL.

communism. Communal ownership of all property. More precise definitions of communism are, however, extremely diverse, in good part due to the ideological implications of the term. It is most often used to refer to revolutionary socialism, that is, socialism brought about by revolution rather than gradual evolution, particularly revolutionary socialism based upon the writings of Karl Marx. Marx advocated the overthrow of the existing order and the abolition of private ownership of the means of production and distribution, and looked forward to the eventual disappearance of the state and the emergence of a classless society where all would be paid according to their needs. In its pure form a Marxian society has never existed, and all contemporary societies based on Marxian socialism have maintained a class system with differential rewards based on criteria other than need; they have also maintained and even greatly strengthened the power of the state. Official ideologists in the U.S.S.R. usually refer to their present socioeconomic system as socialist, and regard communism as an ideal system to be attained in the future.

It should be emphasized, however, that communistic schemes and communities long preceded and have not been limited to Marx and his followers. Non-Marxian communistic schemes include Plato's *Republic,* Sir Thomas More's *Utopia,* and utopian communities founded under the influence of such men as Robert Owen, Charles Fourier, and Étienne Cabet. Christian forms of communism may be found in the communal sharing of property of the early Christians, the communistic organization of medieval monasteries, and more recently communistic sects such as the Shakers and Hutterites.

See BOLSHEVISM; BOURGEOISIE; CAPITALISM; COLLECTIVISM; DIALEC-TICAL MATERIALISM; PROLETARIAT; SOCIALISM.

communism, primitive. A form of COMMUNISM found in certain non-literate societies, in which all the major economic resources (e.g., land, boats) are owned by the community as a whole rather than by individuals, families, kin or other groups.

community. 1. A concentrated settlement of people in a limited territorial area, within which they satisfy many of their daily needs through a system of interdependent relationships. A community is a self-conscious social unit and a focus of group identification. Although a community forms a local geographic and economic unit, providing many of the primary goods and services for its inhabitants, it is not necessarily a political entity, as it is not necessarily contained within or defined by legal boundaries, such as those of a city or town. Community also implies a certain identification of the inhabitants with the geographic area, and with each other, a feeling of sharing common interests and goals, a certain amount of mutual cooperation, and an awareness of the existence of the community in both its inhabitants and those in the surrounding area. For this reason a metropolitan area, which forms an economic and ecological unit, is not necessarily on that basis alone a community. On the other hand, a suburb, which is not economically independent, may, if it meets the criteria given above, be regarded as a community.

2. A number of people who share certain common traditions or interests, such as an ethnic group or a community of scholars. In this sense the term is not associated with a territorial area, as the persons who are considered part of the community may be widely scattered.

3. GEMEINSCHAFT as defined by Ferdinand Tönnies, in contrast to GESELLSCHAFT. Most sociologists, however, use the German term rather than the translation, "community." For this usage see *Gemeinschaft*.

4. The biotic level of human organization as defined by the early human ecologists. See BIOTIC COMMUNITY.

This term has a wide variety of meanings, and is sometimes used without precise definition; however, in sociology the definition given in 1. above is by far the most widely used.

community, metropolitan. See METROPOLITAN COMMUNITY.

community, peasant or **folk.** See PEASANT COMMUNITY.

community, rural. See RURAL COMMUNITY.

community, urban. See URBAN COMMUNITY.

community development. A term used to describe "a process of social action in which the people of a community organize themselves for planning and action; define their common and individual needs and problems; make group and individual plans to meet their needs and solve their problems; execute these plans with a maximum of reliance upon community resources; and supplement these resources when necessary with services and material from governmental and nongovernmental agencies outside the community." (International Cooperation Administration, *Community Development Review,* December 1956.)

community organization. 1. The functional organization of a community, that is, the way the community is organized to provide for the needs of its residents.

2. The pattern of interrelationships among the major groups found in the community.

3. In social work, the process of "bringing together representatives of

all kinds of agencies . . . for the purpose of welfare planning and of coordination of efforts within a given neighborhood or community." (*Social Work as a Profession*, American Association of Social Workers, 1947.)

community planning. See PLANNING, URBAN SOCIAL.

community study method. A method of studying human behavior that focuses upon the thorough analysis of an individual community. It is in fact the application of the CASE STUDY METHOD to the study of a community, the community being the case or unit of analysis. Specific problems of human behavior are studied in terms of the context of a particular community and are analyzed in relation to other aspects of community life. The geographic, historical, and ecological characteristics of the community are studied as well as the social, economic, and political organization, and social and psychological processes are analyzed and interrelated not only to each other but also to these various aspects of the community context in which they operate. The advantage of the community study method is that behavior and attitudes are examined in a natural setting and within the total context of normal social interaction.

commuter zone. See CONCENTRIC ZONE HYPOTHESIS, BURGESS'; SUBURB.

comparative method. Generally, the study of different types of groups (large and small) and societies in order to determine analytically the factors that lead to similarities and differences in specified patterns of behavior. Usually the term includes both the HISTORICAL METHOD and the CROSS-CULTURAL METHOD. Some writers, however, prefer to equate the comparative method with the historical method, and use the term *cross-cultural method* to refer to comparisons of contemporary cultures.

comparative psychology. See PSYCHOLOGY, COMPARATIVE.

comparative religion. See RELIGION, COMPARATIVE.

compartmentalization. The separation of a person's behavior and thought into unconnected categories, frequently referred to as logic-tight compartments, so that the person does not recognize inconsistencies in his thought and behavior patterns. By means of compartmentalization an individual may conform to different and contradictory sets of norms in different situations, without a feeling of inner conflict or confusion. There may be little or no awareness of the inherent contradiction between the two sets of norms because they may seldom or never be thought of in relation to each other. For example, an individual's personal and business ethics may be widely variant. In extreme cases, inconsistencies of thought and behavior, and the refusal of an individual to recognize them, may, quite obviously, be a symptom of a mental disorder. However, from the point of view of a social FRAME OF REFERENCE, much of what may appear to be inconsistencies of behavior and thought to an observer may merely reflect different ROLE patterns expected of the individual in his total social environment. The different roles a person plays in life may each have a certain logic of its own, and often it is clearly normal, healthy and even desirable for the inconsistencies and conflicting logics to remain relatively distinct units.

compartmentalization, mental. See COMPARTMENTALIZATION.

compensation. Emphasis upon an activity or role that is a substitute for another that the individual feels he is unable to perform adequately. Often the individual exerts a particularly strenuous effort to excel in his new activity or role in order to overcome his feeling of failure. Psychologists frequently refer to compensation as a DEFENSE MECHANISM.

competition. 1. The pursuit of goals by individuals or groups the attainment of which depends upon other individuals or groups not attaining the same or related goals. In competition the objects pursued are limited in supply, and demand exceeds supply. Competition is goal- or object-directed. That is, primary concern is directed toward the object sought rather than toward the competitors. Thus, competition differs from CONFLICT, in which defeat of one's opponent is the major concern. In addition competition tends to be continuous until the goal is gained or lost, whereas conflict is intermittent. In this usage competition may be either direct and conscious or indirect and unconscious; for example, a man may or may not be aware that his employment in a job deprives another of employment.

2. An indirect and impersonal process in which individuals or groups attempting to satisfy their needs seek the same limited resources within a given environment. The term was used in this sense by the early human ecologists. The process of competition was seen as occurring without social communication, without personal antagonism, often without even an awareness of the identity of one's competitors. It was seen, in essence, as a basic struggle for existence in a limited environment. The early ecologists regarded competition as the basic process in human organization, determining the spatial and functional distribution of populations. It was regarded as a subsocial process, part of the biotic level of human organization. See BIOTIC COMMUNITY; ECOLOGY, HUMAN; SYMBIOSIS.

complex. In psychology, a number of interrelated, emotionally charged beliefs, attitudes, and memories which an individual has repressed or at least partially repressed but which still actively affect his behavior. See REPRESSION.

complex, culture. See CULTURE COMPLEX.

compromise. A form of ACCOMMODATION between hostile individuals or groups in which each of the contending parties consciously yields some of his original aims in the form of mutual concessions. Usually neither party is completely satisfied, but a relative equality of bargaining power leads to the acceptance of an agreement. Compromise may be relatively permanent or simply a short-lived expedient which ends when either or both parties feel there has been a shift in the balance of power.

compromise reaction or **compromise formation.** A psychological response involving partial acceptance of frustration by an individual. In a compromise reaction, when an individual is frustrated in trying to attain a goal, instead of continuing to try to achieve that goal or abandoning it altogether, he modifies the goal, usually by lowering his level of aspiration or substituting another, related goal.

compulsion. A psychological response to anxiety in which an individual feels impelled to perform some irrational act or series of acts as a way of relieving anxiety. The actor may either fail to understand his act and insist that it is absolutely necessary, or recognize its futility but still be unable to modify his behavior.

compulsive deviance. DEVIANCE that the individual himself cannot control. The individual is compelled to continue or resume his deviant behavior despite the severe social penalties that result from it and despite his attempts to reform. Alcoholism and drug addiction are special forms of compulsive deviance.

concentration. An ecological process in which individuals tend to settle in increasing numbers in an urban area due to favorable conditions there. Concentration may also be viewed as a pattern of density of population settlement, measured by ratio of population to land area. Ecologists who limit this term to the density of residential population use the term CENTRALIZATION to describe the clustering of urban services such as commercial enterprises, churches, theaters, and so forth. However many sociologists use concentration to refer to both density of population and urban services.

concentric zone hypothesis, Burgess'. An ideal construct first proposed by Ernest W. Burgess to describe and summarize the expansion and internal development of a modern city in terms of a series of concentric zones around the central business district. Each of the zones (usually five) is differentiated according to land use, population types, and other physical, economic, and social characteristics. Zone I is the downtown area or the CENTRAL BUSINESS DISTRICT, which is surrounded by Zone II or the ZONE IN TRANSITION. The latter is essentially an interstitial area, a slum area characterized by "social deterioration." It is being invaded by light industry, and its deteriorated buildings provide low-rent housing for poor people; during a period of heavy immigration or internal migration this is an area of first settlement. Zone III is the zone of workingmen's homes. The area is somewhat superior to the slum area in residential accommodations, and rents are higher. It is inhabited primarily by industrial workers, and it is an area of second settlement for immigrants. Zone IV is a zone of better residences and apartment houses, and is inhabited by people having larger incomes and smaller families than the residents of Zone III. Mostly middle-class families but also some highly paid industrial workers occupy this area. Zone V is the commuter or suburban zone. It is usually beyond the city limits, and is an area of economically secure families, living primarily in single-family residences. Numerous modifications, qualifications, and additions are to be found in Burgess' work, as well as in the work of those who have utilized his basic scheme. (E. W. Burgess in *The City*, edited by R. E. Park, E. W. Burgess, R. D. McKenzie, University of Chicago Press, Chicago, 1925.) See AXIATE HYPOTHESIS OF URBAN GROWTH; ECOLOGY, HUMAN; SECTOR HYPOTHESIS.

concept. A word or set of words that expresses a general idea concerning the nature of something or the relations between things, often providing a category for the classification of phenomena. Concepts provide a means of ordering the vast diversity of empirical phenomena, are essential in the process of generalizing, and form the basis of language. However, concepts are not inherent in nature itself, waiting to be discovered, as it were. Concepts, including scientific concepts, are mental constructs reflecting a certain point of view and focusing upon certain aspects of phenomena while ignoring others. Therefore, the concepts a person uses have an important effect upon his perceptions of reality. Scientific concepts form a part of scientific THEORY.

concept, definitive. A concept that "refers precisely to what is common to a class of objects, by the aid of a clear definition in terms of attributes or fixed bench marks. This definition, or the bench marks, serve as a means of clearly identifying the individual instance of the class and the make-up of that instance that is covered by the concept. . . . Whereas definitive concepts provide prescriptions of what to see, sensitizing concepts merely suggest directions along which to look." (H. Blumer, *American Sociological Review*, February 1954.) This term refers to one of the two types of concepts distinguished by Herbert Blumer. See CONCEPT, SENSITIZING.

concept, sensitizing. A concept that lacks "specification of attributes or bench marks and consequently . . . does not enable the user to move directly to the instance and its relevant content. Instead it gives the user a general sense of reference and guidance in approaching empirical instances. . . . The hundreds of our concepts [in sociology]—like culture, institutions, social structure, mores, and personality . . . are sensitizing in nature. . . . I think that thoughtful study shows conclusively that the concepts of our discipline are fundamentally sensitizing instruments." (H. Blumer, *American Sociological Review*, February 1954.) This term refers to one of the two types of concepts distinguished by Herbert Blumer. See CONCEPT, DEFINITIVE.

concepts, paired. See PAIRED CONCEPTS.

conceptual model. See MODEL, CONCEPTUAL.

conceptualist approach, sociological. The general point of view that theoretical concepts are necessary in sociology, and cannot be eliminated and replaced by operational definitions. The proponents of the conceptualist approach do not reject operational definitions; they recognize their importance and use them in research. However, they feel that operational definitions alone are not adequate for the development of a science of sociology. The conceptualist approach, therefore, rejects rigid OPERATIONAL-ISM and stresses the importance both in theory and in research of concepts that provide reasonable, general explanations. It is maintained that only through the use of such concepts are comparison (not only cross-cultural comparison but even comparison within the same culture from one study to another) and generalization possible. See OPERATIONAL DEFINITION.

conciliation. 1. The settlement of a dispute through COMPROMISE, with an emphasis upon the attainment of common objectives. Conciliation brings a lessening of hostility and an agreement is reached, but underlying differences are not removed and varying degrees of hostility may remain.
2. The settlement of a dispute with the help of a third party whose mediation the disputants have willingly agreed to accept. The mediator attempts to get the disputants to reach a compromise themselves, rather than draw up a settlement for them. See ARBITRATION.

concomitant variation. See CORRELATION.

concordance, coefficient of. See KENDALL COEFFICIENT OF CONCORDANCE W.

concrete social class. A group that functions as a social unit, in terms of which the members are directly related to one another. Examples would be political parties, clubs, corporations. (G. H. Mead, *Mind, Self and Society*, University of Chicago Press, 1934.) George Herbert Mead compared concrete social class with ABSTRACT SOCIAL CLASS. This concept is not widely used today. Related but not synonymous concepts in current usage are discussed under ASSOCIATION; COLLECTIVITY; and GROUP, SECONDARY.

concrete sociology. See SOCIOLOGY, CONCRETE.

concreteness, fallacy of misplaced. See REIFICATION, FALLACY OF.

concubinage. 1. A system found in a number of societies in which there is a legally or socially recognized status of concubine. In this type of social arrangement the concubine has a status similar to a wife's, although she and her offspring have lower status than her mate's wife and her children. Children of such unions are considered legitimate, but very often with limited rights. A man may have one or more concubines either instead of or in addition to a wife or wives. When there are both a wife and a concubine, very often the concubine is from a lower social class.

2. In Western society, the cohabitation of a woman with a man without marriage.

condition. See NECESSARY CONDITION; SUFFICIENT CONDITION.

conditioned reflex. See CONDITIONED RESPONSE or REFLEX.

conditioned response or **reflex.** A simple learned reaction to a stimulus acquired through association with a previously existing (frequently biologically based) stimulus-response relationship. In conditioning, a stimulus that does not originally evoke a given response is consistently presented or occurs together with one that does. Through association, the new stimulus comes to evoke the same response. The learned stimulus-response relationship then occurs without the presence of the original unconditioned stimulus. See CONDITIONING.

conditioned stimulus. See STIMULUS, CONDITIONED.

conditioning. The process by which conditioned responses are established. In psychology those who follow the stimulus-response approach regard conditioning as synonymous with learning. Indeed, LEARNING THEORY usually refers to the stimulus-response approach. These psychologists are radical behaviorists, who reject the importance of cognitive mental processes in the analysis of individual behavior. See BEHAVIORISM; COGNITIVE THEORY.

conduct. 1. Behavior consciously oriented to social norms and to the opinions of others.

2. Behavior judged by group norms or social values.

confidence limits. In statistics, two points, one above and one below a STATISTIC, that provide a given degree of confidence that the PARAMETER of the population falls between them. The 95% confidence limits, for example, would be expected to include the parameter 95 times out of 100. The confidence limits can be based on any desired percentage. In a given case the higher the probability that the confidence limits include the parameter, the wider their range will be. For example, in any one case the 99% confidence limits will have a wider range than the 95% confidence limits.

configuration. An organized pattern of interrelated parts. In studying a configuration the parts are analyzed in relation to each other rather than

as isolated individual elements, and the emphasis is upon the total structure—the pattern of the larger whole. This concept is central to the approach of GESTALT PSYCHOLOGY.

configuration, cultural. See CULTURAL CONFIGURATION.

configurational learning. See LEARNING, CONFIGURATIONAL.

conflict. Direct and conscious struggle between individuals or groups
for the same goal. Defeat of the opponent is seen as essential for achieving
the goal. In conflict (unlike COMPETITION), opponents are primarily
oriented toward each other rather than toward the object they seek. In
fact, because of the development of strong feelings of hostility, the
achievement of the goal may at times be considered secondary to the opponent's defeat. In addition, conflict is intermittent rather than continuous.

conflict, class. See CLASS STRUGGLE.

conflict, culture. See CULTURE CONFLICT.

conflict, industrial. See INDUSTRIAL CONFLICT.

conflict, mental. See MENTAL CONFLICT.

conflict, role. See ROLE CONFLICT.

conflict, social. See CONFLICT.

conflict frustration. See MENTAL CONFLICT.

conflict model of society. See CONFLICT THEORY.

conflict theory. Any of various theories of society that view social
phenomena of the past, present, and future as a result of conflict. The social process is viewed primarily not in terms of the cooperation of social
groups but in terms of man's aggressiveness. Emphasis is placed on conflict as a creative or at least an inevitable fact of social life rather than as
merely a destructive and avoidable deviation. There have been many conflict theorists throughout history, including Heraclitus, Polybius, Thomas
Hobbes, David Hume, Georg Hegel, Karl Marx, the social Darwinists, and
others. Ralf Dahrendorf sees the conflict model, which emphasizes
change, conflict, and constraint, as a balance to the recent emphasis in
sociology on the equilibrium or "utopian" model, which emphasizes stability, harmony, and consensus in analyzing societies. (R. Dahrendorf,
American Journal of Sociology, September 1958.)

conformity. Behavior that is in accord with the expectations of a social
group. It reflects acquiescence to the rules or social norms and is expressed in responses that are either similar to those of others or prescribed
by group customs or norms. "Conformity may be defined as the endeavor
to maintain a standard set by a group. It is a voluntary imitation of preva-

lent modes of action, distinguished from rivalry and other aggressive phases of emulation by being comparatively passive, aiming to keep up rather than to excel, and concerning itself for the most part with what is outward and formal." (C. H. Cooley, *Human Nature and the Social Order*, Scribner, New York, 1902.) The term "usually denotes conformity to the norms and expectations current in the individual's *own* membership group. . . . conformity to norms of an outgroup is thus equivalent to what is ordinarily called nonconformity, that is, nonconformity to the norms of the ingroup." (R. K. Merton, *Social Theory and Social Structure*, Free Press, Glencoe, Ill., 1957.) See DEVIANCE; NONCONFORMITY; OVERCONFORMITY.

congeniality group. A small, informal group based on common interests and the personal compatibility and liking of members for each other. Usually the members are engaged in leisure-time activities. The term is not used to refer to a group that is part of a larger, formal organization. See CLIQUE.

congeries. A number of culture traits that are found together within a given culture but are not functionally interrelated to each other, their association being due to mere historical accident, for example, the association of evergreen trees, wreaths, holly, mistletoe, Santa Claus, and gift giving with Christmas. See CULTURE ADHESION; CULTURE COMPLEX; CULTURE TRAIT.

conjugal family. See FAMILY, CONJUGAL.

connotative meaning. The subtle, emotionally toned meaning conveyed by a word, as distinguished from its explicit, denotative meaning. Thus two words with the same definition or reference may have quite different connotations.

consanguine. Related by "blood" or common ancestor. However, the common ancestor in fact may be a social fiction, as is often the case with clans.

consanguine family. See FAMILY, CONSANGUINE.

consanguineal kin group. See KIN GROUP, CONSANGUINEAL.

conscience. Moral standards of behavior internalized by the individual from his social group experience. In the process of SOCIALIZATION the MORES of the social group are incorporated by the individual into his personality. The term conscience is not widely used in sociology. See GENERALIZED OTHER; NORM, SOCIAL; SUPEREGO.

conscious experience. Experience that an individual can at a given time remember, organize, and verbalize. Conscious experience includes inner feelings and thoughts as well as overt behavior of one's SELF and others.

consciousness. The process or state of awareness of subjective experiences at any one moment. Consciousness involves an awareness of one's SELF.

consciousness, class. See CLASS CONSCIOUSNESS.

consciousness, ethnic. See ETHIC IDENTIFICATION.

consciousness of community. See COMMUNITY.

consciousness of kind. A feeling of identification with others who are similar to oneself. This concept was used by Franklin H. Giddings, who maintained that the central social bond of groups is the tendency of people to seek out and establish social relationships with other people who are similar to them—who are of their own kind. This term is not much used in modern sociology.

consensual validation. The concept, central to the work of Harry Stack Sullivan, that meaning is determined by social validation—that is, the meanings of symbols and ideas are derived from a consensus among the community using the symbols and ideas. These socially valid meanings are learned by an individual through communication. In normal development, as a child matures he changes his peculiar individual (autistic) meanings and definitions to meanings in accordance with those accepted by his social group. (See H. S. Sullivan, *Conceptions of Modern Psychiatry*, The William Alanson White Foundation, Washington, D.C., 1947.)

consensus. 1. Delineation of areas of agreement by individuals or groups previously in conflict with each other. In this sense consensus is a means of resolving conflict.

2. The delineation of areas of agreement and common definitions of the situation by persons who are engaged in a joint undertaking.

3. The values, beliefs, attitudes, etc. held in common in a given culture. Cultural consensus is an important factor in social integration.

consequences, latent and **manifest.** See FUNCTION, LATENT; FUNCTION, MANIFEST.

conservatism. An ideological orientation that opposes social change, especially change away from traditional cultural values and mores, and justifies its actions and values on the basis of the presumed accumulated wisdom of the past inherent in traditional forms. The most usual justification for this orientation is that although there are imperfections in existing social institutions, man and society are not perfectible, and established forms at least have a proven value. However, in practice those ideologists who define themselves as conservatives may be dissatisfied with many aspects of the present as well as the past, and desire change and innovation sometimes no less than the liberal; but the appeal for the preservation or reinstatement of selected values and statuses tends to support different interest groups from those supported by the liberals. Nevertheless, the conservatives still tend to believe they adhere to the honored traditions of society and thus they can usually be identified. See LIBERALISM.

consistency, statistical. See RELIABILITY.

consistency, status. See STATUS CONSISTENCY.

conspicuous consumption. The consumption of wealth, goods, and services primarily for the purpose of display. The term was used by Thorstein Veblen in his *Theory of the Leisure Class* (Macmillan, New York, 1899) to point out that people who have a surplus of wealth (above the subsistence level) use it not for constructive or useful purposes, but rather to enhance their social status.

constant. In statistics, a characteristic that is the same for all the individuals being studied. If all the individuals in a particular study have the same value of a given VARIABLE, the variable is a constant in that study. Thus in a study limited to men, sex is a constant.

constellation, ecological. See ECOLOGICAL CONSTELLATION.

constitutional psychology. See PSYCHOLOGY, CONSTITUTIONAL.

construct. A concept devised to aid in scientific analysis and generalization. A construct is generally inferred indirectly from observable phenomena. It is an abstraction from reality, selecting and focusing on certain aspects of reality and ignoring others. It is a HEURISTIC ASSUMPTION designed to guide and suggest fruitful areas of investigation; it is not intended as a direct description of concrete phenomena. Examples of constructs in sociology are STATUS, ROLE, George Herbert Mead's the ME, the I, and the GENERALIZED OTHER. See CONSTRUCTED TYPE; IDEAL TYPE; MODEL.

constructed type. A complex CONSTRUCT that forms a system of interrelated theoretical concepts. "Constructed type" was introduced by Howard Becker as a reformulation of the IDEAL TYPE, and they are very similar. However, Becker suggested that the constructed type, rather than being regarded primarily as a tentative formulation preceding research as in the case of the ideal type, should be regarded as the result of research. "Such types are made up of criteria (so-called elements, traits, aspects, and so on) which have discoverable referents in the empirical world or can legitimately be inferred from empirical evidence, or both. The construction of these types should always take place in relation to an explicit problem and should be oriented toward a clear-cut hypothesis; the type of highest usefulness is not merely classificatory." (H. Becker in *Twentieth Century Sociology*, edited by G. Gurvitch and W. E. Moore, Philosophical Library, New York, 1945.) The constructed type, then, not only provides a means of ordering data, but also serves to facilitate generalization. Various concrete cases may be interrelated to each other in terms of the constructed type. This involves a process of ABSTRACTION, in which certain elements are emphasized and others ignored. Thus the constructed type, like the ideal type, does not describe concrete phenomena. It is a MODEL that provides a framework for the analysis of data and the statement of the probability of certain occurrences, patterns, and interrelationships. Becker used the model of the constructed type in analyzing the distinction between SACRED SOCIETY and SECULAR SOCIETY.

consumer good. See GOOD, ECONOMIC.

consumption, conspicuous. See CONSPICUOUS CONSUMPTION.

contact. The establishment of mutual awareness and communication between two or more persons. Contact is the first stage in the development of a SOCIAL RELATIONSHIP.

contact, categorical. See CATEGORICAL CONTACT.

contact, cultural. See CULTURE CONTACT.

contact, social. See CONTACT.

contagion. See SOCIAL CONTAGION.

content analysis. A research technique used to described and analyze objectively, systematically, and quantitatively the content of written, spoken, or pictorial communications such as novels, editorials, movies, comic books, and public speeches. By systematically classifying analytical components of the material being studied, the researcher can identify specific or general themes that were not evident from simple examination, and, for example, might be able to judge the kind of impact (either intended or unintended) the material is having upon those exposed to the communication.

contingency. 1. An interrelationship or association of any two variables such that the presence, form, or magnitude of one variable is dependent upon the presence, form, or magnitude of the other variable.

2. The term is also used in a more limited sense to refer only to the interrelationship of two qualitative variables. In this case the presence or form of one variable is dependent upon the presence or form of the other variable.

See VARIABLE; VARIABLE, QUALITATIVE.

contingency coefficient C. A nonparametric statistical test used to determine whether the degree of association between two qualitative variables is greater than would be expected by chance. The contingency coefficient C is employed when the data are in the form of unordered categories rather than in continuous numerical series. It is essentially chi square standardized for sample size, and is obtained by the formula

$$C = \sqrt{\frac{\chi^2}{N + \chi^2}}$$. See CHI-SQUARE TEST; PROBABILITY; SIGNIFICANCE, STATISTICAL; VARIABLE, QUALITATIVE.

contingency table. A method of ordering data so that a cross-classification of two variables is presented. The table presents the number of cases falling in each combination of categories of the two variables. A fourfold table (with four cells) is a common example of a contingency table.

continuity, correction for. See CHI-SQUARE TEST.

continuous variable. See VARIABLE, CONTINUOUS.

continuum. An uninterrupted series of gradual changes in the magnitude of a given characteristic, forming a linear increase or decrease through a series of gradual degrees.

contra-acculturative movement. A movement, usually associated with nationalism or an intensifying of ethnic feelings of identification and aspiration, in which a partially acculturated people react against the process of ACCULTURATION and begin to stress and attempt to revive elements of their earlier way of life, for example, nativistic movements among peoples who have experienced partial Westernization, such as the Boxer movement in China in 1900. See NATIVISTIC MOVEMENT.

contract. A formal device for ordering social interaction designed to standardize and enforce agreements between individuals or groups. A contract outlines prescribed reciprocal behavior, attempts to insure predictability of present and future behavior, and attempts to impose community sanctions to insure proper behavior of the parties to the agreement, with, as a last resort, penalties for violation of the formal terms of the agreement.

contraculture. A SUBCULTURE that stands in opposition to important aspects of the dominant culture of the society. The term was introduced by J. Milton Yinger to designate a particular type of subculture in which certain values and social norms of the dominant culture are specifically rejected, and contrary values and norms deliberately accepted. In fact, the value and normative system of the contraculture can really be understood only in terms of its theme of opposition to the dominant culture. "Delinquency and drug addiction often have a contracultural aspect; but somewhat less clearly, political and religious movements among disprivileged groups may also invert the values of the influential but inaccessible dominant group. Thus the concept of contraculture may help us to understand, for example, the Garveyite movement, the Ras Tafari cult, and some aspects of the value schemes of lower-class sects." (J. M. Yinger, *American Sociological Review*, October 1960.)

contrast error. A tendency, found in some social psychological studies, for a person who is asked to rate others to rate them as having characteristics the very opposite of what he believes his own characteristics to be.

contravention. 1. A form of opposition between persons or groups that is intermediate between COMPETITION and CONFLICT. Contravention is more personally directed and involves a greater degree of hostility than competition. On the other hand, the opponent is not so clearly recognized as in the case of conflict. There may be uncertainty regarding his identity, and hostility is often hidden rather than openly expressed as in conflict. The relationship between producers and consumers is often regarded as one of contravention.

2. A one-sided conflict, conflict by one party that is not reciprocated by the other.

control, experimental. See EXPERIMENTAL CONTROL.

control, self-. See SELF-CONTROL.

control, social. See SOCIAL CONTROL.

control culture. Those aspects of culture that make possible the orderly functioning of society by motivating and pressuring individuals to behave in accordance with social expectations. Control culture includes internalized norms and values (CONSCIENCE), religious sanctions, and the whole structure of law and formalized penalties. See SOCIAL CONTROL.

control group. A group of subjects used as a standard for comparison in an experimental design. The control group is identical in all relevant ways to the EXPERIMENTAL GROUP, except that it is not subjected to the independent variable, that is, it does not receive the experimental treatment, is not exposed to whatever factor is being tested. The control group serves as a device with which to compare the experimental group in order to make certain that specific reactions or changes in the experimental group are the result of the effect of the experimental treatment alone and not some irrelevant, uncontrolled element.

controlling a factor. See EXPERIMENTAL CONTROL.

conurbation. 1. A large area of dense urban settlement extending far beyond the boundaries of the central metropolis and including a number of politically separate cities. In this usage conurbation is equivalent to METROPOLITAN AREA. Metropolitan area is the term more frequently used in the United States, while conurbation is preferred in Great Britain. The term conurbation was first introduced by Patrick Geddes.

2. Some writers use the term to refer to a number of towns or cities linked by a continuous string of settlements along a main highway. The

area between the linked towns or cities is primarily rural, and the towns are separate units whose populations do not merge except for the thin line of settlement along the highway. This form of urban development is sometimes referred to as ribbon development.

convention. See FOLKWAY.

conventional behavior. Behavior defined by social norms as appropriate in a given social situation. Once an individual has learned conventional patterns of behavior he knows how to act and what to expect of others, even in a new social situation that he has not previously directly experienced himself. Thus smooth and orderly social relationships are made possible even between strangers. Conventional behavior is defined by folkways, and is considered proper and desirable, but not morally imperative. See FOLKWAY.

conventional sign. See SYMBOL.

convergence, cultural. 1. The development of similar culture traits in two or more cultures either through DIFFUSION or PARALLELISM, that is, either through contact between the cultures or independently.

2. Some writers limit the term to the independent development of similar culture traits in two or more separate cultures. If used in this sense, it is synonymous with PARALLELISM.
See CULTURE TRAIT.

conversion. A striking and relatively sudden change in an individual's view of life. Conversion may involve changes in beliefs, group identification, or personality characteristics. It leads to the reorganization and reorientation of an individual's intellectual and emotional outlook. Conversion may occur in an individual's political, economic, social, or philosophical views, although in traditional general usage it refers most often to religious belief.

conversion reaction or **conversion hysteria.** See HYSTERIA.

cooperation. Social interaction in which individuals or groups engage in joint action to achieve a common goal.

cooperation, antagonistic. The COOPERATION "of two persons or groups to satisfy a great common interest while minor antagonisms which exist between them are suppressed." (W. G. Sumner, *Folkways*, Ginn, Boston, 1906.)

cooperation, direct. COOPERATION involving the performance of like activities carried out side by side because the individuals engaged in these activities want to do them together, even though they could be done individually. Picking berries and hunting in a group would be examples. See COOPERATION, INDIRECT.

cooperation, indirect. COOPERATION based on the performance of unlike activities that complement each other and together achieve a common goal. Indirect cooperation involves a division of labor and the performance of specialized tasks. See COOPERATION, DIRECT.

cooperative stage, Piaget's. The third stage in Jean Piaget's conception of the development of children in relation to the RULES OF THE GAME. The cooperative stage begins at about the age of seven or eight with an incipient form of cooperation. Children in this stage are interested in winning and are anxious to have rules to which all participants conform, but among a group of children playing a game there are considerable differences in their conceptions of the rules. (J. Piaget, *The Moral Judgment of the Child*, Harcourt, Brace, New York, 1932.)

cooptation. A mechanism for maintaining and stabilizing organization by a "process of absorbing new elements into the leadership or policy-determining structure." The term was introduced by Philip Selznick. (P. Selznick, *American Sociological Review*, February 1948.) See COOPTATION, FORMAL; COOPTATION, INFORMAL.

cooptation, formal. Formal recognition that new elements have been incorporated into the leadership of an organization. The persons with whom power is being shared are given official positions of authority. Formal cooptation occurs "when there is a need to establish the legitimacy of authority or the administrative accessibility of the relevant public." The term was introduced by Philip Selznick. (P. Selznick, *T.V.A. and the Grass Roots*, University of California Press, Berkeley, 1949.) See COOPTATION; COOPTATION, INFORMAL.

cooptation, informal. The sharing of power within an organization as a response to specific pressures without formal recognition of the new leaders. The term was introduced by Philip Selznick. (P. Selznick, *T.V.A. and the Grass Roots*, University of California Press, Berkeley, 1949.) See COOPTATION; COOPTATION, FORMAL.

coordinate axes. Two lines, one vertical and one horizontal, perpendicular to each other, which form the base lines of a graph. Their point of intersection is designated as zero or the point of origin for the values on the graph. From that point, values, class intervals, categories, or time periods are arranged along the horizontal axis or ABSCISSA from left to right, and values or frequencies are arranged in increasing order of magnitude along the vertical axis or ORDINATE. When a graph portrays the relationship between two variables, usually the independent VARIABLE is arranged along the abscissa and the dependent variable along the ordinate. When a graph shows a FREQUENCY DISTRIBUTION of a single variable, the class intervals or categories are arranged along the abscissa and the frequencies along the ordinate. When a graph portrays a TIME SERIES, the time periods are arranged along the abscissa and the values of the variable being analyzed are arranged along the ordinate. See CLASS INTERVAL.

coordinate chart. See LINE GRAPH.

coordinates. Two numerical values, one on the ABSCISSA and the other on the ORDINATE, used to plot a point on a graph. See COORDINATE AXES.

Cornell technique of scale analysis. See GUTTMAN SCALE.

corporation. A type of economic formal organization. It is a recognized legal entity with the right to own property, enter into contracts, and otherwise conduct business in the name of the organization. See ORGANIZATION, FORMAL.

correction for continuity. See CHI-SQUARE TEST.

correlation. 1. The interrelationship of two (or more) quantitative variables so that an increase in the magnitude of one of the variables is associated with an increase or decrease in the magnitude of the other. Thus when two variables are highly correlated it is possible to predict with reasonable accuracy the magnitude of one VARIABLE from a knowledge of the magnitude of the other. The term correlation usually is not used to refer to the association of two qualitative variables or of a quantitative variable and a qualitative variable. See specific forms of correlation below. See also COEFFICIENT OF CORRELATION; REGRESSION, STATISTICAL.

2. Occasionally the term correlation is used to refer to the interrelationship of any two (or more) variables whether quantitative or qualitative. See VARIABLE, QUALITATIVE; VARIABLE, QUANTITATIVE.

correlation, biserial. A method of measuring the CORRELATION between two variables when one is expressed in a continuous series of quantitative values and the other is dichotomized, that is, divided into two categories. The biserial correlation assumes that the dichotomous variable is really a variable with a continuous distribution that follows the normal curve which has been constricted into two classes. See FREQUENCY DISTRIBUTION CURVE, NORMAL.

correlation, curvilinear. A CORRELATION in which the rate of change of one variable is at an increasing or decreasing ratio instead of at a constant ratio to the rate of change of the other variable. For example, at first each one-unit increase in variable X may be associated with a one-unit increase in variable Y. Then, at a certain point a one-unit increase in X may be associated with a two-unit increase in Y. This pattern may continue so that a one-unit increase in X is associated with a three-unit increase in Y; or the rate of increase of Y may decline. Many patterns of relationship between two variables are possible. A curvilinear correlation sometimes is referred to as a nonlinear correlation. See CORRELATION, LINEAR.

correlation, direct. See CORRELATION, POSITIVE.

correlation, ecological. A CORRELATION between two variables based on their distribution by geographic areas or by groups. In an ecological correlation, variations in the rate of occurrence or average magnitude of two variables among a set of areas or groups are found to be associated, so that an area or group with a higher level of one variable has a higher (or lower in the case of a negative correlation) level of the other variable. For example, if a correlation were found between average number of years of schooling and average personal income by states for the fifty states, this would be an ecological correlation. W. S. Robinson pointed out that at times ecological correlations have been incorrectly treated as equivalent to individual correlations. (W. S. Robinson, *American Sociological Review*, June 1950.) However, ecological correlations may be of value in and of themselves, and have also been used without being confused with individual correlations. See CORRELATION, INDIVIDUAL.

correlation, individual. A CORRELATION based on individual cases (i.e., persons, objects, acts, or events). The individual correlation, for example, may describe the relationship between personal characteristics, such as the correlation between level of schooling and income for persons in a given population, or between the responses of a sample of individuals to two items on a questionnaire. Unlike the ecological correlation, the data used in determining the individual correlation are not grouped data, and therefore the individual correlation is not based on rates or averages. See CORRELATION, ECOLOGICAL.

correlation, inverse. See CORRELATION, NEGATIVE.

correlation, Kendall partial rank. A nonparametric test of partial correlation for use when the available data for the variables studied are in the form of ranks. It is derived from the Kendall rank correlation test. See CORRELATION, KENDALL RANK; CORRELATION, PARTIAL; NONPARAMETRIC STATISTICS; RANK, STATISTICAL.

correlation, Kendall rank. A nonparametric statistical test, symbolized by the coefficient tau (τ), used to measure the CORRELATION between two variables the data of which are in the form of ranks. It may be used for the same sort of data as the rank difference correlation. The Kendall rank correlation is not so well known or widely used as the rank difference correlation. However, it is particularly useful for small samples. It also has the advantage that it may be extended to a partial correlation coefficient. See CORRELATION, PARTIAL RANK; CORRELATION, RANK DIFFERENCE; NONPARAMETRIC STATISTICS; RANK, STATISTICAL.

correlation, linear. A CORRELATION in which there is a constant ratio between the rates of change of two (or more) quantitative variables. That is, a unit of change in one variable is associated with a set number of units of change in the other variable for the entire range of the observed values of the two variables. Linear correlation between two variables is usually measured by the Pearson product-moment coefficient of correlation, symbolized by r, the most widely used correlation in sociology. See CORRELATION, PEARSON PRODUCT-MOMENT.

correlation, multiple. A measure of CORRELATION between one dependent VARIABLE and a combination of two or more independent variables. Multiple correlation provides an estimate of the combined influence of two or more independent variables on the dependent variable. For example, it could be used to measure the relationship between age and years of schooling combined and hours per week spent watching television. A multiple correlation may be either a linear correlation or a curvilinear correlation. The coefficient of multiple correlation is symbolized by R. See CORRELATION, CURVILINEAR; CORRELATION, LINEAR; CORRELATION, PARTIAL.

correlation, negative. A CORRELATION in which an increase in one variable is associated with a decrease in the other variable. In the case of a negative correlation the COEFFICIENT OF CORRELATION has minus values, ranging from 0 to -1. A negative correlation is also referred to as an inverse correlation. See CORRELATION, POSITIVE.

correlation, partial. A method of measuring the degree of relationship between two variables when the effects of one or more other related variables are removed. Thus if one wishes to study the relationship between two of four interrelated variables, through partial correlation it is possible to remove the effects of two of the variables by holding them constant and then determine the degree of association remaining between the other two.

correlation, partial rank. See CORRELATION, KENDALL PARTIAL RANK.

correlation, Pearson product-moment. The usual method used to measure a linear correlation between two quantitative variables. Symbolized by r, it is the most widely used CORRELATION in sociology. It is in fact so widely used that some writers merely refer to it as the correlation coefficient, assuming that only other measures of correlation need to be specifically named. The Pearson product-moment correlation is a parametric test and depends on the usual parametric assumptions. See CORRELATION, LINEAR; PARAMETRIC STATISTICS.

correlation, positive. A correlation in which an increase in one variable is associated with an increase in the other variable. In the case of a positive correlation the COEFFICIENT OF CORRELATION has plus values, ranging from 0 to 1. A positive correlation is also referred to as a direct correlation. See CORRELATION, NEGATIVE.

correlation, product-moment. See CORRELATION, PEARSON PRODUCT-MOMENT.

correlation, rank difference. A nonparametric statistical test, symbolized by the coefficient rho (ρ), or sometimes r_s, used to measure the CORRELATION between two variables the data of which are in the form of ranks. It is derived from the Pearson product-moment correlation coefficient and is the most widely used correlation for ranked data. It is somewhat easier to compute than the Kendall rank correlation. The rank difference correlation is also known as the Spearman rank correlation. It is linearly related to the KENDALL COEFFICIENT OF CONCORDANCE W. See CORRELATION, PEARSON PRODUCT-MOMENT; NONPARAMETRIC STATISTICS; RANK, STATISTICAL.

correlation, simple. 1. A correlation between two variables, in contrast to a CORRELATION involving more than two variables.

2. A linear correlation in contrast to a nonlinear correlation. See CORRELATION, LINEAR.

3. A linear correlation between two variables, in contrast to a correlation which is either nonlinear or involves more than two variables.

correlation, Spearman rank. See CORRELATION, RANK DIFFERENCE.

correlation, spurious. A CORRELATION between two variables that is due not to a relationship between the variables themselves, but instead to the fact that each of the variables is correlated with a third variable (or variables) that has no connective position between the original two variables. Thus the original correlation does not indicate any real association between the variables, but rather indicates a lack of careful controls in the design of the study. For example, a correlation found among a certain people between eating a particular herb and longevity, would be a spurious correlation if it were due to a third variable, wealth, which does not serve as a link in the association between the first two variables. In other words, in this example, if only the wealthy could afford the herb and only the wealthy could afford a nutritious diet and good medical care, the better diet and better medical care would be the factors that result in greater longevity. The fact that the wealthy class eats the herb is really irrelevant to their greater longevity, making the original correlation spurious.

correlation, tetrachoric. A measure of CORRELATION, symbolized by the coefficient tetrachoric r or r_t, between two variables, each of which is expressed in a dichotomy, or two separate categories. The use of the tetrachoric correlation assumes that each variable is truly continuous, with a normal distribution that has been constricted into a dichotomy. It was originally suggested by Karl Pearson as an estimate of the product-moment correlation coefficient. Its use is limited to the situation in which a researcher has data only in the form of a 2 × 2 table, but knows that the underlying distribution of the two variables is continuous and normal. See CORRELATION, PEARSON PRODUCT-MOMENT.

correlation cluster. A number of intercorrelated variables. A correlation cluster may indicate that the variables represent a single underlying factor. See FACTOR ANALYSIS.

correlation matrix. The arrangement of a series of intercorrelations among a number of variables in the form of a table. The same ordering of the variables is used for the rows and columns of the table. The correlations between each pair of the variables are given in the cells.

correlation ratio. A measure of CORRELATION, symbolized by the coefficient eta (η), used when the relationship between two variables is curvilinear (nonlinear) rather than linear. The correlation ratio may be used for any pattern of curvilinear relationship, and it may be used not only for the association of two quantitative variables, as is the case for most measures of correlation, but also when one VARIABLE is quantitative and one is qualitative. See CORRELATION, CURVILINEAR.

cosmology. The study of the basic nature of the universe—its origin and structure, the nature of time and space, the meaning and essential character of natural laws, and the basic principles underlying the occurrence of events. Cosmology forms a branch of philosophy or theology. Any scientific or religious system rests on certain cosmological assumptions.

cosmopolitan. A person whose sense of involvement and identification is primarily directed toward a larger social world outside of his local organization or community. For example, a professional person who is a cosmopolitan is interested in achieving excellence and recognition at a national or international level. He is relatively unconcerned with local organizational politics and the prestige of local office. While he may remain and actively participate in the local organization for a lifetime, he feels that his primary loyalty is to the larger professional world. The status of a local organization, such as a university, in comparison with similar organizations is largely dependent upon the acquisition and retention of cosmopolitans on its staff. The term was first used by Robert K. Merton, who opposed it to LOCAL. (R. K. Merton, *Social Theory and Social Structure*, Free Press, Glencoe, Ill., 1957.)

council-manager plan of city government. A form of city government consisting of a council and a manager. The executive head, or manager, is not directly responsible to the electorate. He is responsible to an elected city council which hires him to carry out its policies. Ideally, the manager is chosen less for his political popularity or political affiliation than for his ability as a capable executive. See COMMISSION PLAN OF CITY GOVERNMENT; MAYOR-COUNCIL PLAN OF CITY GOVERNMENT.

counseling. The process of using interviews, psychological tests, guidance, and other techniques to help an individual solve his personal problems and plan his future realistically.

counseling, nondirective. A technique used in helping an individual with a personal problem in which the counselor does not make positive suggestions, direct the conversation, or criticize the client. The client is allowed to "talk out" his problem and thereby clarify his problem, see himself objectively, and finally solve his own problem essentially by himself. Any guidance given comes in the form of the counselor's skillfully choosing to repeat or summarize crucial ideas and statements made by the client.

counterformity. A form of NONCONFORMITY in which a person compulsively deviates from the norms of a group toward which he feels negative and hostile. He not only rejects the actions and beliefs of the group, but also tries to have his actions and beliefs as different from those of the group as possible. The term is used by David Krech, Richard S. Crutchfield, and Egerton L. Ballachey. (D. Krech, R. S. Crutchfield, and E. L. Ballachey, *Individual in Society,* McGraw-Hill, New York, 1962.) See REFERENCE GROUP, NEGATIVE.

courtship. Association between an unmarried man and woman, the goal of which is marriage. Courtship practices vary from society to society, and are governed by norms closely interrelated with norms and values regulating the entire marriage and family system.

cousins. See CROSS-COUSINS; PARALLEL COUSINS.

couvade. A custom found in some societies in which after the birth of a child the husband is expected to observe certain taboos and restrictions. Symbolically he may imitate the female experience at childbirth, and in extreme forms even act as though he were suffering all the pains of childbirth.

covariance. A measure of the joint VARIANCE of two or more variables. Each deviation from the arithmetic mean of one VARIABLE is multiplied by the corresponding deviation from the mean of the other variable. The mean of the resulting products is termed the covariance. See MEAN, ARITHMETIC.

covariance, analysis of. The extension of the basic technique of the analysis of VARIANCE to the situation in which there are two or more quantitative variables. The COVARIANCE of the quantitative variables is measured for each of the categories of the qualitative variable, and the resulting measures are compared to see if they differ significantly. The categories of the qualitative variable (or variables) may be referred to as separate samples, and thus it may be said that the covariances of two or more quantitative variables in two or more samples are compared to see if there is a statistically significant difference between the samples. See PROBABILITY; SIGNIFICANCE, STATISTICAL; VARIANCE, ANALYSIS OF.

covariation. See CORRELATION.

covenant, restrictive. See RESTRICTIVE COVENANT.

coyness, ceremonial. See CEREMONIAL COYNESS.

craft union. See UNION, CRAFT.

craze. A novel pattern of behavior that deviates markedly from customary social forms and is followed enthusiastically by a fairly small minority of the members of a community or society with varying degrees of disapproval by the majority. Crazes are of short duration, and often are deliberately stimulated through the use of mass communication for the purpose of economic gain. Those who follow a craze frequently are motivated primarily by a desire for deviance combined with the security of conformity. The craze enables them to deviate from the society as a whole and at the same time to conform to the standards of those who follow the craze. The term craze is usually employed in a sense similar to FAD, but craze often implies a more extreme form of deviance from customary patterns or a pattern that has been deliberately stimulated for economic gain, whereas fad usually implies a spontaneous development. Examples of crazes are hula hoops, Beatle haircuts, and swallowing goldfish. See FASHION.

crime. 1. Any behavior that violates the criminal law.
2. Any behavior that violates any law (criminal, civil, military) that prescribes punitive action against offenders.
3. Any behavior contrary to the group's moral codes for which there are formalized group sanctions whether or not they are laws.
4. Any antisocial behavior harmful to individuals or groups.

crime, folk. A legal violation that is quite common and is not taken seriously by most people within a society. H. Laurence Ross suggests the category folk crime "as a convenient way of thinking about traffic law violations, white collar crime, chiseling, black market dealings, and many other illegal actions that have in common a source in social complexity. As opposed to 'ordinary criminals,' folk criminals are relatively numerous, unstigmatized, and differentially treated in the legal process." (H. L. Ross, *Social Problems*, Winter, 1960–61.)

crime, hypotheses of. See DIFFERENTIAL ASSOCIATION HYPOTHESIS OF CRIME; DIFFERENTIAL GROUP ORGANIZATION HYPOTHESIS OF CRIME; DIFFERENTIAL IDENTIFICATION HYPOTHESIS OF CRIME.

crime, juvenile. See DELINQUENCY, JUVENILE.

crime, organized. Crime committed by members of a formal organization devoted to activities that are in violation of the law. Such criminal organizations have a division of labor with certain roles filled by skilled specialists, a hierarchy of status and authority, their own system of norms, and strict organizational loyalty and discipline. These organizations also often have arrangements with members of the local police and sometimes with certain influential community leaders.

crime, white collar. A "crime committed by a person of respectability and high social status in the course of his occupation. Consequently, it excludes many crimes of the upper class, such as most of their cases of murder, adultery, and intoxication, since these are not customarily a part of their occupational procedures. Also it excludes the confidence games of wealthy members of the underworld, since they are not persons of respectability and high social status." Examples of white collar crime include embezzlement, fraud, graft, illegal combinations in restraint of trade, misrepresentation in advertising, infringement of patents, adulteration of food and drugs, fee-splitting by doctors, and bribery. White collar crimes usually are less severely punished than the more conventional crimes, which are more apt to be committed by members of the lower class, even when the social and economic damage of the white collar crime is greater. There is less public resentment of white collar crime than of other types of crime. The term was introduced by Edwin H. Sutherland. (E. H. Sutherland, *White Collar Crime*, Dryden Press, New York, 1949.)

crime reports, uniform. See UNIFORM CRIME REPORTS.

criminal. 1. A person who is convicted of violating a criminal law. One who is convicted of a felony.

2. A person who commits an antisocial act whether or not he is convicted of committing a crime. This definition would include any person who violates the MORES or behaves in any way that is injurious to society or to other individuals. It would include persons whose violations of the law are not discovered, as well as those whose antisocial acts are not illegal.

3. Because of the varied meanings associated with the term criminal, some writers have attempted to avoid a general definition, and instead focus on types of criminals, such as professional criminals, white collar criminals, those in organized crime, and so forth. They feel that emphasizing types of criminal careers gives a more sociological and less legal orientation to the study of crime. (See W. C. Reckless, *The Crime Problem*, Appleton-Century-Crofts, New York, 1950.)

criminal, accidental. See CRIMINAL, SITUATIONAL.

criminal, legalistic. An individual who violates a law unintentionally either because of ignorance, as in the case of a feeble-minded person, or because the law is so confusing that it is virtually impossible to obey. Persons accused of a crime merely as a pretext to stop them from leading unpopular movements are sometimes also classified as legalistic criminals.

criminal, professional. A career criminal who is highly trained for his work. He often has a philosophy of crime and takes pride in his work. Careers in forgery, counterfeiting, and confidence games are particularly characteristic of professional criminals. For an example of one type of professional criminal see PROFESSIONAL THIEF.

criminal, psychopathic. A person who commits a crime because he is psychologically unable to control his behavior. Psychopathic criminals are psychotics whose psychoses result in illegal acts. They include kleptomaniacs, pyromaniacs, and sexual psychopaths. See PSYCHOPATHIC PERSONALITY; PSYCHOSIS.

criminal, situational. A person who commits a crime because of the overwhelming pressures of an unusual situation in which he finds himself. Criminal behavior is contrary to his normal life pattern, and it is unlikely that he would commit a crime again.

criminal, white collar. See CRIME, WHITE COLLAR.

criminal law. Law enacted by the recognized political authority that prohibits or requires specified behavior by all or by a designated category of persons in the society or community and provides specific punishment, administered by the constituted authority, for violators.

criminality. See CRIME.

criminology. The study of criminal behavior, legal norms, and social attitudes toward various types of crimes and criminals. Criminology includes the sociology of law, the analysis of conflict theories as theoretical explanations for the basic causes of crime in society, the study of the social and psychological determinants of crime, methods of apprehension and punishment, individual and social reform, and the prevention of crime.

criminology, Lombrosian. See LOMBROSIAN THEORY.

crisis. A serious interruption in the normal way of life of an individual or group, resulting from the occurrence of an unexpected situation for which the individual or group is not prepared, and which raises problems for which customary responses are not adequate. A crisis requires the development of new modes of thought and action.

crisis, cumulative. A problem that develops slowly through a long series of events finally reaching a stage where it is so disruptive to the normal life of the individual or group that it can no longer be ignored.

crisis, precipitate. A sudden CRISIS that occurs without warning and that is the result of factors beyond the control of the affected individual or group.

crisis rites. Ceremonies performed at critical times in the life of an individual or group, and in response to immediate needs or anxieties. Examples of crisis rites would include a rain dance performed in times of drought and RITES DE PASSAGE. See CALENDRICAL RITES.

criterion score. In statistics, a score, often based on performance, used to assess the VALIDITY of an INDEX or predictive test score.

critical ratio. A parametric test of statistical significance. Critical ratio, often written C.R. and also referred to as the Z measure, is used to judge whether the difference between two statistics (most commonly—but not necessarily—means) obtained from two groups probably represents a true difference between the groups studied or a meaningless difference due to chance. The critical ratio is obtained by dividing the difference between the statistics obtained from the two groups by the STANDARD ERROR of that difference ($C.R. = \frac{D}{\sigma_D}$). The larger the size of the critical ratio, the less likely it is that the obtained difference is due to chance. Critical ratio is suitable for large samples. For small samples, see t TEST. See also PARAMETRIC STATISTICS; PROBABILITY; SIGNIFICANCE, STATISTICAL.

critical region. See REGION OF REJECTION.

cross-cousins. Children of siblings of the opposite sex, that is, the children of a brother and sister.

cross-cultural index. See HUMAN RELATIONS AREA FILE.

cross-cultural method. The gathering of comparable data from different cultures in order to test hypotheses concerning individual and group behavior. The cross-cultural method is a way of learning which theoretical generalizations or concepts have applicability only within certain cultures, and a method for developing more universal generalizations. See COMPARATIVE METHOD.

cross-fertilization, cultural. A process in which cultures reciprocally influence each other. It may be regarded as one type of acculturation, that is, acculturation in which there is an exchange of culture traits and a mutual modification of the cultures involved in the exchange. The term also implies the stimulation of each culture to further development based on but not limited to the acquisition of the new traits.

cross-hatched map. A map that shows differences in rates of any given phenomenon (for example, birth rates) for geographic areas by grouping the rates into a few classes each of which is represented by a type of cross hatching. A cross-hatched map emphasizes relative rather than absolute frequencies of occurrence. The cross hatching is arranged so that the lowest frequency is lightly hatched or plain white. The hatching increases in density for each higher frequency class to give an increasingly darker impression. The highest frequency is usually represented by solid black. The cross-hatched map is frequently used in ecological studies of the spatial distribution of social phenomena. It is also often used to show the distribution of specified social problems. The cross-hatched map differs from the shaded or CHOROPLETH MAP only in that the latter uses variations in shade rather than cross hatching. The cross-hatched map is usually preferred because it is clearer when only black and white are available.

cross-sectional experimental design. See EXPERIMENTAL DESIGN, CROSS-SECTIONAL.

cross-tabulation. A joint TABULATION of data with regard to two or more variables, each of which is divided into at least two categories. A cross-tabulation indicates the number of cases that occur jointly in each combination of categories of the variables studied. For example, if the variables were sex and marital status, one would tabulate the number of married men, single men, married women, and single women. Cross-tabulation is a basic step in the analysis of data.

crowd. A temporary grouping of individuals with a common focus or interest, in physical proximity, and without a history of previous interaction. Usually when the common interest or activity changes the crowd dissolves. A crowd is a type of AGGREGATE. The term crowd covers a wide variety of forms, all of which sociologists wish to distinguish from the more highly organized COLLECTIVITY and social GROUP. On the other hand, a crowd is also distinguished from an AUDIENCE in that there is a greater degree of emotional stimulation among the individuals involved. It is distinguished from a PUBLIC by the fact that it involves physical proximity. College students at a homecoming football game would be a crowd, and in a minimal sense the aggregate formed when people stand on a street corner and wait for a bus would also be considered a crowd—a casual crowd. Crowd behavior is an elementary form of COLLECTIVE BEHAVIOR. See CROWD, CASUAL.

crowd, acting. A CROWD that is focused on an external objective, and intent upon action to achieve some limited but seemingly important purpose. The acting crowd is often conceived as an instrument for the release of strong emotional tensions felt by the participants in situations where the normal social controls of society have temporarily no effective influence. An acting crowd that is aggressive or destructive is often called a MOB.

crowd, casual. The type of CROWD having the least organization and emotional interaction. Its existence tends to be momentary. The collection of individuals involved have a common object of attention but it is of only passing interest. Window shoppers, people routinely waiting in line for theater tickets or a bus, or people just standing together as they watch the activities of a construction crew putting up a new building are examples of the casual crowd.

crowd, conventionalized. A CROWD whose behavior is directed by established and regularized expectations and characterized by traditional or conventional patterns. Such a crowd may be found, for example, at a baseball game, a wrestling match, or a bull fight.

crowd, expressive. A CROWD that displays unrestrained collective behavior. An expressive crowd has no clearly defined goal or external purpose. Its activity is engaged in as an end in itself, and that end is usually the free expression of emotional feelings, including dancing, weeping, and shouting. The dominant unifying element in such a crowd is the mutual emotional stimulation of the participants. The crowd at Times Square on New Year's Eve and the "dancing crowd" behavior of teen-agers in the 1960's are examples of this phenomenon. Often the behavior of some religious sects is classified as expressive crowd behavior, but it must be pointed out that seemingly uncontrolled forms of religious behavior are usually conventionalized and may even be said to have important individual and group goals. Pentecostal and early Methodist meetings served to release the participants from their usual inhibitions, but they also served to reorient them to new patterns of intuitive religious understanding, as well as to new group identification or religious fellowship. These functions were (and are) often explicitly understood by the participants.

crystallization, class. See CLASS CRYSTALLIZATION.

crystallization, status. See STATUS CONSISTENCY.

cult. An amorphous type of religious organization. Membership in a cult is loosely defined, and usually involves simply the acceptance of certain beliefs and practices. No one is born into a cult, and usually there is no formal system for joining. There may not even be a list of members. Adherence to the beliefs and practices of the cult is voluntary, and there is no system of enforcement or discipline. Theosophy, Spiritualism, and the Churchless Christians of Japan are examples of cults. See DENOMINATION; ECCLESIA; SECT.

cult, cargo. See CARGO CULT.

cultural. Pertaining to CULTURE. See SOCIAL.

cultural absolute. See ABSOLUTE, CULTURAL.

cultural acceleration, hypothesis of. A thesis proposed by Hornell Hart that "over the long sweep of time, man's power to carry out his purposes, in the material, biological, psychological, and sociological realms, has tended to increase at an accelerating rate (though with recurrent stagnations and setbacks), and the rate of acceleration has itself tended to accelerate." (H. Hart in *Symposium on Sociological Theory*, edited by L. Gross, Row, Peterson, Evanston, Ill., 1959.) See EVOLUTION, CULTURAL; EVOLUTION, SOCIAL.

cultural alternatives or **variants.** See ALTERNATIVES, CULTURAL.

cultural anthropology. See ANTHROPOLOGY, CULTURAL.

cultural artifacts. See ARTIFACTS, CULTURAL.

cultural blindness. A predisposition in people to see the world about them in terms of the categories they have been taught and therefore not to be aware of relationships and events that are evident to people of other cultural backgrounds. A way of seeing (made possible by culture) is a way of not seeing, as well.

cultural conditioning. See ENCULTURATION.

cultural configuration. The basic dominant integrative pattern of a culture around which the ways of life of a people are organized. The configuration is composed of interlocking and interdependent beliefs and principles that tend to be elaborated and refined into a distinctive theme. Some anthropologists have attempted to show a relationship between cultural configurations and personality types. See, for example, APOLLONIAN CULTURE; see also NATIONAL CHARACTER.

cultural convergence. See CONVERGENCE, CULTURAL.

cultural cross-fertilization. See CROSS-FERTILIZATION, CULTURAL.

cultural determinism. 1. The view that human behavior and personality are determined primarily by cultural factors.

2. The view that culture basically must be explained in its own terms and on its own level, and cannot be reduced to the study of the individuals who possess it at a particular time. Culture, because it exists before and after the life of a single individual and shapes the thoughts and actions of those who possess it, is not determined by individuals but operates instead on the basis of its own system of laws.

cultural drift. Unplanned culture change resulting from a series of small changes within a culture in the same direction. These changes are cumulative and in time lead to the emergence of new cultural forms. Some anthropologists have used the concept of cultural drift to explain the ready acceptance of, or resistance to, culture traits diffused from other cultures. They suggest that those traits in harmony with the trends of internal drift of a culture will be rapidly accepted, whereas those contrary to these trends will be resisted or rejected.

cultural ethos. The predominant ideas, values, and ideals of a culture or subculture which give it its distinctive character.

cultural evolution. See EVOLUTION, CULTURAL.

cultural focus. A term introduced by Melville J. Herskovits to refer to "the tendency of every culture to exhibit greater complexity, greater variation in the institutions of some of its aspects than in others. So striking is this tendency to develop certain phases of life, while others remain in the background, so to speak, that in the shorthand of the disciplines that study human societies these focal aspects are often used to characterize whole cultures." (M. J. Herskovits, *Man and His Works,* Knopf, New York, 1949.)

cultural heritage. See CULTURE.

cultural hybrid. See MARGINAL MAN.

cultural imperative. A cultural form essential for the survival of any society. Cultural imperatives would include methods of providing food and shelter, of caring for the young, of transmitting knowledge, of limiting internal conflict, and so forth. Cultural imperatives are based on the physiological and social needs of men in all societies. Frequently they are referred to as the functional requisites of any society. See FUNCTIONAL REQUISITE.

cultural inertia. See INERTIA, CULTURAL.

cultural integration. See INTEGRATION, CULTURAL.

cultural lag. See CULTURE LAG.

cultural landscape. A term used by human geographers to refer to the geographical and physical environment as modified by culture.

cultural monism. A doctrine that advocates the assimilation of ethnic minorities into the dominant culture of a society to attain cultural uniformity within the society, and thus eliminate the possibility of internal conflict between ethnic groups. See CULTURAL PLURALISM.

cultural motor habits. See MOTOR HABITS, CULTURAL.

cultural need. See CULTURAL IMPERATIVE.

cultural object. 1. A material object of a culture: an artifact, or material culture trait.

2. Any aspect of the culture (for example, an idea, a value, a custom) to which a person is oriented in a situation and which he regards as part of the situation, that is, as external to himself and not a part of his personality. The concept has been used in this sense in social action theory.

(See T. Parsons, *The Social System,* Free Press, Glencoe, Ill., 1951.) See ACTION THEORY, SOCIAL.

cultural pluralism. Cultural heterogeneity, with ethnic and other minority groups maintaining their identity within a society. Advocates of cultural pluralism hold that cultural differences within a society should be retained insofar as these differences do not conflict with major values and norms of the dominant culture. They believe that culturally diverse groups can live in harmony and that mutual understanding rather than assimilation should be the goal. See CULTURAL MONISM.

cultural possibilities, principle of. A principle, first proposed by Alexander Goldenweiser, which states that the number of possible means of satisfying any cultural need is limited, and therefore the possible variety of cultural forms that may arise in response to a need is limited. See CULTURAL IMPERATIVE; LIMITED POSSIBILITIES, PRINCIPLE OF.

cultural premises. See CULTURE, IMPLICIT.

cultural rationalization. See RATIONALIZATION, CULTURAL.

cultural relativism. The principle that one cannot understand, interpret, or evaluate social and social psychological phenomena meaningfully unless the phenomena under study are seen with special reference to the role they play in the larger social and cultural system. The customs of a culture can be judged or evaluated validly only by considering what values are associated with them, what needs are being satisfied, and their general relationship to other obligations, expectations, and moral codes of the particular culture under study. Thus, cultural relativism holds that the customs of one culture cannot objectively or validly be judged superior to those of another.

cultural residue. See CULTURAL SURVIVAL.

cultural specialties. See SPECIALTIES, CULTURAL.

cultural survival. A CULTURE TRAIT that is maintained even though it no longer performs its original function. Often a trait that originally fulfilled a utilitarian purpose, but in time, due to technological or other changes, has ceased to be of utilitarian importance, is maintained because it is traditional or decorative. Examples of cultural survivals that are readily observable include men's ties, hatbands, coat-sleeve buttons, the use of fireplaces in homes with central heating, and the use of candles where there are electric lights. Cultural survivals are sometimes referred to as cultural residues.

cultural system. A theoretical model of a CULTURE as a system of interrelated parts. This concept is particularly emphasized in FUNCTIONALISM, which is concerned with the analysis of the functional interaction of the parts within the system. The cultural system usually is distinguished from the SOCIAL SYSTEM, the two together being referred to as the sociocultural system.

cultural theme. A major pattern of values within a culture that provides important underlying assumptions upon which systems of belief and standards of behavior are based. Morris E. Opler, who introduced the term, defined it as "a postulate or position, declared or implied, and usually controlling behavior or stimulating activity, which is tacitly approved or openly promoted in a society." (M. E. Opler, *American Journal of Sociology*, November 1945.)

cultural transmission. The process by which accumulated culture is passed down, by both formal and informal methods, from generation to generation through learning. It is the inheritance of the ways of acting, thinking, and feeling of a culture. See SOCIALIZATION.

cultural transmutation. See TRANSMUTATION, CULTURAL.

cultural universals. See UNIVERSALS, CULTURAL.

culture. The way of life of a social group; the group's total man-made environment, including all the material and nonmaterial products of group life that are transmitted from one generation to the next. The classic definition of culture, which most sociological definitions have followed, was stated by Edward B. Tylor: "That complex whole which includes knowledge, belief, art, morals, law, custom, and any other capabilities and habits acquired by man as a member of society." (E. B. Tylor, *Primitive Culture*, Vol. 1, John Murray, London, 1871.) After surveying current definitions of culture, Alfred L. Kroeber and Clyde Kluckhohn concluded that the consensus of most social scientists is that "culture consists of patterns, explicit and implicit, of and for behavior acquired and transmitted by symbols, constituting the distinctive achievements of human groups, including their embodiments in artifacts; the essential core of culture consists of traditional (i.e., historically derived and selected) ideas and especially their attached values." ("Culture: A Critical Review of Concepts and Definitions," *Papers of the Peabody Museum of American Archaeology and Ethnology*, Harvard University, Vol. XLVII, No. 1, 1952.)

It should be noted that some sociologists exclude material objects (artifacts) from their definition of culture. They include technical knowledge about the artifacts, but not the artifacts themselves. See CULTURE, NONMATERIAL.

Other sociologists have suggested combining the concepts culture and SOCIETY on the grounds that all human phenomena are truly sociocultural. However, most prefer to maintain an analytical distinction between culture and society, despite the difficulty, at times, of keeping the terms separate.

culture, adaptive. 1. Those aspects of a CULTURE, the culture traits and complexes, that represent a society's adjustment to its physical environment and enable it to survive. According to this definition, adaptive culture would include methods of agriculture and manufacturing, technical knowledge, norms regulating economic organization, and so forth.

2. Those culture traits and complexes that represent an adjustment of the nonmaterial culture, particularly the values and norms regulating social and institutional life, to the material culture. For example, the norms, values, and patterns of social roles that developed because of the invention and spread of the automobile form part of the adaptive culture. The adaptive culture may not necessarily lead to a perfect adjustment. See CULTURE, NONMATERIAL; CULTURE COMPLEX; CULTURE LAG; CULTURE TRAIT.

culture, Apollonian and Dionysian. See APOLLONIAN CULTURE.

culture, control. See CONTROL CULTURE.

culture, core. See UNIVERSALS, CULTURAL.

culture, covert. See CULTURE, IMPLICIT.

culture, explicit. Those aspects of a CULTURE of which the members of the society are fully aware and which may be directly observed. Explicit culture includes recognized standards of right and wrong, typical patterns of behavior, technology, and all other readily discerned aspects of culture. It is sometimes referred to as overt culture.

culture, idealistic. See IDEALISTIC CULTURE.

culture, ideational. See IDEATIONAL CULTURE.

culture, implicit. Those aspects of a CULTURE of which the members of the society are only partially or not at all aware. Implicit culture consists of assumptions and premises underlying behavior and thought, but not usually verbalized or recognized. Some aspects of implicit culture at times may be more easily recognized by persons from a different culture, because those who share the culture may so thoroughly accept certain assumptions that they are not at all aware of them. Implicit culture is sometimes referred to as covert culture.

culture, mass. See MASS CULTURE.

culture, material. All man-made physical objects. Material culture is sometimes also considered as including natural objects that have meaning to man and are used by him, although not manufactured or modified by him. On the other hand, some sociologists prefer to exclude all material items from the definition of CULTURE. See CULTURE, NONMATERIAL.

culture, nonmaterial. All man-made intangible culture traits, such as technical skills, norms, knowledge, beliefs, attitudes, and language, which are passed down from generation to generation. See CULTURE.

culture, occupational. See OCCUPATIONAL CULTURE.

culture, overt. See CULTURE, EXPLICIT.

culture, sensate. See SENSATE CULTURE.

culture accumulation. The elaboration of a CULTURE by the addition of more new elements to the existing cultural base than are discarded. A culture may build up and transmit from one generation to another an accumulation of such elements as instruments, skills, concepts, and ideas (including ideas about the organization of society).

culture adhesion. The development of an association between two or more aspects of a CULTURE, or culture traits, that do not have an inherent functional connection. The association of the traits is due to certain circumstances in the history of the particular culture or to the fact that the traits were acquired from another culture in association with each other. An example of culture adhesion may be found in the association of many of the traits found in the Christmas complex, that is, the association of Christmas as a religious holiday with snow, evergreen trees, holly, mistletoe, and so forth. See CULTURE TRAIT.

culture area. A geographic region in which the inhabitants share a common CULTURE or CULTURE PATTERN. A culture area may be made up of a number of subcultures, each of which has distinctive and identifiable elements of culture, although sharing the characteristic culture pattern of the larger culture area.

culture base. The total existing CULTURE of a specific society at a given time. The term is most often used in discussions of the development of inventions or innovations of any sort, whether in the material or nonmaterial culture.

culture center. The locality where a CULTURE or distinctive aspect of a culture (a CULTURE PATTERN or CULTURE COMPLEX) is at its point of greatest concentration, and from which the distinctive pattern of a CULTURE AREA is usually diffused. It may also be the culture's point of origin, and the place where the culture is found in its least modified form. It is sometimes referred to as the culture climax.

culture change. Any change in any aspect (material or nonmaterial) of a CULTURE, whether by addition, subtraction, or modification of culture traits or complexes. Culture change may come from many sources, but most often it occurs through contact with other cultures, inventions, or the internal adjustments of a culture.

culture climax. See CULTURE CENTER.

culture complex. Any integrated and patterned system of culture traits that functions as a unit in a society. It is sometimes referred to as culture trait complex or simply trait complex. Such varied examples as the following are possible: the baseball complex in the United States and Japan, the football complex in the United States, the automobile complex, Christmas, and the rice complex in China. See CULTURE TRAIT.

culture conflict. Mental conflict within an individual (or a group of individuals) between two cultures, both of which are partially accepted and which provide certain contradictory standards and opposing loyalties. The term is not usually used to refer specifically to conflict between groups. See MARGINAL MAN.

culture contact. Interaction between members of groups with different cultures that results in the diffusion of culture traits between the cultures involved. Usually, although not always, culture contact results in some modification of both cultures. However, the degree of reciprocal influence may vary greatly. One CULTURE may be profoundly influenced by another culture, while having in return only a slight influence, or there may be a more equal exchange of culture traits. The modification of one culture by another is usually based on contact between individuals from the two cultures who pass on the newly learned trait to others of their own culture. It rarely involves direct contact between entire groups. Culture contact may result from trade, migration, missionary activity, tourism, or war.

culture convergence. See CONVERGENCE, CULTURAL.

culture element. See CULTURE TRAIT.

culture epoch. One of a number of major categories of CULTURE, based primarily on the level of technology, such as the PALEOLITHIC AGE, the NEOLITHIC AGE, the Bronze Age, the Iron Age.

culture-epoch theory. The theory that all cultures pass through a series of stages of development, termed epochs, and that each individual person in his development passes through an essentially similar series of stages. The theory, no longer accepted by sociologists or cultural anthropologists, was related both to the notion in biology that ontogeny recapitulates phylogeny (that the development of an individual retraces the development of the species) and to the belief in cultural evolution. See EVOLUTION, CULTURAL.

culture-fair test. An INTELLIGENCE TEST designed to minimize the influence of cultural differences (either between societies or among subcultures within a society) on comprehension and performance on the test.

culture gradient. The steady decline in the occurrence or importance of a CULTURE TRAIT or CULTURE COMPLEX as one moves away from the culture center.

culture heritage. See CULTURE.

culture hero. See HERO.

culture island. A local community with a CULTURE that is clearly distinct from that of the surrounding area. Culture islands may occur in urban or rural areas. Examples would be an Italian-American neighborhood in a large American city or an Amish farming community in Pennsylvania.

culture lag. A situation in which some parts of a CULTURE change at a faster rate than other, related parts, with a resulting disruption of the integration and equilibrium of the culture. This concept was introduced by William F. Ogburn, who applied it especially to modern, industrial societies in which the material culture, through rapid advances in technology and science, has developed at a much faster rate than that part of the nonmaterial culture which regulates man's adjustment to the material culture (sometimes termed the *adaptive culture*). "The thesis is that the various parts of modern culture are not changing at the same rate, some parts are changing much more rapidly than others; and that since there is a correlation and interdependence of parts, a rapid change in one part of our culture requires readjustments through other changes in the various correlated parts of culture. . . . Where one part of culture changes first, through some discovery or invention, and occasions changes in some part of culture dependent upon it, there frequently is a delay in the changes occasioned in the dependent part of culture. . . . When the material conditions change, changes are occasioned in the adaptive culture. But these changes in the adaptive culture do not synchronize exactly with the change in the material culture. There is a lag which may last for varying lengths of time, sometimes indeed, for many years." (W. F. Ogburn, *Social Change*, Dell, New York, 1966.) The hypothesis of culture lag holds in particular that in modern societies there has been a tendency for changes in the political, educational, family, and religious institutions to fall behind technological changes. See CULTURE, ADAPTIVE; INERTIA, CULTURAL.

culture parallels. See PARALLELISM.

culture pattern. 1. The organization of culture complexes constituting the entire cultural configuration of a society.

2. The predominant values and beliefs that characterize a CULTURE. This is equivalent to the dominant cultural themes or ethos of a society. See CULTURAL THEME; ETHOS.

3. An organization of two or more culture traits that can be viewed as a unit. This usage is synonymous with CULTURE COMPLEX.

culture region. See CULTURE AREA.

culture shock. The often rather severe psychological and social mal-adjustment many individuals experience when they visit or live in a society different from their own. Culture shock involves bewilderment due to new customs, unknown expectations, a feeling of being conspicuous, "different," and foreign, and often a foreign language.

culture trait. The simplest identifiable and significant unit of a culture used in a particular analysis. Thus the size of the simplest unit would be relative to the problem under study. Those who define CULTURE as including material objects would consider such items as the pencil, the cigarette, the football, and the newspaper to be culture traits (but again each of these could be broken down into even smaller units if the analysis demanded it). Those who do not include physical objects as part of culture, as well as those who do, would include such items as specific ideas, beliefs, and customs. Thus the practice of smoking tobacco, using a fork, writing, playing football, wearing shoes (or not wearing them), and the belief in ghosts or spirits would be examples of culture traits. Culture traits are also referred to as culture elements. See CULTURE COMPLEX.

culture trait complex. See CULTURE COMPLEX.

cultures, indexed. See HUMAN RELATIONS AREA FILE.

cumulation, principle of. A process of progressive change in two or more variables resulting from their interrelationship. Cumulation occurs when two or more variables are so related that a change in one results in a change in the same direction in the second, which in turn leads to a further change in the first, and so on. This process is frequently referred to as the vicious circle, but the change may be in any direction—desirable or undesirable—and therefore is not necessarily "vicious." The principle of cumulation was proposed by Gunnar Myrdal as a model of dynamic causation and an attempt to counter notions of stable equilibrium which he felt were too predominant in sociological theory and research. (See G. Myrdal, *An American Dilemma,* Harper, New York, 1944.)

cumulative frequency graph. See OGIVE.

cumulative scale. An attitude scale consisting of a series of attitude statements so related to each other and so arranged that an individual who agrees with a given statement will also tend to agree with all statements arranged below it. The statements (items) are arranged in order of the proportion of respondents agreeing with each of them. The basic idea is that an individual who agrees with a given statement will tend to agree with all statements with which a larger proportion of persons agree. This pattern results from the underlying values and norms which the statements reflect and which assign an order of priorities among them. See GUTTMAN SCALE; SCALE, ATTITUDE; UNDIMENSIONAL SCALE.

curve. See FREQUENCY DISTRIBUTION CURVE.

curve, area under the. See AREA UNDER THE CURVE.

curve, learning. See LEARNING CURVE.

curve chart or **graph.** See LINE GRAPH.

curve, normal. See FREQUENCY DISTRIBUTION CURVE, NORMAL.

curvilinear correlation. See CORRELATION, CURVILINEAR.

curvilinear regression. See REGRESSION, CURVILINEAR.

custom. 1. A FOLKWAY, or form of social behavior, that, having persisted for a long period of time, is well established in a society, has become traditional, and has received some degree of formal recognition.

2. Sometimes the term is used synonymously with *social norm.* See NORM, SOCIAL.

cybernetics. The study of communication among men, animals, and machines, with particular emphasis on the FEEDBACK of information and the function of feedback in the process of control. In cybernetics communication and control are classed together, for as Norbert Wiener, who introduced the term cybernetics in its current usage, explains: "When I control the actions of another person, I communicate a message to him, and although this message is in the imperative mood, the technique of communication does not differ from that of a message of fact. Furthermore, if my control is to be effective I must take cognizance of any messages from him which may indicate that the order is understood and has been obeyed." (N. Wiener, *The Human Use of Human Beings,* Doubleday, Garden City, N.Y., 1954.) Cybernetics was applied originally in the fields of mathematics, engineering, and electronics, and later was extended to other fields, including, recently, the social sciences. In applying cybernetics to the field of sociology the central thesis is that "society can only be understood through a study of the messages and the communication facilities which belong to it; and that in the future development of these messages and communication facilities, messages between man and machines, between machines and man, and between machine and machine, are destined to play an ever-increasing part." (*Ibid.*)

cyclical movement. Repetitious change involving the recurrence of certain conditions or events. The recurrent phases of the cycle may vary in duration. The BUSINESS CYCLE is an example of cyclical movement.

D

D test. See Kolmogorov-Smirnov D test.

Darwinian theory of evolution. As applied to man, the theory that man evolved gradually from animal ancestors through a process of genetic mutation and natural selection resulting from the survival of the fittest, that is, the persistence of those organic changes that provide the greatest competitive advantage for survival in a particular environment. See social Darwinism.

data. Information collected from observation or measurement from which an attempt is made to develop generalizations or conclusions. When the data are without form or organization they are called raw data. See bivariate data; discrete data; qualitative data.

dating. See rating-dating complex.

daydream. A type of mental fantasy that may be but is not necessarily wishful or purposeless thinking or a withdrawal from reality. For most people it is often an important way to preview or experience various possible roles they believe they desire or they expect to play in the future. Hence daydreams may not only be creative but may also play an essential role in the preparation of realistic social behavior, despite a variable proportion of preparatory miscalculations.

daytime population, urban. The actual distribution of an urban population—at work, shopping, etc.—at a particular period of time of the day. The daytime population of an urban area may be contrasted with the nighttime population, and indeed most analyses of population distribution deal with where people sleep. However, there have been a growing number of studies of daytime population patterns. The central business district of a large city may have a small nighttime population (or even smaller resident population), but a large daytime population. See ecology, human.

death rate, age-sex specific. The number of deaths per 1,000 persons in any given age-sex category, for example, the number of deaths per 1,000 men aged fifty in a particular population. See DEATH RATE, SPECIFIC.

death rate, crude. The number of deaths per 1,000 persons occurring within a year period in a particular population. The crude death rate gives the rate at which the members of a population are dying, without regard to any of the characteristics of the population. Its most serious deficiency is its failure to take into account the age and sex structure of the population. See DEATH RATE, SPECIFIC; DEATH RATE, STANDARDIZED.

death rate, infant. The annual number of deaths per 1,000 infants (under the age of one) in the population.

death rate, specific. The number of deaths per 1,000 persons in any given category of a particular population. The most common type of specific death rate is the age-sex specific rate but it is possible to ascertain the death rate for any other category. For example, one could have a race-specific death rate or an education-specific death rate, or a rate specific to a combination of two or more categories, as a race-age-sex specific death rate.

death rate, standardized. A death rate that combines the age-sex specific death rates of a population to give an over-all rate that takes into account the age and sex structure of the population. It is obtained by multiplying the age-sex specific rate of each category by the number of persons in that age-sex category, adding the products, and then dividing the sum by the number of persons in the total population. This provides a death rate that permits the comparison of different populations while controlling on differences in the age and sex distributions of the populations. The standardized death rate is widely used. See DEATH RATE, AGE-SEX SPECIFIC; DEATH RATE, SPECIFIC.

decentralization. An ecological process in which business, industry, and other service agencies tend to move away from the center of a city when land and other costs become too high and congestion becomes too great. The movement is toward secondary centers, or subcenters, located in outlying areas where there is more space and costs are generally lower. This process is the opposite of CENTRALIZATION.

decile. One of the points that divide a FREQUENCY DISTRIBUTION into ten equal parts, so that each part contains ten percent of the cases. Ten percent of the cases in the distribution fall below the first decile. Twenty percent of the total cases are below the second decile, thirty percent below the third decile, etc. See PERCENTILE; QUARTILE.

deconcentration. An ecological process in which there is a decrease in the proportion of people residing near the center of the city and a movement of residences to areas on the outskirts of the city or metropolitan area. See CONCENTRATION.

deduction. The process of reasoning from general principles to particular instances. Deduction is used in the SCIENTIFIC METHOD when specific hypotheses or particular predictions are derived from broader theoretical principles. See INDUCTION.

defense mechanism. Behavior motivated by an individual's attempt to maintain a favorable self image and to avoid embarrassment and expected criticism from other people. Defense behavior is common in normal social interaction, and is important for personality integration as well as social organization.

deference behavior. A type of behavior that is intended to convey respect and appreciation on the part of one person for another. The term was introduced by Erving Goffman, who wrote: "It appears that deference behavior on the whole tends to be honorific and politely toned, conveying appreciation of the recipient that is in many ways more complimentary to the recipient than the actor's true sentiments might warrant. The actor typically gives the recipient the benefit of the doubt, and may even conceal low regard by extra punctiliousness. Thus acts of deference often attest to ideal guidelines to which the actual activity between actor and recipient can now and then be referred." (E. Goffman, *American Anthropologist,* June 1956.) Goffman distinguishes between two types of deference behavior: AVOIDANCE RITUALS and PRESENTATIONAL RITUALS.

deferred gratification pattern. A term introduced by Louis Schneider and Sverre Lysgaard to refer to a pattern of life in which there is emphasis upon the "postponement of gratifications or satisfactions. . . . It may be contended that it does indeed fall into a *pattern,* characteristic of the so-called 'middle class,' members of which tend to delay achievement of economic independence through a relatively elaborate process of education, tend to defer sexual gratification through intercourse, show a relatively marked tendency to save money, and the like. . . . The deferred gratification pattern appears to be closely associated with 'impulse renunciation.' Thus, some of the pertinent current literature emphasizes, by way of example, middle-class renunciation of impulses toward violence. . . . A more important point is the *normative* character of the deferred gratification pattern. Middle class persons feel that they *should* save, postpone, and renounce a variety of gratifications. There are very probably also normative elements in the 'lower class' pattern of non-deferment." (L. Schneider and S. Lysgaard, *American Sociological Review,* April 1953.) See AFFECTIVE NEUTRALITY; AFFECTIVITY-AFFECTIVE NEUTRALITY.

definition, nominal. A statement of the way in which a concept is used. In essence it involves the expression of the concept in another word or words. The purpose of nominal definitions is to provide an agreed-upon set of meanings for the concepts of a discipline, so that persons using the same concepts may understand each other. The value of a nominal definition depends upon its logical consistency with other definitions within a theoretical system and upon its utility as an analytical device. A nominal definition "has no truth claims and it is therefore senseless to ask whether it is true or false. It is merely a resolution, a stipulation, a convention, an agreement, an expression of volition to use a word or other symbol in a particular way. . . . we may not conclude that nominal definitions are unimportant simply because they are not real definitions. Nominal definitions have their own important functions to perform. . . . some sociologists believe the prime task of current methodology in sociology, and indeed in all the social sciences, is to adopt a common system of symbolic notation . . ." (R. Bierstedt in *Symposium on Sociological Theory*, edited by L. Gross, Row, Peterson, Evanston, Ill., 1959.) A nominal definition is sometimes referred to as a verbal definition. See DEFINITION, REAL.

definition, operational. See OPERATIONAL DEFINITION.

definition, real. A definition that is a proposition about the essential nature of a given phenomenon. A real definition can be regarded as "an hypothesis concerning the nature of the phenomenon under investigation." It is "a universal affirmative proposition. . . . no real definition of any concept in any field can be constructed without empirical knowledge of the phenomenon in question." (R. Bierstedt in *Symposium on Sociological Theory*, edited by L. Gross, Row, Peterson, Evanston, Ill., 1959.) See DEFINITION, NOMINAL.

definition of role, personal. See ROLE-DEFINITION, PERSONAL.

definition of the situation. The social-psychological process in which an individual examines and evaluates a situation prior to deciding what attitudes and behavior are appropriate. The way a person interprets a given object or set of circumstances and the meaning it has for him are in great part determined by his culture, particularly his values and social norms. Thus how a person defines a situation and his attitude toward it will be similar to the definition and attitude of those who share common values and experiences. Children, because of incomplete socialization to adult norms, see and react to their environment differently from adults. The adult or group who, for any one of a number of reasons, does not share orientations similar to others' defines situations differently and thus acts inappropriately and is viewed by others as either abnormal or deviant. The term was first used by W. I. Thomas and Florian Znaniecki in *The Polish Peasant in Europe and America* (Vol. I, University of Chicago Press, Chicago, 1918).

deflation. An economic condition characterized by a shortage of available money and purchasing demand relative to the supply of goods available, a decline in prices and wages, a rise in unemployment, and a decline in business activity. See BUSINESS CYCLE; INFLATION.

degrees of freedom. In statistical calculations, the maximum number of values of a VARIABLE (or variables) that are free to vary under a given set of conditions. For example, when the sum of four values is fixed, only three of the values are open to choice, for after the three are chosen the value of the fourth is determined by the sum. Therefore, there are three degrees of freedom for four values of a variable, and in general the degrees of freedom are one less than the number of values of the variable $(N-1)$. In a CONTINGENCY TABLE the degrees of freedom are one less than the number of rows multiplied by one less than the number of columns, usually written $(r-1)(c-1)$.

delinquency. Strictly, any violation of law by an adult or child. Usually, however, delinquency refers to juvenile delinquency. See DELINQUENCY, JUVENILE.

delinquency, juvenile. A violation of a law or ordinance by an individual below the legal adult age of the community. Juvenile delinquency is essentially a legal concept. It does not include all acts of misbehavior or even serious misbehavior by children or youth, but only those acts that violate a law. Adults are considered more responsible for their actions than are children or adolescents, and much juvenile delinquent behavior when performed by an adult is considered criminal behavior. However, there are situations in which juveniles are legally restricted whereas adults are free (e.g., buying liquor or publications judged obscene only for juveniles). The legal age dividing juvenile delinquency from adult crime is most often 18, but varies from state to state. The punishment of delinquent behavior is influenced by the attitudes of the local community and the degree of general tolerance of youthful misbehavior.

delusion. A belief strongly held by an individual even though it is clearly contrary to reality. The belief is maintained by the individual even though there is sufficient evidence that it is false. A persistent delusion is a symptom of PSYCHOSIS, and is especially characteristic of paranoid patients. It may take various forms. In delusion of grandeur the individual believes himself to be a person of great fame or important accomplishments. In delusion of reference he believes that chance events and irrelevant conversations are aimed at him. In delusion of persecution he believes he is the victim of sinister plots. See PARANOIA.

demand mobility. See MOBILITY, DEMAND.

deme. An endogamous kin group. See ENDOGAMY.

democracy. A political system based upon rule by the consent of the governed, i.e., government based directly or indirectly upon the will of the majority of the members of a community or society. In direct democracy, as in ancient Athens, the citizens themselves legislate, that is, vote directly on laws. A more common system, more suited to larger societies, is that of representative democracy, in which the citizens elect representatives who in turn legislate the laws of the society. Essential to true representative democracy are free elections and the secret ballot. Moreover, although democracy is based on majority rule, the protection of minority rights has always been regarded as an essential aspect of the democratic system. Also closely associated with, and usually considered essential to, political democracy are equality before the law, freedom of speech, press, and assembly, and protection from arbitrary arrest. Furthermore, in practice, in a large and varied society democracy also depends on the free competition and balancing of INTEREST GROUPS so that opposing groups may achieve consensus and compromise with minimal conflict. Although democracy is basically a political concept, it is also used in a philosophical sense to denote the inherent equality, worth, and human rights of every individual. In addition, the term economic democracy is used by those who favor greater economic equality, industrial democracy by those who favor control of industries by workers, and social democracy by those who oppose the social class system. Furthermore, groups of any sort may be referred to as democratic or undemocratic depending on the degree of influence over important decision-making by the membership at large of the group.

democratic leadership. See LEADERSHIP, DEMOCRATIC.

demographic gap. The gap between the birth rate and the death rate that occurs during the period of DEMOGRAPHIC TRANSITION. The death rate tends to decline more rapidly than the birth rate causing rapid population growth.

demographic revolution. See DEMOGRAPHIC TRANSITION.

demographic structure. The distribution of a given population by sex, age, marital status, and any other relevant categories (such as race, socioeconomic status, religion).

demographic transition. A process in which, as a result of industrialization (or modernization), there are changes in the rate of population growth that reflect the unequal speed with which the birth and death rates change. Theoretically, there are three phases in this process. In the preindustrial period both birth and death rates are high, resulting in slow population growth. With the introduction of industrialization accompanied by sanitation and modern medicine, the death rate declines. However, during this phase the birth rate remains high, resulting in rapid population growth. In the third phase a low death rate is balanced by a low birth rate and population growth is again slow. See DEMOGRAPHIC GAP.

demography. The study of population size, composition, and distribution, and the patterns of change therein. The narrowest conception of demography views it as the study of vital statistics (the study of birth and death rates and related statistics). However, as vital statistics are analyzed and interpreted, demography develops into social demography or population studies. In the broadest view population composition and distribution include not only such variables as fertility, mortality, age, and sex, but also, marriage, divorce, family size, race, education, illiteracy, unemployment, distribution of wealth, occupational distribution, crime rates, density of population, migration, etc. While some demographers consider demography multidisciplinary, bordering on sociology, biology, and economics, most demographers and other sociologists regard it as a division of sociology and the majority of demographers are sociologists by profession.

demography, formal. The analysis of population statistics and changes in terms of mathematical principles to determine laws of necessary quantitative relationships that would be applicable to any population, and the application of these laws to the specific population being studied. See DEMOGRAPHY.

demography, macro-. DEMOGRAPHY that is concerned with large numbers of people, with the population characteristics and trends of large areas, whole societies or communities, or political units, including international regions, nations, tribes, states, and cities. The study of factors affecting the birth rate and death rate of a population or patterns of migration would be macrodemography. Most demographic research would be classified as macrodemography. See DEMOGRAPHY, MICRO-.

demography, micro-. The branch of DEMOGRAPHY that is concerned with the study of individuals, small groups, and neighborhoods. It is concerned primarily with individual behavior rather than mass trends. For example, microdemography would study the attitudes and behavior patterns that determine the size, health practices, and migration of individual families. See DEMOGRAPHY, MACRO-.

demography, social. See DEMOGRAPHY.

denomination. One of a number of religious organizations that are considered "socially acceptable" by a majority of the members of a society. A denomination accepts the major values and the structure of the society of which it is a part. It emphasizes tolerance and is content to be one of a number of religious organizations in the society. It is also characterized by formal admission procedures, lax membership standards with expulsion rare, a full-time, professionally trained clergy, formalized worship services, a formal system of education for the young, limited and often specialized participation and involvement by the laity with little emphasis on evangelism by the membership at large, wide variations in belief among the members, and support of a variety of nonreligious activities. Denominations frequently develop from sects, which, with the passage of time, tend to become formalized and to accommodate to the secular world. However, it should be kept in mind that the concept of denomination is an IDEAL TYPE, which no specific religious group would conform to in all respects. See CULT; ECCLESIA; SECT.

denotative meaning. See CONNOTATIVE MEANING.

density, building. Within a delimited area, the ratio of the area covered by buildings of any sort to the total size of the area.

density, population. The relative size of a population with reference to the space it occupies. Population density is usually expressed in terms of the number of dwellers per unit area, such as per square mile or per square kilometer.

density of settlement. See DENSITY, POPULATION.

dependent variable. See VARIABLE.

depersonalization. A state in which the individual lacks a clear sense of his personal identity. He feels detached and estranged from himself, and his behavior and personality seem to him to be meaningless and irrelevant to his own needs. See ALIENATION; ANOMIE.

depression, anaclitic. Severe depression occurring in infants who lose their mothers and do not obtain an adequate substitute, particularly in cases where there had been a good mother-child relationship. The term was introduced by René A. Spitz, who, in studying such infants, found that they "developed a weepy behavior that was in marked contrast to their previously happy and outgoing behavior. . . . All showed a greater susceptibility to intercurrent colds or eczema. A gradual decline in the developmental quotient was observed in these cases." If the mother was not restored or an adequate substitute provided "the depression progressed rapidly. Beginning with sadness and weeping, it continued into withdrawal, loss of appetite, loss of interest in the outside world, dejection, retardation, and finally, a condition which could only be described as stuporous." (R. A. Spitz and K. M. Wolf in *The Psychoanalytic Study of the Child,* Vol. II, International Universities Press, New York, 1946.) See HOSPITALISM; MARASMUS.

depression, economic. A severe and prolonged DEFLATION.

deprivation, relative. See RELATIVE DEPRIVATION.

derivations. Rational explanations for nonlogical actions. The term was introduced by Vilfredo Pareto, who maintained that since man usually has conflicting sentiments (called RESIDUES by Pareto), his conduct is often nonlogical. Yet at the same time man feels a need to appear logical to himself as well as to others. The derivations satisfy this need by providing pseudological reasons that give a rational cloak to nonrational actions. The term derivations is essentially equivalent to the more commonly used concept of ideology. (V. Pareto, *The Mind and Society*, tr. by A. Bongiorno and A. Livingston, Harcourt, Brace, New York, 1935.)

derivative influence. An unintended and often unexpected consequence of an act or event that does not follow directly from the act itself but follows from a chain of events set in motion by the original act.

derivative penalizations. Unintended negative "results from the infliction of an intended sanction. Thus imprisonment may (even after release) result in the loss of job, prestige, and associations." (H. Goldhammer and E. A. Shils,.*American Journal of Sociology*, September 1939.)

descent. See BILATERAL or BILENEAL DESCENT; DOUBLE DESCENT; KINSHIP SYSTEM, BILATERAL; LINEAGE; MATRILINEAL DESCENT; PATRILINEAL DESCENT; UNILATERAL or UNILINEAL DESCENT.

descriptive statistics. See STATISTICS, DESCRIPTIVE.

desire. See WANT.

determination, coefficient of. See COEFFICIENT OF DETERMINATION.

determinism. The theory or doctrine that all human behavior is determined by antecedent conditions and events. Determinism is based upon the conception of CAUSE and effect. All events, including all human actions, are seen as the result of a preceding cause or causes. Since the effect invariably follows the cause, all the events of nature, including those involving man, are an invariable series of consequences, each resulting from the preceding and inevitably leading to the following. Man's behavior is determined by the events of the past which resulted in his biological heredity and social and cultural environment. Determinism rejects the notion of FREE WILL or free choice. See CLIMATIC DETERMINISM; CULTURAL DETERMINISM; ECONOMIC DETERMINISM; GEOGRAPHIC DETERMINISM; HISTORICISM; PSYCHOLOGICAL DETERMINISM; SOCIOLOGICAL DETERMINISM.

deterministic system. A SYSTEM the characteristics of which are regarded as the result of its previous characteristics. See DETERMINISM.

deterrence theory. In criminology, the theory that the main purpose of punishment is to prevent crime. According to this theory the knowledge that severe punishment will follow the commission of a crime is the most effective way to discourage potential criminals from committing crimes, and the experience of severe punishment is the most effective way of discouraging criminals from committing additional crimes.

developmental psychology. See PSYCHOLOGY, DEVELOPMENTAL.

deviance. Nonconformity to social norms. The term is preferred by sociologists over the concept of abnormal behavior because of the latter's connotation of psychological illness rather than social maladjustment or conflict. Deviance is a common phenomenon in the life of every human being (even in the so-called "simple societies"). It is always defined from the point of view of a particular normative structure, and in a complex society where there are a multiplicity of groups and conflicting normative standards, each member of the society is at some time liable to be considered deviant by one standard or another. Often deviance simply involves conformity to the standards of a subgroup rather than those of the dominant social group. The consequences of deviance from normative standards are varied and may range from a frown to imprisonment or confinement for mental illness. However, people who deviate from social norms are not necessarily (or necessarily considered) mentally ill, nor does deviance necessarily entail mental illness. The despised deviant from a particular society or social system may be regarded as a martyr or saint by another ethical philosophy or historical period. Thus deviance is not inherent in specific behavior or attitudes but rather is a phenomenon of human interaction in a particular normative setting. See COMPULSIVE DEVIANCE; NONCONFORMITY.

deviation, institutionalized or **systematic.** See PATTERNED EVASION.

deviation, statistical. See MEAN DEVIATION; MEDIAN DEVIATION; QUARTILE DEVIATION; STANDARD DEVIATION.

dialectic. The development of contradictions and their solution as a way of advancing thought. The dialectic approach may be traced back to the ancient Greek philosophers. Of major influence in modern philosophy was Georg Hegel's dialectic involving the theory that reality develops through the conflict of opposites, that is, that every action produces a reaction and then an integration or synthesis. In recent years Llewellyn Gross has been a leading proponent of a neodialectical approach designed to broaden the theoretical framework of sociology and provide more room for new ideas. (See L. Gross, *American Journal of Sociology*, September 1961.)

dialectical materialism. The philosophical approach of Karl Marx and his followers. Marx was very much influenced by the DIALECTIC of Hegel, but rejected Hegel's idealism. Instead Marx emphasized material conditions, that is, economic factors, as the basic causal forces determining both individual motivation and the history of man. He regarded ideology as a rationalization of economic position, and he interpreted history primarily in terms of a series of class struggles. According to Marx, in each period of history there has been a dominant economic class. In time open conflict breaks out between the dominant class and a rising class, resulting in the overthrow of the old ruling class and the establishment of a new dominant class. In this fashion the capitalist class replaced the feudal aristocracy as the dominant class in the West. However, Marx did not regard this as an unending process. He maintained that industrialized, capitalist societies were becoming increasingly polarized into two classes: the dominant capitalist class or BOURGEOISIE and the working masses or PROLETARIAT. He predicted that eventually the proletariat would overthrow the bourgeoisie and establish a classless society. See BOLSHEVISM; COMMUNISM; SOCIALISM.

diaspora. A Greek term meaning dispersion or scattering, originally used to refer to the dispersion of the Jews from ancient Palestine. More recently it has come to be used to refer to any group of persons living in a foreign nation or nations without the protection of their government, e.g., Russian émigrés living in western Europe after the Russian Revolution.

dichotomous population. In statistics, a population that has been divided into two mutually exclusive classes. Thus all cases in one category have a certain characteristic or more than a certain magnitude of a characteristic and no cases in the other category have that characteristic or that magnitude, for example, a population divided into male and female, or over 21 years of age and under 21.

dichotomous question. A question to which there can be only one of two possible answers (e.g., yes or no).

dichotomy. A VARIABLE having only two possible values. Sex is a dichotomous variable, that is, it is composed of just two categories—male and female.

differential aspiration. The phenomenon of different segments of a group or society making unequal attempts to rise to a higher status.

differential association, occupational. The tendency of people to choose their friends from among persons in their own or a related occupational category more than from other occupational categories.

differential association hypothesis of crime. A hypothesis developed by Edwin H. Sutherland holding that criminal behavior is learned in social interaction, rather than being a result of personality traits or the biological or genetic constitution of the individual. The hypothesis maintains that criminal patterns of behavior are learned in interaction with criminals in primary group situations (such as within the family, among school friends) and in relative isolation from anticriminal social norms. Indirect influences, such as television, movies, etc., are considered relatively unimportant. "The hypothesis of differential association is that criminal behavior is learned in association with those who define such behavior favorably and in isolation from those who define it unfavorably, and that a person in an appropriate situation engages in such criminal behavior if, and only if, the weight of the favorable definitions exceeds the weight of the unfavorable definitions." (E. H. Sutherland, *White Collar Crime*, Dryden Press, New York, 1949.)

differential group organization hypothesis of crime. The hypothesis that the activities and social organization of criminals are often complex and well organized, and that criminal behavior is a result of social organization around criminal and antilegal values. Edwin H. Sutherland substituted this term for the term social disorganization "because the organization of the delinquent group, which is often very complex, is social disorganization only from an ethical or some other particularistic point of view. At the suggestion of Albert K. Cohen, this concept has been changed to differential group organization, with organization for criminal activities on one side and organization against criminal activities on the other." (A. K. Cohen, A. Lindesmith, and K. Schuessler, eds., *The Sutherland Papers*, Indiana University Press, Bloomington, Ind., 1956.) See DISORGANIZATION, SOCIAL.

differential identification hypothesis of crime. A hypothesis developed by Daniel Glaser as a reformulation of Edwin H. Sutherland's DIFFERENTIAL ASSOCIATION HYPOTHESIS OF CRIME. It holds, in essence, "that a person pursues criminal behavior to the extent that he identifies himself with real or imaginary persons from whose perspective his criminal behavior seems acceptable." (D. Glaser, *American Journal of Sociology*, March 1956.)

differential psychology. See PSYCHOLOGY, DIFFERENTIAL.

differential reproduction. See FERTILITY, DIFFERENTIAL.

differential scale. A SCALE consisting of items (e.g., attitude statements) that have been ordered on the basis of ratings by judges. See PAIRED COMPARISON SCALE; THURSTONE EQUAL-APPEARING INTERVAL SCALE.

differential status assumption. See STATUS ASSUMPTION, DIFFERENTIAL.

differentiation, social. See SOCIAL DIFFERENTIATION.

diffuseness. The expectation in a social relationship that there should be a wide range of rights and obligations between the persons involved. The extent of their obligations is not specified—they are limited only by obligations to other persons and groups. In a diffuse relationship a wide range of the personality becomes involved in the relationship. Social norms define certain roles as properly diffuse, for example, the roles of husband, wife, father, mother, friend. See DIFFUSENESS-SPECIFICITY; SPECIFICITY.

diffuseness-specificity. A pattern variable, or dichotomy in social behavior, which is concerned with the question of how wide a range of rights and obligations persons in a given social relationship should have toward each other, whether the relationship should cover a broad and undefined range of mutual rights and responsibilities or be limited to a narrow, clearly defined range of expectations. "In confronting an object [i.e., another person], an actor must choose among the various possible ranges in which he will respond to the object. The dilemma consists in whether he should respond to many aspects of the object or to a restricted range of them—how broadly is he to allow himself to be involved with the object? The dilemma may be resolved by accepting no inherent or prior limitation of the scope of the actor's 'concern' with the object, either as an object of interest or of obligations, or by according only a limited and specific type of significance to the object in his system of orientation." This is one of the five PATTERN VARIABLES proposed by Talcott Parsons. (T. Parsons and E. A. Shils, in *Toward a General Theory of Action*, T. Parsons and E. A. Shils, eds., Harvard University Press, Cambridge, Mass., 1951.) See DIFFUSENESS; SPECIFICITY.

diffusion. The process by which culture traits or complexes spread from one society to another, or one part of a society to another.

diffusion, discontinuous. DIFFUSION of culture traits or complexes between spatially separated areas.

diffusion, stimulus. DIFFUSION in which culture traits are borrowed in their general form and not in their concrete content. They are given a unique form in the borrowing culture. The term was introduced by Alfred L. Kroeber, who gave as an example the diffusion of the culture trait of writing from the white settlers to the Cherokee Indians, but in a totally different form. An Indian, seeing the advantages of writing, invented a system, called a syllabary, with eighty-six symbols (including English letters and other signs) to put the Cherokee language into written form. (A. L. Kroeber, *American Anthropologist,* January 1940.)

diffusionism. A theoretical view in anthropology that stresses the importance of DIFFUSION in the development of human culture. Theories of diffusionism emphasize the relative rarity of new inventions and the importance of constant mutual borrowing of culture traits in the history of man. Such theories maintain that, in most cases, similarities found in various cultures are due to borrowing rather than to parallel and independent inventions in the separate cultures. See PARALLELISM.

Dionysian culture. See APOLLONIAN CULTURE.

direct correlation. See CORRELATION, POSITIVE.

disaster studies. Studies of the effects of sudden disasters (such as floods, earthquakes, tornadoes) on social organization and individual behavior. These studies are concerned with such questions as the effects of predisaster social relationships on individual and community adjustment to the disaster, the type of social organization that emerges during and after a disaster, the effects of cultural values on behavior during the disaster, etc.

discourse, universe of. See UNIVERSE OF DISCOURSE.

discoveries, multiple independent. See MULTIPLE INDEPENDENT DISCOVERIES.

discovery. The recognition of phenomena or relationships that previously had not been perceived. To have any social significance a discovery must become interrelated with existing systems of belief and knowledge and thus integrated into the culture. See INNOVATION; INVENTION.

discovery complex. A series of interrelated discoveries (or inventions —see below) of new methods of activity that together form a new system of techniques, such as agriculture or the domestication of animals. The term was proposed by H. S. Harrison, who wrote: "The building up of any discovery-complex, such as agriculture or metal-working, is clearly dependent upon single discoveries, following on each other, and some of them could only emerge at the end of a long sequence." (H. S. Harrison, *Report of the 98th Meeting,* British Association for the Advancement of Science, Bristol, 1930.) It should be noted that Harrison limits the term *invention* to new artifacts, and refers to new techniques as discoveries. This usage is not generally followed. See DISCOVERY; INVENTION.

discrete data. In statistics, data expressed in whole numbers, and representing an enumeration of indivisible units (for example, individuals). See VARIABLE, DISCRETE.

discrete series. See VARIABLE, DISCRETE.

discrete variable. See VARIABLE, DISCRETE.

discrimination. 1. The unequal treatment of individuals or groups on the basis of some, usually categorical, attribute, such as racial, ethnic, religious, or social-class membership. The term is usually used to describe the action of a dominant majority in relation to a weak minority, therefore implying immoral and undemocratic behavior. In this sense discrimination is the active or overt aspect of negative PREJUDICE toward a person or group. The United Nations definition is often quoted: "discrimination includes any conduct based on a distinction made on grounds of natural or social categories, which have no relation either to individual capacities or merits, or to the concrete behavior of the individual person." (*The Main*

Types and Causes of Discrimination, United Nations Commission on Human Rights, Sub-Commission on Prevention of Discrimination and Protection of Minorities, Lake Success, N.Y., 1949.)

It should be noted that in a certain sense discrimination as the unequal treatment of people who are essentially equal, or of the same capacities or merits, is universal. Whether or not discrimination is considered illegitimate depends on societal values, and social rank and social stratification are based firmly on discriminatory principles. Thus the private in the army is legitimately discriminated against (treated unequally) on the basis of his lower rank, even if he has the same or greater capacities than his officers. However, some utopian communities have attempted to abolish such distinctions of social rank, very often on the basis that all believers are equal in the sight of God; and in America the spread of equalitarian political and religious values and profound changes in the structure of society has lead to increasing challenge of any form of discrimination on the basis of religion, race, or even social class. The social criteria for what is considered discriminatory treatment of people and groups are constantly shifting in accordance with social values.

2. In psychology, discrimination refers to the ability of a person to perceive or detect differences between stimuli.

disintegration, social. See SOCIAL DISINTEGRATION.

disorganization, personal. The condition in which an individual cannot function effectively because of inner confusion, usually resulting from his acceptance of contradictory standards of behavior. Personal disorganization may result from the individual's having accepted conflicting roles, social norms, or group loyalties. The disorganized individual lacks a hierarchy of values to determine which standards or obligations should take precedence. Disorganization may be temporary and transitional, due primarily to the immediate situation in which the individual finds himself, or it may be more lasting and deep-rooted in the personality. Personal disorganization often is associated with social disorganization. See DISORGANIZATION, SOCIAL; MENTAL CONFLICT.

disorganization, social. A condition of a society, community, or group characterized by a disruptive increase in certain social problems, such as crime and delinquency, alcoholism, mental illness, and suicide. It is often defined in terms of a breakdown of social control, or a breakdown of social structure or societal order. By contrast, a state of social organization exists when there is within the society or community order, cooperation, common values, unity, discipline, and predictability, and when there is an absence of role conflict, normlessness, social conflict, and demoralization. Thus when a society or group does not seem to be functioning in a desirable way and in accordance with conceptions of social organization, a state of social disorganization is judged to exist. Although the term has very wide usage there is some evidence that it has frequently been applied to what is simply an unfamiliar type of social organization, or differential, that is deviant or nonapproved, group organization. For example, sociologists are apt to view slum life in terms of social disorganization, although a well-established, if not readily visible, form of social organization may exist. This has been discussed by, among others, William F. Whyte in *Street Corner Society* (University of Chicago Press, Chicago, 1955).

dispersion, ecological. The scattering of population, the opposite of CONCENTRATION. Dispersion is the movement of people from an area of concentration to scattered points over a relatively large area, as movement from the center of a city to outlying areas in the countryside.

dispersion, statistical. The degree of variation of the values of a variable from a central point or typical value, such as the mean. Measures that describe dispersion, alternately called scatter or spread, include MEAN DEVIATION, QUARTILE DEVIATION, RANGE, and STANDARD DEVIATION.

displacement, ecological. The process in which a stronger or more advanced group takes over an area (without military conquest—by economic pressure or sheer numbers) formerly occupied by a less advanced or weaker group. The term is not widely used. See SUCCESSION.

displacement, psychological. See AGGRESSION, DISPLACED.

dissociation, psychological. A psychological reaction (in Freudian theory, to a repressed desire) that splits aspects of an individual's behavior or experience away from his normal mental life and actions. Ideas or aspects of the personality that are normally associated form separate functional units. The dissociative behavior or experience may result in MULTIPLE PERSONALITY, amnesia, or inconsistencies in behavior.

dissociation, social. The lessening of interaction between persons or groups usually due to hostility and antagonism.

distance, ecological. See ECOLOGICAL DISTANCE.

distance, latent. See LAZARSFELD LATENT-DISTANCE MODEL.

distance, occupational. See OCCUPATIONAL DISTANCE.

distance, social. See SOCIAL DISTANCE; MOBILITY, SOCIAL DISTANCE.

distribution, binomial. See BINOMIAL DISTRIBUTION.

distribution, frequency. See FREQUENCY DISTRIBUTION.

distribution, sampling. See SAMPLING DISTRIBUTION.

distribution-free methods. See NONPARAMETRIC STATISTICS.

division of labor. A functionally integrated system of occupational roles or specializations within a society. The conception of the division of labor in society has been a theoretical tool used frequently in sociological analyses. It is assumed to exist in all societies. Sex and age are usually the most important bases for differentiating occupational activities in nonliterate societies. In more complex societies the division of labor is more elaborate. Extreme elaboration of the division of labor is one of the outstanding characteristics of industrialization.

division of labor, anomic. One of the major abnormal forms of the division of labor distinguished by Émile Durkheim. The anomic division of labor occurs when extreme specialization is accompanied by a decline in communication between persons performing different functions. Instead of being drawn together by mutual dependence, individuals are separated and isolated from each other by lack of understanding and narrowness of perspective. Moreover, meagerness of communication results in a lack of clearly defined rules regulating the interrelationships of persons isolated in their specializations. The vagueness of these rules, in turn, increases the likelihood of conflict. Durkheim gave as an example of this, conflict between capital and labor, particularly in the early industrial period before there were agreed-upon regulations defining their proper relationship. The anomic division of labor was regarded by Durkheim as abnormal because, like the forced division of labor, it does not promote but rather disrupts social solidarity. (É. Durkheim, *The Division of Labor in Society,* tr. by G. Simpson, Free Press, Glencoe, Ill., 1947.) See ANOMIE; DIVISION OF LABOR, FORCED.

division of labor, forced. One of the major abnormal forms of the division of labor distinguished by Émile Durkheim. The forced division of labor occurs when individuals are compelled to take on occupational roles which they do not like and to which they are not suited. Durkheim regarded caste and social class systems as the principal cause of forced division of labor. Custom or law prevents persons from the lower classes from performing certain functions even if they have the ability. Durkheim regarded this as the primary source of class conflict. "The lower classes not being, or no longer being, satisfied with the role which has devolved upon them from custom or by law aspire to functions which are closed to them and seek to dispossess those who are exercising these functions. Thus civil wars arise which are due to the manner in which labor is distributed." (É. Durkheim, *The Division of Labor in Society,* tr. by G. Simpson, Free Press, Glencoe, Ill., 1947.) See DIVISION OF LABOR, ANOMIC.

divorce. An institutionalized arrangement for terminating the marriage relationship and allowing each partner the right to remarry.

document, personal. See PERSONAL DOCUMENT.

documentary sources of information. Published and unpublished documents that provide data of sociological significance, including census reports, reports of governmental agencies, public and private records, manuscripts, letters, and diaries. Documentary sources are usually divided into PRIMARY SOURCES and SECONDARY SOURCES.

dolichocephalic. A term used by physical anthropologists and biologists to designate a long, narrow head shape with a CEPHALIC INDEX of less than 77 or 80. See BRACHYCEPHALIC; MESOCEPHALIC.

doll-play procedure. A PROJECTIVE TECHNIQUE for studying personality and attitudes, in which a subject is observed acting out a situation with dolls. The subject is usually given dolls representing adults and children of both sexes. He may be instructed as to the situation he is to enact with them, or encouraged to play with them as he chooses. This technique is, of course, particularly suitable for children.

domestic system. A system of production that preceded the development of the FACTORY SYSTEM. Under the domestic system a merchant paid a worker at an agreed-upon rate to produce goods in his home, with the merchant providing the raw materials and sometimes the tools. The finished products belonged to the merchant, who would then market them. The system was prevalent in Europe in the sixteenth and seventeenth centuries, and may still be found in some parts of the world today. Some writers prefer the name putting-out system, which they regard as more precise because the production of goods in the home long preceded and is not necessarily related to this specific system.

domestication. The taming and selective breeding of animals by man to obtain desired characteristics, for example, docility, strength, a high level of food production, disease resistance. The term often is also applied to the cultivation and selective breeding of plants. The domestication of animals and plants enabled man to move from a hunting and gathering economy to a pastoral or agricultural economy.

dominance, ecological. The controlling position of cities or metropolitan areas over the surrounding HINTERLAND due to their strategic location and centralization of specialized services, such as the services found in the CENTRAL BUSINESS DISTRICT and the banking district of large cities. The center of dominance is the focal point of transportation and communication.

dominance, genetic. In the study of heredity, the suppression of the influence of a recessive gene by a dominant gene. The characteristics of the dominant gene become manifested in the individual, whereas the characteristics of the recessive gene are not apparent.

double bind situation. A situation in which an individual is receiving contradictory messages from a highly significant other person. The concept was introduced by Gregory Bateson and his associates in formulating a theory of the origin of schizophrenia as based upon confusion in communication. In the double bind situation an individual is involved in an intense relationship with another person and feels it is vitally important that he understand the message the other person is communicating so that he can respond properly, but the other person is expressing contradictory messages which deny each other. The double bind situation most often occurs in the mother-child relationship when the mother cannot tolerate an affectionate relationship with the child but cannot admit her feelings to herself. The contradictory messages communicated by the mother "can be roughly characterized as (a) hostile or withdrawing behavior which is aroused whenever the child approaches her, and (b) simulated loving or approaching behavior which is aroused when the child responds to her hostile and withdrawing behavior, as a way of denying that she is withdrawing." The consequences of this situation seem to be most severe when a strong father who might help the child to understand the situation is lacking. (G. Bateson, D. D. Jackson, J. Haley, and J. Weakland, *Behavioral Science*, October 1956.)

double descent. A system of descent in which every individual belongs to two groups of kindred, one through his father and one through his mother, both of which are based on UNILATERAL DESCENT.

downtown business district. See CENTRAL BUSINESS DISTRICT.

drift, cultural. See CULTURAL DRIFT.

drive. 1. An internal impulse motivating the individual to activity to reduce feelings of tension or discomfort. The tensions may result from physiological imbalances or socially learned needs. A drive impels an individual toward generalized activity and not toward a specific goal. Today many sociologists prefer the term NEED.

2. A physiological drive. See DRIVE, PHYSIOLOGICAL.

drive, acquired. A DRIVE that has been learned through social interaction rather than inherited as a part of man's physiological make-up. Acquired drives are sometimes referred to as secondary drives, but they may be of equal or greater strength than physiological drives. An example of an acquired drive would be a drive for social recognition or acceptance. However, most sociologists prefer the term *social needs*. See DRIVE, PHYSIOLOGICAL; NEED, SOCIAL; SOCIALIZATION.

drive, basic. See DRIVE, PHYSIOLOGICAL.

drive, biological. See DRIVE, PHYSIOLOGICAL.

drive, innate. See DRIVE, PHYSIOLOGICAL.

drive, physiological. A DRIVE resulting from physical imbalances in the organism. Examples of physiological drives are hunger, thirst, fatigue, and sex. Physiological drives are sometimes referred to as primary or basic drives because in many cases their satisfaction is essential for the survival of the individual. However, an individual may suppress a physiological drive because an acquired drive is of greater importance to him. Physiological drives are highly undifferentiated and the form of their expression and satisfaction depends upon the CULTURE in which the individual has been socialized. See DRIVE, ACQUIRED; NEED; SOCIALIZATION.

drive, primary. See DRIVE, PHYSIOLOGICAL.

drive, psychological. See DRIVE, ACQUIRED.

drive, secondary. See DRIVE, ACQUIRED.

dyad. In sociology, two persons in interaction. This is the simplest sociological unit. Usually the relationship called a dyad is thought of as persisting over a long enough period of time to form a pattern of expectations.

dynamic. Involving motion and change. The term dynamic is used in many ways. In general in sociology it refers to changing relationships within a social or psychological system. In a narrower but often used sense, a dynamic approach to a problem involves the assumption of the instability and constant necessity for readjustment in the social system or human personality with the never reached state of equilibrium as the goal.

dynamic assessment of the situation. An individual's evaluation of a new social situation that results in his following a particular course of action. Robert M. MacIver introduced the term to refer particularly to conscious behavior directed toward a decision to act. Different individuals with different goals or desired ends assess a particular situation differently, because they judge the alternatives from different perspectives, and thus may make different decisions. The dynamic assessment occurs when the decision to act is made on the basis of all the alternatives and contingencies the individual judges relevant to the perceived situation. (R. M. MacIver, *Social Causation*, Ginn, Boston, 1942.) See DEFINITION OF THE SITUATION.

dynamics, group. See GROUP DYNAMICS.

dynamics, social. See SOCIAL DYNAMICS.

dynamism. See ANIMATISM.

dysfunction. Any consequence of the existence or operation of an aspect of a social (or personality) system that is judged to be a disturbance or a hindrance to the integration, adjustment, or stability of the system. However, what may be judged dysfunctional for one part of a system may be judged functional for some other part. For example, in a particular social class system the prevalence of a certain belief may be functional for the upper class but dysfunctional for the lower class. See EUFUNCTION; FUNCTION.

dysgenic trend theory. The theory in EUGENICS that a population may decline in its hereditary qualities as a result of a higher level of reproduction of the biologically inferior than of the biologically superior portion of the population. This is assumed to lead to a generally lower level of intelligence, mental and physical health, and physical strength. The theory is generally rejected by sociologists and other behavioral scientists.

E

ecclesia. A large religious organization that embraces all or almost all the members of a society. The concept was modeled on the medieval European church. Examples of modern churches usually classified as essentially ecclesia-type organizations are the Roman Catholic Church, the Orthodox Church in Greece, and the established Lutheran churches of Germany and Scandinavia. The ecclesia is conservative, allied with the secular authorities, and its members are born into the organization rather than joined to it voluntarily by profession of faith. Its organization may be either national or international. In its pure form the ecclesia tends to attempt domination of an entire population in cooperation with the political authorities. The concept ecclesia frequently is used as part of a fourfold classification of types of religious organization in which it is contrasted with CULT, DENOMINATION, and SECT.

eclecticism. The selecting and combining of aspects of various schools of thought or theories in an attempt to obtain a theoretical system that represents the best elements of each school. In an applied field, eclecticism involves the use of any procedures, concepts, and theoretical principles that seem appropriate to solve a particular problem, whether or not they form an integrated system.

ecological constellation. A grouping of interdependent, specialized areas around a common center. The term was used by R. D. McKenzie, who described the metropolitan area as an ecological constellation. "The metropolitan area, with its various districts of residence, business, and industry integrated around a common center usually called the city, is an ecological constellation." (R. D. McKenzie, *Publications of the American Sociological Society*, XX, 1926.) See ECOLOGICAL UNIT.

ecological dispersion. See DISPERSION, ECOLOGICAL.

ecological displacement. See DISPLACEMENT, ECOLOGICAL.

ecological distance. Distance measured in terms of the costs of moving from one place to another. Whereas spatial distance is measured in terms of spatial units, such as miles or kilometers, ecological distance is measured in terms of the time the trip takes (time-cost) and the other economic costs involved.

ecological dominance. See DOMINANCE, ECOLOGICAL.

ecological organization. See ECOLOGICAL STRUCTURE.

ecological processes. See CENTRALIZATION; CONCENTRATION; INVASION; SEGREGATION; SUCCESSION.

ecological structure. 1. The pattern of spatial distribution and interrelationships of individuals, groups, and services in a community. In this sense ecological structure is the territorial organization of the social and economic systems of the community.

2. The organization of sustenance activities in a community—that is, the organization of a population for survival in a particular environment, including both the resulting spatial distribution and also the nonspatial aspects of that organization. (A. H. Hawley, *Social Forces,* May 1944.)
See ECOLOGY, HUMAN.

ecological unit. 1. A territorially based physical unit that provides a service (or related services) or a place of residence. Examples are a store, a factory, an amusement park, an apartment house, a private residence.

2. "Any ecological distribution—whether of residences, shops, offices, or industrial plants—which has a unitary character sufficient to differentiate it from surrounding distributions." (R. D. McKenzie, *Publications of the American Sociological Society,* XX, 1926.)

ecology. The study of the interrelationships among organisms living in a particular environment, their adjustments to each other and to their environment. Ecology is the study of the network of interrelationships among the organisms (plants or animals), the relationships of members of a given species to each other, to other species of plants and animals, and to other aspects of their natural environment (terrain, climate, etc.). Plant and animal ecology focus on the study of the distributions and mutual adaptations of species to each other and to their habitat in a given geographic area.

ecology, human. 1. The study of the relationship between man and his environment. Traditionally most ecologists have accepted this broad, general definition; however, in attempting a more specific definition, various differences have emerged (see below).

2. The study of community structure through the analysis of the spatial and temporal distribution of persons, groups, and services, under varying specified conditions, and the factors associated with changes in these dis-

tributive patterns. This definition is probably the most widely accepted by sociologists today.

3. The study of the way a population is organized to survive in a given area. This definition was proposed by Amos H. Hawley, who wrote: "This places an emphasis on sustenance relations, . . . the ecologist must be able to trace out the ramifications of sustenance activities and ascertain the degree to which they affect and are in turn affected by other kinds of activities." (A. H. Hawley, *American Sociological Review,* April 1948.) Hawley's definition would include within human ecology the nonspatial as well as the spatial aspects of the organization of sustenance activities.

4. The study of the subsocial (biotic) level of human organization—a level of organization resulting from the struggle for existence and based on impersonal and unplanned competitive cooperation. This is the definition utilized by Robert E. Park and the other "classical ecologists," who, writing in the 1920's and '30's, were the first sociologists to attempt systematically to apply the theoretical scheme of plant and animal ecology to the study of human communities. By this definition, the cultural level of society, based on communication and consensus, was excluded from the province of human ecology. However, even at the outset the classical definition of human ecology was rarely adhered to in ecological research, and it came under such severe attack in the late thirties and forties that today in its pure form it is without proponents. No contemporary ecologist would exclude culture from human ecology, and very few maintain the distinction between a social and a subsocial level of human organization. At present James A. Quinn is the leading proponent of a modified conception of a subsocial level as the province of human ecology. (J. A. Quinn, *Human Ecology*, Prentice-Hall, Englewood Cliffs, N.J., 1950.)

5. The study of human geography. For this definition, which is accepted by many anthropologists and geographers, see GEOGRAPHY, HUMAN.

For a review of the history, theory, and research methods of human ecology, see G. A. Theodorson, ed., *Studies in Human Ecology* (Harper and Row, New York, 1961).

See BIOTIC COMMUNITY; CENTRALIZATION; COMMENSALISM; CONCENTRATION; INVASION; SEGREGATION; SUCCESSION; SYMBIOSIS.

ecology, social. Human ecology considered as a subdivision of sociology rather than as equivalent to human geography. However, sociologists use the term *human ecology* more often than social ecology. See ECOLOGY, HUMAN; GEOGRAPHY, HUMAN.

ecology, work. See WORK ECOLOGY.

economic area. An area the boundaries of which are delimited on the basis of economic criteria, such as a wholesale trade area or an area in which a particular type of economic activity predominates, as a wheat farming area.

economic class. See CLASS, ECONOMIC.

economic determinism. The doctrine that economic factors are the most crucial factors in explaining social behavior. Economic determinism assumes that the acquisition of material goods is the most important source of human motivation and that human behavior is basically rational.

economic good. See GOOD, ECONOMIC.

economic institution. The system of social roles and norms organized about the production, distribution, and consumption of goods and services. The function of the economic institution is to provide for the material needs and demands of the members of a society, ranging from the basic means for survival to goods intended for conspicuous consumption. See INSTITUTION, SOCIAL.

economic man. A theoretical construct of man as a purely rational being motivated solely by his economic self-interests. This view of man was held by the classical economists and is an essential element in the doctrine of ECONOMIC DETERMINISM. See CLASSICAL ECONOMIC THEORY.

economic order. See ECONOMIC INSTITUTION.

economic stratification. See STRATIFICATION, ECONOMIC.

economic theory, classical. See CLASSICAL ECONOMIC THEORY.

economics. The scientific study of the production, distribution, and consumption of goods and services. When economists study the social relations involved in economic behavior their work becomes important for sociological analysis. Hence much of the work of Thorstein Veblen (for example, his *Theory of the Leisure Class,* Macmillan, New York, 1899) is considered as relevant to sociology as it is to economics. In studying economic behavior the sociologist emphasizes the social and cultural framework within which economic activity occurs. Sociological analysis focuses on the forms of social organization, the systems of interrelated roles, and the patterns of norms and values that govern economic activity in a particular society. It is concerned with the relationship between the ECONOMIC INSTITUTION and other aspects of societal organization, with the comparative study of economic systems in different societies, and how they change within a society.

economy. The dominant form of economic activity characterizing a society. Examples of different types of economies are collecting and hunting economy, nomadic pastoral economy, settled agricultural economy, modern industrial economy.

economy, factory. See FACTORY SYSTEM.

economy, handicraft. See HANDICRAFT ECONOMY.

economy, metropolitan. See METROPOLITAN ECONOMY.

economy, principle of. See PARSIMONY, PRINCIPLE OF.

ectomorph. See SHELDON'S BODY TYPES.

education. The transmission of knowledge by either formal or informal methods. The concepts of SOCIALIZATION (the process by which a child learns the culture of his group) and LEARNING are related to, in fact often inseparable from, the concept of education. Although education is often thought of in terms of schooling (formal education), effective training for the individual's role as both a group member and an autonomous person is a constant process. The main function of the educative process is to pass down knowledge from generation to generation—a process that is essential to the development of culture. Formal education is primarily designed to inculcate crucial skills and values central to the survival of the society or to those who hold effective power. Inherent in education, in all periods of man's history, is a stimulus to creative thinking and action which accounts in part for culture change, culture change itself being a powerful stimulus to further innovation.

educational institution. The social institution or system of interrelated social roles and norms that ensures the transmission of knowledge from one generation to another. (Knowledge includes values and patterns of behavior). The educational institution comprises not only formal organizations specifically devoted to education, but also all other socially determined means of transmitting the cultural heritage. See INSTITUTION, SOCIAL.

educational quotient. The ratio between educational age and chronological age. The term is used by psychologists and is similar to INTELLIGENCE QUOTIENT. The educational quotient indicates a child's educational achievement.

educational sociology. See SOCIOLOGY, EDUCATIONAL.

effect, law of. In learning theory, the proposition that responses that are rewarded (i.e., that result in a pleasurable experience or a need satisfaction) tend to be learned, that is, repeated.

efficiency. Effectiveness of action. Ideally, efficiency reflects the use of the most effective means available to secure a given goal. Efficiency is not a quality that inheres in any given course of action. It is determined by the relationship of the means to the goal and the priority of goals.

efficiency, statistical. The extent to which a STATISTIC, or value obtained for a given sample, provides the maximum possible amount of information about one or more characteristics of a population. When there is more than one parameter estimate (a value obtained from a sample) for the same population PARAMETER, then the estimate that has the smallest VARIANCE is called the efficient estimate or efficient statistic. The relative efficiency of any one of the other estimates is determined by dividing its variance into the variance of the efficient estimate. The resulting quotient is called the efficiency, E, of that estimate.

ego. 1. The SELF as perceived by the individual, that is, a person's conception of himself. It is the aspect of the personality that maintains a certain unity and identity for the individual throughout his life. The protection and enhancement of the ego is a constant source of concern for the individual.

2. Sometimes used synonymously with self.

3. In Freudian theory, that aspect of the psyche or personality that is conscious and rational. The ego derives its energy from the ID, the source of instinctual drives, but it checks the impulsiveness of the id by applying the moral restraints urged by the SUPEREGO, which functions in the manner of the traditional conscience. The ego meets the demands of reality and is itself the outcome of reality testing.

4. In kinship analysis, a person (usually a hypothetical adult male) who is the point of reference for identifying kinship relations and terms.

ego-ideal. An ideal self or model of perfection an individual has of himself. It is the standard of what a person feels he should be and toward which he strives.

ego-involved motive. See MOTIVE, EGO-INVOLVED.

egocentric stage, Piaget's. The second of the four stages in Jean Piaget's RULES OF THE GAME, outlining the stages in the development of a child. In this stage, the child is able to see things only from his own point of view. His judgments tend to be absolute because he is unaware of any perspectives other than his own. According to Piaget, the child enters the egocentric stage at about the age of two, when he acquires language and a conception of his self-identity. He leaves the egocentric stage gradually as he learns to take the roles of others in his imagination and understand that their points of view differ from his own. (J. Piaget, *The Moral Judgment of the Child,* Harcourt, Brace, New York, 1932; *The Language and the Thought of the Child,* Harcourt, Brace, New York, 1926.) See GENERALIZED OTHER; SOCIALIZATION.

egoistic suicide. See SUICIDE, EGOISTIC.

eidetic image. An extremely clear and accurate mental image that is almost close to an hallucination in its vividness, but is usually recognized by the person as being imagery. The ability to experience eidetic imagery is characteristic of young children.

Electra complex. In Freudian theory, the excessive emotional attachment of a girl to her father and her consequent jealous rejection of her mother. See OEDIPUS COMPLEX.

element, population. See POPULATION ELEMENT.

elite. 1. The most influential and prestigious stratum in a society.
2. The highest stratum within a field of competence. The elite is composed of those persons who are recognized as outstanding and are considered the leaders in a given field. Thus there are, among others, political, business, artistic, scientific, and religious elites. The members of an elite have an important influence in shaping the values and attitudes held by their segment of society.
See POWER ELITE.

elite, circulation of the. The tendency throughout history for each elite in time to be replaced, either by being penetrated or overthrown, by an elite of the opposite type. The term was introduced by Vilfredo Pareto, who classified elites into two types: speculators and *rentiers*, each characterized by a dominant residue. The speculators, characterized by a residue Pareto termed the instinct for combinations, are schemers, manipulators, and innovators, while the *rentiers*, characterized by the residue termed the instinct for group persistences, are forceful, dogged conservatives. The circulation of the elite refers to the tendency of these two types of elite to alternate in the dominant position in a society. (V. Pareto, *The Mind and Society*, tr. by A. Bongiorno and A. Livingston, Harcourt, Brace, New York, 1935.) See INSTINCT FOR COMBINATIONS and INSTINCT FOR GROUP PERSISTENCES; RESIDUES.

emergent evolution. See EVOLUTION, EMERGENT.

emigration. The departure of individuals or groups from their home country to take up residence in another country. See IMMIGRATION; MIGRATION.

emotion. A complex, conscious experience, involving an arousal of either pleasant or unpleasant psychological and physiological responses, and often characterized by strong feelings, tension, or excitement. Anger, fear, joy, love, and grief are examples of emotions.

emotional contagion. See SOCIAL CONTAGION.

emotional maturity. Emotional behavior in conformity with that expected of an individual's age level within a given society. Emotional maturity depends upon an individual's psychosocial development keeping pace with his physiological development and chronological age. It involves a growing understanding of oneself and others and the ability to control childish impulses.

empathy. The ability to project oneself imaginatively into another's position, that is, to understand or take the role of another person without losing one's objectivity. One may empathize without necessarily sympathizing, that is, sharing the emotions of another person.

empirical. Based on experience, observation, or experimentation.

empirical generalization. An isolated scientific proposition or law. It is a statement of a generalized relationship among facts, verified by empirical observation, but not related to other propositions and not part of an integrated THEORY. "The sociological literature abounds with such generalizations which have not been assimilated to sociological theory. . . . Although propositions of this order are essential in empirical research, a miscellany of such propositions only provides the raw materials for sociology as a discipline. The theoretic task, and the orientation of empirical research toward theory, first begins when the bearing of such uniformities on a set of interrelated propositions is tentatively established." (R. K. Merton, *Social Theory and Social Structure*, Free Press, Glencoe, Ill., 1957.)

empirical method. See EMPIRICISM.

empirical regularity. An observed regularity that has no theoretical explanation.

empirical self. See SELF, EMPIRICAL.

empirical sociology. See SOCIOLOGY, EMPIRICAL.

empirical test. A test of a hypothesis in which the investigator observes the phenomena in question (either under experimental or "natural" conditions) to determine whether the hypothesis is supported or contradicted by these observations. Ideally, the investigator should be as interested in disproving as in verifying the hypothesis, and should consider all other possible explanations for the observed events. Moreover, the scientific validity of any set of observations depends upon their confirmation by other qualified observers. Any other qualified investigator following the specified procedure should reach the same conclusion about a hypothesis as the original investigator.

empirical theory. See THEORY, EMPIRICAL.

empirical trend. See TREND, EMPIRICAL.

empiricism. 1. The philosophical doctrine that all human knowledge is derived from experience. It stands in contrast to IDEALISM and RATIONALISM.

2. In science, the view that generalizations can be held to be valid only when tested by objective techniques and verified by sense experience. Empiricism is based on the belief that only that which can be experienced

by the senses is real, and that the final test of scientific truth is the experience of the senses. Thus all generalizations are to be judged by experiential evidence, i.e., the evidence of observation through the senses. Such observations, however, must be shared by qualified persons in the discipline, and not be idiosyncratic. In this sense empiricism is basic to most scientific thought.

3. In extreme form, sometimes referred to as strict or extreme empiricism, the attempt to eliminate or ignore theoretical models and concepts in scientific investigation. Emphasizing the OPERATIONAL DEFINITION and statistical correlations between variables, strict empiricists claim to study the interrelationships and facts of social life objectively without theoretical abstractions or assumptions. However, since all scientific investigation and analysis inevitably involves a theoretical orientation, strict empiricism in practice has meant the acceptance of theoretical assumptions that are not made explicit. See MODEL; OPERATIONALISM; THEORY.

empiricism, logical. See POSITIVISM, LOGICAL.

employee society. A society based on the relationship of people to impersonal organizations and characterized by a strict system of rank. The term was introduced by Peter F. Drucker to designate "a hierarchical system—a system in which everybody is related to people through his relationship to a strictly impersonal, strictly objective, strictly abstract thing, the 'organization,' the 'corporation,' the 'government agency,' etc. It means, second, that this is a society which is based on, and ruled by, status." Drucker maintained that during the last fifty years American society has become an employee society. (P. F. Drucker, *American Journal of Sociology*, January 1953.)

enculturation. The process of acquiring the cultural traditions of a society. Sometimes the term enculturation is restricted to the acquisition of new cultural patterns in adulthood (with the term SOCIALIZATION being applied to the learning of cultural patterns in childhood). Often, however, socialization and enculturation are used in exactly the same way and when they are, both are considered to occur throughout the life of every normal individual. For obvious theoretical reasons, cultural anthropologists (with their emphasis on the concept of culture) more often use the term *enculturation*, and sociologists the term *socialization*. The term *cultural conditioning* is used synonymously with *enculturation*.

encyclopedic sociology. See SOCIOLOGY, ENCYCLOPEDIC.

endogamy. The custom requiring marriage within one's own social group. Negative sanctions are applied to those who marry outside the group. The endogamous unit may be, for example, a kin unit, a religion, or a social class. See EXOGAMY.

endomorph. See SHELDON'S BODY TYPES.

enumeration district. The smallest territorial unit in a census. "An enumeration district is a small area assigned to one enumerator to be canvassed and reported separately. The average ED contained approximately 200 housing units." (*U.S. Census of Population*, Government Printing Office, Washington, D.C., 1960.)

environment. The effective environment, that is, everything that stimulates and influences the behavior of the individual or group. Many psychologists include internal sources of stimulation, but generally sociologists emphasize and study conditions and events external to the organism, whether they be physical, social, or cultural.

environment, geographic. All aspects of the environment that were not created by man and are not the result of human activity. The geographic environment includes the factors of altitude, terrain, climate, mineral deposits, gravity, the influence of cosmic forces, the natural distribution of plant and animal life, including insects and microorganisms, and all other nonman-made characteristics of an area. The geographic environment is sometimes referred to as the natural environment or the physical environment.

environment, social. That part of the environment consisting of interacting persons and groups, and including social expectations, patterns of social organization, and all other aspects of society. It includes social expectations internalized by the individual, and thus even when the individual is alone he still has a social environment.

epidemic, social. See SOCIAL EPIDEMIC.

epidemiology. The study of the distribution of diseases and the relationship of their distribution to population and environmental characteristics. The epidemiologist seeks to determine which elements of a population have the highest incidence of a particular disease and how this may be related to their physical and social characteristics, their environment, and their way of life.

epiphenomenalism. The doctrine that consciousness and mental phenomena are a result and merely a by-product of physiological or neural processes. Thus mental phenomena are considered to be, at the most, of secondary importance in the study of human behavior. Quite clearly, both sociology and social psychology do not regard mental states (e.g., ideas and thoughts) as epiphenomenal, but regard them as having an importance and a causal logic of their own.

epoch, cultural. See CULTURE EPOCH.

epistemology. The study or theory of knowledge, its origins, nature, and limits.

equal-appearing interval scale. See THURSTONE EQUAL-APPEARING IN-TERVAL SCALE.

equilibrium, social. The concept that social life has a tendency to be and to remain a functionally integrated phenomenon, so that any change in one part of the SOCIAL SYSTEM will bring about adjustive changes in other parts. The initial change creates an imbalance, but a functional adjustment of the parts occurs to re-create an integrated, adjusted, and relatively stable system. This theoretical concept was developed in functional sociology. See FUNCTIONALISM.

error, accidental. See ERROR, CHANCE.

error, alpha. The rejection of a true null hypothesis. Since null hypotheses are accepted or rejected on the basis of statistical probability, the possibility exists that a true null hypothesis may be erroneously rejected. Generally speaking, in the use of statistical probability to accept and reject null hypotheses, the risk of rejecting a true null hypothesis increases as the risk of accepting a false null hypothesis decreases. The level of significance used indicates the probability of making an alpha error, a higher level indicating a greater chance of this type of error. Alpha error is sometimes referred to as a type I error. See ERROR, BETA; HYPOTHESIS, NULL; PROBABILITY; SIGNIFICANCE, STATISTICAL.

error, beta. The retaining of a false null hypothesis. Since null hypotheses are accepted or rejected on the basis of tests of statistical probability, the possibility exists that a false null hypothesis may be accepted. The degree of danger of accepting a false null hypothesis depends upon the level of significance used in testing the hypothesis: the lower the level of significance used, the greater the probability of making a beta error. Beta error is sometimes referred to as type II error. See ERROR, ALPHA; HYPOTHESIS, NULL; PROBABILITY; SIGNIFICANCE, STATISTICAL.

error, chance. In statistics, one of a number of errors that arise from chance and tend to compensate for one another and cancel each other out. Chance errors, sometimes referred to as random or accidental errors, are usually contrasted with constant error or BIAS.

error, constant. See BIAS.

error, contrast. See CONTRAST ERROR.

error, coverage. See SAMPLING ERROR.

error, probable. See PROBABLE ERROR.

error, random. See ERROR, CHANCE.

error, sampling. See SAMPLING ERROR.

error, standard. See STANDARD ERROR.

error, systematic. See BIAS.

error, type I. See ERROR, ALPHA.

error, type II. See ERROR, BETA.

error of estimate, standard. See STANDARD ERROR OF ESTIMATE.

escape mechanism. In psychology, a type of DEFENSE MECHANISM in which an individual who is confronted with an unpleasant or threatening situation, frequently a conflict situation, engages in behavior or thought in which he retreats from reality. He may, for example, escape from reality through fantasy.

esprit de corps. A feeling of unity and closeness on the part of group members. *Esprit de corps* is characterized by the identification of group members with each other, concern for each other's welfare, an emotional feeling of belonging together, and a sense of common purpose. It is an important element in social cohesion. See COHESION, SOCIAL; MORALE.

estate. A social stratum less closed and rigid than a CASTE but more closed than a SOCIAL CLASS. The rights and duties of the members of an estate are defined by law, and membership is based primarily upon inheritance. However, some possibility of upward mobility exists, not so much between estates as within estates, since each estate includes a wide variety of occupations and socioeconomic levels. Medieval European feudal society constitutes the primary model of the estate system.

esteem. The evaluation of a person's performance in a given status, regardless of whether the status is high or low. Whether an individual has high or low esteem depends upon whether, in the judgment of others, he carries out his role well, whatever that role may be. Esteem thus differs from PRESTIGE. A person with a high prestige position may be regarded with low esteem because of his poor performance in that position. On the other hand, a person with a low prestige position may be regarded with high esteem because of his fine performance. However, his prestige remains low.

estimate. See STATISTIC.

ethical relativism. The thesis that values and norms cannot be judged by an absolute or universal standard, but must be understood in terms of varying group standards. Thus standards of morality that differ from one society to another or from one group within a society to another group may be equally valid. Ethical relativism maintains that there is no objective way to determine the relative merit of different systems of morality, since any attempt at evaluation reflects the moral standards accepted by the evaluator. Moreover, specific social norms must be understood in terms of the system of morality of which they are a part. It should be noted that ethical relativism does not deny the importance or meaning of values or norms. It only denies the possibility of universal, nonculturally biased standards of value judgment. See CULTURAL RELATIVISM.

ethnic consciousness. See ETHNIC IDENTIFICATION.

ethnic group. A group with a common cultural tradition and a sense of identity which exists as a subgroup of a larger society. The members of an ethnic group differ with regard to certain cultural characteristics from the other members of their society. They may have their own language and religion as well as certain distinctive customs. Probably most important is their feeling of identification as a traditionally distinct group. Usually the term is applied only to minority groups, but if there are a number of culturally distinct groups in a society some writers also refer to the dominant cultural group as an ethnic group. Ethnic groups should not be confused with racial groups. It is possible for an ethnic group to be a racial group as well, but often this is not the case. See CULTURE; MINORITY GROUP; RACE.

ethnic identification. An awareness of ETHNIC GROUP membership in an individual's relationships with others and also in his own self-conception.

ethnic transposition. The exchange of persons between two national cultures in which each is assimilated into the original culture of the other, for example, Germans becoming Poles and Poles becoming Germans. The term is a translation of the German *Umvolkung*, and has been used primarily by German sociologists.

ethnobotany. The study of the relationship of culture and plant life.

ethnocentrism. An attitude of regarding one's own culture or group as inherently superior. The ethnocentric attitude judges the worth of other cultures in terms of its own cultural standards, and, since other cultures are, of course, different, they are held to be inferior. Ethnocentrism reflects an inability to appreciate the viewpoint of others whose cultures have, for example, a different morality, religion, or language. It expresses an unwillingness or inability to see a common humanity, condition, and problem facing all men in all societies beneath the variations in social and cultural traditions. The term was introduced by William G. Sumner in his *Folkways* (Ginn, Boston, 1906).

ethnography. A division of cultural anthropology devoted to the descriptive study of individual cultures. Ethnography emphasizes description rather than analysis and interpretation. See ANTHROPOLOGY, CULTURAL.

ethnology. See ANTHROPOLOGY, CULTURAL.

ethnomusicology. The comparative study of music in different cultures, preliterate as well as literate.

ethnos. Those distinguishing traits and complexes that characterize a particular culture and differentiate it from other cultures. See CULTURE COMPLEX; CULTURE TRAIT.

ethnozoology. The study of the relationship between culture and animal life.

ethos. See CULTURAL ETHOS.

etiquette. A set of folkways regulating courteous behavior. See FOLK-WAY.

eufunction. Any consequence resulting from the operation of a given pattern of behavior (or any other aspect of a social or personality system) that contributes positively to the survival and stability of the system. Eufunction is sometimes referred to as positive function or simply FUNC-TION. It is contrasted with DYSFUNCTION.

eugenics. The study of human heredity with the goal of improving mankind primarily through selective breeding.

euthenics. The study of means to improve the physical and social environment in such a way that the quality of the population is improved.

evasion, patterned. See PATTERNED EVASION.

event analysis. The analysis of sequences of events under varying cultural conditions to determine common underlying patterns. "It is postulated that events or happenings of various types have genotypical structures independent of local cultural differences; for example, that the sequence of happenings following a severe physical disaster in cities in Japan, the United States, and Germany, will display a uniform pattern, colored but not obscured by local differences in culture." (A. F. C. Wallace, *American Anthropologist,* April 1956.)

evolution. The theory that all existing forms of plant and animal life developed gradually from earlier and generally simpler forms through a long series of small changes. Each change by itself resulted in minor modification of the organism, but the cumulative effect of many changes over a long period of time was the emergence of new, usually more complex, forms. Thus evolution traces the lines of development of vastly different living forms back to common ancestors. See DARWINIAN THEORY OF EVOLU-TION.

evolution, cultural. The theory that cultures develop historically from simpler to more complex forms. The conception of cultural evolution was closely associated with a belief in the inevitability of progress, and in its earlier simple form is no longer widely accepted by sociologists and anthropologists. Today most sociologists and anthropologists reject the notion of the unilineal and uniform development of all aspects of a culture, emphasizing that while some aspects of a culture may become more complex, others may become simpler. See PROGRESS, SOCIAL.

evolution, emergent. The emergence of new forms from unique combinations of pre-existing elements of older forms (physical, biological, social, or cultural). The new forms are qualitatively different from the older forms and cannot be understood by studying the older forms or previous levels. For example, according to this view, although man evolved from lower forms of life, his unique combination of characteristics makes him qualitatively different from the lower animals. It is held, therefore, that very little of importance can be understood about human behavior by studying animal behavior.

evolution, social. A theory of social change that is based upon the assumption that human societies in the long run tend to develop into higher and higher forms. The history of a society is seen as a series of major stages (within which there may be minor, temporary fluctuations), each with a more complex level of social organization, a higher ethical character, and a greater potential for human happiness than the preceding. The theory of social evolution was associated with a belief in the inevitability of social progress. Since a value bias seems to be built into this theory and it is not open to empirical verification, the concept of social evolution is not used by sociologists today. See EVOLUTION, CULTURAL; PROGRESS, SOCIAL; SOCIAL DARWINISM.

ex post facto experimental design. See EXPERIMENT, EX POST FACTO.

ex post facto explanation. An explanation of an event after it has occurred or an explanation of a research finding after the research has been completed. An ex post facto explanation is contrasted with a predictive hypothesis made before research is undertaken or before the occurrence of an event that verifies or contradicts the hypothesis. A predictive hypothesis verified by research is considered scientifically preferable to an ex post facto explanation, but sometimes only the latter is possible. See EXPERIMENT, EX POST FACTO.

ex post facto law. See LAW, EX POST FACTO.

exchange theory. A theory of social structure based on the concept that social exchange is a fundamental process in social life. Although the importance of social exchange has been discussed by many sociologists and cultural anthropologists, the concept has been most thoroughly and systematically developed in a theoretical approach to the analysis of social organization by Peter M. Blau. Blau defines social exchange as consisting in "voluntary actions of individuals that are motivated by the returns they are expected to bring and typically do in fact bring from others." He excludes actions based on coercion or solely on internalized standards with no expectation of any sort of return. In contrast to economic exchange, social exchange "involves favors that create diffuse future obligations, not precisely specified ones, and the nature of the return cannot be bargained about but must be left to the discretion of the one who makes it." Blau relates social exchange to other sociological concepts such as expectations, social norms, values, power, authority, etc., in an attempt to develop the basis for a theory of social structure. (P. M. Blau, *Exchange and Power in Social Life*, Wiley, New York, 1964.)

excitement, collective. See SOCIAL CONTAGION.

existentialism. A modern philosophical movement, with ancient roots in the history of human thought, that stresses the reality of "being" solely as determined by existence, the importance of the particular instance and the disregarding of abstractions, and the uniqueness of individual human experience and existence. The importance of the individual person is stressed particularly in contrast to the collectivism and the emphasis on the good of the organization found in modern corporations, government, and elsewhere in society. Existentialism is also a reaction against extreme rationalistic or scientific approaches to the study of man that attempt to eliminate all subjective phenomena in the study and interpretation of behavior. Existentialism highlights the inevitable subjectivity in man's attempts to be objective, and provides a philosophical counterbalance to theories of behavior (including belief) that stress the supremacy of society and the social group.

exogamy. The custom requiring an individual to marry outside a specific group of which he is a member. The exogamous group may be a kinship group such as a family or a clan, a village group, or other social group. See ENDOGAMY.

expanded family. See FAMILY, EXPANDED.

expectations. See GROUP EXPECTATIONS; ROLE EXPECTATIONS.

expedient rationality. See RATIONALITY, EXPEDIENT.

experience, conscious. See CONSCIOUS EXPERIENCE.

experiment. An investigation in which there is controlled manipulation by the investigator of the variables being studied, and precise observation or measurement of the results. An experiment involves the intervention of the investigator so that the phenomena under investigation may be observed under controlled conditions. Usually the investigator seeks conditions under which the effects of one variable may be observed while other relevant variables are held constant. See EXPERIMENTAL CONTROL; EXPERIMENTAL METHOD.

experiment, after-only. A type of controlled experiment in which both the EXPERIMENTAL GROUP and the CONTROL GROUP are measured with respect to the dependent variable (the factor that is expected to change) only during or after the exposure of the experimental group to the independent variable (the hypothesized cause of change). See EXPERIMENT, CONTROLLED; VARIABLE.

experiment, before-after. A type of controlled experiment in which both the EXPERIMENTAL GROUP and the CONTROL GROUP are measured with respect to the dependent variable (the factor that is expected to change) before as well as after the exposure of the experimental group to the independent variable (the experimental treatment). The before-after type of experiment sometimes is conducted without a separate control group. In this case the same group is compared before and after the experimental treatment, the group before the treatment serving in effect as the control group. See EXPERIMENT, CONTROLLED; VARIABLE.

experiment, contrived. See EXPERIMENT, CONTROLLED.

experiment, controlled. An experiment designed in advance and conducted under conditions in which it is possible to control relevant factors while measuring the effects of an experimentally introduced variable. In a controlled or contrived experiment subjects are divided into two groups, an EXPERIMENTAL GROUP and a CONTROL GROUP, with the subjects in the two groups matched with respect to all relevant characteristics or assigned to the two groups randomly, or, most preferred when practical, matched in pairs and then assigned randomly from each pair. The VARIABLE that is hypothesized to be the independent variable (the effect of which is to be tested) is introduced into the experimental group and withheld from the control group. The experimental group and the control group are then compared to determine whether there are any significant differences between them in regard to the dependent variable (the factor that is expected to change) to determine whether the hypothesized effect of the independent variable has occurred in the experimental group and has not occurred in the control group. On the basis of this comparison the original hypothesis is confirmed or rejected. See EXPERIMENTAL CONTROL; MATCHING; RANDOMIZATION.

experiment, ex post facto. An experiment conducted after the occurrence of the event being studied. The independent variable, or the presumed cause, was not introduced by the investigator, but occurred before the investigation began, and the dependent variable, or the effect, is already present. The investigator must rely on records or the memory of respondents concerning the event being studied. Frequently in an ex post facto experiment the investigator uses previously collected data to test his hypotheses. Experimental controls are introduced through the manipulation of the data, for example, by dividing IBM cards that represent subjects into categories each with specified characteristics. An ex post facto experiment does not permit as rigorous control as an experiment planned in advance. However, it permits the experimental manipulation of data that cannot be obtained through a controlled experiment. For example, an ex post facto experiment might be conducted by analyzing census data previously collected for other purposes. See EXPERIMENT, CONTROLLED.

experiment, factorial. An experiment in which the effects of two or more variables are evaluated simultaneously. The factorial experiment stands in contrast to the usual single-factor experiment. In a factorial experiment the interrelationships of the factors (independent variables whose effects are to be measured) with each other as well as their effects on a resulting characteristic (dependent variable) are studied. Moreover, the effects of various levels of each of the factors and their varied combinations are analyzed. Proponents of the factorial experiment maintain that the findings of this type of experiment are more applicable to concrete situations under natural conditions where a wide variety of factors exist that cannot be reduced to the controlled conditions specified by the single-factor experiment. See EXPERIMENT, SINGLE-FACTOR; VARIABLE.

experiment, laboratory. A controlled experiment in which the investigator creates the entire experimental situation, thus enabling him to determine and manipulate the experimental conditions precisely as he wishes. See EXPERIMENT, CONTROLLED.

experiment, mental. A procedure in which the investigator speculates concerning the results if certain aspects of a social structure were eliminated. This technique is used quite frequently in functional analysis, which is concerned with the functional relationship and interaction of various aspects of a system. See FUNCTIONALISM; SOCIAL SYSTEM.

experiment, natural. A study of causal factors carried out in a social situation not created by the experimenter, but lending itself to experimental investigation. The groups studied exist in society independently of the investigation and are not manipulated by the investigator. The VARIABLE that is hypothesized to be the independent variable, or relevant cause, occurs in the natural course of events and is not introduced by the scientist. In a natural experiment, the scientist must find a group that has experienced the hypothesized independent variable and another group, similar in other respects, that has not been exposed to this variable. The first group is regarded as the EXPERIMENTAL GROUP and the second as the CONTROL

GROUP. The two groups are compared to determine the effects of the independent variable.

experiment, projected. 1. Frequently used synonymously with controlled experiment. See EXPERIMENT, CONTROLLED.

2. Sometimes the term is limited to refer only to a before-after controlled experiment. See EXPERIMENT, BEFORE-AFTER.

3. Occasionally used to refer to any experiment in which an investigator hypothesizes an effect prior to its occurrence.

experiment, self-contained. An experiment designed so that it provides all the evidence upon which the conclusions and interpretations of the study are based.

experiment, single-factor. An experiment in which the effects on a dependent VARIABLE, or characteristic, of the manipulation of one independent variable (the experimental treatment) are studied while all other variables are kept constant. Traditionally most experiments have been of the single-factor type. See EXPERIMENT, FACTORIAL.

experimental bias. See BIAS.

experimental control. The process of holding constant all relevant factors other than the factor being studied in the experiment. In setting up an EXPERIMENTAL GROUP and a CONTROL GROUP, subjects are matched or randomly assigned so that the two groups are known to be the same or assumed to be essentially the same on all relevant characteristics (variables) except the experimental, or independent, variable (the hypothesized cause of change). A factor is said to be controlled when the subjects compared are alike with respect to that factor. See EXPERIMENT, CONTROLLED; MATCHING; RANDOMIZATION.

experimental design, completely randomized. An experimental design in which subjects are exposed or not exposed to the experimental VARIABLE (the hypothesized independent or causal variable), or assigned to the experimental group or the control group, on a completely random basis. RANDOMIZATION is used instead of matching individuals to hold other relevant variables or characteristics constant. See EXPERIMENT, CONTROLLED.

experimental design, cross-sectional. The simultaneous comparison of two (or more) similar groups that differ relevantly only with respect to the factor being studied. See EXPERIMENTAL DESIGN, LONGITUDINAL.

experimental design, longitudinal. The study of the same group over a period of time. The group may be undergoing experimental manipulation by the investigator or it may be experiencing certain changes in its natural social setting. In either case, systematic observations or measurements are made at periodic intervals to determine the precise pattern as well as the direction of the changes that are occurring. See EXPERIMENTAL DESIGN, CROSS-SECTIONAL.

experimental design, randomized complete block. An experimental design in which the subjects are divided into blocks or groups that are as similar as possible. Within each block the experimental treatment, or independent VARIABLE, is randomly assigned (or not assigned) to the subjects. By this method, each block serves as a repetition of the experiment and the blocks can be checked against each other. For this reason a block is referred to as a replicate. See RANDOMIZATION; REPLICATION.

experimental group. In an experiment, the group of subjects into which the experimenter introduces the independent variable (the hypothesized cause, or experimental treatment). The effect of the experimental variable is determined by contrasting the experimental group with the CONTROL GROUP, a group that has not received the experimental treatment but that is similar to the experimental group in respect to all other relevant factors. See EXPERIMENT, CONTROLLED; VARIABLE.

experimental method. The constructing of a body of verified scientific generalizations by testing hypotheses under conditions of carefully controlled observation. See EXPERIMENT; HYPOTHESIS; INDUCTION; SCIENTIFIC METHOD.

experimental psychology. See PSYCHOLOGY, EXPERIMENTAL.

explanation, causal. See CAUSATION; CAUSE.

explanation, ex post facto. See EX POST FACTO EXPLANATION.

exploratory study. A preliminary study the major purpose of which is to become familiar with a phenomenon that is to be investigated, so that the major study to follow may be designed with greater understanding and precision. The exploratory study (which may use any of a variety of techniques, usually with a small sample) permits the investigator to define his research problem and formulate his hypotheses more accurately. It also enables him to choose the most suitable techniques for his research and to decide on the questions most in need of emphasis and detailed investigation, and it may alert him to potential difficulties, sensitivities, and areas of resistance.

extended family. See FAMILY, EXTENDED.

external system. The total system of group activities, sentiments, and social interactions that are directed toward the group's external environment. The term was introduced by George C. Homans, who postulated that the external system constitutes a solution of the problem: "How shall the group survive in its environment? We call it external because it is conditioned by the environment; we call it a system because in it the elements of behavior are mutually dependent. The external system, plus another set of relations which we shall call the INTERNAL SYSTEM, make up the total social system." (G. C. Homans, *The Human Group*, Harcourt, Brace, New York, 1950.) See ACTIVITY; INTERACTION; SENTIMENT.

extinction. In experimental psychology, the gradual disappearance of a CONDITIONED RESPONSE in an organism when it is elicited without REINFORCEMENT. For example, if the conditioned response is salivation when a bell is rung, this response will slowly cease if food is not regularly presented in conjunction with the sound of the bell. The term refers also to the weakening of a habit that occurs when the habit is repeated without reinforcement or reward.

extrapolation. The estimation, from a series of known values, of a variable of unknown values either higher or lower than the entire range of the known values. The estimation is based on the assumption that the distribution of the unknown values will tend to follow the same trend as that shown by the known values.

extrovert. A personality type (proposed by Carl G. Jung) whose conscious interests and energies are directed toward people and events outside himself rather than toward himself and inner experiences. Such a personality tends to talk a great deal, is preoccupied with social life, and requires continual stimulation from the external world. See INTROVERT.

F

F ratio. See F TEST.

F scale. A scale of authoritarian attitudes intended as a measure of both authoritarianism and anti-Semitism. The scale was constructed (by Theodor W. Adorno and associates) so that it would correlate highly with a scale of anti-Semitic attitudes. (T. W. Adorno, E. Frenkel-Brunswik, D. J. Levinson, and R. N. Sanford, *The Authoritarian Personality*, Harper, New York, 1950.) See AUTHORITARIAN PERSONALITY.

F test. A test of whether there is a statistically significant difference between two or more groups, or whether the groups are probably drawn from identical populations (or the same population) with differences between them due only to chance. The F test is based on the analysis of VARI-ANCE or the dispersion of values, and involves the relationship of the variance between groups to the variance within the groups. It is a parametric test, requiring the usual parametric assumptions (primarily concerning the population distribution in the population from which the samples were drawn). See PARAMETRIC STATISTICS; PROBABILITY; SIGNIFI-CANCE, STATISTICAL.

facilitation, social. See SOCIAL FACILITATION.

fact. 1. A statement about a phenomenon that is based upon the observations or experiences of a wide variety of persons.

2. An observed phenomenon itself (a thing, an event, a measurement, a distribution, etc.).

fact, social. See SOCIAL FACT.

factor. 1. One of a number of relatively distinct and basic underlying variables determined through FACTOR ANALYSIS and composed of several highly correlated measures. See VARIABLE.

2. One of two or more variables that combine to bring about a certain result.

3. An independent variable.

factor analysis. A statistical procedure used to determine the basic irreducible variables (factors) underlying a large number of interrelated variables. When measurements of a large number of variables have been obtained (each representing, for example, a test or a test item), factor analysis may be used to reduce them to a smaller number of basic types or factors. Factor analysis, in essence, involves the analysis of the correlations among the variables. Those variables that are highly correlated with each other are regarded as representing the same factor, and the extent to which each variable (e.g., test) has a greater or lesser ability to measure this factor is indicated. The small number of factors obtained in this manner is intended to provide in more economical and comprehensible form all the essential information represented in the large number of original variables. See Q-TECHNIQUE; VARIABLE.

factory farm. See FARM, FACTORY.

factory system. An economic system in which goods are manufactured in specialized establishments where workers gather specifically for the purpose of production. The factory system replaced the system of household production, in which manufacturing was carried on in the home, frequently as an adjunct to farming. The emergence of the factory system was largely the result of the introduction of power-driven machinery which had to be housed in a specialized and centralized location. The development of the factory system was characterized by the emergence of a class of full-time industrial workers, who work for wages and do not own the tools of production or the products they manufacture. The rise of the factory system was an important part of the INDUSTRIAL REVOLUTION.

factual judgment. A statement that asserts a relationship between facts, and which therefore can be empirically confirmed or denied. See EMPIRICAL; FACT.

faculty. 1. A specific ABILITY enabling an individual to excel in a particular type of activity, for example, a faculty for music.

2. In faculty psychology, one of a number of hypothesized mental powers. See PSYCHOLOGY, FACULTY.

fad. An unusual pattern of behavior that spreads rapidly and is adopted with zealous enthusiasm by its adherents, but remains popular for only a short time. The novelty of a fad is an important element in its popularity. A fad differs from a FASHION in that it tends to be more bizarre; its spread is more spontaneous and less planned, and it is of shorter duration. A fad is similar to a CRAZE except that the term craze usually implies either a more extreme form of deviance from customary patterns of behavior or a pattern that has been deliberately stimulated for economic gain.

false class consciousness. See CLASS CONSCIOUSNESS, FALSE.

familiarity, privileged. See PRIVILEGED FAMILIARITY.

familism. A form of social organization characterized by familial values that emphasize the subordination of the interests and personality of individual family members to the interests and welfare of the family group. It is characterized by a strong sense of family identification and loyalty, mutual assistance among family members, and a concern for the perpetuation of the family unit.

family. A basic kinship unit, in its minimal form consisting of a husband, wife, and children. In its widest sense it refers to all relatives living together or recognized as a social unit, including adopted persons.

The U.S. Census defines a family as two or more persons living together who are related to each other by blood, marriage, or adoption. Thus by this definition, a husband and wife, or two sisters living together, would be considered a family.

The family is often called the "basic social institution" because of its important functions of procreation and socialization, and because it is found, in some form, in all societies.

family, atomistic. A type of FAMILY characterized by a higher degree of individuation than either the domestic family or trusteeship family, as distinguished by Carle C. Zimmerman (*Family and Civilization,* Harper, New York, 1947). Individual family members have more freedom from family control, and the welfare of the individual is considered more important than the welfare of the family as a whole. The atomistic family typically is small in size, and centers about a husband, wife, and unmarried children. Usually parents do not live with their married children, and when they do it is not considered a desirable arrangement. The modern American middle-class family in a large urban community is probably the closest approximation to the atomistic family. See FAMILY, DOMESTIC; FAMILY, TRUSTEESHIP.

family, autonomous. A FAMILY that constitutes an economically self-sufficient unit.

family, companionate. See MARRIAGE, COMPANIONATE.

family, companionship. A type of FAMILY in which behavior is based on "the mutual affection and consensus of its members." The companionship family was distinguished by Ernest W. Burgess and Harvey J. Locke as an abstract or IDEAL TYPE contrasted to the ideal type of the institutional family. "The modern American family residing in the apartment-house areas of the city approximates most nearly the ideal type of companion-ship family, in which the members enjoy a high degree of self-expression and at the same time are united by the bonds of affection, congeniality, and common interests." (E. W. Burgess and H. J. Locke, *The Family,* American Book, New York, 1953.) The emergence of the companionship family has been associated with the decline of traditional economic, edu-cational, religious, and recreational functions of the family and with the decline of traditional, neighborhood sources of informal control, especially in the anonymity of the modern city. In the companionship family, affection becomes both the major function of the family and the major source of control over family members. See FAMILY, INSTITUTIONAL.

family, compound. A type of FAMILY resulting from the practice of POLYGYNY or POLYANDRY, in which two or more nuclear families are united through a common husband or wife. See FAMILY, NUCLEAR.

family, conjugal. 1. A type of FAMILY organization in which primary emphasis is placed upon the husband-wife relationship, rather than upon blood relationships. The conjugal family centers about a husband and wife and their unmarried children. If other relatives are found in the family their position is peripheral. The conjugal family usually does not form an extended family. It is the most prevalent family form today among the urban middle class in the Western world. See FAMILY, CONSANGUINE; FAM-ILY, EXPANDED; FAMILY, EXTENDED.

2. See FAMILY, NUCLEAR.

family, consanguine. 1. A type of FAMILY organization in which the primary emphasis is upon the blood relationships of parents and children or brothers and sisters, rather than upon the marital relationship of hus-band and wife. Thus the position of the blood relatives is central while the position of the spouses tends to be peripheral. The consanguine family normally forms an extended family, usually with two or three generations living together. See FAMILY, CONJUGAL; FAMILY, EXTENDED.

2. See FAMILY OF ORIENTATION.

family, democratic. See FAMILY, EQUALITARIAN.

family, domestic. A type of FAMILY that is intermediate between the atomistic family and the trusteeship family, as distinguished by Carle C. Zimmerman (*Family and Civilization,* Harper, New York, 1947). The domestic family has more group unity and less individuation than the atomistic family. Considerable emphasis is placed on the relationship be-tween parents and children even after the children are married, and close contact is maintained between parents and married children and among families of married brothers and sisters. Married children often consult with their parents and visiting is common. However, the domestic family does not form as unified a group as the trusteeship family. See FAMILY, ATOMISTIC; FAMILY, TRUSTEESHIP.

family, equalitarian. A type of FAMILY in which the members of the family are regarded as equal. The husband, in particular, is not regarded as having more authority or privileges than the wife. It is also called the democratic family.

family, expanded. A conjugal FAMILY in which single relatives, such as an unmarried or widowed brother, sister, or cousin of the husband or wife, live with the family. (See D. S. Pitkin, "Land Tenure and Farm Organization in an Italian Village," Ph.D. Dissertation, Harvard University, 1954.) See FAMILY, CONJUGAL; FAMILY, EXTENDED; FAMILY, NUCLEAR.

family, extended. 1. A FAMILY that includes three or more generations. For example, an extended family might include grandparents, their unmarried children, their married sons (or daughters) together with their spouses and children. Consanguine families (organized in terms of blood relationship) usually form extended families, whereas conjugal families (based on the marital relationship), while they may on occasion form very limited extended families, usually do not. According to this definition nuclear families of the same generation joined together, for example through POLYGAMY, would not be considered extended families.

2. A family composed of two or more nuclear families regardless of whether they are of the same or different generations, not united through polygamy.

3. A family composed of more than one nuclear family, including polygamous families.

See FAMILY, CONJUGAL; FAMILY, CONSANGUINE; FAMILY, EXPANDED; FAMILY, NUCLEAR.

family, heteronomous. A FAMILY that is not economically self-sufficient but rather seeks its livelihood within an economic system based on a highly complex division of labor. One or more family members perform specialized services within this economic system. The modern American family is an example of the heteronomous family.

family, institutional. A type of FAMILY in which behavior is based on the fulfillment of traditional role expectations and conformity to traditional norms. Ernest W. Burgess and Harvey J. Locke formulated the abstract or IDEAL TYPE of the institutional family in contrast to the ideal type of the companionship family. "The most extreme theoretical formulation of the institutional family would be one in which its unity would be determined entirely by the social pressure impinging on family members. . . . Of the historical and existing types of families the large-patriarchical type most closely approximates the ideal construction of the institutional family with its combination of the powerful sanctions of the mores, religion, and law, and the practically complete subordination of the individual members of the family to the authority of the patriarch." (E. W. Burgess and H. J. Locke, *The Family*, American Book, New York, 1953.) The use of the term institutional family often implies that the conditions of societal organization are such that the family is the center of education, religion, economic production, recreation, etc. See FAMILY, COMPANIONSHIP.

family, matriarchal. A form of FAMILY organization in which the mother is the formal head and dominant power in the family. A matriarchal family theoretically would be a consanguine family (organized in terms of blood relationship) practicing matrilineal descent and matrilocal residence, and ruled by an older woman such as a grandmother. There is disagreement among anthropologists as to whether there have been any societies with a truly matriarchal family system. Undoubtedly if this family form has occurred it is rare. See FAMILY, CONSANGUINE; FAMILY PATRIARCHAL.

family, matricentric. A FAMILY in which the mother is the central figure and the position of the father tends to be peripheral. The predominant family form among the lower-class rural Negroes in the American South is usually considered matricentric because of the casual and often temporary nature of the father's relationship to the family. The middle-class suburban family is also sometimes classified as matricentric because the father is away from home most of the time and thus many family decisions are made by the wife.

family, matrilineal. See MATRILINEAL DESCENT.

family, matrilocal. See MATRILOCAL RESIDENCE.

family, metronymic. A family form in which the children take the mother's name. See MATRILINEAL DESCENT.

family, monogamous. See MONOGAMY.

family, multilineal. See BILATERAL DESCENT.

family, nuclear. The basic unit of FAMILY organization, composed of a married couple and their offspring. The nuclear family may be a separate family or a part of a larger family. A husband with two wives would be a member of two nuclear families, or a compound family. The term *conjugal family* is sometimes used instead of *nuclear family*. See FAMILY, COMPOUND; FAMILY, CONJUGAL; FAMILY, EXTENDED.

family, patriarchal. A form of FAMILY organization in which the father is the formal head and the ruling power in the family. The authority of the father is absolute and final. The patriarchal family is usually an extended consanguine family (organized in terms of blood relationship) in which the patriarch is the senior male member. Examples of the patriarchal family are the traditional Chinese family, the family in ancient Israel, and the family in ancient Rome. The modern Western family emerged from a modified form of the patriarchal family. See FAMILY, CONSANGUINE; FAMILY, MATRIARCHAL.

family, patrilineal. See PATRILINEAL DESCENT.

family, patrilocal. See PATRILOCAL RESIDENCE.

family, patronymic. The FAMILY form in which children take the father's name. See PATRILINEAL DESCENT.

family, polyandrous. See POLYANDRY.

family, polygamous. See POLYGAMY.

family, polygynous. See POLYGYNY.

family, primary. A FAMILY that has as its family head the person who is the head of the household. In other words, the family is living in its own household. The term is used by the U.S. Census, and all but a small number of American families are classified as primary families. (*U.S. Census of Population,* Government Printing Office, Washington, D.C., 1960.) See FAMILY, SECONDARY.

family, romantic. See FAMILY, COMPANIONSHIP.

family, secondary. A FAMILY that has as its family head a person who is not the head of the household, but who is a lodger or resident employee in the household. In other words, the family is living not in its own household, but in the household of another family. The term is used by the U.S. Census, and only a small number of American families are classified as secondary families. (*U.S. Census of Population,* Government Printing Office, Washington, D.C., 1960.) See FAMILY, PRIMARY.

family, size of completed. The number of children in a FAMILY in which the mother has passed the child-bearing age (usually 45 or over, although sometimes 50 or over is used).

family, stem. 1. A FAMILY comprising one nuclear family plus one or more other relatives who do not form a second nuclear family. See FAMILY, NUCLEAR.

2. A small extended FAMILY that includes two nuclear families of adjacent generations.

3. The term stem family (*famille-souche*) was used by Frederic LePlay to describe a modified type of patriarchal FAMILY in which the family estate is passed on intact to one son chosen by the father. In this way the property is not constantly subdivided from generation to generation, nor is it automatically inherited by the eldest son as in the case of primogeni-

ture. The sons not inheriting the family estate usually are given aid in establishing a livelihood elsewhere, and may return to the family home in case of need. While not as strongly unified as the true patriarchal family, this type of family has more unity than the individualistic, conjugal family. See FAMILY, PATRIARCHAL.

family, trusteeship. A type of FAMILY characterized by a higher degree of group unity than either the atomistic family or domestic family, as distinguished by Carle C. Zimmerman (*Family and Civilization,* Harper, New York, 1947). In the trusteeship family the individual's self-interests are subordinated to the welfare of the family as a whole. The family is regarded as having an identity of its own that is greater than the identities of its living members, and that includes both ancestors and unborn future generations. Living members are regarded as trustees of the family's "blood, rights, property, name and position for their lifetimes." (*Ibid.*) The trusteeship family is usually an extended family (including several living generations) and is typically found in rural cultures where the family forms an economic unit. See FAMILY, ATOMISTIC; FAMILY, DOMESTIC; FAMILY, EXTENDED.

family cycle. The sequence of FAMILY events from the marriage of the spouses to their deaths. It includes the birth and marriage of the first and the last child as well as other important events in the process of child rearing and the period of old age.

family institution. A basic social institution, important to the survival of a society, comprising a system of interrelated social roles and norms organized around the regulation of sexual relations, the rearing of children, and the structuring of kinship relationships. See INSTITUTION, BASIC SOCIAL; INSTITUTION, SOCIAL.

family interaction, law of. See BOSSARD'S LAW OF FAMILY INTERACTION.

family of orientation. The FAMILY into which an individual is born and in which he is socialized. See FAMILY OF PROCREATION.

family of procreation. The FAMILY formed by an individual when he marries and has children. See FAMILY OF ORIENTATION.

fantasy. A sequence of imagined events, usually pleasant and satisfying experiences. Fantasy frequently is a psychological DEFENSE MECHANISM resulting from frustration. When the satisfaction of an individual's wants are blocked in the world of reality, he may escape into a world created by his own imagination. The use of fantasy to relieve frustration may be deliberate and conscious or may occur without full conscious realization by the individual of what he is doing. In extreme cases, fantasy may be associated with SCHIZOPHRENIA. On the other hand, fantasy is common in normal individuals and may lead to creative innovation. See DAYDREAM.

farm, commercial family. A farm, owned and operated by a family, that produces crops for the market. The family lives on the farm and works it themselves with the help of only a small number of hired workers. However, this type of farm, as opposed to a subsistence farm, does not provide all or even most of the family's needs, and a specialized crop is raised for cash. Most family farms in the United States today are of this type. See FARM, SUBSISTENCE.

farm, factory. A large-scale farm operated in the same manner as a large industrial enterprise. The factory farm usually specializes in the production of a single crop. Large numbers of laborers are hired, often on a seasonal basis, and their work is supervised as in a factory. The ownership of the farm is frequently in the form of a corporation, with a manager employed to run the enterprise in the most efficient and profitable manner possible.

farm, family. A farm owned and operated by a family. The family lives on the farm and works it themselves with the help of no more than a small number of hired workers. The family farm may be either a subsistence farm or a commercial family farm. See FARM, COMMERCIAL FAMILY; FARM, SUBSISTENCE.

farm, plantation. A large-scale farm worked by low-cost labor. A plantation does not have the efficient and rational organization of a factory farm. The term is applied to the large-scale cotton-growing agricultural units of the American South both in the pre-Civil War period when they were worked by slaves and in the post-Civil War period when they have been worked by share-cropping and tenant-farming arrangements. It is also used to refer to the large-scale agricultural units found in tropical areas, which usually are controlled by Europeans and worked by native labor. In this form the plantation system has been associated with colonialism. See FARM, FACTORY.

farm, subsistence. A family farm on which crops are produced primarily for home consumption rather than for sale in the market. The farm provides for most of the needs of the family that owns and operates it. Nevertheless, some produce is usually sold in order to purchase certain items that cannot be produced on the farm. See FARM, FAMILY.

farm population. All persons living on farms, whether or not they are engaged in agriculture. In the U.S. Census, this term is distinguished from rural non-farm, which is used for persons living in rural areas but not on farms.

fascism. A political-economic system in which there is rigid regulation of all major aspects of political, economic, and social life by a hierarchically organized and centralized state authority, private ownership of the means of production limited by strict state control, state monopoly of the means of communication, a glorification of the state, and a severe curtailment of individual freedom. The term fascism, originally taken from the name of the Italian Fascist Party, has become a general term for any extreme rightist political-economic movement. The term is often used loosely, frequently as an epithet, but basically it implies the rejection of democracy and belief in a one-party system, rule by an elite class, a totalitarian state, and subjugation of the individual to the state. See TOTALITARIANISM.

fashion. A form of behavior that is socially approved at a given time, but subject to periodic change. Fashion involves patterned changes in certain norms that are culturally permitted and expected to change. Adherence to fashion combines deviation and conformity—deviation from traditional practices and conformity to currently popular standards. The spread of fashions may be regarded as a form of COLLECTIVE BEHAVIOR, and conformity to prevailing fashions is usually enforced through informal forms of social control. See CRAZE; FAD.

fear. A strong, unpleasant emotion or attitude in response to painful, dangerous, or unexpected stimuli—or the anticipation of these. Fear motivates the individual to avoid or escape from the threatening situation, although social norms often require courageous behavior despite fear. Fear certainly occurs no less as a reaction to social situations than it does to physical threats. Usually one's social experiences and culture define what is to be feared and what is not to be feared.

fecundity. The potential physiological capacity of the females of a particular population to reproduce. It is the maximum rate at which women of childbearing age could produce children if the best possible conditions existed for procreation. See FERTILITY.

federalism. A form of government in which powers and functions are divided between a central government and a number of political subdivisions having a significant degree of political autonomy. The realm of authority of the two levels of government is for the most part clearly distinguished. The federal system of government stands in contrast to a centralized system of government, in which all powers lie at the disposal of the central government, with the political subdivisions merely the creations of the central government and having no authority other than that which the central government chooses to delegate to them.

feeble-mindedness. A level of mentality below normal. A consistent I.Q. score of below 70 is the arbitrary point used to identify the feeble-minded. Feeble-minded persons find it very difficult to adjust to normal social situations, particularly without special education. There are degrees of such mental incapacity. Usually the feeble-minded are classified into three levels: idiots, the lowest, with an I.Q. below 25, imbeciles, usually within the I.Q. range 25–49, and morons, usually with an I.Q. of 50–69.

feedback. A process in which knowledge of the results of past performance (by an individual, a group, or a machine) leads to modification of future performance, thereby keeping performance effectively directed toward the attainment of a goal. For an individual, feedback is represented in any return communication in response to previous behavior—that is, knowledge of the results of one's past actions or attitudes—that allows a modification of one's future behavior or attitudes. Feedback is essential in any communications system and is involved in all social interaction. The concept of feedback is central to CYBERNETICS.

feeling. An affective experience of pleasantness or unpleasantness toward something or someone. Feeling is an important aspect of ATTITUDE.

felony. A serious CRIME, punishable by death or imprisonment for more than a year. See MISDEMEANOR.

feminism. A social movement originating in England in the eighteenth century and having as its goal the attainment of certain social, political, and economic rights for women, intended to give them equality with men. The feminist movement generally has followed the spread of the Industrial Revolution and the associated breakdown of traditional norms and the attainment of economic independence by women. In the West today, feminism, having achieved its original objectives, has become more of a psychological state—a constellation of certain attitudes held by individual women—than a social movement. It remains a social movement in its traditional form in certain currently industrializing nations, particularly those in which women have traditionally held a subordinate position.

feral man. 1. A person who, as reported in any of a variety of legends, is reared apart from other humans, usually by animals, and is consequently unsocialized. Myths of children being raised by animals (wolf-boy stories and the like) are common and recurrent and have a wide appeal to the human imagination. The persistence of such beliefs despite evidence to the contrary reflects the durability of ancient beliefs, of romanticism, and totemism. However, human beings require human contact for normal physical as well as mental and social development.
2. Sometimes used to refer to infants who are neglected and who do not receive enough stimulation to develop as normal human beings. However, this usage is generally not preferred since such children are not "wild" but, on the contrary, passive. See MARASMUS.

fertility. The actual rate of reproduction, as measured by the number of births, of a particular population. Fertility is determined by social, economic, and psychological factors as well as by FECUNDITY.

fertility, differential. 1. Differences in the fertility rate of different segments of a population. Comparisons of differential fertility rates may be made on the basis of social class, educational level, occupation, race, religion, rural-urban residence, and so on.

2. In a more limited sense, the lower fertility rate of the upper social classes compared to that of the lower classes. This differential fertility pattern has characterized most industrialized nations, but there is evidence that the differential is declining in countries that have achieved a generally high standard of living. The lower fertility rate of the upper classes has been viewed with alarm by some who see in it a danger that the quality of the population will decline. On the other hand, others have regarded it favorably, for it provides more "room at the top" and increases the opportunities for upward mobility.

fertility rate. An index of the FERTILITY of a population, usually measured by the number of children that have been born to each 1,000 women of childbearing age in the population. Childbearing age is usually defined as 15–44, although 20–44, 20–49, and 15–49 are also used.

fertility rate, total. A hypothetical fertility rate that tells the average total number of children that would be born to a group of women if the births followed a given set of age-specific birth rates and if the entire group lived through the childbearing age. The age-specific birth rates (the birth rate of each age group) of a population may be determined for a given year, and then on that basis the total fertility rate of a group of women may be calculated to indicate what fertility rate would result from this particular set of age-specific birth rates. See BIRTH RATE, SPECIFIC.

fertility ratio. Usually, the number of children under five years of age in a population per 1,000 women of childbearing age. Childbearing age is usually defined as 15–44, although 20–44, 20–49, and 15–49 are also used.

fertility ratio, effective. The number of children under five years of age in a population, divided by the number of women of childbearing age. This is sometimes referred to as the child-woman ratio.

fetish. Any revered object believed to have supernatural or magical power to attain the desired ends of the person who possesses or uses it (for example, a rabbit's foot or a good-luck charm).

fetishism. 1. A religion that emphasizes the worship of fetishes, frequently found in association with ANIMISM.

2. In psychiatry, a type of sexual perversion in which erotic satisfaction is obtained by touching some object (such as shoes) associated with a person who has aroused sexual desire. Love is directed not at the person but at some aspect of the person's behavior, body, or possessions. Its abnormality lies in the compulsively confined and nonsocial character of the sexual relationship.

fetusphilic society. A society characterized by a tender treatment of newborn children that simulates the conditions of the fetal period. In a fetusphilic society infants are bathed in warm water, bundled up warm and tight, fed on demand, and so forth. The term was introduced by Siegfried Bernfeld (*The Psychology of the Infant*, tr. by R. Hurwitz, Brentano's, New York, 1929). See FETUSPHOBIC SOCIETY.

fetusphobic society. A society characterized by a harsh treatment of newborn children that abruptly terminates the conditions of the fetal period. In a fetusphobic society infants are bathed in cold water, dressed lightly, and may be put on a rigid feeding schedule. The term was introduced by Siegfried Bernfeld (*The Psychology of the Infant*, tr. by R. Hurwitz, Brentano's, New York, 1929). See FETUSPHILIC SOCIETY.

feud. A permanent or long-lasting state of hostility, often involving periodic bloodshed, between groups or subgroups. Typically, feuds occur between people who are related to each other by blood, geographical proximity, or traditional ties. Generally feuds are characterized by an inability of either side to dominate or vanquish the other.

feudalism. The dominant system of social organization in Western Europe from the tenth to fifteenth century. Feudalism was based upon a system of land tenure in which land estates of various size (fiefs) were given to hold (not to own) by an overlord to his vassals (knights) in return for military service. The fiefs, which could in turn be subdivided by a vassal among other knights who would then be his vassals, consisted of one or more manors, that is, estates with serfs whose agricultural production provided the economic basis for the existence of the feudal class. When receiving a fief a vassal took an oath of homage and fealty to his lord, and owed him loyalty as well as a specified amount of military service. Upon the death of a vassal the fief would technically revert to the overlord, but it was common practice for the eldest son to take his father's place as vassal of the lord, and thus, in effect, fiefs were passed on through primogeniture. Feudalism was at its height in the eleventh through thirteenth centuries. Its decline was largely the result of the growth of cities, with the accompanying rise of an urban middle class and a commercial economy, and also the rise to power of centralized monarchies.

Although the concept of feudalism is based on the model of the feudal society of Western Europe in the later Middle Ages, the term has also been applied to other societies with a similar system of social organization, particularly to medieval Japan.

fiction. A belief or assumption whose significance is determined by the fact that people accept it as real. People who act as though a fiction were a reality may or may not actually believe in its truthfulness. However, in either case they find the fiction useful. An example would be the belief of clan members that they are descended from a common ancestor. See LEGAL FICTION.

field, psychological. All those factors or variables present in the experienced world of the individual that affect his reactions at any one moment in time. See FIELD THEORY.

field, social. See SOCIAL SITUATION.

field study method. A research technique in which the investigator observes his subjects under their usual environmental conditions of life, rather than under laboratory conditions. The subjects may or may not be aware of being observed. In sociology and anthropology, interviews are often used in such studies.

field theory. A theoretical approach in social psychology based on a conception of the total configuration of an individual's perceptions as opposed to the assumed objective characteristics of his physical and social environment. This approach was developed from GESTALT PSYCHOLOGY primarily through the work of Kurt Lewin. The total psychological environment of an individual (including himself and all other persons significant to him) was referred to by Lewin as the individual's life-space. The life-space is represented diagrammatically and divided into regions, one of which is occupied by the individual himself. Other regions are attractive to the individual (have a positive valence) or unattractive (have a negative valence). This theoretical model is used to explain individual behavior in terms of the total psychological field of forces, the positive and negative valences, operating upon the individual in his particular life-space. (K. Lewin, *A Dynamic Theory of Personality*, McGraw-Hill, New York, 1935.)

figure-drawing test. In psychology, a PROJECTIVE TECHNIQUE in which a subject is asked to draw a person (or a man, woman, child, etc.), on the assumption that such drawings reveal psychological information about the subject.

figure-ground. In GESTALT PSYCHOLOGY the two major aspects of a configuration, the figure being the focus of attention. However, the two aspects are regarded as interdependent parts of one whole, and not separate entities.

filiation. The relationship of child to parent without regard to societal rules of descent or membership in kinship groups. A distinction between descent and filiation occurs when members of a society practice UNILATERAL DESCENT, in which descent is reckoned exclusively through either the mother's or father's line.

filiation, complementary. In a society with a system of UNILATERAL DESCENT, the relationship of a child to the parent through whom he does *not* trace his line of descent.

Fisher exact probability test. A nonparametric statistical technique used for analyzing DISCRETE DATA from two samples that are small in size. The Fisher test is used to determine whether there is a significant difference between two samples in the proportion of cases that fall in each of two mutually exclusive categories. The Fisher test is used in preference to the CHI-SQUARE TEST when the number of cases is small and the data are in a fourfold (2×2) table. See NONPARAMETRIC STATISTICS; PROBABILITY; SIGNIFICANCE, STATISTICAL.

fixation. 1. Excessive, irrational, and compulsive attachment to a person, object, or activity.

2. In psychoanalytic theory, the arrest of an individual's development at an immature stage. The individual's psychosocial development does not keep pace with his physical development and is fixed at a childish or adolescent level.

fixed-alternative question. A question that requires the respondent to select his answer from two or more specified alternatives, for example, "yes," "no," and "undecided." See OPEN-ENDED QUESTION.

fluctuation, periodic. A recurrent pattern of change that follows a regular sequence of time intervals. Seasonal variation of phenomena is an example of periodic fluctuation. Periodic fluctuation is one type of TIME SERIES.

fluctuations, chance. See CHANCE VARIATION.

fluidity. In human ecology, movement of population without change of residence. Daily movement to and from the CENTRAL BUSINESS DISTRICT would be an example of fluidity. The term was used by the early human ecologists, but is seldom used in this technical sense today. See ECOLOGY, HUMAN.

focused interview. See INTERVIEW, FOCUSED.

folk community. See PEASANT COMMUNITY.

folk crime. See CRIME, FOLK.

folk knowledge. See COMMON SENSE.

folk society. An IDEAL TYPE, or abstract model, developed by Robert Redfield to describe a kind of society that contrasts with modern urbanized society. A folk society is "small, isolated, nonliterate, and homogeneous, with a strong sense of group solidarity. . . . Behavior is traditional, spontaneous, uncritical, and personal; there is no legislation or habit of experiment and reflection for intellectual ends. Kinship, its relationships and institutions, are the type categories of experience, and the familial group is the unit of action. The sacred prevails over the secular; the economy is one of status rather than of the market. . . . There is not much division of labor." (R. Redfield, *American Journal of Sociology,* January 1947.) See GEMEINSCHAFT; SACRED SOCIETY; URBAN SOCIETY.

folk-urban typology. A societal TYPOLOGY, or conceptual model for differentiating types of societies, formulated by Robert Redfield, that distinguishes between two contrasting ideal, or generalized, types of society: FOLK SOCIETY and URBAN SOCIETY. (R. Redfield, *American Journal of Sociology,* January 1947.) The typology provides a framework for the comparative analysis of societies and also is useful in the study of social change in a society becoming urbanized. See IDEAL TYPE; POLAR TYPE.

folklore. Unwritten, traditional literature in the form of stories, legends, songs, proverbs, etc. The term is not usually applied to myths or other sacred lore of importance within the culture.

folkways. 1. Social norms, or standards of behavior, that are socially approved but not considered to be of moral significance. Folkways provide traditional definitions of proper ways of behaving in a particular society or social group. Conformity to folkways usually occurs automatically without rational analysis and is based primarily upon custom, passed on from generation to generation through the SOCIALIZATION of children. Folkways are not enforced by law, but by informal SOCIAL CONTROL. They are not held to be as important or obligatory as MORES, or moral standards, and their violation is not as severely sanctioned. The term was introduced by William G. Sumner in his book entitled *Folkways* (Ginn, Boston, 1906).

2. In a broader sense, social norms, including both folkways as defined above and MORES. This definition of folkways is seldom used by sociologists today.

See NORM, SOCIAL; SANCTION.

forbidding. See ORDERING-FORBIDDING.

force. An overt expression of POWER used to compel an individual or group to follow a course or courses of action desired by another individual or group. Force is often referred to as manifest power. It may take the form of physical manipulation (e.g., beating, imprisonment, death) or social pressure. Its legitimacy depends upon whether or not in a specific instance its use is condoned by the society or community as a whole. See AUTHORITY.

forced-choice technique. A technique of formulating a RATING SCALE so as to diminish the HALO EFFECT which results from the tendency of an individual to give consistent responses in rating separate characteristics. In the forced-choice technique, the rating form is composed of a series of tetrads (sets of four statements each). From each set of four statements the respondent is required to choose the statement most true of the person he is rating (himself or another person) and the statement least true. In each tetrad usually two of the statements are favorable and two are unfavorable. Thus a generally favorable respondent is forced to choose between two favorable statements, both of which he might otherwise check. The same is true of a respondent generally unfavorable to the ratee.

formal group. See GROUP, FORMAL.

formal organization. See ORGANIZATION, FORMAL.

formal sociology. See SOCIOLOGY, FORMAL.

formal status. See STATUS, FORMAL.

formal structure. See STRUCTURE, FORMAL.

formalization. In scientific THEORY, the statement of the logical structure by which the propositions of a theory are interrelated. The logical structure of the theory may be stated in mathematical or nonmathematical, symbolic form.

forms-of-sociation. The patterns that are found in social relationships. These patterns or types of social relationships may be seen in a variety of specific social situations. The term was used by Georg Simmel, whose study of the forms-of-sociation was essentially equivalent to contemporary studies of SOCIAL STRUCTURE and SOCIAL PROCESS. See SOCIOLOGY, FORMAL.

formula. A symbolic statement of facts, rules, or principles, usually expressed in algebraic form.

formulative study. See EXPLORATORY STUDY.

fourfold table. A STATISTICAL TABLE with four cells, or places for the entry of data. A fourfold table is formed by the CROSS-TABULATION of two variables each of which has just two categories, so that there are four possible combinations of categories. For example, if the VARIABLE sex, with the two categories men and women, and the variable schooling, divided into just two categories—graduated from high school and did not graduate from high school—were cross-tabulated, there would be four possible combinations of categories: men who graduated from high school, men who did not graduate from high school, women who graduated from high school, and women who did not graduate from high school.

foxes. See INSTINCT FOR COMBINATIONS.

frame of reference. A point of view, standard, or system of concepts held by an individual (or group) that tends to organize experiences, perceptions, and interpretations. One's values and social norms, for example, profoundly influence one's observations, interpretations, and judgments in a social situation.

frame of reference, action. See ACTION FRAME OF REFERENCE.

free association. 1. A technique used in interviewing and probing the thoughts of an individual. The subject is encouraged to respond freely to stimuli presented by the investigator, or to talk freely and to respond to his own comments and thoughts. This technique may be used in sociological case studies and in preliminary investigations where fresh insights are at a premium.

2. In psychoanalysis, a technique in which the subject is encouraged to express thoughts freely on a given theme, expanding and pursuing the theme in any manner that occurs to him.

3. A psychological technique in which the subject responds to a word or phrase with the first word that occurs to him. Some writers, particularly psychoanalysts, prefer to refer to this technique as induced association.

free good. See GOOD, ECONOMIC.

free will. The doctrine that the individual has freedom of choice in determining his actions and that his behavior is not entirely predetermined by factors beyond his control. The social sciences are generally regarded as deterministic in their approach to human behavior in that behavior is seen as caused by cultural, social, psychological, and physiological factors, usually beyond the control of the individual. This is often taken as a denial of the possibility of free will. Moreover, *culture* in particular is often seen as primarily restrictive of the individual's freedom, limiting his freedom of action through social norms, values, sanctions, role expectations, etc. However, it is important to recognize that culture provides man with freedom as well as restriction, and that the social sciences leave room for a modified conception of free will.

Culture provides man with the very conception of freedom, for without culture man has no thoughts or aspirations. Culture also provides man with alternatives. Animals controlled by hereditary physiological mechanisms have little freedom of choice. Their behavior is narrowly determined. Only man, because of his flexible nature and the rich variety of each culture, has alternative paths of action open to him. In addition, cultural, social, and psychological life are so very complex that neither the rigidity and stability of social norms, nor a particular type of personality structure can make human action automatic and simple. Each individual's particular combination of life experiences is unique. At any one moment in time, the individual *self* exists as a unit with volition and personal desires and dislikes. The individual, while a product of a complex series of physiological, psychological, social, and cultural elements, stands at this moment of time as a unique entity faced with a choice of various courses of action. Thus free will from a sociological point of view may be seen as the possibility of conforming to inner motivations (however obtained) rather than immediate external pressures in choosing among the varied alternatives provided by the culture.

It is worth noting that all societies and groups assume that the conduct of the individual is at least partially under his control. Without an assumption of free will in our social expectations, social life probably would be impossible. Social life requires originality and individuality, as well as predictability and conformity.

freedom, degrees of. See DEGREES OF FREEDOM.

frequency. In statistics, the number of occurrences of a particular value, or category of a VARIABLE, in a given set of data. See CLASS FREQUENCY.

frequency distribution. A classification of data showing the number of occurrences of each CLASS INTERVAL (subdivision of a quantitative variable) or CATEGORY of a VARIABLE. In the case of a quantitative variable the class intervals are arranged in order of magnitude. A frequency distribution provides a basic ordering of data, and is usually the first step in statistical analysis. See CLASS FREQUENCY; FREQUENCY DISTRIBUTION CURVE.

frequency distribution, bimodal. A FREQUENCY DISTRIBUTION having two modes or peaks. In a bimodal frequency distribution there are two separated (noncontiguous) class intervals that have the largest number of cases in the distribution of a variable. When presented graphically, the curve has two humps. If the two modes are widely separated an arithmetic mean would have little significance. See CLASS INTERVAL; FREQUENCY DISTRIBUTION CURVE; MEAN, ARITHMETIC; MODE.

frequency distribution, binomial. See BINOMIAL DISTRIBUTION.

frequency distribution, bivariate. The joint presentation of the FREQUENCY DISTRIBUTION of two variables, both for the same sample of individuals. Each CATEGORY or CLASS INTERVAL of one VARIABLE is combined with each category or class interval of the other variable, and the number of cases in each possible combination of categories is determined. For example, if the two variables were religion, with the categories Christian, Hindu, and Moslem, and marital status, with the categories single, married, divorced, and widowed, the combined categories would be single Christian, single Hindu, single Moslem, married Christian, married Hindu, and so forth. In a given sample, the number of cases in each of these combined categories would comprise a bivariate frequency distribution.

frequency distribution, cumulative. A FREQUENCY DISTRIBUTION that presents for each CLASS INTERVAL (subdivision of a quantitative variable) the total number of cases in that interval and below (or above) it. Thus the number of cases given for each class interval includes the cases that fall in that interval and in all preceding intervals. See VARIABLE.

frequency distribution, multimodal. A FREQUENCY DISTRIBUTION with three or more modes. See FREQUENCY DISTRIBUTION, BIMODAL; FREQUENCY DISTRIBUTION, UNIMODAL; MODE.

frequency distribution, Poisson. See POISSON DISTRIBUTION.

frequency distribution, probability. See PROBABILITY DISTRIBUTION.

frequency distribution, single-humped. See FREQUENCY DISTRIBUTION, UNIMODAL.

frequency distribution, symmetrical. A FREQUENCY DISTRIBUTION in which the distribution of cases is identical on both sides of the MODE (most frequent value, or class interval with the greatest number of cases). In a symmetrical frequency distribution the mode, the MEDIAN, and the arithmetic mean coincide. See MEAN, ARITHMETIC.

frequency distribution, unimodal. A FREQUENCY DISTRIBUTION that has one MODE, or peak of frequencies. See FREQUENCY DISTRIBUTION, BIMODAL; FREQUENCY DISTRIBUTION, MULTIMODAL.

frequency distribution curve. The graphic presentation of a FREQUENCY DISTRIBUTION. The frequencies (number of cases) are listed along the vertical axis and the class intervals (divisions of the VARIABLE) or their midpoints are listed along the horizontal axis. The frequency of each CLASS INTERVAL is then plotted, and a line is drawn connecting these points. A frequency distribution curve is often referred to as a frequency polygon.

frequency distribution curve, area under the. See AREA UNDER THE CURVE.

frequency distribution curve, bell-shaped. See FREQUENCY DISTRIBUTION CURVE, NORMAL.

frequency distribution curve, J. See J CURVE.

frequency distribution curve, leptokurtic. A FREQUENCY DISTRIBUTION CURVE having a pronounced peak, or a higher degree of KURTOSIS (peakedness) than a normal frequency distribution curve. See FREQUENCY DISTRIBUTION CURVE, MESOKURTIC; FREQUENCY DISTRIBUTION CURVE, NORMAL; FREQUENCY DISTRIBUTION CURVE, PLATYKURTIC.

frequency distribution curve, Lorenz. See LORENZ CURVE.

frequency distribution curve, mesokurtic. A FREQUENCY DISTRIBUTION CURVE that is neither peaked nor flattened, but is moderately rounded. A normal frequency distribution curve is a mesokurtic curve. See FREQUENCY

DISTRIBUTION CURVE, LEPTOKURTIC; FREQUENCY DISTRIBUTION CURVE, NOR-
MAL; FREQUENCY DISTRIBUTION CURVE, PLATYKURTIC; KURTOSIS.

frequency distribution curve, normal. A FREQUENCY DISTRIBUTION
CURVE in which the highest frequencies are in the center with steadily decreasing frequencies to the right and left of the central value. A normal
curve is unimodal, symmetrical, and bell shaped. It is moderately peaked
(mesokurtic), and is not skewed to the right or left. In an ideal normal
frequency distribution curve the arithmetic mean, the MEDIAN, and the
MODE all have the same value. The normal curve is an important model
in PARAMETRIC STATISTICS. See FREQUENCY DISTRIBUTION, UNIMODAL; KUR-
TOSIS; MEAN, ARITHMETIC; SKEWNESS.

frequency distribution curve, platykurtic. A FREQUENCY DISTRIBUTION
CURVE that is quite flattened. A platykurtic curve has less KURTOSIS (peak-
edness) than a normal frequency distribution curve. See FREQUENCY DIS-
TRIBUTION CURVE, LEPTOKURTIC; FREQUENCY DISTRIBUTION CURVE, MESOKUR-
TIC; FREQUENCY DISTRIBUTION CURVE, NORMAL.

frequency distribution curve, S-shaped. See OGIVE.

frequency distribution curve, skewed. A FREQUENCY DISTRIBUTION CURVE
in which the highest frequencies are to the right or left of the center. The
curve is asymmetrical and the range of cases is greater on one side of the
MODE (the highest point or CLASS INTERVAL with the greatest number of cases)
than on the other. When a curve is skewed, the mode, the MEDIAN, and the
arithmetic mean do not coincide. The arithmetic mean is farthest in the
direction of the skew (farthest to the left if the skew is to the left), followed
by the median and then the mode. See FREQUENCY DISTRIBUTION CURVE, NOR-
MAL; MEAN, ARITHMETIC; SKEWNESS.

frequency distribution curve, U. See U CURVE.

frequency polygon. See FREQUENCY DISTRIBUTION CURVE.

frequency table. A FREQUENCY DISTRIBUTION presented in the form of a
STATISTICAL TABLE. The class intervals, or subdivisions, of a quantitative
VARIABLE are listed from lowest to highest. The cells of the table indicate
the number of occurrences of each CLASS INTERVAL or CATEGORY in a set
of data. Sometimes the original class intervals used in a study are grouped
into a smaller number for convenience in tabular presentation. See CELL.

Friedman χ_r^2 test. A nonparametric statistical test that provides an
analysis of VARIANCE (dispersion of values) based on ranks, or relative position. It is used to test whether the obtained differences between two or
more groups (matched with respect to all relevant variables, including
number of members, other than the independent variable) may be considered statistically significant or whether they are probably due only to

chance. This test may also be used to compare the same group under different conditions. See NONPARAMETRIC STATISTICS; PROBABILITY; RANK, STATISTICAL; SIGNIFICANCE, STATISTICAL; VARIABLE.

fringe. See URBAN FRINGE.

frustration. The prevention or obstruction of an individual's attempts to satisfy his needs or desires. The term is also applied to the resulting emotional state, which is characterized chiefly by anger and anxiety.

frustration-aggression hypothesis. The hypothesis that when a person is frustrated in the attainment of a desire he becomes aggressive, and if he cannot retaliate against the source of his frustration (because he does not know the source, out of fear of the consequences, or the like), he will direct his aggression toward a less threatening substitute person or object. See AGGRESSION, DISPLACED; AGGRESSION, FREE-FLOATING; SCAPEGOATING.

frustration-tolerance. The capacity of an individual to withstand frustration (and anxiety) without developing maladaptive behavior.

function. The consequences of the existence or operation of a unit (a custom, attitude, institution, etc.) for other units in a (social, cultural, or personality) system or for the system as a whole. The function of a CULTURE COMPLEX, such as the Christmas complex, for example, may be analyzed by relating the complex to various other aspects or units of the society, such as toymakers, ministers, churches, religion, socialization practices, secularization, and the like.

Some sociologists regard the term *function* as a general term including and subdivided into *positive* and *negative function,* or EUFUNCTION and DYSFUNCTION. Others, however, use function synonymously with positive function and thus contrast function with dysfunction.

See FUNCTIONALISM.

function, latent. A functional relation that is neither intended nor recognized. The term was introduced by Robert K. Merton, who used it in contradistinction to manifest function. It refers to "unintended and unrecognized consequences . . . for a specified unit (person, subgroup, social or cultural system) which contribute to its adjustment or adaptation." Merton used the Hopi rain dance as an example. The manifest function of the rain dance is to bring rain. However, such ceremonies also "fulfill the latent function of reinforcing the group identity by providing a periodic occasion on which the scattered members of a group assemble to engage in a common activity." (R. K. Merton, *Social Theory and Social Structure,* Free Press, Glencoe, Ill., 1957.) See FUNCTION, MANIFEST.

function, manifest. A functional relation having a recognized value. The term was introduced by Robert K. Merton in contradistinction to latent function. It refers to "those objective consequences for a specified unit (person, subgroup, social or cultural system) which contribute to its adjustment or adaptation and were so intended." (R. K. Merton, *Social Theory and Social Structure*, Free Press, Glencoe, Ill., 1957.) See FUNCTION, LATENT.

function, negative. See DYSFUNCTION.

function, positive. See EUFUNCTION.

function, statistical. A dependent VARIABLE. When each change in one variable results in a corresponding change in a second variable, the second variable is said to be a function of the first.

functional analysis. See FUNCTIONALISM; STRUCTURAL-FUNCTIONAL ANALYSIS.

functional anthropology. See ANTHROPOLOGY, FUNCTIONAL.

functional autonomy. In functional theory, the degree to which the parts of a SOCIAL SYSTEM are self-sustaining and may survive independently of the system of which they originally were a part. The higher the functional autonomy of the parts (specific behavior patterns, roles, social institutions, etc.) of a social system, the lower is their interdependence and the less closely the system is integrated. The parts of a social system need not be integrated and interdependent to a uniform degree, and often vary in degree of functional autonomy.

functional bureaucrat. See BUREAUCRATIC TYPES.

functional disorder. Any impairment of the body's normal functioning not caused by any known organic or structural damage or alteration. Functional mental disorders are often presumed to be caused by the reaction of an individual to his social environment.

functional imperative. A generalized FUNCTIONAL REQUISITE necessary for the survival of *any* SOCIAL SYSTEM, from a society to a small group. Functional imperatives include adaptation to the environment, patterns of organizing interpersonal relations among members, and means of controlling conflict and tension. See STRUCTURAL IMPERATIVE.

functional integration. See INTEGRATION, FUNCTIONAL.

functional psychology. See PSYCHOLOGY, FUNCTIONAL.

functional psychosis. See PSYCHOSIS, FUNCTIONAL.

functional relationship. A social relationship based on interdependence and resulting from the DIVISION OF LABOR. See SOLIDARITY, ORGANIC.

functional requisite. A necessary condition for the survival of a SOCIAL SYSTEM. One type of functional requisite is the FUNCTIONAL IMPERATIVE, which is a necessary condition for the survival of *any* social system, from a society to a small group. More frequently functional requisites are delimited for a particular type of social system. Considerable attention has been paid to analyzing the functional requisites necessary for the survival of societies. The functional requisites of all societies include arrangements to provide for the biological necessities (e.g., food), provision for the socialization of the young, patterns of cooperation, etc.

functional status. See STATUS, FUNCTIONAL.

functionalism. The analysis of social and cultural phenomena in terms of the functions they perform in a sociocultural system. In functionalism, society is conceived of as a system of interrelated parts in which no part can be understood in isolation from the whole. A change in any part is seen as leading to a certain degree of imbalance, which in turn results in changes in other parts of the system and to some extent to a reorganization of the system as a whole. The development of functionalism was based on the model of the organic system found in the biological sciences.

Functionalism has come under considerable criticism because of the assumption of many functionalists of a necessary tendency toward integration of a SOCIAL SYSTEM, an assumption rejected by the critics. Functionalists have also been criticized for tending to be teleological in their explanations and, further, for tending to confuse function and cause.

See FUNCTION; FUNCTION, LATENT; FUNCTION, MANIFEST; MACRO-FUNCTIONALISM; MICRO-FUNCTIONALISM; STRUCTURAL-FUNCTIONAL ANALYSIS; SYSTEM.

fundamentalism. A religious movement that emphasizes Biblical literalism and the final authority of the Bible. The term is sometimes applied to all those who have accepted the literal truth of the Bible even in past centuries. However, most writers prefer to restrict the term to the movement that arose within Protestantism, reaching its peak in the 1920's, as a reaction against "modernism," which rejected certain traditional Christian beliefs and advocated the application of scholarly and scientific criticism to the Bible. In reacting against modernism, fundamentalism espoused an extreme form of Biblical literalism. The term fundamentalist tends to be used loosely with a wide variety of meanings, and frequently as an epithet. Used precisely, it is not synonymous with evangelical or conservative, and many conservative or orthodox Christians resent being referred to as fundamentalists. The term should be reserved for those groups and factions that stress the literal truth of the Bible in its entirety.

fusion process. As defined by E. Wight Bakke, the simultaneous operation of two opposing processes in an organization, which he calls the socializing process and the personalizing process. The socializing process involves the constant pressure on the individual member of an organization to conform to the demands of the organization and be its agent, that is, to model his behavior on the expectations and requirements of his role in the organization. The personalizing process refers to the simultaneous continual effort on the part of the individual member of an organization to realize his own personal objectives, to use the organization as his agency, and to achieve self-expression within it. These two processes operating together Bakke calls the fusion process. (E. W. Bakke, *The Fusion Process*, Yale Labor and Management Center, New Haven, Conn., 1953.)

G

G factor. General intelligence, a basic, underlying factor hypothesized by Charles Spearman as a common component in an individual's performance on all specific tests of intellectual ability.

Gallup poll. A private company engaged in polling public opinion, also known as The American Institute of Public Opinion. See OPINION POLL.

game, organized. A structured social activity in which a number of individuals are involved. The term was used by George Herbert Mead in explaining the conditions in SOCIALIZATION under which the SELF emerges as an object to itself. In order to play an organized game, such as baseball, the maturing child must learn to take the role of every other person who plays in the game. Each of the child's actions is determined by the organization of all the other roles being played. This organization of roles, that is, the total of the roles of all other players as experienced by the child, is called the GENERALIZED OTHER. (G. H. Mead, *Mind, Self and Society,* University of Chicago Press, Chicago, 1934.) See "I"; "ME"; RULES OF THE GAME, PIAGET'S.

game theory. A mathematical method for rationally analyzing the choices available to an individual or group in a situation of conflict or competition with one or more other individuals or groups. Game theory attempts to determine the best strategy or course of action for the individual (or group) to follow in order to maximize the probability of attaining one's goal and to minimize losses. This necessitates prediction of the probable actions of all others in the competitive or conflict situation under various conditions. Game theory assumes that all participants will behave rationally, and makes no provision for irrational behavior. It has been used to analyze a variety of situations which may be regarded as "games of strategy," including such diverse phenomena as poker, military strategy, and collective bargaining.

169

gang. A primary, or intimate, close, group of young people which forms spontaneously, usually in urban areas, for the purpose of friendship, play, or other common activities. The term has been defined in a variety of ways, and there are many types of gangs. Usually gangs are composed of boys, but sometimes of men (criminal gangs), or girls, or even of mixed sexes. While the gang is often defined as a group in conflict with the social order, the activities of many children's gangs are only mildly delinquent, and reflect their age status more than their general deviance. Rural gangs occur, of course, but most gangs studied are from urban areas because of their greater number and the greater likelihood of their coming in contact with the police rather than informal rural sanctions. See GROUP, PRIMARY.

Gemeinschaft. A generalized or IDEAL TYPE of society in which social bonds are based on close personal ties of friendship and kinship. The term was used by Ferdinand Tönnies to distinguish between two basic types of society: *Gemeinschaft* and GESELLSCHAFT. The term *Gemeinschaft* means "community" in German and refers to a society characterized by the predominance of intimate primary relationships and by emphasis upon tradition, consensus, informality, and kinship. This pattern of society is most closely approximated by rural-agricultural societies. See PRIMARY RELATIONS.

generality, glittering. See GLITTERING GENERALITY.

generalization. 1. The formulation of a general statement on the basis of a number of specific observations, for example, "All ravens are black." Generalization is a basic process in INDUCTION. See ABSTRACTION; EMPIRICAL GENERALIZATION; HYPOTHESIS; LAW, SCIENTIFIC; PRINCIPLE.

2. The tendency to think of all persons who belong to the same category as having a wide variety of similar characteristics and therefore to reach general conclusions about the characteristics of all persons in a given category on the basis of the observation of a few individuals. See CATEGORICAL ATTITUDE; STEREOTYPE.

3. In psychology, the tendency for a CONDITIONED RESPONSE to be evoked not only by the stimulus to which the individual was conditioned, but also by all other similar stimuli.

generalization, empirical. See EMPIRICAL GENERALIZATION.

generalized other. A generalized and integrated conception of the expectations, attitudes, and meanings of a group, an ABSTRACT SOCIAL CLASS, or other significant persons in a social situation, that has been incorporated into the thinking of an individual and helps to determine his behavior. An individual develops a generalized other through the process of social interaction, first by taking over the attitudes, expectations, and points of view of significant other persons. These attitudes and expectations then become generalized and interrelated, and in time may no longer represent the specific attitudes of concrete persons. According to George Herbert Mead, who introduced the CONSTRUCT: "The attitude of the generalized other is the attitude of the whole community. Thus, for example, in the case of such a social group as a ball team, the team is the generalized other in so far as it enters—as an organized process or social activity—into the experience of any one of the individual members of it." (G. H. Mead, *Mind, Self and Society*, University of Chicago Press, Chicago, 1934.) Through the generalized other the individual is able to relate himself satisfactorily to a wide variety of other persons, and to react to a complex set of role expectations. It provides the generalized standards and values to which he refers in a new or problematic situation, enabling his behavior to have consistency and his self-image to have a basis for unity. The generalized other not only influences specific behavior, but also provides the basis for abstract thought. See GAME, ORGANIZED; "I"; "ME"; SELF; SIGNIFICANT OTHERS; SOCIALIZATION; SUPEREGO.

generational mobility. See MOBILITY, INTERGENERATIONAL.

genetic. Pertaining to heredity, or to origin and development of any sort.

genetic dominance. See DOMINANCE, GENETIC.

genetic method. The analysis of cultural, social, or psychological phenomena in terms of developmental sequences.

genetic psychology. See PSYCHOLOGY, GENETIC.

genetics. The branch of biology dealing with the study of heredity.

genius. A person who is recognized by at least some segment of a society as having outstanding mental ability. Many psychologists define genius in terms of I.Q. scores. Some regard the minimal I.Q. score for genius as 140, others 145, and still others 160. Since superior intellectual ability is intimately associated with the very complex relations among an individual's psychological, social, and cultural experiences and development, which are only slightly understood, its origins remain almost totally obscure.

genocracy. See GERONTOCRACY.

gens. An exogamous kinship group based on patrilineal descent. Members of a gens claim common descent along the male line from a common ancestor. If a CLAN is defined as either patrilineal or matrilineal, as it most commonly is, a gens would be considered a patrilineal clan, and many anthropologists prefer the term patrilineal clan to gens. However, if clan is defined as matrilineal only, as it sometimes is, a gens would be considered not a clan but its patrilineal equivalent. See EXOGAMY; SIB.

geochronology. The study of the earth's strata for the purpose of deriving time sequences based on rock formations and fossils in order to date eras prior to recorded human history.

geographic determinism. The thesis that culture is shaped by geography, and that variations in human societies are primarily due to variations in the geographic environment. Thus cultural and social phenomena are explained in terms of geographic factors such as climate, rainfall, soil, terrain, and mineral resources. When climate is regarded as the most important factor determining cultural and social variations, this type of geographic determinism is referred to as CLIMATIC DETERMINISM. Geographic determinism was prevalent in the writings of the early human geographers, such as Friedrich Ratzel and Ellen Semple. It is generally rejected today as an oversimplification of the complex interrelationship between culture and the physical environment. See GEOGRAPHY, HUMAN.

geographic environment. See ENVIRONMENT, GEOGRAPHIC.

geography. The study of the physical characteristics of the earth (such as soil types, terrain, climate) and the interrelationship between these characteristics and the nature and distribution of plant and animal life, including patterns of human habitation and man's modifications of his physical habitat.

geography, human. The study of the interrelationship between human culture and the physical environment. Among the early human geographers, such as Friedrich Ratzel and Ellen Semple, GEOGRAPHIC DETERMINISM was a prevalent point of view, but it is rarely advocated today. Contemporary human geographers emphasize the reciprocal interrelationships between man and his geographic environment, including both the impact of the physical environment on human society and also man's modifications and control of his natural environment. Human geography is sometimes referred to by geographers and anthropologists as human ecology. See ECOLOGY, HUMAN.

geometric mean. See MEAN, GEOMETRIC.

geopolitics. The application of the principles of human geography to the analysis of international politics. The political actions of nations are regarded as the result of geographic, economic, and demographic factors, such as the need for natural resources, the pressure to seek more room for a growing population, the drive for an outlet to the sea, etc. Thus certain constant pressures and rivalries are seen as operating throughout the history of a given region. These pressures are regarded as basic to an understanding of the history, present situation, and future course of the nations involved.

The National Socialists in Germany developed an ideological form of geopolitics that was used as a rationale for their policy of expansion. However, there is no inherent ideological bias in the basic orientation and framework of analysis of geopolitics. See GEOGRAPHY, HUMAN.

geriatrics. A branch of medicine specializing in disorders of the aged and their treatment.

gerontocracy. A society in which the old men rule by virtue of the superior wisdom assumed to be associated with their age status.

gerontology. The scientific study of the aged.

Gesellschaft. A type of society in which SECONDARY RELATIONS predominate, that is, in which social relationships are formal, contractual, expedient, impersonal, and specialized. The term _Gesellschaft_ (which means "society" in German) was introduced by Ferdinand Tönnies as an abstract or IDEAL TYPE which he contrasted with GEMEINSCHAFT. Although no actual society exactly matches an ideal type, _Gesellschaft_ is most typically approximated in modern urban society, particularly as it exists in large metropolitan areas. It corresponds to the _Gesellschaft_ type because of its weak family organization, its emphasis on utilitarian goals, and the impersonal and competitive nature of its social relationships.

Gestalt psychology. A school of psychology that emphasizes the organized character of experience and behavior. Gestalt is a German term meaning form, pattern, or configuration. Gestalt theory was developed largely through the works of Kurt Koffka, Wolfgang Köhler, and Max Wertheimer in opposition to ASSOCIATIONISM and elementaristic analysis, the type of theory in which a whole is analyzed in terms of its simplest parts. The Gestalt movement emphasized the study of patterns, wholes, and field properties. According to Gestalt theory, the functioning of the parts is determined by the nature of the whole and the nature and behavior of wholes, or configurations, is such that they are functionally indivisible. Gestalt theory seeks to organize human phenomena in terms of larger units of analysis, rather than the smallest (or atomistic) ones. These larger units are then related to their parts as well as to other configurations. See ATOMISM; FIELD THEORY.

gesture. 1. A physical movement or posture or a facial expression that communicates a culturally standardized meaning, such as raising an eyebrow or waving goodbye.

2. Any physical movement or vocal expression that conveys meaning and evokes a response in another person or persons. The term was used in this sense by George Herbert Mead, who wrote: "The gesture is that phase of the individual act to which adjustment takes place on the part of other individuals in the social process of behavior. The vocal gesture becomes a significant symbol . . . when it has the same effect on the indi-

vidual making it that it has on the individual to whom it is addressed or who explicitly responds to it, and thus involves a reference to the self of the individual making it." (G. H. Mead, *Mind, Self and Society,* University of Chicago Press, Chicago, 1934.) See SYMBOL, SIGNIFICANT; SYMBOLIC GESTURE.

ghetto. In current usage, a segregated community, usually racially or culturally homogeneous, within a larger community. The isolation of the community may either be enforced politically or economically or it may be voluntary.

glittering generality. A PROPAGANDA technique in which a vague, value-laden statement is used to support an idea. The meaning of the value-laden generality (such as "the American way" or "the free enterprise system") is not defined in specific terms, nor is its relationship to the idea being advocated shown. The glittering generality is intended to lead to a favorable emotional reaction and result in uncritical acceptance of the idea with which it is associated.

goal. A condition or object sought by an individual to satisfy a NEED or WANT, thus motivating behavior. See GROUP GOAL; MOTIVATION.

gold coast. A term originally used by Harvey Zorbaugh (*The Gold Coast and the Slum,* University of Chicago Press, Chicago, 1929) to refer to the wealthy residential district along the shore of Lake Michigan in Chicago. Since then it has been used by other writers to refer generally to wealthy urban or suburban residential areas.

good, economic. In economics, anything (an object or a service) that can satisfy a human want, is limited in supply, and is obtained through conscious effort. The term does not imply any moral or ethical quality; an economic good may be harmful to the individual who desires it or used to harm others. An economic good is usually contrasted to a free good. While a free good is also something that can satisfy a human want, it is either in such abundant supply that it cannot command a price or it is by nature not marketable—for example, air. Economic goods are usually divided into consumer goods, or goods used to satisfy wants directly, such as food and clothing, and producer goods, or goods such as tools, used to produce other goods and thereby indirectly to satisfy wants.

good, free. See GOOD, ECONOMIC.

goodness-of-fit test. A type of statistical test used to determine whether a given sample probably was drawn from a POPULATION with certain specified characteristics. The goodness-of-fit test is the usual type of test used with a single SAMPLE. The population with which the sample is compared may be an actual known population or it may be a theoretical distribution, such as the normal frequency distribution curve or a distribution that would be expected if a given hypothesis were true. The population and the sample may be compared in regard to central tendency (see CENTRAL TENDENCY, MEASURE OF), or average value, the shape of the distribution curve (normal, skewed, etc.), the proportion of frequencies in each category, and so forth. The usual goodness-of-fit test in PARAMETRIC STATISTICS compares the sample distribution with the normal frequency distribution curve. There are a number of specific tests of goodness-of-fit, including both parametric and nonparametric tests. See FREQUENCY DISTRIBUTION CURVE, NORMAL; FREQUENCY DISTRIBUTION CURVE, SKEWED; NONPARAMETRIC STATISTICS; PROBABILITY; SIGNIFICANCE, STATISTICAL.

government. That central agency or complex totality of interrelated organizations exercising over-all control over a society or a territorially delimited subdivision of a society. Governments exist in complex societies as formal agencies of social control, in contrast to the informal traditional forms of control in nonliterate or simple societies. See STATE.

governmental institution. See POLITICAL INSTITUTION.

gradient. In general statistical usage, the rate of increase or decrease of a VARIABLE. In sociology the term is most commonly used in ecology to refer to a variable that increases or decreases steadily with distance from a given point. Most frequently gradients are measured from the center of a city outward to the periphery of the urban area. Variables commonly studied as gradients include income, educational level, crime, births, divorce, home ownership, mental illness, newspaper circulation. The concept of gradient is closely related to the concept of ecological dominance, the changes that occur in gradients being used as measures of the pattern and degree of dominance of an urban center over the surrounding areas. See DOMINANCE, ECOLOGICAL; ECOLOGY, HUMAN.

gradient, cultural. See CULTURE GRADIENT.

grand bourgeoisie. See BOURGEOISIE.

graph. The presentation of statistical data in geometric form. This use of visual image facilitates the comprehension of the pattern of distribution of a VARIABLE (a characteristic of the POPULATION studied) or the relationship of two or more variables. Differences in quantities are represented by the area, shape, color, or other differentiating characteristics of the design. See BAR GRAPH; BELT GRAPH; FREQUENCY DISTRIBUTION CURVE; HISTOGRAM; LINE GRAPH; LORENZ CURVE; PIE CHART; POPULATION PYRAMID.

graphic rating scale. See RATING SCALE, GRAPHIC.

gratification. See AFFECTIVE NEUTRALITY; AFFECTIVITY-AFFECTIVE NEUTRALITY; DEFERRED GRATIFICATION PATTERN.

great man theory of history. See HISTORY, GREAT MAN THEORY OF.

greenbelt town. A planned community with a low population density that incorporates in its design a surrounding area of parks, farms, or forests to provide recreation and beauty close to the settlement and to separate it from other communities. The idea of the greenbelt town or garden city was first popularized by the writings of Ebenezer Howard, and Letchworth, England, founded in 1904, was the first attempt to put his ideas into practice. Since then other greenbelt towns have been built in England and the United States, some of them suburbs and others separate new cities.

gregariousness. The tendency and desire of people to make contact and associate with each other. Gregariousness, in man, is neither an instinct nor a drive, but instead the logical outcome of man's SOCIALIZATION and the development of the self, which arises and sustains itself primarily in association with others.

grid pattern. The rectangular street pattern characteristic of most cities in the United States. The grid pattern is a cultural form and of course not the only pattern that cities may have. (See D. Stanislawski, *Geographical Review*, January 1946.)

group. 1. A plurality of persons who have a common identity, at least some feeling of unity, and certain common goals and shared norms. A group is further characterized by direct or indirect communication among its members, standardized patterns of interaction based on a system of interrelated roles, and some degree of interdependence among members. According to this usage, a group is a more developed type of COLLECTIVITY with a distinct sense of identity and a definite social structure based on direct or indirect interaction among its members. Groups range in size and degree of intimacy from a family to a society.

2. In a loose sense, any collectivity or even any plurality of individuals.

3. A small, face-to-face group. This definition has been employed by only a few writers.

See AGGREGATE; AUDIENCE; CROWD; GROUP, PRIMARY; GROUP, SECONDARY; PUBLIC; SOCIAL CATEGORY.

group, allopatric. See ALLOPATRIC GROUP.

group, compound. A GROUP composed of two or more subgroups.

group, concrete social. See CONCRETE SOCIAL CLASS.

group, congeniality. See CONGENIALITY GROUP.

group, contrived. A GROUP formed by an investigator for the purpose of observation or experimentation. Some who prefer to study "natural" groups refer to contrived groups as "artificial" groups. See CONTROL GROUP; EXPERIMENTAL GROUP; GROUP, NATURAL.

group, control. See CONTROL GROUP.

group, cumulative. See GROUP, MULTIBONDED.

group, ethnic. See ETHNIC GROUP.

group, formal. A social GROUP whose structure and activities have been rationally organized and standardized with definitely prescribed group rules, goals, and leaders. Formal groups tend to be either large or a part of a larger organization. An army and a labor union would be examples of formal groups. See GROUP, INFORMAL.

group, functional. A GROUP organized to further some special interest or attain a specific objective, such as a professional or occupational group. Functional groups are usually unibonded groups, that is, they are united by only one purpose or interest. The term is not widely used by sociologists. See INTEREST GROUP.

group, horizontal. A GROUP whose membership is homogeneous in its class or caste composition (for example, a craft union).

group, in-. See IN-GROUP.

group, informal. A GROUP without formally stated group rules, goals, or leaders. It is typically small, and often casually and spontaneously formed. Interaction is based on common interests and intimate contact. Informal groups may or may not have strong group norms, and adherence to group norms rests on personal loyalty rather than on explicit group rules. Children's play groups and gangs, as well as cliques (which might be formed within a formal organization), are examples of informal groups. Informal groups are usually compared with formal groups.

The terms *informal group* and *primary group*, although occasionally used synonymously, should be distinguished from each other. As opposed to an informal group, a primary group may be highly structured by traditional roles (as in the patriarchal family) or by bureaucratic or organizational definitions (as a military platoon). Such a group is not properly an informal group, even though its formal structure may be modified by a spontaneous, informal structure. An informal group does not have standardized and rationalized group goals, and especially not goals imposed from the outside. Its normative structure is a product of face-to-face interaction and is sustained by the close personal relations among the members. See CLIQUE; GANG; GROUP, FORMAL; GROUP, PRIMARY; GROUP, SECONDARY.

group, interest. See INTEREST GROUP.

group, kin. See KIN GROUP.

group, locality. See GROUP, TERRITORIAL.

group, marginal. See MARGINAL GROUP.

group, membership. A GROUP in which an individual is a member. This term is synonymous with the term *group* (or *social group*) but it is usually used strictly in contrast to REFERENCE GROUP. See MULTIPLE GROUP MEMBERSHIP.

group, minority. See GUEST PEOPLE; MINORITY GROUP.

group, multibonded. A GROUP whose members are united by more than one tie (interests, needs, values, etc.). The more ties there are binding group members together, the more likely it is that their relationship to one another will be diffuse, that is, involving a wide range of rights and obligations. The family is an example of a multibonded group. The multibonded group is sometimes referred to as a cumulative group. Pitirim A. Sorokin introduced this term and the term *unibonded group* in his *Society, Culture, and Personality* (Harper, New York, 1947). See DIFFUSENESS; GROUP, UNIBONDED.

group, natural. An ongoing GROUP in society studied in its natural setting without experimental manipulation. The term *natural group* is used as a contrast to a group established and manipulated by an investigator for experimental purposes. See GROUP, CONTRIVED.

group, occupational. See OCCUPATIONAL GROUP.

group, organized. See ORGANIZATION, FORMAL.

group, out-. See OUT-GROUP.

group, peer. See PEER GROUP.

group, pressure. See PRESSURE GROUP.

group, primary. An intimate social GROUP with common values, or basic standards of behavior, and frequent, direct personal contact among its members. The members of a primary group engage in a wide variety of activities with each other and many aspects of each individual's personality are involved in his relations with other members of the group. Primary group is sometimes regarded as synonymous with informal group, but to be precise the terms should be distinguished. An informal group may, in fact, be a primary group, but this is not necessarily the case. A primary group is more permanent and cohesive than are many informal groups. The family and the small, old-fashioned neighborhood or rural community are examples of primary groups. They are considered primary because, in contrast to secondary groups, they have the earliest and most fundamental impact upon the individual's socialization and personality development, thus preparing him for participation in the larger society. Charles Horton Cooley introduced the term and called the primary group the nursery of human nature. (C. H. Cooley, *Social Organization*, Scribner, New York, 1909.) See GROUP, INFORMAL; GROUP, SECONDARY; PRIMARY RELATIONS; SECONDARY RELATIONS.

group, psyche-. See PSYCHE-GROUP.

group, quasi-. See QUASI-GROUP.

group, reference. See REFERENCE GROUP.

group, secondary. An impersonal GROUP that involves only a segment of the members' lives and personalities, although there may be a strong sense of identification with the group. Relationships between members may be either face to face or indirect. The Parent-Teachers Association and most professional, hobby, and political organizations are examples of secondary groups. While the members of a secondary group usually share certain common values, or basic standards of behavior, they do not share as many values as do members of a primary group. Secondary groups usually are united by the specialized interests of their members, and they usually perform specialized functions. Most secondary groups are formal groups (although they may be informal) and most formal groups are secondary groups. See GROUP, FORMAL; GROUP, INFORMAL; GROUP, PRIMARY; PRIMARY RELATIONS; SECONDARY RELATIONS.

group, small. See GROUP RESEARCH, SMALL.

group, social. See GROUP.

group, socio-. See SOCIO-GROUP.

group, status. See STATUS GROUP.

group, sub-. See SUB-GROUP.

group, territorial. A GROUP organized on the basis of residence within a given geographic area. A society, a city, and a neighborhood group are examples of territorial groups. Territorial groups are sometimes referred to as locality groups.

group, they-. See OUT-GROUP.

group, unibonded. A GROUP whose members are united by only one common interest or purpose. Only a small part of each member's life and personality is involved in the group, and relationships among the members are characterized by SPECIFICITY, or a limited range of rights and obligations. See GROUP, MULTIBONDED.

group, we-. See IN-GROUP.

group climate. The general character or inclination of a GROUP based on the attitudes and expectations that directly or indirectly affect the thought and behavior of group members. A similar term is *group atmosphere*, but neither is used widely in sociology.

group cohesiveness. See COHESION, SOCIAL.

group contagion. See SOCIAL CONTAGION.

group dynamics. 1. The study of small groups, of the patterns of interaction within a GROUP, and of the interrelationships between a group and its environment, including other groups. Many sociologists prefer to use the phrase "small group analysis," on the assumption that all aspects of social life are dynamic, and that the study of small groups is an integral part of sociological analysis.

2. The study of the psychological aspects of behavior in small groups.

3. An applied discipline dealing with such concerns as effective leadership, communication, and decision processes, in industry and business.

group expectations. The normative standards or structure of a GROUP as perceived by an observer or by all or some portion of the membership of a group. The social norms of a group enable members to predict each other's behavior and provide continuity and stability. Yet because the norms never precisely define the exact expectations of every specific situation and because the norms of a group are never perfectly integrated, there is always a degree of uncertainty, modification, and change. See GENERALIZED OTHER; NORM, SOCIAL; ROLE EXPECTATIONS.

group goal. An objective sought through GROUP action. A group goal may be the explicitly stated reason for the existence of the group or it may be quite different from the group's official purpose. It may also differ markedly from the primary motivations of most individual members of the group. See GOAL.

group identification. A process in which an individual incorporates within himself the expectations, standards, values, and goals of a GROUP, and utilizes them in the organization, reorganization, or stabilization of his social SELF. A group with which an individual identifies is a positive REFERENCE GROUP for him, and the group's prestige and survival become identified with the individual's own ego. It is not necessary to be a formal member of a group in order to identify with it. See IDENTIFICATION.

group ideology. See IDEOLOGY.

group marriage. See CENOGAMY.

group mind. A collective mind or spirit that exists independently of the individual GROUP members and dominates their behavior. This concept, which appears notably in the writings of Immanuel Kant, Georg Hegel, and William McDougall, is often referred to as the group mind fallacy. Although sociologists may hold that group phenomena are distinct from a simple total of individual acts, they avoid personifying the group. Members of a group are not always aware of the collective consequences of their individual or group-coordinated behavior (see FUNCTION, LATENT), but unintended consequences, no matter how serious, do not add up to an organized and independent entity with a consciousness of its own. See REIFICATION, FALLACY OF.

group morale. See MORALE.

group persistences. See INSTINCT FOR COMBINATIONS and INSTINCT FOR GROUP PERSISTENCES.

group relations. See INTERGROUP RELATIONS.

group research, small. The detailed study of the patterns of interaction in very small, face-to-face groups, usually with fewer than ten members, rarely more than fifteen, and often in an experimental situation, although sometimes in a "natural" setting.

group solidarity. See COHESION, SOCIAL.

group structure. See SOCIAL STRUCTURE; STRUCTURE, FORMAL; STRUCTURE, INFORMAL.

group work, social. See SOCIAL GROUP WORK.

grouping. See SOCIAL CATEGORY.

groups, external and internal systems of. See EXTERNAL SYSTEM; INTERNAL SYSTEM.

groups, sympatric. See SYMPATRIC GROUPS.

"guess who" test. See RATING SCALE, "GUESS WHO" TEST.

guest people. A minority GROUP having a different culture from that of the dominant majority in the society and treated by the dominant group as tolerated outsiders. (See M. Weber, *Gesammelte Aufsatze zur Religions-soziologie,* Vol. II, J. C. B. Mohr, Tübingen, 1921.)

guilt. Anxiety resulting from the sense that one has departed from values and norms that are accepted as having at least some validity. Guilt, however, is not simply the result of individual inadequacy or failure. It arises from conflicting values and demands and thus is a reflection of inconsistencies in the social and cultural environment of the individual. For the individual, guilt is always traumatic to some extent, since the violation of inculcated values involves symbolically (if not always actually) rejection by significant others. But guilt feelings do not just work to encourage conformity; they also may encourage the development of new values or norms that either reject the values or norms that make for feelings of guilt or integrate previously conflicting values into a new system that resolves the previous difficulties.

Guttman scale. A CUMULATIVE SCALE designed to measure the unidimensionality of a series of items (usually statements of attitude), that is, to determine whether the items can be arranged along a single continuum of increasing intensity. When a series of items (attitudes) forms a Guttman scale, acceptance of any item on the scale indicates acceptance of all the items below it—that is, of all the attitude statements of a lesser intensity. Hence from an individual's score it is possible to reproduce his response to each of the items in the scale, and all persons with the same score have the same pattern of responses. If the responses to a set of items are not reproducible in this manner, the items do not form a Guttman scale and are judged to be multidimensional. Thus this scale is a device that permits the ranking of groups or individuals along a unidimensional attitude continuum. See LAZARSFELD LATENT-DISTANCE MODEL; SCALE; SCALE, ATTITUDE; UNIDIMENSIONAL SCALE.

H

H-technique. A technique designed by Samuel A. Stouffer to increase the precision of a CUMULATIVE SCALE. The H-technique "seems to remove some of the most serious practical disabilities in achieving a GUTTMAN SCALE that has high reproducibility and reliability. . . . Actually the H-technique produces a Guttman scale or a Lazarsfeld latent-distance scale with one important modification. Instead of using only one item to determine a given cutting point on the scale, as in the conventional procedure, the H-scale uses two or more items." (S. A. Stouffer, *Social Research to Test Ideas,* Free Press of Glencoe, New York, 1962.) See LAZARSFELD LATENT-DISTANCE MODEL.

H test. See KRUSKAL-WALLIS TEST.

habit. A learned pattern of response that is automatically repeated by an individual in appropriate situations with a minimum of deliberate effort or reflection. Although social customs and patterns of behavior are sometimes termed habitual, it must be remembered that routine social interaction involves complex evaluations of situations, as well as appropriate attitudes and role behavior, and that the resulting uniformities, therefore, are better understood through social and cultural explanations rather than through psychological and physiological ones.

habitat. When applied to human communities, the geographic environment in which a community is located. It includes such factors of the natural environment as climate, altitude, and topography.

halo effect. The tendency of an observer, when judging an individual, to allow his separate observations of the subject's various performances and characteristics to be influenced and distorted by his over-all evaluation of the subject, or by some one other single observation. The halo effect may be either positive or negative. Thus when people observe a positive (or negative) characteristic of another they tend to tie in all their other observations of him to their initial observation. Scientific observation requires that the halo effect be recognized as a normal social-psychological phenomenon, and that observation be specifically designed to avoid this type of error.

hamlet. A small rural service center, smaller than a VILLAGE, with a population of fewer than 250 persons. A hamlet typically has one or two stores, a church, sometimes a school, and a service station. It is frequently located at the juncture of two highways.

handicraft economy. A preindustrial economy based upon the production of goods by artisans or skilled craftsmen without the aid of power-driven machinery. Goods are produced in small shops or in the home rather than in factories, and frequently handicraft activities are combined with agricultural activities. In Europe the handicraft economy was prevalent in the fourteenth and fifteenth centuries, preceding the putting-out or DOMESTIC SYSTEM, and differed from the latter in that the artisan (or the master craftsman in a shop) purchased his raw materials, owned his tools, and sold his finished product.

harmonic mean. See MEAN, HARMONIC.

heading, table. See STATISTICAL TABLE.

headnote, table. See STATISTICAL TABLE.

hedonism. A theory of human motivation holding that behavior can best be understood and explained by the assumption that its ultimate aim is the avoidance of pain and the seeking of pleasure. As a system of normative ethics, it is the doctrine that human pleasure and happiness should be the highest goal of human endeavor. See UTILITARIANISM.

henotheism. The belief that there is one god who is supreme and is to be worshiped above or to the exclusion of other existing gods. Henotheism differs from monotheism, which recognizes the existence of only one God.

herd, human. A temporary AGGREGATE of persons lacking organization but in close physical proximity and following a leader in the manner of dumb animals. This crude term is almost never used by modern sociologists because it implies an unsophisticated view of the complexities of human behavior and culture.

heredity. The transmission of certain physiological characteristics through the genes from parents to their offspring. Most human behavior is not determined by hereditary characteristics (although the relationship is still being studied) but develops as a result of social interaction and the learning of culture.

heredity, social. The transmission of personality patterns and cultural traditions from parents to offspring, from generation to generation, through SOCIALIZATION. This process is essential to human survival, for both stability and variability, or adaptability, of behavior are primarily defined by the social and cultural patterns of one's predecessors, as well as the accident of one's status experience within a particular society or group. See CULTURE.

heritage, biological. See BIOLOGICAL HERITAGE.

heritage, social or **cultural.** See CULTURE.

hero. An individual, either mythical or real, alive or dead, who symbolizes by his past or present social role or deeds some important aspect of the values of a culture or subculture. The individual who becomes a hero may or may not have achieved the deeds associated with him, but in either case those who either worship him (should he come to be regarded as a spirit or supernatural being) or adulate him tend to refine and embellish the legend of his achievements so that they fit in with the ideals of the social group. The hero may be pictured as having human failings as well as extraordinary talents and achievements, and this is sometimes the most beloved type of cultural hero. In some cultures a hero may take the form of an animal. See MYTH; VALUE.

heterogamy. Marriage between persons who are dissimilar in some major respect, for example, cultural background, race, social class, religion, or personality. See HOMOGAMY.

heterophily. See HOMOPHILY.

heteroscedasticity. In statistics, a relationship between two quantitative variables such that there is a changing degree of variation in the values of the dependent VARIABLE for each value of the independent variable. Thus there is a varying degree of dispersion or scatter for different points on the REGRESSION LINE, which shows values representing the relationship between the two variables. For all the values of the independent variable there is not the same VARIANCE in the values of the dependent variable, that is, there is not a uniform degree of relationship between the variables for the range of their values. Heteroscedasticity may follow a clear-cut pattern of decreasing or increasing dispersion with increasing values of the independent variable, or it may take more complex forms. In extreme cases the degree of dispersion may be just random and follow no pattern at all. See DISPERSION, STATISTICAL; HOMOSCEDASTICITY; SCEDASTICITY.

heuristic assumption. An assumption made not because it has been established that it is true but because it is considered useful in the process of investigation. The heuristic assumption is regarded as a utilitarian device that is intended to aid in the discovery of new facts and relationships. For example, although it is known that there is great individual variation in human behavior, the heuristic assumption is made that there are enough similarities to classify individuals into such categories as roles and personality types in order to facilitate analysis. See CONSTRUCT; HYPOTHESIS.

hierarchy. 1. A ranking of statuses within an organization according to some criterion of evaluation accepted as relevant within the system.

2. Any relationship of individuals, groups, or classes involving a system of ranking.

hinterland. 1. The area surrounding a metropolis and dominated or strongly influenced by it. The hinterland extends beyond the metropolitan suburbs and includes rural as well as urban areas. It is a varied area including large and small cities, small towns, and farms. The hinterland communities are not solely oriented to the metropolis. Within the hinterland there are retail shopping, wholesaling, manufacturing, educational, recreational, and other types of centers that serve and influence the areas surrounding them. However, the entire area lies within the sphere of the predominant influence of the metropolis. The hinterland extends beyond the area usually included in the delimitation of a METROPOLITAN AREA, but it is included within a METROPOLITAN REGION, and the boundaries of the hinterland usually determine the boundaries of the metropolitan region.

2. An area dominated or strongly influenced by any urban center whether or not it is a metropolis. The hinterland of a smaller urban center would include small towns, villages, and rural areas.

See DOMINANCE, ECOLOGICAL.

histogram. In statistics, a form of graphic presentation of a FREQUENCY DISTRIBUTION, or distribution of cases, in which a vertical bar is constructed for each CLASS INTERVAL, or subdivision, of the variable being presented. The class intervals are arranged along the horizontal axis and the width of each bar corresponds to the size of the class interval. The frequencies are arranged along the vertical axis and determine the height of the bars. That is, the height of each bar is determined by the number of cases in each class interval. A histogram is similar to a BAR GRAPH except that there are no spaces between the bars.

histogram, area. A modified type of HISTOGRAM in which the frequency, or number of cases in each CLASS INTERVAL (subdivision of the variable), is indicated not by the height of each bar, but instead by the area of each bar. The area of each bar is equal to its height multiplied by its width. Since the width represents the size of the class interval, it follows that, for any given frequency of cases, the larger the class interval the lower will be the height of the bar, and the smaller the class interval the greater will be the height of the bar.

historical method. The evaluation of sources of information about the past to determine their authenticity, and the analysis of authentic sources for detailed data about the period being studied. Sources of information used by historians include written records of all types—laws, public records, reports, business documents, newspapers, diaries, letters, genealogies, travelers' accounts, and literature in all forms—as well as physical survivals in the form of buildings and artifacts. See PRIMARY SOURCE; SECONDARY SOURCE.

historical sociology. See SOCIOLOGY, HISTORICAL.

historicism. 1. A theoretical approach that emphasizes the importance of the historical context in the understanding of social and cultural phenomena. According to this approach, in analyzing any aspect of the social organization or culture of a people at a given time, it is necessary to trace its history to show how the particular form developed and then to relate it to other aspects of the sociocultural system within which it occurs. The emphasis tends to be upon the uniqueness of each historic period, rather than upon recurrent patterns or generalizations for all human behavior. This approach, influenced by the work of Georg Hegel, was developed especially by German historians in the eighteenth and nineteenth centuries. It influenced the writings of Karl Mannheim and his concern with the SOCIOLOGY OF KNOWLEDGE.

2. Historical determinism; the view that any phenomenon is best understood by analyzing its historical development, and that therefore social and cultural phenomena are to be understood primarily through the study of history and the operation of historically determined principles.

historiography. The writing of history; that is, the interpretation of the detailed data gathered by means of the HISTORICAL METHOD, the ordering of these data in terms of a conceptual framework, and the presentation of the data in an account that attempts to reconstruct the period being studied.

history. The study of the events in man's historical past—from the emergence of written records to the present. It is often maintained that history is concerned with the study of specific and unique events largely for their own sake. By contrast, in sociology the emphasis is upon the development of generalized principles of human behavior, and specific events are of sociological significance only insofar as they can be related to patterns of events yielding such principles. Thus history, unlike sociology, tends to be an idiographic science—that is, a primarily descriptive discipline, in which explanation is designed for unique, individual phenomena. See HISTORICAL METHOD; SCIENCE, IDIOGRAPHIC.

history, great man theory of. The theory that the history of a people is shaped primarily by the actions of a small number of outstanding individuals. Thus the political history of a nation is analyzed in terms of the individuals who attained positions of power; scientific development is seen as the result of the discoveries of great scientists; technological development is studied as a series of inventions of individual geniuses; etc. This theory of history does not take into account the gradual and cumulative nature of cultural development or the complexity of economic, geographic, and other nonindividual factors shaping the course of history.

hobohemia. See SKID ROW.

holism. The theoretic principle that a person or group has a totality or Gestalt that is distinct and unique and cannot be understood by studying merely the individual elements or "atoms" composing the whole. See ATOMISM; GESTALT PSYCHOLOGY.

Homo sapiens. The Latin name for the genus (*Homo*) and the species (*sapiens*) to which all modern men belong.

homogamy. Marriage of persons having similar characteristics, either physical, psychological, or social. The tendency of like to marry like is also called assortative (or assortive) mating. See HETEROGAMY.

homophily. The tendency for friendships to form between persons with similar characteristics. Homophily has been contrasted with heterophily, the association of persons having unlike characteristics. The terms were coined by Robert K. Merton in his studies of friendship and were published in his article with Paul F. Lazarsfeld in *Freedom and Control in Modern Society* (M. Berger, J. Abel, and C. Page, eds., Van Nostrand, New York, 1954).

homoscedasticity. In statistics, a relationship between two quantitative variables such that there is a uniform degree of variation in the values of the dependent VARIABLE for each value of the independent variable. Thus there is a uniform degree of dispersion or scatter for all points on the REGRESSION LINE, which shows values representing the relationship between the two variables. In other words, for any given value of the independent variable, there is the same VARIANCE in the values of the dependent variable as there is for every other value of the independent variable; there is a constant degree of relationship between the variables for the range of their values. Homoscedasticity is an implicit assumption in a number of statistical tests. See DISPERSION, STATISTICAL; HETEROSCEDASTICITY; SCEDASTICITY.

horizontal occupational movement. A change in occupational position that does not involve a change in economic or social status level. See VERTICAL OCCUPATIONAL MOVEMENT.

horizontal work group. A work GROUP consisting of individuals whose jobs are essentially similar in level of status, income, skill, and degree of authority. See VERTICAL WORK GROUP.

hospitalism. Severe developmental retardation occurring in infants who at an early age are placed under conditions (as in certain orphanges) in which they are deprived of normal environmental stimulation, social interaction, and affection. The term was used in this sense by René A. Spitz, who, in studying such infants, found that they had low resistance to disease and a high mortality rate (despite good nutrition and sanitary surroundings), far below normal weight and height, very retarded motor and intellectual development, and a high incidence of severe emotional disturbance. This retardation appeared to be progressive and was not reversed by establishing normal human contacts after severe deprivation during the first year of life. (See R. A. Spitz in *The Psychoanalytic Study of the Child*, Vols. I and II, International Universities Press, New York, 1945 and 1946.) See DEPRESSION, ANACLITIC; MARASMUS.

household. As defined by the U.S. Bureau of the Census, all persons who live in the same dwelling unit. The dwelling unit may be a house, an apartment or other group of rooms, or a room. According to the census definition, a household includes not only family members but also persons who are not related to each other, if they share the same dwelling unit. A person living alone is also considered a household. (*U.S. Census of Population*, Government Printing Office, Washington, D.C., 1960.)

household, quasi-. See QUASI-HOUSEHOLD.

human ecology. See ECOLOGY, HUMAN.

human geography. See GEOGRAPHY, HUMAN.

human nature. 1. Those behavioral characteristics that are common to men everywhere, in all societies, past and present. These universal characteristics result from two sources and their combined effects: the physiological nature of man and the requirements of social life. It is obvious that man everywhere has certain biological needs and limitations. It is also true that man everywhere lives in groups, and must make certain adjustments made necessary by group living. When analyzed on a group level, the requirements for the survival of any group have been referred to as functional imperatives and the requirements for the survival of a particular kind of group, such as a society, as functional requisites. The concept of human nature focuses on the individual personality, and in essence deals with the universal human qualities that everywhere result from the impact of the requirements of social life on the human organism. See FUNCTIONAL IMPERATIVE; FUNCTIONAL REQUISITE.

2. All innate biological characteristics of man.

Human Relations Area File. A central repository and file of information about cultures throughout the world. This file contains material on a wide range of cultures and subjects, extracted from original sources or especially secured through area surveys, and compiled and indexed by subjects as well as cultures. The Human Relations Area File was organized by the cooperative effort of a number of universities with the support of the Carnegie Corporation, and was built around the Yale Cross-Cultural Survey, which was founded by George P. Murdock. The Human Relations Area File contributes to the preservation of valuable cultural records and facilitates cross-cultural research.

humanistic coefficient. That aspect of human experience that has meaning to the actor and is nonmaterial and not reducible to sensory manifestations. This would consist of conscious experience, or mental events. The term was introduced by Florian Znaniecki to refer to this type of "primary empirical evidence," whose theoretical utility and significance was denied by orthodox behaviorists. Those who study social action "investigate the data which conscious agents experience and the activities they perform." Because orthodox BEHAVIORISM does not deal with people as conscious beings or with mental processes, its theoretical generalizations, at best, are relevant only in animal and infant studies. Znaniecki regarded the study of personal documents revealing mental and emotional experiences as an important method for sociologists. (F. Znaniecki, *Social Actions*, Farrar and Rinehart, New York, 1936.) See ACTION, SOCIAL; ACTION THEORY, SOCIAL.

humanities. Disciplines concerned with the understanding of human life, human behavior, or human experience. They are not restricted to the limits of SCIENCE or the SCIENTIFIC METHOD, and in certain cases (music and art) are not limited to linguistic or mathematical symbols. Further, they may deal with questions outside the scope of science, such as metaphysical and ethical questions. Moreover, while the humanities may be concerned with generalizing principles, unlike the sciences, they are also frequently concerned with unique, individual events and experiences in and of themselves. Disciplines usually included among the humanities are philosophy, theology, history, literature, music, and art. See SOCIAL SCIENCE.

hybrid, cultural. See MARGINAL MAN.

hypergamy. A custom forbidding the women in a particular social stratum to marry into a lower stratum. They are permitted to marry in their own social stratum or into a higher stratum. However, the term is also often used to refer to the practice of women of lower standing marrying men of higher standing. See HYPOGAMY.

hypnosis. A highly suggestible state or trance. From a social point of view, the hypnotic state can be viewed as a situation in which one partici-

pant accepts a temporarily subordinate role and an extremely limited social definition of the situation as suggested by another person. Within limits, the subject regards as real or relevant only that which is expressly
defined by the other. The phenomenon of hypnosis is related to the ordinary experience of people in social situations, since people always tend to
view a situation in terms of the immediate group activities in which they
are involved. For example, people in mobs often have their perspective
and frame of reference limited by their orientation to one idea or activity.
Normally individuals react to ideas or persons with a many-faceted frame
of reference. That is, they perceive a number of alternate ideas, norms, and
social roles that may be relevant in the situation. When, however, the individual limits his perception of a situation solely to the terms suggested
by another, which is what happens in hypnosis, he loses his objectivity,
flexibility, and the ability to discern and choose among alternate courses
of action.

hypogamy. Marriage of a woman with a man of a lower social
stratum. See HYPERGAMY.

hypothesis. In scientific investigation, a tentative statement asserting
a relationship between certain facts. The statement is intended to be
tested empirically and either verified or rejected. A scientific hypothesis is
derived from a theoretical system and the results of past research. The
clear statement of a theoretically significant hypothesis related to previous
research is crucial to a well-designed scientific study. See EXPERIMENT;
THEORY.

hypothesis, alternative. The HYPOTHESIS that is to be accepted if the
null hypothesis is rejected. As distinguished from the null hypothesis, the
alternative hypothesis is a positive statement that there is a relationship
between the variables being studied. See HYPOTHESIS, NULL.

hypothesis, causal. A HYPOTHESIS stating that a specified event or
condition determines or helps to determine the existence or nature of a
second event or condition. See CAUSATION; CAUSE.

hypothesis, complex. A HYPOTHESIS that relates two or more independent variables to one dependent variable. See CAUSATION, MULTIPLE; VARI-
ABLE.

hypothesis, null. A HYPOTHESIS of no difference or no relationship,
that is, a hypothesis that states that there is no significant difference between two or more groups in regard to a given variable or no relationship
between the variables being studied. It is used most often in experimental
situations, and usually is employed for statistical convenience, being rejected at a given level of statistical significance. When it is rejected, the
investigator turns to an alternative hypothesis. Because the null hypothe-

sis is often formulated with the idea that the data will probably lead to its rejection, some sociologists are critical of its use. Its advocates argue that its use is parsimonious, that is, it states the simplest possible relationship among the data, and contributes to objectivity by starting the experiment with the provisional assumption that the experimental treatment will lead to no real difference between the experimental group and the control group. Because a null hypothesis cannot be proved, strictly speaking it cannot be accepted, and therefore one should speak of it only as being rejected or not rejected. See HYPOTHESIS, ALTERNATIVE; REGION OF REJECTION; SIGNIFICANCE, STATISTICAL.

hypothesis, statistical. A very specific HYPOTHESIS concerning the distribution of a particular population, which tentatively states one or more population parameters (a summary measure of a characteristic of a population). Like other hypotheses, the statistical hypothesis is formulated in order to be tested empirically. Although it is a statement about a total population, it is usually tested by comparison with data drawn from a sample. Unlike the usual scientific hypothesis, the statistical hypothesis refers to a particular population and does not assert a general proposition or suggest a reason for the specified population characteristics. See PARAMETER.

hypothesis, working. A HYPOTHESIS not yet subjected to empirical test. Often the term is used to refer particularly to a hypothesis dealing with phenomena or relationships about which there has been relatively little scientific research. Under these circumstances the hypothesis is necessarily very tentative. Indeed, because of the paucity of available knowledge on which a working hypothesis must sometimes be based, it has been referred to by some writers as a clever guess or perceptive hunch, which it is hoped will provide the basis for investigation that will result in more concrete knowledge.

hysteria. A form of NEUROSIS characterized by the experience of the symptoms of organic disease, such as paralysis, by an individual without evidence of physical disease or injury.

2. what are the cultural elements involved in the way you get ready to go to sleep?

Cultural Uniformity

1 Language
2 Family System
3 Division of labor
4 Economic System
5 Religious System

6 Government - Ruling body, rules
7 Education - Formal or informal
8 Recreation

1 ART

2 Monogamy (Serial Monogamy) one after another marriage divorce + remarry

I

"**I.**" A hypothetical aspect or phase of the total SELF corresponding to what the individual regards as the unique aspect of his self. The term was used by George Herbert Mead, who suggested that the "I" and the "ME" together constitute the personality or self, the "I" being that aspect of the self which a person experiences as a reaction to the other aspect of the self (the "me," which reflects what others expect him to be like). The "I" phase of the personality process is difficult for the individual to know and experience directly. One becomes aware of the "I" only after one has made his individualized and essentially unique response to a social situation. In a sense, what the "I" wants or is, is one of the most difficult things to discover, yet all people, according to Mead, are aware of the existence of an aspect of self separate from that made up of the internalized social values represented in the "me." The "I" would of course be a product of socialization, and develops as a response to the attitudes of the social community, internalized as the "me." (G. H. Mead, *Mind, Self and Society*, University of Chicago Press, Chicago, 1934.) See EGO.

iconic model. See MODEL, ICONIC.

id. In Freudian theory, the aspect of the personality that consists of unorganized, innate, instinctual impulses seeking immediate gratification. The id impulses are primarily sexual and aggressive—and antisocial. The term is little used in sociology. See EGO; SUPEREGO.

ideal, self-. See SELF-IDEAL.

ideal type. A conceptualization or mental construct composed of a configuration of characteristic elements of a class of phenomena used in social analysis. The elements abstracted are based on observations of concrete instances of the phenomena under study, but the resultant construct is not designed to correspond exactly to any single empirical observation. The ideal type was developed as an important methodological technique by Max Weber in conjunction with his method of *verstehen*. It is a heuristic device, that is, a strategy used to describe, compare, and test hypotheses relating to empirical reality. "Economic man," "marginal man," "sect," "church," "*Gemeinschaft*," and "*Gesellschaft*" are examples of ideal types.

There is obviously a similarity between an ideal type and a STEREOTYPE. Stereotypes, however, are not constructed consciously for the purpose of scientifically abstracting reality—indeed, they usually arise spontaneously and may be far from corresponding with reality. Ideal types are constantly examined and refined. Above all, they are not to be regarded as true pictures but as tentative models. See CONSTRUCTED TYPE; HEURISTIC ASSUMPTION; POLAR TYPE; TYPOLOGY; VERSTEHEN, METHOD OF.

idealism. A philosophical orientation covering a wide range of metaphysical and epistemological doctrines that view mind or spirit as the ultimate reality or the basis of experience and knowledge. Kantian idealism holds that what we perceive of the external world and believe to be real or true reflects the internal organization of the mind and thought processes. Hegelian idealism, while agreeing with Kantian idealism that it is impossible to consider the existence of an object apart from its perception, seeks to eliminate the duality of mind and object by regarding an object as an expression of an essential idea. According to Hegelianism, in the perception of an object its specific form is unimportant; significance lies in the suggestion to the perceiver of an essential idea. Thus mind and object are both essentially idea, neither exists in isolation, but both are part of an interrelated whole. See EMPIRICISM; NATURALISM; REALISM.

idealistic culture. A type of culture proposed by Pitirim A. Sorokin that is a synthesis of ideational and sensate values. These two types of cultural elements are integrated so that both spiritual and material values are important, although spiritual values tend to predominate. (P. A. Sorokin, *Social and Cultural Dynamics,* American Book Co., New York, 1937.) See IDEATIONAL CULTURE; SENSATE CULTURE.

ideational attitude. See ATTITUDE, IDEATIONAL.

ideational culture. A type of culture proposed by Pitirim A. Sorokin in which the highest values are nonmaterial, transcendental, and supernatural. Ultimate reality is spiritual and nonutilitarian. Rather than stressing the manipulation of the empirical world to improve the quality of life, as do sensate cultures, the ideational culture emphasizes adjustment to the existing world. (P. A. Sorokin, *Social and Cultural Dynamics,* American Book Co., New York, 1937.) See IDEALISTIC CULTURE; SENSATE CULTURE.

identification. A social-psychological process involving the assimilation and INTERNALIZATION of the values, standards, expectations, or social roles of another person or persons (for example, one's parents) into one's own behavior and self-conception. Identification, therefore, includes modeling one's self after another person, having a sense of "oneness" with him, and being able to put one's self imaginatively into his position. In identifying with a group, one internalizes the interests, standards, and role expectations of the group. Identification is an important process in normal human behavior and is not limited to childhood, nor is it simply a defense mechanism. Both adults and children may identify with others out of anxiety, love, or simply in the course of self-development and normal social adjustment.

Usually the term identification refers to positive identification. However, it should be pointed out that individuals or groups may be taken as negative models, and the standards, interests, and values of people or groups with which one identifies negatively tend to be the mirror image of one's positive identifications. One's negative identifications also provide standards for behavior and definitions of one's self. Groups with which one identifies negatively provide a guide and suggestion of what one does not want to be like, and of policies one does not want to espouse. The interaction of social groups in intense conflict or competition often leads to the development of an explicit normative system centering about their differences and provides complementary points for establishing one's own self and social identity. Thus where there are strong positive identifications with groups or individuals, one may look for their negative social and psychological counterparts. See REFERENCE GROUP; REFERENCE GROUP, NEGATIVE.

identification, ethnic. See ETHNIC IDENTIFICATION.

identification, group. See GROUP IDENTIFICATION.

identity, latent social. See LATENT SOCIAL IDENTITY.

ideograph. A nonphonetic symbol representing an object or idea. Ideographic writing, such as the Chinese characters, uses standardized symbols representing entire objects or ideas instead or phonetically combining letters and syllables to form written words.

ideology. A system of interdependent ideas (beliefs, traditions, principles, and myths) held by a social group or society, which reflects, rationalizes, and defends its particular social, moral, religious, political, and economic institutional interests and commitments. Ideologies serve as logical and philosophical justifications for a group's patterns of behavior, as well as its attitudes, goals, and general life situation. The ideology of any population involves an interpretation (and usually a repudiation) of alternative ideological frames of reference. The elements of an ideology tend to be accepted as truth or dogma rather than as tentative philosophical or theoretical formulations, despite the fact that ideologies are modified in accordance with sociocultural changes.

The term *ideology* was introduced at the beginning of the nineteenth century by Destutt de Tracy, a French philosopher, to refer to the study of ideas. The term, however, soon took on essentially its current meaning of a set of ideas justifying particular interests. The concept was given great prominence in the writings of Karl Marx, who defined it as a system of ostensibly logical ideas that in reality are a justification for the vested interests of a particular social class, the most dominant ideology in a society being that of the ruling class. Karl Mannheim used the term to refer to ideas that are distorted by the historical and social setting of individuals and groups.

See SOCIOLOGY OF KNOWLEDGE.

ideology, open-class. See OPEN-CLASS IDEOLOGY.

idiographic method. The technique of studying human behavior by the thorough analysis of individual cases. The CASE STUDY METHOD may be considered an idiographic method when emphasis is placed upon the complete understanding of each individual case rather than upon deriving analytical generalizations from the common characteristics of a larger number of cases. See SCIENCE, IDIOGRAPHIC; NOMOTHETIC METHOD.

idiographic science. See SCIENCE, IDIOGRAPHIC.

ignorance, pluralistic. See PLURALISTIC IGNORANCE.

image. An abstract mental representation of an object or class of objects. Although images are based on past perceptions they are not simple reflections of these perceptions. Certain aspects of past perceptions may be emphasized while others are forgotten, and still others are reinterpreted in the organization of the image. An image is not necessarily based on direct perception of an object. It may be based on indirect sources of information and elaborated by imagination. An image may be visual, auditory, olfactory, tactual, or verbal or part verbal (verbal and visual, for example). Regardless of the type of image, language is always important in image formation, for language shapes the original perceptions on which the image is based and provides the means for remembering these perceptions. Thus a certain scene may be recalled as "a beautiful lake, surrounded by tree-covered mountains." The picture of this scene in the person's mind in later years will not correspond precisely with the original scene, the differences in large measure being due to the symbols used to remember the scene. See CATEGORICAL ATTITUDE; PERCEPTION; SYMBOL.

image, eidetic. See EIDETIC IMAGE.

image, self-. See SELF.

imagination. The mental recalling and manipulation of ideas, images, and situations, or the reorganization and recombination of ideas, images, and situations to form new patterns.

imaginative reconstruction. A mental construct, essentially the same as IDEAL TYPE. The term is used by Robert M. MacIver.

imitation. A process in which individuals (or groups) copy more or less exactly the behavior of other persons (or groups). Following the example of other people is an important element in LEARNING, ENCULTURATION, and SOCIALIZATION, but use of the term *imitation* suggests a mechanical, automatic process that obscures and distorts the nature of the complex social and psychological processes involved in learning and accepting the social roles that become a part of one's personality and behavior. The term is not often used in contemporary sociology. See IDENTIFICATION; INTERNALIZATION.

immigration. The entrance into a country of individuals or groups who have left their native country to establish a new place of permanent residence. Immigration is international MIGRATION with the focus upon the migrants' country of destination. See EMIGRATION.

imperative. See BIOLOGICAL IMPERATIVE; CULTURAL IMPERATIVE; FUNCTIONAL IMPERATIVE; SOCIAL IMPERATIVE; STRUCTURAL IMPERATIVE.

incapacity, trained. See TRAINED INCAPACITY.

incest. A heterosexual or marital relation between members of a kin group that is forbidden or disapproved because the degree of kinship is too close according to the cultural traditions of that society.

incest taboo. The prohibition of INCEST.

incest taboo, primary. The prohibition of sexual relations and marriage between individuals who belong to the same nuclear family, except for the father and mother—that is, the prohibition of INCEST between father and daughter, mother and son, and brother and sister. This prohibition is sometimes simply termed INCEST TABOO. See FAMILY, NUCLEAR.

incorporated place. As defined by the U.S. Census, a local political unit incorporated, in accordance with the regulations of the state in which it is located, as a city, borough, town, or village "with the exception that towns are not recognized as incorporated places in the New England States, New York, and Wisconsin." (*U.S. Census of Population*, Government Printing Office, Washington, D.C., 1960.)

incorporeal property. Nonmaterial culture traits that are privately owned. Often in nonliterate societies culture traits such as dances, songs, prayers, myths, and magical practices are owned by individuals and may be passed on through inheritance.

independence of judgment. See AUTONOMY.

independent variable. See VARIABLE.

indeterminate sentence. A prison sentence imposed upon an offender that may range from a stated minimum to a stated maximum period of imprisonment (for example, for not less than two years or more than ten years). Within the limits of the sentence, the convict may be released according to his conduct in prison and the estimated probability of his good behavior upon release.

indeterminism. The philosophical position or doctrine that events do not always occur in a fixed pattern of cause-and-effect relationships. Indeterminism rejects the conception of the universe as a totally ordered and predictable system in which phenomena follow upon each other in inevitable sequences, each state being completely determined by the preceding state. Emphasizing the importance of chance, spontaneous occurrence, change, and diversity, indeterminism holds that prediction is limited to statements of probability. In relation to man, it is often maintained that indeterminism, in denying mechanical or strict causation, opens the possibility of a certain degree of FREE WILL. See CAUSATION; DETERMINISM.

index. Any measurable or observable phenomenon (or phenomena) that is used to indicate the presence of another phenomenon that cannot be measured directly or conveniently. Thus one may attempt to determine the social status of individuals in a social system by determining their occupations. Occupation, then, is used as an index of social status. Indexes allow the researcher to quantify or observe aspects of a complex phenomenon, which then are assumed to reveal something about the phenomenon as a whole. For example, frequency of church attendance might be used as a simple index providing one measurement of religiosity. If religiosity is held to mean more than church attendance, another index can be used to add a further dimension to the concept of religiosity. Thus by combining simple indexes, one may develop a composite (or multiple-factor) index. One may also use as an index a phenomenon not conceptually related to the phenomenon being studied, but simply related by correlation. For example, if grades in school were found to be correlated with performance of a certain job, school grades might be used as a predictive index of probable performance, without any analysis of the nature of the relationship. Usually, however, the choice of indexes is related to THEORY, that is, the choice of an index to represent a phenomenon represents some degree of definition of the conceptual nature of that phenomenon. Composite indexes tend to define what the investigator believes are the component parts (the nature) of the phenomenon he cannot measure directly. It should be noted that a number of writers refer to a single measure of an observable phenomenon as an indicator, reserving the term *index* for a more complex combination of indicators.

The use of indexes in the social sciences is an attempt to do objectively, systematically, and with theoretically sophisticated procedures what all human beings do in dealing with social phenomena. Normally people respond to social (and physical) reality in terms of indexes. When people talk about the "status symbols" of our society, they are in essence talking about the various indexes used by others to judge roughly a person's relative status in his society or social group.

index, composite. See INDEX.

index, multiple-factor. See INDEX.

index, simple. See INDEX.

index number. A ratio between two values or two sets of values used to show in simplified and standardized form the changes that have occurred in a variable over time or the differences between two variables. Often the index number is the ratio between a value regarded as a standard or norm or expected value and an observed value.

indicator. See INDEX.

individual psychology. See PSYCHOLOGY, INDIVIDUAL.

individual representation. The private experience of the individual person, in contrast to COLLECTIVE REPRESENTATION. The term was used by Émile Durkheim.

individuation. 1. The breakdown of group ties and the emergence of individuals who lack strong feelings of group loyalty and often have no close, lasting PRIMARY RELATIONS with others. The term is essentially synonymous with ATOMIZATION.

2. In psychology, differentiation, or the development from generalized to specific responses, a process associated with maturation.

induction. The logical process in which generalizations are inferred from specific facts. Essentially, induction is the process of reasoning from individual instances to general principles. The experimental method is basically inductive, in that general conclusions are derived from individual observations. See DEDUCTION.

induction, analytic. A form of INDUCTION distinguished from enumerative induction by Florian Znaniecki, and held to yield universal generalizations. According to Znaniecki, enumerative induction is inadequate because it seeks to formulate generalizations based on statistical PROBABILITY. In analytic induction, particular cases are studied intensively in order to determine their essential characteristics. These essential characteristics are abstracted from the specific cases and generalized on the assumption that if they are essential they must hold in other cases. The resulting generalization is stated so that it will in fact hold in all cases. If any cases are discovered that do not support this generalization, it is modified so that these cases are excluded from its range of applicability. Thus the generalization is stated so that there are no exceptions. (F. Znaniecki, *The Method of Sociology*, Farrar and Rinehart, New York, 1934.)

In defense of the statistical approach, W. S. Robinson has argued that the differences between analytic induction and enumerative induction are differences of degree rather than kind. He maintains that the sophisticated statistician gradually moves toward analytic induction through the constant modification and refinement of his hypotheses. Moreover, Robinson is critical of the assumption of essential characteristics of phenomena, and suggests that analysis in terms of probability is a valuable scientific technique. (W. S. Robinson, *American Sociological Review*, December 1951.) See INDUCTION, ENUMERATIVE; STATISTICAL METHOD.

induction, complete. A form of enumerative induction based on the study of the entire population that is being investigated rather than just a sample. See INDUCTION, ENUMERATIVE; INDUCTION, INCOMPLETE.

induction, enumerative. A form of INDUCTION in which generalizations are based on the analysis and abstracting of similarities from a large number of cases within a defined population, using statistical procedures. The generalizations thus obtained are statements of statistical PROBABILITY. Enumerative induction is the most commonly used method in sociology. See INDUCTION, ANALYTIC; STATISTICAL INFERENCE; STATISTICAL METHOD.

induction, incomplete. A form of enumerative induction based on the study of a sample of the population being investigated rather than the entire population. Most sociological studies are of this type. See INDUCTION, COMPLETE; INDUCTION, ENUMERATIVE.

inductive method. See INDUCTION.

inductive statistics. See STATISTICS, INDUCTIVE.

industrial conflict. Conflict within an industry arising from conflicting interests, most often those of management and labor. The term has been "used loosely to mean at least three things. Sometimes it includes the sources of discontent, the bases of hostility, the grievances, the oppositions of interest. Thus labor and management are said to be in conflict over wage payments or managerial prerogatives in the sense that they have different desires. Sometimes it covers all forms of opposed action, both nonviolent, such as collective bargaining, and violent, such as the strike. In this sense, conflict means not the incompatible views of the parties but the battle between them which finds its source in these views. Sometimes conflict is opposed to peace. Thus a strike is said to constitute industrial conflict, while bargaining is peaceful." (C. Kerr, *American Journal of Sociology*, November 1954.)

industrial psychology. See PSYCHOLOGY, INDUSTRIAL.

Industrial Revolution. The radical changes in methods of production and economic and social organization resulting from the introduction of power-driven machinery and the consequent rise of the FACTORY SYSTEM. The Industrial Revolution is characterized by the replacement of hand production centered in a craftsman's home or small shop by machine production centered in factories, by the production of standardized goods with interchangeable parts, by the rise of a class of factory workers who work for wages and do not own the means of production or the goods they produce, by a great increase in the proportion of the population engaged in nonagricultural occupations, and by the growth of numerous large cities. Industrialization provides a vast quantity of material goods never before available to the majority of the population. The Industrial Revolution began in England in the eighteenth century and spread from there to other countries in western Europe, to the United States, and then to other parts of the world. Industrialization is today a primary goal of many nations in Asia and Africa.

industrial sociology. See SOCIOLOGY, INDUSTRIAL.

industrial union. See UNION, INDUSTRIAL.

industrialism. The system of economic and social organization established by the INDUSTRIAL REVOLUTION.

industrialization. See INDUSTRIAL REVOLUTION.

industry. 1. That branch of economic activity devoted to organized, large-scale manufacturing of goods. In this sense industry is contrasted with agriculture, commerce, finance, and other forms of economic activity.

2. More broadly, any branch of economic activity concerned with one type of product and having a certain degree of organization—including agricultural, extractive, commercial, and financial ventures as well as manufacturing. Examples would be the construction industry, the fishing industry, the lumbering industry, the paper industry.

inequality, social. The existence of unequal opportunities and rewards for different social positions or statuses within a group or society. See STRATIFICATION, SOCIAL.

inertia, cultural. An assumed tendency for culture traits and culture complexes to persist after they have outlived their usefulness. The term is little used in sociology today, probably because of its possible value bias and because as cultural elements or patterns change their meaning or use, their new meanings and functions may not be obvious. Even if old culture traits persist only for sentimental reasons, they cannot be regarded as useless. In addition, culture traits and complexes that persist long past their original uses and meanings do not necessarily simply contribute to stability and stagnation, but may sometimes facilitate innovation. Persistent forms devoid of past meanings often combine with other persistent forms and become elements of new culture complexes with new meanings and functions. The term cultural inertia is similar to CULTURE LAG although cultural inertia is more general. See CULTURE COMPLEX; CULTURE TRAIT.

infanticide. The practice, approved in some cultures under certain conditions, of killing offspring (especially female infants) at birth or soon after.

inference. A process of reasoning by which existing knowledge or truths are used to derive new knowledge or truths. Inference is a mental process in which the person starts with a proposition (or propositions) accepted as true and through the process of logic concludes that therefore a new proposition is true. The truth of the new proposition is seen as logically inherent in the truth of the accepted proposition. Inference may be either valid or invalid. Valid inference is known as implication. Inference may involve either DEDUCTION or INDUCTION.

inference, statistical. See STATISTICAL INFERENCE.

inferential statistics. See STATISTICS, INDUCTIVE.

inferiority complex. A general and exaggerated feeling that one is inadequate, a failure, or in some basic way defective in comparison to other people. This lack of self-confidence may result in compensatory role playing which may show itself, among other ways, in conceit and haughtiness, as well as in timidity.

inflation. An economic condition characterized by an abundance of available money and purchasing demand relative to the supply of goods available, and chiefly manifested in rising prices, frequently, but not necessarily, accompanied by rising wages. The term inflation may refer to a variety of conditions involving a high price level, ranging from a situation in which there is a high level of business activity with high wages and a low rate of unemployment to a situation in which there is a lack of confidence in the nation's currency and a widespread desire to convert the currency into goods. In the latter case, inflation of prices could be accompanied by relatively low wages and high unemployment. See BUSINESS CYCLE; DEFLATION.

influence. The power to effect a voluntary change in a person's attitude or opinion through persuasive action. Robert Bierstedt regards influence as different from POWER in that power is coercive and influence is persuasive. For example, Karl Marx exerted considerable influence, but he had little power. (R. Bierstedt, *American Sociological Review,* December 1950.)

influentials. People who have INFLUENCE within a particular social system. Delbert C. Miller, in an analysis of community power structure, distinguishes between two types of influentials: "The *top influentials* . . . are persons from whom particular members are drawn into various systems of power relations according to the issue at stake. The *key influentials* . . . are sociometric leaders among the top influentials." (D. C. Miller, *American Journal of Sociology,* November 1958.) Robert K. Merton distinguishes between monomorphic and polymorphic influentials. Monomorphic influentials exert "influence, but only in one rather narrowly defined area—*e.g.*, the area of politics, *or* of canons of good taste, *or* of fashion. The monomorphic influentials are the 'experts' in a limited field, and their influence does not diffuse into other spheres of decision." Polymorphic influentials, in contrast, exert "interpersonal influence in a variety of (sometimes seemingly unrelated) spheres." (R. K. Merton, *Social Theory and Social Structure,* Free Press, Glencoe, Ill., 1957.) Merton introduced the term *influentials* into sociology. (R. K. Merton in *Communications Research 1948–49,* P. F. Lazarsfeld and F. Stanton, eds., Harper, New York, 1949.) See ELITE.

informal group. See GROUP, INFORMAL.

informal organization. See ORGANIZATION, INFORMAL.

informal status or rank. See STATUS, INFORMAL.

informal structure. See STRUCTURE, INFORMAL.

information, documentary sources of. See DOCUMENTARY SOURCES OF INFORMATION.

information theory. A mathematical theory of communication concerned with problems relating to the accuracy, efficiency, and effectiveness of communication. It deals with questions such as the extent to which the symbols used in communication convey the intended meaning, the effect of extraneous disturbances (referred to as "noise") in introducing errors in communication, the extent to which there is "redundancy" in communication—that is, portions of a message not needed to convey the intended meaning. Information theory attempts to formulate mathematical postulates and propositions relating to these and other problems in the area of communication. (See C. E. Shannon and W. Weaver, *The Mathematical Theory of Communication,* University of Illinois Press, Urbana, Ill., 1949.)

in-group. Any group (primary or secondary) whose membership has a strong sense of identification and loyalty, and a feeling of exclusiveness toward nonmembers. See OUT-GROUP.

inheritance. See HEREDITY.

inhibition. In social psychology, refraining from or delaying an activity that is desired, due to the expectation of negative consequences somehow connected with the desired activity. In social action, for example, inhibition may be due to conflicting values, fear of social sanctions, or poorly defined social situations in which the individual is not sure what the consequences of action will be.

initiation ritual. A practice of a group or society designed to mark ceremonially an individual's entrance into membership in a group or change from one membership status within the group to another. See RITES DE PASSAGE.

ink blot test. See RORSCHACH TEST.

innate behavior. Inborn or unlearned responses existing in humans at birth (or automatically accompanying biological maturation) and unchanged by experience. Innatism as a theory of human behavior is related to the now discredited conception of human instincts. See INSTINCT.

innate temperament. See TEMPERAMENT, HYPOTHESIS OF INNATE.

inner city. 1. The densely built-up, highly urbanized central area of a large city, including (at least in the large North American city) inner slums, rooming houses, "artistic-intellectual" settlements, and expensive apartment houses located near the center of the city. Some writers consider the CENTRAL BUSINESS DISTRICT as part of the inner city, but others do not. The term has been used primarily with reference to cities in the United States, and often with the implication that in the inner city there is a certain degree of anonymity, transiency, or lack of social organization in both the rich and poor areas. The term is not a technical one and is generally used without precision.

2. The area of deterioration near the CENTRAL BUSINESS DISTRICT, in this sense very similar to the ZONE IN TRANSITION.

inner-directed society. An abstract or IDEAL TYPE formulated by David Riesman, Nathan Glazer, and Reuel Denney, of a society which "develops in its typical members a social character whose conformity is insured by their tendency to acquire early in life an internalized set of goals." (D. Riesman, N. Glazer, R. Denney, *The Lonely Crowd*, Doubleday, New York, 1954.) In common practice the concept of inner-directedness is often applied to an ideal type of individual and termed *inner-directed man*. See OTHER-DIRECTED SOCIETY; TRADITION-DIRECTED SOCIETY.

innovation. The development or recognition of new elements or patterns (either material or nonmaterial) in a culture. Innovation is a broad term including both DISCOVERY and INVENTION, as well as minor changes too small to be classified as inventions. Innovation is always dependent upon a knowledge of the existing culture, for it involves the reinterpretation or new combination of old culture traits or complexes to form new traits or complexes, or the selection of elements from old patterns to create new patterns. It is stimulated by the re-examination of knowledge through, for example, culture contact. Innovation is itself a stimulus to further innovation. See CULTURE COMPLEX; CULTURE TRAIT.

insanity. A legal term for mental disorder or abnormal behavior. A defendant who is judged insane is held to be not responsible for his behavior. The term has been abandoned by psychiatrists and psychologists, who prefer more specific and sophisticated designations.

insect society. The inherited patterns of complex behavior found among such insects as bees, ants, and wasps. In these insect communities there is an interdependence and specialization of activities. Insect societies depend on biological inheritance for their behavior patterns, and because the patterns of interdependence of such societies are specifically and exactly determined by the genetic structure of the species, such societies remain the same for thousands of years and change only as biological changes occur within the species. Learning is at a minimum and of course there is no insect CULTURE. Thus insect societies differ so fundamentally from human societies that their study has given social scientists little insight into the study of human society. Human society involves not only social interaction but also culture, which is to human society what biologically determined behavior is to insect "society."

insecurity, status. See STATUS / SECURITY HYPOTHESIS.

insight. Understanding or solving a problem by mentally grasping the important elements and relationships relevant to the solution. Thus a previously formless, inconsistent, or frustrating situation becomes susceptible of manipulation and control. Insight into one's own behavior often occurs when one is able to view one's behavior objectively, that is, as others see it.

instinct. An unlearned, innate complex of behavior patterns in lower animals that emerges through maturation of the organism. Specific instinctive behavior is universal within a particular species, and it occurs only when the environment provides an adequate stimulus. The nest-building activities of birds and fish have been termed instinctive and provide clear examples of what is meant by the concept.

Some early psychologists, such as Sigmund Freud and William McDougall, applied the term to human behavior, but on the whole modern psychologists and social scientists have abandoned the term when talking about human behavior. Most psychologists prefer the terms REFLEX, DRIVE, and NEED for innate human response patterns.

instinct for combinations and **instinct for group persistences.** Two major forms of motivation (RESIDUES) proposed by Vilfredo Pareto, the former referring to innovative and manipulative behavior and the latter to dogged conservatism and the use of coercion. These concepts were used by Pareto in his analysis of political and economic elites. According to Pareto, both these forms of behavior underlie the actions of elites as they try to maintain their position of ascendancy, but one or the other predominates. When the instinct for combinations is dominant, Pareto refers to these elites as the speculator-fox type. When the instinct for group persistences is dominant, Pareto refers to these elites as the *rentier*-lion type. (V. Pareto, *The Mind and Society*, tr. by A. Bongiorno and A. Livingston, Harcourt, Brace, New York, 1935.) See ELITE, CIRCULATION OF THE.

instinct of workmanship. The tendency in man to seek meaningful activities. The term was used by Thorstein Veblen, who wrote, "[Man] is an agent seeking in every act the accomplishment of some concrete, objective, impersonal end. By force of his being such an agent he is possessed of a taste for effective work, and a distaste for futile effort. He has a sense of the merit of serviceability or efficiency and of the demerit of futility, waste, or incapacity. This aptitude or propensity may be called the instinct of workmanship." (T. Veblen, *The Theory of the Leisure Class*, Macmillan, New York, 1899.)

institution. See INSTITUTION, SOCIAL.

institution, basic social. A social institution that satisfies a basic human need, and thus is necessary for the survival of society. Usually the family, the economic, the political, and the religious institution are regarded as basic institutions. See INSTITUTION, SOCIAL.

institution, crescive social. A social institution that has developed slowly and spontaneously through the gradual accretion of social norms. William G. Sumner distinguished between crescive institutions and enacted institutions. His conception of crescive institution was similar to the general conception of social institution held by sociologists today. (W. G. Sumner, *Folkways*, Ginn, Boston, 1906.) See INSTITUTION, ENACTED SOCIAL; INSTITUTION, SOCIAL.

institution, enacted social. An organization established at a particular time for a specific purpose. This definition proposed by William G. Sumner, who distinguished between enactive and crescive institutions, is at variance with the definition of social institution most commonly accepted by sociologists today, and is similar to the usual definition of an ASSOCIATION or a formal organization. (W. G. Sumner, *Folkways*, Ginn, Boston, 1906.) See INSTITUTION, CRESCIVE SOCIAL; INSTITUTION, SOCIAL; ORGANIZATION, FORMAL.

institution, primary social. See INSTITUTION, BASIC SOCIAL.

institution, social. 1. An interrelated system of social roles and norms organized about the satisfaction of an important social need or function. The social roles and norms comprising the social institution define proper and expected behavior oriented to the fulfillment of the particular social need, such as the provision of food and other material goods. The economic institution, for example, provides the social norms that define proper behavior for the roles of business manager, factory worker, retail clerk, customer, farmer, and all others concerned with economic relationships, and also provides the basic values on which the particular economic system (socialist, capitalist) is based. Many groups are involved in a given social institution. For example, within the economic institution may be included business organizations, labor unions, consumer organizations, family farms, and so forth. In addition, roles performed by individuals not in groups, such as unorganized consumers, also form part of the social institution. It should be emphasized, however, that social institution is an analytic concept. Specific groups may be analyzed in terms of a number of institutions, and of course all individuals play a variety of roles falling within the scope of various institutions. Commonly defined institutions are the family institution, the economic institution, the educational institution, the political institution, the religious institution, etc. Among sociologists who essentially follow this definition, there is variation in emphasis in the discussion of social institutions. Some emphasize the satisfaction of needs or wants, others the system of reciprocal role relationships, and still others the complex of interrelated norms. See NORM, SOCIAL; ROLE. See also ART INSTITUTION; ECONOMIC INSTITUTION; EDUCATIONAL INSTITUTION; FAMILY INSTITUTION; MILITARY INSTITUTION; POLITICAL INSTITUTION; RECREATIONAL INSTITUTION; RELIGIOUS INSTITUTION.

2. Any traditional cultural pattern or interrelated complex of social norms, such as private property, trial by jury, etc. This definition is similar to the concept of CULTURE COMPLEX.

3. An organized social group. Some writers have used the term in this way to refer to any relatively permanent group, whereas others define it so that it is equivalent to ASSOCIATION.

institution, total. A place of confinement or partial confinement where persons of a specified type live, following a formalized life routine under the control and direction of a bureaucratic staff, and having limited contact with the rest of society. Examples of total institutions are prisons, hospitals, army camps, boarding schools, etc. This term is entirely distinct from and should not be confused with the usual sociological sense of social institution.

institutional agency. An organized group carrying out a particular institutional function. For example, a specific religious denomination would be an institutional agency of the religious institution, an industrial corporation would be an institutional agency of the economic institution, etc. See INSTITUTION, SOCIAL.

institutional capitalist. A member of the highest level of management of a very large corporation. The institutional capitalist is a top administrative official. He usually does not own a controlling share of the stock of the corporation, frequently not even being the largest stockholder, but he has power to control or at least substantially affect the operations of the corporation. It is often said that the institutional capitalist is more interested in power than money.

institutional order. A number of institutions serving a similar social function. This term was used by Hans Gerth and C. Wright Mills, and essentially refers to a major social institution. They defined a social institution, in turn, as a role clustering organized about a central role. The basic institutional orders of society according to Gerth and Mills are the political order, the economic order, the military order, the kinship order, and the religious order. (H. Gerth and C. W. Mills, *Character and Social Structure: The Psychology of Social Institutions,* Harcourt, Brace, New York, 1953.) See INSTITUTION, SOCIAL.

institutional pattern. A pattern of interrelated social norms that defines the expected and legitimate mode of behavior in a social situation in a given society. It is a normative pattern which in a given society is stable and structured and has definite social sanctions attached to it. See INSTITUTIONALIZATION; NORM, SOCIAL; SANCTION.

institutional specialization. The condition characteristic of complex societies in which each social institution fulfills a specialized function and thus may be distinguished quite readily from the other social institutions. In such a society specialized organizations exist that predominantly fulfill particular social functions, and specific behavior of individuals can often be classified as primarily economic, religious, or the like, even though there is a certain degree of overlap. Institutional specialization is lacking in nonliterate societies, which, in contrast to complex societies, are characterized by institutional integration. In a nonliterate society specific individual behavior often has simultaneously economic, religious, and kinship significance. Specialized organizations are generally lacking, and the family performs a wide range of social functions. See INSTITUTION, SOCIAL.

institutionalization. The development of stable patterns of social interaction based on formalized rules, laws, customs, and rituals. Institutionalization makes social behavior predictable by defining the behavior that is expected and considered legitimate in specific social roles, such as parent, employee, priest, and so forth. A system of sanctions is associated with institutionalization, such that conformity to institutionalized expectations is rewarded and deviance is punished. Institutionalization provides an orderly system of social relationships. It is found in all societies, but there are varying degrees of institutionalization of behavior in different aspects of social life within a society. See INSTITUTIONAL PATTERN; ROLE; SANCTION.

institutionalized evasion. See PATTERNED EVASION.

institutionalized priority. An institutionalized social norm that defines which norm shall take precedence in case of a conflict between two or more social norms. For example, in case of conflict between a social norm against killing and a social norm that one should fight (and kill if necessary) for one's country, an institutionalized norm holding that the latter should take precedence would be an institutionalized priority. See NORM, INSTITUTIONALIZED SOCIAL; NORM, SOCIAL.

institutionalized social norm. See NORM, INSTITUTIONALIZED SOCIAL.

instrumentalism. The orientation which holds that the concepts and propositions comprising a THEORY should be empirically verifiable and useful for research. Instrumentalism, while influenced by OPERATIONALISM, represents a more moderate position than the latter, for while it holds that concepts must be susceptible to empirical testing it does not seek to define them solely in terms of the procedures used to test them or exclude a conceptual level of analysis. It is sometimes regarded as an intermediate position in degree of emphasis on empirical research on the one hand and theory on the other hand. It is an approach characteristic of many contemporary sociologists. The term originally was introduced in philosophy by John Dewey to refer to his form of PRAGMATISM.

insulation, role. See ROLE INSULATION.

integralism. See SOCIOLOGICAL MYSTIC INTEGRALISM.

integration, cultural. The mutual adjustment of diverse or conflicting culture traits to form a harmonious cultural system. For example, through culture DIFFUSION new traits may be absorbed into a culture which are in conflict with certain traditional culture traits; the resolution of this conflict through the modification and coordination of the new and old traits would be cultural integration. See CULTURE TRAIT.

integration, functional. Unity or harmony within a system based on the interdependence of specialized parts. As applied to groups, this term refers to group unity resulting from the fact that the members perform interrelated, specialized activities and thus are dependent upon each other. The members' diverse activities complement each other, fitting together to form an integrated whole. See SOLIDARITY, ORGANIC.

integration, normative. See NORMATIVE INTEGRATION.

integration, personality. See PERSONALITY INTEGRATION.

integration, social. 1. The uniting of formerly separate groups into one group with the obliteration of any previous social and cultural group differences as well as the obliteration of separate group identifications. In this sense social integration is similar to ASSIMILATION. The main difference is that assimilation assumes the groups had major cultural differences to begin with, whereas social integration may occur between groups in the same culture that had been separated primarily by the group loyalties of their members.

2. See COHESION, SOCIAL.

3. The acceptance of an individual by the other members of a group.

intellectuals. Those members of a society who are devoted to the development of original ideas and are engaged in creative intellectual pursuits. The intellectuals constitute a small, creative segment of the INTELLIGENTSIA. They provide the intellectual leadership for the remainder of the intelligentsia.

intelligence. The capacity of an individual to learn, think in abstract terms, solve problems, and generally adapt himself to his environment and to new situations as they arise. Some psychologists feel that intelligence is the sort of elusive phenomenon that can be defined only operationally— as a score on an intelligence test. See INTELLIGENCE QUOTIENT.

intelligence quotient (I.Q.). The ratio between an individual's mental age and his chronological age (or for adults, a fixed denominator) multiplied by 100. The mental age of a person is determined by a standardized intelligence test. An I.Q. score of 90–109 is considered normal.

intelligence test. Any standardized set of questions or problems that allow the tester to discriminate between various individuals' ability to solve given verbal or nonverbal problems. See CULTURE-FAIR TEST; STANFORD-BINET TEST.

intelligentsia. The members of the educated stratum of society, mostly with professional or managerial occupations, who have an interest in ideas and a certain degree of consciousness of themselves as a social stratum. See INTELLECTUALS.

intensiveness of utilization, hypothesis of. An ecological hypothesis concerning the distribution of businesses and industries in an urban community, which holds that in the competition for a given location the unit that uses the location most intensively will tend to occupy it. The hypothesis of intensiveness of utilization is one of a series of locational hypotheses formulated by James A. Quinn. (J. A. Quinn, *Human Ecology*, Prentice-Hall, Englewood Cliffs, N.J., 1950.) See ECOLOGY, HUMAN; MEDIAN LOCATION, HYPOTHESIS OF; MINIMUM COST, HYPOTHESIS OF.

interaction. 1. In general, a dynamic interplay and relationship of joint determination between two or more variables. It is the mutual influencing of variables so that the value of each variable influences the value of the other variables involved in the relationship. For an example of one type of interaction between variables, see CUMULATION, PRINCIPLE OF. See INTERACTION, SOCIAL.

2. Behavior directed toward or influenced by another person. This is one of the three basic concepts used by George C. Homans in his analysis of groups. It is similar to the usual definition of social interaction. (G. C. Homans, *The Human Group*, Harcourt, Brace, New York, 1950.) See ACTIVITY; INTERACTION, SOCIAL; SENTIMENT.

interaction, social. The basic social process represented in communication and a mutual relationship between two or more individuals (or groups). Interaction between persons is social behavior. Through language, symbols, and gestures people exchange meanings and have a reciprocal effect upon each other's behavior, expectations, and thought.

interaction, symbolic. See SYMBOLIC INTERACTION.

interactionism. A sociological approach to social psychology emphasizing the action and reaction of persons and groups to each other. The expectations and influences of people on each other, rather than the reactions of single individuals to impersonal and nonsocial stimuli, are seen as the primary data of social psychology. Thus interactionism is more concerned with social norms and social roles than with stimulus-response explanations of human behavior. See SYMBOLIC INTERACTIONISM.

interaction recorder. A device developed by Robert F. Bales for the systematic analysis of social interaction in small groups by trained observers. The observers classify any verbal or nonverbal behavior of group members into one of twelve categories (such as, shows solidarity, shows tension release, agrees, etc.) and also indicate which member originates the interaction and to whom it is directed. (See R. F. Bales, *Interaction Process Analysis*, Addison-Wesley, Cambridge, Mass., 1950.)

interest. 1. A favorable disposition toward an object or an activity and a consistent preference for that object or activity over others. In this sense interest implies that the object or activity of interest is a focus of attention for the individual. See NEED; WANT.

2. Particularly in the plural, economic or other objectives that would be beneficial to a particular group or segment of society. Sometimes these are referred to as objective interests, for it is presumed that the members of a group or stratum may not be aware of their self-interests and may at times act contrary to them. See INTEREST GROUP.

interest, vested. See VESTED INTEREST.

interest group. A GROUP organized to secure certain objectives which the members value or regard as beneficial to themselves. Interest groups, sometimes referred to as special interest groups or pressure groups, frequently represent particular economic interests—for example, organized labor, large manufacturers, small businessmen, farmers, professional organizations. At times larger interest groups may be divided into more specifically oriented smaller groups. Thus for certain purposes all manufacturers may form one interest group, whereas at other times the objectives of one type of manufacturer may conflict with those of another. Interest groups also may be organized to secure noneconomic objectives or objectives that are not purely economic. An interest group may, for example, be a religious group, an ethnic or racial group, antivivisectionists, an association concerned with saving historic landmarks, a rifle association, etc. Interest groups play a particularly important role in a large, representative democracy, where they seek to exert influence over the passage of legislation and the actions of governmental agencies.

interest theory of social class. See SOCIAL CLASS, SUBJECTIVE CONCEPTION OF.

interests, objective. See CLASS INTEREST CONSCIOUSNESS; INTEREST (2); MANIFEST INTERESTS.

intergroup relations. In general, the interaction of social groups or the study of this. However, very often the term is used to refer quite specifically to the study of the contact, coexistence, or conflict of ethnic, religious, or racial groups. Clearly, the general principles that apply to the interaction of all social groups also apply to intergroup relations that are considered "social problems."

intermarriage. Marriage between persons belonging to two social groups or categories, the members of one or both of which normally disapprove, at least to some extent, of marriage with members of the other, thereby creating possible difficulties between the husband and wife and/or between them and their respective groups or families of origin. Usually intermarriage is described as involving persons from different religious, racial, or ethnic backgrounds. See ENDOGAMY.

internal system. In George C. Homans' schema for the analysis of groups, the organization of group activities, sentiments, and interactions directed toward the members themselves; that is, the organization of their attitudes and behavior toward each other. The internal system together with the EXTERNAL SYSTEM constitutes the total social system. (G. C. Homans, *The Human Group,* Harcourt, Brace, New York, 1950.) See ACTIVITY; INTERACTION; SENTIMENT.

internalization. The acceptance by an individual as part of his own SELF of an attitude, belief, or value held by another person or group. Personality structure is formed primarily by the IDENTIFICATION of an individual with significant others (individuals and groups) and the internalization of their standards, as well as by the rejection of the standards of negative reference groups or figures. The term INTROJECTION is not synonymous with internalization, in that internalization usually refers to the formation and modification of the self (EGO or PERSONALITY structure).

internalized role. See ROLE, INTERNALIZED.

interpersonal relations. The patterns of personal relationships that develop out of sustained social interaction.

interpolation. The process of calculating an unknown value of a variable that is between two or more known values in the series. When the known values are plotted on a graph, the process of interpolation assumes that the unknown value lies on the line of the graph.

interpretation. The application of a conceptual scheme or MODEL to observed data in order to relate a fact logically to other facts and explanations. The interpretation of what is observed serves to associate one observation with other current and past observations or even with hypothetical occurrences or relationships. Data must be interpreted if they are to lead to further hypotheses and research. Indeed, every fact stands in a relationship to other facts. Hence, interpretation and fact finding are aspects of the same process.

interpretive method. See VERSTEHEN, METHOD OF.

interstimulation, social. See INTERACTION, SOCIAL.

interstitial area. See ZONE IN TRANSITION.

interval, class. See CLASS INTERVAL.

interval scale. A SCALE in which the distance between each of the numbers or units on the scale is equal. The construction of such a scale assumes that the intervals can be quantified, that they are equal, and that the direction (greater, equal, or less) is known. A ruler and a thermometer are interval scales. The THURSTONE EQUAL-APPEARING INTERVAL SCALE is an attempt to approximate an interval scale.

intervening opportunities, hypothesis of. See STOUFFER'S HYPOTHESIS OF INTERVENING OPPORTUNITIES.

intervening variable. See VARIABLE, INTERVENING.

interview. A conversation between an investigator and an informant for the purpose of gathering information. A number of the social sciences use the interview as one of their methods of data gathering.

interview, depth. An intensive and detailed INTERVIEW usually designed to allow for the free exploration of unknown variables, the study of the larger social or psychological context of the informant's responses, and, hopefully, the emergence of new insights. Depth interviews may be either guided or nondirective. See INTERVIEW, GUIDED; INTERVIEW, NONDI-RECTIVE.

interview, focused. An INTERVIEW that concentrates the investigation on selected aspects of a specific event or situation experienced by the respondent. Focused interviews are usually held with a number of respondents who have had a common experience—for example, having read the same propaganda leaflet, seen the same movie, or having been involved in the same event. Focused interviews generally must be carefully prepared to concentrate on the most relevant aspects of the problem being studied, and therefore tend to be quite structured. The term was introduced by Robert K. Merton, Marjorie Fiske, and Patricia L. Kendall in *The Focused Interview* (Free Press, Glencoe, Ill., 1956).

interview, guided. An INTERVIEW in which the interviewer asks a set of questions carefully prepared in advance. In such an interview previously defined problems are investigated. New insights are expected to be derived in the analysis of the data being collected, but not on the basis of informal discussion with the respondent.

interview, nondirective. An unstructured INTERVIEW in which the respondent is given a maximum amount of freedom to engage in spontaneous conversation, that is, to discuss material he thinks is most crucial. The interviewer asks a minimum of questions and gives few suggestions.

interview, therapeutic. An interview designed not so much for eliciting information as for allowing the respondent to express his hostilities and frustrations or to develop greater self-understanding.

interview, unguided. See INTERVIEW, NONDIRECTIVE.

interview guide. A list of topics for use in relatively unstructured interviews that serves to order and assure the coverage of important subjects by an interviewer. The interview guide differs from an INTERVIEW SCHEDULE in that it does not consist of a set of fixed questions, and therefore allows for greater flexibility and informality between the respondent and the interviewer.

interview schedule. A list of questions used by an interviewer to structure and guide his questioning of a respondent. The interviewer asks the questions and records the answers himself. It is a QUESTIONNAIRE filled out by the interviewer instead of the respondent. The use of an interview schedule allows the respondent to ask for clarification and explanation of unclear or difficult questions. It also allows the interviewer to record responses not directly anticipated in the design of the study. However, interview schedules may be highly structured with the interviewer simply reading the questions and recording answers based on predetermined alternatives, such as yes or no, or agree or disagree. The latter technique may be useful, for example, when literate but otherwise untrained interviewers are interviewing nonliterate or illiterate respondents.

interviewer's effect. See BIAS.

introception. See INTERNALIZATION.

introjection. 1. A process in which a person incorporates into his thinking and behavior the attitudes, beliefs, values, or other characteristics of other individuals or groups. Some writers use the term synonymously with INTERNALIZATION. In the most usual usage, however, introjection is defined as a more limited or incipient process in which the introjected characteristic, while influencing behavior, has not been assimilated as a part of the personality or self. Introjection may then be a first step leading to internalization and IDENTIFICATION.
2. In psychoanalytic theory, the direction of impulses and responses toward an internalized, subjective image of an object rather than toward the external object itself. The object becomes absorbed in the subject's ego.

introspection. A form of observation in which a person considers his own subjective experiences. Introspection is a major source of the person's evaluation of social reality. In an analysis of his past and present behavior and experience or his reaction to a social situation a person reflects upon and evaluates the roles he has played in various social situations, and then may act on the basis of this analysis. Introspection is also often considered a source of information in social research; however, the scientific approach to the study of human behavior involves numerous techniques of observation to supplement, enhance, transform, and at times to supplant investigation by introspection.

introspection, sympathetic. See SYMPATHETIC INTROSPECTION.

introvert. A personality type (proposed by Carl G. Jung) having a tendency to be occupied with himself, his own thoughts and inner experiences, rather than with other people. An introvert tends to withdraw from social and emotional interaction with others, especially during periods of emotional stress. See EXTROVERT.

intuition. The immediate understanding of an idea or problem without meditation or an awareness of the logical or empirical reasons for one's judgment.

invariant. See CONSTANT.

invasion. An ecological process involving the movement of one type of population or land use into an area already occupied by or subject to a different type of population or land use. Invasion may involve, for example, the movement of a new racial, cultural, or status group into an area, or the penetration of a residential area by commercial enterprises. When the invading type predominates over or displaces the previous type SUCCESSION has occurred. See ECOLOGY, HUMAN.

invention. A creative innovation in the relationship between either material or nonmaterial culture traits, often defined as the synthesis of existing culture traits or complexes into new culture traits or complexes. The new cultural forms in turn become a part of the cultural heritage and thereby a potential element in further combinations and inventions. Inventions include not only technological and scientific innovation, but also social inventions, such as new forms of government. See CULTURE COMPLEX; CULTURE TRAIT; DISCOVERY; INNOVATION.

invention, parallel. The occurrence of the same invention in two or more cultures not as a result of DIFFUSION or cultural borrowing, but rather as a result of independent development. Parallel inventions that occur in diverse cultures are assumed to be a result of common needs and circumstances found in these cultures. When an invention emerges from the work of different men within the same or closely related cultures, there is less of a theoretical problem in explaining such occurrences, because the creative act of each inventor stems from an identical cultural environment in which all the elements necessary to the invention may have been familiar to any number of people. See MULTIPLE INDEPENDENT DISCOVERIES.

inverse correlation. See CORRELATION, NEGATIVE.

iron law of oligarchy. See OLIGARCHY, IRON LAW OF.

isolate. A person who appears to be a participant in a small group but who upon investigation is found to consider no one in the group a friend, nor does anyone in the group consider him a friend. The isolate is a peripheral member. There is not necessarily an isolate in every group. The term is used especially in SOCIOMETRY.

isolation. A degree of separation of individuals or groups from one another in terms of interaction, communication, cooperation, and social and emotional involvement. The prolonged isolation of an individual from satisfying social and psychological involvement with others usually leads to or is a result of a mental disorder. From a social-psychological point of view, a person is isolated in a community, such as a large city, if he feels alienated from the people with whom he interacts in his neighborhood and at his job. A group may also be isolated in a community, that is, live in physical proximity to other groups and either because of choice or rejection (or both) have culturally and socially a minimum of communication and interaction with them. Groups of this type often produce very strong feelings of group identification on the part of their members, with strong social and emotional commitment to their values, customs, and disciplines.

isometric map. A map showing the geographic distribution of rates of occurrence of a variable, such as birth rates. Lines connect points on the map having the same rate. The shape and pattern of the lines show the pattern of distribution of the variable. The isometric map is an alternative to the CROSS-HATCHED MAP or CHOROPLETH MAP (shaded map). It has the advantage of giving the impression of a gradual change in the rate of occurrence of a variable, rather than clearly demarcated areas. However, it does not provide as visually clear a picture as does a cross-hatched map.

item analysis. A process of evaluating individual items (for example, questions, attitude statements) on a questionnaire by comparing responses to these items with an external or internal criterion in order to test the items' VALIDITY or RELIABILITY. An external criterion might be the comparison of the known attitudes or characteristics of a group of respondents with their responses to the items being analyzed. An internal criterion might be the intercorrelation of scores on individual items through FACTOR ANALYSIS or the comparison of scores on individual items with scores for the total set of items or all those items on the questionnaire that are interrelated.

item replication. See REPLICATION, ITEM.

J

J curve. A FREQUENCY DISTRIBUTION CURVE in which the greatest frequency of cases, the MODE, falls in the first CLASS INTERVAL, or subdivision of the variable. In the subsequent class intervals the frequency declines sharply. When presented graphically the distribution gives the general impression of a reversed J.

James-Lange theory. A classical psychological theory of emotion, proposed by William James and Carl G. Lange, holding that an emotion is a set of physiological changes and sensations, particularly in the skeletal-muscular structure and the visceral organs. According to this view, one's consciousness of an emotion does not precede but rather follows the motor response and physiological experience.

jargon. 1. The body of specialized terms used by various subgroups of a society, such as a trade or professional group.

2. A primitive type of language, such as pidgin English, with a relatively simple grammar and limited vocabulary, usually formed because of the need for immediate communication between peoples with different languages who have had no formal language training. It usually involves the selection, adaptation, and rearrangement of elements of one or more foreign languages into a related, though highly modified, specialized language, which in time develops its own internal organization and grammar. Jargon develops among island people who have frequent but unenduring contacts with sailors and traders of one or several linguistic groups.

job bureaucrat. See BUREAUCRATIC TYPES.

joking relationship. A socially approved and standardized pattern of interaction which allows certain relatives or people with specific social statuses to joke, tease, trick, or otherwise express privileged familiarity with one another, without offense or impropriety.

judgment, independence of. See AUTONOMY.

judgment, value. See VALUE JUDGMENT.

juvenile court. A court of law that deals only with illegal acts by children under the legal age of adulthood (in the U.S., depending on the state, anywhere from under 16 to under 21).

juvenile delinquency. See DELINQUENCY, JUVENILE.

K

Kahn test. A PROJECTIVE TECHNIQUE for eliciting psychological information. The subject is shown assorted pictorial symbols with culturally defined significance, such as a star, a flag, or an arrow, and is asked to arrange them in order and explain the meaning they have to him.

karyokinesis, social. See SOCIAL KARYOKINESIS.

Kendall coefficient of concordance W. A nonparametric statistical measure of the degree of similarity among several sets of rankings of individuals or objects. The separate sets of rankings may have been obtained in a variety of ways. They may represent scores on different variables or they may be rankings on one variable by different judges. In the latter instance, the W coefficient enables the investigator to determine the degree of consensus among judges or observers in attempting to obtain a ranking when no objective standard of rank order is available. See NONPARAMETRIC STATISTICS; RANK, STATISTICAL.

Kendall tau test. See CORRELATION, KENDALL RANK.

kin group. A group united by ties of blood or marriage. Most kin groups, other than the family, are consanguineal. See KIN GROUP, CONSANGUINEAL.

kin group, consanguineal. A group consisting of persons related by blood, not all residing in a common household. Their relationship is socially determined—that is, it is based upon the fact that the group members believe they are all descended from a common ancestor, even though this may not really be the case. Which blood relatives are included in consanguineal kin groups depends upon culturally defined rules of descent.

kind, consciousness of. See CONSCIOUSNESS OF KIND.

kindred. A type of consanguineal kin group that is vaguely defined and loosely organized. Based on BILATERAL DESCENT, it includes all those consanguineous relatives to whom an individual feels some sense of obligation, however limited. The kindred is the characteristic type of kin group found in the United States today.

kinship. A social relationship based upon family relatedness, as culturally defined. The culture determines which family relationships are considered significant, what the rights and obligations of specific types of related persons are, and what forms of organization exist among related persons. Some anthropologists limit the term kinship to consanguineal relationships, that is, relationships based on ties of blood, but affinal relationships, that is relationships based on marriage, form an essential part of any KINSHIP SYSTEM. See FAMILY; MARRIAGE.

kinship, ritual. A KINSHIP relationship established on the basis of some functional social relationship (as godfather or godmother) rather than upon blood or marriage ties.

kinship institution. See FAMILY INSTITUTION.

kinship order. See FAMILY INSTITUTION.

kinship system. The customary system of statuses and roles that acts as a model for and governs the behavior of people who are considered to be related to each other through marriage or descent from a common ancestor.

kinship system, bilateral. A KINSHIP SYSTEM in which an individual is considered to be equally related to both his father's and mother's relatives. The bilateral system of kinship, which predominates in the United States, is neither patrilineal nor matrilineal.

kinship terminology, classificatory. The use of the same kinship term, uncle, for example, to refer to persons who stand in different biological relationships, thus emphasizing the social rather than the biological or lineage aspect of the relationship. Classificatory kinship terminology is sometimes contrasted with descriptive terminology, which defines a precise biological relationship. Some systems of kinship terminology are more classificatory in character, while others are more descriptive.

knowledge, folk. See COMMON SENSE.

knowledge, sociology of. See SOCIOLOGY OF KNOWLEDGE.

Kolmogorov-Smirnov D test. A nonparametric statistical test designed to measure whether the difference between two frequency distributions probably is significant or is merely due to chance. The two frequency distributions being compared may be the distributions of two independent samples or the comparison may be between the distribution of one sample and a theoretical distribution. In the Kolmogorov-Smirnov test the cumulative percentages of the two distributions in each category or CLASS INTERVAL are compared. The test may be either a ONE-TAILED TEST or a TWO-TAILED TEST, that is, it may be used when the direction of the difference between the two distributions is hypothesized or when it is not. See FREQUENCY DISTRIBUTION; PROBABILITY; NONPARAMETRIC STATISTICS; SIGNIFICANCE, STATISTICAL.

Kruskal-Wallis test. A nonparametric statistical test used to compare several samples in order to determine whether the samples probably come from the same population, that is, whether the differences between them probably are significant or merely due to chance variations. The Kruskal-Wallis test, also known as the H test, is an extension of the Wilcoxon test for use with more than two samples. It is used with data in the form of ranks, and involves the analysis of VARIANCE for one variable, which is assumed to have an underlying continuous distribution. See NONPARAMETRIC STATISTICS; PROBABILITY; SIGNIFICANCE, STATISTICAL; WILCOXON MATCHED-PAIRS SIGNED RANKS TEST.

kurtosis. In statistics, the shape of a FREQUENCY DISTRIBUTION CURVE, specifically the degree of flatness or peakedness. The normal distribution is mesokurtic; the curve with a higher degree of kurtosis (peakedness) is leptokurtic; and the curve with a flat top (compared to the normal curve) is platykurtic. See FREQUENCY DISTRIBUTION CURVE, LEPTOKURTIC; FREQUENCY DISTRIBUTION CURVE, MESOKURTIC; FREQUENCY DISTRIBUTION CURVE, PLATYKURTIC.

L

labor. 1. As a general term, any work or effort directed toward the attainment of a specific goal.

2. Manual workers, including factory, farm, mining, and construction workers, and all others whose work is primarily physical rather than social or intellectual, including skilled, semiskilled, and unskilled workers.

3. In economics, one of the three basic factors in production, the other two being land and capital. In this sense it includes mental as well as manual work.

labor, division of. See DIVISION OF LABOR; DIVISION OF LABOR, ANOMIC; DIVISION OF LABOR, FORCED.

labor, professionalization of. See PROFESSIONALIZATION OF LABOR.

labor dispute. As defined by Section 2 (9) of the National Labor Relations Act, "any controversy concerning terms, tenure or conditions of employment, or concerning the association or representation of persons in negotiating, fixing, maintaining, changing, or seeking to arrange terms or conditions of employment, regardless of whether the disputants stand in the proximate relation of employer and employee."

labor force. 1. The total number or proportion of the population actually working, employed although temporarily not working, or unemployed but able to work and seeking employment. The U.S. Census sets the minimum age of persons included in the labor force at fourteen. It also includes all members of the armed forces.

2. Less often, persons employed and paid for their services.

labor turnover. The percent of all of any given set of employees (for example, all steel workers or the employees of one particular company) who during a given period of time leave their employment and are replaced by others.

labor union. See UNION.

laissez-faire. A doctrine, policy, or ideal holding that government should not interfere with economic activity either with assistance or control. It is assumed that competition is capable of acting as the supreme regulator of the economy, preventing restrictions on trade or production and promoting efficiency and progress. The term was introduced in France in the eighteenth century and before long spread to England, where it was elaborated in the writings of Adam Smith. Smith used the doctrine of laissez-faire to argue against the prevalent theory of mercantilism and the governmental restrictions and regulations of economic activity characteristic of his day. In the nineteenth century it became a conservative doctrine supported by industrial and commercial interests in various parts of the world who sought to avoid government regulation of their activities. It found support in the writings of John Stuart Mill, who argued that government interference in the economic realm should be limited to activities clearly demonstrated to be absolutely essential. In the twentieth century laissez-faire ceased to be a seriously advocated economic doctrine. See CLASSICAL ECONOMIC THEORY.

language. A universal form of human behavior involving symbolic communication through a culturally accepted system of sound patterns having standardized meanings. Language is a part of and expresses the cultural heritage. In language arbitrary sounds are formed into cultural symbols capable of communicating ideas, desires, meanings, experiences, and traditions from one generation to another. Language is a social product. Each individual in the culture develops language through prolonged interaction with members who are already socialized, and language represents the accumulated and current experiences, feelings, and meanings that can be communicated and stabilized within the culture. Language is essential to human perception, thinking, awareness of self, awareness of others, and to the existence of the social community itself.

language, constructed. A deliberately created logical system of symbols, designed for clarity and internal consistency. Each symbol has a specific meaning and there are precise rules defining the relationships between symbols. Mathematics and formal logic are examples of constructed languages.

language, sociology of. See SOCIOLINGUISTICS.

language, special. See ARGOT; JARGON.

latency. 1. In LEARNING THEORY, a measure of response referring to the time between the presentation of the stimulus and the occurrence of the response. See CONDITIONED RESPONSE.

2. Occasionally in psychological usage, a currently inappropriate attitude or habit pattern which was adjustive at some period in the past.

latency period. In psychoanalytic theory, the middle period of childhood, that is, between the ages of five and twelve. Presumably, in this period sexual interest is low and aggression relatively subdued.

latent consequences. See FUNCTION, LATENT.

latent-distance model. See LAZARSFELD LATENT-DISTANCE MODEL.

latent function. See FUNCTION, LATENT.

latent social identity. A social identification or ROLE held by a member of a formal organization that is officially regarded as irrelevant to the organization but which nevertheless influences the organization's functioning. For example, sex, religious, and ethnic identifications may influence the behavior of persons in a formal organization, and thus affect the functioning of the organization, even though such identifications are not recognized by the organizational rules nor regarded as significant to the organization according to the prevailing cultural values. The concept is discussed by Alvin W. Gouldner, who also uses the terms *latent organizational identity* and *latent social role.* The identities and roles that are considered relevant and are prescribed by organizational rules and cultural values are called manifest social or organizational identities. (A. W. Gouldner, *Administrative Science Quarterly,* December 1957.)

latent structure analysis. The study of the latent attitude structure underlying expressed (manifest) attitudes. The latent structure is a theoretical model proposed by Paul F. Lazarsfeld. Observed correlations between expressed attitudes are explained in terms of their relationship to the latent structure. This structure, conceived of as a continuum of attitudes, is inferred from the overt, expressed attitudes, using a form of FACTOR ANALYSIS especially suited for qualitative data. The GUTTMAN SCALE is conceived of as a particular and limited case of latent structure analysis. (See S. A. Stouffer, *et al., Studies in Social Psychology in World War II,* Vol. IV, Princeton University Press, Princeton, 1950.) See LAZARSFELD LATENT-DISTANCE MODEL.

law. A system of standardized norms regulating human conduct, deliberately established for the purpose of social control. Laws are interpreted and enforced by formal public (political) authority, rather than by custom.

law, civil. See CIVIL LAW.

law, class. See CLASS LAW.

law, criminal. See CRIMINAL LAW.

law, customary. An early form of law that is primarily a codification of traditional practices although it provides some formalization of rules of behavior, enforcement procedures, and punishment for violators. Essentially equivalent to common law, customary law may be either written or unwritten. It may be systematized and codified, but when it is, it is a codification of established traditional practices, such as the Justinian Code. Customary law never breaks with tradition. William G. Sumner distinguished customary law from enacted law. (W. G. Sumner, *Folkways*, Ginn, Boston, 1906.) See LAW, ENACTED.

law, enacted. Law that is brought into existence through a formalized procedure and proclaimed at a specific time by recognized authorities. The term was used by William G. Sumner, who distinguished enacted law from customary law. He regarded enacted law as a more fully developed form of law, which no longer depends entirely on custom, and at times may even contradict certain customs. "Enactment is not possible until reverence for ancestors has been so much weakened that it is no longer thought wrong to interfere with traditional customs by positive enactment. . . . When an enactment is made there is a sacrifice of the elasticity and automatic self-adaptation of custom, but an enactment is specific and is provided with sanctions. Enactments come into use when conscious purposes are formed, and it is believed that specific devices can be framed by which to realize such purposes in the society. Then also prohibitions take the place of taboos, and punishments are planned to be deterrent rather than revengeful." (W. G. Sumner, *Folkways*, Ginn, Boston, 1906.) See LAW, CUSTOMARY.

law, ex post facto. A law that is retroactive. It penalizes acts that were committed before the law was passed and were not illegal at the time they occurred.

law, regulatory. Law not based on custom and tradition but enacted to meet new needs in a rapidly changing society. When there is rapid technological and social change, new conditions that require regulation emerge for which there are no or inadequate traditional norms on which to base such regulations.

law, scientific. A precise statement of a relationship among facts that has been repeatedly corroborated by scientific investigation and is generally accepted as accurate by experts in the field. A scientific law, also referred to as a scientific principle, is a HYPOTHESIS that has been sufficiently well verified to be considered probably true. A law is frequently referred to as a universal and predictive statement. It is universal in the sense that the stated relationship is held always to occur under the specified conditions, although these conditions may be quite limiting. And it is predictive in that if the specified conditions are found the relationship may be predicted to follow. See SCIENTIFIC METHOD.

law, sociology of. See SOCIOLOGY OF LAW.

law, statistical. A statement of the specific PROBABILITY (p) that a given relationship will occur or that two (or more) events will be associated with each other in a specified way. See LAW, SCIENTIFIC.

law, universal. See LAW, SCIENTIFIC.

Lazarsfeld latent-distance model. A model, or hypothetical system of relationships, developed by Paul F. Lazarsfeld for use in attitude studies. It is conceived of as a CONTINUUM along which respondents may be ordered on the basis of their attitudes on a particular subject. In any given study the continuum is divided into classes, the number of classes being one more than the number of items (attitudes) being studied (since that is the number of possible combinations of positive and negative responses; for example, three items provide four possible combinations: three positive, two positive and one negative, one positive and two negative, three negative). Each item is assigned a probability that a positive response places the respondent in a given latent class, and it is possible to compute the probability that the members of a given latent class will give a positive response to a certain number of items in the study. See LATENT STRUCTURE ANALYSIS.

leader. A person who occupies a central ROLE or position of dominance and influence in a group. See LEADERSHIP.

leader, bureaucratic. A person whose AUTHORITY stems primarily from his office or position in a bureaucratic hierarchy, rather than from his personality or personal characteristics. See BUREAUCRACY; CHARISMATIC LEADERSHIP.

leader, cosmopolitan. See COSMOPOLITAN.

leader, local. See LOCAL.

leader, nominal. A person who holds an official or publically acknowledged status as a leader, but who in fact does not perform the leadership role. The implication in the use of the term is that one or more other people provide the actual leadership.

leader, opinion. See OPINION LEADER.

leadership. The exercise of influence and AUTHORITY within a social relationship or group by one or more members. The leadership function is primarily the coordination of group activities toward group goals. The dominance and prestige associated with the leadership role result from its being the focus of coordination and unification of activities, information, and decisions.

leadership, authoritarian. A form of LEADERSHIP in which the leader or body of leaders determines the goals and rules of behavior of a group. Absolute authority is invested in the leader, and he is not required to consult the members of the group or to take their opinions into account in making decisions. The composition and functions of the leadership hierarchy (if the group is large enough to have a well-developed hierarchy) are determined from the top down. The major requirement of the membership at large is obedience to the leaders, and those in the leadership hierarchy are in turn expected to obey their superiors. Authoritarian leadership may be found, for example, in armies, dictatorships, industrial and commercial organizations, patriarchal families, and some youth gangs. See LEADERSHIP, DEMOCRATIC.

leadership, charismatic. See CHARISMATIC LEADERSHIP.

leadership, democratic. A form of leadership in which the leader or body of leaders believes in and acts in accordance with a social role that supports certain democratic attitudes, beliefs, and values. The democratic leader or leaders accept and value the right of all members of the group to participate in decision making that has an effect upon them. Democratic leadership is based on an acceptance of the belief that all members of the group have an essential dignity, and an acceptance of the values of co-operation, discussion, and consensus. This form of leadership has confidence in and commitment to the greater efficiency and practicality of the democratic process over the efficiency and practicality of authoritarian leadership. It is quite possible for democratic leadership to emerge in scattered subgroups of an authoritarian hierarchy, just as it is possible for authoritarian leaders to emerge in more democratic organizations, although it is more normative for each type of leadership to predominate in its own type of environment. As with every social ROLE, the incumbents of the role may believe in the ideals of the role to a greater or lesser extent. Thus in a democratic social environment, a person in a leadership position will, at a minimum, have to espouse democratic ideals and follow certain democratic procedures, whether he really accepts the democratic ideology or not. The extent to which authoritarian leaders emerge and are tolerated within the structure of democratic organizations is probably a good index of the weakness and superficiality of the democratic ideology within the larger social organization. The reverse of this proposition is also probably valid. Certain groups within a society are without doubt more likely to demand democratic leadership than others; thus the modern urban family is more likely to be under (male) democratic leadership than is an industrial work group or a small military unit. See LEADERSHIP, AUTHORITARIAN.

learning. The process of adjusting previous response patterns to newly experienced or perceived environmental changes. Learning involves the modification and reorganization of a person's behavior (perceptions, attitudes, self-image, and so forth) as a result of new experience. Learning may also include relatively permanent changes in behavior due to repetition or practice.

learning, configurational. The immediate and direct perception of complex patterns or configurations. See GESTALT PSYCHOLOGY.

learning, personal-social. See PERSONAL-SOCIAL LEARNING.

learning curve. A graphic presentation of an individual's progress in learning new material after successive periods of practice.

learning plateau. A temporary stage that sometimes occurs in the process of learning (and is indicated by a flat stretch in the LEARNING CURVE) when there is little or no improvement in learning. The learning plateau is preceded and followed by measurable progress.

learning theory. Usually, the theory that learning is based on a direct stimulus-response relationship, although there are other psychological theories of learning. Sociologists generally have not found the type of results obtained by learning theorists to be fruitful in the study of social behavior or society. See CONDITIONED RESPONSE; CONDITIONING.

least squares, principle of. The principle that in fitting a mathematical line (on a graph) to a series of observed values, the line of best fit is the one for which the sum of the squared differences between the actual values and the values of the line is the least. In other words, for each possible line the difference between the line values and the observed values are squared and summed and the line for which the sum of these squared deviations is the lowest is the line of best fit.

legal fiction. An assumption held to be true under the law even though in fact it may be false. An example would be the fiction that a law remains as it has always been while in fact the law has been modified considerably in its interpretation and application.

legend. A folktale, based in part on historical events concerning some person or incident, but with embellishments that tend to glorify and emphasize certain cultural values. Legends dealing with the supernatural are sometimes classified as myths. See MYTH.

legitimate power. See AUTHORITY.

leisure. Temporary withdrawal from routine activity that is based on outwardly imposed social constraints and is not fully satisfying to the individual. Leisure involves the substitution of a preferred activity that provides diversion and pleasure by satisfying strongly internalized values and sentiments in a situation free of the everyday pressures of social obligation. Leisure may be productive and entail social reciprocity and obligations, but it does not carry the social responsibility related to one's routine social role. The playing of games, as a leisure-time activity, involves cooperative social interaction and even competition, but winning or losing is, ideally, separate from one's general status in the community. In the playing of leisure-time games, a person may become fully involved in social interaction without fear of the sanctions and judgments imposed in his normal social roles.

leptokurtic curve. See FREQUENCY DISTRIBUTION CURVE, LEPTOKURTIC.

leviathan. See "BIG ANIMAL" THEORY OF SOCIETY; ORGANICISM.

levirate. A custom in which a widow marries one of her husband's brothers. The levirate may take a number of forms, and the obligations on the brother differ from one culture to another. The ancient Hebrews and Greeks each had a type of levirate.

liberalism. An ideological orientation based on a belief in the importance of the freedom and welfare of the individual, and the possibility of social progress and the improvement of the quality of life through change and innovation in social organization. Liberalism developed in the eighteenth and nineteenth centuries as a movement for individual liberty in many realms of life—political, economic, and religious. Thus it supported the growth of democracy, the spread of the universal franchise, the freedom of expression, the abolition of slavery, and the increase in civil liberties. It opposed the domination of the individual by the government and also by the upper class. In the economic realm, liberalism supported free competition and it also opposed all but the most essential governmental interference in economic activities. However, in the late nineteenth and twentieth centuries liberals came to believe that freeing the individual from autocratic control is not sufficient, but that the government, as the collective representative of society, must take positive steps to ensure each person's welfare. Thus twentieth-century liberalism has supported the growth of such government regulations as minimum-wage laws, pure food and drug acts, antitrust laws, civil rights legislation, and so forth. Thus in attempting to ensure the welfare of the individual, liberalism has come to support certain curtailments on the freedom of the individual. However, liberalism has continued to emphasize the justification of actions in terms of social progress rather than on the basis of an appeal to tradition. In practice, however, liberals, often no less than conservatives, appeal to selected values of both the past and the present, except that they tend to represent different interest groups from those represented by the conservatives. The terms *liberal* and *conservative* help us to distinguish two ideologies, in a general way, though they do not enable us to validate sociologically, on all or most issues, the special claim of either to prefer change or tradition. See CONSERVATISM; LAISSEZ-FAIRE; PROGRESS, SOCIAL.

liberties, civil. See CIVIL LIBERTIES.

libido. In Freudian theory, an undifferentiated life-energy, an instinct or drive toward sexuality (or more general love impulses), found in all individuals.

life, web of. See WEB OF LIFE.

life chances. The probability that an individual in a given status (social class, race, etc.) will attain or fail to attain certain goals or experiences, such as a happy marriage, a certain income, or a certain amount of education.

life cycle. The life of an individual seen in terms of a series of stages, such as infancy, childhood, adolescence, active adulthood, old age, death. Erik H. Erikson uses the concept to emphasize the importance of all stages of life and the totality of a person's life as an integrated psychosocial phenomenon, in contrast to the tendency in much of psychoanalysis and psychiatry to place primary emphasis on infancy and early childhood in the shaping of personality. Erikson also stresses the importance of the meaning attached to the total life cycle by the culture (for example, as part of an unending process of reincarnation or a struggle for material success ending in oblivion) and the cultural definition of the stages of life and the behavior deemed proper for each stage, in the understanding of individual personality and behavior. (E. H. Erikson, *Insight and Responsibility,* W. W. Norton, New York, 1964.)

life expectancy. The average number of years that persons in a given population born in a particular period of time can, on the average, be expected to live. Mortality rates for specific age groups are used to determine life expectancy for any group or category of people. See DEATH RATE, SPECIFIC.

life-history method. A technique of investigation in which the subject gives a full and detailed personal account of his life experiences, including his significant feelings, emotions, observations, and a general analysis of himself. The document may be written by the subject, or recorded by the investigator (or both) for later analysis.

life organization. The structure of an individual's attitudes and values, derived from his social experience and revealed and expressed in his self-conception, his social status, and his role behavior. The term was used by W. I. Thomas and Florian Znaniecki. (W. I. Thomas and F. Znaniecki, *The Polish Peasant in Europe and America,* University of Chicago Press, Chicago, 1918.)

life span. The biological age limit of man, that is, the life expectancy of the average human being if he does not die as a result of accident, injury, disease, or disaster. The life span of man is not an exact figure. It is usually considered to be approximately 100 years.

life table. A statistical table that presents the death rate and life expectancy of each of a series of age-sex categories of a particular population at a given time or over a period of time. The population may be divided into other categories, such as race, in which case the death rate and life expectancy of each age-sex-race category would be given. From a life table it is possible to calculate the probability of a person in a specified category (for example a male or a white male) living from any given age to any other given age. A life table may be either a current life table or a generation life table. See DEATH RATE, AGE-SEX SPECIFIC; LIFE TABLE, CURRENT; LIFE TABLE, GENERATION.

life table, current. A hypothetical LIFE TABLE for a population or a segment of a population constructed on the basis of the current age-sex specific death rates of all age-sex groups in the population. The current life table shows what the mortality and life expectancy of given population would be if present age-sex specific death rates were to remain unchanged. If the age-sex death rates used in constructing the table do remain stable, the current life table would then be the same as the generation life table. Under changing mortality conditions, they would, of course, differ. See DEATH RATE, AGE-SEX SPECIFIC; LIFE TABLE, GENERATION.

life table, generation. A LIFE TABLE showing the history of the actual mortality of the members of one cohort, or persons born in a given year, over the years from the death of the first to the last member. The generation life table is not used very often. See LIFE TABLE, CURRENT.

Likert scale. A summated attitude scale consisting of a series of items (attitude statements) each of which is rated by the respondent to indicate his degree of agreement or disagreement. Typically each statement has five possible responses: strongly agree, agree, uncertain, disagree, strongly disagree. The responses are assigned weights, for example, strongly agree, 1, agree, 2, uncertain, 3, etc. A total score for each respondent is obtained by summing his scores on all the individual items. ITEM ANALYSIS may then be used to compare scores on individual items with total scores, or FACTOR ANALYSIS to analyze interrelationships among the items. Those items that are most consistent with each other are included in the final scale. The scale was developed by Rensis Likert. See SCALE; SCALE, ATTITUDE; SUMMATED SCALE.

limited possibilities, principle of. The principle, proposed by Alexander A. Goldenweiser, that the fewer the possibilities of variation in the final form of a given culture trait, the greater is the probability that similarities in the form of the trait in separated cultures are the result of parallel development rather than of cultural diffusion. The principle states that "wherever a wider range of variability in origins and developments co-exists with a limitation of end results, there will be reduction in variability, decrease in dissimilarity, and increase in similarity or convergence." Goldenweiser illustrated this principle with the example of oars. Oars might originate in a variety of ways, and at first be made of many different materials, and have various shapes, but eventually they have to develop "certain relatively fixed features determined by conditions of effective use." (A. A. Goldenweiser, *History, Psychology, and Culture*, Knopf, New York, 1933.) See CULTURAL POSSIBILITIES, PRINCIPLE OF; DIFFUSIONISM; PARALLELISM.

limits, principle of. The principle that a particular relationship found between two variables may occur only within certain limits. Beyond those limits there may be no relationship between the variables or even a re-verse relationship. This principle was related to social variables and social change by Pitirim A. Sorokin: "there is no logical reason whatever to assume that the observance or discovery of causal relationships for certain values of the phenomena warrants a conclusion that the same connection will necessarily exist whatever values the variable assume. . . . We know that within certain limits improved nutrition tends to accelerate growth and increase stature, but beyond a certain point no additional improve-ment, quantitative or qualitative, in food will be followed by a further in-crease in stature. Poverty, below the physiological minimum, has an ad-verse effect on fertility, but above this line comparative poverty does not necessarily have the same result. At some point, compared with a state of relative comfort, it may serve as a stimulus or be associated with increased fertility. Similar statements may be made regarding the relations between poverty and criminality, urbanization and mental disease, marriage and suicide. . . . there is scarcely any causal tie between societal variables which holds for all values given to them." (P. A. Sorokin, *Publications of the American Sociological Society*, August 1932.)

line caption. See ROW CAPTION.

line chart. See LINE GRAPH.

line graph. A GRAPH in which values are arranged along a horizontal axis and a vertical axis, points are plotted with reference to the values on the two axes, and a line is drawn to connect the points. A line graph may show the relationship between two quantitative variables, which are ar-ranged along the two axes in order of increasing magnitude. Frequently a line graph shows changes in one variable over time, with values of the variable along the perpendicular axis and time sequences along the hori-zontal axis. When a FREQUENCY DISTRIBUTION is presented in the form of a line graph it is known as a FREQUENCY DISTRIBUTION CURVE or a frequency polygon.

The line graph is sometimes referred to as a curve line graph, a curve graph, a line chart, a curve chart, or a coordinate chart. It is the most commonly used type of graph. See COORDINATE AXES.

line graph, broken-. A type of LINE GRAPH in which points are connected by a series of straight lines instead of one smooth, curved line.

line of regression. See REGRESSION LINE.

line official. See MANAGEMENT, MIDDLE.

line organization. See ORGANIZATION, LINE.

lineage. A consanguineous unilateral descent group whose members trace themselves from a known common ancestor. A lineage is based on more precise and specific genealogy than a CLAN, of which it may be a subgroup. A lineage may be either patrilineal or matrilineal. See UNILATERAL OR UNILINEAL DESCENT.

linear correlation. See CORRELATION, LINEAR.

linear regression. See REGRESSION, LINEAR.

linear trend. See TREND, LINEAR.

linguistics. The comparative study of the nature and structure of languages. Linguistics includes the study of phonetics, vocabulary, grammar, sentence and word formation, and the origins and interrelationships of languages. It includes the classification of languages into major families (for example, Indo-European) and subgroupings, and the analysis of the history and distribution of these language groups, as well as the analysis of specific contemporary languages. Although linguists are found in a number of fields, linguistics is usually classified as a branch of anthropology. Recently there has been considerable interest among linguists and other social scientists in the interrelationships between language and sociocultural forms.

linguistics, sociological. See SOCIOLINGUISTICS.

lions. See INSTINCT FOR COMBINATIONS and INSTINCT FOR GROUP PERSISTENCES.

literature, sociology of. See SOCIOLOGY OF LITERATURE.

loaded question. A question asked of a respondent in such a way as to suggest a biased or desired answer.

local. A person who is primarily involved and identified with his local organization or community, in which he strives to gain office, leadership, and prestige. He does not seek recognition and honor in the larger profession, and his leadership contributions are in the local community rather than the national or international professional community. Robert

K. Merton differentiates between local community leaders and the cosmopolitans, both of these classifications being considered as generalized or ideal types. (R. K. Merton, *Social Theory and Social Structure*, Free Press, Glencoe, Ill., 1957.) See COSMOPOLITAN; IDEAL TYPE.

locality group. See GROUP, TERRITORIAL.

locational hypotheses. A series of ecological hypotheses developed by James A. Quinn. See INTENSIVENESS OF UTILIZATION, HYPOTHESIS OF; MEDIAN LOCATION, HYPOTHESIS OF; MINIMUM COST, HYPOTHESIS OF. (J. A. Quinn, *Human Ecology*, Prentice-Hall, Englewood Cliffs, N.J., 1950.)

logic. The discipline dealing with the methods and criteria of correct reasoning.

logic of the sentiments. Reasoning of the sort that characterizes pseudological explanations used to justify and rationalize behavior or beliefs based on sentiments or values. The term was used by Vilfredo Pareto in discussing the fact that people often do not apply the principles of strict logic to situations in which objective logical analysis would be disturbing to their accustomed point of view, but rather develop forms of thinking that tend to overlook contradictions and support their values. (V. Pareto, *The Mind and Society*, tr. by A. Bongiorno and A. Livingston, Harcourt, Brace, New York, 1935.)

logic-tight compartment. See COMPARTMENTALIZATION.

logical empiricism. See POSITIVISM, LOGICAL.

logical positivism. See POSITIVISM, LOGICAL.

logistic surges, law of. As stated by Hornell Hart, "progress with respect to specific purposes, as expressed in individual inventions and in the growth of specific social organizations and culture complexes, has tended to take place in the form of surges, progressing slowly at first, then speeding up, and finally slowing down to a stop or a collapse. In scores of instances, the indexes of these surges can be fitted mathematically with logistic curves." (H. Hart in *Symposium on Sociological Theory*, edited by L. Gross, Row, Peterson, Evanston, Ill., 1959.)

Lombrosian theory. A theory in criminology, set forth by Cesare Lombroso in the late nineteenth century, holding that criminal behavior is the result of biological rather than social, psychological, or environmental factors. Lombroso regarded criminals as being essentially physiologically degenerate and animalistic, and believed that criminal types could be detected through such measures as head shape. This theory has no standing in modern research on criminal behavior. (C. Lombroso, *Crime, Its Causes and Remedies*, Little, Brown, Boston, 1911.)

longevity, total immediate ancestral. A measure developed by Raymond Pearl to predict longevity of an individual. The figure is arrived at by totaling the ages at death of an individual's parents and four grandparents. If any of these persons are still living either their present ages or their expected ages at death (derived from a LIFE TABLE) are used.

longitudinal study. A study of individuals over a period of time or at successive stages. The longitudinal method allows the researcher to study trends or the effect of a stimulus, training, event, or experience with "before" and "after" observations.

looking-glass self. A person's perception of himself as determined by the way he imagines he appears to others. It is the conception of self that is formed as a consequence of the attitudes other people have toward him. This self idea carries with it a certain kind of self feeling, such as pride or mortification. The term was introduced by Charles H. Cooley, who also called it the reflected self. (C. H. Cooley, *Human Nature and the Social Order,* Scribner, New York, 1902.)

Lorenz curve. A graph showing the relationship between the percentages of the cumulated values of a variable and the percentages of the cumulated frequencies. The percentages of the cumulated values of the variable are shown on the vertical axis, and the percentages of the cumulated number of cases on the horizontal axis. For example, if the variable being presented were income, it would be arranged along the vertical axis in cumulative fashion as: 10% of the total income received by all the cases studied, 20% of the total income, 30%, etc. The frequencies would be arranged along the horizontal axis also in cumulative fashion as: 10% of the total number of cases, 20% of the total number of cases, 30%, etc. The resulting curve would show what percent of the cases studied receive what percent of the income. See OGIVE.

love. A strong emotional identification with another that is the basis of a gratifying or potentially gratifying social relationship. The identity of self with another involves a merging of a person's self with devotion to another's welfare. The lover identifies himself with the self of the loved one. Love is a dynamic social-psychological process that has many phases. As a social relationship, love takes many forms, including the husband-wife relationship, parent-child relationship, and sibling relationship.

love, conjugal. Love between husband and wife based upon a mutually satisfactory performance of reciprocal marital role obligations as defined by the society. Conjugal love may take on different forms in different societies. In middle-class American society, conjugal love would involve some elements of the romantic pattern which might be missing in other cultures where marriages are arranged and primarily held together by extended kinship ties. See LOVE, ROMANTIC.

love, romantic. Love between man and woman based on personal preference and intense social-psychological identification and involvement. The intensity of the emotional attachment is in part a function of the small-family system, high social mobility and social change, the psychological and social isolation of the unmarried, and the absence of a stable social and moral universe.

lower class. A rough designation of social-class status determined in general by the low income and educational levels of its members as well as by how they view themselves and how others view them in terms of the class system of the society. The lower class is sometimes divided into two parts: the lower-lower class and the upper-lower class. See LOWER CLASS, LOWER-; LOWER CLASS, UPPER-; SOCIAL CLASS and the entries listed with it.

lower class, lower-. In the Yankee City studies of W. Lloyd Warner and Paul S. Lunt, the class of people who are semiskilled and unskilled workers (when they can get work), tend to be on relief, live in the worst sections of town, and are considered to be immoral by the other social classes. The lower-lower class category is often reserved for the people of a community who are the poorest and most alienated from middle-class values. (W. L. Warner and P. S. Lunt, *The Social Life of a Modern Community*, Yankee City Series, Vol. I, Yale University Press, New Haven, 1941.) See LOWER CLASS, UPPER-; MIDDLE CLASS, LOWER-; MIDDLE CLASS, UPPER-; UPPER CLASS, LOWER-; UPPER CLASS, UPPER-; SOCIAL CLASS.

lower class, upper-. In the Yankee City studies of W. Lloyd Warner and Paul S. Lunt, the class of "respectable" people who live in the less desirable sections of town, and who are factory operatives and service workers. The term usually refers to people who, while poor, have certain attitudes of the middle class, such as cleanliness, and a sense of responsibility toward their work. They are not regarded as the lowest people on the social ladder, as judged by middle-class standards, although they are relatively poor and uneducated. Clearly the term is not meant to be precise, and is used only in a general way to distinguish roughly between two general types of lower status categories in a community. (W. L. Warner and P. S. Lunt, *The Social Life of a Modern Community*, Yankee City Series, Vol. I, Yale University Press, New Haven, 1941.) See LOWER CLASS, LOWER-; MIDDLE CLASS, LOWER-; MIDDLE CLASS, UPPER-; UPPER CLASS, LOWER-; UPPER CLASS, UPPER-; SOCIAL CLASS.

lower-middle class. See MIDDLE CLASS, LOWER-.

lower-upper class. See UPPER CLASS, LOWER-.

M

macro-functionalism. A sociological theoretical orientation stressing the functional analysis of large-scale social systems. This approach assumes the functional unity of societies and proposes that analysis should start with a society (or civilization) and extend downward to smaller subsections and groups in society. The term was introduced by Don Martindale, who includes in this category such writers as Vilfredo Pareto, Florian Znaniecki, Talcott Parsons, and Robert K. Merton. (D. Martindale, *The Nature and Types of Sociological Theory*, Houghton Mifflin, Boston, 1960.) See FUNCTIONALISM; MICRO-FUNCTIONALISM; SOCIAL SYSTEM.

macro-sociology. The study of large-scale social systems and patterns of interrelationships within and between these systems, including, for example, national and international forms of social organization. See MICROSOCIOLOGY.

magic. Techniques for manipulating supernatural or natural forces by the application of certain ritual performances that are believed to compel or assure desired results. In modern society magic is not part of an organized system of beliefs and roles. However, in other societies magic has been or is more organized and involves a specialized status of magician. The magician in such societies plays a role not always distinct from that of a religious and medical specialist. Where religion and science fail to satisfy human desires to solve pressing problems, magic probably tends to act as a substitute adjustment. Crude and intellectually unsophisticated applications of religious and scientific philosophies often are considered to become or border on magical practices. Not all ritual behavior is magic, however, even though it may be performed automatically and the primary effect is emotional satisfaction. Magical rituals may symbolically represent, as religious behavior does, a system of cherished values and beliefs.

magic, black. Magical practices that are harmful in intent, such as practices aimed at destroying or injuring others. See MAGIC, WHITE.

magic, contagious. A type of sympathetic MAGIC based on the assumption that once objects (or forms of behavior) have been associated or in contact with each other a connection will continue to exist thereafter. Thus it is believed that a magical practice performed on an object will have an effect on another object with which it was formerly associated, or on its previous owner. For example, magic might be performed on a lock of hair in order to harm the person to whom it previously belonged. See MAGIC, IMITATIVE; MAGIC, SYMPATHETIC.

magic, homeopathic. See MAGIC, IMITATIVE.

magic, imitative. A type of sympathetic MAGIC based on the assumption that a magical practice symbolically enacting a desired effect can produce that effect. Thus it is believed that by enacting a rain storm, a person can cause it to rain, or by putting an evil spell on a doll made to look like a certain person, one can harm the person himself. Basically, imitative magic assumes magical transference from one object or occurrence to another because of their similarity. Imitative magic is also referred to as homeopathic magic. See MAGIC, CONTAGIOUS; MAGIC, SYMPATHETIC.

magic, repetitive. MAGIC based on the assumption that if events happen simultaneously or in sequence, then they will continue to follow the same pattern. Belief in omens is based on repetitive magic.

magic, sympathetic. MAGIC based on the belief that a magical practice performed on one object (or in one situation) can have an effect upon another object (or situation), either because the two objects were once associated with each other or because they are similar. Sympathetic magic includes contagious magic and imitative magic. See MAGIC, CONTAGIOUS; MAGIC, IMITATIVE.

magic, white. MAGIC used to do good rather than harm. Magic that helps to protect people from evil forces, bad luck, or an enemy who is outside the group is considered white magic. See MAGIC, BLACK.

maladjustment. A condition or process involving the inability or unwillingness of an individual or group to conform to prevailing psychological, social, or cultural standards—either their own or those of an external system. Maladjustment of an individual, group, or institution is not necessarily an absolute condition. Maladjustment in one aspect of one's behavior or life may be counterbalanced by compensations that are a direct result of the maladjustive condition. While maladjustment may result in conflict or conditions that are destructive of cherished feelings and values, it must also be recognized that maladjustment is as constant a personal and social phenomenon as is ADJUSTMENT. Social and psychological life is a process of continual change. Adjustment is often a temporary state of stability following a previous period of maladjustment or the threat of maladjustment.

Malthusian theory. A theory of population growth, formulated by Thomas R. Malthus in the late eighteenth century, holding that population tends to grow at a faster rate than the food supply. Malthus maintained that population tends to increase in a geometric ratio, whereas the food supply increases in an arithmetic ratio. He saw famine and disease as the two main checks on population growth. However, he argued, these checks would not be sufficient to permit a rise in the standard of living, and therefore the mass of the world's population would necessarily exist at the edge of subsistence. (T. R. Malthus, *An Essay on the Principles of Population*, Macmillan, London, 1926.) In time, Malthusian theory came to be regarded as out of date and unduly pessimistic. It was felt that population growth could be limited through birth control and the food supply increased more rapidly, through technological and scientific developments in agriculture, than Malthus could have imagined. In recent years, however, there has been a renewed interest in Malthus and a development of neo-Malthusianism, as world population has grown at an unprecedented rate, a rate with which increasing food production has been unable to keep pace.

man, economic. See ECONOMIC MAN.

man, marginal. See MARGINAL MAN.

man, organization. See ORGANIZATION MAN.

man-land ratio. See DENSITY, POPULATION.

mana. An impersonal, supernatural power or influence. This force may be attributed to individuals, objects, or actions. If a charm or ritual is felt to have the mysterious quality of mana, it is usually thought to bring good luck. Mana is a Melanesian term. Other terms designating the same power include *orenda, wakan,* and *manitou.* See ANIMATISM.

management. The process of planning, organizing, coordinating, and directing the productive process in an economic enterprise. The term is also applied to those persons, organized in a hierarchy, who carry out the management process, that is, who perform these tasks or functions. The management hierarchy of a formal organization "derives its authority and its responsibilities squarely from function, that is, from its status relationship to the organization, and not from anything it possesses such as property, birth, inherited magical power, or military force. Nor does it derive its position from the authority of superior knowledge or through socially accepted objective tests of achievement or accomplishment; in other words, it is not based on the standing of a profession. Its position, its power, and its responsibilities rest solely on indispensable function. This is equally true incidentally in a free-enterprise society such as ours as in a society of democratic socialism or in a totalitarian state." (P. F. Drucker, *American Journal of Sociology,* January 1953.)

management, middle. The intermediate level of management, excluding the top executives on the one hand and the first-line supervisors on the other hand, sometimes referred to as junior executives, line officials, or line officers.

manager, professional. See PROFESSIONAL MANAGER.

manic-depressive psychosis. A PSYCHOSIS characterized by alternation between extreme emotional states of elation (mania) and depression. Either phase may vary in severity. In the manic phase there may be extreme excitement, hyperactivity, delirium, or occasionally violence. The depressive phase may involve sadness and feelings of inferiority, severe depression, suicidal tendencies, or occasionally stupor. Some patients alternate only between manic and normal states or only between depressive and normal states. Manic-depressive psychosis has been shown to vary by such social characteristics as sex and ethnic group.

manifest consequence. See FUNCTION, MANIFEST.

manifest function. See FUNCTION, MANIFEST.

manifest interests. Self-interests that are common to members of a group, profession, social class, etc., and that are recognized as such and openly sought. Manifest interests constitute collective objectives that are actively pursued, sometimes through formal organizations. See INTEREST; INTEREST GROUP; ORGANIZATION, FORMAL.

manifest social identity. See LATENT SOCIAL IDENTITY.

manipulation. A type of exercise of POWER in which the power-holder "influences the behavior of others without making explicit the behavior which he thereby wants them to perform. Manipulation may be exercised by utilizing symbols or performing acts. Propaganda is a major form of manipulation by symbols." Although a legitimate power-holder may exercise manipulation, manipulation is not a form of legitimate power, "since in the case of manipulation there is no recognition by the subordinated individual that an act of power has been effected." (H. Goldhamer and E. A. Shils, *American Journal of Sociology,* September 1939.) See AUTHORITY; FORCE.

manitou. See MANA.

Mann-Whitney U test. A nonparametric statistical test based on rank order. When data from two samples are in the form of ranks, or relative position in terms of magnitude, this test may be used to determine whether one sample has significantly higher ranks than the other sample. On this basis the test indicates whether the two samples probably are drawn from different populations or from the same population with the observed differences due merely to chance. The Mann-Whitney U test is generally regarded as one of the most powerful nonparametric tests available for determining differences in central tendency in a series of data. It provides a nonparametric alternative for the parametric t TEST. See CENTRAL TENDENCY, MEASURE OF; NONPARAMETRIC STATISTICS; PROBABILITY; RANK, STATISTICAL; SIGNIFICANCE, STATISTICAL.

Mann-Whitney U test, Whitney extension. An extension of the MANN-WHITNEY U TEST for use with three samples instead of two. The Whitney extension tests the rank order of central tendency of the three samples. See CENTRAL TENDENCY, MEASURE OF.

maps. See BASE MAP; CENTROGRAM; CHOROPLETH MAP; CROSS-HATCHED MAP; ISOMETRIC MAP; SPOT MAP.

marasmus. A condition in which there is a progressive physiological and emotional decline in an infant, sometimes resulting in death or in permanent physical, mental, or emotional damage. This "wasting away" may be due to physiological or social causes. It can result from malnutrition or from depriving the infant of social interaction or mothering (stimulation by regular and frequent handling). Without the social stimulation of human interaction, infants may not only fail to mature emotionally and physically, but actually regress seriously. See DEPRESSION, ANACLITIC; HOSPITALISM.

marginal. In a STATISTICAL TABLE, the sum of all the entries in a COLUMN or ROW. In a CROSS-TABULATION of two variables, each marginal would give the total number of cases in one category or class interval of one of the variables without regard to their distribution in the categories or class intervals of the other variable. For example, if the variables sex and nationality were being cross-tabulated, the marginals would give the number of men, the number of women, and the number of each nationality without regard to sex (for example, the number of Americans, the number of Canadians, and the number of Mexicans) in the sample. Marginals are sometimes referred to as marginal totals.

marginal area. Territory at the periphery of a CULTURE AREA where two or more cultures meet, and where culture traits of the neighboring cultures are to be found. Marginal areas are the farthest areas one can possibly include within a particular culture area. See CULTURE TRAIT.

marginal group. A culture group that has relinquished some of its traditions and separate identity and partially accepted the values and ways of life of a culture it is in the process of adopting.

marginal man. A person in a dilemma, or state of mental conflict, by reason of his participation in two different, distinct cultural groups. He is not fully loyal and committed to the values and standards of either, nor is he fully acceptable to either of the groups with which he identifies. Moreover, the two groups may have certain conflicting values or norms, both of which the individual accepts to some degree. The term was introduced by Robert E. Park (*The American Journal of Society,* May 1928).

marital exchange, generalized. A type of preferential marriage in which three or more groups provide each other with marriage partners in a circular pattern. For example, if three groups were involved in the circle, the men in the first group would marry women from the second group; the men in the second group would marry women from the third group; and the men in the third group would marry women from the first group. Sometimes the pattern is more complicated, since a group may belong to several marriage circles at the same time. The groups involved in such systems of marital exchange may be kin groups, such as families, territorial groups, such as villages, or other social groups. See MARITAL EXCHANGE, RESTRICTED; MARRIAGE, PREFERENTIAL.

marital exchange, restricted. A type of preferential marriage in which two groups exchange marriage partners. The men of one group are required to marry women from the second group, while the men of the second group are required to marry women from the first group. The groups involved in such a relationship are often kin groups larger than families. The system is found in various parts of the world, but is particularly widespread among the aboriginal inhabitants of Australia. See MARITAL EXCHANGE, GENERALIZED; MARRIAGE, PREFERENTIAL.

market system. The formalized system of exchange of goods and services necessitated by the specialization of economic functions characteristic of complex societies and regulated by institutionalized social norms. While a market system is found in all societies in which economic functions are specialized, the specific nature of the system differs according to the predominant form of economic organization, such as capitalist, socialist, and so forth.

marketing orientation. A type of personality orientation, described by Erich Fromm, characterized by a dominant need to be as attractive as possible to others in order to win acceptance. The person with a marketing orientation quickly shifts his behavior and attitudes according to the requirements of the "market." (E. Fromm, *Man for Himself,* Farrar and Rinehart, New York, 1947.) See OTHER-DIRECTED SOCIETY.

Markov chain. See STOCHASTIC PROCESS.

marriage. An institution or complex of social norms that sanctions the relationship of a man and woman and binds them in a system of mutual obligations and rights essential to the functioning of family life. The marriage ceremony, when performed publicly or by some representative of the community, is a ritual that announces or signifies the recognition by both the husband and wife of their new status in the community, and also signifies the social approval and support of the new status being contracted. See NORM, SOCIAL.

marriage, arranged. The pairing of marriage partners by persons other than the mates-to-be. In arranged marriages the parents (or other members of the family) play an important role in selecting a mate for their offspring. Arranged marriages may completely exclude the participation of the persons to be married in the choice of spouses, or they may be consulted, with varying degrees of consideration being given to their opinions by parents and family.

marriage, beena. A form of marriage in which the husband lives with his wife's clan or family, usually with the children and property being identified with the wife's family.

marriage, companionate. A type of trial marital arrangement in which the couple agrees not to have children until they are certain their marriage is going to be successful. If the marital relationship does not prove to be harmonious, the marriage is dissolved by mutual consent. When children result from the marriage the union is considered binding. This form of marriage has been proposed in the past as a type that might be legalized; the main proponent of this idea was Judge Ben B. Lindsey.

marriage, companionship. See FAMILY, COMPANIONSHIP.

marriage, consensual. Marriage by common consent, rather than by religious, legal, or written agreement. Wherever such unions are a common form of marriage there is usually informal community recognition of the union, so that traditional elements of social control and permanence are involved.

marriage, cross-cousin. A type of marriage, prescribed or preferred in certain societies, in which there is a union between the children of a brother and a sister; in other words, marriage between cousins related to each other through parents who are siblings of the opposite sex.

marriage, group. See CENOGAMY; POLYGAMY.

marriage, interfaith. See INTERMARRIAGE.

marriage, matrilateral cross-cousin. A type of cross-cousin marriage in which the preferred form of marriage is between a sister's son and a brother's daughter; in other words, marriage in which the husband's mother is the sister of his wife's father. See MARRIAGE, CROSS-COUSIN.

marriage, mixed. See INTERMARRIAGE.

marriage, monogamous. See MONOGAMY.

marriage, morganatic. A form of marriage contract between a person of high social rank and a person of low social rank under which the children are legitimate but neither the children nor the low-status parent inherits or assumes the wealth or titles of the high-status parent.

marriage, polyandrous. See POLYANDRY.

marriage, polygamous. See POLYGAMY.

marriage, polygynous. See POLYGYNY.

marriage, preferential. A rule or custom that encourages or prescribes marriage between people of some specifically defined status, such as in the LEVIRATE, SORORATE, or cross-cousin marriage. See MARITAL EXCHANGE, GENERALIZED; MARITAL EXCHANGE, RESTRICTED; MARRIAGE, CROSS-COUSIN.

marriage, selection in. See NEEDS IN MATE-SELECTION, THEORY OF COMPLEMENTARY.

marriage, sequential. See POLYGAMY, SERIAL.

marriage rate. The number of marriages per 1,000 population for a one-year period.

Marxian theory of stratification. See STRATIFICATION, MARXIAN THEORY OF.

Marxism. See DIALECTICAL MATERIALISM.

mass. A large number of people constituting the audience or consumers of some standardized communication, such as one of the MASS MEDIA. A mass is a very diverse population that has no social organization and yet responds to common cultural stimuli in a relatively uniform manner. See MASS BEHAVIOR.

mass behavior. A form of COLLECTIVE BEHAVIOR based on impersonal and indirect communication among members of a large, heterogeneous, and nontraditional population. MASS COMMUNICATION plays a crucial role in the development of mass behavior by providing specific communication among individuals who have no personal contact with each other and who may have very little in common. Mass behavior includes a wide range of behavior, beliefs, and interests, from new political movements to fads and fashions in popular dances, songs, and styles of dress. See CRAZE; CROWD; FAD; FASHION; MASS; PUBLIC.

mass communication. Any message or cultural stimulus, such as a mass medium, that influences large and heterogeneous populations. See MASS MEDIA.

mass culture. Elements of culture that develop in a large, heterogeneous society as a result of common exposure to and experience of the mass media, such as popular songs and dances. The emergence of mass culture is a part of the process of the development of common unifying cultural values and attitudes in the new and vast populations of modern national social units. Mass culture is inherent in a complex, industrial society and objections that it results in the "standardization" of culture and represents the "lowest common denominator" of cultural values, although valid complaints, ignore the enriching effects of mass media on many levels of the society.

mass media. Any means or instrument of communication reaching large numbers of people, such as books, periodicals, radio, television, and motion pictures.

mass movement. Any large-scale, spontaneous behavior on the part of large numbers of people toward some similar goal, without over-all planning or coordination. Examples of this phenomenon include mass migrations and religious or political upheavals that have spontaneous mass support.

mass society. Large, modern political-social units, such as nations, that have developed with the rise of industrialization and the breakdown of local folk societies and parochial and regional identities, and are characterized by mass behavior and mass culture. The rise of a sense of unity and identity with the larger social unit is related to the development of modern transportation and MASS COMMUNICATION. Often the term mass society is used to emphasize such elements in modern society as one-way communication from the mass media to the individual, ANONYMITY, loneliness, impersonal SECONDARY RELATIONS among people, high MOBILITY, conformity, bureaucratization, loss of (folk) community ties, stereotyped values, extreme specialization, etc. While modern society involves special problems, as does every form of society, concentration on its disadvantages can distort its character. A large-scale society such as the United States is honeycombed with a great variety of primary group structures from the family to the local units of national organizations (e.g., professional, fraternal, and youth organizations). Such informal, intimate, and enduring group structures proliferate and help to organize a highly specialized society's adjustment from provincial rural life to large-scale cosmopolitan social structures. It should be added, however, that it is quite possible that many of the negative characteristics of mass society are not inherent in the nature of a developing modern, complex society, but are due to certain unwitting as well as deliberate economic, political, and social policies. Perhaps as the evolution of this new form of society becomes better established and understood, we shall not refer to mass society, but shall find some other, more accurate term to refer to our modern, complex society. See BUREAUCRACY; GEMEINSCHAFT; GESELLSCHAFT; GROUP, PRIMARY; URBAN SOCIETY.

matching. A form of EXPERIMENTAL CONTROL in which the subjects selected for the EXPERIMENTAL GROUP are similar to the subjects selected for the CONTROL GROUP in regard to those variables that the experimenter considers relevant to his study. Matching may be based on either FREQUENCY DISTRIBUTION or pairing. In matching by frequency distribution, the experimental group and the control group have the same proportions of subjects with given characteristics, for example, the same proportion of men and women, whites and Negroes, married, single, and divorced, etc. However, the subjects in the two groups do not necessarily have the same combinations of these characteristics. For example, one group may have more married men, and the other group more married women. In paired or precision matching, individual subjects are matched in regard to the relevant variables—for example, two single white men would be matched. One member of each pair is then (usually randomly) placed in each group. Paired matching is obviously more precise than matching by frequency distribution, but its disadvantage is that many more potential subjects must be rejected. See RANDOMIZATION.

materialism, dialectical. See DIALECTICAL MATERIALISM.

mate-selection, theory of complementary needs in. See NEEDS IN MATE-SELECTION, THEORY OF COMPLEMENTARY.

mathematical model. See MODEL, MATHEMATICAL.

mathematical value. See VALUE, MATHEMATICAL.

mating, assortative. See HOMOGAMY.

mating, preferential. See MARRIAGE, PREFERENTIAL.

matriarchy. See FAMILY, MATRIARCHAL.

matrilineal descent. Descent (and sometimes inheritance) traced unilaterally through the mother and the female line.

matrilocal residence. The custom found in some societies for a married couple to reside in the wife's parental household or community.

matri-patrilocal residence. A type of patrilocal residence, distinguished by George P. Murdock, in which the bride and groom first live with the bride's family, with the groom contributing his services to her family for a specified period of time. Later, the couple moves and stays permanently at the groom's parental home or community.

matripotestal. Pertaining to the authority of the mother or maternal grandmother within the household.

matrix. In statistics, the tabular arrangement of data in rows and columns. This arrangement facilitates the comprehension of relationships among variables being studied. See COLUMN; CORRELATION MATRIX; ROW; STATISTICAL TABLE.

maturation. 1. The growth and development of an individual physically, emotionally, intellectually, and socially, through physiological development, LEARNING, and SOCIALIZATION.

2. In psychology, sometimes restricted to the unfolding of innate or biological processes, not involving learning or socialization.

maturation hypothesis. The HYPOTHESIS that many behavior patterns developed from infancy to adolescence can be better explained as a result of the process of physical maturation than as a result of experience, LEARNING, and SOCIALIZATION. This hypothesis is generally not accepted by sociologists and social psychologists, who emphasize the inevitable and necessary influence of social and cultural factors in the maturation of an individual.

maturity, emotional. See EMOTIONAL MATURITY.

mayor-council plan of city government. A form of municipal government in which an elected city council governs a city together with an elected mayor. This form of city government is an attempt to separate the executive and legislative functions in a system of checks and balances. See COMMISSION PLAN OF CITY GOVERNMENT; COUNCIL-MANAGER PLAN OF CITY GOVERNMENT.

McNemar test. A nonparametric statistical test that may be used to determine whether changes in a variable for a given set of individuals are statistically significant or probably due merely to chance. The McNemar test is particularly suitable for use with before-after experiments, in which the same subjects are studied before and after an experimental treatment and the investigator wishes to determine whether the observed changes in the subjects which follow the experimental treatment are statistically significant. For the McNemar test the data need only be in categories (that is, in a NOMINAL SCALE). The variable studied may be a qualitative variable, since no assumption of a continuous variable is needed. See EXPERIMENT, BEFORE-AFTER; NONPARAMETRIC STATISTICS; PROBABILITY; SIGNIFICANCE, STATISTICAL; VARIABLE, QUALITATIVE.

"me." A hypothetical phase or aspect of the total SELF. The term was introduced by George H. Mead, who suggested that the "I" and the "me" together constitute the self or personality, with the "me" representing the internalized social attitudes that a person assumes in a social situation. The "me" phase of the self organization is the one that creates self-consciousness and integrates the person into the social community, and also reflects the attitudes of the community. (G. H. Mead, *Mind, Self and Society*, University of Chicago Press, Chicago, 1934.) See GENERALIZED OTHER; INTERNALIZATION.

mean, arithmetic. The sum of a set of mathematical values divided by the number of values. The arithmetic mean is the most commonly used measure of central tendency of a series of data. In fact, the word "mean" is often used alone to refer to the arithmetic mean, and, although correctly the arithmetic mean is only one type of average, the term average is sometimes used as if it were synonymous with arithmetic mean. See CENTRAL TENDENCY, MEASURE OF; MEAN, GEOMETRIC; MEAN, HARMONIC; MEAN, QUADRATIC; MEDIAN; MODE.

mean, geometric. A measure of the central tendency of a set of mathematical values, computed by multiplying the (N) values and then taking the Nth root of their product. In other words, if there are two values, the geometric mean is the square root of their product; if there are three values, it is the cube root; four values, the fourth root; etc. The geometric mean is most often used in studying average rates of change. It is used less often than the arithmetic mean. See CENTRAL TENDENCY, MEASURE OF; MEAN, ARITHMETIC; MEAN, HARMONIC; MEAN, QUADRATIC; MEDIAN; MODE.

mean, harmonic. An infrequently used measure of central tendency of a series of data that is the reciprocal (1 divided by a quantity) of the arithmetic mean of the reciprocals of a set of values. To compute the harmonic mean, first each value is divided into 1 in order to obtain the reciprocals of the values. These reciprocals are then summed and the sum is divided by the number of reciprocals to obtain their arithmetic mean. The resulting arithmetic mean is divided into 1 to obtain its reciprocal, which is the harmonic mean. The harmonic mean is used primarily in averaging rates. See CENTRAL TENDENCY, MEASURE OF; MEAN, ARITHMETIC; MEAN, GEOMETRIC; MEAN, QUADRATIC; MEDIAN; MODE; RATE.

mean, quadratic. A measure of central tendency of a series of data that is the square root of the arithmetic mean of the squares of a set of values. To compute the quadratic mean of a set of values, first each value is squared. These squares are summed and divided by the number of values to obtain their arithmetic mean. The square root of this arithmetic mean is the quadratic mean. The quadratic mean is used primarily in computing STANDARD DEVIATION. See CENTRAL TENDENCY, MEASURE OF; MEAN, ARITHMETIC; MEAN, GEOMETRIC; MEAN, HARMONIC; MEDIAN; MODE.

mean deviation. A measure of the dispersion of a set of values from a measure of their central tendency. The mean deviation is the arithmetic mean of the deviations from any measure of central tendency (frequently the arithmetic mean, but sometimes the MEDIAN, or occasionally the MODE). It is computed by adding the deviations of a set of values from a measure of central tendency (ignoring their positive or negative signs) and dividing the sum by the number of deviations. The mean deviation is sometimes referred to as the average deviation. It is used much less frequently than the STANDARD DEVIATION. See CENTRAL TENDENCY, MEASURE OF; DISPERSION, STATISTICAL; MEAN, ARITHMETIC.

meaning. An interpretation of the significance of a situation, act, idea, or object with reference to how one should respond. Social interaction and social organization are made possible by the existence of culturally shared meanings. However, the subjective significance of the behavior of other persons to an actor (person) is determined by his individual past experiences as well as by his internalized culturally defined meanings. Hence the meaning of a social situation varies to a certain extent from one person to another even in the same culture. Each participant may have subjective meanings that are unique, but at the same time have shared meanings that make interaction and communication possible. See CONNOTATIVE MEANING.

measure. 1. A standardized mathematical unit used in the MEASUREMENT of a specific characteristic.

2. See INDEX.

measure, standard. See Z SCORE.

measure, unobtrusive. See UNOBTRUSIVE MEASURE.

measure, Z. See CRITICAL RATIO; Z SCORE.

measurement. The quantification of observations. Measurement involves the expression of observed characteristics or relationships in numerical form. The process of measurement may range from the simple tabulation of the number of cases in each of a set of categories to the use of complex statistical procedures.

mechanical solidarity. See SOLIDARITY, MECHANICAL.

mechanism. 1. The doctrine that human behavior can be explained in terms of the principles of physics or chemistry. A few sociologists refer to the law of thermodynamics, the law of inertia, etc., in explaining human behavior.

2. A psychic structure or set of acquired responses that operates to protect the integrity of the EGO or SELF. See DEFENSE MECHANISM.

mechanistic analogy. The conceptualization of society, or aspects of social life, as a machine. The structure of society is viewed in terms of gears, friction, stresses, and the like. See MECHANISM; ORGANICISM.

media, mass. See MASS MEDIA.

median. A positional measure of central tendency (see CENTRAL TENDENCY, MEASURE OF) of a series of data that is the middle value in a series of mathematical values. If all the values in a series are arranged in order of magnitude, the median is the value that divides the series in half; half the values lie above the median and half below it. See MEAN, ARITHMETIC; MODE.

median deviation. The MEDIAN value of the deviations from a measure of central tendency (see CENTRAL TENDENCY, MEASURE OF) of a series of data.

To find the median deviation the deviations from a measure of central tendency are arranged in order of magnitude (ignoring their positive or negative signs). The value that exceeds half the deviations and is exceeded by half is the median deviation. The median deviation is an infrequently used measure of dispersion. See DISPERSION, STATISTICAL; MEAN DEVIATION; STANDARD DEVIATION.

median location, hypothesis of. An ecological hypothesis concerning the distribution of businesses, industries, and other services within an urban community, based on the assumption that an important factor in this distribution is the accessibility of a location to those who must reach it. The most efficient location is held to be the median distance from the persons who will travel to it and the sources or destinations of goods that will be transported to it or from it. The hypothesis of median location is one of a series of locational hypotheses formulated by James A. Quinn. (J. A. Quinn, *Human Ecology*, Prentice-Hall, Englewood Cliffs, N.J., 1950.) See ECOLOGY, HUMAN; INTENSIVENESS OF UTILIZATION, HYPOTHESIS OF; MINIMUM COST, HYPOTHESIS OF.

median test. A nonparametric statistical test used to determine whether two samples differ significantly in central tendency (see CENTRAL TENDENCY, MEASURE OF), that is, whether or not they probably come from populations with the same MEDIAN. In order for the median test to be used, the data must be in at least an ORDINAL SCALE, that is, they must be at least in ranks, although they may be in actual scores. In this test the common median of the two samples combined is found, and then the number of scores above and below the common median in each sample separately is counted and placed in a fourfold (2 × 2) CONTINGENCY TABLE. The data in the contingency table are analyzed with either the FISHER EXACT PROBABILITY TEST, or the CHI-SQUARE TEST, depending on the number of cases. See NONPARAMETRIC STATISTICS; PROBABILITY; SIGNIFICANCE, STATISTICAL.

median test, extension of. A modification of the MEDIAN TEST for use with more than two samples.

mediation. A technique used for settling disputes, in which a disinterested third party attempts to bring together two conflicting parties. The disputants are not committed in advance to take the advice of the mediator as they are in ARBITRATION or CONCILIATION.

medical sociology. See SOCIOLOGY, MEDICAL.

mediopolis. A medium-sized city, neither a small town nor a large metropolitan city. The term was proposed by Murray H. Leiffer.

membership group. See GROUP MEMBERSHIP.

memory. The capacity to retain, recall, reorganize, and reproduce past experiences, events, and ideas. The remarkable memory of man is due primarily to the human ability to use symbols, and ultimately human memory depends upon the existence of LANGUAGE and CULTURE.

mental ability. See ABILITY, PRIMARY MENTAL.

mental age (M.A.). A score used by psychologists to estimate the mental ability or development of a person (usually a child). If a child's chronological age is 3 and his INTELLIGENCE TEST score is as high as that of an average child of 4 years of age, then his M.A. is 4, and he is above average in his mental ability or intelligence.

mental conflict. The social-psychological state of frustration and indecision resulting from the inability of an individual to act in a situation because he feels he cannot act without precipitating unpleasant consequences. Mental conflict may result when, for example, all of the possible alternative choices are undesirable, or when all are desirable and to choose one is to lose the advantages of the omitted choices. Inconsistent ROLE EXPECTATIONS and values are a common source of mental conflict. Mental conflict is to some degree inherent in human life. However, much mental conflict is a result of rapid social change, social mobility, and culture conflict, as well as of complex social organization and the ordinary experiences in the process of socialization. No human society can be organized so as to eliminate mental conflict, but the constant individual and collective effort to do so is a crucial, dynamic factor in the social, cultural, and psychological processes. See VALUE.

mental deficiency. A general condition of an individual who is unable to learn sufficiently well to communicate adequately with others and to adjust to the various social roles, routine demands, and requirements of social life. Mental deficiency cannot be equated with psychosis or personality disorganization. Rather it refers to a condition that, although in many cases it seems to have no known organic origin, appears at birth or at an early age. Persons with an I.Q. below 70 are defined by many psychologists as being mentally deficient. With special training, however, such persons are sometimes able to learn to take care of their own welfare and participate adequately in society. Thus mental deficiency is not without environmental determinants.

mental disorder. A serious personality disorganization, MENTAL ILLNESS, or PSYCHOSIS that is manifested in deviation from social norms. A person with a mental disorder finds it difficult to adjust to his social environment. Some writers also include less severe disturbances of personality, particularly NEUROSIS. See DISORGANIZATION, PERSONAL.

mental hygiene. The study and application of social and psychological principles in the prevention of mental disorders and the promotion of mental health.

mental illness. A nonorganic, social-psychological disorder in which the individual is unable to protect his EGO or social SELF sufficiently to participate in ordinary social life and obtain at least a minimal degree of social and psychological rewards.

mental illness, sociology of. See SOCIOLOGY OF MENTAL ILLNESS.

mental set. A mental orientation expressing the readiness of an individual to respond in a specified way to his environment (objects, individuals, or social situations) in terms of previously learned or organized interests and expectations. Thus, for example, culture and social experiences prepare people to perceive phenomena in a way that is consistent with the concerns of their social roles and individual personality patterns. A mental set may make us see only what we want to see or what fits in with our prejudices, but it also serves the necessary function of categorizing diverse phenomena into perceived cultural uniformities or classes without which effective response would generally be impossible. In addition, one's social role in society involves mental sets (viewpoints and concerns) that are crucial in an efficient system of specialization and division of labor.

mesocephalic. In physical anthropology a medium-sized head or skull with a CEPHALIC INDEX of approximately 80. See BRACHYCEPHALIC; DOLICHO-CEPHALIC.

mesokurtic curve. See FREQUENCY DISTRIBUTION CURVE, MESOKURTIC.

mesomorph. See SHELDON'S BODY TYPES.

messiah. In the widest sense, a prophet and charismatic leader who claims or is assumed by his followers to have supernatural guidance or powers and the mission to save his people from destruction or tragedy.

mestizo. In Latin America a person of mixed white and Indian ancestry. The term is used occasionally so that persons of any racial mixture (in Latin America) are included.

meta-anthropology. The study of the philosophical, conceptual, and methodological bases of anthropology.

metahistory. A philosophical orientation as to the meaning or underlying principles of history that provides a framework within which history is analyzed and interpreted. The framework of a metahistorical orientation is not constructed simply from the objective analysis of the specific details of historic events—although these details are often used as evidence to support the generalizations on which the framework is based—it comprises a body of theoretical generalizations that are meant to explain and be applicable to all history. Interpretations of history in terms of linear evolution or of cycles are examples of metahistory. Karl Marx's interpretation of history was based upon a metahistorical framework.

metaphysics. That branch of philosophy which studies the nature of ultimate reality.

metasociology. The branch of sociological theory that is concerned with the methods and logic of sociological inquiry, rather than with propositions, principles, and generalizations about social life. Robert Bierstedt refers to metasociology as metasociological or methodological theory, which he contrasts with substantive theory. (R. Bierstedt in *Symposium on Sociological Theory*, edited by L. Gross, Row, Peterson, Evanston, Ill., 1959.) See THEORY, SUBSTANTIVE.

method. See METHODOLOGY; SCIENTIFIC METHOD. See also CASE STUDY METHOD; COMMUNITY STUDY METHOD; COMPARATIVE METHOD; CROSS-CULTURAL METHOD; EXPERIMENTAL METHOD; FIELD STUDY METHOD; GENETIC METHOD; HISTORICAL METHOD; IDIOGRAPHIC METHOD; LIFE-HISTORY METHOD; NOMOTHETIC METHOD; SUBJECTIVE METHOD; TYPOLOGICAL METHOD; VERSTEHEN, METHOD OF.

method, deductive. See DEDUCTION.

method, empirical. See EMPIRICISM.

method, inductive. See INDUCTION.

method, longitudinal. See LONGITUDINAL STUDY.

method, sociometric. See SOCIOMETRY.

method, statistical. See STATISTICS.

methodology. 1. The logic of scientific investigation. In this sense, methodology in sociology includes the analysis of the basic assumptions of science in general and of sociology in particular, the process of theory construction, the interrelationship of theory and research, and the procedures of empirical investigation. Methodology is not concerned with building substantive knowledge, but rather deals with the procedures by which knowledge is built—conceptual, logical, and research procedures. See METASOCIOLOGY; SCIENTIFIC METHOD.

2. The procedures of research, or research techniques, including methods of collecting and handling data.

metronymic system. See FAMILY, METRONYMIC.

metropolis. A large city that economically and culturally dominates the surrounding area with its satellite cities and towns. A metropolis is the central city of a METROPOLITAN AREA.

metropolitan area. A contiguous territorial unit economically and socially integrated around a large central city or metropolis. Such areas tend to be functional units tied together by a network of transportation and communication lines radiating from the metropolis. They are not, however, politically integrated. That is, a metropolitan area may encompass or cross the governmental boundaries of cities, towns, and states. However, political parties, corporations, and churches sometimes attempt to organize their economic and political activities around the metropolitan unit, and social planners usually view the metropolitan area as a unit.

metropolitan area, standard. As defined by the U.S. Census, an area with at least one central city of at least 50,000 inhabitants, the county in which the central city is located, and one or more contiguous counties that are dependent upon the central city for services and employment. (In New England, towns and cities are used rather than counties.) While the standard metropolitan area has certain urban characteristics, the total area is not urban. The 1960 census used the term standard metropolitan statistical area and designated 212 such areas in the United States. See URBAN COMMUNITY.

metropolitan city. See METROPOLIS.

metropolitan community. A METROPOLITAN AREA viewed as a functional whole despite the many boundaries that separate political units and tend to obscure the interdependence of all subdivisions of the area.

metropolitan district. An area with at least one central city of 50,000 or more population and contiguous civil divisions having a density of 150 or more per square mile. This term was used in the U.S. Census of 1940 and earlier, but in the 1950 census the metropolitan district was replaced by the standard metropolitan area. See METROPOLITAN AREA, STANDARD.

metropolitan economy. The "organization of producers and consumers mutually dependent for goods and services, wherein their wants are supplied by a system of exchange concentrated in a large city which is the focus of local trade and the center through which normal economic relations with the outside are established and maintained." (N. S. B. Gras, *An Introduction to Economic History*, Harper, New York, 1922.)

metropolitan region. A large area that is economically and culturally dominated by a metropolis. A metropolitan region is larger than a METROPOLITAN AREA and extends well beyond the suburbs of the metropolis. The metropolitan region is often divided into the metropolis and its HINTERLAND. Within the hinterland are found smaller cities, towns, and rural areas. The boundary of the metropolitan region is not clear-cut, and varies according to the criterion used. Criteria used to delimit metropolitan regions include the range of metropolitan newspaper circulation, wholesale trade, retail trade, and banking areas, freight shipment routes, the volume of long-distance telephone calls to points varying distances from the metropolis, public transportation routes—frequency of service and volume of passengers, etc. See DOMINANCE, ECOLOGICAL.

micro-functionalism. A sociological theoretical orientation focusing on the functional analysis of small-scale social systems. The term was introduced by Don Martindale. (D. Martindale, *The Nature and Types of Sociological Theory*, Houghton Mifflin, Boston, 1960.) See FUNCTIONALISM; MACRO-FUNCTIONALISM.

micro-sociology. The study of small groups. See GROUP RESEARCH, SMALL; MACRO-SOCIOLOGY.

middle class. That segment of a system of economic and social stratification of a society which does not have either exceptionally low status or exceptionally high status. There is no agreement on the exact definition of middle class on the part of all the members of a large complex society such as the United States. Given the OPEN CLASS SYSTEM in the United States, middle-class status is not uniformly conceived by everyone. As many as 80% of the American people, according to public opinion polls, consider themselves middle class. See the various definitions of middle class below, and SOCIAL CLASS, and its related entries.

middle class, lower-. In the Yankee City studies of W. Lloyd Warner and Paul S. Lunt, a social stratum of a community including those people who have a limited but modestly adequate amount of money and education (usually through high school). It includes a variety of occupational groups such as skilled workers, clerical, sales, and other white collar workers, small businessmen, farmers, foremen, etc. The dominant values tend to stress responsibility, respectability, hard work, thrift, and cleanliness. (W. L. Warner and P. S. Lunt, *The Social Life of a Modern Community*, Yankee City Series, Vol. I, Yale University Press, New Haven, 1941.) See LOWER CLASS, LOWER-; LOWER CLASS, UPPER-; MIDDLE CLASS; MIDDLE CLASS, UPPER-; SOCIAL CLASS; UPPER CLASS, LOWER-; UPPER CLASS, UPPER-.

middle class, new. The large new middle class that has emerged in contemporary society, and has characteristics differing from those of the old middle class. The new middle class is a product of large-scale social organization. Particularly in the United States, the rise of vast industrial and governmental complexes and other forms of bureaucracy resulted in the rise of a salaried class of managerial, professional, technical, and clerical workers in a new system of identity and prestige. Local small-town values and prestige symbols, including ownership of small businesses and property holdings, have been replaced by those based on one's role in the economic, governmental, political, medical, and educational agencies of a large, complex, and heterogeneous society. Even in the old professions the individual entrepeneur is giving way to the corporate employee (such as the corporation lawyer) of the new middle class. See MIDDLE CLASS, OLD.

middle class, old. The middle class of a preindustrial society, composed primarily of small businessmen, farmers, and independent professionals (doctors, lawyers, etc.), whose status and power were primarily in local communities rather than national in orientation. The old middle class occupations and prestige systems of rural America are being replaced by those of the new middle class. See MIDDLE CLASS, NEW.

middle class, upper-. In the Yankee City studies of W. Lloyd Warner and Paul S. Lunt, the stratum of the community that includes the relatively prosperous business, professional, and governmental occupations. The members of the upper-middle class obtain their income from their occupation, are active in community affairs, send their children to college, live in the better residential areas, etc. As with other concepts of SOCIAL CLASS, the concept of upper-middle class is a variable one because each community and each stratum within the community views the criteria for social class quite differently. See LOWER CLASS, LOWER-; LOWER CLASS, UPPER-; MIDDLE CLASS; MIDDLE CLASS, LOWER-; SOCIAL CLASS; UPPER CLASS, LOWER-; UPPER CLASS, UPPER-.

middle management. See MANAGEMENT, MIDDLE.

middle range theory. See THEORY, MIDDLE RANGE.

migrant. A person who changes his place of residence and in so doing crosses a political boundary and settles in a new political area, such as a state or a nation.

migrant worker. A worker who finds employment in different places in different seasons of the year. The migrant worker is frequently an agricultural worker who follows the path of the harvest. For example, in the United States migrant workers, often with their families, spend the winter in Florida and Georgia and move north through the Atlantic states in the summer, moving south again in the late fall. Other paths of migrant workers extend from Texas, where the workers spend the winter, through the Central States and from the Southwest north along the Pacific coast.

migration. A relatively permanent movement of a person or population across a political boundary to a new residential area or community. See EMIGRATION; IMMIGRATION.

migration, internal. Migration within a single nation or political unit.

migration, international. See EMIGRATION; IMMIGRATION.

migration, selective. The migration of a particular class or category of people from one area to another. Thus the migrants moving from one area to another may be primarily Negro, upper class, Protestant, etc., with other population categories being less involved in the migration.

migration hypotheses. See PUSH-PULL MIGRATION HYPOTHESIS; ZIPF MIGRATION HYPOTHESIS.

milieu, social. Man's social environment. When humans respond to their environment, they respond not merely to physical and spatial stimuli, but also to their social surroundings, that is, the norms and expectations of other persons involved in any situation.

military institution. An interrelated system of social roles and norms organized around activities of the dominant political elite of a state in applying force in its most extreme form. The military institution legitimizes and depersonalizes the taking of life of the defined enemy. It is concerned with the suppression of external or internal threats to the survival, power, influence, interests, or structure of a society or a dominant stratum of a society. See INSTITUTION, SOCIAL; NORM, SOCIAL; ROLE.

military order. See MILITARY INSTITUTION.

millenarian movement. A SOCIAL MOVEMENT based on the expectation of a sudden transformation of society through the intervention of the supernatural. For an example of a millenarian movement, see CARGO CULT. See also NATIVISTIC MOVEMENT; REVITALIZATION MOVEMENT; VITALISTIC MOVEMENT.

milling. A typé of physical behavior found in an early stage of certain types of CROWD formation, characterized by restless, random movement of the crowd's members. This uncoordinated movement reflects the sensitivity of the members to each other and the diffuse interstimulation based upon a feeling of physical proximity and a sense of crisis.

mind. That organized abstract entity which is revealed by the social and psychological activity of an individual. Mental processes can be said to be a part of the social process and therefore to have a constantly changing character. The mind is formed largely through social interaction, is inseparable from the social process, and is revealed and its organization understood only within the context and with reference to a social and cultural environment.

mind, group or **collective.** See GROUP MIND.

minimum cost, hypothesis of. An ecological hypothesis concerning the location of businesses, factories, etc., in an industrial-capitalistic urban community. According to this hypothesis, when other costs are fixed, these units will tend to be located so as to minimize the time and other costs of transporting people and goods to and from the location. The hypothesis of minimum cost is one of a series of locational hypotheses formulated by James A. Quinn. (J. A. Quinn, *Human Ecology*, Prentice-Hall, Englewood Cliffs, N.J., 1950.) See ECOLOGY, HUMAN; INTENSIVENESS OF UTILIZATION, HYPOTHESIS OF; MEDIAN LOCATION, HYPOTHESIS OF.

minimum equation, hypothesis of. See ZIPF MIGRATION HYPOTHESIS.

minority group. Any recognizable racial, religious, or ethnic group in a community that suffers some disadvantage due to PREJUDICE or DISCRIMI-

NATION. This term, as commonly used, is not a technical term, and indeed it is often used to refer to categories of people rather than groups, and sometimes to majorities rather than minorities. For example, though women are neither a group (but rather a SOCIAL CATEGORY) nor a minority, some writers call them a minority group because supposedly a male-oriented society discriminates against women. On the other hand, a group which is privileged or not discriminated against but which is a numerical minority would rarely be called a minority group. Thus, as the term is often used, a minority group need be neither a minority nor a group, so long as it refers to a category of people who can be identified by a sizable segment of the population as objects for prejudice or discrimination.

minority relations. See INTERGROUP RELATIONS.

miscegenation. INTERMARRIAGE or interbreeding of two socially recognized races, such as whites and Negroes in the United States.

mob. A very active and emotionally aroused aggregation of people or CROWD with a common purpose or interest that motivates them to acts of destruction, violence, or aggression.

mobility. Movement or change in relative position, whether it be physical or social.

mobility, demand. Intergenerational mobility within a society due to changes in the occupational structure of the society. Thus much of the intergenerational mobility in American society is due to the expansion of the proportion of positions in professional, managerial, and other white collar categories and a general decline in the demand for positions in unskilled, semiskilled, and factory work. The term was introduced by Natalie Rogoff to refer to one of two important sources of intergenerational mobility. (N. Rogoff, *Recent Trends in Occupational Mobility,* Free Press, Glencoe, Ill., 1953.) See MOBILITY, INTERGENERATIONAL; MOBILITY, SOCIAL DISTANCE.

mobility, ecological. The movement of persons from one physical location to another, usually used with reference to a change in residence. Thus, for example, daily movement of population in and out of the central business district and temporary movement to another location for a short period of time are not usually considered mobility. Ecological mobility is sometimes referred to as geographical mobility. See ECOLOGY, HUMAN; FLUIDITY.

mobility, generational. See MOBILITY, INTERGENERATIONAL.

mobility, horizontal social. A change in one's social position without a corresponding change in one's general position in a prestige hierarchy or social-class level. This might occur in the case, for example, of a change of jobs from one type of skilled work to another, both of which are at the same general prestige level.

mobility, intergenerational. A vertical change of social status from one generation to the next. In studying upward or downward mobility, usually the son's occupational status is compared with his father's. See MOBILITY, VERTICAL SOCIAL.

mobility, social. 1. The movement of an individual or group from one social class or social stratum to another. In the more usual usage, social mobility refers to movement up or down a system of stratification, that is, it is synonymous with vertical social mobility.

2. A general term including both horizontal and vertical social mobility.

See MOBILITY, HORIZONTAL SOCIAL; MOBILITY, VERTICAL SOCIAL.

mobility, social distance. Intergenerational mobility within a society that is not a result of demand mobility but instead represents a change in one's social class position which places one higher than one's parents in the relative status hierarchy. Thus if most factory workers' sons become semiprofessional workers due to a general societal need for semiprofessionals and the decline of factory positions, the son of a factory worker who becomes a semiprofessional has shown demand mobility but not real social distance mobility since he is still in the same relative position in the status system of society. The term was introduced by Natalie Rogoff to refer to one of two important sources of intergenerational mobility. (N. Rogoff, *Recent Trends in Occupational Mobility*, Free Press, Glencoe, Ill., 1953.) See MOBILITY, DEMAND; MOBILITY, INTERGENERATIONAL.

mobility, vertical social. Movement between different social classes or status levels of a society or social system, that is, upward or downward mobility, involving a gain or loss of class status or prestige.

modal personality. See PERSONALITY TYPE, BASIC.

mode. A measure of central tendency (see CENTRAL TENDENCY, MEASURE OF) of a series of data which is the value that occurs more frequently than any other in a series of mathematical values. In a FREQUENCY DISTRIBUTION the mode is the class interval (subdivision of a variable) that has the greatest number of cases. Portrayed graphically, it is the highest point on the FREQUENCY DISTRIBUTION CURVE. See MEAN, ARITHMETIC; MEDIAN; MODE, CRUDE; MODE, TRUE.

mode, crude. In a FREQUENCY DISTRIBUTION in which data are grouped into class intervals, the midpoint of the class interval which has the largest number of cases. For example, in the distribution of the variable age, if the largest number of cases in a particular sample fell into the CLASS INTERVAL 20 to 24 years, the crude mode would be 22 years. See MODE, TRUE.

mode, true. That value in a series of values which is the actual point of highest frequency, and not merely an estimation or approximation of it. In the case of a FREQUENCY DISTRIBUTION, the true mode is the specific value with the greatest frequency of occurrence and not simply the midpoint of the most frequent class interval. The true mode is also known as the theoretical mode. See MODE, CRUDE.

model. A pattern of relationships, either conceptual or mathematical, which is found in some way to imitate, duplicate, or analogously illustrate a pattern of relationships in one's observations of the world, such as patterns in social behavior or social structure. The world of perceived reality is a product of the organization of perceptions according to some previously learned pattern. Scientists consciously attempt to discover order in nature by relating observations and data by analogy to previously developed patterns of relationships already in use for observing and ordering other types of data. Thus science has attempted, for example, to order the "facts" of society by using the evolutionary model, the organic model, the causal model, stimulus-response model, mathematical models, etc. Models may be very simple or very complex. Since the world we observe cannot be observed in its totality, each model reflects only a limited aspect of the total world. Hence each model is an ordering of only selected aspects of reality. No single model or combination of models reveals the truth of the structure of reality. Each model reveals and orders reality from a particular perspective. The value of a model is determined by its usefulness for guiding study. Models are tentative and limited, yet they are the building blocks of theory, interpretation, empirical discoveries, prediction, and general scientific progress.

model, analogue. A MODEL based on an analogy between certain characteristics of the phenomena being studied and similar characteristics of very different phenomena. In sociology the most common analogue models have been the mechanical and organic models. The analogue model is usually contrasted with the iconic model and the symbolic model. See MECHANISTIC ANALOGY; MODEL, ICONIC; MODEL, SYMBOLIC; ORGANICISM.

model, causal. A MODEL based on the assumption that two or more events or patterns of events occur so that one event is prior in time to the occurrence of one or more other events and is necessary for and leads to the occurrence of the second event. A causal model assumes a one-way dependence of events in a cause-effect relationship. However, it need not assume a single cause or a simple relationship in which one cause necessarily and inevitably leads to one effect. Causal models may be quite complex. See CAUSATION; CAUSE.

model, conceptual. A MODEL composed of a pattern of interrelated concepts not expressed in mathematical form and not primarily concerned with quantification. Ideal types and functional models (including the organic and mechanical) are conceptual models used in sociology. See FUNCTIONALISM; IDEAL TYPE; MECHANISTIC ANALOGY; ORGANICISM.

model, iconic. A MODEL based directly on the representation of the phenomena being studied. However, while the iconic model attempts to represent the characteristics of empirical phenomena, it is, like all models, necessarily an abstraction, thereby differing in some respects from the actual phenomena being represented. The level of abstraction of iconic models varies greatly; the more abstract types involving a great deal of simplification and possibly exaggeration of the characteristics of the phenomena being portrayed. A SOCIOGRAM and an IDEAL TYPE would be examples of iconic models. Iconic models are usually contrasted with analogue models and symbolic models. See MODEL, ANALOGUE; MODEL, SYMBOLIC.

model, mathematical. A quantified MODEL that, in sociology, expresses the interrelationships among persons, actions, and events in numerical form. Many sociologists tend to feel that mathematical models, which have been useful in the physical sciences, are not meaningfully applicable to the logic and patterns of social life. Some sociologists, however, are vigorously continuing work in this area of scholarship.

model, statistical. See STATISTICAL MODEL.

model, symbolic. A MODEL based on the logical and theoretical interrelationships of a set of concepts. The concepts form a theoretical system, and are derived from each other rather than directly from the characteristics of empirical phenomena. The symbolic model is usually contrasted with the analogue model and the iconic model. See MODEL, ANALOGUE; MODEL, ICONIC.

moiety. In cultural anthropology, each of two mutually exclusive social subdivisions of a tribal or clan society. While some writers define moiety as any one of two subdivisions of a society divided into two mutually exclusive groups regardless of type, others limit the term to one of two mutually exclusive kinship groups. When a moiety is a kinship group, it is usually composed of interrelated clans, and frequently moiety EXOGAMY is practiced. See CLAN.

monism, cultural. See CULTURAL MONISM.

monogamy. A form of marriage in which one man is married to one woman. Western society in general holds to monogamous norms for each current marriage. However, widowed persons may replace a spouse by remarriage, and, in addition, approved religious and secular separation of spouses permits what has been called serial polygamy. In societies whose norms do not prescribe monogamy the most common form of marital relationship is nevertheless monogamous. See POLYGAMY; POLYGAMY, SERIAL.

monogenetic hypothesis. In sociology and anthropology, the hypothesis that all living races of man are descended from the same ancestral stock and geographic region. Racial differences, such as skin, hair, and eye color, and body, head, hair, lip, nose, and eye shape are assumed to be due to the geographic isolation of the descendants of migrants from the original habitat and the attendant selective effects of environment, culture, and chance mutations. This has also been called the monogenetic theory and monogenism. See POLYGENETIC HYPOTHESIS.

monopoly. The control of an industry or market by a single organization. See OLIGOPOLY.

monotonic sequence. A sequence of mathematical values in which each value is larger (or smaller) than the one preceding it.

mood. In psychology, a temporary and often recurrent emotional feeling (happiness, anger, sadness, etc.) that is relatively mild but persists beyond the situation that created or aroused it.

moral code. The ideas of right and wrong held by an individual, group, or society. This very general term is used only occasionally in sociology, and rarely in any technical sense. See MORAL SYSTEM.

moral dilemma. A situation that is perceived by an individual (or individuals) as calling for a decision that involves at least two alternative actions, either of which would result in the violation of an ethical value held by the person being forced to make the decision. Since moral standards are abstract guides to ethical behavior, concrete situations often seem to evoke actions that have elements that support one's ethical standards as well as elements that violate them. Moral dilemmas are resolved in many ways, but a person's hierarchy of values, group loyalties, social status, and self-interests (or role-interests) help him to rationalize one choice over another. The study of moral dilemmas is crucial in the study of societal organization and process.

moral norms. See MORES.

moral obligation. A recognized social expectation that some specific and defined behavior is called for in a given situation. An individual is most aware of a moral obligation when the obligation is at variance with what he regards as his duty to a less immediate but contradictory moral demand (perhaps one which the immediate moral community would call "selfish"). Selfishness and nonconformity to the moral obligations imposed by a particular situation often reflect socially learned norms that have no perceived group reference point in the immediate social situation. Thus immediate social situations impose strong moral obligations on participants because the immediate situation tends to obscure or even deny the relevance of other obligations the participants have to other social norms and moral principles.

moral realism, stage of. As defined by Jean Piaget, an early stage in a child's development of a moral sense, when the child uncritically regards norms of right and wrong behavior as absolute. (J. Piaget, *The Moral Judgment of the Child*, Harcourt, Brace, New York, 1932.) At this stage of SOCIALIZATION the child views complex situations that call for the consideration of a variety of social norms as involving only a single social norm. The child's tendency to apply a single norm to a complex situation is a result of his inability to evaluate the important competing social definitions of "rightness" and his inability to see the total situation, which for an adult involves moral issues and definitions as yet impossible for a child to perceive. The child tends to see the parts rather than the whole, which explains why sometimes children see things that adults do not, and seem wise, as well as why children are not as responsible for deviance as are adults.

moral statement. A public statement or announcement that expresses an individual or group's definition of a situation in a way that rejects competing moral definitions of the same situation. Moral statements attempt to legitimize certain individual and group interests. Moral statements that are used to influence the behavior of others may unify a social group by clarifying for group members the dominant moral issue or issues, or they may cause conflict if alternate definitions of the situation are accepted by various segments of the group. It is possible for a group to maintain a sense of unity, despite the divergent perspectives of its members, through the general acceptance of common abstract moral statements, which members interpret differently in concrete situations.

moral system. A relatively large, complex, and integrated system of ideas of right and wrong, as, for example, the moral principles of a religion, of an ideology, or of a particular culture. The term system implies that individual moral judgments are dominated by a limited number of principles around which all other values are organized, modified, and evaluated. The various moral systems of the world may include many of the same moral ideas. The differences among men concerning moral issues often are a result of the problem of which moral values predominate and are the basis for the hierarchical ordering of other moral values and choices within a particular system.

morale. Commitment to group goals on the part of group members, confidence in the group's eventual attainment of these goals, and satisfaction with the group experience. High morale involves belief in the rightness and importance of a group's goals, willingness to work for these goals, and belief in their ultimate achievement. When morale is high, group goals are compatible with the individual members' ideals and values, and group members feel satisfaction in working for these goals, which they believe the group will succeed in attaining. Morale may be distinguished from ESPRIT DE CORPS, which depends upon a strong sense of identity among group members. Although high morale is usually associated with high *esprit de corps,* it is possible to have high *esprit de corps* and low morale. Both morale and *esprit de corps* are important factors in social cohesion. See COHESION, SOCIAL; GROUP GOAL.

morals. Standards of right and wrong. See MORES.

morbidity rate. The number of cases of a disease (or diseases) for a given unit of population (for example, per 100,000) within a given period.

mores. Those social norms that provide the moral standards of behavior of a group or society. Conformity to the mores is not optional, and nonconformity is severely sanctioned. Group members feel an emotional attachment to the mores and their preservation is considered essential to the group's welfare. Usually the term is limited to those standards of behavior that depend upon informal sanctions and have not been enacted into law. However, a few writers regard as mores all rules of behavior accepted by the members of a society (or group) as standards of moral conduct whether or not they have been enacted into law. The term was introduced by William G. Sumner in *Folkways* (Ginn, Boston, 1906). See FOLKWAYS; NORM, SOCIAL; SANCTION.

morphology. The study of form and structure. Morphology may involve the study of somatic, linguistic, or social structure.

morphology, social. The study of the relationship between SOCIAL STRUCTURE and the physical environment and the material form manifested by the social structure of a community or society in a particular physical environment, in terms of, for example, the patterns of spatial distribution of types of population and services, population density, and so forth. The term was introduced by Émile Durkheim, and is similar to the usual sociological conception of human ecology. See ECOLOGY, HUMAN.

mortality rate. See entries beginning DEATH RATE.

mos. The correct singular form of mores. In practice, the singular of mores is often avoided.

Moses test. A nonparametric statistical test used to compare the span of the scores in two samples. The Moses test indicates whether one sample has significantly more extreme scores (opposite extremes combined) than the other sample. It could be used, for example, to determine whether an experimental treatment significantly increased both extremely favorable and extremely unfavorable attitudes on a given subject by comparing the number of extreme responses in the EXPERIMENTAL GROUP and the CONTROL GROUP. To use the Moses test, the data must be at least in an ORDINAL

SCALE, that is, have an order of magnitude. See NONPARAMETRIC STATIS-TICS; PROBABILITY; SIGNIFICANCE, STATISTICAL.

mote-beam mechanism. The tendency of people to project personal characteristics they have upon others and to exaggerate the degree to which others have these characteristics. Thus an ambitious and competitive individual might tend to see those around him as excessively ambitious and competitive, yet deny that he has these characteristics. The term was introduced by Gustave Ichheiser.

mother-in-law taboo. A custom found in some societies that formally prohibits or substantially restricts interaction between a husband and his wife's mother.

motivation. The recognition by a person of a situation that he feels stimulated to complete or which stimulates him to contribute to its stability or modification. Motivation is a general term used to refer to any arousal of an individual to goal-directed behavior. The term motivation when applied to humans is a social-psychological concept, and motivation cannot be considered apart from the individual's conception of himself, his social statuses and roles, and the existence of society and culture, which define situations and appropriate and desirable behavior.

motivation, extrinsic. Motivation based on an expectation of indirect fulfillment of one's desires in a situation. The task undertaken has no inherent source of motivation for the individual, but is seen as instrumental in attaining his desired goals. There is no intrinsic relationship between the goals that are the source of motivation and the task itself. An example would be a student learning a foreign language not because of any interest in knowing the language, but solely to fulfill a language requirement for a degree. See MOTIVATION, INTRINSIC.

motivation, intrinsic. Motivation based on an expectation of direct and immediate fulfillment of one's desires in a situation. The motivation stems directly from the task undertaken and is inherent in the task itself. An example would be a person learning a foreign language because he wants to know that language. See MOTIVATION, EXTRINSIC.

motivational research. Research designed to discover what psychological or social factors motivate people to buy various products, so that advertising and sales techniques can be made more effective.

motive. An impulse to act in a specific manner. A motive is more specifically goal-directed than a DRIVE or a NEED. Although a motive may stem from "unconscious" sources not recognized by the individual himself, there is awareness of the goal that is sought. A motive involves the recognition of a situation or state, either external or internal, that is perceived as requiring completion or modification. Human motives in any particular situation, while often predictable, may vary considerably, since it is not only the external situation that determines the motive, but also the internal meaning attributed to it by the individual, in whom social and psychological processes are in constant flux. See MOTIVATION.

motive, biogenic. See BIOGENIC MOTIVE.

motive, ego-involved. A motive primarily concerned with the defense or enhancement of one's image in the eyes of others (or as one believes he will be judged by others). While much behavior proceeds without acute anxiety or self-analysis, most social-psychological motives are ego-involved at least to some degree.

motive, hidden. A motive possessed by an individual, the operation of which he does not directly perceive. Since the values and norms of an individual tend to pervade his perceptions of many situations, it is possible for a person to perceive his motives in a situation according to one value system which in effect justifies behavior that he would disapprove under other sets of values he holds. Thus, when a person's motives are couched in terms of one set of personal values but at the same time serve his self-interest and are contrary to other values he possesses, his motives may be said to be hidden. An example would be a parent who, purportedly for the child's "own good," bullies the child into achievements that are in fact more rewarding for the parent than the child.

motive, vocabulary of. See VOCABULARY OF MOTIVE.

motive pattern, acquired. See ACQUIRED MOTIVE PATTERN.

motor habits, cultural. Those learned and patterned bodily movements and stances that are peculiar to particular cultures or social roles.

motor stage, Piaget's. A stage in the development of a child in which social rules and norms of behavior are not understood or examined but are ritually followed by automatic and habitual compliance. This is the first of the four stages of Jean Piaget's RULES OF THE GAME.

movement. See MOBILITY.

movement, cyclical. See CYCLICAL MOVEMENT.

movement, mass. See MASS MOVEMENT.

movement, millenarian. See MILLENARIAN MOVEMENT.

movement, nativistic. See NATIVISTIC MOVEMENT.

movement, occupational. See HORIZONTAL OCCUPATIONAL MOVEMENT; VERTICAL OCCUPATIONAL MOVEMENT.

movement, revitalization. See REVITALIZATION MOVEMENT.

movement, social. See SOCIAL MOVEMENT.

movement, vitalistic. See VITALISTIC MOVEMENT.

multidimensional. See UNIDIMENSIONAL SCALE.

multilineal descent. See BILATERAL DESCENT.

multiple causation. See CAUSATION, MULTIPLE.

multiple factor analysis. See FACTOR ANALYSIS.

multiple group membership. Membership by an individual in more than one GROUP. This is a typical occurrence, and in the analysis of social structure or social behavior the student of society must be aware of the fact that social groups share their members with other groups and of the implications this has for societal integration, deviance, conflict, value conflict, etc. Social behavior involves multiple reference groups and individual behavior can rarely be understood merely in terms of any one of an individual's many group memberships. See REFERENCE GROUP.

multiple independent discoveries. Identical discoveries or inventions that occur independently of each other either in the same or different cultures. Often in the same culture multiple independent discoveries occur simultaneously. Sometimes referred to in abbreviated form as *multiples,* the term was introduced by Robert K. Merton (*Proceedings, American Philosophical Society,* October 1961). See INVENTION, PARALLEL.

multiple nuclei pattern. A pattern of city land use in which a number of business centers or districts develop, each with its own special activities and influences, instead of the entire city being organized around one CENTRAL BUSINESS DISTRICT. Frequently the separate nuclei are the centers of relatively separate communities within the city. In some cases this pattern is the result of the uniting of two or more independent communities into a single city. In other cases separate communal areas develop within a city, sometimes because of ethnic, class, or other differences. Paris is an example of a city with a multiple nuclei pattern.

multiple personality. A PSYCHOSIS characterized by the division of the personality into two or more distinct and often very different subpersonalities, each with a fairly complete organization of its own. Multiple personality is sometimes incorrectly referred to as SCHIZOPHRENIA.

As in the case of most psychoses, the difference between the psychotic condition of multiple personality and a normal personality is one of degree and not of kind. Many normal individuals experience pronounced changes in personality as they move back and forth between social situations requiring widely divergent types of role behavior. For some people their various social roles can be and are comfortably performed according to a relatively consistent set of basic norms and expectations. For others their lives are organized about two (or sometimes more) vastly different social patterns, and they develop different patterns of behavior to adjust to each. But even in a less extreme bifurcation of one's social life, different social situations demand different behavior, and, in a sense, each person presents subpersonalities to others and even "feels like a different person" in certain groups and situations. Yet the personality retains sufficient unity not to disintegrate into the psychotic state of multiple personality.

multiple-phase sampling. See SAMPLING, MULTIPLE-PHASE.

multiple-stage sampling. See SAMPLING, MULTIPLE-STAGE.

multivariate analysis. The analysis and interpretation of the interrelationships of three or more variables. This may be done by introducing an intervening variable into the analysis of the relationship between two variables, by successively controlling on a series of variables, or by the use of techniques such as FACTOR ANALYSIS or the factorial experiment. See EXPERIMENT, FACTORIAL; EXPERIMENTAL CONTROL; VARIABLE; VARIABLE, INTERVENING.

municipal government. See under CITY GOVERNMENT.

mutually exclusive events. Events that cannot occur simultaneously, the occurrence of one event preventing the occurrence of the other; for example, if the toss of a coin turns up heads it cannot turn up tails. Whether or not events are mutually exclusive is important in statistical analysis.

mystic integralism. See SOCIOLOGICAL MYSTIC INTEGRALISM.

myth. A highly symbolic account or story of a supernatural or extraordinary event within a culture or subculture. The myth is continually retold and contemplated for its wisdom, philosophy, inspiration, or practicality. See HERO.

N

N. The total number of measures in a series of data. N may be equal to the number of individuals in a sample, or it may exceed the number of individuals if there is more than one observation or response for each individual.

name calling. A PROPAGANDA technique by which a negative label or name is assigned to a person or idea to discredit it and discourage people from considering the facts or developing identification with the person or idea.

nation. An autonomous, territorially delimited political grouping whose members have a loyalty to shared institutions that gives a sense of unity as a community. A nation need not have a common origin, language, religion, or race, although nationhood often is formed around a common history and other cultural similarities.

national character. The PERSONALITY structure hypothesized to be typical of members of the same society. This concept assumes that the different cultural patterns of a society produce distinguishable personality types, each dominant within a culture area or society. See PERSONALITY TYPE, BASIC.

nationalism. An IDEOLOGY in which patriotism is a central social value and which promotes loyalty to one's nation as a conscious emotion. Nationalism involves a sense of common destiny, common goals, and common responsibilities for all citizens of the nation.

nationality. 1. Membership in and identification with a particular NATION. In this sense of the term, which is essentially political, nationality often, but not always, involves the sharing of a common culture, including a common language.

2. Membership in and identification with a group that shares common culture traits, usually including a common language and a common history. See ETHNIC GROUP.

nativistic movement. An organized attempt by members of a society to eliminate foreign elements from their culture, and very often to remove foreign persons from their society. An example would be the Boxer movement in China around 1900. See MILLENARIAN MOVEMENT; REVITALIZATION MOVEMENT; VITALISTIC MOVEMENT.

natural area. A territorial area with some common, unifying characteristic. The term has been used primarily in human ecology, and usually refers to an area that emerges without planning from the operation of ECOLOGICAL PROCESSES. It is frequently contrasted with an ADMINISTRATIVE AREA having arbitrarily delimited boundaries, and has been most often applied to specialized areas of a city—areas characterized by distinctive land use or population type, such as a CENTRAL BUSINESS DISTRICT, SLUM, wholesale district, ROOMING HOUSE AREA, financial district, Negro district, Italian district, etc. Some ecologists also refer to metropolitan areas and the economic regions of a nation as natural areas, because they are identifiable areas that have not developed from planning or legislation and are not delimited by political boundaries. See ECOLOGY, HUMAN.

natural environment. See GEOGRAPHICAL ENVIRONMENT.

natural increase, rate of. The birth rate minus the death rate of a population.

natural science. One of the older, more traditional sciences, such as physics, chemistry, biology, and geology, as contrasted to one of the behavioral or social sciences. The term is, however, misleading, since sciences such as sociology and psychology obviously deal with natural phenomena and, moreover, strive to develop a body of theory that has been verified by scientific procedures. See BEHAVIORAL SCIENCE; SCIENCE; SCIENTIFIC METHOD; SOCIAL SCIENCE.

natural selection. See DARWINIAN THEORY; EVOLUTION.

natural sign. See SIGN, NATURAL.

naturalism. The philosophical doctrine that all phenomena, whether physical, mental, or social, are determined by and explainable in terms of the laws of nature. Naturalism rejects both supernatural and anthropocentric explanations of the universe. The human mind is regarded as merely a by-product of the operation of natural laws, and man's behavior is to be explained entirely by deterministic laws without assuming the existence of human purpose or freedom. The doctrine of naturalism stands in direct opposition to philosophical IDEALISM. See EMPIRICISM; POSITIVISM; REALISM.

naturalization. A legal procedure that confers formal citizenship on a person who is regarded as previously having been a citizen of another nation.

nature, human. See HUMAN NATURE.

nature, original. See ORIGINAL NATURE.

nature-nurture problem. The controversy in the behavioral sciences as to whether certain aspects of human behavior—intelligence, for example—are primarily due to hereditary (genetic) factors or to environmental factors.

necessary condition. A condition that must exist if a given event is to occur. The event can never occur unless the necessary condition occurs first. However, the existence of the necessary condition does not assure the occurrence of the event. If the necessary condition exists, the event may or may not occur. An example would be a FUNCTIONAL REQUISITE, such as the provision of an adequate food supply, which is a necessary condition for the survival of any society and yet in itself does not assure the survival of a society. The concept of necessary condition is used in the analysis of CAUSATION. See SUFFICIENT CONDITION.

need. A state of tension or dissatisfaction felt by an individual that impels him to action toward a goal he believes will satisfy the impulse. Although sometimes equated with DRIVE, the term need usually implies a more channeled impulse with a more articulated goal. It does not necessarily imply that fulfillment of the need contributes to the survival or well-being of the individual. A person may feel a need that is harmful to himself as an individual, for example, a need to sacrifice his life for his group. Examples of social-psychological needs are those for personal recognition, affection, autonomy; examples of physiological needs are hunger, thirst, and SEX. See MOTIVE; WANT.

need, physiological. A NEED resulting from the biological structure of the organism. Physiological needs are sometimes termed primary needs because often their fulfillment is necessary for the survival of the individual and because most are present at birth and thus precede the development of social needs. Physiological needs, however, do not necessarily take primacy over social needs in the behavior of the individual. Moreover, the expression and specific form of physiological needs are determined by the process of SOCIALIZATION and by the individual's culture and social relationships.

need, primary. See NEED, PHYSIOLOGICAL.

need, social. A need learned by the individual through social interaction. See NEED, PHYSIOLOGICAL.

needs in mate-selection, theory of complementary. "The basic hypothesis of the theory of complementary needs in mate-selection is that in mate-selection each individual seeks within his or her field of eligibles for that person who gives the greatest promise of providing him or her with maximum need-gratification. It is not assumed that this process is totally or even largely conscious." This theory was formulated by Robert F. Winch to explain the process of mate-selection in modern American society, particularly within the middle class. (R. F. Winch, T. Ktsanes, and V. Ktsanes, *American Sociological Review*, June 1954.) Winch hypothesizes that those marriages are most successful in which the personality needs of the husband and wife do in fact complement each other, whatever their needs may be. If personality needs are complementary, then "as the husbands engage in the behavior which their own needs arouse, this behavior is found to gratify the relevant needs of their wives; and similarly, the wives acting out their, say, masochistic needs are hypothesized to be gratifying the hostile needs of the husbands." (R. F. Winch, *Mate-Selection*, Harper, New York, 1958.)

negative correlation. See CORRELATION, NEGATIVE.

negative reference group. See REFERENCE GROUP, NEGATIVE.

negativism. An attitude of noncooperation and nonconformity in a social situation where those in authority, or the dominant norms and expectations, call for compliance. Negativism is common where conformity to prevailing norms is overwhelming but not felt to be in the interest of the actor. All humans develop negative attitudes when conformity threatens their values, status, or self-conception. Young children periodically show negativism because their parents simultaneously demand conformity and obedience and independence and responsibility. The negativism of the mentally ill may stem from several sources, one being the fact that they organize norms and values differently from others.

neighborhood. 1. A small territorial unit, usually a subdivision of a larger community, in which there is some sense of local unity or identity. Because the neighborhood is small, contacts are face to face, and many relationships tend to be primary, that is, close and enduring. However, according to this definition, a neighborhood also includes families that have little if any interaction with each other. The neighborhood usually provides essential services for the local residents. See PRIMARY RELATIONS.

2. An informal primary group found within a limited area. In this sense, a neighborhood includes only those families within a limited area who are friendly with each other. Thus a given neighborhood would include some families living farther away than others who are not included in the neighborhood. Although in this sense the neighborhood is not delimited primarily on the basis of physical proximity, it is nevertheless limited to a

local area small enough to permit frequent face-to-face contact. See GROUP, PRIMARY.

Neolithic Age. A period or stage of cultural and economic development in the history of man, also called the New Stone Age, characterized by the development of polished stone tools, the domestication of plants and animals, and the development of weaving and pottery. The use of metal tools had not yet developed during this period. In different parts of the world the Neolithic Age appeared at different times. See PALEOLITHIC AGE.

neolocal residence. A social custom according to which married couples are normally expected not to live with either of the families of origin, but to establish a separate or new residence. See MATRILOCAL RESIDENCE; PATRILOCAL RESIDENCE.

neopositivism. A methodological approach in sociology holding that social research should be based upon the procedures of the physical sciences, and emphasizing the study of overt behavior and the use of operational concepts and quantitative, mathematical techniques. A neopositivistic approach to sociological analysis tends to regard relatively nonquantitative approaches to the study of human behavior as peripheral in sociological analysis. See OPERATIONAL DEFINITION; OPERATIONALISM; POSITIVISM.

neurosis. Any of a group of mild personality disorders or chronic emotional difficulties. A neurosis (or psychoneurosis) is less serious than a PSYCHOSIS, and it is considered to be functional in character rather than organic.

neutrality. See AFFECTIVE NEUTRALITY; AFFECTIVITY-AFFECTIVE NEUTRALITY.

New Stone Age. See NEOLITHIC AGE.

nighttime population. See DAYTIME POPULATION, URBAN.

nomad. A person belonging to a group that changes its place of residence periodically according to the seasonal advantages of each location, for example, better hunting, grass for cattle, better weather. Generally nomadic groups are limited to a certain area and tend to return to traditional locations. They do not wander aimlessly. A large-scale migration of nomadic tribes occurs when overpopulation, invasion, famine, or other catastrophe makes it impossible for them to utilize their traditional seasonal camps.

nominal leader. See LEADER, NOMINAL.

nominal scale. A simple scheme of measurement consisting of two or more categories used to classify and differentiate observed data. The classes distinguished by a nominal scale may be symbolically designated by a word, letter, or number. However, the categories have no inherent rank order or any other mathematical significance, even when designated by numbers. The categories of Protestant, Catholic, and Jewish would be an example of a nominal scale. The nominal scale is often called a classificatory scale.

nominalism. A philosophical doctrine holding that general or abstract concepts and terms are merely names, referring to particulars. Reality is regarded as composed of particular things, and universal ideas or abstract conceptions, such as "goodness" or "the state," have no independent or distinct identity. The nominalist position in modern science is that of extreme EMPIRICISM, which in the study of human behavior would involve an emphasis upon the study of sensory data using operational concepts and statistical correlations. General concepts such as society, group, culture, and values would not be regarded as useful in the study of human behavior, for they would be rejected as not being real entities or objects for study. See OPERATIONAL DEFINITION; OPERATIONALISM; POSITIVISM; REALISM; REDUCTIONISM.

nomothetic method. Analysis directed toward the formulation of general principles. In the study of behavior, application of this method would entail that individual events are studied not for their own sake but for their significance insofar as they contribute to the formulation of generalizations. See IDIOGRAPHIC METHOD; SCIENCE, NOMOTHETIC.

nomothetic science. See SCIENCE, NOMOTHETIC.

nonconformity. Behavior perceived as divergent from social expectations in a particular situation. Creative nonconformity is sometimes rewarded. Usually, however, failure to comply with the expected patterns of behavior is negatively sanctioned, even by those individuals who regard nonconformity as a positive value. Nonconformity is a relative concept, and an act that violates the norms in one situation or group may be in conformity with norms of other groups. The members of a group will define an individual as a nonconformist and will apply sanctions to him even if he merely inconveniently demands conformity to the same group's highest values. This is especially likely to happen if the group is at the time strongly concerned with another group value and is ignoring the higher values that are not convenient to recall. Thus punishment is as hard on the "saint" as on the "sinner."

nondirective technique. See COUNSELING, NONDIRECTIVE; INTERVIEW, NONDIRECTIVE.

nonlinear association or correlation. See CORRELATION, CURVILINEAR.

nonlinear regression. See REGRESSION, CURVILINEAR.

nonlinear trend. See TREND, NONLINEAR.

nonliterate. Without a written language. A nonliterate culture has no written language. Sometimes the term *preliterate* is used as synonymous with nonliterate; however, preliterate is associated with certain theoretical assumptions concerning the evolutionary development of societies that are no longer accepted. It should be noted that literate societies, that is, those that have a written language, may be composed primarily of illiterate persons.

nonnumerical variable. See VARIABLE, QUALITATIVE.

nonparametric statistics. That branch of statistics comprising techniques of statistical analysis that do not entail assumptions about the exact form of the distribution of the POPULATION. The use of nonparametric statistical tests does not require that the SAMPLE being analyzed be from a population with a normal distribution or with any other specified distribution (that is, the exact shape of the distribution of the population need not be known). Therefore, nonparametric statistics is sometimes referred to as distribution-free statistics. The term nonparametric itself refers to the fact that these techniques do not make stringent assumptions or assertions about population parameters (but only some limited, less restrictive assumptions about the nature of the population), and deal primarily with the sample data. Moreover, whereas data must be in the form of absolute scores or values to be used in PARAMETRIC STATISTICS, there are nonparametric techniques that may be used with data in the form of ranks (ORDINAL SCALE), techniques for use with data classified as plus or minus (higher or lower), and techniques for data simply in categories (NOMINAL SCALE). Nonparametric statistics is a more recent development in statistics than parametric statistics. Generally, the power of nonparametric tests is less than that of parametric tests, but the nonparametric techniques have been growing in popularity because of the difficulty of meeting the stringent assumptions of the parametric model. See FREQUENCY DISTRIBUTION; PARAMETER; POWER, STATISTICAL.

nonparticipant observation. See OBSERVATION, NONPARTICIPANT.

nonprobability sample. See SAMPLE, NONPROBABILITY.

nonreactive research. See UNOBTRUSIVE MEASURE.

norm. 1. See NORM, SOCIAL.
2. See NORM, STATISTICAL.

norm, institutionalized social. A social norm supported universally or widely within a society or social system. It is supported by a broad societal consensus and sanctions for violations. See NORM, SOCIAL.

norm, social. A rule or standard of behavior defined by the shared expectations of two or more people regarding what behavior is to be considered socially acceptable. Social norms provide guidelines to the range of behavior appropriate and applicable to particular social situations. Thus, one's ROLE obligations in a social group are defined by that group's social norms. Social norms are studied by observing overt behavior (what people do), as well as by observing what people say their norms are. Many sociologists regard society, social institutions, social roles, moral systems, etc., as normative structures based on shared expectations of behavior. See FOLKWAYS; MORES.

norm, statistical. A mathematical value, measure, or score used as a standard for comparison. A norm may be derived from observed data. For example, it may be an average score of a large number of persons of a given type with which the scores of individuals or subdivisions are compared. It is also possible to derive a norm from a theoretical distribution. In the latter case observed data are compared with hypothetical norms based on the assumption of specified conditions.

normal curve. See FREQUENCY DISTRIBUTION CURVE, NORMAL.

normative integration. The interrelationship of the social norms of a group into a consistent pattern so organized that there are relatively few seriously conflicting social or psychological expectations or obligations on the members that stem directly from the norms of the group. Normative integration within a social group is a function of its members' values. Hence if the membership of a group changes over time, the formal norms of a group might not be viewed as integrated by new members who do not share exactly the same values as the long-time members. See NORM, SOCIAL.

normative pattern. An interrelated set of social norms held by the members of a group. See NORM, SOCIAL; NORMATIVE INTEGRATION.

normative score. See SCORE, NORMATIVE.

normative theory. See THEORY, NORMATIVE.

normless suicide. See SUICIDE, ANOMIC.

normlessness. A condition characterized by the absence of an organized system of social norms or values that enable an individual to choose the most desirable action in a situation. Without a guiding system of norms, the consequences of action or inaction or of one action as against an alternate action are judged to be of equal value or harm. Normlessness often may be a result not of too few norms, but of an awareness of too many that could apply in a situation, leading to an inability on the part of the individual to accept one norm as superior to another, and causing him to withdraw and refuse to commit himself to any single norm or set of norms. See ANOMIE.

North-Hatt scale of occupational prestige. A SCALE used to rank occupations according to prestige by assigning them scores within a specified range (originally from 33 to 96). The occupational prestige scores of respondents may be compared with the scores of their fathers to study trends in social mobility. (C. C. North and P. K. Hatt, *Opinion News,* September 1947). See MOBILITY, SOCIAL.

nouveaux riches. The newly rich, those who have acquired wealth in their own lifetime. The term implies that these persons lack familiarity with the customs of those who have had wealth for several generations and that they feel an insecurity regarding social status, usually compensated for by the ostentatious display of wealth. The term is used primarily as a stereotype or an epithet, or by way of asserting one's superior status over those who may have greater wealth but lack one's "family background," manners, or other characteristics. It is not a technical sociological term. See UPPER CLASS, LOWER-.

nuclear family. See FAMILY, NUCLEAR.

nucleation. See CENTRALIZATION.

null hypothesis. See HYPOTHESIS, NULL.

number, absolute value of. See ABSOLUTE VALUE OF A NUMBER.

O

object, cultural. See CULTURAL OBJECT.

object, social. See SOCIAL OBJECT.

objective analysis. See OBJECTIVITY.

objective interests. See CLASS-INTEREST CONSCIOUSNESS; INTEREST (2); MANIFEST INTERESTS.

objective social classes. See SOCIAL CLASS, OBJECTIVE CONCEPTION OF.

objectivism. The philosophical view that the objects of knowledge have their own existence in reality. See SUBJECTIVISM.

objectivity. In scientific reaserch, the quality that is expressed in the effort to eliminate distortions in perception or explanation due to the relatively temporary social or psychological biases of a group or individual, and to achieve the most unbiased and universal generalizations possible under the conditions of knowledge at the time. In an objective analysis, one utilizes the best available theoretical framework and methods of observation. The SCIENTIFIC METHOD attempts to develop techniques to maximize objectivity. See SUBJECTIVITY.

obligation. See MORAL OBLIGATION; SOCIAL OBLIGATION.

observation. 1. In more general usage, the examination of behavior directly by an investigator or by persons who serve as observers. Usually the observed items of behavior are recorded, enumerated, or classified by the observer or observers. Recording devices or other tools may be used to simplify this process. Observation of complex phenomena usually requires some degree of analysis, synthesis, or interpretation of the data. Those who use the second definition of observation (below) would refer to this usage as "direct observation."

2. The examination, recording, or enumeration of events or phenom-

ena. According to this definition, observation may be either direct and personal or indirect and impersonal; for example, gathering data through mailed questionnaires would be regarded as observation. In fact, in this usage, any data collection is considered observation, including the collection of data from records. Thus in statistics any individual score or response is referred to as an observation.

observation, direct. See OBSERVATION (2).

observation, nonparticipant. A method of OBSERVATION in which an investigator directly observes a group without becoming a functioning member of the group or taking part in its activities. The group members may or may not know that the investigator is observing them. If they do know, they regard him as an outsider who is interested in watching and recording their activities, but not interested in becoming a regular member of the group. See OBSERVATION, PARTICIPANT.

observation, participant. A method of OBSERVATION in which an investigator participates as a member of the group he is studying. Participant observers are sometimes known by the group members to be observers, though they have joined the activities and taken on the obligations of a group member. In other cases, the observer is believed to be an ordinary member, and the group members are not aware that they are being observed. The concept was introduced by Eduard C. Lindeman in his book *Social Discovery* (Republic Publishing Co., New York, 1924). See OBSERVATION, NONPARTICIPANT.

observation, systematic. A method of OBSERVATION based on the use of a prepared schedule of categories designated to assure the deliberate and controlled observation of important aspects of behavior. For example, see INTERACTION RECORDER.

Occam's razor. See PARSIMONY, PRINCIPLE OF.

occupation. A set of activities centered on an economic ROLE and usually associated with earning a living—for example, a trade or profession. An occupation is a social role that is determined by the general division of labor within a society. As a specialization of an individual's function in society, it is an important factor defining a person's prestige, class position, and style of life.

occupation, primary. An OCCUPATION concerned with the production or extraction of raw materials. The primary occupations include those in agriculture, fishing, hunting, lumbering, and mining. In nonindustrial societies the overwhelming majority of the population are engaged in primary occupations. See OCCUPATION, SECONDARY; OCCUPATION, TERTIARY.

occupation, secondary. An OCCUPATION concerned with the production of man-made goods or the processing of raw materials. Secondary occupations include those involved in all forms of manufacturing, food processing, and handicrafts. Nonindustrial societies usually have only a small proportion of the population engaged in secondary occupations, primarily handicrafts. In the early stage of industrialization there is a great growth of manufacturing and thus a striking increase in the proportion of the population in secondary occupations and an accompanying decline in the proportion in primary occupations. See OCCUPATION, PRIMARY; OCCUPATION, TERTIARY.

occupation, tertiary. An OCCUPATION concerned with the provision of services rather than the production of goods. The tertiary occupations include those in government, management, medicine, religion, transportation, communication, personal services, etc. A wide variety of occupations fall into this category, including such diverse occupations as bus driver, barber, lawyer, actor, clergyman, and newspaper reporter. In nonindustrial societies only a very small proportion of the population is involved in tertiary occupations. In the early stage of industrialization there is an expansion in the tertiary occupations, but it is not as great as the expansion in the secondary occupations. (In this stage both secondary and tertiary occupations expand at the expense of the primary occupations.) In the later stage of industrialization, however, there is a marked expansion in the tertiary occupations, and not only does the proportion of the population in the primary occupations continue to decline, but there is also a decline in the proportion engaged in secondary occupations. One of the striking characteristics of advanced industrial societies is the greatly increased proportion of the population in the tertiary occupations. See OCCUPATION, PRIMARY; OCCUPATION, SECONDARY.

occupational categories. Classifications of the chief types of occupations. Many different sets of occupational categories have been devised for sociological studies. One that is widely used is the set of categories utilized by Richard Centers: business executives, professionals, small businessmen, white collar workers, skilled manual workers, semiskilled manual workers, and unskilled manual workers. (R. Centers, *International Journal of Opinion and Attitude Research,* Fall 1950.) See OCCUPATION.

occupational culture. A set of subculture traits traditionally associated with a particular OCCUPATION and passed on to those who newly enter the occupation. The occupational culture may include beliefs, attitudes, rituals, jargon, and other elements. See CULTURE TRAIT.

occupational differential association. See DIFFERENTIAL ASSOCIATION, OCCUPATIONAL.

occupational distance. The distance between the OCCUPATIONAL CATEGORIES into which any two occupations fall, when occupations are classified in a hierarchy of status and prestige. The concept of occupational distance is used in studies of social stratification and vertical mobility. See MOBILITY, VERTICAL SOCIAL; STRATIFICATION, SOCIAL.

occupational group. A GROUP organized on the basis of the common (or similar) OCCUPATION of its members. All persons engaged in a common occupation do not necessarily form an occupational group, for an occupational group is united by an awareness of common interests, a feeling of identity with the occupation and with others in that occupation, certain common goals and values, leadership, and group organization. Professional associations and labor unions are examples of occupational groups.

occupational hierarchy. The ranking of occupations on the basis of prestige, income, or other criteria. Usually occupations are classified into categories and the categories are ranked in a hierarchy. Such occupational hierarchies are used in studies of social class structure and social mobility. See MOBILITY, SOCIAL; OCCUPATION; OCCUPATIONAL CATEGORIES; SOCIAL CLASS.

occupational movement. See HORIZONTAL OCCUPATIONAL MOVEMENT; VERTICAL OCCUPATIONAL MOVEMENT.

occupational prestige scale. See NORTH-HATT SCALE OF OCCUPATIONAL PRESTIGE.

occupational situs. See SITUS.

occupational sociology. See SOCIOLOGY, OCCUPATIONAL.

Ockham's razor. See PARSIMONY, PRINCIPLE OF.

Oedipus complex. A very strong attachment of a son to his mother and a strong feeling of rivalry with his father for his mother's affections. Psychoanalytic theory often defines the Oedipus (and Electra) complex as more biological and incestuous than it is regarded to be by sociologists. See ELECTRA COMPLEX.

office. A position within a formal organization. An office confers upon its occupant specific rights and duties defined by standardized rules.

official, line. See MANAGEMENT, MIDDLE.

ogive. A LINE GRAPH showing the cumulative frequency distribution of a VARIABLE. The cumulative class intervals, or subdivisions, of the variable are arranged along the horizontal axis, and the cumulative frequencies are arranged along the vertical axis. Each CLASS INTERVAL along the horizontal axis includes all the cases below (or above) a certain level (for example, less than $1,000, less than $1,500, less than $2,000, etc.) and thus each class interval includes all the cases in the class intervals below it. The vertical axis is in essence a percentile scale (although it may be expressed in numbers of cases), as it shows the increasing proportion of cases in each cumulative class interval. The term *ogive* is taken from architecture, where it refers to a type of Gothic arch that has somewhat the shape of an S. This shape occurs only in the case of the cumulative curve of a normal frequency distribution, and technically, therefore, only this curve is an ogive. Some writers insist on thus limiting the use of the term; however, frequently it is used to refer to any cumulative frequency distribution curve plotted in the manner described above, regardless of the shape of the distribution. See FREQUENCY DISTRIBUTION; FREQUENCY DISTRIBUTION, CUMULATIVE; FREQUENCY DISTRIBUTION CURVE; FREQUENCY DISTRIBUTION CURVE, NORMAL.

oligarchy. A form of government in which a small group rules and holds supreme power over a larger society.

oligarchy, iron law of. A principle of social stratification, used by Roberto Michels, holding that it is functionally necessary for power eventually to come into the hands of a small group of people, whether the form of government is democratic, socialist, communist, or any other. (R. Michels, *Political Parties,* Free Press, Glencoe, Ill., 1949.)

oligopoly. The effective control and domination of a market or industry by a few powerful firms.

one-tailed test. A statistical test used to test a HYPOTHESIS when the direction of the difference between samples or the relationship between variables is predicted in the hypothesis. That is, the alternative hypothesis specifies which sample will be further in a given direction (score higher, be more favorable, etc.) if there is a significant difference between them, or if there is a relationship between the variables, whether it will be positive or negative. Such a prediction, of course, must be based on adequate theoretical and logical grounds. The term *one-tailed* refers to the fact that the REGION OF REJECTION of the null hypothesis (the hypothesis that there will be no significant difference) is located entirely at one end (or tail) of the SAMPLING DISTRIBUTION. See HYPOTHESIS, ALTERNATIVE; HYPOTHESIS, NULL; TWO-TAILED TEST.

ontogenesis or **ontogeny.** The development, history, or life cycle of an individual organism from conception to death.

ontology. The branch of METAPHYSICS that deals with the nature of ultimate reality and the theory of being itself.

open-class ideology. A system of beliefs centered on the idea that any person can rise to any position and social class in society by hard work and ability, regardless of his class of origin and his present condition or status.

open-class system. A SOCIAL CLASS system in which there is freedom of vertical mobility, that is, one in which an individual can readily increase or decrease his social-class position. No legal or traditional restrictions are placed on upward or downward mobility, and rising to a higher social class is positively valued in the society. In an open-class system, movement of persons up and down the social-class structure is frequent both within the lifetime of individuals and between generations. In an IDEAL TYPE of open-class system, persons would be distributed in social classes primarily on the basis of achievement. See CLOSED-CLASS SYSTEM; MOBILITY, VERTICAL SOCIAL.

open-ended question. A question that does not force the respondent to answer in terms of predetermined and fixed alternatives, such as "yes" or "no," but allows him to answer the question freely in his own words and from his point of view. See FIXED-ALTERNATIVE QUESTION.

open shop. A plant or other enterprise in which employees are not required to join a union.

operational definition. A definition of an abstract concept in terms of simple, observable procedures. The measuring procedure constitutes the full extent of the definition as well as the method of observation of the phenomenon. An example would be the definition of intelligence in terms of I.Q. score or social class in terms of income. Thus, concepts are tied to readily measurable and readily communicated phenomena and, in a sense, one determines what one wishes to define by finding an acceptable way of measuring it empirically. The operational definition is very important in social research, but many concepts relating to human values and role behavior are extremely complex—too complex to be expressed fully and adequately in simple operational terms. Rigid operational definitions have a limited, though important, role in social research. See CONCEPT, SENSITIZING.

operationalism. A position in the philosophy of science holding that scientific concepts and research procedure are inseparable. Thus the only scientifically valid concepts are OPERATIONAL DEFINITIONS—definitions so constructed that the means of measuring the concept constitute the definition of the concept.

opinion. 1. A conclusion or judgment about a specific event, object (including a person or group), or situation. An opinion is a very specific manifestation of an ATTITUDE in relation to a particular problem. For example, a person may have an attitude favoring maximum public support for education and an opinion that the local school tax in his community should be raised immediately.
2. A verbal expression of an attitude.
See BELIEF; VALUE.

opinion, public. See PUBLIC OPINION.

opinion leader. An individual within a community who has an important impact on the opinion of others. Others in the community tend to look to the opinion leaders for information and advice. The opinion leader does not necessarily hold any official position of leadership, and may not be immediately known to an investigator studying the community. Such leaders are important in shaping public opinion with regard to new ideas, for example, the fluoridation of water.

opinion poll. A method of systematically questioning people to study their opinions about topics or issues, usually using a SAMPLE of the population being studied.

opportunities, intervening. See STOUFFER'S HYPOTHESIS OF INTERVENING OPPORTUNITIES.

opposition. A universal process found in social interaction in which individuals or groups struggle in COMPETITION or CONFLICT with each other for control of leadership or domination of the conditions of social life. Opposition to the goals and values of other individuals or groups is usually justified in terms of a higher good or value. Opposition is as much a fact of social life as is COOPERATION.

optimum estimate. The best available estimate of a population PARAMETER. See STATISTIC.

oral tradition. CULTURE that is transmitted from one generation to the next by word of mouth rather than through written accounts. The term is usually used with reference to folk societies without a written language. Nevertheless it should be recognized that even in modern industrial society there are many informal traditions (games, for example) that persist among adults as well as children and survive generation after generation without ever being written down. Folklorists can study modern as well as primitive society.

order. See SOCIAL ORDER.

order statistics. See STATISTICS, ORDER.

ordering-forbidding. A social technique that involves "meeting a crisis by an arbitrary act of will decreeing the disappearance of the undesirable or the appearance of the desirable phenomena, and using arbitrary physical action to enforce the decree. This method corresponds exactly to the magical phase of natural technique [technique to control natural phenomena such as weather, disease, etc.]. In both, the essential means of bringing a determined effect is more or less consciously thought to reside in the act of will itself by which the effect is decreed as desirable and of which the action is merely an indispensable vehicle or instrument; in both, the process by which the cause (act of will and physical action) is supposed to bring its effect to realization remains out of reach of investigation; in both, finally, if the result is not attained, some new act of will with new material accessories is introduced, instead of trying to find and remove the perturbing causes. A good instance of this in the social field is the typical legislative procedure of today." (W. I. Thomas and F. Znaniecki, *The Polish Peasant in Europe and America,* Vol. I, University of Chicago Press, Chicago, 1918.)

ordinal sampling. See SAMPLE, SYSTEMATIC.

ordinal scale. A SCALE in which the categories have an inherent order of magnitude according to which they are arranged. The categories represent degrees of magnitude of a given characteristic, and may be ranked from greatest to least, highest to lowest, or first to last. There is no implication that there is an equal distance between succeeding categories or that the categories represent a uniform rate of increase or decrease. That is, there may be twice as great a distance between the first and second categories as there is between the second and third categories. An ordinal scale provides only a rank order of categories. Ordinal scales are used frequently in social research. Most attitude scales and scales of socioeconomic status are ordinal scales. Ordinal scales are sometimes referred to as ranking scales or rank order scales. See INTERVAL SCALE; NOMINAL SCALE; RANK, STATISTICAL; RATIO SCALE.

ordinate. The vertical axis on a GRAPH. The ordinate is perpendicular to the ABSCISSA, or horizontal axis. See COORDINATE AXES.

orenda. See MANA.

organic solidarity. See SOLIDARITY, ORGANIC.

organicism. The view that society is structurally similar to a biological organism. Society is viewed as being essentially analogous to a human or animal system, with its interdependent parts (or organs) making up the totality or the body of society. The organic model and the MECHANISTIC ANALOGY of society have been widely used in social theory. The most influential sociologist to use the organic analogy was Herbert Spencer. Others include Albert Schaeffle, Paul von Lilienfeld, and René Worms.

organization. 1. See ORGANIZATION, SOCIAL.
2. See ORGANIZATION, FORMAL.

organization, complex. A large-scale formal organization. Complex organizations include corporations, labor unions, universities, professional associations, religious denominations, and government agencies. Although complex organizations are formal organizations, the study of complex organizations treats the informal as well as the formal aspects of their social organization. See BUREAUCRACY; ORGANIZATION, FORMAL.

organization, corporate. See CORPORATION.

organization, ecological. See ECOLOGICAL STRUCTURE.

organization, formal. 1. A highly organized GROUP having explicit objectives, formally stated rules and regulations, and a system of specifically defined roles, each with clearly designated rights and duties. Usually the term is more restricted in its usage than is formal group. Thus while all formal organizations are formal groups, not all formal groups are considered formal organizations, only those that are highly formalized, impersonal, and fairly large. Formal organizations include schools, hospitals, voluntary associations, corporations, government agencies, etc. The study of formal organizations usually includes both the formal and informal aspects of their social organization. See BUREAUCRACY; GROUP, FORMAL; ORGANIZATION, COMPLEX; ROLE.

2. The formal aspects of social organization: the rationally ordered systems of norms and roles governing the relationships of persons in groups or in specified social situations. Thus it may be said that a GROUP that is a formal organization (definition 1.) has both a formal and an informal social organization. See ORGANIZATION, INFORMAL; ORGANIZATION, SOCIAL; STRUCTURE, FORMAL.

organization, informal. 1. The system of personal relationships that develops spontaneously as individuals interact within a formal organization. Every formal organization has an informal aspect to its social organization, which is not planned and not formally stated. The informal social organization includes social norms, rituals, traditions, sentiments, and subgroups that influence the functioning of the formal organization but are not officially recognized.

2. Occasionally, informal aspects of any social organization, regardless of whether or not it is a formal organization. See ORGANIZATION, FORMAL; ORGANIZATION, SOCIAL.

organization, line. That segment of a large-scale organization, such as an industrial corporation, that has the authority and direct responsibility for the production of goods or services. The line organization consults and is advised by the staff organization. See ORGANIZATION, STAFF.

organization, social. 1. A relatively stable pattern of social relationships of individuals and subgroups within a society or group, based upon systems of social roles, norms, and shared meanings that provide regularity and predictability in social interaction. In this sense social organization is essentially synonymous with SOCIAL STRUCTURE. See MEANING; NORM, SOCIAL; ROLE.

2. Sometimes, a formally organized social group. More often, such a group is referred to as a formal organization. See ORGANIZATION, FORMAL.

3. See SOCIETY.

organization, staff. The staff of specialists and technicians who perform research and advisory services for the line officials or production segment of a formal organization, such as a large industrial corporation. See ORGANIZATION, LINE.

organization man. A business or professional person who dedicates himself to the tasks, norms, and goals defined by the leaders who control and dominate the formal organization of which he is a part. He is loyal and conforming and does not stress individuality, innovation, originality, or concern with a wider range of interests than those encompassed by the organization. He is more dedicated to the organization than to abstract ideals or principles. When there is a conflict of abstract ideals with organizational demands and requirements, he easily rationalizes the primacy of organizational demands. The term was introduced by William H. Whyte (*Organization Man,* Simon and Schuster, New York, 1956). See ORGANIZATION, FORMAL.

organizational effectiveness. The extent to which an organization is able to attain its currently stated goals without jeopardizing its future material or organizational resources (for example, morale) or long-range interests.

organized crime. See CRIME, ORGANIZED.

organized research. See RESEARCH, ORGANIZED.

original nature. The primitive bodily or organic characteristics found in infants before human interaction, culture, and general environmental conditions begin to modify innate reflexes. Sometimes original nature is defined as the sum of all hereditary factors and tendencies that emerge as a person matures. This latter definition is generally rejected by sociologists and social psychologists because hereditary tendencies and characteristics developed through physical maturation are not in any "original" form, that is, not in a form determined solely by hereditary factors. All personal characteristics are modified according to the experiences of the individual in his psychological, social, and cultural environment. Original nature must not be confused with the concept of HUMAN NATURE. Human nature is usually used with reference to mature individuals and thus assumes the impact of SOCIALIZATION upon the socially and culturally unorganized reflexes of the child's original nature.

ossification. A condition of society in which there is resistance to "progress" and social change. The term is now obsolete, but ossification was considered to be one of the "diseases" of society. See CULTURE LAG; ORGANICISM.

other, generalized. See GENERALIZED OTHER.

other-directed society. A generalized or IDEAL TYPE of society, formulated by David Riesman, Nathan Glazer, and Reuel Denney, which "develops in its typical members a social character whose conformity is insured by their tendency to be sensitized to the expectations and preferences of others." According to Riesman, Glazer, and Denney, other-directedness is characteristic of modern urban, industrial, and bureaucratic society, where getting along with others in a mobile and impersonal world demands a sensitivity to the norms of the immediate social situation. (D. Riesman, N. Glazer, R. Denney, *The Lonely Crowd*, Doubleday, New York, 1954.) In common practice the concept of other-directedness is often applied to an ideal type of individual and termed *other-directed man*. See INNER-DIRECTED SOCIETY; TRADITION-DIRECTED SOCIETY.

others, significant or **relevant.** See SIGNIFICANT OTHERS.

out-group. 1. All persons who are considered as being excluded from or outside of an IN-GROUP—that is, all nonmembers of an in-group.

2. A group whose members are considered to be in opposition, or to be in some way alien, to an IN-GROUP.

overconformity. Excessive or compulsive insistence on conformity to a social norm or set of social norms. Excessive devotion to social norms is often punished, or in some way negatively sanctioned. Overconformity is often called "hypocritical" or "fanatical." This negative response to overconformity is probably due to the fact that to overconform to one social norm (patriotism, religiosity, generosity, etc.) is to erode or deviate from some other important social norm or obligation. The limits of conformity to any social norm are determined by the other norms and obligations in the situation. Thus overconformity to one social norm (or norms) involves the neglect of or deviance from other important duties, obligations, and norms.

overt behavior. See BEHAVIOR, OVERT.

overt culture. See CULTURE, EXPLICIT.

ownership, absentee. See ABSENTEE OWNERSHIP.

P

paired-comparison scale. A SCALE constructed by comparing each item in the study with every other item. For every pair of items a judgment is made as to which is higher in the characteristic being measured by the scale. On the basis of all the paired judgments, the items are arranged in an ORDINAL SCALE.

paired concepts. Concepts used to organize the analysis of social phenomena into sets of dichotomies, for example, FOLK SOCIETY/URBAN SOCIETY, PRIMARY RELATIONS/SECONDARY RELATIONS. Paired concepts are the names used to designate a pair of polar types. See IDEAL TYPE; POLAR TYPE.

pairing method. See MATCHING.

Paleolithic Age. A period or stage of cultural and economic development in the history of man, also called the Old Stone Age, characterized by the use of chipped stone tools and pressure-chipped tools in the latter part of the epoch, and having an economy based on hunting and gathering. The Paleolithic Age is the earliest known period of culture. See NEOLITHIC AGE.

panel technique. An interviewing technique in which the sample or population is interviewed repeatedly over an extended period of time.

paradigm. Generally, a MODEL or schema. The term has been used by Robert K. Merton to refer to a device for presenting a succinct codification of an area of sociological analysis. A paradigm is a compact outline of the major concepts, assumptions, procedures, propositions, and problems of a substantive area or a theoretical approach in sociological analysis. Merton hoped that the use of the paradigm would give to qualitative analysis some of the precision of quantitative analysis by cutting through pages of discursive exposition to the "hard skeleton of fact, inference, and theoretic conclusion" concisely and explicitly stated. It "should be noted that the paradigm does not represent a set of categories introduced *de novo*, but rather a *codification* of those concepts and problems which have been forced upon our attention by critical scrutiny of current research and theory" in a given field. (R. K. Merton, *Social Theory and Social Structure*, Free Press, Glencoe, Ill., 1957.) See IDEAL TYPE.

parallel cousins. Children of siblings of the same sex, that is, two or more brothers' children, or two or more sisters' children. A person's paternal uncle's children or his maternal aunt's children would be his parallel cousins. In some societies parallel cousins are forbidden to marry because they are considered brothers and sisters. See CROSS-COUSINS.

parallelism. The independent development of similar or identical inventions or cultural forms in widely separated cultures. The term also refers to the theoretical view holding that all cultures tend to follow the same lines of development. See DIFFUSIONISM.

parameter. A summary measure of a characteristic of a POPULATION. A parameter may be a measure of central tendency, such as a mean, a MEDIAN, or a MODE, a measure of dispersion such as a STANDARD DEVIATION, a measure of association between two variables such as a COEFFICIENT OF CORRELATION, or any other measure of the distribution of one or more characteristics in a population. It is important to note that a parameter is a measure of an entire population, or universe, and not a measure of a SAMPLE. Since most social research deals with samples, true parameters are usually unknown and must be estimated from sample data. A parameter is sometimes referred to as a population parameter or a universe parameter. See ASSOCIATION, STATISTICAL; CENTRAL TENDENCY, MEASURE OF; DISPERSION, STATISTICAL; FREQUENCY DISTRIBUTION; MEAN, ARITHMETIC; STATISTIC.

parameter estimate. See STATISTIC.

parametric statistics. That brand of statistics comprising techniques of statistical analysis which require that the data being analyzed be drawn from a population distribution with a specified form. Usually parametric techniques assume that the POPULATION from which the SAMPLE was drawn has a normal frequency distribution. In addition, parametric techniques require that each case included in the sample has been included independently of every other case (that is, the inclusion of one case does not automatically lead to the inclusion of another case), that when samples have been drawn from two or more populations these populations have the same VARIANCE or in some cases a known ratio of variances, and that the data be in arithmetic form (so that they can be added, divided, multiplied) and not in the form of ranks. Parametric statistics developed earlier than NONPARAMETRIC STATISTICS. When the above conditions are met, parametric techniques usually provide greater power than nonparametric techniques. See FREQUENCY DISTRIBUTION; FREQUENCY DISTRIBUTION CURVE, NORMAL; PARAMETER; POWER, STATISTICAL; RANK, STATISTICAL.

paranoia. A PSYCHOSIS characterized by a systematic, well-organized, and enduring DELUSION, most commonly a delusion of persecution or a delusion of grandeur.

parole. The release of a person from prison prior to the expiration of the maximum period of time for which he was sentenced, on the condition that he submit to certain supervision and specified restrictions on his behavior. If he violates the conditions of his parole, he may be returned to prison. Parole is often granted for "good behavior" in prison and when the authorities feel it will contribute to the prisoner's rehabilitation.

parsimony, principle of. The principle, also called Ockham's razor, holding that the simplest and least complicated explanations and hypotheses are the best. When two explanations seem equally good, the one with the least complicated set of assumptions should be chosen.

participant observation. See OBSERVATION, PARTICIPANT.

participation, social. 1. The participation of an individual in social groups. See GROUP.

2. Sometimes restricted to participation in voluntary organizations, particularly those engaged in some type of community activity or project, outside of an individual's professional or occupational work situations.

particularism. The orientation of an individual to another individual in terms of the special nature of their relationship to each other (for example, their membership in the same group) rather than in terms of abstract standards of behavior. For example, if a judge sentences a defendant leniently because the defendant is his nephew, he is applying particularistic standards. In all societies there are social situations in which particularism is expected and approved. However, in specific situations particularistic norms may be approved in one group and not in another. See PATTERN VARIABLE; UNIVERSALISM; UNIVERSALISM-PARTICULARISM.

particularism-universalism. See UNIVERSALISM-PARTICULARISM.

particularistic fallacy. The unwarranted generalization of certain particular facts so that broad conclusions about complex phenomena are based on certain specific facts that support a particular point of view while other facts are ignored or unknown. Thus the conclusions are based on insufficient or incomplete data.

party, political. See POLITICAL PARTY.

pastoralism. A type of economy centered about domesticated animals.

paternalism. A type of LEADERSHIP in which those who are superordinate provide for the needs of the subordinates in return for loyalty and obedience.

path analysis. The analysis of causal relationships among a series of variables. Path analysis attempts to determine the plausibility of a causal ordering among variables, based upon regression analysis. In a simplified example, variable b may be dependent on variable a, and variable c, in turn, may be dependent on variable b. However, the models developed in path analysis are usually much more complex than this. They are frequently presented diagrammatically and are referred to as path diagrams. Relationships between independent and dependent variables are asymmetric (one-way) and are shown by an arrow. (Independent variables may be symmetrically related to each other and this is shown by a two-way arrow.) Path analysis can be particularly useful in analyzing causal relationships among variables over a prolonged period of time. (See O. D. Duncan, *American Journal of Sociology*, July 1966.) See CAUSATION; REGRESSION, STATISTICAL; VARIABLE.

pathology, social. See SOCIAL PATHOLOGY.

patriarchy. See FAMILY, PATRIARCHAL.

patrilineal descent. Descent (and sometimes inheritance) traced unilaterally through the father and the male line.

patrilocal residence. The custom in some cultures for a married couple to reside in the husband's parent's (father's) home or locality.

patronymic system. See FAMILY, PATRONYMIC.

pattern variables. Five dichotomies or pairs of variables proposed by Talcott Parsons for the purpose of classifying types of social relationships. Each pattern variable provides two mutually exclusive alternatives, one of which must be chosen by an individual before he can act in a social situation. According to Parsons, the five pattern variables represent the basic dilemmas a person faces in orienting to another person. Social roles in a society may be classified according to those alternatives of the pattern variables that predominate in the normative expectations that define the appropriate role behavior. The five pattern variables are: AFFECTIVITY-AFFECTIVE NEUTRALITY; SELF-ORIENTATION—COLLECTIVITY ORIENTATION; UNIVERSALISM-PARTICULARISM; ASCRIPTION-ACHIEVEMENT (also referred to as quality-performance); DIFFUSENESS-SPECIFICITY. (See T. Parsons and E. A. Shils, eds., *Toward a General Theory of Action*, Harvard University Press, Cambridge, Mass., 1951.) See ACTION THEORY, SOCIAL; ROLE; VARIABLE.

patterned evasion. A regularized way of deviating from an established social norm which is tolerated and in fact becomes part of the culture. Examples of patterned evasions include income tax cheating, fee-splitting among physicians, nepotism, gambling, prostitution, bribery, and graft. The term was introduced by Robin M. Williams, Jr., as an alternative to Robert K. Merton's *institutionalized evasion*. (R. M. Williams, Jr., *American Society*, Knopf, New York, 1951.)

Pearson product-moment correlation coefficient. See CORRELATION, PEARSON PRODUCT-MOMENT.

peasant community. A rural, agricultural community with a simple technology and a cultural tradition relatively distinct from that of the larger society of which it is a part. Peasant communities are often nonliterate, but lie within a literate, politically organized society. Although the peasant community maintains its traditional distinctiveness from the larger society and sophisticated elite, it is nevertheless part of the economic, political, and religious structure of the society as a whole.

pecking order. The pattern found in the pecking behavior of chickens, in which each bird has a relative position of dominance within the flock by virtue of its ability to peck at other birds. Each bird learns which members of the flock it can and cannot peck at successfully. Often the least successful birds are eventually pecked to ill-health or death. Some writers refer to the competitive aspects of human life as evidence of a human pecking order. As with all analogies from animal to human behavior, this is an oversimplification.

peer group. A primary group, that is, a close, intimate group, composed of members who have roughly equal status. Children's play groups are peer groups and are important to children in forming models for identification because they are relatively free from adult definitions and adult authority. While the term is most often used to refer to children's or teenage groups, it also applies to adult groups in which the members have approximately equal status. See GROUP, PRIMARY.

penalizations, derivative. See DERIVATIVE PENALIZATIONS.

penology. The branch of criminology that studies the punishment and treatment of criminals in various societies and at various historical periods, and the effects of different types of treatment.

perceived role. See ROLE, PERCEIVED.

percentage. A proportion or fraction multiplied by 100. A percent expresses a proportion as a part of a hundred, telling how much the proportion would be if the whole were one hundred.

percentile. One of one hundred points dividing a FREQUENCY DISTRIBUTION into one hundred equal parts. A particular percentile tells the percent of the total number of cases in the frequency distribution that fall below that point. For example, the tenth percentile is the point below which 10% of the cases lie, the 16th percentile the point below which 16% lie, the 73rd percentile the point below which 73% lie, etc. See DECILE; QUARTILE.

percentile range. A measure of dispersion of values in a FREQUENCY DISTRIBUTION, sometimes used instead of the total RANGE. The PERCENTILE range gives the range between two percentile points, usually the 10th and 90th percentiles between which 80% of the cases fall. When the 10th and 90th percentiles are used, the percentile range is found by subtracting the value of the 10th percentile from the value of the 90th percentile. Thus, for example, if 10% of a sample had scores of 50 or lower and 90% had scores of 150 or lower, the 10th–90th percentile range would be 100. The 10th–90th percentile range is used most often in educational research. See DISPERSION, STATISTICAL; QUARTILE DEVIATION.

perception. 1. The selection, organization, and interpretation by an individual of specific stimuli in a situation, according to prior learning, activities, interests, experiences, etc. Perception is a process and a pattern of response to stimuli. It is a function of the situational field, that is, of the total configuration of stimuli, as well as of previous social and cultural conditioning.
   2. Recognition or awareness of an object or event through the sense organs.
   See SENSATION.

perception, selective. The tendency of individuals to perceive those elements of a situation which support previous expectations. All PERCEPTION is selective, in the sense that all individuals learn to select relevant stimuli and organize them in standard ways, both for understanding and for communication with others.

performance. In Talcott Parsons' scheme of PATTERN VARIABLES, one of the dichotomous categories of the pattern variable quality-performance. This pattern variable is more commonly known by its original name of ASCRIPTION-ACHIEVEMENT, and performance is equivalent to achievement.

performance test. A nonverbal test (of intelligence, aptitude, interest, etc.) used to test the responses of a person to actual situations, problems, objects, and so forth, in contrast to a verbal test.

permissiveness. Tolerance in certain situations of deviance, rebellion, or the expression of hostility, without negative judgments or sanctions. For example, excessive emotionalism, irrationality, and incompetence during periods of mourning are tolerated in many societies.

permutation. The arrangement of objects in a particular order. Each possible ordering of a number of objects is a permutation. The permutations of a given set of objects are all the possible sequences of those objects. Thus ABC is one permutation of the letters A,B, and C. The other permutations are ACB, BAC, BCA, CAB, and CBA. See COMBINATION.

persistences, group. See INSTINCT FOR COMBINATIONS and INSTINCT FOR GROUP PERSISTENCES.

person. A self-conscious being capable of choosing between alternative modes of behavior on the basis of reflection. The person as a unit of sociological analysis is a social object, has a particular STATUS, and performs social roles involving responsibilities to himself and others as a member of society and participant in its cultural ideals and traditions. See ROLE.

personal disorganization. See DISORGANIZATION, PERSONAL.

personal document. Any written or recorded document, such as an essay, diary, autobiography, or letter, which is an account of the social and psychological experiences of an individual. Such documents are called "personal" because they are organized by the individual himself and are essentially a self-analysis or self-documentation, recording and stressing what is most salient to the individual rather than to the interests of an interviewer.

personal-social learning. Learning that is not culturally determined, but which for the most part grows out of more individualized social relationships and experiences. The term was used by Kimball Young (*Personality and Problems of Adjustment,* Appleton-Century-Crofts, New York, 1952).

personality. The relatively organized configuration of typical patterns of behavior, attitudes, beliefs, and values characteristic of a person, and recognized as such by himself and others. Personality is a product of individual experiences in a cultural environment and social interaction. We identify the structure of an individual's personality by observing the general pattern of his behavior, how he thinks, feels, and acts (including his role behavior and value system). Individual personalities reflect the structure and processes of the person's SOCIETY and CULTURE. In a sense we arrive at our notion of culture by studying individual behavior and its products, and thus personality can be viewed as the subjective aspect of culture. However, social and cultural life is so complex, changing, inconsistent, and unstable that personalities are infinitely diverse despite their relatively uniform conformity to cultural definitions and social roles. See PERSONALITY TRAIT; ROLE; SELF.

personality, abnormal. See ABNORMAL BEHAVIOR.

personality, authoritarian. See AUTHORITARIAN PERSONALITY.

personality, basic. See PERSONALITY TYPE, BASIC.

personality, modal. See PERSONALITY TYPE, BASIC.

personality, multiple. See MULTIPLE PERSONALITY.

personality, psychopathic. See PSYCHOPATHIC PERSONALITY.

personality, segmentalized. A PERSONALITY comprising social roles that are very diverse and not consistent with each other. The individual's values and attitudes do not form an integrated and satisfying self-conception. Values and adjustive responses that are valid and applicable in certain segments of the individual's life are maladaptive or irrelevant in other aspects of his life. The segmentalized personality is presumably more characteristic of large, complex, modern societies than of small, simple, rural societies. See ROLE.

personality, status. See STATUS PERSONALITY.

personality absorption. The domination of a child's activities by a parent or parents in such a way and to such extent as to forestall and discourage exploratory and independent action on the part of the child. Such children are often considered "spoiled" because of their emotional and social dependence (for example, their ineptitude in competently making independent judgments). Personality absorption is a form of social domination and suppression of autonomy and freedom of the child by a possessive parent or parents.

personality configuration. See PERSONALITY.

personality disorder. See MENTAL DISORDER.

personality disorganization. See DISORGANIZATION, PERSONAL.

personality integration. The harmonious coordination of the various aspects of the PERSONALITY with each other, and of the personality as a whole with its environment, so that the individual experiences relatively few inconsistent and frustrating demands from within the self or from the social environment. Perfect personality integration is impossible, and certainly not normal for persons in social interaction. It probably is, however, a constant goal of every individual—one that cannot be reached and stabilized, since the nature of the social demands and social roles faced by each individual is constantly changing as he matures and ages. There is, however, considerable status in successfully presenting an image of an integrated personality to others.

personality trait. A relatively consistent and enduring pattern of behavior or other aspect of an individual's PERSONALITY which is manifested in many situations and which can be used to distinguish one personality from another. Honesty and aggressiveness are examples of personality traits.

personality type, basic. A pattern of common personality traits presumed to be characteristic of persons in a particular culture. The basic personality type distinguishes the personality of individuals in that culture from the type of personality prevalent in other cultural groups. Differences in basic personality types are presumably due to differences in child-rearing practices and other characteristics of the social and cultural life of each group. The concept is controversial but of great theoretical interest for sociology, cultural anthropology, and social psychology. It is sometimes referred to as modal personality. See NATIONAL CHARACTER.

personalizing process. See FUSION PROCESS.

personification. 1. Imputing to social groups or social structures human qualities.

2. In psychiatry, the tendency to blame some person for the frustrating events and situations experienced by an individual.

3. See ANTHROPOMORPHISM.

perspective. The values, beliefs, attitudes, and meanings that provide the framework and point of view from which an individual views a situation. A perspective consists of assumptions that are usually not consciously defined, but which influence what the individual perceives and how he interprets his perceptions. See FRAME OF REFERENCE.

petty bourgeoisie. See BOURGEOISIE.

phenomenalism. The philosophical doctrine that we cannot know reality or the ultimate nature of things, but only appearances. Thus we can only know objects as they appear through our senses.

phenomenological approach. In psychology and social psychology an approach that attempts to suspend the biases and judgments of the observer, and to observe and describe faithfully the phenomena involved in the behavior of the individual, emphasizing perception and consciousness. It is held that the phenomena shaping individual behavior are phenomena as perceived by the acting individual. Objects are recognized as existing as objective phenomena, but it is maintained that their meaning for behavior derives from the individual's relationship and reaction to the objects. Psychological phenomenology may be regarded as an approach in COGNITIVE THEORY.

phenomenon. Any object or event that can be observed or experienced through the senses. See SOCIAL PHENOMENON.

phi coefficient. A statistical test used to determine whether there is a statistically significant association between two dichotomous variables. The phi coefficient (ϕ) is used with data in a fourfold (2×2) table. The variables may be dichotomous qualitative variables or quantitative variables that have been compressed into dichotomies. Phi coefficient has the advantage that it is mathematically related to the Pearsonian product-moment coefficient of correlation (r). It is most useful when the set of marginals (totals for each category) of the two variables are similar. When the marginal sets are very dissimilar, phi provides a weak measure of association. See ASSOCIATION, STATISTICAL; CONTINGENCY; CORRELATION, PEARSON PRODUCT-MOMENT; PROBABILITY; SIGNIFICANCE, STATISTICAL; VARIABLE.

philosophical idealism. See IDEALISM.

philosophical sociology. See SOCIOLOGY, PHILOSOPHICAL.

philosophy. A broad discipline concerned with the nature of reality, knowledge, meaning, and truth, the ultimate nature of man and his relation to the universe, the problem of value, or ethics, and aesthetics. Philosophy uses the findings of the empirical sciences, but philosophical inquiry is primarily concerned with the clarification of those conceptual problems that are seen as underlying all other disciplines. Thus, in addition to concern with the fundamental problems mentioned above, philosophy is also concerned with the analysis of the basic assumptions, concepts, and procedures of specific fields of inquiry.

philosophy, social. See SOCIAL PHILOSOPHY.

phratry. An exogamous group of two or more clans which have a special bond between them and which associate for various activities. The various phratries within a tribe or society sometimes may be the result of the splitting of a large clan into several units or sometimes of the uniting of two distinct clans into a phratry. See CLAN; EXOGAMY.

phrenology. A PSEUDO SCIENCE based on the discredited assumption that mental faculties or talents are located in different areas of the brain and that therefore a person's talents can be determined by examining the shape (particularly the bumps) of his skull.

physical anthropology. See ANTHROPOLOGY, PHYSICAL.

physical environment. See ENVIRONMENT, GEOGRAPHIC.

physiological hypothesis. The notion that behavior is determined by changes in the physiology of the organism.

physiological need. See NEED, PHYSIOLOGICAL.

physiological psychology. See PSYCHOLOGY, PHYSIOLOGICAL.

Piaget's rules of the game. See RULES OF THE GAME, PIAGET'S.

pictograph. 1. In cultural anthropology, a simple, stylized picture used in an early form of writing. The pictograph conveys meaning through the picture portrayed, and is not used as a conventionalized symbol with which to construct words or sentences. Pictographic writing preceded the development of hieroglyphics, which utilizes a more conventionalized symbolic form. See IDEOGRAPH.

2. In statistics, a pictorial presentation of a horizontal BAR GRAPH. Rows of pictorial symbols are used instead of horizontal bars. The symbols represent the phenomenon whose distribution or quantity is being presented, the number of symbols indicating the quantity in each CATEGORY or time period.

picture-frustration study. See ROSENZWEIG TEST.

pidgin. A simplified form of a language (such as pidgin English, pidgin French) developed by a people, having a different native language, who have a practical need for limited communication in the foreign language. The pidginized language develops a standardized form influenced by the grammatical structure of the speakers' native tongue, and in time is stabilized and learned as a second language by its users. "A pidgin is defined as a stable form of speech that is not learned as a first language (mother tongue) by any of its users, but as an auxiliary language by all; whose functions are sharply restricted (e.g., to trade, supervision of work, administration, communication with visitors), and whose vocabulary and overt structure are sharply reduced, in comparison with those of the languages from which they are derived." (D. Hymes, *Items*, Social Science Research Council, June 1968.)

pie chart. A GRAPH or graphic illustration (also called circle chart) consisting of a circle divided into pie-shaped sectors that add up to 100% of the whole. The radius is arbitrary and drawn to a convenient size. The pie chart graphically shows the percent or proportion of each component sector (or CATEGORY) to the whole.

place grouping. See GROUP, TERRITORIAL.

plain-folks technique. A PROPAGANDA technique in which a speaker or writer attempts to convey the impression that he is really not the high-status, wealthy, or powerful individual he seems, but rather an ordinary person with the same interests, values, and identities as the lower-status group he is trying to deceive to gain their political or economic favor. Large corporations and governments may also personify their organization and be "folksy" to their customers in an effort to win their loyalty.

planning, city or **community.** See PLANNING, URBAN SOCIAL.

planning, social. Any conscious and relatively large-scale, coordinated effort to recognize old or anticipate new problems or opportunities and to propose solutions and programs for the benefit of a society, community, or organization. Social planning is inherent in large-scale organization. Governments, corporations, armies, and other large organizations engage in social planning for the future activity of their members. Objections to social planning stem not from any real objections to planning but rather from objections to who shall direct the planning. Various political, economic, and other groups oppose planning when they are not in a position to control the planning to their advantage and for their protection; for, since social planning involves the statement of basic objectives and values and the sacrifice of other, lesser values, those who are not directing social change fear their interests may be damaged for the "higher" goals.

planning, urban social. Social planning for a city or larger urban area, directed or coordinated by a municipal or regional agency. Urban planning dates back to ancient times. It may include regulations concerning zoning, sanitation, health, communications, transportation, or any other area that a community or its leadership considers significant for the achievement of important goals.

plantation farm. See FARM, PLANTATION.

plateau, learning. See LEARNING PLATEAU.

platykurtic curve. See FREQUENCY DISTRIBUTION CURVE, PLATYKURTIC.

play. 1. As defined by George Herbert Mead, a childhood activity, preceding and less socially complicated than the organized game, in which the young child invents make-believe situations and takes the attitude of others toward himself. Thus the young child can pretend to be "mommy" or "daddy" and take on the expectations of his parents to some extent, although he is not yet able to generalize his role playing to form the organized set of perceptions concerning the expectations of others that Mead calls the GENERALIZED OTHER. (G. H. Mead, *Mind, Self and Society,* University of Chicago Press, Chicago, 1934.) See GAME, ORGANIZED.

2. Activity to amuse oneself, to entertain oneself, and to relax some usual inhibition. Play is often creative and may also have a purpose and a usefulness, but the player is not anxious about the activity or its precise outcome. See LEISURE.

play, doll. See DOLL-PLAY PROCEDURE.

pluralism, cultural. See CULTURAL PLURALISM.

pluralistic ignorance. A situation in which individual members of a group believe incorrectly that they are each alone or the only deviants in believing or not believing in particular values, while in reality many others, if not the majority, secretly feel exactly as they do. When traditional values become impractical or when one influential segment of a group dominates, such a situation is common. Much seemingly sudden and revolutionary change in social life is due to a sudden exposure of the widespread deviance in the acceptance of official or traditional attitudes. The term was introduced by Floyd H. Allport, and is discussed in his *Institutionalized Behavior* (University of North Carolina Press, Chapel Hill, N.C., 1933).

plurel. A number of persons. A general term that may be applied to any plurality of persons, including any type of aggregate, collectivity, group, etc.

point biserial coefficient of correlation. See CORRELATION, BISERIAL.

point estimate. See STATISTIC.

point scale. In statistics, an ORDINAL SCALE (one with the categories arranged according to magnitude) that is converted into numerical form by assigning a numerical value to each CATEGORY. Although the numerical values are selected arbitrarily (for example, 1,2,3,4,5), they are assigned to the categories in sequential order in accordance with the categories' rank order, thus expressing in numerical form the increasing (or decreasing) magnitude of the categories. See RANK, STATISTICAL.

Poisson distribution. A limited form of the BINOMIAL DISTRIBUTION (a theoretically expected distribution of a series of random samples drawn from a population with two categories or classes) that occurs when the number of cases in the samples is large and drawn from a very large population and the proportion in one of the two categories is very small.

polar statuses. See STATUSES, POLAR.

polar type. One of a pair of concepts in a dichotomous conceptual MODEL comprising two opposite and contrasting ideal types, such as FOLK SOCIETY and URBAN SOCIETY. The term is also sometimes used to refer to each of the two extreme points of a conceptual model that is in the form of a CONTINUUM. See IDEAL TYPE; PAIRED CONCEPTS.

polemology. The study of human aggressiveness and group CONFLICT. A newly developed field, it is based on the assumption that group conflict is abnormal or unhealthy, and attempts to determine the causes and means of preventing such conflict, particularly wars. Polemology has been developed largely in Europe by biological scientists and experimental psychologists who attempt to explain human behavior primarily on the basis of studies of animals, implying the existence of human instincts and tending to neglect the role of CULTURE in shaping human behavior. See CONFLICT THEORY; ETHNOCENTRISM; IDEOLOGY; INSTINCT; MILITARY INSTITUTION; WAR.

"policy" theory. A type of social theory "concerned with analyzing a given social situation, or social structure, or social action as a basis for policy or action. It might be an analysis of communist strategy and tactics, or of the conditions that sustain racial segregation in an American city, or of the power play in labor relations in mass production industry, or of the morale potential of an enemy country. Such theoretical analysis is not made in the interests of empirical science. Nor is it a mere application of scientific knowledge. Nor is it research inquiry in accordance with the canons of empirical science. The elements of its analysis and their relations have a nature given by the concrete situation and not by the methods or abstractions of empirical science. This form of social theorizing is of obvious importance." (H. Blumer, *American Sociological Review,* February 1954.)

political class. See CLASS, POLITICAL.

political institution. The social institution, or complex of social norms and roles, that serves to maintain social order, to exercise power to compel conformity to the existing system of authority, and to provide the means for changes in the legal or administrative systems. The political institution includes the traditions and laws by which a society is coordinated and administered and is the major repository of force. The modern STATE is one type of social structure in which the political institution finds much of its formal expression and codification. See INSTITUTION, SOCIAL.

political order. See POLITICAL INSTITUTION.

political party. An organization of people interested in and working to control or influence the power structure of a community or society in a way they regard as best for their interests and presumably for the best interests of the community.

political power. See POWER, POLITICAL.

political science. The branch of the social sciences that studies the organization and administration of government, its history and theory.

political sociology. See SOCIOLOGY, POLITICAL.

politics. The process of creating public policy through influencing or controlling the sources of POWER and AUTHORITY. The process involves competition and usually conflict.

polling. See OPINION POLL.

pollyanna response. A DEFENSE MECHANISM for warding off anxiety in which the individual attempts to interpret a negative occurrence positively. For example, a man who is fired from his job might assert that his health would have been ruined if he had worked one more day under those conditions.

polyandry. A form of polygamous marriage in which one woman may be married to several men at the same time. This practice is extremely rare. See POLYGAMY.

polyandry, fraternal. A form of POLYANDRY in which the woman's husbands must be brothers. Where polyandry is practiced, it usually takes this form.

polygamy. Plural marriage, or marriage involving more than one spouse simultaneously. The term includes both POLYANDRY and POLYGYNY, as well as CENOGAMY.

polygamy, serial. A form of marriage which permits a person to have more than one legal mate, but not at the same time. Actually serial polygamy is usually considered MONOGAMY, since strict monogamy (one spouse for eternity) is rare as an obligatory and absolute marriage custom.

polygamy, tandem. See POLYGAMY, SERIAL.

polygenetic hypothesis. An evolutionary hypothesis holding that the human race evolved from several distinctly different species of apelike creatures in different parts of the world. In time, the different forms came in contact with each other and intermixed. This has also been called polygenism and the polygenetic theory. See MONOGENETIC HYPOTHESIS.

polygon, frequency. See FREQUENCY DISTRIBUTION CURVE.

polygyny. A form of POLYGAMY in which a husband has more than one wife at the same time. It is the most common form of polygamy.

polygyny, sororal. A form of POLYGYNY in which custom requires that the several wives of a man must be sisters. In some cases a man may be required to marry his wife's sister if she becomes a widow or has no husband.

population. 1. All the people residing within a delimited geographic area, for example, within a nation, a geographic region, a state, a metropolitan area, a city.

2. In statistics, the total number of cases with a given characteristic (or characteristics), or all members of a given set or class. A population may be an existing, finite number of cases, as all the children attending first grade in the United States at a given time, or it may be a theoretical and infinite number of cases, as all the possible tosses of a coin. Whether the population is finite or infinite, it is from this totality of cases that a SAMPLE is drawn. A population is sometimes referred to as a universe, because it includes the entire existence of a specific characteristic or combination of characteristics. See PARAMETER; POPULATION, FINITE; POPULATION, INFINITE.

population, closed. A POPULATION into which there is no immigration and from which there is no emigration. Population change, therefore, is determined entirely by the relationship between the birth rate and the death rate.

population, daytime. See DAYTIME POPULATION, URBAN.

population, dichotomous. See DICHOTOMOUS POPULATION.

population, finite. In statistics, an existing (or previously existing) POPULATION with a fixed number of cases. A finite population may, but does not necessarily, consist of persons. For example, all the automobile accidents in the United States during a given five-year period would be a finite population. See POPULATION, INFINITE.

population, infinite. In statistics, a theoretical POPULATION with an unlimited number of cases. An example of an infinite population would be all the possible tosses of a coin. See POPULATION, FINITE.

population, nighttime. See DAYTIME POPULATION, URBAN.

population, optimum. The population size that is most conducive to the attainment of a particular social value. Most often those who deal with the concept are interested in determining the population size that will probably result in the highest standard of living (or real per capita income) in a society (or other specified population), given the natural resources of the area, the level of technology, and the forms of social organization. Optimum population size is necessarily a theoretical estimate and cannot be precisely determined. Moreover, optimum size is not constant, it changes as cultural and social forms change. Nevertheless it has been found to be a useful concept, particularly in analyzing probable trends in national economic development. Optimum population may also be considered with reference to other social goals, such as military strength, the advancement of science, and so forth.

population, stable. A population in which the age-sex distribution (distribution of males and females by age) remains unchanged over a period of time. Such a population would be a closed population, that is, have no in- or out-migration to change the age-sex structure, and would have unchanging birth and death rates over a long period of time. A stable population may be either a stationary population or an increasing population. If it is an increasing population, the annual rate of increase is constant. Actual populations are never perfectly stable, but the conception of a stable population provides an abstract or IDEAL TYPE with which actual populations may be compared. See POPULATION, CLOSED; POPULATION, STATIONARY.

population, stationary. A population whose size remains unchanged over a period of time.

population, statistical. See POPULATION (2).

population, sub-. See STRATUM, SOCIAL.

population center. The geographic point about which the POPULATION of a given area is numerically balanced in each direction, so that, for example, the same number of persons live north of the point as south of it, the same number east of it as west of it.

population change theory. See DEMOGRAPHIC TRANSITION.

population composition. See DEMOGRAPHIC STRUCTURE.

population density. See DENSITY, POPULATION.

population element. An individual in a given statistical population.

population growth. See DEMOGRAPHIC TRANSITION; MALTHUSIAN THE-ORY; NATURAL INCREASE, RATE OF.

population parameter. See PARAMETER.

population pyramid. A technique of graphically portraying in the form of a pyramid the composition of a given POPULATION. Population pyramids are used primarily to show the age and sex distribution of a population. However, other aspects of the DEMOGRAPHIC STRUCTURE, for example, race, ethnic composition, economic characteristics, may also be portrayed in a population pyramid. See AGE-SEX PYRAMID; GRAPH.

population studies. Usually, DEMOGRAPHY. However, some writers who limit the term demography to the study of vital statistics use the term population studies to refer to the study of the interrelationship between population composition and distribution and a wide variety of social and economic variables. Sometimes this is referred to as social demography.

position. The location or place of an individual or SOCIAL CATEGORY (class or category of people, such as professional men) within a social system or system of social relationships. The term is usually used synonymously with STATUS, hence every position involves ROLE EXPECTATIONS.

position, social. See POSITION.

position centrality. The degree to which a position within a system of social relationships receives, transmits, or originates communications to other positions. A LEADER would have high centrality of position and an ISOLATE would have low centrality.

positional psychology. The study of individual personality primarily on the basis of the individual's order of birth within his family of origin. Thus one might study the special stresses experienced by an oldest child.

positive function. See EUFUNCTION.

positivism. The philosophical position holding that knowledge can be derived only from sensory experience. Metaphysical speculation, subjective or intuitive insight, and purely logical analysis are rejected as outside the realm of true knowledge. The methods of the physical sciences are regarded as the only accurate means of obtaining knowledge, and therefore the social sciences should be limited to the use of these methods and modeled after the physical sciences. Auguste Comte is regarded as the founder of positivism, but he was influenced by the writings of David Hume and Claude H. Saint-Simon. (See H. Martineau, *The Positive Philosophy of Auguste Comte*, George Bell, London, 1896.) See NEOPOSITIVISM; POSITIVISM, LOGICAL; RATIONALISM; SCIENCE.

positivism, logical. A philosophical position that developed from POSI-
TIVISM, holding that the truth of any statement lies in its verification
through sensory experience. Any statement that cannot be verified
through sensory experience, such as theological or metaphysical statements, is held to be meaningless. Moreover, ethical and aesthetic statements are regarded as merely expressions of subjective emotions. According to this position, logical analysis is needed to clarify meanings that have
been verified or falsified through sense experience, but such analyses
should be closely associated with empirical observation and THEORY building should be kept to a minimum. Logical positivism is sometimes referred
to as logical empiricism. See EMPIRICISM; NEOPOSITIVISM; OPERATIONALISM.

possibilities, limited. See LIMITED POSSIBILITIES, PRINCIPLE OF.

post hoc fallacy. The fallacy inherent in the argument that because
one event follows another, the earlier one is the cause of the later event.
The term comes from the phrase *post hoc ergo propter hoc.*

postulate. A proposition within a science that is assumed to be self-
evident or a true statement of fact, or is stipulated to be true. Although not
proved, it is not contradicted by any facts or principles of the science, and
is a reasonable and necessary assumption.

potlatch. A custom among the Indians of the northwest coast of North
America in which a ceremonial feast was held at which people gained
prestige by destroying or giving away wealth and property. The more
goods a person destroyed or gave away the greater was his prestige, and
each competed to outdo his rivals.

poverty. A low STANDARD OF LIVING that lasts long enough to undermine
the health, morale, and self-respect of an individual or group of individuals. The term is relative to the general standard of living in the society,
the distribution of wealth, the status system, and social expectations.

power. The ability of an individual or group to carry out its wishes or
policies, and to control, manipulate, or influence the behavior of others,
whether they wish to cooperate or not. The agent who possesses power has
resources to force his will on others. These resources often stem from social relationships and the individual's position in a group or society. One
need not have formal AUTHORITY to force one's will on others, for a person
may be able to force others to conform through the MANIPULATION of social
norms, exploitation of ignorance, etc. The threat of FORCE is the basis of
some forms of power, but more genteel and prevalent forms of power depend on deception and deceit. Power of the latter type does not resort to
brute force, but rather to the manipulation of the morality of others for the
selfish ends of the person wielding this type of power. Thus those who are
able to detach themselves emotionally from the normative system, but still

remain very sensitive to the involvement of others in the normative and moral system, may wield power without formal authority. This type of power is difficult to uncover, because it selectively uses the legitimate system of social norms to coerce compliance to a covert plan of action whose individual steps taken separately appear to be legitimate and in the interest of the common good.

The most effective form of power is found legitimized in AUTHORITY, but it is not always possible to institutionalize power. Power is really inherent in a relationship between social units (persons or groups), and on rare occasions even the lowest-status persons in a hierarchy may have the power to coerce persons of the highest statuses. That power is a social relationship is true to such an extent that it is often spoken of as a reciprocal relationship—that is, the person who exerts power over another does not necessarily completely escape obligations, commitments, and some limitations to his own freedom of action as a result of his power relationship.

Robert Bierstedt distinguishes between power which is legitimate as authority and power as latent force. (R. Bierstedt, *American Sociological Review*, December 1950.)

power, legitimate. See AUTHORITY.

power, political. Power exercised through the formal and informal structures of the POLITICAL INSTITUTION of a society, including governmental organizations.

power, scarcity theory of. Robert S. Lynd's hypothesis that within a society there is a limited amount of power available to be manipulated. If one group increases its advantages and power, this immediately entails some other group's giving up or losing power. In the same way, if one group seems to be losing its authority or power, then we must expect some other group to be gaining power. (R. S. Lynd in *Problems and Power in American Society*, edited by A. Kornhauser, Wayne State University Press, Detroit, 1957.) Talcott Parsons refers to this idea as the zero-sum concept of power, employing the concept of the zero-sum relationship developed in GAME THEORY to refer to a particular type of relationship in which an increase in the power of, or improvement in the position of, one participant in regard to a certain factor necessarily results in a corresponding decrease in the power of the position of one or more other participants. This hypothesis might also be applied to international power relations.

power, social. See POWER.

power, statistical. The probability that a given statistical test will reveal a statistically significant relationship when such a relationship really does exist. Put in other words, it is the probability that the test will reject the null hypothesis (that there is no significant relationship) when it is false, leading to the acceptance of the alternative hypothesis, which states a true relationship. Statistical tests differ in their power. Generally, in choosing among a number of suitable statistical tests to analyze the data in a particular study, with other factors being equal, the most powerful test for which the requirements and assumptions are met by the data is the test selected. On the whole, the power of a statistical test is greater with a larger number of cases and a higher level of significance. See ERROR, BETA; HYPOTHESIS, NULL; PROBABILITY; SIGNIFICANCE, STATISTICAL.

power act, substitute. As defined by Herbert Goldhamer and Edward A. Shils, an act exercising POWER which follows an originally unsuccessful attempt to exercise power. The substitute power act is intended to attain the same basic goal as the previously unsuccessful act of power. (H. Goldhamer and E. A. Shils, *American Journal of Sociology*, September 1939.)

power elite. Those "political, economic, and military circles which as an intricate set of overlapping cliques share decisions having at least national consequences. In so far as national events are decided, the power elite are those who decide them." (C. W. Mills, *The Power Elite*, Oxford University Press, New York, 1956.) See ELITE; ELITE, CIRCULATION OF THE.

power figure. A person, real or imaginary, whom one identifies with and imitates because of his AUTHORITY and POWER. In social groups obedience to leadership is both normative and expedient, but conformity and loyalty to those in authority or LEADERSHIP positions is often aided by the psychosocial need of many people to identify (in various degrees) with a father figure, that is, a power figure.

power organization. See POWER STRUCTURE.

power relationship, bilateral. A power relationship in which two parties (either individuals or groups) are able to exercise POWER over each other. Each party is in a position to bargain with the other and influence the other party in a desired direction. Parties may manipulate each other without either letting the other know specifically in what way he is trying to influence him. The outcome of a bilateral power relationship may be a mutually satisfying compromise, or the eventual domination of one party by the other. In the latter case the relationship has changed into a unilateral power relationship. (H. Goldhamer and E. A. Shils, *American Journal of Sociology*, September 1939.)

power relationship, unilateral. A social relationship in which one person or group can exercise POWER over another person or group, with relatively little expectation of reciprocal acts of power from the subordinate. The term was used by Herbert Goldhamer and Edward A. Shils (*American Journal of Sociology*, September 1939.)

power strategy. An "act designed to influence the behavior of another, but an act that is *oriented to* rather than in *conformity with* institutionalized normative orders." The act is not prescribed by the norms of the organization, but it is an attempt to utilize relationships within the organization to achieve the desired change. An example would be the case of an employee who goes to a superior in the hope of persuading him to order another employee to change his behavior or work methods. (W. A. Rushing, *The Psychiatric Professions,* University of North Carolina Press, Chapel Hill, N.C., 1964.) See POWER.

power structure. The total network of power relations within a community, both formal and informal, which determines major decisions and actions. The power structure, then, is more than the official leaders and the recognized political structure, and includes, for example, influential individuals and interest groups.

powerlessness. The psychological state of an individual when he feels deprived of any protection, control, influence, or involvement in the social events that are determining his fate. Powerlessness is closely related to ALIENATION.

pragmatism. A philosophical theory of meaning, truth, and value, in which the empirically ascertainable consequences implied by an idea or statement are held to constitute the meaning of the statement and (in some forms of pragmatism) also to be the criterion for the truth of the statement. The pragmatic theory of value presents utility as the chief criterion of value. Exponents of pragmatism include Charles S. Peirce, William James, and John Dewey. See INSTRUMENTALISM; OPERATIONALISM; UTILITARIANISM.

precoding. See CODING.

prediction. The foretelling of an event or set of events. In the sciences, the term is usually used with reference to cases where the antecedent factors leading to the event are known, controllable, or mechanical. Prediction of human behavior and social life in controlled experiments is more difficult than prediction in the physical sciences. However, human life is based on the predictability of the behavior of others. The sophistication of man in attempting to predict his own behavior is ancient and just as crucial to his survival as his understanding of the physical universe. While the process of prediction is central to the existence of social life, prediction of behavior is not absolute but is necessarily stated in terms of probabilities.

One of the reasons why human behavior cannot be precisely predicted is that often predictions of social events are made for the purpose of assuring outcomes different from the predictions. In other words, man predicts the future course of social life in part to reverse predicted trends or to make changes in line with his changing needs. Sociology attempts to increase the probabilities of predictions, at the same time that society must act to insure the conditions for desirable predictions and to prevent predicted undesirable situations. The utility of sociology does not rest on its accurate predictions of the future, but on its ability to analyze social life intelligently so that desirable trends may be enhanced by providing the necessary conditions for their success and the undesirable trends discouraged by changing the conditions leading society in that direction. See EXPERIMENT, CONTROLLED; PROBABILITY.

preferential mating. See MARRIAGE, PREFERENTIAL.

preferential shop. A place of work in which nonunion workers are employed only if there are no union workers available to fill the positions. See CLOSED SHOP; OPEN SHOP.

preferential sociometry. See SOCIOMETRY, PREFERENTIAL.

prehistoric anthropology. See ARCHAEOLOGY.

prehistory. The study of societies that existed prior to recorded history, that is, prior to the development of writing.

preindustrial civilization. See CIVILIZATION, PREINDUSTRIAL.

prejudice. 1. An unfavorable attitude toward any category or group of people based on one or an elaborate series of negative traits assumed to be uniformly distributed among the people toward whom one is antagonistic. Prejudice is usually regarded as a characteristic of the majority, but minorities, including persecuted minorities, are not necessarily less prejudiced toward out-group members than oppressive majorities. Prejudice exists wherever there is hostility toward an OUT-GROUP. It is in good part due to a lack of communication and not sharing a common life. Prejudice is a universal phenomenon and a perennial problem in social life. Racial, ethnic, and religious prejudices are the most often discussed as social problems. There is, however, prejudice in many other areas of social life, such as class prejudice and occupational prejudice, and an infinite variety of prejudices between various status categories.

2. Any oversimplified and overgeneralized belief about the characteristics of a group or category of people, either favorable or unfavorable. Prejudice then means to prejudge any individual in an OUT-GROUP on the basis of his supposed similarity to the stereotype of his group. In this sense the person who sees all the members of a persecuted minority as uniformly kind, generous, noble, etc., rather than as ordinary fallible human beings like those of his in-group, is prejudiced; the oppressed minority is denied ordinary human characteristics.

See DISCRIMINATION; MINORITY GROUP; STATUS; STEREOTYPE.

preliterate. See NONLITERATE.

prescribed role. See ROLE, PRESCRIBED.

presentational deference. See PRESENTATIONAL RITUALS.

presentational rituals. Prescribed patterns of polite behavior that serve to promote social interaction. Presentational rituals are one of two types of DEFERENCE BEHAVIOR distinguished by Erving Goffman. Whereas the other type of deference behavior (AVOIDANCE RITUALS) is based on consideration of what one must not do to other people out of respect for their autonomy and individuality, presentational rituals are concerned with involving the individual in social interaction. Four very common forms of presentational deference are "salutations, invitations, compliments and minor services. Through all of these the recipient is told that he is not an island unto himself and that others are, or seek to be, involved with him in his personal private concerns. . . . social intercourse involves a constant dialectic between presentational rituals and avoidance rituals. A peculiar tension must be maintained, for these opposing requirements of conduct must somehow be held apart from one another and yet realized together in the same interaction." (E. Goffman, *American Anthropologist,* June 1956.)

pressure group. Any group that attempts to influence legislative or governing agencies in behalf of its own special interests or the interests of a larger public that it represents. See INTEREST GROUP.

prestation. A formal exchange of goods or services within a society which is regarded not quite as the free giving of gifts and not quite as an economic exchange. The term is a French word meaning "payment," which was adopted by cultural anthropologists.

prestige. A general type of social status that carries with it social recognition, respect, admiration, and some degree of deference. Different groups may grant prestige for the achievement or possession of different values.

pretest. A final trial use of a questionnaire prior to its large-scale administration. The pretest usually involves interviewing a relatively few respondents to see if the questions used need revision or additions.

prevalence. In EPIDEMIOLOGY, the total number of cases of a specific physical or mental disease or disorder active in a given population during a specific interval or at a specific point of time.

priest. In cultural anthropology, a religious specialist who is a functionary and representative of an organized church or cult. The magico-religious or religious work performed by a priest stems from his official position within the organized religious community. The general term *priest* is used to differentiate such functionaries from the SHAMAN, who has special or private power derived directly from a supernatural source.

primary group. See GROUP, PRIMARY.

primary mental ability. See ABILITY, PRIMARY MENTAL.

primary need. See NEED, PHYSIOLOGICAL.

primary occupation. See OCCUPATION, PRIMARY.

primary relations. Social relations that are lasting, are based on frequent and direct contact, and are characterized by deep personal and emotional involvement. A primary relationship is not limited to the performance of one specific activity, but involves a variety of common interests and activities. Individuals in such a relationship are concerned about a wide range of aspects of each other's lives. Persons in a primary relationship have a great deal of information about each other, and a broad range of mutual rights and duties. Thus the relationship is diffuse (see DIFFUSE-NESS). Persons in a primary relationship value each other as individuals, and thus a member cannot simply be replaced by another person equally competent to perform a particular role, as is the case in a secondary relationship, where the emphasis is on the impersonal functions the members perform. Members of a primary relationship are more likely to regard each other as ends rather than means, and thus are not likely to use each other in a purely instrumental fashion. See GEMEINSCHAFT; GROUP, PRIMARY; SECONDARY RELATIONS.

primary source. A source of information that is an original document of research data, or a first-hand account or recording of events. Examples of primary sources of information include census reports, diaries, autobiographies, letters, deeds, all public records, records of business transactions and accounts, newspapers, etc.

primate. The highest order of mammals, which includes man, apes, monkeys and other related species, all of which have certain similarities in physical structure.

primitive society. A NONLITERATE society. However, cultural anthropologists and sociologists occasionally use the term to refer roughly to cultures that have a relatively simple technology, relative cultural homogeneity, and relative isolation from larger cultural influences, whether such cultures have a written language or not. The term, however, is now somewhat antiquated.

primogeniture. A system of inheritance in which the first-born son inherits the entire estate (and the title, if any) of the father, with none of the inheritance going to the other children. Primogeniture was practiced by the upper class in western Europe in the Middle Ages, where it provided a means of keeping large estates intact. Modified forms of primogeniture have also been found in various societies. See, for example, FAMILY, STEM (3).

principle. 1. A statement of a basic relationship among facts that has been well verified by empirical evidence, is widely accepted as true, and is used to derive hypotheses and uncover new facts.

2. An accepted rule of procedure, for example, of scientific procedure.

principle of least squares. See LEAST SQUARES, PRINCIPLE OF.

prison sentence, indeterminate. See INDETERMINATE SENTENCE.

privilege. An advantage guaranteed for a person or group and withheld from other persons within the group or society. Many privileges are primarily symbolic of the exclusiveness or higher status of those who have the privilege.

privileged familiarity. A cultural practice of allowing or even prescribing a high frequency of interaction and special forms of familiarity (for example, joking) between people of certain statuses. The AVUNCULATE would be such a relationship. See JOKING RELATIONSHIP.

probability. The likelihood that out of a specified number of equally likely and mutually exclusive occurrences a given event or relationship will occur. Probability, thus, refers to a proportion—the proportionate frequency with which a given outcome is expected out of the total frequency of all outcomes. For example, one can state the probability of obtaining heads in a large number of coin tosses or the probability that a baby born in a given year to a family with specified characteristics (of income, occupation, race, etc.) will in time go to college. Probability, which is closely related to the concept of chance, is very important in statistical analysis. There are many statistical tests designed to determine the probability that observed occurrences, relationships, or differences are due to chance. Statistical probability, often written p, may range from 0 to 1 and usually is expressed in decimal form as greater or less than a given level. Thus, for example, $p < .05$ means that the probability is less than 5 out of 100 that a given result would occur by chance alone, or, put another way, on a purely chance basis one could expect this outcome fewer than 5 times out of 100. See SIGNIFICANCE, STATISTICAL.

probability distribution. A theoretically expected FREQUENCY DISTRIBUTION. A probability distribution gives the probable frequency of occurrence of each CATEGORY or CLASS INTERVAL (subdivision) of a given VARIABLE. See PROBABILITY.

probability sample. See SAMPLE, PROBABILITY.

probable error. A statistical measure of the error that results from the differences between a SAMPLE and the total POPULATION from which the sample was drawn. The probable error of the mean (P.E.) is the interval in a FREQUENCY DISTRIBUTION that centers about the arithmetic mean and includes 50% of all the cases in the distribution, extending from that point which includes half the cases below the mean (25% of all the cases) to that point which includes half the cases above the mean (25% of all the cases). In a normal frequency distribution, this is equal to the QUARTILE DEVIATION. (The use of the probable error is not considered suitable in skewed distributions.) The chances are regarded as even (50%) that the true population mean falls within the interval of the probable error or that the mean of another sample from the same population would fall within this interval. In a normal distribution, the probable error of the mean is equal to .6745 times the STANDARD ERROR. The latter is generally preferred today. See FREQUENCY DISTRIBUTION CURVE, NORMAL; MEAN, ARITHMETIC; SKEWNESS.

probation. The suspension of a convicted lawbreaker's imprisonment on the condition that the offender remain on good behavior when released. Should the person not conform to the conditions prescribed by the court, the sentence becomes active. Probation is often used with first offenders who give promise of reform, and usually a probation officer or adviser is assigned to supervise and assist the rehabilitation of the convicted person.

problem, social. See SOCIAL PROBLEM.

procedure. In scholarly investigation, any established pattern for conducting research. See SCIENTIFIC METHOD.

process. 1. A series of events forming a recognizable pattern that recurs often enough so that one may observe the pattern over and over again, for example, the process of SOCIALIZATION.

2. Any sequence of events following a logical pattern toward some predictable goal or outcome.

process, cognitive. See COGNITION.

process, social. See SOCIAL PROCESS.

producer good. See GOOD, ECONOMIC.

product-moment correlation coefficient. See CORRELATION, PEARSON PRODUCT-MOMENT.

product theorem. The principle that if in a given trial or occurrence, the occurrence of each of two or more events is independent of the other (that is, whether or not one occurs does not affect whether the other occurs), the PROBABILITY that both (or all) will occur is the product of their individual probabilities. For example, in the tossing of a coin, the probability is .5 that a head will appear. In a second toss of the coin, the probability of obtaining a head is again .5. Thus, according to the product theorem, the probability of obtaining heads in both tosses is .25. This is also known as the multiplication theorem or multiplication rule. See ADDITION THEOREM.

production. All economic activity involving the creation of goods or services. See DOMESTIC SYSTEM; FACTORY SYSTEM; HANDICRAFT ECONOMY.

profession. In the strictest sense of the term, a high-status occupation composed of highly trained experts performing a very specialized role in society. A profession has exclusive possession of competence in certain types of knowledge and skills crucial to society and its individual clients. The special intensive education and necessary discipline develops a strong in-group solidarity and exclusiveness. Every profession, on the basis of its monopoly of knowledge and skills and its responsibility for the honor and perpetuation of the profession, tends to feel that it is by itself capable of formulating its ethics and judging the quality of its work. Thus professional groups tend to reject the control of the public or clients they serve. Nevertheless, a profession is, of course, influenced by the public it professes to serve, and it is shaped by the needs of other interest groups and by the demands of other professional organizations.

professional authority. The competence of professionals to judge or analyze matters relating to their profession. Professional authority tends to be unchallengeable within its sphere, but is severely limited outside its area of competence. As the division of labor and the process of PROFES-SIONALIZATION spread in society, the area of professional competence narrows, producing results not yet fully explored by sociologists. One question of interest, for example, is the relationship between democratic (or autocratic) social organization (for example, in the professional structure of universities) and the growing degree of professional specialization.

professional manager. A salaried manager who pursues his occupation as a PROFESSION. He has been prepared for a managerial position with formalized training during which he acquires a body of technical skills and a code of professional ethics. The professional manager is usually distinguished from the owner manager.

professional thief. A criminal who pursues thievery as a profession. "The professional thief has a complex of abilities and skills, just as do physicians, lawyers, or bricklayers. The abilities and skills of the professional thief are directed to the planning and execution of crimes, the disposal of stolen goods, the fixing of cases in which arrests occur, and the control of other situations which may arise in the course of the occupation. Manual dexterity and physical force are a minor element in these techniques. The principle elements in these techniques are wits, 'front,' and talking ability. The thieves who lack these general abilities or the specific skills which are based on the general abilities are regarded as amateurs, even though they may steal habitually. Also, burglars, robbers, kidnappers and others who engage in the 'heavy rackets' are generally not regarded as professional thieves, for they depend primarily on manual dexterity or force." (E. H. Sutherland, *The Professional Thief,* University of Chicago Press, Chicago, 1937.) See CRIMINAL, PROFESSIONAL.

professionalization. The tendency of an occupational group to take on the characteristics of a PROFESSION, or the process by which this occurs.

professionalization of labor. The tendency for manual occupations to rise in status and increasingly assume professional characteristics through SPECIALIZATION, supported by a body of technical theory, a career pattern, an association of colleagues, and community recognition of their status. The concept of the professionalization of labor was developed by Nelson N. Foote. (N. N. Foote, *American Journal of Sociology,* January 1953.)

progress, social. Social change of a desirable nature. In sociology this term is regarded as somewhat antiquated, and is seldom used today. It is not that we cannot talk of social progress in specific areas of change within a society or generally within the world. Certainly there are trends that can be regarded as desirable, from one point of view or another. However, there is no way of determining whether the totality of man's social life has improved over the past—or deteriorated, for that matter. Also, the idea of social progress as an inevitable evolutionary trend toward a better world society is not widely accepted among social scientists. Social progress is an ideal and a goal that permeates many ideologies, and as an ideal it refers to plans for social change and is not descriptive of a process of natural evolution. See EVOLUTION, SOCIAL.

projected experimental design. See EXPERIMENT, PROJECTED.

projection. A psychological process in which an individual unwittingly attributes his own unacceptable thoughts, shortcomings, fears, desires, attributes, etc., to other persons or objects as a way of protecting himself from guilt and self-blame, and as a way of justifying his behavior. Projection is a type of DEFENSE MECHANISM and a way by which a person escapes the recognition and acceptance of his shortcomings and unacceptable attitudes. See PROJECTIVE TECHNIQUE.

projective technique. A method of studying personality or attitudes in which the subject is asked or encouraged to react to a standardized set of ambiguous or neutral stimuli. The unstructured stimuli allow the subject to project, read into, or interpret the material inadvertently so that his feelings and attitudes are revealed. There are many types of projective techniques, using photographs, words, stories, ink blots, and the like. See DOLL-PLAY PROCEDURE; FIGURE-DRAWING TEST; KAHN TEST; PROJECTION; RORSCHACH TEST; ROSENZWEIG TEST; SENTENCE-COMPLETION TEST; THEMATIC APPERCEPTION TEST; TOMKINS-HORN PICTURE ARRANGEMENT TEST; WORD ASSOCIATION TEST.

proletariat. In its most general usage, a Marxian term referring to a modern type of lower class consisting of wage earners who do not own the means of production but instead sell their labor. The term is not widely used in general sociology.

promiscuity. Sexual intercourse with many partners, outside of and contrary to culturally institutionalized patterns governing relations between the sexes.

promiscuity, stage of. A hypothetical stage of social evolution discussed by some early thinkers in sociology, in which supposedly a family system had not developed, sexual relations were not guided by familial or marital norms, and everybody mated freely with everyone else, with no social regulation of sex. This hypothesis is not widely accepted today.

propaganda. A conscious, systematic, and organized effort designed deliberately to manipulate or influence the decisions, actions, or beliefs of a large number of people in a specified direction on a controversial issue. Usually propaganda is considered to be an attempt to manipulate group opinion by concealing the true purpose of the propaganda and presenting only one side of debatable issues. For examples of propaganda techniques, see BANDWAGON TECHNIQUE; CARD STACKING; GLITTERING GENERALITY; NAME CALLING; PLAIN FOLKS TECHNIQUE; TESTIMONIAL; TRANSFERENCE.

property. A socially sanctioned recognition of a group or individual's rights, privileges, and responsibilities with relation to an object, resource, or activity. The rights an individual has to most types of private property are limited, for society always reserves the right to some control over a person's or group's property, and owners of property are required by others to reciprocate in some way for their rights of ownership. Politically powerful groups tend to work to weaken public control over their own property; in addition they tend to seek to increase control over other types of property holders and to multiply their obligations.

property, incorporeal. See INCORPOREAL PROPERTY.

prophecy, self-fulfilling. See SELF-FULFILLING PROPHECY.

prophet. A charismatic leader who claims a divine insight into the form of future events and values on the basis of a renewed and enhanced dedication to the central traditional values of the culture. The ROLE of prophet may be viewed as a way of satisfying the "need" of society for a new and creative future through a reinterpretation and fulfillment of the deeply engrained social traditions of the past.

propitiation. An act performed to propitiate or please a supernatural force, and thus to avoid harm or to bring good fortune.

proportion. A summarizing measure, and a special type of ratio in which the denominator is the sum of the total number of cases in all the categories of the group being studied. The numerator is the number of cases in one (or more) of the categories. Thus if the number of divorced persons within a group of 100 members is 10, the proportion of divorced persons is 10/100 or 1/10.

proposition. A generalized statement of a relationship among facts. Most often in sociological usage the term refers to a HYPOTHESIS that has been affirmed by empirical research but is not sufficiently established to be considered a scientific law. Thus, the generalizations found in theories are frequently referred to as propositions. However, some writers use the term synonymously with hypothesis. See LAW, SCIENTIFIC; THEORY.

Protestant ethic. The ethical milieu, or set of values and attitudes, embodied in Protestantism, which has been hypothesized as being very favorable to the development of modern, rational capitalism. The concept was developed by Max Weber, who tried to show the ideological compatibility of rational capitalism and Protestantism, particularly Calvinism of the seventeenth century. John Calvin and the other reformers taught that salvation is a pure gift from God and cannot be earned, but also that one who is in God's grace and among the elect manifests in his behavior systematic self-control and obedience to the will of God. The Calvinist was dedicated to a constant examination of the condition of his soul and an examination of his life for signs of grace. Calvinism also emphasized the notion of one's calling; that is, a person's worldly occupation was regarded as the sphere in which he was to serve God through his dedication to his work. The man of property was to act as a steward of worldly goods, that is, to use them for some betterment rather than for luxurious enjoyment. This unlimited demand for self-discipline, self-examination, hard work, dedication to duty and one's calling survived in secular form when its religious motivations were lost. These values promoted the ascetic dedication to systematic profits, reinvestment of earnings, thrift and hard work, characteristic of the early development of capitalism. (M. Weber, *The Protestant Ethic and the Spirit of Capitalism*, tr. by T. Parsons, Scribner, New York, 1930.)

pseudocommunication. Communication between individuals or groups in which each party assumes that the other party understands the major elements of his message or communication, whereas in fact, because of divergent interests and perspectives, each party is focusing upon and emphasizing different aspects of the conversation. Much of human communication involves some pseudocommunication, but this usually does not generate problems. Indeed, it often creates an illusion of social harmony and agreement on unimportant matters, and it probably tends to smooth social interaction. However, when accurate communication is crucial to cooperation, decision making, or the like, pseudocommunication causes conflict and distrust.

pseudoscience. A system of beliefs that claims to be objective and scientific but that in fact does not seriously value or attempt to apply the procedures of logic or the scientific method to its endeavors. Astrology, palmistry, and phrenology are examples of pseudosciences.

psyche. Mind, or mental processes, considered as a functional system.

psyche-group. A membership group one chooses for private, personal reasons (for example, a bridge club) rather than because the group serves some social function (as a work group). The term was used by Helen H. Jennings, who distinguished the psyche-group from the SOCIO-GROUP, although the two may overlap. (H. H. Jennings, *Leadership and Isolation*, Longmans, Green, New York, 1950.)

psychiatry. The branch of medicine dealing with the genesis, diagnosis, and treatment of mental disorders. See PSYCHOLOGY, ABNORMAL; PSYCHOLOGY, CLINICAL; SOCIAL PSYCHIATRY.

psychoanalysis. A theory of the structure and development of personality, and a method of psychotherapy for the treatment of neurosis, originated by Sigmund Freud. Psychoanalysis is particularly concerned with problems of repression and inner conflict, and is designed to bring unconscious desires into consciousness. The analysis of dreams and the techniques of free association are used in freeing the patient from the "tyranny of the unconscious."

psychobiology. The analysis and treatment of psychological disorders through a study not only of the psychology of an individual but also of contributing biological and social factors. Adolph Meyer first used the term, and he sometimes called it "objective psychobiology."

psychodrama. The use of play-acting as a way of reducing psychological tensions or for the analysis of personality. Developed by J. L. Moreno, this technique requires the subject to act out certain crucial psychosocial situations before a trained observer. The psychodrama may be either a soliloquy or acted out with other participants. There are some writers who define psychodrama as play-acting without interaction, that is, not in a group setting. In this way they contrast psychodrama with SOCIODRAMA (second definition). Others differentiate the two by defining psychodrama as the acting out of the person's own role and sociodrama as acting out the role of another. More often though, if the aim of the psychodrama is to give an individual insight into his own (internal) personal problems, that is, if the focus is on the individual, it is regarded as a psychodrama. See SOCIO-DRAMA; SOCIOMETRY.

psychogenic. Pertaining to the psychological origins or causes of behavior or behavior disorders, as opposed to somatic or organic causes.

psychological determinism. The view that in the study of human behavior there are no significant individual, self-determined choices, and that the psychologist needs only to study universal psychological factors to understand and predict behavior. Psychological determinism thus denies the possibility of significant, unique individual choices that are not predictable from known psychological patterns. It also denies or tends to ignore the importance of cultural and group influences on individual behavior. See SOCIOLOGICAL DETERMINISM.

psychological feedback. See FEEDBACK.

psychological field. See FIELD, PSYCHOLOGICAL.

psychological phenomenology. See PHENOMENOLOGICAL APPROACH.

psychologism. The tendency to overemphasize the psychological point of view to the neglect of other forms of analysis, as, for example, by analyzing philosophical problems in purely psychological terms. The term is intended as one of reproach.

psychology. 1. The science of the behavior of living organisms, both animal and human, with an emphasis on the study of individual behavior and its relationship to environmental stimuli.
2. The science of the mind and mental processes.

psychology, abnormal. The branch of psychology that deals with unusual, deviant, and maladjustive individual behavior.

psychology, analytic. Carl G. Jung's system of psychology as distinguished from Sigmund Freud's PSYCHOANALYSIS. Essentially Jung deemphasized sex and introduced mystical and religious concepts into the study of the unconscious.

psychology, applied. The application of the tools, methods, and findings of psychology to practical problems in such areas as business management and advertising.

psychology, clinical. That branch of psychology which is concerned with the diagnosis and treatment of individual personality disorders, using such techniques as psychological testing and PSYCHOTHERAPY. Often clinical psychologists work in hospitals and in collaboration with medical doctors.

psychology, comparative. The comparative study of the differences and similarities in the behavior of different animals and man.

psychology, constitutional. A theoretical approach to the study of personality that emphasizes the relationship of the physical structure of the human body to the structure of personality. Such theories of personality place greater emphasis on the process of physiological maturation in explaining the development of human personality than upon explanations based on the process of SOCIALIZATION.

psychology, developmental. The study of the total development of the individual from birth to adulthood. Not only psychological but also physiological and social processes are taken into account.

psychology, differential. The study of variations between individuals that are revealed by various tests and measurements and the study of the factors that cause these differences—for example, studies designed to attempt to differentiate inherited from learned characteristics.

psychology, experimental. 1. In its broadest sense, psychological investigation based on the application of the scientific method, that is, psychological research utilizing the control of variables.
2. The branch of psychology that studies behavior under controlled laboratory conditions. It deals primarily with the behavior of animals, and with simple human reflexes.

psychology, faculty. A now discredited system of psychology, which held that the human constitution or mind was organized into a limited and fixed number of distinct entities or faculties that were the source of an individual's actions and mental activities. Feeling, will, and intellect are examples of such faculties.

psychology, field. See FIELD THEORY.

psychology, functional. A theoretical approach in psychology, holding that the study of individual behavior should focus on psychological processes of adjustment to the environment rather than psychological structures, such as sensations and feelings. Functional psychology replaced the older structural psychology. George H. Mead, William James, and John Dewey rejected the atomistic approach to the study of the human mind and emphasized the function of conduct and the necessity to study the mind through the study of behavior. (See G. H. Mead, *Movements of Thought in the Nineteenth Century*, University of Chicago Press, Chicago, 1936.) See PSYCHOLOGY, STRUCTURAL.

psychology, genetic. The branch of psychology that studies the development of the individual's mental life and behavior from birth onward. It also traces the development from animal to human life.

psychology, Gestalt. See GESTALT THEORY.

psychology, individual. The theoretical approach of Alfred Adler, based on the analysis of the individual as a distinct, organized entity, with the various forms of behavior of an individual forming a composite whole.

The Adlerian approach views the individual as feeling insecure, and constantly struggling for power and superiority to compensate for his inferiority feelings.

psychology, industrial. A field of applied psychology that studies the adjustment problems of the individual worker to his work. See SOCIOLOGY, INDUSTRIAL.

psychology, physiological. The branch of experimental psychology that studies the relationship between organic processes (e.g., neural stimulation, visceral activity, hormonal secretions) and psychological processes (such as learning, feeling, thinking).

psychology, social. See SOCIAL PSYCHOLOGY.

psychology, structural. A theoretical approach in psychology that holds that the study of individual behavior should involve the study of conscious experience through introspection, and should focus on the atomistic or elementary mental states such as sensations, images, and feelings. This approach is associated with the writings of E. B. Titchener. (E. B. Titchener, *A Textbook of Psychology*, Macmillan, New York, 1910.) See PSYCHOLOGY, FUNCTIONAL.

psychology, topological. See FIELD THEORY.

psychometrics. Mental testing or the measurement of psychological factors based on the application of standardized psychological devices such as intelligence and personality tests.

psychoneurosis. See NEUROSIS.

psychopathic criminal. See CRIMINAL, PSYCHOPATHIC.

psychopathic personality. A personality type that generally lacks ethical character, morality, emotional stability, and a sense of responsibility to persons and social norms. A psychopath does not appear to be obviously mentally deranged—he appears intelligent and even normal at first glance. This category of personality is one that fits a number of observed cases, but it is very difficult to define precisely. Some writers think it results from poor SOCIALIZATION or a deficiency in role-playing abilities. The calculated ruthlessness of normal people who possess power over subordinates would not be psychopathic because the ruthless individual is capable of understanding social norms, moral rules, the needs of others, and notions of personal responsibility. His cruelty is intellectually justified in terms of other social values which he may righteously uphold.

psychophysics. The study of the relationship between physical stimuli (such as light) and psychological sensations.

psychosis. A severe mental or personality disorder in which the person loses contact with reality. It is legally and popularly known as insanity. The person usually requires hospitalization because of his inability to participate in ordinary social life. The cause may be classified as either organic or functional. PARANOIA, SCHIZOPHRENIA, and MANIC DEPRESSIVE PSYCHOSIS are examples of psychoses.

psychosis, functional. A PSYCHOSIS for which no physiological base has been established. Usually the psychosis is assumed to stem from social and psychological sources.

psychosocial need. See NEED, SOCIAL.

psychosomatic. Pertaining to physical illnesses that are related to a personality problem. Psychosomatic medicine assumes the interdependence of mind and body, of the physical and the mental.

psychotherapy. The treatment of personality problems by psychological and psychiatric techniques (suggestion, hypnosis, etc.) rather than by medical methods (such as drugs or shock treatments).

puberty. That period of life at which the individual reaches reproductive maturity, that is, when the individual is capable of fathering or bearing a child. Secondary sex characteristics appear during this period. In many societies there are special puberty rites to acknowledge not only the physiological changes in the individual but also the changes in his social STATUS and ROLE. See RITES DE PASSAGE.

public. A considerable number of individuals who share a common interest of which they and others are aware. Because of their common interest, the members of a public have some sense of unity and identification, which varies in degree from one public to another. Publics are usually large, physically separated, and often quite diverse. Major issues of a society, particularly a large complex society, stimulate the formation of publics, their formation being greatly facilitated by the mass media of communication. Most members of a public usually are not in direct communication with each other, but they may seek out common reading material, common sources of information, and common activities. Golfers, antivivisectionists, conservationists, animal lovers, and atheists may be considered publics insofar as they are not all members of an organized group (although they may give informal support or financial contributions to groups and activities dedicated to their values or interests). The formal groups that are concerned with issues of importance serve as reference groups for the wider public. Publics have an impact through their voting, buying, noncooperation, financial contributions, letters to the editor, etc. Thus a public functions more as a unit than a SOCIAL CATEGORY, which simply constitutes a class of people, such as working women or college graduates. See REFERENCE GROUP.

public opinion. 1. The prevailing and predominant attitudes and judgments of the members of a community on given issues of general controversy as determined by public opinion polls.

2. The active or potentially active interests and values of a community that are asserted forcefully when threatened or promoted.

public opinion poll. See OPINION POLL.

punishment. A negative sanction constituting an aggressive form of disapproval, which functions as a device for SOCIAL CONTROL. Punishment involves the withdrawal of support and a denial of the protection from aggressive impulses that is normally provided for those who comply with the demands of social life. The person who is punished is made to endure some sort of painful treatment, whether symbolic or physical. In a sense, punishment is a kind of institutionalized cruelty. Normally social norms attempt to prevent cruelty, and most cruelty is not engaged in openly. Punishment, however, is always to some extent given a social justification and its impact is not simply in the degree of pain inflicted, for people often suffer from man's informal inhumanity to man, but in the fact that the sanction is public and implies the disapproval of the entire social group.

purposive sample. See SAMPLE, PURPOSIVE.

push-pull migration hypothesis. The demographic hypothesis that MIGRATION is due to differences in the social and economic desirability of communities. The migrant leaves one community for another because of the unfavorable conditions (push) of his old community and the attractive (pull) conditions in the new community.

putting-out system. See DOMESTIC SYSTEM.

pyramid, age-sex. See AGE-SEX PYRAMID.

pyramid, population. See POPULATION PYRAMID.

pyramid, social. See SOCIAL PYRAMID.

Q

Q-technique. A statistical technique that may be used in FACTOR ANAL-
YSIS instead of the more common R-TECHNIQUE. Sometimes referred to as
inverted factor analysis, the Q-technique analyzes intercorrelations (of
test results) among subjects instead of among tests (or variables). As a result, basic types of subjects (for example, if individuals—upwardly mobile
type; if groups—highly adhesive type, etc.) rather than basic variables
(factors) are obtained. The Q-technique was developed by William Ste-
phenson. See VARIABLE.

quadratic mean. See MEAN, QUADRATIC.

qualitative data. Data that are not in numerical form. Qualitative
data are data in the form of descriptive accounts of observations, interviews, or written material. Data in qualitative form may be possible to
quantify. See QUANTITATIVE DATA.

qualitative variable. See VARIABLE, QUALITATIVE.

quality-performance. See ASCRIPTION-ACHIEVEMENT.

quantitative data. Data in numerical form. Quantitative data are obtained through enumeration and measurement. Data may be collected
directly in quantitative form, or data originally in qualitative form may be
quantified. See QUALITATIVE DATA.

quantitative variable. See VARIABLE, QUANTITATIVE.

quartile. One of three points dividing a FREQUENCY DISTRIBUTION into
four equal parts, that is, four parts each with the same number of cases.
The first quartile is the 25th PERCENTILE, the second the 50th percentile, and
the third the 75th percentile. In other words, 25% of the cases in the distribution fall below the first quartile, 50% below the second quartile, and
75% below the third quartile. Thus the second quartile is at the MEDIAN.
See DECILE.

quartile, lower. In a FREQUENCY DISTRIBUTION, the first QUARTILE or 25th PERCENTILE, below which lies one quarter of the cases.

quartile, upper. In a FREQUENCY DISTRIBUTION, the third QUARTILE or 75th PERCENTILE, below which lie three-quarters of the cases and above which lies one-quarter of the cases.

quartile deviation. In a FREQUENCY DISTRIBUTION, one half the range of values from the first to the third QUARTILE. It is obtained by subtracting the value of the first quartile from the value of the third quartile, and then dividing by two. The quartile deviation, also referred to as the semi-interquartile range, is a measure of dispersion (see DISPERSION, STATISTICAL) used as an alternative to the total RANGE of the distribution. It is intended to minimize the effect of extreme values by using only the middle 50% of the range. The quartile deviation may be used as a measure of dispersion when the MEDIAN is used as the measure of central tendency. In a normal frequency distribution the quartile deviation is equal to the PROBABLE ERROR. See CENTRAL TENDENCY, MEASURE OF; FREQUENCY DISTRIBUTION CURVE, NORMAL; STANDARD DEVIATION.

quasi group. An unstructured and unorganized collection of people, such as an AGGREGATE, SOCIAL CATEGORY, CROWD, or PUBLIC, whose members have a potential for GROUP formation, although they may not be necessarily fully aware of it or prepared to join or form a group.

quasi household. As defined by the U.S. Census, a group of persons living in a residence that is not classified as a dwelling unit, for example, a large hotel, a fraternity, a rooming house, or a military barrack.

questionnaire. 1. A form or document having a set of questions the answers to which are to be filled in personally by the respondents. If an interviewer writes or records the responses on the form, it is called an IN-TERVIEW SCHEDULE.

2. In a wider usage, a QUESTIONNAIRE (as defined above) or an INTER-VIEW SCHEDULE.

questions. See DICHOTOMOUS QUESTION; FIXED-ALTERNATIVE QUESTION; LOADED QUESTION; OPEN-ENDED QUESTION.

quintile. One of four points dividing a FREQUENCY DISTRIBUTION into five equal parts. The first quintile is the 20th PERCENTILE, the second the 40th percentile, the third the 60th percentile, and the fourth the 80th percentile. Quintiles are not used very frequently. See DECILE; QUARTILE.

quota control. See SAMPLE, QUOTA.

R

R-technique. A statistical technique commonly used in FACTOR ANALYSIS in which the intercorrelations among a number of tests administered to the same subjects are arranged in a MATRIX (a tabular arrangement in rows and columns). From the matrix of intercorrelations, the basic underlying variables or factors are extracted and arranged in some meaningful order or structure. See Q-TECHNIQUE.

race. 1. An anthropological classification dividing mankind (HOMO SAPIENS) into several divisions and subdivisions (or subraces). The criteria for labeling the various races are based essentially on physical characteristics of size, the shape of the head, eyes, ears, lips, and nose, and the color of skin and eyes. The hereditary characteristics, such as skin color (widely used as a criterion of race), are not exclusive to any racial group, but rather overlap from one racial category to another. The characteristics used in classification are determined on a statistical basis, that is, according to frequency of occurrence, with a higher percent of certain characteristics in each classification. The interest in racial differences stems largely from the relative geographical, national, social, and cultural isolation and variations among the peoples of the world. The awareness and relevance of racial distinctions found in any part of the world is related to the social and cultural history of the society; as social and cultural conditions change, so quite obviously do the awareness and relevance of racial varieties. The major racial groups are usually identified as Caucasoid, Mongoloid, Negroid, and Australoid.

2. In popular and in antiquated usage, any distinct group, whether it be racial, ethnic, national, etc. Such usage was based on early beliefs that social and cultural differences were biological and inherited, rather than learned and the result of different values and patterns of SOCIALIZATION.

race awareness. A consciousness of physical differences between the members of one's own group and others, which is associated with the feeling that these differences indicate differences in status. Physical differences between people come into awareness as they symbolize the necessity for special behavior toward a social group different in some way from one's own. Racial (or color) nonconformity is associated very often with status and other types of sociocultural nonconformity, so that where racial differences are associated with sociocultural differences, race awareness is a guide to social interaction. Race awareness probably declines as sociocultural differences decline.

race consciousness. See RACE AWARENESS.

race prejudice. See PREJUDICE.

race relations. The interaction of individuals and groups that conceive of themselves with relation to each other as races. Thus Negro-white relations would be a part of the study of race relations in the United States.

Because ethnic and cultural groups are confused with races, the relations between ethnic and cultural groups have been considered a part of the study of race relations. This latter usage has been largely abandoned in the United States, and other terms have been substituted, such as minority relations or INTERGROUP RELATIONS.

racial monogenetic hypothesis. See MONOGENETIC HYPOTHESIS.

racial polygenetic hypothesis. See POLYGENETIC HYPOTHESIS.

racism. An ideological orientation and form of ETHNOCENTRISM, in which it is maintained that one's own group is a distinct race that is inherently superior to other races.

racket. An organized commercial activity that is illegal and not fully institutionalized, although it may be informally supported by a significant part of the population. Examples are gambling, bootlegging, and prostitution. Rackets exist outside the usual web of community controls, and they need not, and in fact cannot, conform even to the most minimal of the restrictions and ethical principles imposed by public opinion and legitimate businessmen on other commercial activities. The leaders of rackets often tend to be of the lower class, because of the very high risks involved and the unsophisticated techniques in the use of power. As with the slave, rum, and gun runners of the past, if the modern racketeer prospers, he and his family often turn to safer and more legitimate business enterprises.

radex analysis. An approach to FACTOR ANALYSIS, proposed by Louis Guttman, that is concerned with analyzing the complexity of factors. Models are constructed of factors ordered according to their degree of complexity and the complexity of their interrelationships. (L. Guttman in *Mathematical Thinking in the Social Sciences,* edited by P. F. Lazarsfeld, Free Press, Glencoe, Ill., 1954.) See MODEL.

radicalism. 1. A nonconformist approach to social and political problems characterized by extreme dissatisfaction with the status quo and a call to change society as quickly as possible and by vigorous means. The extreme leftist and extreme rightist would be considered radicals. Both desire to make fundamental changes in society and its leadership, although they would each change different things.

2. Nonconformist ideologies centered on innovation, change, and the concept of progress, rather than an ideology based on the values of the past, that is, extremism of the left rather than the right.

random numbers, table of. A printed table listing numbers in random order that may be used in selecting a random sample. The arrangement of the numbers in the table is random in all directions. To use such a table, the investigator first numbers all the units in the population from which the sample is to be selected. Starting at any point in the table (the point having been decided upon before looking at the table to prevent the possibility of bias), the investigator selects for his sample those units whose numbers follow in order from that point. The use of a table of random numbers enables the investigator to select a sample in which units are included on a purely chance basis, each unit having an equal chance of inclusion without reference to its characteristics. For tables of random numbers, see L. H. C. Tippett, *Tracts for Computers, No. 15, Random Sampling Numbers*, Cambridge University Press, London, 1927; R. A. Fisher and F. Yates, *Statistical Tables*, Oliver and Boyd, Edinburgh, 1953. See SAMPLE, RANDOM.

random selection. See SAMPLE, RANDOM.

randomization. The use of chance to control extraneous variables in an experiment. Randomization is often used in addition to MATCHING in controlled experiments. Subjects are matched in pairs on those variables which the experimenter seeks to control, and then one member of each pair is assigned to the EXPERIMENTAL GROUP and one to the CONTROL GROUP on a random basis, such as the toss of a coin. Thus, randomization is used to equalize on a chance basis the factors (often unknown) that are not specifically controlled but that might affect the outcome of the experiment. Randomization is also used sometimes without matching. That is, subjects are assigned to the experimental and control groups on a purely random (chance) basis. In addition, it may be possible to use randomization at other points in an experiment to minimize the possibility of bias. See EXPERIMENT, CONTROLLED; EXPERIMENTAL CONTROL; EXPERIMENTAL DESIGN, COMPLETELY RANDOMIZED; EXPERIMENTAL DESIGN, RANDOMIZED COMPLETE BLOCK.

randomization test. A nonparametric statistical test used to determine whether an observed difference between two samples is statistically significant or probably due to chance, or, in other words, whether the two samples probably come from the same or different populations. When the two samples consist of matched pairs the randomization test may be used to analyze the sum of the differences between the pairs. When the two samples are unrelated to each other, and possibly even differ in size, the randomization test may be used to analyze the difference between the means of the two samples. In either case, the randomization test requires that the data be in the form of numerical scores that may be treated mathematically (and not in any other form, such as ranks). Because the computation becomes long and involved with large samples, the randomization test is usually limited to use with small samples. However, under specified conditions methods have been proposed to avoid the long computations when using the randomization test with large samples. See MEAN, ARITHMETIC; NONPARAMETRIC STATISTICS; PROBABILITY; RANK, STATISTICAL; SIGNIFICANCE, STATISTICAL.

randomized design. See EXPERIMENTAL DESIGN, COMPLETELY RANDOMIZED.

randomness. The occurrence of events in an unpredictable order. The occurrence of one event does not affect the occurrence of the other events: each occurs independently. Moreover, the occurrence of an event is not in any way related to its characteristics. Random occurrences cannot be predicted in any formula, for they depend entirely on chance. Thus in a series of coin tosses one cannot predict or state in a formula in what order heads and tails will appear, as the outcome of each toss is independently determined by chance. See SAMPLE, RANDOM.

range. The total spread of values in a FREQUENCY DISTRIBUTION. The range is the difference between the highest value and the lowest value in the distribution. If the data are grouped, the range is obtained by subtracting the midpoint of the lowest CLASS INTERVAL (subdivision of the variable) from the midpoint of the highest class interval. The range is the simplest and most easily obtained measure of dispersion; however, it has the serious disadvantage of being determined entirely by the most extreme values in the distribution. See DISPERSION, STATISTICAL; QUARTILE DEVIATION; STANDARD DEVIATION.

range, percentile. See PERCENTILE RANGE.

range, semi-interquartile. See QUARTILE DEVIATION.

rank, informal. See STATUS, INFORMAL.

rank, percentile. See PERCENTILE.

rank, statistical. Position in a series arranged in order of magnitude. The rank of a case tells where it stands in the magnitude of a given variable relative to the other cases in the sample. Ranking does not assume equidistance between cases. For example, in a set of scores, the score that ranks first may be twice the score that ranks second, but the score that ranks second may be only slightly higher than the score that ranks third. Therefore when only ranks are available they cannot be treated mathematically as scores. In statistical analysis there are nonparametric tests available for use with data in the form of ranks. See CORRELATION, KENDALL PARTIAL RANK; CORRELATION, KENDALL RANK; FRIEDMAN χ^2_r TEST; KENDALL COEFFICIENT OF CONCORDANCE W; KOLMOGOROV-SMIRNOV D TEST; KRUSKAL-WALLIS TEST; MANN-WHITNEY U TEST; MEDIAN TEST; MEDIAN TEST, EXTENSION OF; MOSES TEST; WILCOXON MATCHED-PAIRS SIGNED RANKS TEST. See also NONPARAMETRIC STATISTICS; ORDINAL SCALE; PERCENTILE.

rank difference correlation. See CORRELATION, RANK DIFFERENCE.

rank order scale. See ORDINAL SCALE.

rank status. The position an individual has within a particular HIERARCHY or RANK SYSTEM.

rank system. The arrangement and interrelationships of the rank statuses within a particular social hierarchy, such as an ecclesiastical or military organization. See RANK STATUS.

ranking scale. 1. An ORDINAL SCALE.
2. A type of PAIRED-COMPARISON SCALE in which the subjects themselves make comparative judgments between pairs of items. On the basis of these comparisons an ORDINAL SCALE is constructed.

rapport. As used in sociology and cultural anthropology, a sympathetic and harmonious relationship between an investigator and his subject or subjects. To achieve rapport the investigator usually tries to gain the confidence of his subjects by showing them that his investigation is not going to cause them harm. People often resist answering personal questions because they are fully aware that such information, in the hands of hostile neighbors, colleagues, or exploiters of various sorts, could be used to their disadvantage. When rapport is gained, the researcher has convinced his subject that personal data will not be revealed in any way that can be used to embarrass or injure him. The researcher in addition tries to show his respondents that the information gained will be used to improve understanding of the respondents' community or group, or of all mankind.

rate. 1. A type of ratio in which the numerator gives the number of occurrences of an event within a specified period of time and the denominator gives the number of units to which the event could occur or the total number of possible occurrences of the event. An example would be a birth rate, which gives the number of births per year in relationship to the number of women of childbearing age in a given population. Usually the quotient is multiplied by 100 or 1,000. Unlike a proportion, which describes a given moment of time, a rate refers to events occurring over a period of time.

2. Simply the number of occurrences of an event (or quantity of a variable) per unit of time, as a rate of speed of 50 miles per hour.

3. A number of units of one type stated in terms of a number of units of another type, as a rate of currency exchange.

rate, crude. A rate (birth rate, death rate, crime rate, etc.) that refers to a total population without taking into account the composition of the population. A crude rate is contrasted to a specific rate, which gives the rate for a specific category or categories of the population. For example, a rate may be age-sex specific or specific to economic and social divisions within the population. A crude rate is of minimal comparative or predictive value. See BIRTH RATE, CRUDE; BIRTH RATE, SPECIFIC; DEATH RATE, CRUDE; DEATH RATE, SPECIFIC.

rate of change. A ratio in which the numerator is the number of units of change (the amount of change) and the denominator is the number of units there were (the quantity) before the change occurred. Frequently the quotient is multiplied by 100 or 1,000.

rating. A method used in social research in which persons judge and record the characteristics of others or of themselves. Ratings may be made by specialized judges or observers, by group members of each other, or they may be self-ratings. Ratings may be used in a variety of social and psychological studies, including, for example, studies of social class, studies of small-group interaction, and personality studies. Raters may be given a prepared form on which they simply check categories or they may be asked to respond in their own words.

rating-dating complex. As defined by Willard Waller in a study of college students (primarily in sororities and fraternities), a pattern of dating that is not focused on preparation for true courtship and marriage, but based on a desire for prestige and material values. In this study, dates were found to be chosen according to the prestigeful characteristics of the date (manners, money, etc.). Dating was essentially an exploitative relationship, free from entanglements, and undertaken more to satisfy the ego than to find friendship or love. The rating-dating complex has not been found to be universal among college students. On large, impersonal campuses, where strong group organization is minimal, the pressure to date on the basis of a system of ratings is probably not widespread. (See W. Waller, *The Family*, Dryden, New York, 1938.)

rating scale. A graduated series of categories arranged in sequential order (from highest to lowest, most favorable to least favorable, greatest degree to least degree, and so forth) for use in rating the characteristics of others or oneself. Rating scales may consist of personality traits, social characteristics (such as socioeconomic status), or types of interpersonal relationships (such as friend, acquaintance, etc.). The rating scale may be used by judges or observers to rate subjects or by the subjects to rate each other or themselves.

rating scale, check list. A RATING SCALE composed of a list of short, concrete descriptions of the characteristic being rated. These descriptions are selected from a large number that are given to judges to rank. Those descriptions that the judges consistently place in the same rank position are included in the check list and given a scale value based on the judges' decisions. After the check list is constructed, the rater simply checks the categories (descriptions) that he feels apply to the person being rated. On the basis of the categories checked, a score may be obtained for each person rated.

rating scale, compound. A RATING SCALE consisting of two or more individual rating scales, the scores on which are combined to form a total score for each subject. The characteristics measured by the individual scales are considered components of one variable. The total variable is measured by the compound scale, which is the sum of the compound parts.

rating scale, forced-choice. See FORCED-CHOICE TECHNIQUE.

rating scale, graphic. A type of RATING SCALE used to determine the intensity of the respondent's positive or negative feelings toward certain attitudes (or individuals). In this form of rating scale, an attitude statement is followed by a line that extends from a negative to a positive response. One end of the line indicates strong disagreement with the stated attitude while the other end indicates strong agreement. The center of the line indicates uncertainty or indifference. The respondent may check any point on the line that most closely reflects his feeling. When the scale is used in rating an individual, a personal quality may be followed by a line that extends from the absence of the quality to its presence in a strong degree.

rating scale, "guess who" test. A RATING SCALE in which brief descriptions of different types of personalities are presented to the respondents, who are asked to name the person within the group or set of persons being rated who best fits each description. Each description has a scale value assigned before the descriptions are given to the respondents. Thus it is possible to determine the total score of each individual being rated on the basis of the descriptions assigned to him by all the other respondents.

rating scale, itemized. A RATING SCALE in which the rater is required to select one of a number of specific categories that have been arranged in order of magnitude (highest to lowest, most favorable to least favorable, etc.). The number of categories from which the rater must choose varies, but in most studies is between five and ten.

rating scale, point. See POINT SCALE.

ratio. A relationship between two quantities expressed in the form of a fraction or a quotient. In a ratio the size of two numbers is compared by expressing one as a fraction of the other or dividing one by the other. Thus a ratio may be written 3:2, 3/2, or 1.5. The quantity that is the base of comparison is placed in the denominator. Either the numerator or the denominator may be the larger quantity.

ratio, critical. See CRITICAL RATIO.

ratio scale. An INTERVAL SCALE (that is, one in which the units are equal) that has an absolute zero point of origin. The measurements on the scale start at a true, known (not arbitrary) zero and increase in units with equal intervals between them. Scales of weight and length are examples of ratio scales. Ratio scales are sometimes referred to as absolute scales.

rational behavior. Behavior consistent with some system of logical thought. In social behavior the actions of others are usually judged as rational when the others apply the same system of logic to the situation as the actor. Thus most people regard themselves as very rational because their behavior is consistent with the logical patterns of thought they associate with a particular situation. The further another person is from one's own reference groups and culture, the more illogical his behavior seems. A liberal formal education presumably gives a person an awareness and appreciation for a greater number of logical approaches to a problem and a greater tolerance for behavior patterns different from his own.

rational trend. See TREND, RATIONAL.

rational uniformity. As defined by Hans Gerth and C. Wright Mills, a uniformity in patterns of conduct that results not from ethical considerations but from the fact that it is expedient and in the individual's rational self-interest not to deviate from the general pattern. Thus everyone is motivated to conform. This type of conformity and uniformity in society is based not on people's desire to uphold cherished values and norms, but on their sense of the advantage to be gained in exploiting the social and normative system by "playing the game" through overt conformity. (H. Gerth and C. W. Mills, *Character and Social Structure*, Harcourt, Brace, New York, 1953.)

rationalism. The doctrine that reason itself and systematic thinking yield truth and knowledge, and are for this purpose superior to experience or empirical investigation. See EMPIRICISM.

rationality, expedient. Behavior that is expedient and directed toward fulfilling one's self-interest, with no consideration of ethical values. See RATIONAL UNIFORMITY.

rationalization. 1. The development of greater standardization, consistency, and coordination in organizational structure. With reference to political structures, rationalization may consist in the substitution of a system of consistent rules for the arbitrary decisions of erratic rulers. In industry the term has been used to refer to the principles of "scientific management."

2. A form of self-justification in which an individual (or group) presents to himself or others a socially acceptable argument for behavior that he or others regard as unacceptable or foolish. Sometimes rationalization implies that the individual engaged in rationalizing is, to some extent at least, aware consciously or unconsciously of the falseness of his arguments. However, this need not mean that he is being totally dishonest or hypocritical. For example, a person may have spontaneously performed an act that he feels is quite innocent, although he could not specify his motive. If later he is made to feel that his action is unacceptable or wrong and he is faced with possible censure (from others or himself), he may search for motives and reasons that are favorable to himself. His rationalization may not represent his true reasons for acting as he did, but it may be no less true than the charge that his reasons were disreputable.

rationalization, cultural. A RATIONALIZATION provided by a culture or subculture to explain away inconsistencies in its norms. Cultural rationalization provides apparently reasonable justifications for group approval of conflicting social norms and values. For example, in a culture with strong equalitarian values mistreatment of a minority group might be rationalized by declaring that they are not quite fully human. Group members are provided with an excuse they can present both to themselves and to nonmembers. Such justifications of contradictory standards might be difficult for individual members to develop on their own, for often they do not understand the value system well enough to develop their own personal rationalizations. In many situations, however, group members still must rationalize for themselves, as, for example, when they as individuals deviate from group norms. Clearly a personal rationalization may be incorporated into more broadly applicable cultural rationalizations.

raw data. See DATA.

raw score. See SCORE, RAW.

reaction, circular. See CIRCULAR INTERACTION OR REACTION.

reaction formation. A psychological DEFENSE MECHANISM, that is, a method of defending one's self-esteem, in which an individual strives to develop behavior and attitudes that are opposite to and counteract certain strongly felt emotions and attitudes that he feels must be repressed or disguised. His real feelings are covered by a display of opposite feelings. Thus, an aggressive and hostile person may try to act kindly, speak softly, and emphasize a concern for the needs of the community. Reaction forma-

tion, however, is not usually fully successful in repressing or even concealing the underlying emotions, and often they break out into the open. Some
unexpected inconsistencies in human behavior, such as a vicious action
performed by an otherwise kindly person, come about in this way.

   realism. 1. As opposed to NOMINALISM, the metaphysical doctrine
that universals, or abstract concepts, have a real existence as entities. In
sociology this would be associated with the claim that concepts such as
society, culture, group, value, etc., refer to real entities that may be empirically investigated.

   2. As opposed to epistemological IDEALISM, the doctrine that the external world exists in reality independently of perception and the mind, and
is reflected with reasonable accuracy in sensory experiences.

   reality, social. See SOCIAL REALITY.

   reasoning. The organization of all relevant experiences or relationships with reference to a particular problem or situation. Reasoning helps
the person to fit a problem or situation into familiar social, cultural, or
psychological patterns so that his decisions and actions have continuity
and are understood by others.

   recall. The mental reproduction of previously learned knowledge or
skills.

   recidivism. Repeated return to criminal behavior, especially following imprisonment. Recidivists are sometimes called "repeaters" or habitual criminals.

   reciprocal roles. See ROLES, RECIPROCAL.

   recognition. 1. The positive evaluation or favorable regard of a person, or some characteristic of a person, by others. Recognition is one of
the four basic wishes proposed by W. I. Thomas. See WISHES, THOMAS'
FOUR.

   2. The awareness of having experienced some event, situation, or object previously.

   recreation. A nonwork activity engaged in for pleasure. Recreational
activities are often culturally and socially structured, and within a culture
people tend to want to engage in similar recreational activities. Activities
defined as recreational provide easily identifiable situations that give immediate sanctions for people to relax. Games are one such structured device for defining a situation as a time to relax from normal work, serious-
ness, and routine responsibility.

   recreational institution. The interrelated system of roles and norms
that fulfills the need in a society for recreation. A study of the recreational
institution in the United States would include an analysis of professional

and amateur sports, the complex of physical education at all levels of schooling, and a great many other formal and informal recreational activities and organizations. See INSTITUTION, SOCIAL.

redintegration. The recalling or re-establishing of a whole experience or event by experiencing some single aspect of the original experience or event. Examples of redintegration in social life are the phenomena of college alumni who like to return to reunions in fraternity and sorority houses for the purpose of arousing the experiences or feelings of their youth, and the married couple returning to the scene of their honeymoon to share a recaptured portion of their more youthful romantic past.

reductionism. In sociology, the view that all explanations of social behavior are reducible to psychological or physiological explanations. In essence it denies the reality of social phenomena as a distinct level of analysis.

reference, frame of. See FRAME OF REFERENCE.

reference cycle. The period of time between two successive low points (or high points) in a cyclical time series (for example, from a low point through a high point to the next low point), that is, the period of one complete cycle in a series of cycles. See CYCLICAL MOVEMENT.

reference group. A GROUP or SOCIAL CATEGORY that an individual uses to help define his beliefs, attitudes, and values and to guide his behavior. The individual has some sense of identity with his reference group, but he need not be an actual member of it, he may not even wish to join it, and his conception of the group and its values may be inaccurate. The term reference group may be used to designate a real, distinct group, such as a political organization, or it may be used to designate a social category that functions as a reference group. Thus one may identify as being Protestant. This is a social category, but it also represents a body of values and traditions shared by individual Protestant churches and also by numerous other groups and persons, including many who are not formally associated with any church. The term positive reference group is synonymous with reference group. The concept of reference group was introduced by Herbert H. Hyman (*Archives of Psychology*, June 1942).

reference group, aspirational. A REFERENCE GROUP in which a person desires to be accepted as a member. Such a reference group, like any concrete social group, has specific norms and requirements for membership. An aspirational reference group is, of course, not the membership group of the individual who aspires to it—the aspirant presumably does not have or is not sure he has the necessary qualifications to join. Identification with an aspirational reference group obviously requires a different type of conformity to norms than does identification with a group in which one is a member or with a group that one does not aspire to join. See GROUP, MEM-BERSHIP.

reference group, negative. A group whose norms and activities an individual uses as a guide to what he shall reject and oppose. A negative reference group motivates behavior as does a positive reference group, but it motivates behavior directly opposed to the group's values. Often people who are uncertain of their views on an issue will look to a negative reference group to discover the "incorrect" views on the subject, which helps then to formulate their "own" point of view.

reference group, positive. See REFERENCE GROUP.

reference individual. An individual with whom a person identifies and on whose behavior he patterns his own behavior in a variety of situations and roles. Many of the values, norms, and attitudes of the reference individual are internalized by the identifying person. See IDENTIFICATION; REFERENCE GROUP; ROLE MODEL; SIGNIFICANT OTHERS.

reflex. A relatively simple, innate, and automatic response to a stimulus. This is probably the only behavior in man that is determined almost purely by his biological composition and it is the closest man comes to the more complex INSTINCT. A human infant has a number of reflexes (such as breathing, shivering when cold, grasping, contracting the pupils, blinking the eyes, etc.) that provide for a biologically coordinated organism, but that do not, in their original state, form a psychological or social unity capable of complex human behavior.

reflex, conditioned. See CONDITIONED REFLEX.

reflexive role-taking. See ROLE-TAKING, REFLEXIVE.

regimentation. A form of standardization in social groups that is designed to symbolize and display the organizational uniformity and unity of the group and that is glorified as a value in itself. Thus in most large military organizations many aspects of the soldiers' appearance and behavior must be identical for each rank and function in the organization. Hair must be cut in one or a very limited number of styles, ties tucked in the same way, hats worn at the same angle, and salutes made as precisely alike as possible. Regimentation reflects centralized control and the ability of hierarchical organizations to plan and direct the behavior of subordinates. Outside of rigid, hierarchical organizations, standardized behavior, appearance, and even values may come about spontaneously simply as result of fashion, a sense of social solidarity, similarity of experience, or the like, but regimentation is not spontaneous and it goes beyond practicality—it is a prime instrument of discipline and control and cleaved to as a value even in situations where it is not practical.

region. A large territorial area that is homogeneous in certain respects. The common element or elements on the basis of which the region is delimited may be geographic, economic, cultural, or a combination of these. Thus a geographic region may be characterized by a certain type of climate, terrain, soil, flora and fauna (a desert region, a tropical rain forest region). An economic region may be distinguished on the basis of the predominant economy (a wheat-farming region, a coal-mining region) or on the basis of its economic interdependence and its center of dominance (a METROPOLITAN REGION). A cultural region would be characterized by certain culture traits that distinguish it from surrounding regions. Regional boundaries are usually not sharply demarcated, but rather vary depending on the criteria used. See CULTURE TRAIT.

region of rejection. In statistics, that portion of the distribution of all the possible outcomes of a particular statistical test that, if a given sample outcome falls therein, would indicate that the null hypothesis (the hypothesis of no significance) should be rejected. The values in the region of rejection are sufficiently extreme for the PROBABILITY that they would occur by chance to be small. The size of the region of rejection depends on the level of significance desired. The lower the level of significance is, the lower is the probability that a result falling within the region of rejection is due to chance, and the smaller is the region of rejection. Thus for a given statistic, the region of rejection for a chance probability of 1 out of 100 (.01 level of significance) or less would be smaller than the region of rejection for a chance probability of 5 out of 100 (.05) or less. The region of rejection is also referred to as the critical region. See ERROR, ALPHA; ERROR, BETA; HYPOTHESIS, NULL; SIGNIFICANCE, STATISTICAL.

regional city. See METROPOLIS.

regionalism. An approach to the study of behavior that emphasizes the geographic REGION as the unit of analysis, stressing the relationship between man and his immediate physical environment. Economic, social, and cultural organizations are analyzed in terms of their interrelationships and functions within the geographic region. See GEOGRAPHY, HUMAN.

regression. A DEFENSE MECHANISM that is a form of psychological adjustment to anxiety and conflict in which an individual retreats to an earlier, less mature, and less adequate, but seemingly more secure, pattern of behavior.

regression, curvilinear. A relationship between two (or more) variables in which there is not a constant ratio of change between them. A unit of change (increase or decrease) in the independent VARIABLE (or variables) does not always result in the same number of units of change in the dependent variable. The REGRESSION LINE is curved rather than straight.

There are numerous forms a curved regression line may take, depending on the nature of the relationship between the two variables. The analysis of curvilinear regression involves finding the curve that best fits the data. See CORRELATION, CURVILINEAR; REGRESSION, LINEAR; REGRESSION, STATISTICAL.

regression, linear. The regression of one VARIABLE on another variable (or variables) in a constant ratio, so that each unit of increase or decrease in the independent variable (or variables) is associated with a fixed number of units of change in the dependent variable. The REGRESSION LINE is a straight line. See CORRELATION, LINEAR; REGRESSION, STATISTICAL.

regression, nonlinear. See REGRESSION, CURVILINEAR.

regression, statistical. The analysis of the relationship between two or more correlated quantitative variables. Whereas CORRELATION provides a summary statistic of the total relationship between the variables, regression gives a detailed analysis of the value-for-value relationship between the variables. With regression analysis, it is possible to predict the average values of the dependent VARIABLE from the values of the independent variable (or combined independent variables) when the COEFFICIENT OF CORRELATION is known. Thus when the values of only one of two correlated variables are known, it is possible to predict the average value of the second variable for each of the values of the first variable. See REGRESSION COEFFICIENT; REGRESSION LINE.

regression analysis. See REGRESSION, STATISTICAL.

regression coefficient. In a linear regression between two variables, the average unit of change in the dependent VARIABLE associated with each unit of change in the independent variable. The regression coefficient is obtained by dividing the STANDARD DEVIATION of the dependent variable by the standard deviation of the independent variable and multiplying the quotient by the COEFFICIENT OF CORRELATION. The regression coefficient defines the slope of the REGRESSION LINE (illustrating the relationship between the two variables). See REGRESSION, LINEAR; REGRESSION, STATISTICAL.

regression estimate. The estimate of a value of a dependent VARIABLE from a known value of an independent variable using the REGRESSION LINE. See REGRESSION, STATISTICAL.

regression line. A line showing a value-for-value relationship between two (or more) correlated variables. For each value of the independent VARIABLE (or combined independent variables) the average value of the dependent variable is given. In simple regression (a linear relationship between two variables) the values of the dependent variable are obtained by multiplying each value of the independent variable by the REGRESSION CO-

EFFICIENT. The regression line is usually plotted on a graph. For any pair of correlated variables, two regression lines may be obtained. The second regression line is obtained by using the variable that was considered the dependent variable in constructing the first line as the independent variable and the variable that was the independent variable as the dependent variable. In the case of a perfect CORRELATION, the regression lines coincide. See REGRESSION, LINEAR; REGRESSION, STATISTICAL.

regularity, empirical. See EMPIRICAL REGULARITY.

reification, fallacy of. The error of regarding an abstraction as a real phenomenon. The source of the error lies in the fact that in analysis it is necessary to simplify the complex phenomena of the real world, and in developing analytic concepts certain aspects of a given phenomenon must be ignored in order to focus on other aspects. There may be a deliberate exaggeration of certain characteristics in order to formulate a useful conceptual MODEL or an IDEAL TYPE. Thus, although an ideal type, such as FOLK SOCIETY or AUTHORITARIAN PERSONALITY, is a useful model with which actual cases may be compared, it is essentially an abstraction and should not be regarded as a description of any real society or individual. The fallacy of reification is essentially what Alfred North Whitehead refers to as the fallacy of misplaced concreteness. (A. N. Whitehead, *Science and the Modern World,* Macmillan, New York, 1925.)

reinforcement. 1. The process of increasing the strength of a learned habit or response. Reward and punishment are both methods of reinforcement.

2. More specifically, in CONDITIONING the reintroduction of the original unconditioned stimulus in order to strengthen the CONDITIONED RESPONSE. For example, Pavlov's dogs' conditioned response (salivating at the sound of a bell) was reinforced by periodically reintroducing the food (the unconditioned stimulus) with the bell.

rejection. In social behavior, the act of depriving someone of appropriate and normal social interaction. Rejection takes place not only when someone is excluded from a social group or social relationship, but also when a person is denied an appropriate social ROLE or set of relationships. Thus a person who has been allotted a lower social status (in the family, occupational group, etc.) than is clearly appropriate for him (according to his age, sex, etc.) is a person who has to some extent been rejected. In this sense a "spoiled child," who is not granted appropriate responsibility and adult status, is not a child who is too greatly loved and accepted, but a child who is rejected—he has been deprived of appropriate and normal social interaction.

rejection region. See REGION OF REJECTION.

relation, social. See SOCIAL RELATION.

relations, primary. See PRIMARY RELATIONS.

relations, secondary. See SECONDARY RELATIONS.

relations, sustenance. See SUSTENANCE RELATIONS.

relationship. A reciprocal influence between two or more elements such that together they form a distinct unit.

relationship, avoidance. See AVOIDANCE RELATIONSHIP.

relationship, curvilinear. See CORRELATION, CURVILINEAR.

relationship, linear. See CORRELATION, LINEAR.

relationship, social. See SOCIAL RELATIONSHIP.

relationship, spurious. See SPURIOUS CORRELATION.

relationship, statistics of. See STATISTICS OF RELATIONSHIP.

relationship, symmetrical. A noncausal relationship between two variables in which they mutually influence each other. One VARIABLE may not be said to be the cause and the other the effect, for one does not precede and result in a change in the other. Rather the relationship is reciprocal. In contrast, causal relationships are asymmetrical or one way. Most statistical measures of CORRELATION do not in themselves indicate whether a given relationship is symmetrical or asymmetrical. They show only that the variables vary together, that a change in one is associated with a change in the other. See CAUSATION.

relative, affinal. See AFFINAL RELATIVE.

relative deprivation. Deprivation or disadvantage measured not by objective standards but by comparison with the relatively superior advantages of others, such as members of a REFERENCE GROUP whom one desires to emulate. Thus the mere millionaire can feel relatively disadvantaged among his multimillionaire friends, as can the man with only a small yacht, or the one-star general, and so forth. The term was used originally by Samuel A. Stouffer in *The American Soldier* (S. A. Stouffer, ed., Princeton University Press, Princeton, N.J., 1950).

relativism, cultural. See CULTURAL RELATIVISM.

relativism, ethical. See ETHICAL RELATIVISM.

relevant others. See SIGNIFICANT OTHERS.

reliability. The consistency, objectivity, and lack of ambiguity of a statistical test or a set of measurements. Reliability may be measured by giving a test (or questionnaire) to the same subjects more than once to see if the same results are obtained or by comparing different sections of a test that are supposed to measure the same thing. Reliability deals with the problem of whether a measuring instrument is accurately measuring whatever it is measuring. It is not concerned with the problem of VALIDITY, that is, with whether it is measuring what it purports to measure. A test may be reliable but not valid.

reliability coefficient. See COEFFICIENT OF RELIABILITY.

religion. A system of beliefs, practices, and philosophical values concerned with the definition of the SACRED, the comprehension of life, and salvation from the problems of human existence. Religion is essentially an institutionalized or traditional path to salvation. All men in all societies ultimately must face certain of life's problems essentially alone, despite all efforts of others to help. Religious traditions are the result of man's attempt to capture and enshrine his philosophical and spiritual insights so that they are available to the individual as he faces life and its stresses, confusions, and complexities. Religion is a social phenomenon (as well as a psychological one) because it necessarily stresses fellowship in the development, teaching, and perpetuation of religious insight and knowledge. It is concerned with the common plight of all people at all times, regardless of age, sex, or status within society. The concept of the supernatural or a path of salvation may work to bind man to the dictates of limited contemporary social values and social groups, or it may serve to provide the wisdom and techniques by which man may free himself from contemporary groups and values—it may give him periodic freedom to achieve values that transcend the demands of the social present. Thus religion is both intensely personal and intensely social.

Specific religious beliefs vary considerably, and moreover, even within a particular religion the variety of religious experience is considerable. For many it is peripheral, for others it is central. Religious groups are important social groups and significant reference groups. See REFERENCE GROUP; RELIGIOUS INSTITUTION.

religion, aleatory element in. The influence of chance happenings or unforeseen and uncontrollable events in promoting the development of and adherence to religion. This concept was discussed at length by William G. Sumner as an important explanatory factor in the use and persistence of religion. They reasoned essentially that no matter how man works to adjust to his natural and social environment, his fate is often determined by bad luck or some chance fortune over which he has no control. Religion, they argued, has been developed to deal with these elements that cannot be explained or manipulated by ordinary methods. (W. G. Sumner, *Folkways*, Ginn, Boston, 1906.)

religion, comparative. The objective study of all religions for the purpose of understanding their role in human life. Since religion is a universal phenomenon, it is assumed to fulfill important human needs. Comparative religion attempts to discover what these needs are, how different religions satisfy these needs, and how religion influences other social behavior. Sociologists, cultural anthropologists, social psychologists, philosophers (religious or otherwise) are all contributors to this area of study.

religion, sociology of. See SOCIOLOGY OF RELIGION.

religiosity. Interest and participation in religious activities. A general definition is difficult, since different religions emphasize different behaviors and values. Operationally, religiosity may be defined in terms of the degree of participation of an individual in religious rituals or a sum of various behaviors and attitudes judged to be religious within a group or society. See OPERATIONAL DEFINITION.

religious institution. The system of social norms and roles organized about the need to answer ultimate questions concerning the purpose of life and the meaning of death, suffering, and fortuitous occurrences. The religious institution answers these questions by defining the supernatural and the nature of man's relationship to the supernatural. In so doing it defines what is SACRED and what the proper relationship is between the sacred and the secular. The religious institution includes those customs, rituals, prohibitions, standards of conduct, organizational forms, and roles primarily concerned with or justified in terms of the supernatural and the sacred, whether within or without formal religious organizations. See CHURCH; INSTITUTION, SOCIAL; NORM, SOCIAL; RELIGION; ROLE.

religious leaders, types of. As defined by Max Weber, there are three types of religious leader: the bureaucratic, the charismatic, and the traditional. The last is a leader whose authority stems from a hereditary or time-honored custom for selecting religious leaders. The authority of a charismatic religious leader depends upon his personal or charismatic qualities, and such leaders typically emerge during periods of revolution or renewal. The bureaucratic religious leader derives his authority from his legal status within a religious hierarchy. (M. Weber, *The Theory of Social and Economic Organization*, tr. by A. M. Henderson and T. Parsons, Oxford University Press, New York, 1947.)

religious order. See RELIGIOUS INSTITUTION.

rentier-lion type. See ELITE, CIRCULATION OF THE; INSTINCT FOR COMBINATIONS and INSTINCT FOR GROUP PERSISTENCES.

reorganization, social. See SOCIAL REORGANIZATION.

replication. Repetition of the same basic study or experiment to check its accuracy or to estimate the experimental error.

replication, item. The use of several items to obtain basically the same information (for example, several items on a questionnaire that ask essentially the same question in different words). Item replication may be used as a test of RELIABILITY or as a means of shedding light on different facets of an ATTITUDE.

representation, collective. See COLLECTIVE REPRESENTATION.

representation, individual. See INDIVIDUAL REPRESENTATION.

representative government. See DEMOCRACY.

representative sample. See SAMPLE, REPRESENTATIVE.

repression. 1. A DEFENSE MECHANISM involving the exclusion from a person's memory or self-image of painful or unpleasant thoughts that conflict with social norms. Psychiatrists speak of "unconscious forgetting."
2. A dominant group or groups' limiting the freedom of action of another group or groups.

reproducibility, coefficient of. A statistical measure used in connection with the GUTTMAN SCALE to determine the extent to which an individual's response to a single item (attitude statement) in the scale can be predicted (reproduced) from his total scale score.

reproduction, differential. See FERTILITY, DIFFERENTIAL.

reproduction rate, gross. A rate of population reproduction based on the number of female births and not taking into account the death rate. To obtain this rate, one first determines the total number of daughters that would eventually be born to a COHORT of newborn females if the present age-specific birth rates for females remained constant and if all the newborn females lived through the childbearing period. The gross reproduction rate is the ratio of this estimated number of daughters to the number of newborn females in the cohort (the future mothers). This rate does not take into account the fact that a certain number of the newborn females will not live through the childbearing period. See BIRTH RATE, SPECIFIC; REPRODUCTION RATE, NET.

reproduction rate, net. A rate of population reproduction based on the number of female births and taking into account the death rate. To obtain this rate, one starts with a COHORT of newborn females and determines the total number of daughters they may be expected eventually to have on the basis of present age-specific birth rates modified by present age-specific death rates (some of the newborn females will not live through the childbearing period). The net reproduction rate is the ratio of this number of expected daughters to the number of newborn females in the original cohort (the future mothers). A rate of 1 indicates a stationary population, over 1 a growing population, under 1 a declining population. However, the net reproduction rate indicates a population trend only if the birth rate and death rate remain constant. The net reproduction rate is more frequently used than the gross reproduction rate because it is a more realistic measure of population replacement. See BIRTH RATE, SPECIFIC; DEATH RATE, SPECIFIC; REPRODUCTION RATE, GROSS.

republic. 1. A system of government in which ultimate sovereignty is held to reside in the people rather than in a hereditary monarch. In this sense republic is opposed to monarchy. The ultimate sovereignty of the people may amount to little more than a theoretical assertion (such as, "the state embodies the will of the people"), and does not necessarily imply any effective popular control over the government. Thus a republic is not necessarily a DEMOCRACY. The United States and the Soviet Union would both be considered republics, whereas Great Britain (a constitutional monarchy) would not.

2. Sometimes used synonymously with representative democracy.

reputational social classes. See SOCIAL CLASS, REPUTATIONAL CONCEPTION OF.

requisite, functional. See FUNCTIONAL REQUISITE.

requisite, structural. See STRUCTURAL REQUISITE.

research. A systematic and objective attempt to study a problem for the purpose of deriving general principles. The investigation is guided by previously collected information and aims to add to the body of knowledge on the subject. Man's knowledge grows from studying what is already known and revising past knowledge in the light of new discoveries. All honest attempts to study a problem systematically or to add to man's knowledge of a problem may be regarded as research. See SCIENTIFIC METHOD.

research, action. See ACTION RESEARCH.

research, applied. RESEARCH directed to the formulation or discovery of scientific principles that can be used to solve some practical problem (of business, government, labor unions, etc.).

research, basic. RESEARCH conducted for the purpose of developing scientific theories or the basic principles of a discipline, rather than for the purpose of solving some immediate problem. Basic research, of course, lays the essential foundations for applied research. Technology advances ever more rapidly because there has been a corresponding advance in the development of general theories and principles from basic research.

research, individual. RESEARCH carried out by a single scholar following his own interests independently of bureaucratic or organizational direction. Individual research is oriented to what other scholars are doing, as is all good research, but the individual research scholar is coordinated with the rest of the scholarly community by virtue of his own knowledge, insights, interests, and self-discipline. If two or more scholars are given financial grants to work on similar or related problems, but left to follow their own hunches and interests, this would still be considered individual research. See RESEARCH, ORGANIZED.

research, motivational. See MOTIVATIONAL RESEARCH.

research, organized. RESEARCH carried out by a group of investigators working on the same problem or a set of interrelated and coordinated problems. It is also called group research, as contrasted to individual research. Usually, organized research involves a research director or directors and a number of subordinates, both professional and clerical, located in the same organization (university, business, government, etc.). See RESEARCH, INDIVIDUAL.

research, small group. See GROUP RESEARCH, SMALL.

research, social. Any RESEARCH that focuses on the study of human groups or the processes of social interaction.

research design. Any plan for the collection, analysis, and evaluation of data. The controlled experiment and the field study are types of research design. See EXPERIMENT, CONTROLLED; FIELD STUDY METHOD.

research group. See RESEARCH, ORGANIZATIONAL.

residence. See AVUNCULOCAL RESIDENCE; BILOCAL RESIDENCE; MATRILOCAL RESIDENCE; MATRI-PATRILOCAL RESIDENCE; NEOLOCAL RESIDENCE; PATRILOCAL RESIDENCE.

residential mobility. See MOBILITY, ECOLOGICAL.

residue, cultural. See CULTURAL SURVIVAL.

residues. The underlying sentiments or emotions that motivate man's nonlogical or nonrational actions. The term was introduced by Vilfredo Pareto, who sought to explain why it is that men often behave in a fashion that is nonrational. That aspect of human behavior which Pareto sought to explain in terms of residues essentially would be explained by sociologists today in terms of values and social norms. (V. Pareto, *The Mind and Society*, tr. by A. Bongiorno and A. Livingston, Harcourt, Brace, New York, 1935.) See DERIVATIONS; INSTINCT FOR COMBINATIONS and INSTINCT FOR GROUP PERSISTENCES; NORM, SOCIAL; SENTIMENT; VALUE.

resource. Any part of man's physical environment, living or nonliving, or any human skill or knowledge that can be used in the production of goods or services.

response. The reaction or activity of an individual aroused by a STIMULUS.

response, conditioned. See CONDITIONED RESPONSE OR REFLEX.

responsibility, collective. See COLLECTIVE RESPONSIBILITY.

restrictive covenant. An agreement restricting the sale of property in an area to members of specified groups or social categories. Such restrictions are usually based on race, religion, or ethnic group, but may also be based upon other agreed-upon indexes of socioeconomic status. Restrictive covenants may be either unwritten, informal agreements or written into property deeds. See SOCIAL CATEGORY.

retail trade area. The area served by the retail stores of a city or town. It includes the city itself and that part of the surrounding area having residents who shop frequently in the city. The retail trade area is often defined in terms of the area provided with free delivery service by the city's major stores, for example, department stores and furniture stores.

retreatism. A form of deviant behavior in which the individual rejects the culturally defined goals of success and the institutionalized means of attaining them. Retreatism is a mode of adaptation to the frustration of being unable to attain culturally valued goals. Examples of retreatism may be found in the behavior of psychotics, hobos, alcoholics, and drug addicts. The term was used by Robert K. Merton in his TYPOLOGY of individual modes of adaptation to patterns of cultural goals and institutional norms to refer to one of five modes of adaptation. (R. K. Merton, *Social Theory and Social Structure,* Free Press, Glencoe, Ill., 1957.) See RITUALISM.

revitalization movement. As defined by Anthony F. C. Wallace, a "deliberate, organized, conscious effort by members of a society to construct a more satisfying culture. Revitalization is thus, from a cultural standpoint, a special kind of culture change phenomenon." (A. F. C. Wallace, *American Anthropologist,* April 1956.) See MILLENARIAN MOVEMENT; NATIVISTIC MOVEMENT; SOCIAL MOVEMENT; VITALISTIC MOVEMENT.

revolution. 1. Any large-scale change in the leadership of a society (or of some fundamental part or institution of society, such as the political institution) and a successful restructuring of those aspects of society in a way deemed in the interests of the new ruling class. Revolutions may have profound effects upon a society, but not all aspects of a culture are changed immediately. When a revolution is described as a change in the power structure of society, this implies that the new interest groups, in making expedient changes, are also inadvertently causing other changes in society that they can only partially control and often do not understand.

2. Any change in society that brings about basic changes, even if they occur over a relatively long period of time—for example, the industrial, scientific, commercial, and agricultural revolutions. See AGRICULTURAL REVOLUTION; COMMERCIAL REVOLUTION; INDUSTRIAL REVOLUTION.

revolution, demographic. See DEMOGRAPHIC TRANSITION.

reward system. The ways in which any particular society or group through its members or through the holders of power or authority sanctions conformity. Such a system involves not only the awarding of honors and advantages, but also the withholding of negative sanctions. Reward systems do not necessarily represent the influence of the group as a whole, but may be primarily operated for those who hold power and authority. Leaders justify their control of much of the reward system on the basis of their claim to represent and express the will or best interests of the group or society. See SANCTION; SANCTION, NEGATIVE; SANCTION, POSITIVE.

rho. The Greek letter (written ρ), usually used to symbolize the rank difference coefficient of correlation. See CORRELATION, RANK DIFFERENCE.

ribbon development. See CONURBATION.

Riesman's categories of directedness. See INNER-DIRECTED SOCIETY; OTHER-DIRECTED SOCIETY; TRADITION-DIRECTED SOCIETY.

right. A legitimate or socially recognized moral or legal justification for an individual to be allowed specified behavior or to demand specified behavior of others with regard to himself. Rights of individuals or groups are constantly being redefined, withdrawn, or extended. For example, a person's rights change drastically if he becomes a criminal, and most ordinary citizens' rights are routinely denied to conscripts in modern military organizations, particularly during periods of warfare. Many rights are given up voluntarily when people join groups that demand special discipline, sacrifice, and conformity. Rights are situational, and a social group may recognize a general right of an individual to act in a specified way but sanction him for exercising his right in the immediate situation. For example, the right of free speech is not equally the same for an individual in his various social roles. All rights are limited or enlarged by obligations entailed in group membership, particular social situations, and social roles that are associated with the exercise of the particular right.

ring, urban. See URBAN RING.

rite. See CEREMONY; RITUAL.

rites. See CALENDRICAL RITES; CRISIS RITES; RITES DE PASSAGE; RITES OF INTENSIFICATION.

rites de passage. Ceremonies that mark a critical transition in the life of an individual from one phase of the life cycle to another. These ceremonies, often religious in nature, provide an institutionalized means of ending one social STATUS and starting another. They give emotional support to the individual (and those close to him) entering the new status and at the same time signify to all who interact with him that he now has new rights and obligations. *Rites de passage* include ceremonies associ-

ated with birth, puberty, marriage, and death. The term was used originally by Arnold van Gennep in his *Les Rites de Passage* (Nourry, Paris,
1909). Sometimes the term is translated from the French and referred to
as rites of passage. See CEREMONY.

rites of intensification. Ceremonies having as their primary purpose
the strengthening of group unity. The term was introduced by Eliot D.
Chapple and Carleton S. Coon to refer to CRISIS RITES directed toward a
group crisis, CALENDRICAL RITES, and any other ceremonies performed by
members of a group that tend to counteract disturbances to the equilibrium of the group, intensify interaction among group members, and solid-
ify the group. Examples would be family grace, harvest ceremonies, and
war ceremonies. (E. D. Chapple and C. S. Coon, *Principles of Anthropology*, Henry Holt, New York, 1942.)

rites of passage. See RITES DE PASSAGE.

ritual. 1. A culturally standardized set of actions with symbolic significance performed on occasions prescribed by tradition. The acts and
words that comprise a ritual are precisely defined and vary very little if at
all from one occasion to another. Tradition also determines who may perform the ritual. Rituals often involve the use of sacred objects, and are
usually expected to result in the emotional involvement of the participants. The ritual may be believed to have power in itself to produce certain results. In this case it is a magical ritual. Religious rituals usually symbolize a basic belief and are intended to induce a feeling of reverence and
awe. Rituals also are used to promote group unity, as in nationalistic rituals. Rituals may also provide a means of relieving feelings of anxiety in
times of crisis. Ritual is usually distinguished from CEREMONY, in that
ceremony implies a more elaborate sequence of behavior, usually consisting of a standardized series of rituals. Moreover, a ceremony is necessarily
social, involving more than one person, whereas a ritual may be collective
or individual.

2. Symbolic behavior that is repeated at appropriate times, expressing
in a stylized, overt form some value or concern of a group (or individual).
In this meaning of the term, small and relatively temporary social groups
may develop rituals that are not traditional in the culture but are unique
to the particular group.

ritual, initiation. See INITIATION RITUAL.

ritual kinship. See KINSHIP, RITUAL.

ritualism. As defined by Robert K. Merton, a type of individual
adaptation in which the individual rejects culturally defined goals because he feels he cannot succeed in attaining them, but continues to cling
to the institutionalized routines and norms that are supposed to lead to
these goals. The individual finds security in compulsively following the

safe routines prescribed for success. Even though he does not think he will ever be a success or enter a much higher status, the process of ritually conforming to the institutionalized means protects him from the anxiety that is ordinarily provoked by failure to achieve these goals. Ritualism is one of five modes of adaptation used by Merton in his TYPOLOGY of the modes of individual adaptation to patterns of cultural goals and institutional norms. The other modes of adaptation are: conformity, in which the individual accepts the cultural goals as well as the institutionalized means of achieving them; innovation, in which he accepts the goals of the culture but rejects the institutionalized means of achieving them (as in white collar crime); RETREATISM, in which he rejects the cultural goals as well as the institutionalized means of obtaining them; and rebellion, involving the rejection of both the culturally prescribed goals and the institutionalized means of achieving them, with a substitution of new goals and means (as in adolescent subculture). (R. K. Merton, *Social Theory and Social Structure*, Free Press, Glencoe, Ill., 1957.) See CRIME, WHITE COLLAR.

rituals, avoidance. See AVOIDANCE RITUALS.

rituals, presentational. See PRESENTATIONAL RITUALS.

rivalry. A type of COMPETITION or CONFLICT in which the groups or individuals involved are in communication with each other, and continually adjust their behavior on the basis of the success or failure of the opposing party.

role. A pattern of behavior, structured around specific rights and duties and associated with a particular STATUS position within a group or social situation. A person's role in any situation is defined by the set of expectations for his behavior held by others and by the person himself. Ralph Linton has referred to role as the dynamic aspect of status; a role is the totality of all the cultural patterns associated with a particular status. (R. Linton, *The Study of Man*, Appleton-Century-Crofts, New York, 1936.)

The SOCIAL STRUCTURE has certain requirements and these are reflected in how people are expected to act in a particular position, and how, in fact, they more or less do act. There are variations in the expectations associated with a status position (of father, physician, husband, wife, etc.), but only within a certain range of culturally acceptable behavior. Any given role within a group tends to vary according to the individual who occupies the status, as well as the general membership composition of the group, but if the performance of a role deviates very much from the expected range of behavior, the individual will be negatively sanctioned.

Each individual has many status positions within a society, and therefore he performs a variety of roles. Since the unity of SELF requires a degree of value and behavioral integration, and frequently even a hierarchy of role priorities (according to which is most central to the self), the particular combination of statuses a person has tends to influence the way he performs his various roles. His performance will never exactly correspond to the expectations of others, nor will it meet all the expectations he may have of himself. See ROLE EXPECTATIONS.

role, achieved. A ROLE that an individual has because he has either chosen or earned it. It is the result of his efforts and his actions. See ROLE, ASCRIBED; STATUS, ACHIEVED.

role, ascribed. A ROLE that an individual acquires automatically at birth or on the attainment of a certain age. The most universal ascribed role is one's sex role—male or female. Different age levels are also associated with different expectations. Roles based on one's birth as a member of a particular racial or religious group are ascribed, as are inherited upper-class roles. See ROLE, ACHIEVED; STATUS, ASCRIBED.

role, assumed. See ROLE, ACHIEVED.

role, counterfeit. A ROLE that an individual pretends is his own, but that in reality has only been assumed as a cover to protect him from the penalties associated with his actual role. The epileptic who prefers to be known as an alcoholic and the divorced woman who pretends to be a widow would be examples. (E. M. Lemert, *Social Pathology*, McGraw-Hill, New York, 1951.)

role, internalized. A ROLE or ROLE-SET observed by an individual and adopted by him as a part of his self-conception or self-image. Usually an individual's personal role definition stems from roles he has internalized, or adopted from others as his own. See INTERNALIZATION; ROLE DEFINITION, PERSONAL; SELF.

role, perceived. The ROLE expectations that a person believes others have of him in a situation. It is the role that a person believes others expect him to play. It may or may not correspond to the ROLE DEMANDS (actual expectations of others) or his own personal role definition. See ROLE DEFINITION, PERSONAL.

role, prescribed. A ROLE as defined by cultural standards. Theodore M. Newcomb uses the term to refer to a set of behaviors expected for all occupants of a particular role. The prescribed role sets the limits of the behavior within a particular role. Newcomb distinguishes this from ROLE BEHAVIOR, which refers to the behavior of a single individual in a role. (T. M. Newcomb, *Social Psychology*, Dryden-Holt, New York, 1950.)

role, representative. A ROLE which an individual plays that conforms to his and his group's view of the type of behavior that typifies and represents the standards and values of the group. Any member who, in his interaction with persons outside the group, represents the group by behaving in a manner characteristic of the group would be regarded as playing a representative role. Siegfried F. Nadel holds that the concept of the representative role is the only way that there is to give meaning to the idea of interrelationships between groups. (S. F. Nadel, *The Theory of Social Structure*, Free Press, Glencoe, Ill., 1957.)

role, social. See ROLE.

role anticipation. See ROLE EXPECTATIONS.

role behavior. 1. Behavior that is socially expected in a particular ROLE, or behavior that is performed as part of a role.
2. The behavior of a particular individual in a certain role. Theodore M. Newcomb distinguishes between prescribed role, which he regards as a sociological concept, and role behavior in this sense, which he regards as a psychological concept. (T. M. Newcomb, *Social Psychology*, Dryden-Holt, New York, 1950.) See ROLE, PRESCRIBED.

role cluster. See ROLES, MULTIPLE.

role conflict. Incompatibility between two or more roles that an individual is expected to perform in a given situation. The performance of one role interferes with or is antagonistic to the other. The state of conflict may last only a short time and the conflicting demands may be met without much difficulty or it may be a persistent problem facing someone all of his life. The analysis of role conflict and its resolution is important in the study of values, social processes, and SOCIAL STRUCTURE in general. Possible sources of role conflict may be found in the combined roles of the young career mother or of the military chaplain. See SOCIAL PROCESS; VALUE.

role definition, personal. An individual's own definition of his ROLE in a situation. Daniel J. Levinson suggests that the concept of role be divided into personal role definition and ROLE DEMANDS. (D. J. Levinson, *Journal of Abnormal and Social Psychology*, March 1959.)

role demands. The expectation of others with reference to a person playing a ROLE in a situation. The actor may or may not, once aware of the role demands, wish or be able to fulfill them. See ROLE DEFINITION, PERSONAL.

role discontinuity. A lack of congruity between the expectations associated with social roles taken on consecutively by an individual. The changes from the courtship to the marriage role, and the occupational role to the retirement role are examples of situations involving a degree of role discontinuity.

role expectations. 1. The entire set of responses or behavior anticipated and desired in relation to a certain ROLE. By this definition, role expectations include the actor's expectations of himself as well as the expectations of others.

2. Role expectations as defined above but excluding those expectations a person has of himself.

role insulation. A state of relative isolation of the occupants of a ROLE that results from the tendency for persons occupying a given role, particularly an occupational role, to have more informal social interaction with each other than with persons occupying other roles. This tends to reinforce their own particular role perspective and decrease their understanding of other points of view.

role model. An individual whose behavior in a particular ROLE provides a pattern or model upon which another individual bases his behavior in performing the same role. The role model provides a standard used by the other person in determining the appropriate attitudes and actions of an occupant of the role. The role model differs from the REFERENCE INDIVIDUAL in that the INTERNALIZATION of the standards of behavior and attitudes of the role model is limited to one or a very few roles, whereas IDENTIFICATION with a reference individual is more comprehensive, including a wide range of roles. For example a person may have a role model for an occupational role (nurse, lawyer, or the like), but not identify with or emulate that individual in any other aspect of life. A role model need not be personally known to the individual, not living, nor necessarily real, and may include public figures, historical figures, and legendary heroes.

role performance. The way a person actually plays his ROLE in a situation.

role playing. 1. Acting in a manner one considers proper for his ROLE. In role playing the individual conforms to the social norms that define the appropriate behavior for a given role. Walter Coutu distinguishes between role playing, which he defines as enacting what one considers his appropriate role in a situation, from playing at a role, which he conceives of as enacting a role as a form of pretense. (W. Coutu, *American Sociological Review*, April 1951.)

2. A technique used in SOCIODRAMA and PSYCHODRAMA in which a person enacts a part in an improvised dramatization of a life situation.

role primacy. The precedence of one ROLE over another. Every individual must play a number of roles, and sometimes the demands of one role conflict with the demands of another. In the case of ROLE CONFLICT, an order of precedence must be established. The primacy of a role is determined by the extent to which it is important or essential to the individual's self-conception or self-image. Role primacy, however, is not simply an individual matter. The primacy of a particular role varies by historical, cultural, and situational factors, and the structure of a society or a social group is crucial in the determination of role primacy for its members. For example, the culture may demand the primacy of certain occupational roles, such as physician or priest, over other normal role obligations of persons who play these important social roles. See SELF.

role-set. As defined by Robert K. Merton, a set of roles (a role complex) that centers around a particular social STATUS. Any given social status involves an individual actor (person) in a number of social relationships that are always or usually found to be necessary for persons in that particular status. For example, the status of university professor frequently involves the roles of teacher, research technician, adviser to students, consultant to industry and government, administrator, clerk, author, specialist in a professional discipline, and so forth. Thus various social statuses in a society may require common associated roles which continually bring functionally different statuses together. In such an overlapping of associated roles people who have different positions in society may often meet and interact in a manner that promotes social integration. (See R. K. Merton, *Social Theory and Social Structure*, Free Press, Glencoe, Ill., 1957.) See ROLES, MULTIPLE; STATUS SEQUENCE; STATUS-SET.

role strain. As defined by William J. Goode, a feeling of difficulty or stress in fulfilling the demands of one's ROLE obligations.

role-taking. The taking of the attitudes or point of view of another person by imagining oneself as the other person, in order to anticipate his actual behavior. In essence, it is as if a person said to himself, "Knowing him and his situation, and putting myself in his shoes, what would I myself do?" Often, but not always, role-taking involves EMPATHY or SYMPATHY.

role-taking, reflexive. As defined by George H. Mead, a taking of the ROLE of another by viewing oneself from the point of view of the other. Thus a person sees himself as he is evaluated by someone else. Reflexive role-taking allows a person to become an object to himself, to see himself as others see him. Mead was interested in the idea that man cannot experience himself as a person directly, but only indirectly by taking the attitudes of others toward himself in a social context. The concept of reflexive role-taking is similar to Charles H. Cooley's concept of the LOOKING-GLASS SELF. (G. H. Mead, *Mind, Self and Society*, University of Chicago Press, Chicago, 1934.)

roles, multiple. The roles associated with the various statuses (the STATUS-SET) held by an individual at a given time, for example, the roles associated with the statuses of husband, father, lawyer, church elder, and so forth. See ROLE-SET.

roles, reciprocal. Social roles that define the patterns of interaction between two or more related statuses. Reciprocal roles are related and inseparable. The teacher-student, husband-wife, father-daughter, son-father relationships are reciprocal. The understanding of reciprocal roles is crucial in the study of the structure (and processes) of social life. See ROLE; STATUS.

romantic family. See FAMILY, COMPANIONSHIP.

romantic love. See LOVE, ROMANTIC.

rooming-house area. An area of the city in which there are many unattached, highly mobile individuals living in rooming houses. The rooming-house area is characterized by a rapid turnover in population, a high degree of ANONYMITY, an absence of primary group ties, a predominance of impersonal or secondary relationships, and a lack of community identification. It is often an area with a high rate of personal as well as social disorganization, as evidence by a high incidence of divorce, alcoholism, mental illness, ANOMIE, and so forth. See DISORGANIZATION, PERSONAL; DISORGANIZATION, SOCIAL; GROUP, PRIMARY; NATURAL AREA; SECONDARY RELATIONS.

Rorschach test. A PROJECTIVE TECHNIQUE used in analyzing personality, developed by Hermann Rorschach. In this test a series of standardized ink blots are presented to a subject for his interpretation of what the ink blots look like. The subject's imaginative responses are used to analyze his personality. The Rorschach test is often simply called the ink-blot test.

Rosenzweig test. A PROJECTIVE TECHNIQUE for studying the way a person tends to direct blame and aggression in a frustrating situation. The subject is presented with a series of cartoons, each of which consists of a line drawing of a person in a frustrating situation, with the frustrated person's "balloon" empty, to be filled in by the subject taking the test. The subject fills in what he thinks the cartoon character is saying. Responses are classified according to whether the subject, identifying with the frustrated persons, tends to direct blame and aggression toward an external source (outside himself), blame himself, or be impersonal and objective. The test was developed by Saul Rosenzweig, and is sometimes called picture-frustration study.

routinization, ecological. The recurrent pattern of daily movement of population within a METROPOLITAN AREA. Routinized population movement includes movement back and forth between place of residence and place of work, patterns of movement to retail shopping districts, to service centers, and to places of amusement. The term is often also applied to recurrent patterns of movement of goods within a metropolitan area, for example, from the wholesale district to the retail district.

row. In statistics, a horizontal listing of data in a series of categories all of which have a common classification. A STATISTICAL TABLE is composed of horizontal rows and vertical columns. See COLUMN.

row caption. A title that descriptively indicates the common classification of the data listed in a ROW.

rules of the game, Piaget's. The stages of normative and moral development through which children progress as they grow older and as they participate in social interaction and finally achieve an adult understanding of social rules. Jean Piaget studied children and the way they regard rules in their playing of games. He was primarily interested in the formation of the SELF and the development of morality. He outlined four general stages of moral development of children: the motor stage, in which the child complies with social rules, but only ritually and with little understanding; the egocentric stage, in which the child becomes dogmatic about social rules and tends to see them primarily from his own point of view; the cooperative stage, in which the child develops an incipient form of cooperation; and finally the codification of the rules stage, in which the child begins to understand the logic of rules and morality. (J. Piaget, *The Moral Judgment of the Child,* Harcourt, Brace, New York, 1932.) See CODIFICATION OF THE RULES STAGE, PIAGET'S; COOPERATIVE STAGE, PIAGET'S; EGOCENTRIC STAGE, PIAGET'S; MOTOR STAGE, PIAGET'S; SOCIALIZATION.

rumor. A usually inaccurate or untrue report that is informally communicated from person to person (generally by word of mouth). Rumors are usually about people or events of intense interest to the public which passes on the rumor, and about which they desire additional information. In crisis situations, under censorship, under repression, or when people are subject to any other type of emotional or intellectual stress, they are apt to respond to any shred or pretense of information, and tend to either believe or half-believe in rumors. See SOCIAL CONTAGION.

rumor intensity formula. A formula $(R \sim i \times a)$ suggested by Gordon W. Allport and Leo Postman to symbolize the relationship between the intensity of a rumor and the importance and ambiguity of the subject with which it deals (with R standing for "rumor," "i" for "intensity," and "a" for "ambiguity"). "In words this formula means that the amount of rumor in circulation will vary with the importance of the subject to the individuals concerned *times* the ambiguity of the evidence pertaining to the topic at issue. The relation between importance and ambiguity is not additive but multiplicative, for if either importance or ambiguity is zero, there is *no* rumor." (G. W. Allport and L. Postman, *The Psychology of Rumor,* Henry Holt, New York, 1947.)

run. In statistics, a series of identical symbols, either numerical or nonnumerical (for example, 6, 6, 6 or + + +), which may or may not be preceded or followed by different symbols.

runs test. A nonparametric statistical test that may be used with a single SAMPLE to test whether that sample is random, that is, whether the cases included represent a random sample of the POPULATION from which they were drawn. The one-sample runs test is based on the analysis of the occurrence of runs in a sequence of scores or observations (for example, a comparison of the number of runs in scores above and below the median score). From the sequence of scores or observations, that is, the number of runs, the probability that the sample is random is determined. For a runs test used with two samples, see WALD-WOLFOWITZ RUNS TEST. See also NONPARAMETRIC STATISTICS; PROBABILITY; RUN; SAMPLE, RANDOM.

rural community. As defined by Dwight Sanderson, "that form of association maintained between the people and their institutions in a local area in which they live on dispersed farmsteads and in a village which usually forms the center of their common activities." (D. Sanderson, *Rural Sociology and Rural Social Organization*, Wiley, New York, 1942.)

rural nonfarm. As used by the U.S. Census, the rural population that is not living on farms.

rural place. According to the U.S. Census, any place that is not defined as an URBAN PLACE, that is, any place that is unincorporated, or open country, or incorporated places having a population under 2,500. However, unincorporated places on the fringe of large urban areas are classified as urban if they have a population density of 1,000 inhabitants or more per square mile. In addition, incorporated places with a population under 2,500 on the fringe of large urban areas are also classified as urban if they have a closely settled area of 100 dwelling units or more. Other countries use different arbitrary standards for distinguishing rural and urban places.

rural sociology. See SOCIOLOGY, RURAL.

rural-urban fringe. See URBAN FRINGE.

rurban area. See URBAN FRINGE.

rurbanization. A term introduced by Charles J. Galpin to refer to the blending of urban and rural life through the dispersion of urban populations into rural areas and the resulting development of large fringe areas, or mixed rural-urban areas, that are neither truly rural nor truly urban. (C. J. Galpin, *Rural Life*, Century, New York, 1918.) See URBAN FRINGE.

S

S-shaped curve. See OGIVE.

S theory. The formalized sociological theory expressed in mathematical terms that was developed by Stuart Dodd in *Dimensions of Society* (Macmillan, New York, 1942).

sacred. Culture traits or aspects of a culture that symbolize important cultural values and evoke attitudes of great respect or awe. Sacred culture traits may be either material or nonmaterial. Those that are material are referred to as sacred objects; examples would be a Christian cross, a statue of Buddha, a Hindu sacred cow, or a national symbol such as a flag. Nonmaterial sacred traits would include supernatural beings, abstract conceptions of a group (such as the nation), beliefs, and ideals. The common element in these diverse traits inheres in the attitude of the members of a group or society. That which is sacred is not judged by utilitarian or rational standards. It evokes sentiment and emotion, embodies tradition, and is not considered to be properly subject to the critical evaluation that may be directed at that which is secular. The sacred is often associated with religion and is sometimes considered synonymous with the holy. But the ideas or objects that become the focus of sacred values and emotions need not be religious in the usual meaning of the term. Religion attempts to institutionalize the sacred, but formal religions, being bound by past definitions and traditions, sometimes neglect or fail to assimiliate new interpretations of the sacred and instead become engrossed in secular and profane concerns. Thus, particularly in modern society, much that is considered sacred remains separate from the RELIGIOUS INSTITUTION. See CULTURE TRAIT; VALUE.

sacred society. A society that because of its homogeneity, integration, and stability has a great many values and customs that are regarded as sacred and unchangeable. In a sacred society the value system and social relationships are regarded as more absolute, natural, and unchallengeable than they are in a SECULAR SOCIETY. The meanings or interpretations of objects and activities are shared widely and therefore seldom questioned. Nonliterate societies are usually considered examples of societies that most typify the sacred type, although the concept of sacred society was developed by Howard Becker as a CONSTRUCTED TYPE, or abstract model to which no actual society corresponds exactly. He developed this constructed type as part of a sacred-secular societal TYPOLOGY. (H. Becker in *Modern Sociological Theory*, edited by H. Becker and A. Boskoff, Dryden Press, New York, 1957.)

salience. In the study of attitudes, the prominence of an ATTITUDE or group IDENTIFICATION in the thought and behavior of an individual. If an attitude or group identification is salient for an individual, it is in the forefront of his awareness. He thinks of it often, regards it as relevant in many situations, and is easily reminded of it.

sample. In statistics, a portion of the total number of cases having a given characteristic (or characteristics). A sample consists of a limited number of cases selected for study from a particular POPULATION. Most sociological research deals with samples rather than total populations. The extent to which generalizations based on sample data may be considered applicable to the total population from which the sample was drawn depends on the method used to select the cases included in the sample and the size of the sample. There are numerous statistical techniques concerned with the problem of making inferences about a population from the data of a sample or samples. See entries for kinds of samples, listed alphabetically below.

sample, accidental. A SAMPLE selected purely on the basis of convenience and accessibility without regard to the extent to which it is representative of the POPULATION from which it is drawn.

sample, area. A type of SAMPLE selected on the basis of geographic areas. The total region to be surveyed is divided into geographic areas from which a designated number of areas are randomly chosen. These in turn are subdivided into smaller areas from which a designated number again are randomly selected. Within the finally selected subareas, all or a specified proportion (randomly chosen) of the households are studied.

sample, biased. A SAMPLE selected in such a manner that certain types of cases have a greater chance of being included than other types of cases. Thus the sample is not representative of the POPULATION from which it was drawn, but differs from the population in some systematic fashion.

sample, cluster. A SAMPLE selected by using clusters or groupings of cases rather than selecting individual cases directly from the total POPULA-

TION. In cluster sampling, the total population is divided into clusters of some type (for example, geographic areas or schools) and a certain number of clusters are randomly selected. All of the cases within the selected clusters may be used, or a certain number of cases within each cluster may be randomly selected on an individual basis, or each cluster may be subdivided into smaller clusters from which a random selection of subclusters is made. An area sample is a type of cluster sample. See SAMPLE, AREA.

sample, nonprobability. A SAMPLE so selected that it is not possible to determine the PROBABILITY each case in the POPULATION has of being included in the sample. Therefore it is not known whether each case in the population had a chance of being included in the sample. For examples of nonprobability samples, see SAMPLE, ACCIDENTAL; SAMPLE, PURPOSIVE; and SAMPLE, QUOTA.

sample, probability. A SAMPLE so selected that the PROBABILITY each case in the POPULATION has of being included in the sample is known or may be determined. Thus it is known that each case has a chance of being included in the sample, and moreover it is possible to specify the probability that the sample results do not vary more than a determined amount from the true population values. For examples of probability samples, see SAMPLE, AREA; SAMPLE, RANDOM; SAMPLE, STRATIFIED; and SAMPLE, SYSTEMATIC.

sample, proportional. See SAMPLE, STRATIFIED.

sample, purposive. A SAMPLE composed of cases deliberately selected individually on the basis of certain variables so that they will be representative of the population from which they are drawn. The selection of a purposive sample assumes a knowledge of the population characteristics of which the sample is to be representative. Because this method involves the risk of unrecognized biases in regard to other variables that may also be relevant, generally the proportional stratified random sample is preferred. See SAMPLE, STRATIFIED.

sample, quota. A SAMPLE selected by dividing a population into categories on the basis of certain variables and choosing a certain number (a quota) of cases from each category. No attempt is made to select the individual cases within each category (quota) randomly. They may be chosen on any basis including convenience. The quota sample has been most widely used in public opinion sampling. The usual procedure in the use of the quota sample is to select geographic areas on a random basis, assign the interviewers quotas of individuals with specified characteristics within each selected area, and leave the selection of specific individuals to fill the quotas to the interviewers' discretion. A quota sample is the same as a stratified nonrandom sample. See SAMPLE, STRATIFIED.

sample, random. A SAMPLE selected purely on the basis of chance. In the selection of a random sample, each case is independently chosen, that is, the selection of one case in no way affects the likelihood of any other case's being selected. In addition, in choosing a random sample every case in the POPULATION has the same probability of being included in the sample. Moreover, if enough samples of a given size were chosen in a random manner from a population, eventually every possible combination of cases would occur, and in the long run every combination would occur about the same number of times. A random sample can be drawn by placing cards in a container—one card for each case in the population—thoroughly mixing the cards, and then selecting the desired number of cases. To avoid the tediousness this procedure involves, particularly with large populations, and for greater convenience, a computer or a table of random numbers is usually used instead of drawing lots. In using a table of random numbers, the investigator numbers all the cases in the population, and then, starting at any point on the table selects those cases whose numbers follow in successive order. The random sample, in which each individual case is drawn from the population as a whole, is frequently referred to as a simple random sample to distinguish it from samples in which random selection is combined with another sampling technique, as in the stratified random sample or the area sample. See RANDOMNESS; RANDOM NUMBERS, TABLE OF.

sample, representative. A SAMPLE that has essentially the same distribution of relevant characteristics as the POPULATION from which it was drawn. In order to generalize sample findings to the population as a whole, the sample must be representative of that population. For the most popular methods of attempting to assure the representativeness of a sample, see SAMPLE, AREA; SAMPLE, RANDOM; SAMPLE, STRATIFIED; and SAMPLE, SYSTEMATIC.

sample, simple random. See SAMPLE, RANDOM.

sample, stratified. A SAMPLE selected by dividing a POPULATION into categories (strata) on the basis of certain relevant variables and selecting a determined number of cases from each category, thus assuring that each category will be represented in the sample. If the proportion of cases in each category is the same in the sample as in the population as a whole, the sample is known as a proportional stratified sample, or sometimes simply a proportional sample. If the cases included in the sample are selected randomly within each category (a random sample of specified size being taken of each category), the sample is a stratified random sample. If the cases chosen within each category are not selected randomly, the sample is a stratified nonrandom sample, usually referred to as a quota sample. A proportional stratified random sample provides an efficient means of obtaining a representative sample when sufficient information about the characteristics of the population is available. See SAMPLE, QUOTA; SAMPLE, RANDOM.

sample, stratified nonrandom. See SAMPLE, QUOTA.

sample, stratified random. See SAMPLE, STRATIFIED.

sample, systematic. A SAMPLE obtained by selecting every nth case from an arbitrary list (for example, an alphabetical list) of all the cases in the POPULATION. The size of n is determined by dividing the size of the population by the size desired for the sample. Thus if a sample of 100 is desired from a population of 1,000, every tenth case would be selected. The first case is selected at random between 1 and n. Thus if n were 10, the first case selected at random between 1 and 10 might be 4. Then included in the sample would be the 4th case, the 14th, the 24th, etc. In selecting a systematic sample the investigator must be careful that cases with a certain characteristic or characteristics do not occur in regular intervals on the list. This method is also referred to as sampling by regular intervals and ordinal sampling.

sample, unbiased. See SAMPLE, REPRESENTATIVE.

sample statistic. See STATISTIC.

sampling. See SAMPLE.

sampling, multiple-phase. A technique of statistical analysis in which basic information is gathered from a sample in the first phase of the study; and, in the second phase, a subsample is given more intensive analysis.

sampling, multiple-stage. Sampling carried out in two or more stages. In the first stage larger units are selected, and in the second stage smaller units (or the individual cases, depending on the number of stages) are selected from within the larger units. Cluster samples involve multiple-stage sampling if a sample is taken within each of the selected clusters, that is, if not all of the cases within clusters are used, which is most often the procedure followed. The area sample is a widely used type of cluster sample that is based on multiple-stage sampling. See SAMPLE, AREA; SAMPLE, CLUSTER; SAMPLING UNIT.

sampling, ordinal. See SAMPLE, SYSTEMATIC.

sampling by regular intervals. See SAMPLE, SYSTEMATIC.

sampling distribution. A PROBABILITY DISTRIBUTION (theoretically expected distribution) of a statistical measure (chi-square, the product-moment coefficient of correlation r, t, a mean, or any other STATISTIC) for random samples of a specified size. The sampling distribution gives the probable distribution of values of the statistic that would be obtained if an extremely large number of random samples of a specified size were taken from the same population. In other words, while a particular sample yields a specific value for the statistic, the sampling distribution shows theoretically the probable distribution of values that would be obtained from a great many samples. At the same time it gives the probability of obtaining each specified value. See CHI-SQUARE TEST; MEAN, ARITHMETIC; SAMPLE, RANDOM.

sampling error. The difference between the true population PARAMETER and the PARAMETER ESTIMATE obtained from a SAMPLE of the POPULATION. Most sociological research deals with samples rather than total populations, and therefore is subject to sampling error. The attempt is made to minimize sampling error by obtaining a sample that is as representative as possible of the population. However, even with the best sampling techniques there is always some difference between the characteristics of a total population and the characteristics of a sample. When proper sampling procedures are followed, statistical techniques may be employed to estimate the size of the sampling error. For the most widely employed techniques for obtaining a representative sample, see SAMPLE, AREA; SAMPLE, RANDOM; SAMPLE, STRATIFIED (especially a proportional stratified random sample); and SAMPLE, SYSTEMATIC. See also STANDARD ERROR.

sampling statistics. See STATISTICS, INDUCTIVE.

sampling unit. A unit used in selecting a SAMPLE. In many types of samples, as the simple random sample, the sampling units are simply the individual cases that comprise the sample. In multiple-stage sampling, however, the first stage or primary sampling units are aggregates or clusters of cases (such as geographic areas) from within which the final sampling units, that is, the individual cases, are selected. See SAMPLE, RANDOM; SAMPLING, MULTIPLE-STAGE.

sampling variation. See CHANCE FACTORS.

sanction. A penalty or reward directed at a person (or group) in order to discourage or encourage certain types of behavior. Among negative sanctions, the firing squad would be an extreme form, and a look of disapproval relatively mild. Examples of positive sanctions would include praise, applause, and medals. Although drastic sanctions are often (though not always) successful in enforcing rules of behavior, other sanctions may fail altogether, or succeed only partially. A look of disapproval may hurt the person sanctioned very much or not at all, depending on the extent to which the sanction appears to enforce social norms, that is, depending on whether or not it is believed to reflect the attitude of the group or society to which the person belongs. Negative sanctions are directed at the deviant's presumed refusal to conform as well as at the disapproved act itself. They have less legitimacy when the deviant did not intend nonconformity—if his act was accidental or somehow beyond his control. See NORM, SOCIAL; PUNISHMENT; REWARD SYSTEM; SOCIAL CONTROL.

sanction, diffuse. As defined by A. R. Radcliffe-Brown, a SANCTION applied by a single individual as a spontaneous expression of his approval or disapproval of some deviance from societal norms. The expression of such sanctions provides a widespread, informal system of SOCIAL CONTROL. (A. R. Radcliffe-Brown in *Encyclopedia of the Social Sciences*, Macmillan, New York, 1934.) See SANCTION, ORGANIZED.

sanction, formal. See SANCTION, ORGANIZED.

sanction, informal. See SANCTION, DIFFUSE.

sanction, legal. A SANCTION that is part of a formalized code of justice backed by some form of authority.

sanction, moral. A SANCTION that is intended to support the ethical values of a society. Negative moral sanctions consist of reactions of disapproval and reprobations evoked by the violation of moral norms. See MORES.

sanction, negative. A SANCTION intended to punish rather than reward. See PUNISHMENT.

sanction, organized. As defined by A. R. Radcliffe-Brown, a SANCTION that is carried out by a recognized, traditional procedure by the whole community or by its representatives. Imprisonment, fines, and exile are examples of organized negative sanctions. Medals, monetary rewards, and titles are examples of organized, positive (or premial) sanctions. (A. R. Radcliffe-Brown in *Encyclopedia of the Social Sciences*, Macmillan, New York, 1934.) See SANCTION, DIFFUSE.

sanction, positive. A SANCTION intended to reward rather than punish. See REWARD SYSTEM.

sanction, premial. A positive organized sanction. See SANCTION, ORGANIZED.

sanction, satirical. A SANCTION imposed by ridicule.

sanction, social. See SANCTION.

satellite city. See CITY, SATELLITE.

scalar status. See STATUS, SCALAR.

scale. A series of numerical units or nonnumerical categories used to measure or classify data. Scales range from the NOMINAL SCALE, consisting simply of a series of nonordered categories for classifying data, to the RATIO SCALE, which is the most precise instrument for the quantitative measurement of degrees of magnitude. See SCALE, ATTITUDE; SCALES.

scale, attitude. A device for quantitatively measuring the intensity with which an ATTITUDE is held (for example, an attitude toward an ethnic group). There are several types of attitude scales which differ considerably in form and method of construction. However, all attitude scales are designed to obtain a numerical score for each respondent that indicates his position on an attitude continuum, that is, the degree of favorableness or unfavorableness with which he regards a person, group, idea, or pattern of behavior. An attitude scale consists of a series of related attitude statements. The respondent indicates his agreement or disagreement with each statement, or, depending on the type of scale, his degree of agreement or disagreement. Attitude scales are widely used in sociological and social psychological research. See BOGARDUS SOCIAL DISTANCE SCALE; CUMULATIVE SCALE; GUTTMAN SCALE; LIKERT SCALE; SUMMATED SCALE; THURSTONE EQUAL-APPEARING INTERVAL SCALE; UNIDIMENSIONAL SCALE.

scales. See BOGARDUS SOCIAL DISTANCE SCALE; CHAPIN SOCIAL STATUS SCALE; CUMULATIVE SCALE; DIFFERENTIAL SCALE; F SCALE; GUTTMAN SCALE; INTERVAL SCALE; LIKERT SCALE; NOMINAL SCALE; NORTH-HATT SCALE OF OCCUPATIONAL PRESTIGE; ORDINAL SCALE; PAIRED COMPARISON SCALE; POINT SCALE; RANKING SCALE; RATING SCALE; RATING SCALE, GRAPHIC; RATIO SCALE; SUMMATED SCALE; THURSTONE EQUAL-APPEARING INTERVAL SCALE; UNIDIMENSIONAL SCALE.

scaling. The ordering of a number of related items (descriptive characteristics or attitude statements) to form a CONTINUUM in order to provide a means of quantitative measurement of qualitative variables. See SCALE, ATTITUDE; SCALES; VARIABLE, QUALITATIVE.

scalogram analysis. See GUTTMAN SCALE.

scapegoating. Placing the blame for one's troubles, frustration, or sense of guilt on some convenient but innocent person or group. (The ancient Hebrews, once a year, symbolically placed their sins on a goat and then drove the goat into the wilderness—hence the term.) Scapegoating is often used as a PROPAGANDA technique by those with national political power. A foreign enemy or some subgroup within the society is blamed for bad conditions, in order to divert hostility away from the ruling class or elite.

scarcity theory of power. See POWER, SCARCITY THEORY OF.

scatter. See DISPERSION, STATISTICAL.

scatter diagram. A diagram that shows by means of dots on a graph the value-for-value relationship between two quantitative variables. The values or class intervals of one VARIABLE (customarily the independent variable) are arranged along the horizontal axis and the values or class intervals of the other variable are arranged along the vertical axis. Dots are placed on the graph to show each pair of values for the two variables. That is, for each occurrence of the two variables a dot is plotted on the graph showing the values of the two variables. The greater the degree of association between the two variables (i.e., the higher the correlation) the more the dots will fall within a narrow range of a straight line or curve. The less the association between the two variables (i.e., the lower the correlation) the less the dots will tend to follow a straight line or curve and the more widely they will be scattered. See DISPERSION, STATISTICAL; VARIABLE, QUANTITATIVE.

schedasticity. In the relationship between two quantitative variables, the dispersion or scatter of the values of one VARIABLE for the values of the other variable. Analyzing scedasticity involves comparing the dispersion of the values of the dependent variable for each of the values of the independent variable and determining the extent to which the degree of dispersion remains uniform throughout the values of the independent variable. See DISPERSION, STATISTICAL; HETEROSCEDASTICITY; HOMOSCEDASTICITY; VARIABLE, QUANTITATIVE.

schedule. See INTERVIEW SCHEDULE.

schismogenesis. CLEAVAGE within a group resulting from the type of behavior associated with different social roles. The process of cleavage is cumulative as the role behavior tends to continue to produce reactions that intensify the corresponding patterns of behavior. Schismogenesis may develop, for example, between the sexes, as shown by Gregory Bateson, who introduced the term in his study of the Iatmul of New Guinea. Among the Iatmul, the masculine role calls for extremely aggressive, competitive, boasting behavior, while the feminine role is quiet, submissive, and cooperative. Bateson referred to this type of schismogenesis, in which the cleavage involves reciprocal patterns of behavior, as complementary schismogenesis, and distinguished it from symmetrical schismogenesis, in which a like kind of behavior is stimulated (for example, aggressive behavior stimulating aggressive behavior). (G. Bateson, *Naven*, Cambridge University Press, Cambridge, 1936.) See ROLE.

schizophrenia. A functional PSYCHOSIS, at one time called dementia praecox, which is characterized by the progressive inability to make adequate and appropriate emotional responses, a loss of contact with the world of reality, and often the presence of hallucinations and the development of a highly individualized logic, with inappropriate intellectual reactions.

science. An approach to the problem of human knowledge based on the attempt to develop general principles about a delimited range of phenomena derived from empirical observations (that is, from the experience of the senses) and so stated that they can be tested by any competent person. The interrelated generalizations that constitute the body of knowledge of a science do not reflect idiosyncratic, individual experiences, but rather the consensus of the scientific community. Science is based on the assumption that it is possible to derive objective knowledge about the world through the senses and that the truth of this knowledge is confirmed by the similar observations of many persons. It is also based on the assumption that the biases and values of the observer can be relatively controlled so that a reasonable degree of objectivity is possible. However, facts do not order themselves and thus any science necessarily involves a logical interrelating of observations and cannot be limited to the mere collecting of observations. Scientific principles and theories are constantly open to criticism, further testing, and revision within an accumulating tradition of nondogmatic knowledge. See RESEARCH; SCIENTIFIC METHOD; THEORY.

science, applied. 1. The application of known scientific principles to a practical problem, with a simultaneous concern with the development of new principles based on insights developed in the study and solution of the practical problem.

2. The application of known scientific principles to a practical problem with no systematic or serious attempt to add to scientific knowledge.

science, behavioral. See BEHAVIORAL SCIENCE.

science, idiographic. A discipline that is primarily descriptive and concerned with individual, unique facts. History is regarded as an idiographic discipline because it is more concerned with studying particular events and configurations of events in specific settings than with deriving general principles and scientific laws. The distinction between idiographic science and nomothetic science was developed by Wilhelm Windelband. (W. Windelband, *Geschichte und Naturwissenschaft*, Heitz, Strassburg, 1904.) It has been suggested that the term idiographic discipline would be more appropriate than idiographic science, since a SCIENCE is usually defined as a generalizing discipline. See HUMANITIES; SCIENCE, NOMOTHETIC.

science, natural. See NATURAL SCIENCE.

science, nomothetic. A discipline that is primarily concerned with studying the general rather than the particular and is concerned less with description than with the development of scientific laws. Sociology and the physical sciences are regarded as nomothetic sciences because their primary goal is to abstract generalizations from specific events and individual facts. However, all scientific disciplines involve both nomothetic and idiographic knowledge, and thus sociology has its idiographic aspect.

The distinction between nomothetic science and idiographic science was developed by Wilhelm Windelband. (W. Windelband, *Geschichte und Naturwissenschaft,* Heitz, Strassburg, 1904.) See LAW, SCIENTIFIC; SCIENCE; SCIENCE, IDIOGRAPHIC.

science, pseudo-. See PSEUDOSCIENCE.

science, pure. Scientific investigation devoted exclusively to the pursuit of knowledge for its own sake, with no immediate concern for practical problems and applications. Scientific effort bent on the development of basic principles is crucial for the development of science, presumably because it is more efficient in the long run, less corruptible, more under the control of scientists rather than of politicians, administrators, and managers, and therefore more objective and systematic. See SCIENCE, APPLIED.

science, social. See SOCIAL SCIENCE.

scientific law. See LAW, SCIENTIFIC.

scientific method. The building of a body of scientific knowledge through observation, experimentation, generalization, and verification. The scientific method is based on the assumption that knowledge is based on what is experienced through the senses, and that if a statement concerning natural phenomena is to be accepted as meaningful or true it must be empirically verifiable. Thus any scientific law must be based on empirical evidence. The scientific method also assumes that when there are differences in what is observed, the judgment of the community of qualified experts determines which empirical observations are to be accepted. Thus individual, idiosyncratic observations not shared by other scientists are not regarded as scientific facts. Although the scientific method depends on the collection of empirical facts, it extends beyond this. Facts alone do not constitute a science. To have any meaning, facts must be ordered in some fashion, analyzed, generalized, and related to other facts. Thus THEORY construction is a vital part of the scientific method. A theoretical framework provides the means for organizing and interpreting empirical observations and for relating them to previous findings of other investigators. Also, the building of a body of scientific knowledge is a cumulative process, and therefore a crucial part of the scientific method involves the interrelating of the findings of scientists working in different times and places. Although the scientific method is usually regarded as an inductive method because its purpose is to build generalizations on the basis of specific facts, in the interplay of research, theory construction, and verification, both INDUCTION and DEDUCTION are used.

Specifically, the application of the scientific method to a particular problem involves the following steps. First, the problem is defined. Second, the problem is stated in terms of a particular theoretical framework and related to relevant findings of previous research. Third, a hypothesis (or hypotheses) relating to the problem is devised, utilizing previously accepted theoretical principles. Fourth, the procedure to be used in gathering data to test the hypothesis is determined. Fifth, the data are gathered. Sixth, the data are analyzed to determine if the hypothesis is verified or rejected. Finally, the conclusions of the study are related to the original body of theory, which is modified in accordance with the new findings. See RESEARCH; SCIENCE; THEORY.

scientific theory. See THEORY.

scientism. 1. A term of criticism directed toward the view that science can provide mankind with an all-embracing philosophy of life and the solution to all problems. The term scientism is applicable when science is presented as an ideology, embodying the highest values.

2. A term of criticism directed toward the view that the techniques used in the physical sciences can be used to solve any problem, and that those disciplines that do not use the same research techniques as the physical sciences are not really scientific. This view represents a type of traditionalism, or belief that what came first and is oldest is best and cannot be changed. Creative innovation and the adaptation of techniques and methods to the nature of the empirical phenomena being studied are crucial for scientific work and thought.

score, criterion. See CRITERION SCORE.

score, normative. A score expressed in terms of the population distribution. The conversion of a raw score into a normative score reveals the individual's (or group's) relative standing in a given population. Percentiles and I.Q. scores are examples of normative scores. See SCORE, RAW; T SCORE; Z SCORE.

score, raw. A numerical score in the original form that is obtained from a test. It has not been standardized in any way or related to the other scores on the test in the population, and therefore is not comparable with scores from other tests. See SCORE, NORMATIVE; T SCORE; Z SCORE.

score, standard or **sigma.** See Z SCORE.

score, T. See T SCORE.

score, Z. See Z SCORE.

seasonal ceremony. See CALENDRICAL RITES.

seasonal variation. A recurrent pattern of change in a variable associated with the changing seasons. The variable (for example, unemployment rate) regularly increases in certain seasons and decreases in other seasons. Seasonal variation is a type of CYCLICAL MOVEMENT.

secondary group. See GROUP, SECONDARY.

secondary occupation. See OCCUPATION, SECONDARY.

secondary relations. Social relations that are impersonal, without emotional involvement, and specialized, that is generally limited to the performance of a specific activity or activities (for example, a buyer-seller relationship). The mutual rights and duties of the individuals involved in the relationship are clearly defined, and other aspects of their lives are considered irrelevant. (Thus the relationship is characterized by SPECIFIC-ITY.) Secondary relations are frequently of short duration. The persons involved are simply regarded as performing a function, and thus are replaceable by any other person who can perform the role competently or who fulfills certain requirements. There is no attachment to a particular individual. Modern urban society is characterized by a large number of secondary relations. See GESELLSCHAFT; GROUP, SECONDARY; PRIMARY RELATIONS.

secondary source. A source of information or data that presents material that has been copied or compiled from a PRIMARY SOURCE or from another secondary source, rather than collected by the person or agency who publishes the information. Secondary sources are not original sources, and, since they often present only a portion or summary of the original source, they may fail to include all the information of interest to a researcher. Biographies, almanacs, and most textbooks are examples of secondary sources.

sect. An exclusive, highly cohesive ascetic group of religious believers whose membership is voluntary (especially by conversion) rather than hereditary. A sect tends to ignore or repudiate the existing order, whether it be ecclesiastical or secular. It usually stresses equalitarian ideals among its adherents, and expects active participation, conformity, and personal commitment on the part of its members. Since sects tend to deviate from established norms (sometimes because of dedication to what are regarded as higher values) and also tend to attract low-status people (who have the least to lose by nonconformity), they are very likely to suffer harassment. The concept of sect is an abstract or IDEAL TYPE, which has been distinguished from three other ideal types of religious organization: the DENOMINATION, the CHURCH or ECCLESIA, and the CULT. The Jehovah's Witnesses, the Pentecostals, and the early Quakers, Methodists, Adventists, and Christian Scientists are examples of the sect type of movements. See CHURCH-SECT TYPOLOGY.

sector hypothesis. A hypothesis of urban growth proposed by Homer Hoyt as a modification of Burgess' concentric zone hypothesis. According to the sector hypothesis, specialized areas of the city develop in the form of sectors rather than concentric zones. As the city grows, each specialized sector expands at its periphery and thus each type of land use (for example, high-cost residential) tends to extend outward from the center of the city in a wedge-shaped sector rather than surrounding the center in a circular zone. Hoyt emphasized the importance of lines of transportation in urban growth, particularly in their impact on industrial and commercial development. In essence he combined Burgess' concentric zone hypothesis with Galpin's AXIATE HYPOTHESIS OF URBAN GROWTH. (H. Hoyt, *The Structure and Growth of Residential Neighborhoods in American Cities*, Government Printing Office, Washington, D.C., 1939.) See CONCENTRIC ZONE HYPOTHESIS, BURGESS'.

secular. Of or pertaining to that which is not SACRED.

secular society. A society whose primary values are utilitarian and rational, and that accepts and even promotes change and innovation. As contrasted with SACRED SOCIETY, a secular society is characterized by a lack of concern with the sacred, the supernatural, or the values associated with traditionalism and conservatism. The concept of secular society was developed as a CONSTRUCTED TYPE by Howard Becker as part of his sacred-secular societal TYPOLOGY. He further distinguished two types of secular society, one in which change is permissible in support of principles, and a more extreme type in which change is valued in and of itself. Modern American society is usually considered to be an example of a secular society. However, since the concept is a constructed type, no actual society corresponds to the type in all details, and there is variation within any society. The extreme type of secular society is apt to be highly unstable, and it is possible for a sacred society to arise from a secular society. Becker regarded Nazi Germany as a type of sacred society that arose from the instability of an extreme secular society. (H. Becker in *Modern Sociological Theory*, edited by H. Becker and A. Boskoff, Dryden Press, New York, 1957.)

secular trend. See TREND, SECULAR.

segmentation, social. The process in which a group (usually a large group such as a society or formal organization) develops within it subgroups that are relatively isolated from each other, that is, have barriers preventing full communication between them, and that may have mutual antagonisms. Segmentation may result from extreme SPECIALIZATION of function, in which persons in different specializations lose understanding of each other, through rigid stratification or through SEGREGATION and ethnic hostilities. See CLEAVAGE; ROLE INSULATION; STRATIFICATION, SOCIAL.

segregation. 1. An ecological process in which the areas of a city become specialized in type of land use, services, or population. Thus segregation includes the emergence of retail-business districts, industrial districts, financial districts, slums, apartment-house areas, upper-class residential areas, ethnic districts, and so forth. In other words, any basis on which an area is differentiated from other areas, whether by function (commercial, residential, etc.), type of housing, or population characteristics (including social class as well as race, religion, or ethnic group) is referred to as segregation. See ECOLOGY, HUMAN; INVASION; SUCCESSION.

2. The voluntary or involuntary separation of residence areas, services, or other facilities, on the basis of race, religion, or ethnic characteristics of the people using them.

selection, natural. See DARWINIAN THEORY; EVOLUTION.

selection, social. An antiquated term denoting a process, assumed to be similar to biological selection, by which persons, groups, or culture traits emerge and become dominant or at least survive weaker competitors. Interest in this concept reflected the influence of biological Darwinism. It is certainly still of interest to sociologists to study which groups and sociocultural patterns survive and which decline, but the term selection implies that whatever survives is superior and survives for some simple and naturally determined goal—that is, the survival of the strongest, best, most rational, etc. In human society the bases of selection are many and they constantly change. No simple principle similar to the biological one of the survival of the fittest has been developed for social selection. See SOCIAL DARWINISM.

selective perception. See PERCEPTION, SELECTIVE.

selectivity, cognitive. See COGNITIVE SELECTIVITY.

self. That aspect of the PERSONALITY consisting of the individual's conception of himself. The way a person perceives himself is a result of his experiences with other people, the way they act toward him, and the impression he gets of their view of him. The self develops during the process of SOCIALIZATION, through social interaction. The young child does not at first have an organized conception of his own identity and characteristics. By internalizing the definitions others have of him and his place in society, the child comes to have a conception of who he is and what he is like. However, the self does not develop solely in childhood and reach a final, unchangeable form upon the attainment of adulthood. While the self normally maintains a certain degree of stability and consistency, it nevertheless is constantly subject to modification in its ever changing social environment. The self undergoes a constant process of comparison, assessment, and reinterpretation as the individual's statuses and roles change (for example, the progression of age statuses) along with related definitions and expectations. See GENERALIZED OTHER; "I"; INTERNALIZATION; LOOKING-GLASS SELF; "ME"; ROLE; STATUS.

self, empirical. As defined by William James, a concept similar to George Herbert Mead's "ME."

self, ideal. A person's conception of what he should be like, rather than what he actually judges himself to be like.

self, social. See SELF.

self-conception. See SELF.

self-consciousness. 1. Having social attitudes toward oneself and thus being aware of oneself in terms of what others expect. See SELF.

2. Embarrassed self-awareness due to an acute sense of the evaluation of others. If a person anticipates negative attitudes toward himself, he becomes more self-conscious, in this sense of the term, whereas if he is relaxed and is not judging himself, he is not likely to be self-conscious.

self-control. 1. Internalized SOCIAL CONTROL, that is, conformity to social norms not because of the expectation of sanctions by others but because the individual himself accepts the norms as valid and proper. See INTERNALIZATION.

2. The regulation of one's behavior such that one adheres to the forms and standards of behavior that one regards as most practical and desirable in terms of achieving some ideal or goal relating to oneself or one's social group.

self-esteem. A person's evaluation of himself in terms of the way he perceives others' opinions of him.

self-fulfilling prophecy. A false definition of a situation, or belief regarding a social situation, which, because one believes it and one acts upon it, actually manifests itself as a truth, further strengthening the belief. If, for example, an outgroup is believed to be hostile, and if people act as though it were hostile, the outgroup will most likely show hostility in response. The concept was developed by Robert K. Merton, based on W. I. Thomas' statement: "If men define situations as real, they are real in their consequences." This is also known as the Thomas theorem. (R. K. Merton, *Social Theory and Social Structure*, Free Press, Glencoe, Ill., 1957.) See DEFINITION OF THE SITUATION.

self-image. See SELF.

self-orientation–collectivity orientation. The opposition between personal interests and group interests in social situations. For the individual in a given situation this is the dilemma of whether to pursue his own personal interests and goals or subordinate his private interests to the interests and welfare of a group or other individuals. This dichotomy is one of the five PATTERN VARIABLES proposed by Talcott Parsons, and is described by him as the "dilemma of private versus collective interests, or the distribution between private permissiveness and collective obligation."

(T. Parsons and E. A. Shils, eds., *Toward a General Theory of Action*, Harvard University Press, Cambridge, Mass., 1951.)

selves, abandoned. A term used by William James to refer to models a person once tried to incorporate into his SELF—that is, conceptions of the sort of person he wanted to be like—and later abandoned.

semantics. The study of the meanings of words, their historical development, the structure of word usage, and the relationship of words to human thought and behavior.

semi-interquartile range. See QUARTILE DEVIATION.

semiskilled manual worker. A manual worker whose work requires some skill but not a high degree of skill. It is a classification intermediate between SKILLED MANUAL WORKER and UNSKILLED MANUAL WORKER, requiring more training, knowledge, and ability than the latter but less than the former. Usually included in this category are production workers in factories, truck drivers, etc.

senicide or **senilicide.** The killing of the aged and infirm members of a society.

sensate culture. A type of culture proposed by Pitirim A. Sorokin in which materialistic and empirical values predominate. In such a culture, ultimate reality is seen as comprising only natural phenomena, subject to empirical investigation: no reality exists beyond what can be revealed in sense perception. Its value system is not concerned with absolutes, and agnosticism and atheism prevail. Empiricism, rationalism, and the pursuit of science outweigh interest in art. (P. A. Sorokin, *Social and Cultural Dynamics*, American Book Co., New York, 1937.) See IDEALISTIC CULTURE; IDEATIONAL CULTURE.

sensation. A conscious experience aroused by the stimulation of one of the sense organs (eyes, ears, etc.).

sensory adaptation. See ADAPTATION, SENSORY.

sensory aphasia. A form of APHASIA, in which there is an inability to perceive words in a conversation, although the person can hear the sound of the flow of speech. This disorder is also called "word deafness."

sentence-completion test. A PROJECTIVE TECHNIQUE for the study of personality in which the respondent is asked to complete sentences that are partially written.

sentiment. 1. An enduring pattern of emotional dispositions held by an individual in relation to another person, an object, or an idea. Emotionally toned beliefs and attitudes form a part of any sentiment. Patriotism and romantic love are examples of sentiments.

2. As defined by Vilfredo Pareto, a nonrational, fundamental motivating emotion. It is essentially the same as his concept of residue. He sometimes used the two terms synonymously but at other times spoke of RESIDUES as manifestations of sentiments.

3. As defined by George C. Homans, an internal, emotionally toned, psychological state of an individual that influences his social behavior. The concept of sentiment is one of the three basic concepts he used in his analysis of groups. (G. C. Homans, *The Human Group*, Harcourt, Brace, New York, 1950.) See ACTIVITY; INTERACTION.

sentiments, logic of. See LOGIC OF THE SENTIMENTS.

sequential analysis. A research procedure in which the total number of cases to be studied or observations to be made is not determined in advance, but is decided as the research proceeds through a process of periodic analysis of the data thus far gathered. At each stage the data are analyzed to determine if the hypotheses may be accepted or rejected or if more data are needed or possibly if more of a specific type of data are needed.

sequential marriage. See POLYGAMY, SERIAL.

serendipity. In science, the chance discovery of theoretically important facts in the course of research, leading the scientist to new discoveries he did not anticipate.

serial polygamy. See POLYGAMY, SERIAL.

service bureaucrat. See BUREAUCRATIC TYPES.

service center. A city, town, or village that provides services for the surrounding area. The services provided may be economic, medical, recreational, religious, educational, and so forth.

set. 1. In psychology, a predisposition to respond in a particular way to a situation or a problem. See MENTAL SET.

2. As a mathematical concept, a set is a clearly defined collection of people, objects, ideas, or symbols (including other sets). A set is the totality of the elements or members of a specified type, for example, the members of a small group, all the college-educated women living in a certain area, all the favorable responses on a questionnaire. A set may be finite, infinite (the set of all even numbers), or empty. An empty set (sometimes referred to as a null set) is a set (category) that contains no elements (for example, the set of all female presidents of the United States).

set, role-. See ROLE-SET.

set, status-. See STATUS-SET.

set-theoretic model. The MODEL of the SET used as the basis for the mathematical analysis of data. In essence, use of this model means that the data are divided into sets or categories and subcategories on the basis of some classification (types of individuals, types of responses, types of experimental situations, group membership, etc.). Certain logical axioms and propositions about the relationship between sets and subsets are then applied to the observed data and used to test hypotheses about the data.

sex. From a sociological point of view, the elaboration of the biological division of function between male and female into two major statuses upon which behavior is differentiated in all societies. Sex is the first element in the division of labor in society and the social STATUS most central to self-identity, particularly in adults. The sexual relationship is a social relationship, and is organized only partially around biological sexual needs. In all societies, social needs for acceptance, companionship, approval, and affection, as well as economic needs, are very closely tied to the conception of the sexual relationship. Even the more purely biological aspect of sex is never a simple expression of a physiological drive. The methods and sources of sexual gratification, the meanings attached to sexual relationships, and the essential significance of sex are derived by the individual from the customs and definitions of his culture or subculture and his unique social experiences. See FAMILY INSTITUTION; NEED.

sex ratio. In the United States, the number of males per 100 females within a specified population. A sex ratio of 100 means there is an equal number of males and females. If there are more males than females in a population the sex ratio will be over 100, and the higher the sex ratio, the greater is the proportion of males to females.

sexual relationship. See SEX.

shaded map. See CHOROPLETH MAP.

shaman. An unspecialized medical, magic, and religious practitioner, often also called a medicine man or witch doctor. See PRIEST.

Sheldon's body types. A system of classification of human body types, hypothetically related to personality types, devised by William H. Sheldon and his associates. It is one of the most ambitious attempts of its kind. By means of a technique he referred to as somatotyping, Sheldon classified man into three basic constitutional types: the endomorph, who is round and fat—particularly in the abdominal region; the mesomorph, who has large muscles and bones; the ectomorph, who is tall and thin with much skin surface, a large brain, and a sensitive nervous system. Sheldon then attempted to relate these body types to temperament and behavior. He maintained that endomorphs are primarily viscerotonic—extroverted, fond of physical pleasures, and sociable; mesomorphs primarily somatotonic—fond of vigorous physical activity; and ectomorphs primarily cerebrotonic—introverted, cautious, and studious. Acceptance of such a simplified explanation of human behavior and personality is very rare among sociologists or social psychologists. A constitutionally determined schema such as Sheldon's does not take into account any of the social and cultural factors that shape human behavior.

Shevky typology. See SOCIAL AREA ANALYSIS.

shock, cultural. See CULTURE SHOCK.

shop. See CLOSED SHOP; OPEN SHOP; PREFERENTIAL SHOP; UNION SHOP.

shop production. See FACTORY SYSTEM.

sib. A unilateral KIN GROUP that may be either matrilineal or patrilineal. The members of a sib believe they are all descended from a common ancestor along either the male or female line (depending on the culture), although they may not have any genealogical proof of common descent. If a CLAN is defined as either patrilineal or matrilineal, as it most commonly is, sib is synonymous with clan. If, however, a clan is defined as matrilineal only, as it sometimes is, a sib would be considered a broader category of which a clan and a GENS are subdivisions. In the latter case a clan would be a matrilineal sib and a gens would be a patrilineal sib. A sib is usually exogamous. See UNILATERAL DESCENT.

sibling. A brother or sister. All the offspring of the same mother and father are siblings.

sigma. In statistics; the capital sigma, Σ, is the symbol for summation; i.e., the sum of. The lower case sigma, σ, is the symbol for standard deviation.

sigma score. See Z SCORE.

sign. An object or event that stands for something else. Any cue or stimulus that evokes a response to, or is associated with, something not physically present at the time is a sign. A sign may be experienced through any of the senses, that is, it may be something seen, heard, felt, tasted, or smelled. Signs range from the very simple to the very complex, and include conditioned stimuli to which animals may be trained to react as well as abstract linguistic symbols understood only by humans. The major distinction is between the natural sign, or signal, and the conventional sign, or SYMBOL. See SIGN, NATURAL.

sign, conventional. See SYMBOL.

sign, natural. A SIGN that has or has had a physical association with the thing for which it stands. The association may be inherent, as in the case of an odor that indicates the presence of a certain type of food or smoke as a sign of fire. This, however, is not necessarily the case. A conditioned stimulus introduced by an experimenter is also regarded as a natural sign because it becomes a substitute for an unconditioned stimulus through the physical association of the two. Both animals and humans respond to natural signs. Natural signs are sometimes referred to as signals. See CONDITIONING; SYMBOL.

sign test. A nonparametric statistical test that may be used when data are in the form of paired observations divided into a dichotomized ranking, that is, divided into plus and minus categories indicating more and less or higher and lower. With data in this form the sign test may be used to determine whether the two matched samples (i.e., each sample consisting of one member of each pair) differ significantly in the proportion of cases in the plus and minus categories. The sign test may be used to compare an EXPERIMENTAL GROUP and a CONTROL GROUP when precise quantitative measurement is not possible. See NONPARAMETRIC STATISTICS; PROBABILITY; SIGNIFICANCE, STATISTICAL.

signal. See SIGN, NATURAL.

significance, statistical. The PROBABILITY that an observed SAMPLE characteristic or relationship, or difference between samples, represents a true POPULATION characteristic, relationship, or difference and is not merely due to chance sampling variation. There is always a certain amount of variation among samples drawn from the same population. Tests of significance attempt to determine whether observed relationships and differences (between variables in a sample, between samples, or between a sample and a specified type of population) are merely a result of these chance differences among samples or whether they reflect characteristics of the population or populations from which the samples were drawn. If the latter is the case, repeated samples, despite the variations among them, would continue to show the same essential pattern. The level of significance refers to the degree of probability of chance that is accepted as sufficiently low to declare a relationship significant. Commonly used levels of significance are .05 and .01. A significance level of .05 (often written $p < .05$, i.e., the probability is less than .05) means that by chance alone a relationship or difference of the observed magnitude could be expected to occur five times out of a hundred. The smaller the probability is that an observed relationship would occur by chance, the more statistically significant the relationship is. Tests of statistical significance are used to determine whether to accept or reject the null hypothesis (that there is no significance). If a relationship is judged to be significant, the null hypothesis is rejected. Statistical significance should not be confused with substantive significance. The statistical significance of a relationship, which depends on the magnitude of the relationship and the size of the sample, does not in itself tell whether the relationship has theoretical significance. See ERROR, ALPHA; ERROR, BETA; HYPOTHESIS, NULL; PARAMETER; REGION OF REJECTION; STATISTIC.

significant others. Those people who have the greatest influence on an individual's evaluation of himself and who have the greatest impact on his acceptance or rejection of social norms. In the SOCIALIZATION of a child, the significant others generally include his parents, teachers, and playmates. In evaluating and guiding their behavior, people look not only to abstract principles, standards, and reference groups, but also to individual persons. The term was originally used by Harry Stack Sullivan, and is essentially the same as George Herbert Mead's *the others*. Ralph H. Turner prefers the term *relevant others*.

significant symbol. See SYMBOL, SIGNIFICANT.

silent trade. A practice among some societies with simple economies in which goods are exchanged without social contact. Goods to be exchanged are left at a certain place for inspection and pick-up, with only one party present at a time.

singularism. See SOCIOLOGICAL SINGULARISM.

situation, definition of the. See DEFINITION OF THE SITUATION.

situation, dynamic assessment of. See DYNAMIC ASSESSMENT OF THE SITUATION.

situation, social. The total configuration of social factors influencing an individual's behavior or experience within a system of interaction at a particular time. An individual's behavior varies from one social situation to another, and thus situational social factors are crucial in the understanding of an individual's behavior and his self-conception or self-image.

situation, tendency in. See TINSIT.

situation, unstructured. See UNSTRUCTURED SITUATION.

situs. A category or segment of a society differentiated from other categories or segments on the basis of criteria that do not involve any rank or hierarchical evaluation, that is, the categories or segments are of equal rank and prestige. Émile Benoît-Smullyan introduced the concept of situs, which he distinguished from stratum (based on the hierarchical differentiation of society), in order to have a term that refers specifically to horizontal differentiation of a society. He analyzed clan and sex differentiation as examples of situs distinctions. (É. Benoît-Smullyan, *American Sociological Review*, April 1944.) Paul K. Hatt and subsequent writers have found the concept to be particularly useful when applied to occupations. When occupations are classified into categories that are of equal prestige, each category including occupations from various strata, these categories are referred to as occupational situses. For example, the occupational situs of manufacturing occupations would include occupations ranging from corporation president to production worker and as a category is neither higher nor lower than the occupational situs of law-enforcement occupations, with occupations ranging from judge to prison guard. See STRATUM, SOCIAL.

skewness. Lack of symmetry in a FREQUENCY DISTRIBUTION CURVE. A normal frequency distribution curve is symmetrical, with an equal number of cases above and below the MODE. When the number of cases above the mode and the number of cases below the mode of a frequency distribution are not equal, the distribution is said to be skewed in the direction of the greater number of cases (the longer tail of the curve). If the greater number of cases is in the higher values above the mode, the distribution is said to be skewed to the right. If the greater number of cases is in the lower values below the mode, the distribution is said to be skewed to the left. In a skewed distribution, the mode, the mean, and the MEDIAN do not coincide as they do in a symmetrical distribution. The greater the degree of skewness, the farther apart are these three measures of central tendency. See CENTRAL TENDENCY, MEASURE OF; FREQUENCY DISTRIBUTION CURVE, NORMAL; FREQUENCY DISTRIBUTION CURVE, SKEWED; MEAN, ARITHMETIC.

skewness, negative. SKEWNESS in which there are more extreme values (the long tail of the curve) in the lower values, below the MODE, than in the higher values above the mode. In other words, a FREQUENCY DISTRIBUTION that is skewed to the left is referred to as a negatively skewed distribution. See SKEWNESS, POSITIVE.

skewness, positive. SKEWNESS in which there are more extreme values (the long tail of the curve) in the higher values, above the MODE, than in the lower values, below the mode. In other words, a FREQUENCY DISTRIBUTION that is skewed to the right is referred to as a positively skewed distribution. See SKEWNESS, NEGATIVE.

skid row. An area found in large cities that is predominantly inhabited by homeless men and characterized by a concentration of prostitutes, alcoholics, thieves, flophouses, strip-tease joints, and rescue missions. It is an area of physical deterioration where the demoralized poor who are mentally or physically ill find cheap rent and partial escape from middle-class ridicule and censure. The term was used often by classical ecologists. See ECOLOGY, HUMAN.

skill. A complex organization of behavior (physical or verbal) developed through learning and directed toward a particular goal or centered on a specific activity. Sometimes the term also is used to refer to social skills or skill in evaluating situations and manipulating or influencing the behavior of others.

skilled manual worker. A manual worker whose work requires specialized training, knowledge, ability, and experience to acquire a high level of proficiency. Usually included in this category are plumbers, machinists, bricklayers, printers, barbers, etc. See SEMISKILLED MANUAL WORKER; UNSKILLED MANUAL WORKER.

sleeper effect. The delayed or hidden impact of a message in teaching, propaganda, or mass communications. In testing people who are exposed to efforts to influence their attitudes or teach them some material, sometimes it at first appears that little or no impact has been made. Later testing, however, may reveal that, in fact, the message did have the desired effect. The influence of a message may become clearer after a period of time has elapsed. The term was introduced by Carl I. Hovland. (C. I. Hovland, A. A. Lumsdaine, and F. D. Sheffield, *Experiments on Mass Communication*, Princeton University Press, Princeton, N.J., 1949.)

slogan. An appealing, short, easy-to-remember statement that expresses a stereotyped idea, value, or objective—as the old regimental slogan of "death before dishonor."

slum. A residential area inhabited primarily by poor, often demoralized families, and characterized by substandard, unsanitary conditions, overcrowding, and usually social disorganization.

small group research. See GROUP RESEARCH, SMALL.

sociability. The inclination to associate with others for the sheer pleasure of human interaction, without thought of practical aims or for other serious purposes. Georg Simmel regarded it as a "play" form of SOCIATION.

social. Having to do with interrelationships between individuals or groups. A social factor is said to exist when the behavior of even one individual is affected by another person or group, whether that person (or persons) is physically present or not. The term social is distinguished from cultural in that social pertains to relations between persons, whereas cultural pertains to beliefs, standards of behavior, values, knowledge, and all other aspects of culture. See BEHAVIOR, SOCIAL; INTERACTION, SOCIAL; SOCIAL SYSTEM; SOCIETY.

social action. See ACTION, SOCIAL; ACTION THEORY, SOCIAL.

social action theory. See ACTION THEORY, SOCIAL.

social adaptation. See ADAPTATION, SOCIAL.

social anthropology. See ANTHROPOLOGY, CULTURAL.

social area analysis. An approach to the ecological study of urban areas based on the analysis of census tract data, developed primarily through the work of Eshref Shevky, Wendell Bell, Marilyn Williams, and Robert Tryon. In social area analysis, the census tracts of a city are classified according to three indexes, termed by Shevky social rank, urbanization, and segregation. The index of social rank is based on measures of occupation and education; the index of urbanization on measures of fertility, women in the labor force, and single family dwellings; the index of segregation on measures of spatial isolation of ethnic or racial groups. Using the same measures for each index, Bell prefers the terms economic status for social rank, family status for urbanization, and ethnic status for segregation. After census tracts are classified according to these three indexes, they may then be analyzed in terms of other variables. (See E. Shevky and W. Bell, *Social Area Analysis: Theory, Illustrative Application and Computational Procedure*, Stanford University Press, Palo Alto, Calif., 1955.) See ECOLOGY, HUMAN; SOCIOECONOMIC STATUS.

social base map. See BASE MAP.

social behavior. See BEHAVIOR, SOCIAL.

social behaviorism. See BEHAVIORISM, SOCIAL.

social category. A plurality of persons who are not organized into a system of social interaction (and therefore do not form a GROUP) but who do have similar social characteristics or statuses. Examples of social categories would be working women, carpenters, those over 65 years of age, males, females, millionaires, teen-agers, etc. Persons may be classified as members of a common social category without themselves having a sense of common identity. If the members of a social category develop a sense of common awareness and identity, leadership may emerge and the category may become the basis for the formation of a group. However, most social categories do not develop into groups. See AGGREGATE; COLLECTIVITY; STATUS.

social causation. See CAUSATION, SOCIAL.

social change. Any modification in the social organization of a society in any of its social institutions or patterns of social roles. Usually social change refers to a significant change in social behavior or a change in some larger SOCIAL SYSTEM rather than to minor changes within a small group. Thus social change refers to changes in the established patterns of social relationships—for example, in family, religious, or economic life. See CULTURE CHANGE; INSTITUTION, SOCIAL; ORGANIZATION, SOCIAL; ROLE; SOCIAL STRUCTURE.

social class. A large category of people within a system of social stratification who have a similar socioeconomic status in relation to other segments of their community or society. A social class is not organized, but the individuals and families who compose it are relatively similar in educational, economic, and prestige STATUS. Those who are classified as part of the same social class have similar LIFE CHANCES. Some sociologists regard social classes as being primarily economic in nature, whereas others tend to stress factors such as prestige, style of life, attitudes, identification, etc. The term social stratum is sometimes used instead of social class. See CASTE; CLASS STRUCTURE HYPOTHESIS; SOCIOECONOMIC STATUS; STATUS CONTINUUM HYPOTHESIS; STRATIFICATION, SOCIAL; STRATUM, SOCIAL; and the definitions of various conceptions of social class listed below.

social class, abstract. See ABSTRACT SOCIAL CLASS.

social class, concrete. See CONCRETE SOCIAL CLASS.

social class, interest theory of. See CLASS-INTEREST CONSCIOUSNESS; SOCIAL CLASS, SUBJECTIVE CONCEPTION OF.

social class, lower. See LOWER CLASS.

social class, middle. See MIDDLE CLASS.

social class, objective conception of. Definition of SOCIAL CLASS in terms of objective criteria decided upon by the sociologist, for example, income, occupation, and education. The criteria chosen by the sociologist are usually based on observations and studies of how the people in the COMMUNITY view the system of stratification. This approach may be combined with other approaches to social class in any study. See SOCIAL CLASS, REPUTATIONAL CONCEPTION OF; SOCIAL CLASS, SUBJECTIVE CONCEPTION OF; STRATIFICATION, SOCIAL.

social class, reputational conception of. Definition of SOCIAL CLASS in terms of how the members of a COMMUNITY rank each other with regard to class position and power in the community. Thus an individual's position in the class system is determined by the attitudes and judgments of the other members of the community. The reputational approach may be used together with the objective and subjective approaches in a single study of stratification. See SOCIAL CLASS, OBJECTIVE CONCEPTION OF; SOCIAL CLASS, SUBJECTIVE CONCEPTION OF.

social class, self-identified. See SOCIAL CLASS, SUBJECTIVE CONCEPTION OF.

social class, self-rating. See SOCIAL CLASS, SUBJECTIVE CONCEPTION OF.

social class, subjective conception of. Definition of SOCIAL CLASS in terms of how people place themselves within the society. People may be asked what social classes exist in their community and then asked to place themselves in one of these classes, or they may be asked to rate themselves within a system of classes presented by the investigator, for example, LOWER CLASS (or working class), MIDDLE CLASS, or UPPER CLASS. This approach to social class may be combined with other approaches. See SOCIAL CLASS, OBJECTIVE CONCEPTION OF; SOCIAL CLASS, REPUTATIONAL CONCEPTION OF.

social class, upper. See UPPER CLASS.

social class system, closed. See CLOSED CLASS SYSTEM.

social class system, open. See OPEN CLASS SYSTEM.

social climate. See GROUP CLIMATE.

social collective. A group of "individuals or families, who are tied to one another by virtue of shared traditions or because of their common interests and their common perspective. They are aware of a certain ideological unity, though this would not result by itself in a collective will, because they are not (as individuals or families) capable to decide and act by means of established organizations. These social collectives are capable merely of a tacit consensus, which may manifest itself, though it need not, in a variety of ways, given certain conditions or occasions. This consensus remains a latent one, as long as there are no stimuli which would force it into consciousness. I regard the political party as the ideal type of a *societal* collective." (F. Tönnies in *Class, Status and Power*, edited by R. Bendix and S. M. Lipset, Free Press, Glencoe, Ill., 1953.)

social contagion. The spread of ideas, moods, or forms of behavior in a rapid, emotionally toned manner, as in the case of rumors and fads. The search for more sophisticated understanding of CROWD behavior has rather limited the use of this term and of the similar term *social epidemic*.

social control. Any social or cultural means by which systematic and relatively consistent restraints are imposed upon individual behavior and by which people are motivated to adhere to traditions and patterns of behavior that are important to the smooth functioning of a group or society. Probably the most basic form of social control depends upon the individual's acceptance of the standards of behavior defined by social norms and ROLE EXPECTATIONS as being right and proper. Thus SOCIALIZATION with the accompanying INTERNALIZATION of social norms and values provides an essential source of positive social control. Social control may be positive or negative, and either of these may be formal or informal. Formal social control involves systems of AUTHORITY, and laws, rules, and regulations that specify rewards (organized positive sanctions, such as diplomas, money, medals) or punishments (organized negative sanctions, such as death, imprisonment, banishment) for conformity or violation. Organized RELIGION also provides a system of formal social control. Informal social control may be manifested in such forms as PUBLIC OPINION and FASHION, and enforced by diffuse (informal) sanctions such as praise or ridicule.

The term is usually defined so that the end of social control is seen as order and the attainment of social values, and not exploitation, selfish gain, or the benefit of those who have POWER. However, it must be noted that the values of a society may reflect the needs of a ruling class, an elite, or a dominant cultural or racial group, and thus social control may be directed toward supporting special interests. See LAW; NORM, SOCIAL; ROLE; SANCTION; SANCTION, DIFFUSE; SANCTION, ORGANIZED; SOCIAL CONTROL, NEGATIVE; SOCIAL CONTROL, POSITIVE; VALUE.

social control, negative. SOCIAL CONTROL that depends on punishment or fear of punishment, ranging from laws (threatening death, imprisonment, or fines) to folkways, the violation of which brings ridicule, social disapproval, and rejection. Negative forms of social control may be formal or informal, but in either case they are regarded by the individual as imposed from without and he conforms so that he may avoid unpleasant consequences. See FOLKWAY; LAW; SOCIAL CONTROL, POSITIVE.

social control, positive. SOCIAL CONTROL that depends on the positive motivation of the individual to conform. This may be effected simply through the promise of rewards, ranging from tangible material benefits to social approval. A more fundamental form of positive social control depends on the individual's INTERNALIZATION of social norms, values, and role expectations during the process of SOCIALIZATION. As a result of this process, the individual is motivated to conform because he believes in the social norm. He feels it is the right thing to do. Rewards and punishments then serve as a reinforcement rather than the primary source of motivation. Internalization of the social norms and values by the members of a society is essential to the stability of a society. See NORM, SOCIAL; REWARD SYSTEM; ROLE; SOCIAL CONTROL, NEGATIVE.

social Darwinism. The attempt to apply by analogy the evolutionary theories of plant and animal development to the explanation of social phenomena. Social life is conceived of as governed by laws of competition and conflict, with natural selection leading to the survival of the fittest and the elimination of the weak. Despite its simplicity as an explanatory model of social interaction, this explanation did not long survive in its struggle with the more powerful and sophisticated theories of modern sociology and social science. See DARWINIAN THEORY OF EVOLUTION; EVOLUTION, CULTURAL; EVOLUTION, SOCIAL; SELECTION, SOCIAL.

social demography. See DEMOGRAPHY; POPULATION STUDIES.

social differentiation. The process by which different statuses, roles, strata, and groups develop or persist within a society. The most basic stage in this process is the differentiation of sex roles, which divides the society into two functional parts. Differentiation and SPECIALIZATION also result in different role behavior for people of different ages, occupations, skills, influence, income, etc. Social differentiation in the form of some degree of division of labor or functional division of roles is essential to social organization; however, the basis and nature of differentiation change over time, with changes in traditions and values. See ORGANIZATION, SOCIAL; ROLE; STATUS.

social disintegration. The breakdown of group structure due to a lack of common norms, leadership, and consensus. This term is no longer widely used, and its decline may be due to its negative-value implication. The development of an emphasis on a more general theory has led to the recognition that the dissolving of a group may be as much a constructive as a destructive event in that it may be part of a process of integration in a larger group or society. Social disintegration is less likely to occur in whole societies or communities than in small groups.

social disorganization. See DISORGANIZATION, SOCIAL.

social distance. A feeling of separation or actual social separation between individuals or groups. The greater the social distance between two groups of different status or culture, the less sympathy, understanding, intimacy, and interaction there is between them. Discussions of social distance are often concerned with relationships between statuses and groups with different social ranks, but social distance may also be the result of vigorous *mutual* repudiation. When the structure of a society is based on a hierarchy of statuses, as in a CASTE system, social distance is a part of the ROLE structure of the society and may be regarded as desirable and legitimate within a traditional and stable system of SOCIAL STRATIFICATION. The term was first used by Georg Simmel (*The Sociology of Georg Simmel*, edited by K. Wolff, Free Press, Glencoe, Ill., 1950). See STATUS.

social distance, Bogardus scale of. See BOGARDUS SOCIAL DISTANCE SCALE.

social distance, horizontal. SOCIAL DISTANCE between persons or groups with social statuses of equal rank. See SOCIAL DISTANCE, VERTICAL.

social distance, vertical. SOCIAL DISTANCE between persons or groups of unequal status levels. See SOCIAL DISTANCE, HORIZONTAL.

social distance scale. See BOGARDUS SOCIAL DISTANCE SCALE.

social dynamics. The study of social processes. The term was used by Auguste Comte to refer to the study of society in terms of interrelated social processes and the successive stages of social change. Comte regarded the study of social processes as well as the study of SOCIAL STATICS as necessary in the analysis of society. (H. Martineau, *The Positive Philosophy of Auguste Comte*, George Bell, London, 1896.)

social ecology. See ECOLOGY, SOCIAL.

social engineering. The application of sociological principles to the solution of specific problems. The term, now largely abandoned by sociologists, had been variously used to include social reform, social planning, and applied sociology. See PLANNING, SOCIAL; SOCIOLOGY, APPLIED.

social environment. See ENVIRONMENT, SOCIAL.

social epidemic. An antiquated term similar to SOCIAL CONTAGION.

social equilibrium. See EQUILIBRIUM, SOCIAL.

social evolution. See EVOLUTION, SOCIAL.

social expectations. See ROLE EXPECTATIONS.

social facilitation. The stimulating effect of the presence or activity of other people on an individual's motivation or performance.

social fact. As defined by Émile Durkheim, a social phenomenon as distinct from an individual phenomenon. "Here, then, is a category of facts with very distinctive characteristics: it consists of ways of acting, thinking, and feeling, external to the individual, and endowed with a power of coercion by reason of which they control him. These ways of thinking could not be confused with biological phenomena, since they consist of representations and of actions; nor with psychological phenomena, which exist only in the individual consciousness and through it." (É. Durkheim, *The Rules of Sociological Method,* translated by S. A. Solovay and J. H. Mueller, edited by G. E. G. Catlin, University of Chicago Press, Chicago, 1938.) See FACT; SOCIAL PHENOMENON.

social field. See SITUATION, SOCIAL.

social force. In early usage, anything that influences social behavior, or that results from social interaction. Today, the term is seldom used; however it remains as the title of a major journal of sociology, *Social Forces.*

social group work. In social work, the technique of sponsoring and working with voluntary social groups, such as clubs and gangs, in order to develop socially desirable qualities.

social heredity. See HEREDITY, SOCIAL.

social heritage. See CULTURE.

social identity, latent. See LATENT SOCIAL IDENTITY.

social imperative. Any of several basic requirements of social organization that provide for the resolution of problems inherent in interpersonal relations. These are requirements that must be met by all forms of social organization if the organization is to persist. The social imperative is one type of FUNCTIONAL IMPERATIVE and is usually included in discussions of functional imperatives without being specifically distinguished.

social inequality. See INEQUALITY, SOCIAL.

social insects. See INSECT SOCIETIES.

social institution. See INSTITUTION, SOCIAL.

social integration. See INTEGRATION, SOCIAL.

social interaction. See INTERACTION, SOCIAL.

social karyokinesis. A process by which societies or groups develop, presumably similar to the biological process of karyokinesis or mitosis. The concept was developed by Lester F. Ward, Paul Lilienfeld, Ludwig Gumplowitz, and Gustav Ratzenhofer. The term was used, for example, to describe the hypothetical process of the development of a society or nation, starting with the cross-fertilization of races through the conquest and domination of the more passive and submissive races by the stronger and more active races. It was held that caste structure and inequality result, but that in time there is a development of law and legal rights. Eventually there is a greater homogenation of peoples and the development of a nation. This term and its biological analogy are not used by sociologists today. (See L. F. Ward, *Pure Sociology,* Macmillan, New York, 1903.) See OR-GANICISM.

social milieu. See MILIEU, SOCIAL.

social mobility. See MOBILITY, SOCIAL.

social morphology. See MORPHOLOGY, SOCIAL.

social movement. An important form of COLLECTIVE BEHAVIOR in which large numbers of people are organized or alerted to support and bring about or to resist SOCIAL CHANGE. Revolutions and reformations are general types of social movements. Participation in a social movement is for most people only informal or indirect. Usually large numbers of sympathizers identify with and support the movement and its program without joining any formal organizations associated with the movement.

social necessity. See FUNCTIONAL IMPERATIVE; FUNCTIONAL REQUISITE.

social need. See NEED, SOCIAL.

social norm. See NORM, INSTITUTIONALIZED SOCIAL; NORM, SOCIAL.

social object. 1. A person.
2. Any object or phenomenon that is the focus of social behavior in a given situation. A social object, then, could be a person, a group, an attitude, a goal.

social obligation. Behavior recognized as required to satisfy social expectations.

social order. 1. The total complex of the social institutions of a society and their interrelationships. See INSTITUTION, SOCIAL.
2. A condition of a society or group characterized by the predominance of harmonious social relationships and a relative lack of conflict among social norms. Social order depends upon the successful interrelation and coordination of ROLE behavior between individuals, individuals and groups,

and between social institutions. However, change and disharmonies are present even in the most orderly societies.

social organization. See ORGANIZATION, SOCIAL.

social participation. See PARTICIPATION, SOCIAL.

social pathology. Any "diseased" condition of society, such as crime, vice, or alcoholism; this term was used by some early sociologists, but is obsolescent today. It implies a biological analogy in which society is conceived of as an organism that can be either sick or healthy. It has been largely replaced by such terms as social disorganization and SOCIAL PROBLEM, which are not associated with the organic MODEL of society. See DISORGANIZATION, SOCIAL; ORGANICISM.

social phenomenon. Any PHENOMENON that stems from the influence of one or more persons on another person. This would include all types of interpersonal behavior (physical or verbal) and all interpersonal situations. Social phenomena are the observable, empirical occurrences in the social life of man—the pattern of events, behavior, and thought—that form the basic data of sociology. Expectations with regard to behavior, uniformities in the behavior of persons in a certain SOCIAL CATEGORY, STATUS, or GROUP, attitudes and beliefs about persons, groups, or modes of behavior, and the status structure of a group are examples of social phenomena. The great multiplicity of social phenomena are ordered, interpreted, and given meaning by the concepts and FRAME OF REFERENCE of the observer. Some writers regard a phenomenon as synonymous with a FACT, whereas others define a fact as a statement about a phenomenon.

social philosophy. The analysis of society and social life using philosophical concepts and insights. The term social philosophy is frequently applied to social thought prior to the development of modern sociology (for example to the works of such thinkers as Confucius, Plato, and John Locke), often in a way that implies that a philosophical orientation in sociology leads to unscientific and biased results. However, the social philosophy of the past, despite admitted shortcomings, has had and still has profound effects on current sociological thought. Moreover, as an intellectual and scientific discipline, sociology is inevitably influenced by advances in philosophical thought, just as philosophy is influenced by new concepts in science.

social physics. Auguste Comte's term for the new science of society, which he later (1839) replaced with the term *sociology* (See H. Martineau, *The Positive Philosophy of Auguste Comte*, George Bell, London, 1896.)

social planning. See PLANNING, SOCIAL.

social position. See POSITION.

social power. See POWER.

social pressure. See PRESSURE GROUP; SOCIAL CONTROL.

social problem. Any undesirable condition or situation that is judged by an influential number of persons within a community to be intolerable and to require group action toward constructive reform. Examples are juvenile delinquency, drug addiction, crime, prostitution, divorce, chronic unemployment, poverty, and mental illness.

social process. Any identifiable, repetitive pattern of social interaction. The traditional listing of major social processes includes CONFLICT, COMPETITION, ASSIMILATION, ACCULTURATION, ACCOMMODATION, consensus, COOPERATION, specialization, differentiation, and stratification. However, many sociologists regard all of sociology as a study of social interaction and therefore a study of social process. See STRATIFICATION, SOCIAL.

Social process is an observable pattern of social interaction over a period of time. A pattern observable at any one moment of time is usually designated as STRUCTURE. See SOCIAL STRUCTURE.

social progress. See PROGRESS, SOCIAL.

social psychiatry. The study of the role of social factors in the development of mental illness.

social psychology. The branch of sociology that deals with the study of individual behavior as explained in terms of social factors and with the study of group structure in terms of the behavior of the individuals who comprise it. It is concerned with the study of the individual as a unit in a social group, and emphasizes the analysis of individual behavior in terms of statuses and roles, and the relationship of an individual's statuses and roles to the total pattern of statuses and roles of a group or community. Thus if an individual student is interviewed, one may study his student ROLE, his fraternity role and STATUS, as well as other statuses and roles he plays within his university environment. Sociologists are not interested primarily in the individual's mind or psyche, but rather in the pattern of his relations in his social group. The social psychologist views individual behavior as, in good part, a reflection of the various status positions of the individual in the numerous social groups that have had an influence on him.

Social psychology is so fundamental in sociology that some sociologists do not regard it merely as a branch of sociology but as inseparable from many phases of sociology. Social INTERACTIONISM provides an important theoretical framework for sociological social psychology.

Many psychologists are also interested in the field of social psychology, and in studying the influence of social factors on individual behavior. Psychologists have always been aware of the importance of interpersonal relations, and many psychologists are engaged in small-group research. On their part, sociologists have shown increasing interest in the field of mental health and in other traditional psychological problems, viewed from a social psychological point of view. At universities, courses in social psychology are often taught in both the sociology and psychology departments, and both the American Sociological Association and the American Psychological Association have sections or divisions of social psychology. Each discipline tends to have a different emphasis due to the different traditions from which they stem and the theoretical problems to which they address themselves.

social pyramid. Social strata conceived of as roughly forming a pyramid, with the more numerous lower strata at the bottom of the pyramid and the less numerous upper classes or strata at the top (the narrowest part) of the pyramid. See POPULATION PYRAMID; STRATUM, SOCIAL.

social reality. The reality, or conception of what actually exists, that is established and maintained by the consensus of the group. A stable worldview with regard to existence of phenomena requires the validation of other people. To completely lose faith in the reality expressed by social consensus is to cut oneself off from the possibility of associating meaningfully with others. The nature of reality as expressed in culture is a part of one's social heritage and is as essential to man's survival as is instinctive behavior in insects, although human conceptions of reality are more subject to change than are the realities of animal life.

social relation. A reciprocal pattern of interaction that persists over a period of time so that a stable set of social expectations develops. It is a long lasting SOCIAL RELATIONSHIP. The reciprocal ROLE relationship between husband and wife and the relationship between a psychiatrist and his patient are examples of social relations.

social relationship. A pattern of social interaction between two or more persons. It is the simplest unit of sociological analysis, and it involves meaningful communication and awareness of the probable behavior of the other person. A social relationship may be of short duration (a driver trying to convince a policeman that he wasn't speeding) or of a more permanent nature (the husband-wife relationship). The more permanent social relationship may be called a SOCIAL RELATION.

social reorganization. The process of cooperative action to counteract undesirable conditions in society. It has been seen as the opposite of social disorganization, or as the reaction to social disorganization when conditions become intolerable. See DISORGANIZATION, SOCIAL.

social role. See ROLE.

social science. Any discipline that studies social INTERACTION, SOCIETY, or CULTURE. The social sciences are composed of the disciplines of sociology and social psychology, cultural anthropology, political science, economics, and aspects of geography. History may be regarded as among the social sciences, but many historians prefer to consider it part of the HUMANITIES. See SCIENCE; SCIENTIFIC METHOD.

social segmentation. See SEGMENTATION, SOCIAL.

social selection. See SELECTION, SOCIAL.

social self. See SELF.

social situation. See SITUATION, SOCIAL.

social solidarity. See SOLIDARITY.

social space. The persons and groups of which an individual is aware and toward which he orients his behavior. Social space is determined by the individual's perception of his social world and not by the objective description of his social relationships by any observer. The social space of an individual changes as his social relationships change. New persons and groups become significant to him and some who were formerly significant may be forgotten. Thus an individual's social space may become broader or narrower. The organization of his social space changes not only as there are actual changes in the relationships among the relevant persons and groups, but also as his perceptions of relationships change.

social stability. See STABILITY, SOCIAL.

social statics. As defined by Auguste Comte, the study of SOCIAL STRUCTURE and the interrelations of its various parts at a moment of time. In Comte's system, the study of social statics complemented the study of SOCIAL DYNAMICS; the term *social statics* is not currently in wide use. (See H. Martineau, *The Positive Philosophy of Auguste Comte*, George Bell, London, 1896.)

social status. See STATUS.

social status, Chapin scale of. See CHAPIN SOCIAL STATUS SCALE.

social stigma. 1. A mark of disgrace imposed on an individual by other individuals or a social group. In popular usage it often refers to any negative SANCTION or to disapproval for nonconformity, such as having dandelions in the lawn in a middle-class American suburb. See SANCTION, NEGATIVE.

2. An undesirable differentness of an individual that disqualifies him from full social acceptance. It is an attribute or stereotype that departs negatively from the expectations of others. The individual with social de-

formities (hangman, ex-convict, prostitute) or physical deformities (amputation, scars) is not accorded the respect given to "normal" individuals. Other aspects of the stigmatized individual's social identity are distorted to conform with the stereotypes associated with the particular stigma. (E. Goffman, *Stigma: Notes on the Management of Spoiled Identity*, Prentice-Hall, Englewood Cliffs, N.J., 1963.)

social stimulus. See STIMULUS, SOCIAL.

social stratification. See STRATIFICATION, SOCIAL.

social stratum. See STRATUM, SOCIAL.

social structure. The pattern of interrelated statuses and roles found in a society or other group at a particular time and constituting a relatively stable set of social relations. It is the organized pattern of the interrelated rights and obligations of persons and groups in a system of interaction as analyzed in terms of statuses, roles, social norms, and social institutions. The term *social organization* is sometimes used synonymously with social structure. See GROUP; INSTITUTION, SOCIAL; NORM, SOCIAL; ORGANIZATION, SOCIAL; ROLE; SOCIAL RELATION; SOCIAL SYSTEM; STATUS.

social survey. A systematic and comprehensive study of a particular community with a view to the analysis of a social problem and the presentation of recommendations for its solution.

social system. 1. A social GROUP or set of interacting persons or groups, conceived of as distinct from the particular persons who compose it. A social system includes a SOCIAL STRUCTURE of interrelated statuses and roles and the functioning of that structure in terms of patterns of actions and interactions. Thus the social system includes process and change and the active consequences and modifications of interaction as well as structure and stable forms. The various interrelated status and role obligations of interacting persons, whether in a dyad, a family, a community, or a society, may be regarded as constituting a social system because they form a unitary whole reflecting many common values, social norms, and objectives. A study of the family as a social system might begin with the analysis of husband-wife, brother-sister, parent-child roles, etc., within a particular cultural environment. The hospital, the prison, the university, the nation, etc., can be analyzed as social systems. Analysis in terms of social systems is particularly characteristic of FUNCTIONALISM. See NORM, SOCIAL; ROLE; STATUS; SYSTEM.

2. A GROUP.

social technique. See TECHNIQUE.

social telesis. The conscious and rational control of societal development in an orderly and intelligent way to attain purposive social goals.

The term was used by Lester F. Ward in discussing the idea that it is possible for man to control not only the physical world for social ends, but also the social world for social ends. (L. F. Ward, *Pure Sociology*, Macmillan, New York, 1903.)

social theory. See THEORY; THEORY, SOCIOLOGICAL.

social thought. 1. The ideas of social thinkers, from the earliest times (in Babylonia, Egypt, Israel, Greece, China, India, Japan, etc.) up to the development of scientific sociology (roughly in the late nineteenth century). Social thought and SOCIAL PHILOSOPHY are both sometimes used in this sense.

2. Any relatively systematic attempt to theorize about society and social life, whether it be classical or modern, scientific or nonscientific.

social time. See TIME, SOCIAL.

social trend. See TREND, SOCIAL.

social type. See TYPE, SOCIAL.

social welfare programs. Programs of formal agencies, either governmental or private, designed to aid poor and disadvantaged individuals.

social work. A specialized professional field concerned with the application of sociological and psychological principles to the solution of specific community problems and the alleviation of individual distress. Social workers deal with a variety of problems related to the adjustment and functioning of the social organization of the community and the integration of the individual into this social organization. Specific areas dealt with include poverty, unemployment, youth guidance and organization, recreation, delinquency, family disorganization, health, drug addiction, and mental illness. Social work is often classified into case work (with individuals or families), group work (for example, with youth gangs), and work in community organization.

socialism. Generally, an economic and political system based on state ownership and operation of the means of production and distribution. It usually includes rational societal planning to achieve desired goals. The term is used with a wide range of meanings. For example, some writers regard socialism as a democratic system and thus distinguish it from COMMUNISM, whereas others equate socialism with communism. See BOLSHEVISM; CAPITALISM; COLLECTIVISM; DEMOCRACY; DIALECTICAL MATERIALISM.

socialization. 1. The basic social process through which an individual becomes integrated into a social group by learning the group's culture and his ROLE in the group. By this definition socialization is a lifelong process. A critical phase occurs in childhood as the child internalizes the values, attitudes, skills, and roles that shape his personality and result in his integration into his society. This process is essential to the formation of the child's SELF, for he develops a conception of himself as a person through the behavior and attitudes of others and it is through learning to play various social roles that a well-developed social self emerges. However, the learning of any new social role enabling a person to function as a group or community member is also considered socialization. Thus a candidate for the police force, the Boy Scouts, or any new STATUS group, who has to learn the appropriate values, attitudes, folkways, and social roles, is involved in socialization. Indeed, the learning of new social roles is a constant process, and adulthood is not easily identified (except ritually). Teen-agers in a sense have to socialize their parents to the facts of their own changed status and their parents' changed status in modern society.

2. As defined by some authors, the process that occurs in childhood by which the individual initially develops his personality and becomes integrated into his society. The writers who limit the term thus would refer to any new acquisition of or change in culture or group membership that occurs in adulthood as ENCULTURATION. See INTERNALIZATION.

socialization, anticipatory. The learning of the rights, obligations, expectations, and outlook of a social ROLE preparatory to assuming it. As a person learns the proper beliefs, values, and norms of a STATUS or GROUP to which he aspires, he is learning how to act in his new role. Anticipatory socialization makes a person's adjustment to a change in status easier and makes his acceptance into the new status possible. Often each status that a person holds includes as part of its required behavior learning in preparation for the next step upward, particularly in hierarchies having regular promotions or opportunities for advancement. The term was introduced by Robert K. Merton and Alice S. Kitt. (R. K. Merton and A. S. Kitt in *Continuities in Social Research*, edited by R. K. Merton and P. F. Lazarsfeld, Free Press, Glencoe, Ill., 1950.)

socializing process. See FUSION PROCESS.

sociation. The development of stable patterns of relationships among individuals through social interaction and communication. The term was used by Georg Simmel in his analysis of the processes of group formation and the basic structure of society. Sociation is a translation from the German *Vergesellschaftung*. An earlier translation of the term by Albion Small as "socialization" is not in accordance with the current definition of SOCIALIZATION. (G. Simmel, *The Sociology of Georg Simmel*, ed. and tr. by K. H. Wolff, Free Press, Glencoe, Ill., 1950.)

sociation, forms of. See FORMS-OF-SOCIATION.

societal. Pertaining to social characteristics that exist throughout a society.

societal structure. The SOCIAL STRUCTURE of a society.

society. 1. A group of people with a common and at least somewhat distinct CULTURE who occupy a particular territorial area, have a feeling of unity, and regard themselves as a distinguishable entity. Like all groups, a society has a structure of interrelated roles with proper ROLE behavior prescribed by social norms. However, a society is a special type of group with a comprehensive social system that includes all of the basic social institutions required to meet basic human needs. It is independent, not in the sense that it is necessarily completely economically self-sufficient, but in that it includes all of the organizational forms necessary for its own survival. In addition, a society has the means to survive for a long period of time, and recruits its members at least in part by biological reproduction within the group itself. See INSTITUTION, SOCIAL; NORM, SOCIAL; SOCIAL STRUCTURE.

2. As defined by the early human ecologists, such as Robert E. Park, a level of human organization based on COMMUNICATION and CULTURE and regarded as superimposed on and distinguished from a lower, subsocial level of organization that was referred to as community, or BIOTIC COMMUNITY. See ECOLOGY, HUMAN.

society, "big animal" theory of. See "BIG ANIMAL" THEORY OF SOCIETY.

society, class. See CLASS SOCIETY.

society, classless. See CLASSLESS SOCIETY.

society, closed. See CLOSED-CLASS SYSTEM.

society, employee. See EMPLOYEE SOCIETY.

society, fetusphilic. See FETUSPHILIC SOCIETY.

society, fetusphobic. See FETUSPHOBIC SOCIETY.

society, folk. See FOLK SOCIETY.

society, inner-directed. See INNER-DIRECTED SOCIETY.

society, insect. See INSECT SOCIETY.

society, mass. See MASS SOCIETY.

society, mechanical. See SOLIDARITY, MECHANICAL.

society, open. See OPEN-CLASS SYSTEM.

society, organic. See SOLIDARITY, ORGANIC.

society, other-directed. See OTHER-DIRECTED SOCIETY.

society, primitive. See PRIMITIVE SOCIETY.

society, sacred. See SACRED SOCIETY.

society, secular. See SECULAR SOCIETY.

society, static. A society that experiences little or no change from one generation to the next. It was a belief, at one time, that simple nonliterate societies were static societies that had remained the same for thousands of years. However, while one society may change faster than another, it is very doubtful that it is possible for a society to remain static. Even in the simplest societies change occurs, due to such factors as changes in technology, new knowledge and insights, culture contact, disasters, rivalries, depletion of resources, and migration to new environments.

society, tradition-directed. See TRADITION-DIRECTED SOCIETY.

sociocentrism. See ETHNOCENTRISM.

sociocultural system. See CULTURAL SYSTEM; SOCIAL SYSTEM.

sociodrama. 1. A technique developed by J. L. Moreno, similar to the PSYCHODRAMA, in which the subjects engage in an improvised dramatic presentation of significant social roles (such as husband and wife) for the purpose of gaining insight into the culture of another social group or the expectations of a different social role. Sociodramas focus on exploring new social roles and giving the subjects an understanding of other groups and situations. Sociodramas also allow sociologists and social psychologists to study attitudes of one group toward another which might not be expressed or revealed in an interview situation.

2. A psychodrama carried out in a group setting, rather than as a soliloquy.

socioeconomic class. See SOCIAL CLASS; SOCIOECONOMIC STATUS.

socioeconomic status. In a system of social stratification, a combination of various social and economic indexes of rank that are used in research studies. The term is often used to deal with stratification in a society without the need for the assumption that there are distinct social classes. Social characteristics (family background, education, values, prestige of occupation, etc.) and economic status (income) are combined into one SES rating. See SOCIAL CLASS; STRATIFICATION, SOCIAL.

sociogenic. Derived from the social (and cultural) environment, through attitudes, values, norms, social expectations, etc. For example, one might study the sociogenic factors in juvenile delinquency.

sociogram. In sociometry, a diagrammatic presentation of the patterns of attraction and antagonism among members of a small group.

sociography. The detailed quantitative description of a specified problem of social relations within a delimited spatial environment, for example, a detailed description of crime and the distribution of crime rates in a particular area. The term was introduced by Roberto Michels in *Il proletariato e la borghesia nel movimento socialista italiano: Saggio di* *scienza sociografico-politica* (Turin, 1908). Michels was an Italian, but the concept was adopted by Sebald R. Steinmetz in the Netherlands, and then by Ferdinand Tönnies in Germany. Under the influence of Tönnies, sociography developed primarily in Germany. See ECOLOGY, HUMAN.

socio-group. A group a person joins, not because of his own private personal choice for psychological satisfaction, but because of the social importance of the group. The term was used by Helen H. Jennings to contrast with a PSYCHE-GROUP. (H. H. Jennings, *Leadership and Isolation*, Longmans, Green, New York, 1950.)

sociolinguistics. The study of the interrelationships between linguistics and sociology, that is, between language and social relationships. It includes the study of the effects of the social context on the structure and use of language, for example, the distinctive linguistic characteristics of regions, ethnic groups, social classes, and occupations in a society and how these are perpetuated through SOCIALIZATION. It also includes the study of culturally determined patterns of language use, such as whispering or shouting in certain situations. Still another area of concern in sociolinguistics is the effects of language on patterns of social relationships, such as the effects of early linguistic influences on a child's performance in school and eventual position in the socioeconomic structure of society. Sociolinguistics is sometimes referred to as the sociology of language.

sociological determinism. The view that individual behavior is completely determined by cultural and group influences. This view tends not to take into account the significance of individual variations or the influence of psychological, biological, or geographic factors. Other forms of DETERMINISM are biological determinism, CLIMATIC DETERMINISM, GEOGRAPHIC DETERMINISM, and PSYCHOLOGICAL DETERMINISM. They also tend to assume that behavior can be explained entirely in terms of a single causative schema, and ignore the possibility of modifying factors.

sociological mystic integralism. As defined by Pitirim A. Sorokin, any theory that attempts to combine the nominalist or reductionist view that only individuals have reality with the realist view that the social phenomena denoted by abstract concepts, such as society or group, have a reality that is distinct from the individual constituents. This approach "attempts to give a harmonious synthesis of individualistic singularism with universalism. . . . the individual is the singularistic incarnation of the societal reality; society is the *universalia* of all the individuals, permeating all of them; it is the condition without which the individual is impossible." (P. A. Sorokin, *Social and Cultural Dynamics*, American Book, New York, 1937.) See NOMINALISM; REALISM; REDUCTIONISM; SOCIOLOGICAL SINGULARISM; SOCIOLOGICAL UNIVERSALISM.

sociological singularism. As defined by Pitirim A. Sorokin, any nominalist theory holding that concepts such as society or group have no reference in reality besides their individual members. See NOMINALISM; REDUCTIONISM; SOCIOLOGICAL MYSTIC INTEGRALISM; SOCIOLOGICAL UNIVERSALISM.

sociological theory. See THEORY, SOCIOLOGICAL.

sociological universalism. As defined by Pitirim A. Sorokin, any theory holding that the concepts society and group refer to entities that have a real and distinct identity apart from their individual members. See REALISM; SOCIOLOGICAL MYSTIC INTEGRALISM; SOCIOLOGICAL SINGULARISM.

sociologist, proposed civil service definition of. The American Sociological Association Committee on Sociologists in the Federal Government proposed to the Civil Service Commission a definition for a new, separate series of career positions with the title of sociologist. "The proposed definition states: 'This series includes positions the duties of which are to advise on, administer, supervise, or perform professional work requiring a knowledge of sociology and sociological methods, relating to the culture, structure or functioning of groups, organizations or social systems; to the relationships between groups, organizations or social systems; to the demographic characteristics, and ecological patterning of communities and societies; or to human behavior in social situations.'" (N. Z. Medalia and W. S. Mason, *American Sociological Review*, April 1963.) See SOCIOLOGY.

sociology. The scientific study of human social behavior. Sociology studies the processes and patterns of individual and group interaction, the forms of organization of social groups, the relationships among them, and group influences on individual behavior. Although sociology includes the study of all forms of social interaction and interrelationships, it has focused on the understanding of group or other collective factors in human behavior. Traditionally particular emphasis has been placed on the study of society, so that in fact some writers have referred to sociology as the science of society. However, sociological research may deal with any social system, including the small group, or any aspect of social organization or social behavior. Sociology seeks to develop a body of interrelated scientific propositions, or generalizations, that explain social behavior and that may under specified conditions predict or aid in understanding behavior. Verification of all generalizations depends upon empirical observation. On the other hand, the meaningful interpretation of data and the cumulation and integration of knowledge from various sources require THEORY construction and the application of theory to empirical problems.

sociology, applied. The application of sociological principles and insights to the analysis and understanding of a concrete social situation or system of social relationships. Applied sociology is not to be confused with either SOCIAL WORK or social reform. See SOCIOLOGY, EMPIRICAL.

sociology, clinical. See SOCIOLOGY, CONCRETE.

sociology, concrete. Sociological investigation that "deals not with trends of the broad social order, but rather with a total situation within restricted limits of time and space. The limits are usually imposed by the group or organization under consideration, and the aim is to understand the situation in its entirety or the 'system' as a functioning unit. The concepts that prove useful for this range of study are those that give the investigator a general sense of reference in approaching concrete situations. [Herbert] Blumer has aptly labeled these 'sensitizing' concepts, distinguishing them from more 'definitive' concepts. A variety of specific methods may be used in concrete sociology, but in any case skilled observation must play the major role. Indeed, the area of concrete sociology can be delineated as the area in which 'participant observation' may be used as a key method of research." This approach has also been termed *clinical sociology.* (J. A. Shellenberg, *American Sociological Review,* December 1957.) See CONCEPT, DEFINITIVE; CONCEPT, SENSITIZING; OBSERVATION, PARTICIPANT.

sociology, educational. A substantive area of sociology that treats the EDUCATIONAL INSTITUTION and its relationship to other social institutions that make up society. There are no special principles of educational sociology —the subject is studied with the usual theoretical and methodological tools of sociology. There is a section of the American Sociological Association devoted to educational sociology and a journal of the Association with the name of *Sociology of Education.*

sociology, empirical. The empirical investigation of social phenomena, using the concepts developed by pure sociology to provide the theoretical orientation. This is one of the three divisions of sociology proposed by Ferdinand Tönnies. For the other two divisions see SOCIOLOGY, APPLIED; SOCIOLOGY, PURE. (F. Tönnies, *Community and Society,* tr. and ed. by C. P. Loomis, Michigan State University Press, East Lansing, Mich., 1957.)

sociology, encyclopedic. The conception of sociology as a broad, synthesizing science that includes and integrates all of the social sciences. Thus economics, political science, history, and psychology would be regarded as branches of sociology. This conception of sociology is not common in modern sociology.

sociology, formal. A type of sociological analysis, originated by Georg Simmel, that attempts to differentiate the forms of social interaction from the content of interaction, and to analyze the former independently of the latter. The forms of interaction are seen as comprising the basic structure of society independently of the concrete characteristics (the content) of specific societies. Formal sociology thus is highly abstract and generalized. An example of formal analysis would be the study of two- and three-person groups in terms of the principles governing the structure of dyads and triads, or the analysis of art and play as societal forms. Simmel distinguished formal sociology from general sociology and philosophical sociology. He regarded formal sociology as the essence of the science of sociology, and therefore also referred to it as pure sociology. (G. Simmel, *The Sociology of Georg Simmel,* tr. and ed. by K. H. Wolff, Free Press, Glencoe, Ill., 1950.) See SOCIOLOGY, PHILOSOPHICAL.

sociology, historical. The analysis of historical data to obtain sociological generalizations. The historical approach may involve an attempt to uncover broad trends in the development or change of a society or civilization or it may be limited to the analysis of a specific problem. In the latter case the historical approach may simply involve an attempt to test specific limited hypotheses about social behavior, using the data of the past.

sociology, industrial. The application of sociological theory and research methods to the study of industrial organization, such as factory or business organization. The study of work groups in industry and the study of industrial occupations are important areas of research in industrial sociology.

sociology, medical. A substantive area of sociology dealing with the social aspects of illness. It deals with the study of attitudes toward illness, its distribution, the relationship of illness to the organization of society, and so forth. It also includes the study of the organizational structure of the hospital, the various social roles (patient, doctor, nurse, etc.) played by those who are sick or who deal directly and indirectly with the sick. There is a journal of the American Sociological Association entitled *Journal of Health and Social Behavior.* See ROLE.

sociology, meta-. See METASOCIOLOGY.

sociology, occupational. The application of principles of sociology to the analysis of professions and occupations. The study of career patterns is a part of occupational sociology.

sociology, philosophical. The study of philosophical concerns of interest to sociology, such as the problem of reality, and the sources, standards, and limits of man's thought and knowledge. The term was used by Georg Simmel, who distinguished philosophical sociology from general sociology and formal sociology. See SOCIOLOGY, FORMAL; SOCIOLOGY OF KNOWLEDGE.

sociology, political. The sociological study of the POLITICAL INSTITUTION and its relationship to the other social institutions of society. Political sociology is concerned, for example, with political movements and ideologies. Such phenomena are studied primarily as constituent parts of the structure of society and of social processes, which is what differentiates political sociology from traditional political science. See INSTITUTION, SOCIAL.

sociology, psychological. See SOCIAL PSYCHOLOGY.

sociology, pure. 1. As defined by Lester F. Ward, the objective, scientific, unbiased study of society for the purposes of pure knowledge and theoretical advance. Pure sociology is not interested in practical applications to solve particular problems or even to bring about societal improvement. Some present-day critics of sociology (usually sociologists themselves) object to its lack of adequate concern with the solution of pressing national and international problems, contending that sociology already has enough knowledge to apply to basic world problems, and that sociologists are morally obliged to apply their knowledge. The term is not widely used today. (See L. F. Ward, *Pure Sociology*, Macmillan, New York, 1903.)

2. See SOCIOLOGY, FORMAL.

3. The development of ideal types (abstract, generalized types) that contribute to the analysis and understanding of social phenomena by providing the theoretical orientation for the investigation of empirical data. This is one of the three divisions of sociology discussed by Ferdinand Tönnies. See IDEAL TYPE; SOCIOLOGY, APPLIED; SOCIOLOGY, EMPIRICAL.

sociology, rural. The sociological study of rural communities and rural life in both agricultural and industrialized societies. In this area of sociology there is emphasis both on the development of general principles and on the application of sociological principles to solving the problems of rural communities. At universities, rural sociology is often taught in schools of agriculture. See SOCIOLOGY, URBAN.

sociology, substantive area of. Any area of sociological analysis that is designated as an area of specialization on the basis not of special theoretical principles but of a convenient breakdown of subject matter. See, for example, SOCIOLOGY, EDUCATIONAL; SOCIOLOGY, INDUSTRIAL; SOCIOLOGY, MEDICAL; SOCIOLOGY, OCCUPATIONAL; SOCIOLOGY, POLITICAL; SOCIOLOGY, URBAN; SOCIOLOGY OF RELIGION.

sociology, systematic. A consistent, comprehensive, and self-sufficient body of sociological principles to account for all social phenomena.

sociology, urban. A substantive area in sociology devoted to the study of urban social life and organization. Most American sociologists today are in practice involved in at least some aspect of urban sociology since they live and work in a very highly urbanized society. Often sociologists who are involved in research on urban situations do not particularly think of themselves as studying urban sociology but simply as studying a special area, such as race relations or political sociology. See SOCIOLOGY, RURAL.

sociology of art. The study of the influence of society on art and the role and influence of art in society. The analysis of art as a social institution would include the analysis of the network of social roles and norms involved in the creation, evaluation, use, and distribution of art in society.

sociology of knowledge. The aspect of sociology that is concerned with the relationship between knowledge or systems of thought (scientific, religious, philosophical, aesthetic, political, legal, etc.) and social and cultural factors. One problem dealt with by sociologists in this area is the way the culture and society of the present or past shape knowledge and thought. For example, see Karl Mannheim, *Ideology and Utopia* (tr. by L. Wirth and E. A. Shils, Harcourt, Brace, New York, 1936). See HISTORICISM.

sociology of language. See SOCIOLINGUISTICS.

sociology of law. The study of the legal institution in terms of sociological concepts. The study of social norms is central to sociology and so the sociological analysis of legal codes is a long-standing concern. The analysis of the social roles of criminal, lawyer, judge, juror, etc., and how they relate to the general structure of society, is a major aspect of the sociology of law. See INSTITUTION, SOCIAL; ROLE.

sociology of literature. The sociological study of literature either to derive the insights of writers concerning society or to relate literature to the structure of society, in the manner of the SOCIOLOGY OF KNOWLEDGE. With respect to earlier literate societies or to contemporary societies that have not been or (for political reasons) cannot be directly and comprehensively studied, literature enables us to learn something about the society on the basis of comparative sociological analysis. Thus if a society was (or is) presumably without class distinctions, it would not take a sociologist long to apply many of his various subtle indicators of stratification to be able to indicate the existence of this phenomenon and its specific nature.

sociology of mental illness. Essentially "the study of the social norms and processes which have a marked bearing upon the production or course of various forms of psychic disturbance (especially as such disturbance impairs the individual's ability to carry out usual roles), or which govern the ways in which disturbed persons are perceived, defined, and dealt with during and after acute disturbance." (J. A. Clausen in *Sociology Today*, edited by R. K. Merton, L. Broom and L. S. Cottrell, Jr., Basic Books, New York, 1959.)

sociology of religion. The sociological analysis of the RELIGIOUS INSTITUTION and the study of the SOCIAL PSYCHOLOGY of religious phenomena. Religion is viewed in terms of social interaction and is studied with reference to the general concepts of sociology, including LEADERSHIP, stratification, and SOCIALIZATION. See STRATIFICATION, SOCIAL.

sociometric choice. See SOCIOMETRIC TEST.

sociometric diagram. See SOCIOGRAM.

sociometric method. See SOCIOMETRY.

sociometric test. The basic technique of SOCIOMETRY, which is used to measure and study interpersonal relations and social organization in small groups based on sociometric choices—who wants to associate with whom in particular situations. In a sociometric test, each group member is asked to choose which members he would want to be with, work with, etc., on the basis of liking, and which he would reject on the basis of disliking. Sociometric choice might also involve choosing persons on other bases, for example, on the basis of trust, or of who has the greatest concern for each member of the group. See SOCIOGRAM.

sociometrics. The systematic attempt to quantify interpersonal relations. Some writers have defined SOCIOMETRY in this sense, rather than in the more limited, usual usage. See SOCIOMETRY, PREFERENTIAL.

sociometry. The study of group structure and SOCIAL DISTANCE in terms of the personal preference of the members of a group for each other, in some specific type of situation. Sociometry, developed by J. L. Moreno and Helen H. Jennings, studies an important aspect of the network of relations among the members of a group. The technique has been used in varied types of groups in which all the members personally know each other, for example, in classrooms, prisons, factories, army units. See SOCIOGRAM; SOCIOMETRIC TEST.

sociometry, preferential. A term used by Ake Bjerstedt to refer to what is defined in this dictionary as SOCIOMETRY. He uses the term *sociometry* for what is here defined as SOCIOMETRICS, except that he includes not only human interaction, but interaction between all forms of animal life. Bjerstedt's usage is not shared by the majority of sociologists.

sociopath. 1. A person who usually tends to act in an antisocial way. See ANTISOCIAL BEHAVIOR.

2. See PSYCHOPATHIC PERSONALITY.

sociotype. See TYPE, SOCIAL.

socius. The individual person conceived of as a unit in a system of social interaction and as a point of convergence of the various social and cultural patterns of society.

solidarity. 1. That condition within a group in which there is social cohesion plus cooperative, collective action directed toward the achievement of group goals.

2. Synonymous with social cohesion. See COHESION, SOCIAL.

solidarity, mechanical. As defined by Émile Durkheim, societal SOLI-DARITY based upon a homogeneity of values and behavior, strong social constraint, and loyalty to tradition and kinship. The term applies to small, nonliterate societies characterized by a simple division of labor, very little specialization of function, only a few social roles, and very little tolerance of individuality. (É. Durkheim, *The Division of Labor in Society*, tr. by G. Simpson, Free Press, Glencoe, Ill., 1947.) See SOLIDARITY, ORGANIC.

solidarity, organic. As defined by Émile Durkheim, a type of societal SOLIDARITY typical of modern industrial society, in which unity is based on the interdependence of a very large number of highly specialized roles in a system involving a complex division of labor that requires the cooperation of almost all the groups and individuals of the society. In contrast to solidarity that is mechanical, that is, based on a homogeneity of values, beliefs, and loyalties, this type of solidarity is called organic because it is similar to the unity of a biological organism in which highly specialized parts, or organs, must work in coordination if the organism (or any one of its parts) is to survive. (É. Durkheim, *The Division of Labor in Society*, tr. by G. Simpson, Free Press, Glencoe, Ill., 1947.) See ROLE; SOLIDARITY, MECHANICAL.

solidarity, social. See SOLIDARITY.

somatic anthropology. See ANTHROPOLOGY, PHYSICAL.

somatology. See ANTHROPOLOGY, PHYSICAL.

somatotonia. See SHELDON'S BODY TYPES.

somatotype. See SHELDON'S BODY TYPES.

sorcery. 1. See WITCHCRAFT.
2. The practice of divination, or prophesying future events, with the aid of evil spirits.

sororate. 1. The custom of a widower's marrying the sister of his deceased wife. Often it is a younger sister who marries her deceased older sister's husband. In some cultures this practice may be just an expectation without undue pressure; in other cultures it may be required. See LEVIRATE.
2. See POLYGYNY, SORORAL.

source, primary. See PRIMARY SOURCE.

source, secondary. See SECONDARY SOURCE.

sources of information. See DOCUMENTARY SOURCES OF INFORMATION.

sovereignty. The supreme and final authority that nations are regarded as having over their citizens in all territories within their legitimate jurisdiction.

space, social. See SOCIAL SPACE.

Spearman-Brown formula. A formula used to predict approximately the COEFFICIENT OF RELIABILITY (degree of consistency in measurement, for example, between different applications of a test or between two parts of the test) that would result if the number of similar measurements (for instance, the number of items on a questionnaire measuring one thing or the number of observers observing one situation) were increased to a given number. In the Spearman-Brown formula, the CORRELATION (rNN) between two measurements is multiplied by the number of measurements (N) for which the reliability coefficient is to be predicted and the resulting product is divided by $1 + (N-1) r : I_{NN} = \dfrac{N r}{1 + (N-1)r}$. See RELIABILITY.

Spearman rank correlation. See CORRELATION, RANK DIFFERENCE.

specialist bureaucrat. See BUREAUCRATIC TYPES.

specialization. The DIVISION OF LABOR or territorial areas of a group, community, or society into a number of interrelated and specialized functions. Occupational specialization and ecological specialization are types of specialization. The latter refers, for example, to the specialization of districts within a city, such as the business district, the banking district, the wholesale district, the theater district.

specialization, institutional. See INSTITUTIONAL SPECIALIZATION.

specialties, cultural. Those "elements of culture which are shared by the members of certain socially recognized categories of individuals but which are not shared by the total population. . . . Under this head come the patterns for all those varied but mutually interdependent activities which have been assigned to various sections of the society in the course of its division of labor." Thus men and women within a particular society will be familiar with different occupations and techniques. Various occupational groups, such as plumbers, doctors, lawyers, teachers, carpenters, and clergymen, share within their own specialties certain elements of culture that are only vaguely understood by the general population. "Although such elements are not shared by the entire society, the benefits arising from them are shared, and all members of the society will have a fairly clear idea as to what the end product of each specialized activity should be." (R. Linton, *The Study of Man*, Appleton-Century-Crofts, New York, 1936.) See ALTERNATIVES, CULTURAL; UNIVERSALS, CULTURAL.

species. Populations of organisms that are genetically similar to the extent that they are capable of interbreeding with each other. One species cannot breed and produce offspring with another species. See HOMO SAPIENS.

species, survival of. See EVOLUTION.

specificity. The expectation that a social relationship be limited to a narrow and clearly defined range of rights and obligations, and that only a limited aspect of the individuals' personalities be involved in the relationship. Social norms define certain roles as properly specific. Usually behavior regarded as appropriate in occupational roles is characterized by the expectation of specificity. The opposing term is DIFFUSENESS. See also DIFFUSENESS-SPECIFICITY.

speculator-fox type. See ELITE, CIRCULATION OF THE; INSTINCT FOR COMBINATIONS and INSTINCT FOR GROUP PERSISTENCES.

speech. See LANGUAGE.

spending unit. As defined by the Survey Research Center of the University of Michigan, "a group of persons . . . living in the same dwelling and related by blood, marriage or adoption, who pool their incomes for their major items of expense. In some instances a spending unit consists of only one person." (*Federal Reserve Bulletin,* June 1949.)

spiritism. The belief in freely moving spirits, such as spirits of the dead who are able to communicate with the living. In evolutionary theories of the origins of religion, spiritism was regarded as a stage following ANIMISM.

spontaneity. The quality of being free from feelings of restraint due to situational obligations and duties. It is a release from or unconcern with social demands. Spontaneous behavior requires a feeling of escape from the usual and immediate or relatively immediate social restraints. Without a feeling of restraint, spontaneity would be impossible to achieve, for restraint is the reference point for doing what one feels like doing as opposed to what one's obligations are judged to be at a particular time and place.

spot map. A map that portrays the geographic distribution of the phenomenon (or phenomena) being illustrated or studied, by using dots, squares, etc. (or a combination of symbols for more than one phenomenon) to indicate the frequency of its occurrence.

spread. See DISPERSION, STATISTICAL.

spurious correlation. See CORRELATION, SPURIOUS.

squares, least. See LEAST SQUARES, PRINCIPLE OF.

stability, social. Continuity of the social and cultural patterns within a community or society without sudden or radical change in any major segment of these patterns. Social stability does not necessarily mean a static society, although a static society, if it were to exist, would be stable. A society in which changes occur gradually and slowly enough to permit readjustment of other aspects of the culture and social structure without serious disruption and disorganization would be regarded as stable.

In modern society change is an essential ingredient in conserving basic values and maintaining a continuity of broad traditional patterns. Just as an individual must adjust his behavior and values in the process of socialization and in his effort to achieve his desired goals, so social stability in modern society is possible only within a context of change. See SOCIETY, STATIC.

stable population. See POPULATION, STABLE.

staff organization. See ORGANIZATION, STAFF.

standard consolidated area. A term introduced by the U.S. Census of 1960 to designate any vast metropolitan area consisting of two or more standard metropolitan statistical areas. In the 1960 census two standard consolidated areas were delimited in the United States: New York–Northeastern New Jersey and Chicago–Northwestern Indiana. See METROPOLITAN AREA, STANDARD.

standard deviation. In statistics, the most widely used measure of the dispersion of values. Standard deviation may be used as a measure of the dispersion of a FREQUENCY DISTRIBUTION when the arithmetic mean is used as the measure of central tendency. To obtain the standard deviation, each observed value in the frequency distribution is subtracted from the arithmetic mean of all the values. Each of the differences is squared (eliminating the signs—plus or minus), and the arithmetic mean of these squared differences is obtained. The square root of their mean is the standard deviation. Thus the standard deviation is usually defined as the square root of the mean of the squared deviations from the mean. The symbol for the standard deviation is the lower case sigma, σ, although occasionally s or SD is used. Some writers use σ to refer to the standard deviation of a POPULATION and s to refer to the standard deviation of a SAMPLE. See CENTRAL TENDENCY, MEASURE OF; DISPERSION, STATISTICAL; MEAN, ARITHMETIC; VARIANCE.

standard error. An estimate of the deviation of a summarizing measure of a SAMPLE from the true population PARAMETER, for example, the extent to which a sample mean differs from the population mean. The standard error is based on the STANDARD DEVIATION of the SAMPLING DISTRIBUTION of a statistical measure. If a large number of samples were available, the standard error might be computed directly from their standard deviation. However it is usually estimated from the data of a single sample, using a formula based on the standard deviation and the size of the sample. The standard error may be used to construct CONFIDENCE LIMITS. The chances are approximately 68% that the true population parameter lies within one standard error on either side of the sample measure. The 95%

confidence limits are 1.96 standard errors on either side of the sample measure. The standard error may be obtained for any statistical measure—the standard error of the mean, the standard error of the MEDIAN, the standard error of a percentage, the standard error of the STANDARD DEVIATION, the standard error of a difference between samples. The standard error is symbolized by the symbol for standard deviation (or sometimes SE), followed by the symbol for the summarizing statistic; for instance, the standard error of the mean may be symbolized $\sigma_{\bar{x}}$. See MEAN, ARITHMETIC; PROBABLE ERROR; STATISTIC.

standard error of estimate. A measure of the approximate error in predicting the values of one variable from those of a correlated variable. In the regression analysis of two correlated variables, for each value of one variable a value is predicted for the other variable. The standard error of estimate attempts to estimate the error involved in such predictions. Symbolized $\sigma_{y \cdot x}$ or $s_{y \cdot x}$, it is derived from a formula based on the STANDARD DEVIATION of the known values of the predicted variable (the dependent variable), the size of the correlation coefficient, and the size of the sample. The chances are approximately two out of three that an actual value will be within one standard error of a predicted value. See COEFFICIENT OF CORRELATION; REGRESSION, STATISTICAL; STANDARD ERROR.

standard measure. See Z SCORE.

standard metropolitan area. See METROPOLITAN AREA, STANDARD.

standard of living. The economic level on which an individual or group lives. The term is usually used broadly to refer to the over-all level of goods and services economically available to an individual or group, including type of housing, food, clothing, medical care, recreation, education, etc. In any study involving standard of living, specific indexes are used which must be clearly specified.

standard score. See T SCORE; Z SCORE.

standardization. 1. The establishment of uniform modes of behavior in an organization. Large, formal organizations usually attempt to standardize procedures of operation throughout the organization by adopting formal rules. This is particularly characteristic of a BUREAUCRACY.

2. In testing, the establishment of uniform procedures for the administering, scoring, and interpreting of tests, so that the results from different administrations of the test may be compared.

Stanford-Binet test. Revision of the Binet-Simon INTELLIGENCE TEST by Lewis M. Terman of Stanford University. Later (1937) revised again by Terman and Maud A. Merrill, it is the most widely used intelligence test in the United States. It is a verbal test of intelligence. See INTELLIGENCE; INTELLIGENCE QUOTIENT.

state. A political form of human association by which a society is organized under the agency of a government that claims legitimate sovereignty over a territorial area, AUTHORITY over all of the members of the society, and the right to use physical force when necessary to insure the effective exercise of its legitimate control. Two meanings of the term may be distinguished: that of NATION (an autonomous, politically organized people) and that of national GOVERNMENT (the political agency ruling the nation). However, in most actual usage these two meanings are combined and thus state comes to refer to the nation as symbolized by the government or the government as the symbol of the nation.

stateway. A social norm that has been enacted into law. The term is seldom used today. See LAW; NORM, SOCIAL.

static society. See SOCIETY, STATIC.

statics. See SOCIAL STATICS.

statism. See TOTALITARIANISM.

statistic. A mathematical value that summarizes a characteristic of a SAMPLE. A statistic may be a measure of central tendency, of dispersion (see DISPERSION, STATISTICAL), of CORRELATION, of a difference between two samples, or any other summarizing measure based upon sample data. It is used to estimate a PARAMETER of the POPULATION from which the sample was drawn, and is sometimes referred to as a parameter estimate. Since most social research deals with samples rather than entire populations, most research yields a statistic rather than a parameter. See CENTRAL TENDENCY, MEASURE OF.

statistic, sufficient. A STATISTIC that utilizes all available sample data in attempting to estimate a PARAMETER.

statistical artifact. See ARTIFACT, STATISTICAL.

statistical association. See ASSOCIATION, STATISTICAL.

statistical attenuation. See ATTENUATION, STATISTICAL.

statistical class. See CLASS INTERVAL.

statistical dispersion. See DISPERSION, STATISTICAL.

statistical efficiency. See EFFICIENCY, STATISTICAL.

statistical induction. See STATISTICAL INFERENCE.

statistical inference. The process of inferring generalizations about a POPULATION on the basis of SAMPLE data. Statistical inference includes the estimation of population parameters and the testing of statistical hypotheses about populations, using data obtained from samples. Statistical inference is based upon PROBABILITY theory. A wide variety of statistical techniques is available to test sample data and determine probable degree of accuracy of generalizations about the population from which the sample was drawn. Generalizations based on statistical inference always are probability statements and are never statements of absolute certainty. Statistical inference is also referred to as statistical induction. See HYPOTHESIS, STATISTICAL; PROBABILITY; STATISTIC; STATISTICS, INDUCTIVE.

statistical law. See LAW, STATISTICAL.

statistical method. See STATISTICS.

statistical model. A set of assumptions underlying a statistical test. Every statistical test assumes that certain conditions are met. Usually these assumptions refer to the form of the data, the nature of the sample, the nature of the population from which the sample was drawn, and the character of the variables being studied. The test is valid only if these conditions are met, and thus it is important to know the statistical model on which a test is based before that test is used. In addition to the various assumptions of individual statistical tests, tests may be grouped into parametric and nonparametric, with certain basic assumptions characteristic of each group. These assumptions are sometimes referred to as the parametric statistical model and the nonparametric statistical model. See MODEL; NONPARAMETRIC STATISTICS; PARAMETRIC STATISTICS.

statistical norm. See NORM, STATISTICAL.

statistical population. See POPULATION (2).

statistical population, dichotomous. See DICHOTOMOUS POPULATION.

statistical power. See POWER, STATISTICAL.

statistical rank. See RANK, STATISTICAL.

statistical regression. See REGRESSION, STATISTICAL.

statistical reliability. See RELIABILITY.

statistical significance. See SIGNIFICANCE, STATISTICAL.

statistical table. A systematic arrangement of numerical data into a series of rows and columns in order to facilitate the comprehension and comparison of the data. The presentation of data in a statistical table involves the classification of the data into the categories or class intervals specified in the column and row headings. (For example, the column headings might represent the categories of the variable *type of occupation* and the row headings might represent the class intervals of the variable *income*.) The columns are the vertical arrangements of data and the rows are the horizontal arrangements of data. At the top of the table is the table heading, which includes the number and title of the table, and the subtitle and headnote (an explanatory note) if any. Below the table heading are the column headings or captions, which are sometimes regarded as part of the table heading. At the extreme left of the table is the list of row headings, referred to as the stub of the table. The data themselves comprise the field of the table, with the place for each entry referred to as a CELL. Sometimes columns and rows are enclosed with straight lines, so that there is actually a square box for each cell. However, often the lines are omitted. The number of columns and rows may be two or more. Their number need not be equal. There may be more columns or more rows. A table with two columns and two rows is referred to as a FOURFOLD TABLE (sometimes written 2×2). It is the simplest type of statistical table. See CLASS INTERVAL.

statistical tables. See CONTINGENCY TABLE; CORRELATION MATRIX; FOURFOLD TABLE; FREQUENCY TABLE; LIFE TABLE.

statistical technique. See STATISTICAL TEST.

statistical technique, descriptive. See STATISTICS, DESCRIPTIVE.

statistical technique, generalizing. See STATISTICS, INDUCTIVE.

statistical test. A procedure used with quantitative SAMPLE data to estimate the probable truth of a hypothesis about the population from which the sample was drawn. The formulas used are based on certain principles, assumptions, and rules of mathematical logic. A wide range of statistical tests is available for a variety of purposes and various types of data. See PROBABILITY; STATISTICS. See also BINOMIAL TEST; CHI-SQUARE TEST; COCHRAN Q TEST; CORRELATION, KENDALL PARTIAL RANK; CORRELATION, KENDALL RANK; CORRELATION, RANK DIFFERENCE; CORRELATION, PEARSON PRODUCT-MOMENT; F TEST; FISHER EXACT PROBABILITY TEST; FRIEDMAN χ_r^2 TEST; GOODNESS-OF-FIT TEST; KOLMOGOROV-SMIRNOV D TEST; KRUSKAL-WALLIS TEST; MCNEMAR TEST; MANN-WHITNEY U TEST; MEDIAN TEST; MOSES TEST; ONE-TAILED TEST; RANDOMIZATION TEST; RUNS TEST; SIGN TEST; t TEST; TWO-TAILED TEST; WALD-WOLFOWITZ RUNS TEST; WILCOXON MATCHED-PAIRS SIGNED RANKS TEST.

statistics. 1. A body of methods for collecting, tabulating, presenting, and analyzing quantitative data. The data may consist of enumerations or measurements. Statistical techniques provide descriptive procedures for classifying and summarizing data so that a mass of quantitative facts may be converted into a comprehensible form. Statistics also provides inductive techniques for using principles of mathematical probability to obtain generalizations from sample data that may be applied to the larger population. See NONPARAMETRIC STATISTICS; PARAMETRIC STATISTICS; POPULATIONS; SAMPLE; STATISTICS, DESCRIPTIVE; STATISTICS, INDUCTIVE; STATISTICS OF RELATIONSHIP.

2. In popular usage, numerical data. In this usage the term is plural.

statistics, complex. See STATISTICS OF RELATIONSHIP.

statistics, descriptive. Statistical techniques used to condense and summarize quantitative data, for the purpose of converting a mass of numerical data into a form that may be more readily comprehended and discussed. Frequently used techniques of descriptive statistics are measures of central tendency, measures of dispersion, PERCENTAGE, RATE, RATIO, and FREQUENCY DISTRIBUTION. See CENTRAL TENDENCY, MEASURE OF; DISPERSION, STATISTICAL; STATISTICS; STATISTICS, INDUCTIVE.

statistics, inductive. Statistical techniques based on the theory of mathematical PROBABILITY and used to induce generalizations about a POPULATION from a SAMPLE of that population. Inductive statistics provides techniques for estimating population parameters and testing statistical hypotheses about populations on the basis of sample data. These techniques enable the investigator to arrive at probability statements about a population. Inductive statistics is also referred to as inferential statistics or, sometimes, generalizing statistics. See HYPOTHESIS, STATISTICAL; PARAMETER; STATISTIC; STATISTICAL INFERENCE; STATISTICS; STATISTICS, DESCRIPTIVE.

statistics, inferential. See STATISTICS, INDUCTIVE.

statistics, order. Statistical techniques used with data in the form of ranks rather than absolute values, that is, data in the form of an ORDINAL SCALE (greatest to least, highest to lowest, etc.). There are a number of nonparametric statistical tests that can be used when one has information only about the relative rank of each case. See NONPARAMETRIC STATISTICS; RANK, STATISTICAL.

statistics, sampling. See STATISTICS, INDUCTIVE.

statistics, vital. See VITAL STATISTICS.

statistics of relationship. Statistical methods used to analyze the simultaneous distribution of two or more variables, showing the relationship between them. The body of techniques to measure the CORRELATION of variables is an example of statistics of relationship. Statistics of relationship may be used either as descriptive statistics (if they are used solely to describe a relationship among the cases studied) or as a part of inductive statistics (if PROBABILITY theory is used to generalize from the relationship of the variables in a SAMPLE to a larger POPULATION). Statistics of relationship are sometimes referred to as complex statistics, in contrast to simple statistics used to analyze the distribution of a single VARIABLE. See STATISTICS, DESCRIPTIVE; STATISTICS, INDUCTIVE.

status. 1. A defined position in the SOCIAL STRUCTURE of a group or society that is distinguished from and at the same time related to other positions through its designated rights and obligations. Because each status position in a social structure (for instance, GROUP, BUREAUCRACY) can be viewed in terms of its superiority or inferiority (advantages, disadvantages), people tend to equate status with rank and prestige or hierarchical position. However, status in the usual sociological sense does not necessarily imply a rank in a hierarchy. Thus widow, musician, student, boy scout, and husband would all be examples of statuses. Each status position is expressed in terms of a ROLE, that is, a pattern of behavior expected of the occupant of the status. Ralph Linton, who developed the classic statement of the distinction between status and role, referred to role as the dynamic aspect of status. Thus status refers to a location in a system of social relationships, while role refers to the behavior associated with that location (that is, with a given status). (R. Linton, *The Study of Man*, Appleton-Century-Crofts, New York, 1936.)

2. A rank in a hierarchy.

3. A person's total standing in society, that is, the combination of his known statuses. This usage is vague, but tends to be related to the concept of SOCIAL CLASS.

status, achieved. A STATUS acquired by an individual through his efforts, often through competition and the use of special abilities, knowledge, and skill. It is a status that is not an ascribed status. Many occupational statuses are considered to be achieved, for example, physician, lawyer, artist. Any status open to competition, the major criteria for the status being based on personal abilities rather than on factors present or inherent at birth (such as sex, family, race, ethnic group), would be considered an achieved status. The distinction between achieved and ascribed status is a rough but often useful type of classification. There are obviously ascriptive elements in many statuses defined as achieved (especially for some persons), and many achieved elements in ascribed statuses. Ralph Linton contrasted achieved status with ascribed status in *The Study of Man* (Appleton-Century-Crofts, New York, 1936). See STATUS, ASCRIBED.

status, ascribed. Any STATUS that is based not on individual ability, skill, effort, or accomplishment, but on inherited position in the society. An ascribed status is either acquired at birth or acquired automatically on reaching a certain age. Many statuses are ascribed in society. Sex and age statuses are the most obvious and universal. Race can be considered an ascribed status. The occupational statuses within a CASTE system are also ascribed. The term was used by Ralph Linton to contrast with achieved status. (R. Linton, *The Study of Man*, Appleton-Century-Crofts, New York, 1936.) See STATUS, ACHIEVED.

status, assigned. See STATUS, ASCRIBED.

status, assumed. See STATUS, ACHIEVED.

status, Chapin scale of social. See CHAPIN SCALE OF SOCIAL STATUS.

status, consciousness of. See CLASS-STATUS CONSCIOUSNESS.

status, formal. A formally designated position in a group with offi-cially specified rights and duties, such as a personnel manager in a cor-poration or a deacon in a church. The term is used primarily in contrast to informal status. See STATUS, INFORMAL.

status, functional. STATUS within a group viewed in terms of the func-tions performed, rather than in terms of prestige or authority. In the func-tional status system of an army a low-ranking medical officer or chaplain may have a functionally more important and dominant role in certain situ-ations than a higher-ranking line officer.

status, general. See STATUS (3).

status, informal. A STATUS in an organized group that is different from the occupant's formal status in the group. A person with a relatively low status in a formal hierarchy of status positions may be very popular or may achieve prestige because of some skill or because of another status held outside the group. A person whose formal status grants him no AUTHORITY, may, through his informal status, be very influential and even wield POWER. See STATUS, FORMAL.

status, scalar. STATUS conceived in terms of hierarchical positions, superiority and inferiority, or in terms of a structure of AUTHORITY.

status, social. See STATUS.

status, socioeconomic. See SOCIOECONOMIC STATUS.

status assumption, differential. The assumption that all lasting social groups have a system of statuses, each STATUS tending to have distinctive characteristics. In small groups the differential statuses do not necessarily entail higher or lower prestige. In the case of large-scale organizations or societies, it is assumed, however, that status differentiation inevitably in-volves an unequal distribution of power, prestige, and advantages. See SO-CIAL DIFFERENTIATION; SOCIAL STRUCTURE.

status consistency. Similarity of social and cultural expectations di-rected toward the various statuses occupied by an individual. When cer-tain statuses are related in such a way that one position tends to lead to or reinforce the assumption of other statuses of a particular type and to dis-courage the assumption of those of a different type, this is called status crystallization, and it promotes status consistency. Inconsistent statuses lead to anxiety (as may be the case with the military chaplain) or disap-proval of those who occupy such positions (for example, the doctor-undertaker). The acquisition of a particular STATUS is often followed auto-matically by other consistent statuses. For example, people who achieve great wealth often gain positions of power, influence, and honor as a result. See CLASS CRYSTALLIZATION; ROLE CLUSTER.

status continuum hypothesis. The hypothesis that the social stratification system of a society is not necessarily composed of distinct social classes (lower, middle, upper), but instead may be composed of a continuous spectrum of statuses without any clearcut structural breaks. Some writers contend that in the United States there is such a continuum of status—that social status differences are gradual and do not clearly divide the society into social classes. Werner S. Landecker termed this the status continuum hypothesis and contrasted it with the CLASS STRUCTURE HYPOTHESIS. (W. S. Landecker, *American Sociological Review*, December 1960.) See STRATIFICATION, SOCIAL.

status crystallization. See STATUS CONSISTENCY.

status discrepancy. Prestige differences between the statuses held by one person in two status systems, particularly when the status systems overlap in a social situation, for example, a racketeer may have high prestige for his status of a very wealthy man and low prestige for his status of criminal. See STATUS CONSISTENCY.

status equilibrium. See STATUS CONSISTENCY.

status group. 1. A number of people who share a specific style of life and a common STATUS HONOR (code of behavior) view each other as equals, have a sense of awareness as a GROUP, and have some group organization (such as criteria for determining membership in the group, leaders, or rules). A CASTE would be an example of a (closed) status group. A status group may be either a large, formal group or a small, informal group. See GROUP, FORMAL; GROUP, INFORMAL.

2. A number of persons who occupy the same status in society and share the same style of life, but who do not really form a GROUP. They would more accurately be referred to as a status category. See SOCIAL CATEGORY.

status honor. A code of behavior required of all members of a STATUS GROUP if they wish to remain in good standing. Marrying within the status group would be one example of a requirement of status honor.

status judgment, total. See STATUS (3).

status organization. See STATUS SYSTEM.

status personality. The set of personality characteristics deemed appropriate for any given status in a society (for example, an occupational status). The individual who occupies a particular social status has to have or to develop the appropriate attitudes and emotions necessary to fit that status. Many different personality types (such as introverts and extroverts) may occupy a status and acquire the appropriate status personality either permanently or just while performing the role attached to the status. Sometimes an individual's personality type will be very similar to the particular status personality he is required to assume. At other times it may be quite different, as for example when an introverted person is required to assume an extroverted status personality (such as that of a politician). Status has an effect on personality structure, but quite obviously status positions are not uniformly filled by specific psychological types. There are variations in the way a single social role is played due to personality differences. The term was introduced by Ralph Linton. (R. Linton in *Culture and Personality*, edited by S. S. Sargent and M. W. Smith, The Viking Fund, New York, 1949.)

status/security hypothesis. The hypothesis, proposed by Anthony Richmond, that prejudice and out-group hostility on the part of an individual are due to a feeling of insecurity or rejection in his own membership reference group. (A. Richmond, *Colour Prejudice in Britain*, Routledge & Kegan Paul, London, 1950.)

status sequence. A "succession of statuses occurring with sufficient frequency as to be socially patterned . . . as in the case, for example, of the statuses successively occupied by a medical student, intern, resident, and independent medical practitioner. In much the same sense, of course, we can observe *sequences of role-sets and status-sets*." (R. K. Merton, *Social Theory and Social Structure*, Free Press, Glencoe, Ill., 1957.) See ROLE-SET; STATUS-SET.

status-set. As defined by Robert K. Merton, the complex of different and distinct statuses occupied by a single individual. A person's status-set therefore changes when any one of his various statuses changes, and thus represents a person's statuses only at one particular moment of time. (R. K. Merton, *Social Theory and Social Structure*, Free Press, Glencoe, Ill., 1957.) See ROLE-SET.

status symbol. Any visible mark, object, word, or activity that is intended to convey to others an individual's or group's social status or status aspirations. Usually the term refers to social display to enhance one's prestige—to make it either equal or superior to the prestige of those persons one desires to impress. Sociologists do not widely use the term, but the general public finds it useful.

status system. An interconnected system of statuses found within a SOCIAL SYSTEM. See STATUS.

statuses, polar. Statuses that exist in pairs by virtue of the fact that each is defined in terms of its relationship to the other—for example, husband-wife, student-teacher, doctor-patient.

stereotype. 1. A set of biased generalizations about a group or category of people that is unfavorable, exaggerated, and oversimplified. Stereotyping is a form of categorizing, that is, it follows from the CATEGORICAL ATTITUDE—the tendency, characteristic of all human thought, to put things in categories. Thus there is a tendency to categorize people and to generalize, often beyond the facts, about the characteristics of the members of the category. However, stereotyping differs from other categorizing in that negative characteristics of the members of the category are emphasized, and preconceived beliefs are often emotionally toned and not susceptible of modification through empirical evidence. Although inaccurate, a stereotyped belief is maintained because it is a shared belief receiving strong support from one's reference groups. See REFERENCE GROUP.

2. A set of exaggerated and inaccurate generalizations about a group or category of people that is either favorable or unfavorable.

See PREJUDICE.

stigma, social. See SOCIAL STIGMA.

stimulus. Any factor or event that arouses a response in an organism. A stimulus may arise in either the internal or external environment.

stimulus, conditioned. A stimulus associated with a CONDITIONED RESPONSE.

stimulus, social. Any STIMULUS that is an element in the behavior of one or more persons and influences the behavior of some other person or group (for example, an attitude or expression of approval). Sociologists ordinarily do not use the term because they prefer concepts based on a more sociologically oriented MODEL rather than the stimulus-response model. See CONDITIONED RESPONSE.

stimulus, unconditioned. A stimulus that arouses a reflexive response. See REFLEX.

stimulus diffusion. See DIFFUSION, STIMULUS.

stimulus-response learning. See CONDITIONED RESPONSE; CONDITIONING.

stochastic process. A series of systematically changing probabilities of the occurrence of a particular event through time. The occurrence of an event is regarded as a PROBABILITY function of its occurrences at earlier periods. One type of stochastic process is known as a Markov chain or process. In a Markov chain, all previous periods of time are ignored except the one immediately preceding the event being analyzed, and the probability of the event is regarded as solely a function of the probability of the immediately preceding stage.

Stone Age, New. See NEOLITHIC AGE.

Stone Age, Old. See PALEOLITHIC AGE.

Stouffer's hypothesis of intervening opportunities. The ecological hypothesis that "the number of persons going a given distance is directly proportional to the number of opportunities at that distance and inversely proportional to the number of intervening opportunities." (S. A. Stouffer, *American Sociological Review,* December 1940.) This hypothesis provides a mathematical formula for population movement (migration).

strategy, power. See POWER STRATEGY.

stratification. See STRATIFICATION, SOCIAL.

stratification, economic. Stratification in a society or community expressed in the differential distribution of LIFE CHANCES, as determined by wealth and related economic advantages. In its simplest form, individuals and groups are hierarchically arranged according to their income. Since occupation is related to income, this variable is sometimes used in rough judgments of income levels. See STRATIFICATION, MARXIAN THEORY OF; STRATIFICATION, SOCIAL.

stratification, Marxian theory of. The theory, developed by Karl Marx, in which social stratification was explained primarily in economic terms. The distribution of power, prestige, styles of life, ideologies, and attitudes in a society were all regarded as essentially determined by the relationship of the various social strata to the means of production and distribution. See BOURGEOISIE; DIALECTICAL MATERIALISM; PROLETARIAT; STRATIFICATION, SOCIAL; STRATUM, SOCIAL.

stratification, social. 1. A relatively permanent ranking of statuses and roles in a SOCIAL SYSTEM (ranging from a small group to a society) in terms of differential privileges, prestige, influence, and power. Social stratification involves inequality, arising either from the actual functions performed by the persons involved or from the superior power and control of resources possessed by certain individuals or groups, or both. Societal systems of social stratification, although differing greatly in degree of emphasis on achievement or ascription, are never identical with an objective system of functional differentiation or social contribution. The advantages of power and authority (which are or tend to be inherited) serve to develop systems of stratification based, to some degree at least, on group membership (family, class, caste, race) rather than solely on a person's actual or potential functional contribution to society. See ROLE; STATUS; STATUS, ACHIEVED; STATUS, ASCRIBED.

2. The hierarchical arrangement of social strata in a society. In this sense social stratification refers specifically to the SOCIAL CLASS or CASTE system of a society. See STRATUM, SOCIAL.

stratified sample. See SAMPLE, STRATIFIED.

stratifying factor. A variable used to divide a population into strata in the selection of a stratified sample. See SAMPLE, STRATIFIED.

stratum, social. 1. A number of individuals having a relatively similar STATUS, rank, or other socially relevant characteristic or set of characteristics. The term has been used to designate any division of a population into segments or subpopulations, including not only castes and social classes, but also nonhierarchical divisions, for example, divisions based on sex, religion, age, or marital status, with no implication of ranking.

2. A segment of a population divided on a hierarchical basis. In this sense the term is limited to a population segment differentiated from other segments on the basis of prestige, power, wealth, or other criteria of rank order. Castes and social classes would be social strata in this sense. See CASTE; SOCIAL CLASS.

stress. Any unpleasant and disturbing emotional experience due to frustration (expressed, for example, in anger, anxiety, confusion, discomfort, etc.). Stress often results from an alteration of or interference with an individual's usual pattern of behavior.

stress-strain concept. The concept that a SOCIAL SYSTEM is never in a state of perfect equilibrium but always has inconsistencies among its component parts (role expectations, social institutions, etc.) producing stresses and strains. These internal stresses and strains may hinder the achievement of goals or in extreme cases threaten the survival of the system. The stress-strain concept was proposed by Alvin L. Bertrand as a means of reconciling theories emphasizing the importance of conflict and change in social organization (CONFLICT THEORY) with the emphasis on the integration, balance, and equilibrium of social systems characteristic of FUNCTIONALISM. (A. L. Bertrand, *Social Forces*, October 1963.)

structural-functional analysis. A methodological and theoretical framework for the analysis of social phenomena in terms of both the structure of the society and the functional relation of its parts. This approach is similar to the perspective of the biologist, who views the operation of the body in terms of both its structural parts and the functions they perform in the total system. Structural-functional analysis presumes that social units (groups, institutions, etc.) that are in interaction mutually influence and adjust to each other, so that through the various social processes, including cooperation, competition, conflict, and accommodation, the various groups and segments of a society form a relatively unified social system. Structural-functionalism is essentially synonymous with FUNCTIONALISM. However, the term structural-functionalism usually implies a greater emphasis on the formalistic analysis of the structural aspects of society and social systems. For examples of structural-functional analysis, see Talcott Parsons, *The Social System* (Free Press, Glencoe, Ill., 1951) and Marion J. Levy, *The Structure of Society* (Princeton University Press, Princeton, N.J., 1952). See SOCIAL STRUCTURE.

structural imperative. A pattern of behavior necessitated in a SOCIAL SYSTEM by the existence of a particular dominant pattern or structure. Given the dominant pattern (and if it is to survive), only certain other patterns of behavior or a limited range of other patterns is possible. Thus, for example, the classical Chinese Confucian bureaucracy could not have been accompanied by a system of capitalism. Structural imperatives are also called imperatives of compatibility. (See T. Parsons, *The Social System*, Free Press, Glencoe, Ill., 1951.) See FUNCTIONAL IMPERATIVE.

structural requisite. The structural counterpart of FUNCTIONAL REQUISITE.

structuralism. See PSYCHOLOGY, STRUCTURAL.

structure. The underlying and relatively stable relationship among elements, parts, or patterns in a unified, organized whole. See SOCIAL STRUCTURE.

structure, ecological. See ECOLOGICAL STRUCTURE.

structure, formal. That part of the SOCIAL STRUCTURE of a group or organization that is defined by explicitly stated rules and expectations. See STRUCTURE, INFORMAL.

structure, informal. That part of the SOCIAL STRUCTURE of a group or organization which is not explicitly stated in terms of rules and official expectations, but which results from expectations inherent in generally accepted ways of thinking or acting. The informal structure of a group, although it is not codified or readily apparent, is nevertheless significant in the patterning of behavior. See STRUCTURE, FORMAL.

structure, social. See SOCIAL STRUCTURE.

structure of attitudes, latent. See LATENT STRUCTURE ANALYSIS.

stub. See STATISTICAL TABLE.

Student's t distribution. See t TEST.

subcentralization. An ecological process in which secondary service centers develop in a large urban area. These secondary centers provide limited, basic services for their surrounding areas, but do not threaten the dominance of the CENTRAL BUSINESS DISTRICT over the entire urban area. Subcentralization is really a limited form of DECENTRALIZATION. See DOMINANCE, ECOLOGICAL; ECOLOGY, HUMAN; SERVICE CENTER.

subconscious. 1. On the fringe of consciousness; either conscious but not the focus of conscious attention, or not quite conscious but readily made so.
2. Synonymous with UNCONSCIOUS.
See CONSCIOUS EXPERIENCE.

subculture. The culture of an identifiable segment of a society. A subculture is part of the total culture of the society but it differs from the larger culture in certain respects—for example, in language, customs, values, or social norms. The extent to which a system of social norms or other cultural patterns must be distinctive to be regarded as forming a subculture has not been specifically defined. It is agreed that ethnic groups have subcultures, but writers also refer to the subcultures of occupations, adolescents, criminals, social classes, etc.

subfamily. As defined by the U.S. Census Bureau, a "married couple with or without children, or one parent with one or more own single children under 18 years old, living in a HOUSEHOLD and related to, but not including the head of the household or his wife. The most common example of a subfamily is a young married couple sharing the home of the husband's or wife's parents. Members of a subfamily are also members of a primary family. The number of subfamilies, therefore, is not included in the number of families." ("Population Characteristics," *Current Population Reports,* June 1968.) See FAMILY, PRIMARY.

subgroup. A GROUP that is part of a larger group. A subgroup may operate as a functional unit of the larger group (by performing some task considered beneficial to the group as a whole) or it may be disruptive or divisive.

subjective conception of social class. See SOCIAL CLASS, SUBJECTIVE CONCEPTION OF.

subjective method. In the analysis and evaluation of data, the application of principles that the scholar feels are justified on the basis of his knowledge but that are not completely objectively verifiable. Where there is no absolute evidence pointing to a particular solution of a problem, the scholar may marshal all of his knowledge, training, and analytical skills to reach an answer or evaluation. In a sense, the scholar regards his brain as a super-electronic computer that enables him to arrive at answers by a process too complex for programming in the relatively simple electronic computers devised by man. The subjective method is used notably in the analysis of history. See VERSTEHEN, METHOD OF.

subjective social class. See SOCIAL CLASS, SUBJECTIVE CONCEPTION OF.

subjectivism. The philosophical view that our knowledge of reality is determined entirely by our subjective experience or mind.

subjectivity. The quality that reflects the private and unique experience of an individual. The term sometimes implies that the private individual experience is not open to verification by others, and therefore it is sometimes used to refer to the biased and unscientific. However, when a number of individuals agree that their separate subjective experiences coincide, then subjective experience becomes shared, culturally objective reality. Social agreement, of course, is not necessarily final truth or reality, but what is real is known to man only in terms of what other people agree is real. The objective is necessarily a truncation of the subjective experiences of many individuals, because it consists only of what a number of people share and can agree to in common. The subjective is more complex than the objective, and for that reason it is an important source of insight and innovation. However, without the objective, the shared, and the socially verifiable, there can be no social life and therefore no human life or subjective experience. See OBJECTIVITY.

sublimation. A psychological process of adjustment to frustration in which an individual satisfies a desire for a socially unacceptable goal or activity by expressing it indirectly in a socially approved activity.

subliminal communication. A communication or message that is received by a person without his full or specific awareness. Frequently, it is apprehended as a part of a more central message and therefore it is not critically examined. In a sense, it is a hidden message. When responding to complex stimuli, a person's critical evaluations are focused on only a part of what he is experiencing. However, he also may be influenced by secondary messages that he may recall long after the experience and become "aware" of for the first time. If the secondary message is not specifically recalled but influences the person's behavior without his full awareness, or if it can be recalled but not in its original context, the message is called subliminal. Subliminal advertising as a technique is a new device for the manipulation of the public, but the use of secondary messages is really as old as human communication. All humans communicate not merely a central message, but a series of secondary messages that are not explicit, but that have an impact.

subordination. The act or process by which an individual or group is placed or treated as lower in rank in relation to another person (or group) that exercises greater authority, power, or influence. See SUPERORDINATION.

subpopulation. See STRATUM, SOCIAL.

substantive theory. See THEORY, SUBSTANTIVE.

substitution. The replacing of an unattainable goal or satisfaction with one that is possible to obtain.

substructure. A subdivision of a SOCIAL STRUCTURE. See ORGANIZATION, SOCIAL.

suburb. A relatively small community that is part of the urbanized area adjacent to and dependent on a central CITY. It may be attached to a METROPOLIS or to a nonmetropolitan city. A suburb is politically independent from the central city, but economically dependent upon it for either employment, goods, services, or workers (or a combination of these). The exact nature of the relationship between the suburb and the central city depends upon the type of suburb. The term *suburb* implies some degree of community awareness and organization as contrasted to the more amorphous "URBAN FRINGE." See CITY, SATELLITE; HINTERLAND; METROPOLITAN AREA.

suburb, employing. A SUBURB that serves as a center of employment, as contrasted to the predominantly residential suburb. Employing suburbs include industrial suburbs as well as those that are centers for mining, education, recreation, or any other activity that gives rise to jobs. See SUBURB, INDUSTRIAL; SUBURB, RESIDENTIAL.

suburb, industrial. A SUBURB that is a manufacturing center. In large metropolitan areas heavy industry is frequently located outside of the central city because of the lower cost of land and taxes and greater ease of transportation, thus forming suburban communities that are predominantly industrial in character. The industrial suburb is the most common type of employing suburb. See SUBURB, EMPLOYING.

suburb, residential. A SUBURB that serves primarily as a residential area. It does not provide employment for most of its population and is not a center of employment for persons residing elsewhere. Most of its population is dependent upon employment in the central city or in other suburbs. Residential suburbs are sometimes referred to as dormitory or bedroom suburbs because the working population sleep there and spend most of the day elsewhere. The residential suburbs form the commuters' zone of the METROPOLITAN AREA.

suburbanization. The movement of population and services from large cities to the areas surrounding these cities, with the result that the cities are ringed by an array of suburbs beyond their political limits. Suburbanization is a reflection of the processes of DECONCENTRATION and DECENTRALIZATION. It has been made possible on a vast scale by the development of the automobile, which permits a dispersed population to commute to work in scattered parts of the metropolitan area. Suburbanization has resulted in a proliferation of small, independent political units in vast metropolitan areas. See METROPOLITAN AREA; SUBURB.

succession. An ecological process involving the replacement of one type of occupancy of an area by another type. Succession is the completion of the process begun by INVASION (in which a new type of land use or population challenges the established occupants). Succession occurs when the invaders become the dominant occupants of the area. It may involve the supplanting of residential land use by commercial use, of single family dwellings by multiple dwelling units, of one socioeconomic level by another socioeconomic level, of one racial or ethnic group by a different racial or ethnic group, and so forth. See ECOLOGY, HUMAN.

sufficient condition. In CAUSATION, a condition whose existence always results in the occurrence of a given event. The condition is sufficient to produce the event. A sufficient condition may or may not be necessary (that is, have to exist if the event is to occur). In other words, there may be more than one condition sufficient to produce the same event. See NECESSARY CONDITION.

sufficient statistic. See STATISTIC, SUFFICIENT.

suggestion. A psychological process in which one person influences the attitude or behavior of another person indirectly, so that the person being influenced is uncritical and unaware of the reasons for his acceptance of the communication.

suicide. Death resulting either from a deliberate act of self-destruction or from inaction when it is known that inaction will have fatal consequences.

suicide, altruistic. A type of SUICIDE in which an individual who is very closely integrated into a group or society kills himself for the welfare of the group. Altruistic suicide is motivated by a desire to serve the needs of the group. It is suicide based on self-sacrifice and tends to occur in social systems that deemphasize the importance of the individual. The Japanese hara-kiri is a way to destroy oneself rather than disgrace one's family or group. A soldier who throws himself on a grenade to save others is also committing altruistic suicide. Altruistic suicide is one of the three types of suicide distinguished by Émile Durkheim. It should be noted that in both altruistic and egoistic suicide a strong personal value system exists in the individual, as it does not in anomic suicide. (É. Durkheim, *Suicide*, tr. by J. A. Spaulding and G. Simpson, Routledge & Kegan Paul, London, 1952.) See SUICIDE, ANOMIC; SUICIDE, EGOISTIC.

suicide, anomic. A type of SUICIDE that results from normlessness or social and personal disorganization. The value system of the group no longer has meaning for the individual, and he feels isolated, lonely, and confused. Any disruption of a way of life may lead to this type of suicide. For a rich man suddenly to become poor—or a poor man suddenly to become rich—might lead to a catastrophic breakdown in the established normative integration of the individual's personality. Anomic (*anomique*) suicide, then, is a result of not being properly integrated into a system of cultural values, and thus feeling isolated and regarding the social norms as meaningless. The incidence of anomic suicide would presumably be greater in societies that experience a high rate of social change, with a rapid disintegration of traditional social expectations. It would also tend to be higher among certain categories of individuals, such as the divorced and unmarried. Émile Durkheim distinguished anomic suicide, which is also called normless suicide, from altruistic suicide and egoistic suicide. (É. Durkheim, *Suicide*, tr. by J. A. Spaulding and G. Simpson, Routledge & Kegan Paul, London, 1952.) See ANOMIE; DISORGANIZATION, PERSONAL; DISORGANIZATION, SOCIAL; SUICIDE, ALTRUISTIC; SUICIDE, EGOISTIC.

suicide, egoistic. SUICIDE that is due to the existence of strong social norms for which the individual is made to feel personally responsible, resulting in an overwhelming burden on the individual. The group itself is not strong enough to provide the individual with a sufficient source of support and strength outside himself. Nor is it sufficiently integrated to be able collectively to mitigate the individual's feeling of responsibility and guilt for moral weaknesses and failure. Egoistic suicide is due to a strong value system, weak group integration, and an overpowering sense of personal responsibility. This type of suicide was distinguished by Émile Durkheim. Durkheim found the suicide rate in the latter half of the nineteenth century highest for Protestants and lowest for Jews, with Catholics in between. For Durkheim's other two types of suicide, see SUICIDE, ALTRUISTIC and SUICIDE, ANOMIC. (É. Durkheim, *Suicide*, tr. by J. A. Spaulding and G. Simpson, Routledge & Kegan Paul, London, 1952.)

suicide, normless. See SUICIDE, ANOMIC.

summated scale. An attitude scale consisting of a series of items (attitude statements, a list of objects) to each of which an individual indicates a positive or negative response (agreement or disagreement, favorableness or unfavorableness). The number of possible responses to each item may be limited to two (such as "agree" or "disagree") or may comprise a series of graded categories (for example, from "strongly agree" to "strongly disagree"). The individual's response to each item is given a numerical value (or plus or minus if there are only two possible responses to each item) that indicates its favorableness or unfavorableness. The sum of the respondent's scores on the individual items gives his total score, which is used to place him on a positive-negative scale on the particular attitude. The most frequently used type of summated scale is the LIKERT SCALE. See SCALE, ATTITUDE.

superego. According to Freudian theory, the aspect of the self that has internalized social norms. It is similar to the concept of conscience, or the ethical or moral self. Sigmund Freud viewed personality or self as composed of EGO (SELF), ID (innate impulses), and superego. Presumably the superego develops between two and one-half and six years of age.

Through the ego, the superego acts to control the impulses of the id. See INTERNALIZATION; SOCIALIZATION.

superordination. The act or process by which an individual or group is placed or treated as higher in rank or position in relation to another individual or group. See SUBORDINATION.

superorganic. Of or pertaining to cultural phenomena, as distinguished from biological or organic phenomena. The term emphasizes the social and cultural nature of social life as against purely biological interpretations of behavior.

superstition. A belief about natural phenomena that depends upon a magical or occult interpretation of events and that is widely held to be true in spite of objectively demonstrable facts to the contrary.

surplus value. In Marxian theory, the economic value created by the productivity of the proletariat that is not returned to the laborer (who receives the barest subsistence wage), but is appropriated as profit by the entrepreneur, who supports himself in luxury.

surrogate. A social role in which a person becomes a substitute parent or relative.

survey. See SOCIAL SURVEY.

survival, cultural. See CULTURAL SURVIVAL.

survival of species. See EVOLUTION.

sustenance relations. Those social relations in a population that are directly related to survival in a particular habitat. Sustenance relations provide the social organization for the production and distribution of goods and services. The term has been used primarily in human ecology. See ECOLOGY, HUMAN.

syllogism. A logical formula used to test the validity of reasoning, consisting of a major premise, a minor premise, and a conclusion. From the two premises the conclusion necessarily follows (and is therefore necessarily true if the premises are granted to be true). The syllogism is used to simplify complex reasoning into its simplest logical parts.

symbiosis. In sociology, relation of mutual dependence between unlike and distinct groups within a community that works to their mutual advantage. See COMMENSALISM; ECOLOGY, HUMAN.

symbol. An arbitrary SIGN that evokes a uniform social response. The meaning of a symbol is arbitrary in the sense that it is not inherent in the sound, object, event, etc., but is derived from the common learning and consensus of the people who use it in communication. Human beings communicate with each other symbolically with words, gestures, and actions.

A word, a flag, a wedding ring, and a number are examples of symbols. Symbols are not within the experience of animals. A symbol is sometimes referred to as a conventional sign. See CULTURE; LANGUAGE.

symbol, collective. See COLLECTIVE REPRESENTATION.

symbol, significant. As defined by George H. Mead, a GESTURE or learned symbol that is used consciously to convey a meaning from one person to another, and that has the same meaning for the person transmitting it as for the person receiving it. It is a mutually understood symbol. (G. H. Mead, *Mind, Self and Society,* University of Chicago Press, Chicago, 1934.)

symbolic gesture. 1. A physical GESTURE that performs an essentially linguistic function by communicating an emotional feeling or attitude, as for example, a handshake, a salute, clapping.
2. As used by George H. Mead, a conscious gesture (either physical or verbal) whose meaning is understood by the individual using it. See SYMBOL, SIGNIFICANT.

symbolic interaction. The typical form of communication and interaction characteristic of human social life, involving either LANGUAGE or symbolic gestures. See SYMBOL; SYMBOLIC GESTURE.

symbolic interactionism. A form of social behaviorism in the social-psychological branch of sociology (particularly the approach of George H. Mead) that stresses linguistic and gestural communication, especially the role of language in the formation of the mind, the self, and society. This theoretically important approach to social psychology can be found in the writings of such sociologists as Charles H. Cooley, W. I. Thomas, Florian Znaniecki, Kimball Young, Herbert Blumer, Nelson N. Foote, and Walter Coutu. (See J. G. Manis and B. N. Meltzer, eds., *Symbolic Interaction,* Allyn & Bacon, Boston, 1967.) See BEHAVIORISM, SOCIAL.

symbolic model. See MODEL, SYMBOLIC.

symbolic values, ecological hypothesis of. The hypothesis proposed by Walter Firey that land not only has economic value, but also may have symbolic value and that the symbolic value may at times be more important than economic factors in determining its use. Thus land use cannot always be explained in purely rational, economic terms. Firey supported this hypothesis with data from Boston. (W. Firey, *Land Use in Central Boston,* Harvard University Press, Cambridge, Mass., 1947.) See ECOLOGY, HUMAN.

symmetrical curve. See FREQUENCY DISTRIBUTION, SYMMETRICAL.

symmetrical relationship. See RELATIONSHIP, SYMMETRICAL.

sympathetic introspection. As defined by Charles H. Cooley, a method of social analysis (similar to Max Weber's method of *verstehen*) by which a person tries to experience the feelings and attitudes of others through intimate contact and participation in their way of life, and then to analyze how they think and feel, using his insight into his own motivations and nature as well as his understanding of those he has studied. (C. H. Cooley, *Social Organization,* Scribner, New York, 1909.) See VERSTEHEN, METHOD OF.

sympathy. A compassionate sharing of another's feelings, emotions, and attitudes by imaginatively putting oneself in the position of the other person. See EMPATHY.

sympatric groups. Two or more cultural groups that occupy the same or overlapping territorial areas, without a loss of their separate identities. See ALLOPATRIC GROUP.

syncretism. The union of distinct elements drawn from different systems into a new whole or system. Cultural syncretism is the fusion of distinctive beliefs and practices of one culture into another. See CULTURE CONTACT; DIFFUSION.

syndicalism. A radical form of SOCIALISM, strong at the turn of the century, that aimed to overthrow the existing society and economy completely through general strikes and to put both in the hands of syndicates or unions of workers. It opposed government ownership of the means of production and distribution and all forms of state power, and favored instead the cooperation in a loose federation of the separate autonomous syndicates for the general welfare. See ANARCHISM.

synergy. 1. Combined effort; the total amount of effort or energy available to a group for a given purpose.

2. Unplanned and unrecognized cooperation; the combined effect of behavior that is individually motivated but nevertheless results in social organization.

system. An organization of interrelated and interdependent parts that form a unity. A system is a conceptual MODEL used to facilitate investigation and analysis of complex phenomena. Systems are usually treated as though they are not part of larger systems, but in reality a system is usually an abstraction from a larger system (and usually contains smaller systems), particularly in the case of social systems. Thus, in reality, systems are never stable, in perfect equilibrium, or completely predictive.

system, social. See SOCIAL SYSTEM.

systematic sample. See SAMPLE, SYSTEMATIC.

systematic sociology. See SOCIOLOGY, SYSTEMATIC.

systems analysis. A theoretical approach of importance in many scientific disciplines, in which emphasis is placed on analysis in terms of organization and interrelationships rather than on the study of separate units or entities. In sociology, systems analysis focuses on the MODEL of the socio-cultural system and the analysis of society and culture in terms of this model. However, the proponents of systems analysis emphasize that their model does not involve the fallacies of the older mechanical or organismic models. In contrast to earlier mechanical- or organismic-type models, modern systems models emphasize the integration of the sociocultural system in terms of networks of information and communication. Thus systems analysis in sociology is closely allied with CYBERNETICS and INFORMATION THEORY. Another important characteristic of systems analysis is that, by conceiving of systems as involved in a constant process of adaptation to their environment and internal reorganization, the attempt is made to build into the model conceptions of conflict, change, and process. Thus systems analysis attempts to avoid the criticisms of excessive emphasis on equilibrium and integration leveled at FUNCTIONALISM. (See W. Buckley, *Sociology and Modern Systems Theory*, Prentice-Hall, Englewood Cliffs, N.J., 1967.) See MECHANISTIC ANALOGY; ORGANICISM.

T

t distribution, Student's. See t TEST.

T score. A Z SCORE (standard score) that has been modified by multiplying it by ten and adding fifty in order to eliminate negative, zero, and decimal scores.

t test. A statistical test used to determine the PROBABILITY that a STATISTIC (summarizing value for a sample) obtained from SAMPLE data is merely a reflection of a chance variation in the sample(s) rather than a measure of a true population PARAMETER. In other words, t, which is based upon the ratio of a statistic to its STANDARD ERROR, is used to determine the level of significance of a statistic of a certain size obtained from a sample of a certain size. The t test is used instead of the CRITICAL RATIO when the size of the sample is small. The SAMPLING DISTRIBUTION of t, sometimes referred to as Student's distribution or Student's t distribution, does not exactly coincide with a normal frequency distribution curve because, with a small sample, the probability of more extreme deviations is greater than with a large sample. As the size of the sample increases, the distribution of t approaches a normal curve. With very large samples the t distribution becomes a normal probability curve. The calculation of t for any statistic takes into account the size of the sample from which the statistic was obtained. See FREQUENCY DISTRIBUTION CURVE, NORMAL; PROBABILITY; SIGNIFICANCE, STATISTICAL.

T test, Wilcoxon. See WILCOXON MATCHED-PAIRS SIGNED RANKS TEST.

table. See STATISTICAL TABLE.

taboo (tabu). A strong social norm prohibiting certain actions that are punishable by the group or community, by the supernatural, or by magical consequences.

taboo, mother-in-law. See MOTHER-IN-LAW TABOO.

taboo, universal. A taboo found in all societies. The incest taboo is generally regarded as the only universal taboo; however, definitions of IN-CEST vary in different societies.

tabula rasa fallacy. The "myth that the true scientist starts by observing the facts without any conceptual anticipations." (J. C. McKinney in *Modern Sociological Theory*, edited by H. Becker and A. Boskoff, Dryden Press, New York, 1957.)

tabulation. In statistics, the enumeration of the number of cases that fall in each CATEGORY or CLASS INTERVAL (subdivision) of a VARIABLE. Tabulation is often the first step in the analysis of data. See CROSS-TABULATION.

TAT. See THEMATIC APPERCEPTION TEST.

tau test. See KENDALL TAU TEST.

technicways. A term used by Howard W. Odum to refer to the modern behavior patterns of a scientific and technological civilization that have replaced the traditional folkways and mores. According to Odum, the technicways lack the stabilizing and cumulative character of the folkways and MORES and are specific technical responses to specific technical problems. (H. W. Odum, *Understanding Society*, Macmillan, New York, 1947.) The term has not been widely adopted in sociology. See FOLKWAY.

technique. A specific, culturally patterned means of attaining a given end. Techniques are learned, and may require the acquisition of specialized skills. Techniques may be simple or complex. They may involve manual actions, as in the techniques of a skilled craft; or they may be primarily intellectual, as in the case of statistical techniques; or social, as in the techniques of leadership.

technological unemployment. Unemployment due to the introduction of automation or other technological changes into industry or other work places.

technology. That segment of culture, including knowledge and tools, that man uses to manipulate his physical environment in order to achieve desired practical ends. Scientific knowledge applied to practical problems of providing goods and services is part of modern technology.

teknonymy. The custom or practice of identifying a parent through one of his children, as "father of Robert."

telesis. See SOCIAL TELESIS.

telic change. Change due to human planning to achieve some purpose, in contrast to change that occurs without an over-all control of its nature and direction. See SOCIAL TELESIS.

temperament. The general, prevailing, and characteristic emotional attitudes or mood of a person, perhaps partly innate but clearly and strongly influenced by the process of socialization.

temperament, hypothesis of innate. The as yet to be demonstrated hypothesis that each person's basic temperament stems from biological factors reflected in observed differences in the behavior of infants. Placid infants should, by this hypothesis, become placid adults. In evaluating this hypothesis some care would need to be exercised in the study of the way the mother handles her baby—which could reflect the mother's attitude toward the child, rather than the inborn character of the child's temperament.

temporocentrism. The "unexamined and largely unconscious acceptance of one's own century, one's own era, one's own lifetime, as the center of sociological significance, as the focus to which all other periods of historical time are related, and as the criterion by which they are judged." (R. Bierstedt, *American Journal of Sociology*, July 1948.) See ETHNOCENTRISM.

tendency. 1. A recurrent behavior sequence; a pattern in which a certain action is usually followed by another particular action or reaction.

2. In statistical analysis, essentially equivalent to PROBABILITY, but sometimes used synonymously with TREND.

tendency in situation. See TINSIT.

tension. A state of emotionally charged stress due to frustrated or conflicting motivations and an inability to act in a manner that resolves the problem.

territorial group. See LOCALITY GROUP.

tertiary occupation. See OCCUPATION, TERTIARY.

test. 1. A device for the systematic measurement and comparison of individuals in regard to a specified characteristic.

2. See STATISTICAL TEST.

test, empirical. See EMPIRICAL TEST.

test, performance. See PERFORMANCE TEST.

test, projective. See PROJECTIVE TECHNIQUE.

test, statistical. See STATISTICAL TEST.

test, verbal. See VERBAL TEST.

test of aptitude. See APTITUDE TEST.

test of intelligence. See INTELLIGENCE TEST.

test score. See SCORE, NORMATIVE; SCORE, RAW; T SCORE; Z SCORE.

testimonial. A PROPAGANDA technique in which a famous or prestigeful person of the past or present (or an infamous and disliked person) is claimed to support or have supported (or oppose or have opposed) an idea, movement, or the like that the propagandist wishes to promote (or discourage).

thematic apperception test. In psychology, a PROJECTIVE TECHNIQUE for the study of personality in which the subject is asked to respond to a series of ambiguous pictures by creating stories about each of them. An analysis of each of the stories is used to study the attitudes, values, and role conflicts the subject is experiencing or has experienced in actual social interaction, which he may not wish or be able to discuss directly. The test is often referred to as the TAT.

theme. See CULTURAL THEME.

theorem. An established and accepted GENERALIZATION based on empirical observations or derived by logical reasoning from postulates, other theorems, or laws. A theorem thus may be derived by deduction or INDUCTION or both. See LAW, SCIENTIFIC; POSTULATE.

theoretic bias. A methodological approach, suggested by Robert Bierstedt, in which the theorist deliberately uses exaggeration as a heuristic device in his theory construction. A particular interpretation of social phenomena is developed and extended to its limit, in order to shed illumination on theoretical problems that cannot be adequately handled by current methods and interpretations. "Thus, Marx used the theoretic bias to support the role of the economic factor, Buckle the geographic factor, Freud the psychological, Weber the ideological, Durkheim the sociological (in a special sense), and so on. Each of these thinkers was lured into excess by his enthusiasm for his own bias and each was surely guilty of exaggeration. The greatest thinkers, however, have not been the neutral and objective ones, but those who have turned their biases to good account." (R. Bierstedt, *American Sociological Review*, February 1960.) See HEURISTIC ASSUMPTION.

theoretical mode. See MODE, TRUE.

theory. 1. A set of interrelated principles and definitions that serves conceptually to organize selected aspects of the empirical world in a systematic way. A theory includes a basic set of assumptions and axioms as the foundation, and the body of the theory composed of logically interrelated, empirically verifiable propositions. Although usage varies, the propositions that comprise a theory may be regarded as scientific laws if they have been sufficiently verified to be widely accepted, or as hypotheses if they have not been that well verified. In either case the propositions that comprise a theory are constantly subject to further empirical testing and revision. Through the process of DEDUCTION a theory provides specific hypotheses for research, and through INDUCTION research data provide generalizations to be incorporated into and to modify a theory. The essence of theory is that it attempts to explain a wide variety of empirical phenomena in a parsimonious way.

The philosophical and methodological assumptions that underlie theory (for example, assumptions concerning the nature of causation) are a part of theory primarily because they are related to the same empirical facts. Methodological and philosophical assumptions are higher level generalizations about the empirical world and are crucial in the ordering of empirical reality. See AXIOM; HYPOTHESIS; LAW, SCIENTIFIC.

2. As defined by some writers, either theory related to or theory embodying empirical propositions. See METASOCIOLOGY; THEORY, SUBSTANTIVE.

3. A generalization intermediate in degree of verification between a law and a HYPOTHESIS. See LAW, SCIENTIFIC.

4. Sometimes, loosely, a HYPOTHESIS.

theory, broad. In sociology, a THEORY that includes a large number of interrelated propositions and provides a major conceptual scheme in terms of which a wide range of human behavior can be explained. See THEORY, MIDDLE-RANGE.

theory, cumulative. THEORY built upon a succession of previous theories that have been steadily revised through the extension, modification, and refinement of the propositions that comprise the theory. This process of revision is based on the accumulation of new empirical data as well as the application of logical analysis to the propositions and the nature of their interrelationships.

theory, empirical. THEORY that attempts to avoid value judgments and describe the empirical world as objectively and accurately as possible. Scientific theory is empirical theory. See THEORY, NORMATIVE.

theory, methodological. See METASOCIOLOGY.

theory, middle-range. In sociology, a theory that is "intermediate to the minor working hypotheses evolved in abundance during the day-by-day routines of research, and the all-inclusive speculations comprising a master conceptual scheme from which it is hoped to derive a very large number of empirically observed uniformities of social behavior." (R. K. Merton, *Social Theory and Social Structure,* Free Press, Glencoe, Ill., 1957.) A middle-range theory attempts to explain a limited area of human behavior. It is sometimes referred to as a miniature theory. See THEORY, BROAD.

theory, miniature. See THEORY, MIDDLE-RANGE.

theory, normative. A theory consisting of interrelated propositions that prescribe the means of attaining certain goals. The goals are determined by the values (axioms) upon which the theory is based. The acceptance of these values is assumed. Normative theory may be used in an attempt to provide a systematic course of action for the solution of a social problem or in some other applied field. Normative theory is not scientific theory. It selects principles from scientific theory and formulates them in a value- and action-oriented framework. See THEORY, EMPIRICAL.

theory, scientific. See THEORY.

theory, sociological. THEORY that attempts to provide systematic explanations and predictions relating to the nature, patterns, and dynamics of human social interaction. A sociological theory integrates into a coherent pattern individual observations and insights about social life. The ideas about society expressed by early sociologists such as Max Weber, Émile Durkheim, George H. Mead, and Georg Simmel, are often spoken of as theoretical because much of their work dealt with basic assumptions and principles of social structure and process, and forms the logical and conceptual framework of modern sociological thought. Sociological theory may be regarded in its broadest sense as dealing with methodological and philosophical assumptions, as well as substantive propositions. However, some writers regard it as essentially substantive in nature. See METASOCIOLOGY; THEORY, SUBSTANTIVE.

theory, substantive. In sociology, THEORY that relates directly to the empirical social world—that makes truth claims concerning social reality, as opposed to theory that is concerned with methodological assumptions. This distinction between substantive theory and METASOCIOLOGY is made by Robert Bierstedt. (R. Bierstedt in *Symposium on Sociological Theory,* edited by L. Gross, Row, Peterson, Evanston, Ill., 1959.)

theory, systematic. A system of propositions or laws that is especially well integrated, with logical or causal connections between all of the individual propositions and all the possible logical interrelationships between the propositions and the implications of each proposition for every other proposition explicitly recognized and accounted for.

thief, professional. See PROFESSIONAL THIEF.

thinking. The process of mental manipulation of cultural and social images, symbols, and ideas.

thinking, autistic. See AUTISTIC THINKING.

Thomas' four wishes. See WISHES, THOMAS' FOUR.

Thomas theorem. See SELF-FULFILLING PROPHECY.

thought, social. See SOCIAL THOUGHT.

Thurstone equal-appearing interval scale. A type of attitude scale, developed by Louis L. Thurstone, consisting of a series of items (attitude statements) that the respondent rates, either as agree/disagree or by choosing the two or three he most agrees with. To construct a Thurstone scale, the investigator gathers a large number of statements (usually several hundred) relating to the attitude being studied. These statements are given to from fifty to several hundred judges, who individually and independently classify the statements into eleven categories, from one extreme (such as most favorable) to the opposite (most unfavorable). The middle (sixth) category is regarded as neutral. The classifications of the judges are compared. Those statements on which there is a great deal of disagreement among the judges are discarded. The investigator then selects a certain number of statements (usually about twenty) on which there is sufficient consensus among the judges and which provide an even representation of the categories. Each statement is given a scale value that is the value of the median category of the categories to which it was assigned by the judges. The respondent's scale score is the median or mean value of the statements with which he agrees. In developing this scale Thurstone was attempting to approximate an INTERVAL SCALE (in which the units are equally spaced); however, most writers feel that it is more accurate to regard it as an ORDINAL SCALE. See SCALE, ATTITUDE.

time, social. Time perceived according to social and cultural reference points. "The category of astronomical time is only one of several concepts of time. . . . social phenomena are frequently adopted as a frame of reference so that units of time are often fixed by the rhythm of collective life. The need for social collaboration is at the root of social systems of time. Social time is qualitatively differentiated according to the beliefs and customs common to the group." (P. A. Sorokin and R. K. Merton, *American Journal of Sociology*, March 1937.)

time series. The arrangement of a series of measures or observations of a variable in the sequence of their occurrence at successive points of time. Various categories of time may be used (weeks, months, years, etc.). The data are arranged to show the number of occurrences or the magnitude of the variable in each period of time, for example, size of per capita income in each month of a given year. See CYCLICAL MOVEMENT; FLUCTUATION, PERIODIC; SEASONAL VARIATION; TREND, SECULAR.

tinsit. An abbreviation for tendency-in-situation. The term was introduced by Walter Coutu to refer to the probable behavior of an individual in a given situation. "The tinsit is an inference based on frequency of a given behavior in a given situation, or on frequency of type-response in a type-situation, or on frequency of related responses in type-situations. It thus involves the application of statistical operations to the study of individual, as well as group, behavior." (W. Coutu, *Emergent Human Nature*, Knopf, New York, 1949.) Coutu distinguished two types of tinsit: somatic tinsit and personic tinsit. Somatic tinsit refers to physiologically determined behavior tendencies, while personic tinsit refers to socially and psychologically determined behavior tendencies.

tolerance limits. See CONFIDENCE LIMITS.

toleration. A form of ACCOMMODATION in which opposing groups that cannot agree take the attitude that despite differences and disagreements with each other, harmony and avoidance of conflict is the most acceptable and practical solution. "Live and let live" is a minimal statement of toleration.

Tomkins-Horn picture arrangement test. In psychology, a PROJECTIVE TECHNIQUE for studying personality in which the subject is given a set of pictures and asked to arrange them in the most logical sequence. Interpretations about the subject's personality are made on the basis of his arrangement of the pictures.

topological psychology. See FIELD THEORY.

totalitarianism. A form of society in which the state controls and regulates all phases of life considered essential for perpetuating its power and for carrying out programs arbitrarily deemed best for the society. Centralized authority is stressed over the autonomy of individuals or subgroups within the society. The state is in practice represented by a politically powerful ruling class or elite that dominates all other interest groups. Various types or doctrines of government have been described as totalitarian (notably Nazi Germany and Stalinist Russia).

totem. A class of objects, usually a species of animal (sometimes a type of plant or inanimate object), that is regarded by a CLAN, LINEAGE, or other social group as having a special relationship to the social unit. See TOTEMISM.

totemism. A complex of beliefs organized about a TOTEM. The totem is regarded as having a special relationship to the members of the totemic group. Often the members of a CLAN or LINEAGE believe that they are in some way descended from a totem animal. The mystical relationship with the totemic object is frequently an important principle in the social organization of a group. Émile Durkheim suggested that totemism was an early and elementary form of religion that provided a collective religious object which was a powerful factor in developing social cohesion within early society. (É. Durkheim, *The Elementary Forms of the Religious Life*, tr. by J. W. Swain, Free Press, Glencoe, Ill., 1947.)

town. 1. A small urban settlement, larger than a HAMLET or VILLAGE and smaller than a CITY. It often is a focal point of a rural trade area.

2. In certain states of the U.S., a township, that is, an administrative area that is unincorporated but has definite boundaries.

tract. See CENSUS TRACT.

trade, silent. See SILENT TRADE.

trade area. A geographical area economically dominated by a CITY, TOWN, or VILLAGE that serves as a finance and TRADE CENTER.

trade center. A CITY, TOWN, or VILLAGE that serves as the marketing and financial center of a geographic area (TRADE AREA).

trade union. See UNION, TRADE.

trade village. See VILLAGE, CRAFT.

tradition. A social custom passed down from one generation to another through the process of SOCIALIZATION. Traditions represent the beliefs, values, and ways of thinking of a social group. Folkways, MORES, and myths are examples of traditions. See FOLKWAY; MYTH.

tradition, oral. See ORAL TRADITION.

tradition-directed society. An abstract or IDEAL TYPE of society which "develops in its typical members a social character whose conformity is insured by their tendency to follow tradition." (D. Riesman, N. Glazer, R. Denney, *The Lonely Crowd*, Doubleday, New York, 1954.) In common practice the concept of tradition-directedness is often applied to an ideal type of individual and termed *tradition-directed man.* See INNER-DIRECTED SOCIETY; OTHER-DIRECTED SOCIETY.

traditional authority. See AUTHORITY, TRADITIONAL.

traditionalism. The attitude or philosophy that the established patterns of the past are the best guides in deciding behavior in the present and the future. See CONSERVATISM.

trained incapacity. A reduction in personal flexibility that takes place when the very training and experience that give an expert competence in his specialized field also act to narrow his range of perception, make him unable to envision new possibilities, and render him ineffective under changed conditions. The term was derived from the writings of Thorstein Veblen, who used it primarily with reference to large-scale businessmen, particularly the financiers of capitalism, but since his time sociologists have used it to refer to any inadequacy or "blindness" due to specialization. (T. Veblen, *The Engineers and the Price System*, Viking, New York, 1933.)

trait, culture. See CULTURE TRAIT.

trait, personality. See PERSONALITY TRAIT.

trait complex. See CULTURE COMPLEX.

transference. The displacement of emotions and feelings (positive or negative) from one person (or object) to another. In psychotherapy a patient may transfer feelings of admiration or hostility to the therapist. In PROPAGANDA, one may try to manipulate public attitudes by associating an admired (or disliked) person or object with an idea, product, or the like toward which the propagandist wishes to stimulate a given attitude, with the hope that transference of affect will achieve the desired result.

transition, demographic. See DEMOGRAPHIC TRANSITION.

transition, zone in. See ZONE IN TRANSITION.

transmission. See CULTURAL TRANSMISSION.

transmutation, cultural. CULTURE CHANGE that occurs inadvertently because of the difficulty each generation has in exactly reproducing the behavior and ideas of the preceding generation. Thus some changes in language are presumably due to the cumulative effect of the imperfect imitation by children of their parents' vowels and consonants. The term was introduced by Edward A. Ross. (E. A. Ross in *Social Control and the Foundations of Sociology*, edited by E. F. Borgatta and H. J. Meyer, Beacon, Boston, 1959.)

transportation hypothesis, break in. See BREAK IN TRANSPORTATION HYPOTHESIS OR THEORY.

transposition, ethnic. See ETHNIC TRANSPOSITION.

trauma. A mental shock, as, for example, when a person is unexpectedly disgraced in the eyes of his friends, or when a situation occurs in which a person's self-conception is radically challenged by his actual performance or by the attitudes of others, or when a social relationship is destroyed, as in the case of death or divorce.

trend. In statistics, a steady change in a VARIABLE or set of related variables in a certain direction (for example, a steadily increasing magnitude or frequency of occurrence of a variable) for a period of time. See TREND, SECULAR.

trend, empirical. A TREND found in a set of data for which the investigator has no logical or theoretical explanation. Such a trend is usually identified simply to eliminate its influence from consideration in the analysis of CYCLICAL MOVEMENT. See TREND, RATIONAL.

trend, linear. A TREND in which the rate of change remains constant. If it were plotted on a graph, it would form a straight line. See TREND, NONLINEAR.

trend, nonlinear. A TREND in which the rate of change is not constant but varies from one period of time to another. If it were plotted on a graph, it would not form a straight line. Most trends are nonlinear. See TREND, LINEAR.

trend, rational. A TREND for which the investigator has a logical or theoretical explanation and which he is interested in analyzing. See TREND, EMPIRICAL.

trend, secular. A long-term TREND, that is, a trend that persists for a long enough period of time so that it is clearly not merely a phase in a CYCLICAL MOVEMENT. Cyclical fluctuations may occur in the course of a secular trend, but there is always a clear, long-range movement in a certain direction despite the short-run variations.

trend, social. Any observable gradual and persistent change in social behavior and social structure over a specified period of time. There are trends in family size, participation in religious organizations, urbanization, suburbanization, etc.

trial and error. An effort to learn a skill or solve a problem by exploring alternate possibilities without establishing a planned, systematic procedure. The leads that fail are discarded and those that are successful are followed.

tribal analogy. An analogy in which the social structure of a modern industrial community is treated as similar to that of a tribe. The term was used by Walter Goldschmidt in criticizing the practice of certain theorists of using a few informants in studying a modern community, in the same way anthropologists use a few informants to study a small, isolated tribe. Goldschmidt argues that, in fact, a modern community is not analogous to an isolated tribe, and therefore the same techniques are not properly applicable. (W. Goldschmidt, *American Anthropologist,* October–December 1950.)

tribe. In most usage, a nonliterate community or a collection of such communities occupying a common geographic area and having a similar language and culture.

trickle effect. The "tendency in U.S. society (and perhaps to a lesser extent in Western societies generally) for new styles or fashions in consumption goods to be introduced via the socioeconomic elite and then to pass down through the status hierarchy, often in the form of inexpensive, mass-produced copies." (L. A. Fallers, *Public Opinion Quarterly,* Fall 1954.)

truce. A form of ACCOMMODATION in which persons or groups in active conflict temporarily or permanently suspend hostile actions without the conflict's being resolved or the issues settled.

turnover. See LABOR TURNOVER.

twin cities. An AGGLOMERATION comprised of two cities bordering each other and forming a single ecological community, but remaining administratively separate. Minneapolis–St. Paul and Kansas City, Kansas–Kansas City, Missouri are examples of twin cities divided by rivers.

twins, dizygotic. Fraternal twins, or twins that develop from two separate eggs. Dizygotic twins are no more alike than are siblings in general, and may therefore be of different sexes. See TWINS, MONOZYGOTIC.

twins, fraternal. See TWINS, DIZYGOTIC.

twins, identical. See TWINS, MONOZYGOTIC.

twins, monozygotic. Identical twins, or twins that develop from a single fertilized egg and thus have the same hereditary structure. See TWINS, DIZYGOTIC.

twins, separated one-egg. Monozygotic twins socialized (raised) separately from a very early age so that their social and psychological experiences differ. Separated one-egg twins are often studied to attempt to determine the differential effects of environmental and hereditary factors in personality development. See SOCIALIZATION; TWINS, MONOZYGOTIC.

two-tailed test. A STATISTICAL TEST used to test a hypothesis when the direction of the difference between samples or relationship between variables is not predicted in the hypothesis. That is, the null hypothesis merely states that there will not be a significant difference between the samples, or relationship between the variables, and the alternative hypothesis does not specify which sample will be further in a given direction (score higher, be more favorable, etc.) if there is a difference, or if there is a relationship between the variables whether it will be positive or negative. The term *two-tailed* refers to the fact that there is a REGION OF REJECTION of the null hypothesis at both ends (or tails) of the SAMPLING DISTRIBUTION. See HYPOTHESIS, ALTERNATIVE; HYPOTHESIS, NULL; ONE-TAILED TEST; SIGNIFICANCE, STATISTICAL.

type. 1. A pattern of traits of an individual, group, or culture that distinguishes it from other individuals, groups, etc. Types are used on the assumption that they provide a means of classification of persons or cultures that is useful for the purpose of analysis.

2. An IDEAL TYPE or CONSTRUCTED TYPE.

type, constructed. See CONSTRUCTED TYPE.

type, ideal. See IDEAL TYPE.

type, personality. See PERSONALITY TYPE, BASIC.

type, polar. See POLAR TYPE.

type, social. 1. A consensual or group-shared conception of a ROLE (such as clown, operator, social climber, playboy) that is not fully rationalized or structured by formal definitions. The apprehension of social types helps the individual to perform knowledgeably within the social system. Social types, according to Orrin E. Klapp, are essentially "a chart to role-structures otherwise largely invisible and submerged." They "are needed for effective participation in modern secondary society, and are characteristically applied within the system to promote insightful relations." (O. E. Klapp, *American Sociological Review*, December 1958.)

2. A TYPE defined on the basis of social characteristics, such as types of social relations, types of groups, types of roles, etc.

type I error. See ERROR, ALPHA.

type II error. See ERROR, BETA.

types, body. See SHELDON'S BODY TYPES.

typological method. The use of typologies in sociological analysis. See TYPOLOGY.

typology. A classificatory schema composed of two or more ideal types (or constructed types). The ideal types provide abstract categories in terms of which individual or group phenomena are analyzed. The differences between the ideal types may be conceptualized as a gradual CONTINUUM or as discrete. In psychology the distinction between INTROVERT and EXTROVERT, in sociology the distinction between GEMEINSCHAFT and GESELLSCHAFT or SACRED SOCIETY and SECULAR SOCIETY, or the fourfold classification of ECCLESIA, DENOMINATION, SECT, and CULT are examples of typologies. Typologies are used to organize data and are an important kind of conceptual MODEL, useful in guiding research and in developing theory. See CONSTRUCTED TYPE; IDEAL TYPE; POLAR TYPE.

typology, church-sect. See CHURCH-SECT TYPOLOGY.

typology, folk-urban. See FOLK-URBAN TYPOLOGY.

typology, Shevky. See SOCIAL AREA ANALYSIS.

U

U curve. In statistics, a FREQUENCY DISTRIBUTION CURVE in which the highest frequencies are at the two extreme ends of the curve and the lowest frequencies are in the middle. In other words, the U curve represents a bimodal distribution in which the largest number of cases is concentrated in the lowest and highest values of the variable, and the smallest number in the middle values. It is the reverse of a normal frequency distribution curve. See FREQUENCY DISTRIBUTION, BIMODAL; FREQUENCY DISTRIBUTION CURVE, NORMAL.

U test. See MANN-WHITNEY U TEST; MANN-WHITNEY U TEST, EXTENSION OF.

unbiased estimate. See STATISTIC.

unbiased sampling. See SAMPLE, REPRESENTATIVE.

unconditioned response. See REFLEX.

unconditioned stimulus. See STIMULUS, UNCONDITIONED.

unconscious. A psychoanalytic term referring to mental processes that are presumed to exist but of which the individual is not entirely aware. Some writers distinguish between the SUBCONSCIOUS and the unconscious, defining the subconscious as the fringe of consciousness or that which is partially conscious and the unconscious as mental processes of which the individual is totally unaware. However, other writers use the two terms interchangeably, either referring to mental processes ranging from the fringe of consciousness to the total absence of conscious awareness. In Freudian theory the ID is said to reside in and form an important part of the unconscious.

Unconscious processes may be analyzed from a social frame of reference in terms of concepts such as ROLE and ROLE EXPECTATIONS, social norm, and DEFINITION OF THE SITUATION. An older person, for example, may retain certain habitual childhood patterns in one set of roles and more mature patterns of behavior in other roles and social situations. Thus, from a social framework unconscious behavior may in part be explained in terms of habitual or residual role patterns of response that persist in an outmoded and unsophisticated form from an earlier period of life side by side with more adaptive definitions of the situation and appropriate role responses. In the PSYCHODRAMA and SOCIODRAMA, where social roles are analyzed and manipulated, inappropriate patterns of thought and behavior, which were adaptive in childhood or in other situations, are often exposed. They are brought into consciousness by getting the individual to examine his various habitual patterns of social behavior, to sort them out logically and rationally in terms of their appropriateness in his present statuses, perhaps to discard inappropriate or outdated social responses and self-images, and to integrate previously separate patterns of thought and behavior. See NORM, SOCIAL; REFERENCE GROUP.

underdeveloped area. A region or country that is not highly industrialized, is primarily rural rather than urban, and lacks mechanized and scientific agriculture. The term also implies a lack of development of natural resources, a lack of modern medicine for most of the population and an accompanying high death rate, and often a high rate of illiteracy and poverty.

understanding, method of. See VERSTEHEN, METHOD OF.

unemployment, technological. See TECHNOLOGICAL UNEMPLOYMENT.

unidimensional scale. An attitude scale in which all the items measure the intensity of only one underlying dimension of an attitude. All the attitude statements that comprise the scale may be ranked along a single continuum of increasing intensity of the underlying attitude dimension. Thus on a unidimensional scale a person's pattern of response to the individual items can be predicted from his total score and those persons who agree with an item high on the scale will also agree with all items that rank below it. Any ORDINAL SCALE assumes a unidimensional CONTINUUM. See SCALE, ATTITUDE.

uniform crime reports. Bulletins issued by the Federal Bureau of Investigation which contain statistical data on crime that have been systematically and regularly collected from police agencies all over the United States. These reports are used as a source for the study of comparative rates of crime among various regions and cities of the United States.

uniformity, rational. See RATIONAL UNIFORMITY.

unilateral or **unilineal descent.** Descent or inheritance regarded as determined exclusively by either the mother's line or the father's line. See BILATERAL DESCENT; MATRILINEAL DESCENT; PATRILINEAL DESCENT.

unilateral power relationship. See POWER RELATIONSHIP, UNILATERAL.

unilineal descent. See UNILATERAL DESCENT.

unilocal residence. A custom prescribing that married couples reside in or near the household of one of the spouse's relatives. Tradition dictates whether within a particular culture the pair live with the husband's or the wife's family. See AVUNCULOCAL RESIDENCE; MATRILOCAL RESIDENCE; PATRILOCAL RESIDENCE.

union. An association of workers organized to advance the special interests of its members.

union, business. A union that sees its only function as one of bargaining for higher wages and better working conditions. Ideology and social activities are not regarded as important.

union, craft. See UNION, TRADE.

union, industrial. An association of workers organized on an industry-wide basis rather than along craft or trade lines. An industrial union is composed of all the various skilled and unskilled workers within an industry. Thus, for example, carpenters, electricians, and machine operators who are employed in a single industry would belong to the same industrial union. The United Auto Workers of America (U.A.W.) is an industrial union. See UNION, TRADE.

union, trade. An association of workers organized around a particular skill, craft, or occupation. It is also called a craft union. See UNION, INDUSTRIAL.

union shop. A plant or enterprise that requires its employees to join the union within a specified period of time if they are not already members.

univariate data. Data consisting of measurements or observations of only one VARIABLE.

universal law. See LAW, SCIENTIFIC.

universalism. The orientation of a person to another person (or persons) in a situation in terms of generalized standards of behavior rather than in terms of any special relationship that may exist between them. This pattern of behavior arises when it is prescribed and expected that an individual regard the other person as a member or representative of a SOCIAL CATEGORY or social STATUS that is relevant to the situation at hand and behave toward him as he would toward any member of that category in that situation. If a special relationship exists between persons in a situation defined as properly universalistic, they are expected to ignore this relationship. For example, if a student were a nephew of his professor, universalism would require that the professor ignore this relationship in the classroom and treat his nephew only as a member of the general social category of student, applying the same standards to him as to other students. In some societies universalism is a more widely expected pattern of behavior than in others. See PARTICULARISM; UNIVERSALISM-PARTICULARISM.

universalism, sociological. See SOCIOLOGICAL UNIVERSALISM.

universalism-particularism. A pattern variable, or dichotomy in social behavior, that is concerned with the problem of whether a person in a given situation should be oriented to another person (or persons) in terms of generalized standards of behavior or in terms of the special nature of their relationship to each other. "In confronting any situation, the actor faces the dilemma whether to treat the objects [other persons] in the situation in accordance with a general norm covering *all* objects in that class or whether to treat them in accordance with their standing in some particular relationship to him or his collectivity, independently of the objects' subsumibility under a general norm. This dilemma can be resolved by giving primacy to norms or value standards which are maximally generalized and which have a basis of validity transcending *any* specific system of relationships in which ego is involved, or by giving primacy to value standards which allot priority to standards *integral* to the *particular* relationship system in which the actor is involved with the object." This dichotomy, or dilemma, is one of the five PATTERN VARIABLES proposed by Talcott Parsons. (T. Parsons and E. A. Shils, eds., *Toward a General Theory of Action*, Harvard University Press, Cambridge, Mass., 1951.) See PARTICULARISM; UNIVERSALISM.

universals, cultural. Those "ideas, habits, and conditioned emotional responses which are common to all sane, adult members of the society. . . . this terminology applies only to the content of a particular culture. An element classed as a Universal in one culture may be completely lacking in another." Ralph Linton cites as examples the use of a particular language, particular "patterns of costume and housing, and the ideal patterns for social relationships." (R. Linton, *The Study of Man*, Appleton-Century-Crofts, New York, 1936.) See ALTERNATIVES, CULTURAL; SPECIALTIES, CULTURAL.

universe. See POPULATION (2).

universe of discourse. The shared symbols of communication and conceptions of reality that are peculiar to a group or society. Words, phrases, and ideas have special meanings within a group that make interaction more efficient and give the members a sense of identity and belonging. Outsiders or new members must learn the language and assumptions of the culture or subculture before they can understand the subtleties of communication or feel secure as members.

universe parameter. See PARAMETER.

unobtrusive measure. A research technique that can be used without the awareness of the subjects being studied. Unobtrusive measures include the study of records (such as birth, death, and marriage records, scientific directories, political and judicial records, tombstones, sales records), the study of physical evidence (such as wear on library books, fingerprints on exhibits, the setting on automobile radio dials), unnoticed observers, and hidden cameras and tape recorders. Although many of these techniques have been used in social research for some time, they were named unobtrusive measures and systematically presented by Eugene J. Webb, Donald T. Campbell, Richard D. Schwartz, and Lee Sechrest (*Unobtrusive Measures*, Rand McNally, Chicago, 1966). The authors also refer to the use of these techniques as nonreactive research.

unskilled manual worker. A manual worker whose work requires very little training, knowledge, or experience. Any worker with average or even somewhat below average intelligence and normal health can perform work of this type without specialized training. Usually included in this category are janitors, porters, sanitation workers, bell hops, construction laborers, etc. See SEMISKILLED MANUAL WORKER; SKILLED MANUAL WORKER.

unstructured situation. A situation in which an individual cannot organize conceptually the great variety of stimuli into a meaningful pattern for the purpose of responding. In an unstructured social situation, one usually cannot define the appropriate ROLE EXPECTATIONS. If a person is unfamiliar with the behavior expected of him in a situation he obviously cannot organize his behavior to adjust to what is expected. Interaction is the usual process by which unstructured social situations evolve into social situations in which people know what to expect of each other.

upper class. That stratum of a society that is able to dominate the lower strata by virtue of its greater power, authority, wealth, and prestige. Upper classes vary in their characteristics from one society to another, and the term has to be defined in relation to a particular society, its values, its power structure, its pattern of wealth distribution, etc. Often the upper class is regarded primarily as a prestige class, and such criteria as royal and aristocratic blood, number of generations one's family is removed from its immigrant origins in new countries, style of life, etc., are used. Socialist countries usually officially discourage reference to their own upper classes for ideological reasons, but hierarchical differentiation of strata in terms of power, prestige, and wealth remain. See ELITE; SOCIAL CLASS; STRATIFICATION, SOCIAL; UPPER CLASS, LOWER-; UPPER CLASS, UPPER-.

upper class, lower-. In the Yankee City studies of W. Lloyd Warner and Paul S. Lunt, an upper class stratum of the community that has most of the characteristics of the upper-upper class, but is regarded by the upper-upper class and perhaps others as on a lower level of prestige—primarily due to the lack of inherited wealth or prestigeful ancestors. It is the belief system (for example, beliefs regarding mystical identity with one's dead ancestors, inherited status, selective standards of social prestige, the superiority of specific social manners, recreations, affectations, etc.) that separates an upper-upper from a lower-upper class as a rule. Both usually have wealth and power, and even authority. (W. L. Warner and P. S. Lunt, *The Social Life of a Modern Community,* Yankee City Series, Vol. I, Yale University Press, New Haven, 1941.) See LOWER CLASS, LOWER-; LOWER CLASS, UPPER-; MIDDLE CLASS, LOWER-; MIDDLE CLASS, UPPER-; SOCIAL CLASS; UPPER CLASS, UPPER-.

upper class, upper-. In the Yankee City studies of W. Lloyd Warner and Paul S. Lunt, that stratum (see STRATUM, SOCIAL) of the UPPER CLASS which is able to determine the standards of the prestige system of a community, particularly with regard to those social classes nearest it. The upper-upper class uses its authority, power, wealth, and prestige to protect or attempt to protect its pre-eminence by the creation of elaborate prestige beliefs that exclude those who otherwise have all the characteristics of their class—power, authority, and wealth. (W. L. Warner and P. S. Lunt, *The Social Life of a Modern Community,* Yankee City Series, Vol. I, Yale University Press, New Haven, 1941.) See LOWER CLASS, LOWER-; LOWER CLASS, UPPER-; MIDDLE CLASS, LOWER-; MIDDLE CLASS, UPPER-; SOCIAL CLASS; UPPER CLASS, LOWER-.

upper-lower class. See LOWER CLASS, UPPER-.

upper-middle class. See MIDDLE CLASS, UPPER-.

urban community. A COMMUNITY with a high population density, a predominance of nonagricultural occupations, a high degree of specialization resulting in a complex division of labor, and a formalized system of local government. Urban communities also tend to be characterized by a heterogeneous population, a prevalence of impersonal SECONDARY RELATIONS, and dependence on formal social controls. See RURAL COMMUNITY.

urban daytime population. See DAYTIME POPULATION, URBAN.

urban ecology. See ECOLOGY, HUMAN.

urban fringe. 1. The area beyond the established suburbs of a city where urban and rural characteristics converge. It is an area of mixed land use, and is less politically organized than the suburbs. Because of an absence of zoning regulations and the relatively lower land cost, types of land use that are considered undesirable (such as automobile junk yards) are often found in fringe areas. This area is also referred to as the rural-urban fringe.

2. As defined by the U.S. Census, the built-up area surrounding a large city, which is continuous with the city and has an average density of 2,000 persons per square mile. In this sense the urban fringe includes the suburbs and the fringe as defined above.

See HINTERLAND; SUBURB.

urban growth, axiate hypothesis of. See AXIATE HYPOTHESIS OF URBAN GROWTH.

urban growth, concentric zone hypothesis of. See CONCENTRIC ZONE HYPOTHESIS, BURGESS'.

urban growth, sector hypothesis of. See SECTOR HYPOTHESIS.

urban place. According to the U.S. Census, any place that has a population of 2,500 or more and is incorporated. In addition, unincorporated places that have a population density of 1,000 or more inhabitants per square mile and are located on the fringe of large urban areas are classified as urban. Incorporated places with a population under 2,500 located on the fringe of large urban areas are also classified as urban if they have a closely settled area of 100 or more dwelling units. In other countries other criteria are used to define urban place. Minimum population standards vary greatly. In a number of countries 2,000 is regarded as the minimum size for a place to be designated as urban. However, in some countries the minimum is lower than this, and in others considerably higher. For example, in Denmark the minimum is 200, whereas in the Netherlands a minimum population of 20,000 is required for a place to be designated as urban. In some countries whether or not a place is incorporated is important in determining whether it is considered urban, whereas in other countries the question of incorporation is disregarded. In addition, whether a place has a local government, whether it is a chief town in a district, and other criteria of urban status are used in various national definitions. The varying criteria used to define urban make international comparisons of national census reports of urban and rural population proportions extremely difficult. See INCORPORATED PLACE; RURAL PLACE.

urban renewal. "A term applied to an approach to urban development which became popular after the passage of the Federal Housing Act of 1954. Three things are stressed in urban renewal:

1. Prevention of the spread of blight into good areas.

2. The rehabilitation and conservation of areas that can be economically restored.

3. Clearance and redevelopment of areas that cannot be saved." (W. E. Cole, *Urban Society,* Houghton Mifflin, Boston, 1958.)

See BLIGHTED AREA.

urban ring. The area surrounding a city, including the suburbs and the URBAN FRINGE. See SUBURB.

urban social planning. See PLANNING, URBAN SOCIAL.

urban society. An abstract or IDEAL TYPE, developed by Robert Redfield as part of his folk-urban societal typology. Urban society is characterized by a large, heterogeneous population, close contact with other societies (through trade, communication, etc.), a complex division of labor, a prevalence of secular over sacred concerns, and the desire to organize behavior rationally toward given goals, as opposed to following without question traditional standards and norms. Many social relationships are impersonal and contractual, and there is a formal system of social controls. Urban society is contrasted to FOLK SOCIETY. (R. Redfield, *American Journal of Sociology*, January 1947.) See GESELLSCHAFT; SECULAR SOCIETY.

urban sociology. See SOCIOLOGY, URBAN.

urban zones. See CONCENTRIC ZONE HYPOTHESIS, BURGESS'.

urbanism. Patterns of culture and social interaction resulting from the concentration of large populations into relatively small areas. Urbanism reflects an organization of society in terms of a complex division of labor, high levels of technology, high mobility, interdependence of its members in fulfilling economic functions, and impersonality in social relations. See URBAN SOCIETY; URBANIZATION.

urbanization. 1. The movement of population from rural to urban areas, and the resulting increasing proportion of a population that resides in urban rather than rural places. While cities, including great cities, have existed since ancient times, until the modern period they represented only a relatively small proportion of the population. The lives of the great majority of people in all parts of the world were predominantly shaped by the rural community or village. The massive growth of cities and metropolitan areas and the striking shift in the proportion of the population that is urban has been a characteristic phenomenon of the modern era. Modern urbanization has resulted from the INDUSTRIAL REVOLUTION, which created a demand for large numbers of workers at centralized locations, and the AGRICULTURAL REVOLUTION, which permitted a smaller proportion of the population to be engaged in the production of food and raw materials. See FACTORY SYSTEM; METROPOLITAN AREA; URBAN PLACE.

2. The spread of urban patterns of behavior and modes of thought. The MASS MEDIA play an important role in spreading urban culture into rural areas. Thus in highly urbanized societies cultural differences between urban and rural populations tend to decline. See GESELLSCHAFT; URBAN SOCIETY.

urbanized area. As defined by the U.S. Census, an area that "contains at least one city which has 50,000 inhabitants or more . . . as well as the surrounding closely settled incorporated places and unincorporated areas. . . . An urbanized area may be thought of as divided into the cen-

tral city, or cities, and the remainder of the area, or the urban fringe."
(U.S. Bureau of the Census, *U.S. Census of the Population: 1960*, Vol. I.)
See INCORPORATED PLACE; METROPOLITAN AREA, STANDARD; URBAN FRINGE;
URBAN PLACE.

usage, social. A uniform or customary way of behaving within a social
group. Max Weber used the term *social usage* as a more general term than
CUSTOM, which he regarded as a subtype.

uterine descent. See MATRILINEAL DESCENT.

utilitarianism. The ethical and social doctrine, originated by Jeremy
Bentham, that the sole aim and criterion for judging all human conduct
and all laws is the amount of happiness produced for the greatest number
of people.

utopia. A conception of an ideal or perfect society which eliminates
all of the aspects of prevailing societies that are regarded as undesirable.
Highly idealized utopias represent societies in which people live without
interpersonal conflict, without rivalry, without competition—in fact,
without any of the potentially painful experiences realistically involved in
human interaction in every human society of both the past and the
present.

uxorilocal residence. See MATRILOCAL RESIDENCE.

V

valence. As defined by Kurt Lewin, the quality of an object or goal that attracts (positive valence) or repels (negative valence) an individual. See FIELD THEORY.

validation, consensual. See CONSENSUAL VALIDATION.

validity. 1. In statistics, correspondence between what a measuring device is supposed to measure and what it really measures. For example, if one were to ask whether a particular survey of voter preference really measures the preferences of voters or whether a particular intelligence test actually measures intelligence, one would be raising the question of the validity of the survey or the test. The validity of a measuring device is usually determined by comparing the results obtained from that device with an independent and accepted measure of the same characteristic. The independent measure used for comparison may be a test the validity of which has been established, or an accepted objective criterion (income as a criterion of economic success, grades as a criterion of academic success, etc.). If a measuring instrument is not valid it may be consistently measuring something quite different from what it purports to measure. See RELIABILITY.

2. In logic, that which is logically correct, so that one's reasoning follows logically from one's premises. Validity is formal correctness. One could assume false premises and arrive at a valid conclusion.

validity coefficient. See COEFFICIENT OF VALIDITY.

value. 1. An abstract, generalized principle of behavior to which the members of a group feel a strong, emotionally toned positive commitment and which provides a standard for judging specific acts and goals. Values are accepted not merely as overt statements to which each group member assents, but as the individual commitment of each member, who has internalized them in the process of SOCIALIZATION. Values provide the general-

455

ized standards of behavior that are expressed in more specific, concrete form in social norms. Because of the generalized nature of values, it is possible for individuals who share the same values to disagree on specific norms embodying these values. Examples of values are justice, freedom, patriotism, and romantic love.

Values provide essential organizing principles for the integration of individual and group goals. Because of the strong emotional feeling attached to values and because they serve as standards for judging concrete rules, goals, or actions, they are often regarded as absolute, although the formation and apprehension of values evolve in the normal process of social interaction. Since values guide choices of objects and behavior, the study of values involves the study of attitudes, behavior, interaction, and social structure.

2. A desired object or goal.

See INTERNALIZATION; NORM, SOCIAL.

value, economic. 1. The exchange relationship of one good to another (or others), that is, how much one good can command of another (or others) when they are exchanged at a given time and place. This is usually expressed in terms of money (the usual medium of exchange), and thus is represented by the relative price of the goods.

2. The utility of a good.

See GOOD, ECONOMIC.

value, mathematical. A quantity or magnitude, represented by a number.

value, social. See VALUE.

value, surplus. See SURPLUS VALUE.

value, ultimate. A VALUE or ideal that a society or subgroup in a society regards as fundamental, unchallengeable, and unchanging.

value judgment. A judgment of what is desirable or worth while. Value judgments are essential in all human activities except where they lead to rigidities and dogmatism. Value judgments are undesirable in sociology only if they exclude or obscure available or obtainable facts, knowledge, or insights. In science value judgments influence the selection of problems for investigation and the practical application of scientific findings. Moreover, even in the course of scientific investigation itself, it is impossible to eliminate all value judgments. However, the SCIENTIFIC METHOD constantly strives to maximize OBJECTIVITY. The control of value judgments allows sociologists and social scientists of diverse value systems to communicate and cooperate with each other in the attempt to increase our understanding of social life.

value-orientation. 1. A VALUE to which an individual is committed and which influences his behavior. Value-orientation is distinguished from value, by those writers who make this distinction, in that value-orientation focuses on an individual, whereas value focuses on a group. It may be said that the members of a group share a certain value, and yet this value will not be equally important to all group members. When referring to a value to which a particular member is personally committed, that is, when emphasizing the point of view of a specific individual rather than the group as a whole, some writers use the term value-orientation.

2. Used by some writers synonymously with value.

value system. An organized pattern of values of a society or group in which individual values are interrelated so as to reinforce each other and form a coherent whole. A value system provides a framework for the analysis of social norms, ideals, beliefs, and behavior.

values, ecological hypothesis of symbolic. See SYMBOLIC VALUES, ECOLOGICAL HYPOTHESIS OF.

variability. See DISPERSION, STATISTICAL.

variability, coefficient of. See COEFFICIENT OF VARIATION.

variable. In statistics, a characteristic that is common to a number of individuals, objects, groups, events, etc., and that has different degrees of magnitude or different categories (for example, positive or negative) so that individual cases differ in the extent to which they possess the characteristic (expressed in numerical values) or in the CATEGORY of the characteristic into which they fall. In a controlled experiment certain variables may be made into constants by being made uniform for all the subjects being studied so that the relationship of other variables, usually the independent and dependent variable, may be more accurately observed and tested.

An independent variable (also called the X variable) is one whose occurrence or change results in the occurrence or change in another variable (the dependent variable). In terms of the cause-effect schema, the independent variable is the cause. In a controlled experiment the independent variable is the experimental variable, that is, the variable introduced into the experimental group and withheld from the control group. When the values of an independent variable are known, they may be used to predict the values of the variable that is dependent upon it.

A dependent variable (also called the Y variable) occurs or changes in a regular, determinable pattern related to the occurrence of or changes in another variable or variables. In terms of the cause-effect schema, the dependent variable is the effect.

See CONSTANT; EXPERIMENT, CONTROLLED; VARIABLE, QUALITATIVE; VARIABLE, QUANTITATIVE.

variable, continuous. A quantitative VARIABLE that increases continuously in magnitude, with an uninterrupted series of gradations of possible values. Between the lowest and the highest possible values of the variable, any value or fractional value may occur. A continuous variable increases by a series of unlimited gradations, and theoretically may be subject to indefinite refinement. Examples of continuous variables are height, weight, and age. Continuous variables are arbitrarily divided into class intervals for the purpose of analysis. See CLASS INTERVAL; VARIABLE, DISCRETE; VARIABLE, QUANTITATIVE.

variable, dependent. See VARIABLE.

variable, dichotomous. See DICHOTOMY.

variable, discrete. A VARIABLE that is composed of a series of distinct and separate units or categories. All qualitative variables are discrete variables, and those quantitative variables consisting of values that are indivisible units (such as individuals) are also discrete variables. There are no values possible in between the units of a discrete variable. The magnitude of a discrete quantitative variable increases by definite steps. For example, in numbers of individuals one must go from one to two. It is not possible to have anything intermediate. Examples of discrete variables are sex, family size, number of college graduates, etc. See CATEGORY; VARIABLE, CONTINUOUS; VARIABLE, QUALITATIVE; VARIABLE, QUANTITATIVE.

variable, independent. See VARIABLE.

variable, intervening. A VARIABLE regarded as the explanatory link in the apparent CORRELATION of two other variables. In the case in which there is an intervening variable, a correlation found between two other variables (perhaps originally regarded as an independent variable and a dependent variable) is due not to any genuine relationship between these variables, but rather to the fact that each is correlated with a third variable, referred to as the intervening variable. If the intervening variable were controlled (held constant), the correlation between the other two variables would disappear.

variable, nonnumerical. See VARIABLE, QUALITATIVE.

variable, qualitative. A VARIABLE that consists of categories rather than numerical units. A qualitative variable has two or more categories that are distinguished from each other on a nonnumerical basis. Examples of qualitative variables are sex, race, and religion. See CATEGORY; VARIABLE.

variable, quantitative. A VARIABLE consisting of a series of numerical units. The units of a quantitative variable differ from each other in magnitude rather than in kind. A quantitative variable may be continuous or discrete. Examples of quantitative variables are age, income, and family size. See VARIABLE, CONTINUOUS; VARIABLE, DISCRETE.

variables, correlated. See CORRELATION.

variables, cumulative change in. See CUMULATION, PRINCIPLE OF.

variables, pattern. See PATTERN VARIABLES.

variance. A measure of dispersion of statistical values that is the arithmetic mean of the squared deviations from the mean. It is obtained by subtracting each value in a FREQUENCY DISTRIBUTION from the arithmetic mean of the distribution to obtain the deviations from the mean. Each deviation is squared (thus eliminating positive and negative signs). The arithmetic mean of these squared deviations is the variance. Thus the variance is the STANDARD DEVIATION squared. It is usually symbolized by σ^2. See DISPERSION, STATISTICAL; MEAN, ARITHMETIC.

variance, analysis of. The analysis and comparison of the variances in two or more samples to determine whether or not the samples probably are from the same POPULATION, or put in other words, whether there is a statistically significant difference between two or more samples. The techniques for analyzing VARIANCE provide a means of analyzing the relationship between a qualitative variable (or variables) and a quantitative variable. The separate samples represent a division of the cases on the basis of a qualitative variable or variables. (Usually other relevant variables are controlled.) The distribution of the quantitative variable within each of these divisions (samples) is then compared by means of techniques using variance. For example, if the relationship between nationality (a qualitative variable) and scores on a particular test (a quantitative variable) were being studied, each nationality (that is, each category of the qualitative variable) would be considered a sample and the distribution of test scores in each sample (for each nationality) would be compared using variance. See F TEST; PROBABILITY; SAMPLE; SIGNIFICANCE, STATISTICAL; VARIABLE, QUALITATIVE; VARIABLE, QUANTITATIVE.

variants, cultural. See ALTERNATIVES, CULTURAL.

variate. 1. Any of the specific values of a quantitative variable, for example, age 10 would be a variate of the VARIABLE age. A quantitative variable consists of a series of variates.

2. Either a value of a quantitative variable or a CATEGORY of qualitative variable.

See ATTRIBUTE; VARIABLE, QUALITATIVE; VARIABLE, QUANTITATIVE.

variation. 1. A measure of dispersion of statistical values that is the sum of the squared deviations from the mean. To obtain the variation, each value in a FREQUENCY DISTRIBUTION is subtracted from the arithmetic mean. Each of the resulting deviations is squared (thus eliminating the plus and minus signs). The sum of these squared deviations is the variation. Variation is not used as frequently as VARIANCE or STANDARD DEVIATION. See DISPERSION, STATISTICAL; MEAN, ARITHMETIC.

2. See VARIABLE.

3. In the study of cultures, differences among the forms of CULTURE traits and patterns within a given culture (usually reflecting a process of culture change) or differences between the norms, values, and other characteristics of one culture and those of another culture. See CULTURE TRAIT.

> **variation, categorical.** See VARIABLE, QUALITATIVE.
>
> **variation, chance.** See CHANCE FACTORS.
>
> **variation, coefficient of.** See COEFFICIENT OF VARIATION.
>
> **variation, concomitant.** See CORRELATION.
>
> **variation, continuous.** See VARIABLE, CONTINUOUS.
>
> **variation, discontinuous.** See VARIABLE, DISCRETE.
>
> **variation, qualitative.** See VARIABLE, QUALITATIVE.
>
> **variation, quantitative.** See VARIABLE, QUANTITATIVE.
>
> **variation, sampling.** See CHANCE FACTORS.
>
> **variation, seasonal.** See SEASONAL VARIATION.
>
> **verbal definition.** See DEFINITION, NOMINAL.

verbal test. A TEST that depends on the use of language. The person being tested is not asked to perform any tasks but to respond in words. See PERFORMANCE TEST.

verstehen, method of. As defined by Max Weber, the use of personal knowledge and insight gained in social interaction and through ROLE TAKING as a tool in the understanding of the social behavior of others. An observer of social interaction is capable of inferring the participants' DEFINITION OF THE SITUATION (their understanding of and expectations in a situation) through his knowledge of how he would define the situation. Participant observation as a methodological technique requires the use of a complex and flexible conceptual framework or system in order to organize the many otherwise unrelated observations, and the success of the method of *verstehen* depends upon the observer's understanding of the culture and social norms within which the behavior being observed occurs. The method is essential in sociology and social psychology. *Verstehen* is a German term meaning understanding, insight, or comprehension. (See M. Weber, *The Theory of Social and Economic Organization*, tr. by A. M. Henderson and T. Parsons, Oxford University Press, New York, 1947.) See NEOPOSITIVISM; OBSERVATION, PARTICIPANT; OPERATIONALISM; POSITIVISM; SYMPATHETIC INTROSPECTION.

vertical occupational movement. A change in occupational position that involves a change (upward or downward) in economic or social status level. See HORIZONTAL OCCUPATIONAL MOVEMENT; MOBILITY, VERTICAL SOCIAL.

vertical work group. A work GROUP consisting of individuals whose jobs differ in degree of prestige, income, skill, or authority. See HORIZONTAL WORK GROUP.

vested interest. An INTEREST GROUP having special, established advantages that it seeks to maintain by opposing policies that threaten its position within the social system.

vice. Disapproved behavior that violates an important social norm within a society. In American studies of "vice," the term usually refers to illegal activities that are considered personally or socially harmful, such as prostitution, gambling, and narcotic traffic.

vice area. An urban area in which there is a concentration of prostitutes, drug addicts, alcoholics, and other social deviants. It is an area of physical deterioration and is often part of a ZONE IN TRANSITION. It is also characterized by a high crime rate, a lack of community organization, a high rate of personal disorganization, and the prevalence of a wide variety of social problems.

vicious cycle. See CUMULATION, PRINCIPLE OF.

vill. A term proposed by George A. Hillery, Jr., to refer to a community when one means to designate a territorial unit (a village, a city, etc.). Hillery proposes the use of this term because of the confusion resulting from the various usages of the term community. See COMMUNITY (1).

village. A small community, larger than a HAMLET, but usually rural rather than urban. Precise definitions vary. Some writers limit the size of the village to 1,000 population, others to 2,500. Villages may be incorporated or unincorporated. When it is incorporated, a community may be officially classified as a village even though its population exceeds 2,500. Official criteria for the designation of village vary from state to state as well as from one country to another. Today many communities incorporated as villages are suburban rather than rural. See INCORPORATED PLACE; RURAL PLACE; SUBURB; TOWN; URBAN PLACE.

village, agricultural. A small rural VILLAGE that is an area of residence for the farm families whose farms are located outside the village. It serves as a center for family life, recreation, and trade. As a pattern of settlement, the agricultural village is in contrast to the isolated farmstead that is typical of North American farming communities.

village, craft. A VILLAGE that specializes in a specific craft. For example, in rural parts of upper Burma there are villages that specialize in silverwork and others that specialize in silk weaving. It is also called a trade village.

village, industrial. A VILLAGE, surrounded by a rural farming area, whose inhabitants are primarily engaged in manufacturing or other industrial pursuits. An industrial village is not rural in character despite its small size. The population consists primarily of wage earners whose lives are organized about the schedule demanded by the local industry (or small industries)—textile manufacture, mining, lumbering, or the like. It may provide a few services to farmers, but this is not a major source of its income.

village, rural nonfarm. A VILLAGE that is primarily rural in character, in the sense that it exists on the income derived from goods and services provided to farmers in the surrounding rural area. Few of its residents are active farmers, although retired farmers are a part of the community. It may be a very small community providing a general store, a mill, a church, a school, and a doctor's office, or it may be larger. See VILLAGE, AGRICULTURAL.

village, suburban. See SUBURB.

village, trade. See VILLAGE, CRAFT.

virilocal residence. See PATRILOCAL RESIDENCE.

viscerotonia. See SHELDON'S BODY TYPES.

vital statistics. Numerical data, usually in the form of public records, dealing with birth, marriage, death, and other recorded information about local, national, and international populations.

vitalism. 1. The doctrine that living organisms have a unique life-principle which cannot be explained in physical or chemical terms.

2. See ANIMATISM.

vitalistic movement. "Any conscious, organized attempt on the part of a society's members to incorporate in its culture selected aspects of another culture in contact with it." (M. Smith, *Man*, August 1954.) See MILLENARIAN MOVEMENT; NATIVISTIC MOVEMENT; REVITALIZATION MOVEMENT.

vocabulary of motive. An individual's explanation of his own motivation or the motivation of others. Hans Gerth and C. Wright Mills proposed this concept as a sociological alternative to the psychological conception of MOTIVE. "Sociologically, as Max Weber put it, a motive is a term in a vocabulary which appears to the actor himself and/or to the observer to be an adequate reason for his conduct. This conception grasps the intrinsically social character of motivation: a satisfactory or adequate motive is one that satisfies those who question some act or program, whether the actor questions his own or another's conduct. The words which may fulfill this function are limited to the vocabulary of motives acceptable for given situations by given social circles. . . . Along with the conduct patterns appropriate for various occasions, we learn their appropriate motives, and these are the motives we will use in dealing with others and with ourselves. The motives we use to justify or to criticize an act thus link our conduct with that of significant others, and line up our conduct with the standardized expectations, often backed up by sanctions, that we call norms. Such words may function as directives and incentives: they are the judgments of others as anticipated by the actor." (H. Gerth and C. W. Mills, *Character and Social Structure*, Harcourt, Brace, New York, 1953.)

vocabulary, special. See ARGOT; JARGON.

voluntarism. In the study of human behavior, the orientation that emphasizes individual choice and decision making in determining behavior. Human behavior is viewed as rational and purposive and not entirely determined by external forces. The voluntaristic MODEL of human behavior is in contrast to the deterministic model. See DETERMINISM.

voluntary association. See ASSOCIATION, VOLUNTARY.

W

W coefficient. See Kendall coefficient of concordance W.

wakan. See mana.

Wald-Wolfowitz runs test. A nonparametric statistical test used to determine whether two samples differ significantly in any respect. On the basis of the number of runs obtained when the scores of the two samples are put in a single series, the test indicates whether the two samples probably come from the same or different populations. Unlike some tests that are designed for a specific type of difference, this test indicates whether there is a significant difference of any sort between two samples—in central tendency, dispersion, skewness. For the use of a runs test with one sample see runs test. See also central tendency, measure of; nonparametric statistics; probability; run; significance, statistical.

want. A motivating impulse impelling an individual to act either to attain a desired goal or to prevent an undesired event from occurring. It is essentially similar to the concepts need and drive.

war. A state of collective physical conflict between politically organized groups (nations or subnations) that are not bound together by social bonds of interdependence and a degree of interaction sufficient to make the settlement of disputes by peaceful means the most practical and rational alternative (for both sides) to armed conflict. In this sense war is a form of international disorganization, for the various nations of the world have not developed sufficiently diverse patterns of interdependence to make less violent alternatives not only the most obvious choice, but the only possible one. War is a result of the concentration of conflict and cooperation in the hands of a few representatives of the opposing isolated territorial units. When groups interact primarily on a political-diplomatic level, collective conflict becomes a possible form of conflict resolution. The process of cooperation and conflict, both personal and organizational, be-

464

tween territorial groups on a great variety of levels keeps conflict from becoming concentrated in the hands of two (or more) unified political representatives of the separate parties to the dispute. Peace involves not only cooperation, but the intertwining and diffusing of a multiplicity of opposing groups throughout the two social systems. See POLEMOLOGY.

we-feeling. Sociological slang for a feeling of identification with a group. The term is seldom used seriously.

we-group. See IN-GROUP.

web of life. A term, borrowed from biology, used in early studies of human ecology to refer to the interdependence of organisms (such as humans) on their physical environment and each other. The community is conceived of as a system having a unity resulting from complex interdependent connections between its various parts. Changes in the community lead to intricate readjustments in the organization of its parts tending to maintain a state of equilibrium. See BIOTIC COMMUNITY; ECOLOGY, HUMAN.

welfare programs. See SOCIAL WELFARE PROGRAMS.

Weltanschauung. The world view or philosophy of life of a cultural community.

white collar crime. See CRIME, WHITE COLLAR.

white collar worker. A "large heterogeneous category of clerical and technical workers, such as stenographers, bookkeepers, typists, draftsmen, sales-people, and others whose work is primarily non-managerial and non-manual." (R. Centers in *Class, Status and Power*, edited by R. Bendix and S. M. Lipset, Free Press, Glencoe, Ill., 1953.)

Wilcoxon matched-pairs signed ranks test. A nonparametric statistical test that may be used to determine whether there is a statistically significant difference between two samples, each composed of one member of each of a series of matched pairs. This test can be used when it is possible to determine which member of each pair is higher in the variable being tested and to rank the differences between the pairs in order of magnitude. The test uses data in the form of ranks, and does not require data in the form of precise quantities. When the necessary data are available, the Wilcoxon test is considered preferable to the SIGN TEST because it treats information not only on the direction of the differences between the pairs but also on the relative magnitude of these differences. This test is symbolized by T, and is sometimes referred to as the Wilcoxon T test. See MATCHING; NONPARAMETRIC STATISTICS; PROBABILITY; SAMPLE; SIGNIFICANCE, STATISTICAL.

wish. A WANT or NEED. See WISHES, THOMAS' FOUR.

wishes, Thomas' four. W. I. Thomas' suggested classification of four universal and basic human desires or wishes: (1) the desire for new experience, (2) the desire for security, (3) the desire for response (friendship), and (4) the desire for recognition (approval). (W. I. Thomas, *The Unadjusted Girl*, Little, Brown, Boston, 1923.)

witch. See WITCHCRAFT.

witchcraft. The practice of black magic or sorcery. The existence of witches is an accepted belief in many societies. They are believed to have supernatural powers employed for evil and harmful purposes and frequently derived from a compact with an evil spirit.

Technically the term *witch* refers to females (males being wizards), and in some societies the practice of witchcraft is considered limited to females. However, in most usage, witch and witchcraft may refer to either sex. Thus in Europe the term witch was often used to refer to males as well as females, and men as well as women were executed during the witch burnings of the fourteenth to sixteenth centuries. See MAGIC, BLACK.

withdrawal. A psychological reaction, or type of DEFENSE MECHANISM, in which a person attempts to adjust to a frustrating situation by avoiding it. People may withdraw from frustrating social situations by refusing to participate actively in group activities and by exhibiting noncooperative attitudes. Severe withdrawal may involve the avoidance of all social interaction, the heavy use of alcohol or drugs, or other radical behavior, but withdrawal from social participation may also be partial, tentative, and strategic. It can, for example, be used as a form of social protest. In this sense it is a form of sanctioning available to most group members and does not necessarily involve genuine ALIENATION. See SANCTION.

wolf children. See FERAL MAN.

word association test. In psychology, a PROJECTIVE TECHNIQUE for studying personality in which the subject is presented with a list of words and asked to respond to each word with the first word that comes to his mind.

word deafness. See SENSORY APHASIA.

work. 1. Disciplined and persistent activity devoted to achieving a goal, with the actual activity only instrumental to the accomplishment of the final goal of the activity. This definition contrasts work to LEISURE or PLAY.

2. Work that is related to economic necessity.

work culture. See OCCUPATIONAL CULTURE.

work ecology. The ecological study of the spatial distribution of workers in a factory, business office, or the like, and the relationship of this distribution to the patterns of work relationships and informal social relationships.

work group. See HORIZONTAL WORK GROUP; VERTICAL WORK GROUP.

worker, blue collar. See BLUE COLLAR WORKER.

worker, migrant. See MIGRANT WORKER.

worker, semiskilled manual. See SEMISKILLED MANUAL WORKER.

worker, skilled manual. See SKILLED MANUAL WORKER.

worker, unskilled manual. See UNSKILLED MANUAL WORKER.

worker, white collar. See WHITE COLLAR WORKER.

working class. Loosely, the category of skilled and unskilled manual workers, sometimes extended to include low-paid clerical workers and other white collar workers. Because it is so vague, the term is seldom used in sociology, except in cases where subjects are being asked to rate themselves on the basis of social class. "Working class" is a more acceptable term for oneself than "lower class." See LOWER CLASS; SOCIAL CLASS; SOCIAL CLASS, SUBJECTIVE CONCEPTION OF.

workmanship, instinct of. See INSTINCT OF WORKMANSHIP.

workmanship, sense of. A feeling on the part of a craftsman of pride in his work and identification with his trade. The craftsman with pride of workmanship desires to create a fine product because of the satisfaction this gives him in and of itself and because his self-esteem is related to his workmanship. It is usually maintained that mass production, by breaking up the production of a product into many small component processes, tends to destroy the sense of workmanship.

world view. See WELTANSCHAUUNG.

worship, ancestor. See ANCESTOR WORSHIP.

X, Y, Z

x axis. See ABSCISSA.

X variable. See VARIABLE, INDEPENDENT.

xenocentrism. "Rejection of the culture of one's own group." (P. Horton, *Sociology and the Health Sciences*, McGraw-Hill, New York, 1965.)

y axis. See ORDINATE.

Y variable. See VARIABLE, DEPENDENT.

Yale Cross-Cultural Survey. See HUMAN RELATIONS AREA FILE.

Yates' correction for continuity. See CHI-SQUARE TEST.

Z measure. See CRITICAL RATIO.

Z score. A statistical score expressed in terms of its relative position in the FREQUENCY DISTRIBUTION of which it is a part. A score is converted to a Z score so that it may be compared with scores from other tests or measuring instruments. A Z score is obtained by subtracting a raw score from the arithmetic mean of the distribution of scores, and dividing this difference (the deviation from the mean) by the STANDARD DEVIATION of the distribution. The Z score is often referred to as the standard score, and occasionally as the sigma score. See MEAN, ARITHMETIC; SCORE, NORMATIVE; SCORE, RAW; T SCORE.

    zero-sum concept of power. See POWER, SCARCITY THEORY OF.

    Zipf migration hypothesis. An hypothesis in ecology, proposed by George K. Zipf, that states that, other factors (such as income level, unemployment) being equal, the number of persons who migrate between two communities (in both directions) will be equal to the product of the population of the two communities divided by the shortest distance between the communities. The hypothesis is often expressed in terms of the formula $P_1 \cdot P_2 / D$, in which P_1 is the population of one community, P_2 the population of the other community, and D the shortest distance between the two communities. It is sometimes referred to as the P_1P_2/D hypothesis, and also the hypothesis on the intercity movement of persons and the minimum equation hypothesis. (G. K. Zipf, *American Sociological Review*, December 1946.) See ECOLOGY, HUMAN; MIGRATION.

zonal hypothesis. See CONCENTRIC ZONE HYPOTHESIS, BURGESS'.

zone in transition. The second of E. W. Burgess' five concentric zones: an area immediately surrounding the CENTRAL BUSINESS DISTRICT of a large city that is being invaded by business and industrial expansion. Land value is high and expected to become higher when the area eventually becomes part of the central business district. Because of this there is intense real estate speculation. Buildings are old and deteriorated, and landlords, who are often land speculators, have little incentive to repair or improve them. This is the area of the slums, and in Burgess' concentric zone hypothesis the existence of slums is explained primarily in terms of this process of transition in land use. See CONCENTRIC ZONE HYPOTHESIS, BURGESS'; SLUM.

zone of commuters. See CONCENTRIC ZONE HYPOTHESIS, BURGESS'; SUBURB.

zone of residential hotels and apartments. See CONCENTRIC ZONE HYPOTHESIS, BURGESS'.

zone of workingmen's homes. See CONCENTRIC ZONE HYPOTHESIS, BURGESS'.

zoning. The public regulation of land and building use in order to control the character of the community. Ideally, areas of the city or town are restricted to specialized usage for the benefit of the public welfare, for example, so that residential areas will not become interspersed with industry. Zoning is an aspect of community planning. See PLANNING, SOCIAL; PLANNING, URBAN SOCIAL.